CRIME IN CALIFORNIA

A Case Reader in California Criminal Law

Laurie Kubicek

SECOND EDITION

Kendall Hunt
publishing company

Cover design © Eamonn Fitzmaurice

Kendall Hunt
publishing company

www.kendallhunt.com
Send all inquiries to:
4050 Westmark Drive
Dubuque, IA 52004-1840

Copyright © 2007, 2011 Laurie Kubicek

ISBN 978-0-7575-9134-1

Printed in the United States of America
10 9 8 7 6 5 4 3

DEDICATION

Many thanks to my husband Matt and my sons Ty and Wyatt for their love and loyalty.
I am inspired by them. I also want to thank the many family members, friends,
and colleagues who made the completion of this work possible.

office hours   M/W/F : 8:30-9:45 A.M.

CONTENTS

CASES

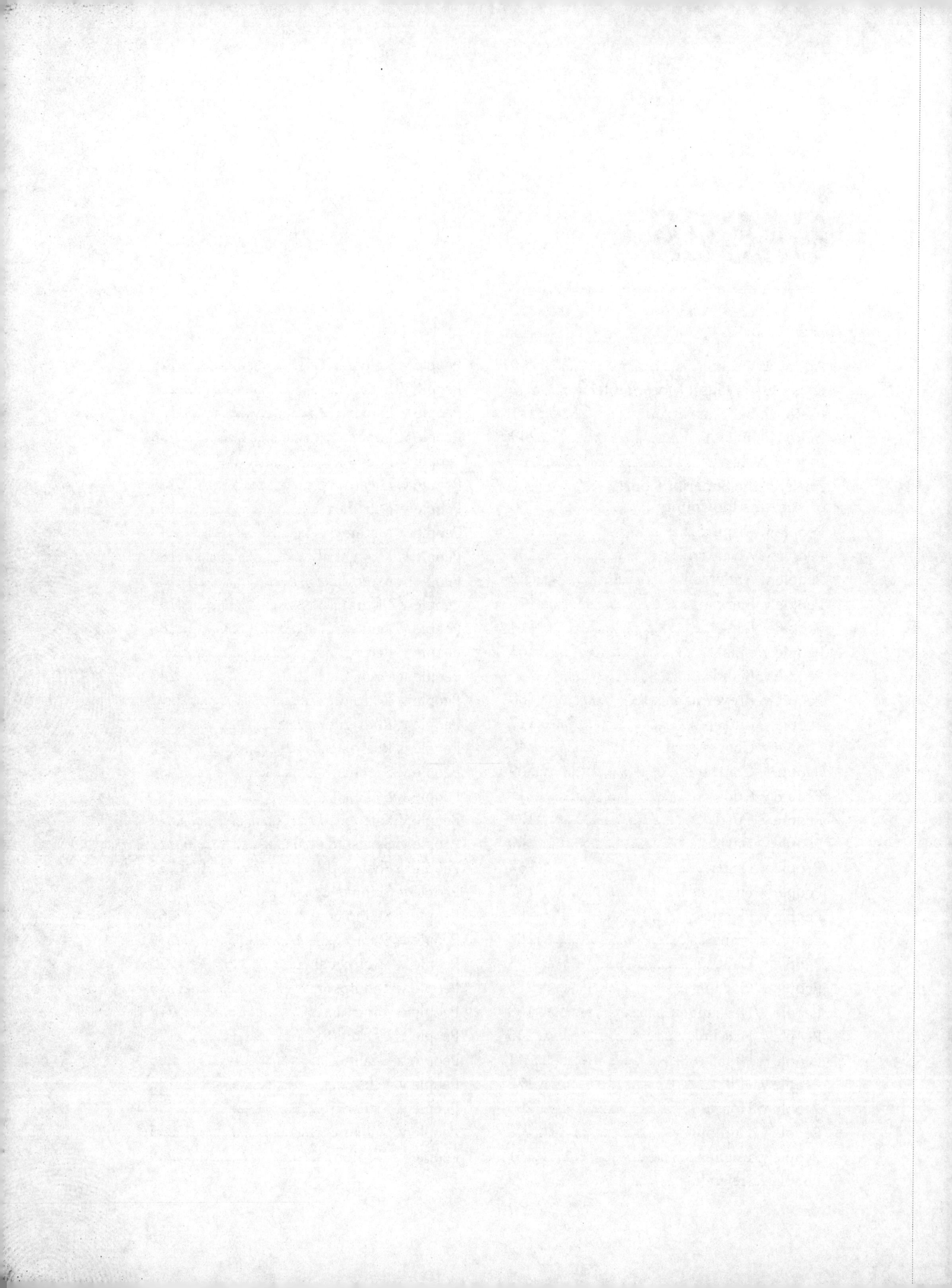

ACKNOWLEDGMENT

I am grateful to Julie Mumma for her important contributions to this new edition of *Crime in California*.

CHAPTER 1

Introduction to Criminal Law

THE AMERICAN COURTS

The American court system consists of two separate but similar types of organizations. One is the federal court system, which is responsible for hearing federal claims and disputes, and the other is the state court system. Each state has its own independent court system that is responsible for hearing disputes arising from matters of state law. In many ways, the state and federal systems are a mirror image of each other. Both have trial courts, appellate courts, and courts of last resort, or supreme courts. There are two main categories of American law: **civil** and **criminal.** Civil cases arise out of disputes between public or private parties over alleged wrongdoing. Typical examples of types of civil law are family law, personal injury, and probate (estates, wills, and trusts). In civil disputes, the **plaintiff** is the party who originates or files the lawsuit and the **defendant** is the party who is being sued and is expected to answer the allegations made in the plaintiff's complaint. In contrast, criminal law involves the government bringing criminal charges on behalf of the people against a person suspected of violating a criminal code or statute. The government is represented in criminal prosecutions by a **prosecutor.** In state courts, the prosecutor is the county district attorney's office, while in federal court, the prosecutor is the United States Attorneys' Office.

Criminal **trial courts** are tasked with determining the guilt of a person charged with committing a crime. They are obligated through a **fact finder,** either a judge or jury, to evaluate evidence presented during the trial and reach a conclusion. A judge serves as the fact finder in **bench trials** and the jury serves as the fact finder in jury trials. The American system of jurisprudence is **adversarial,** meaning that at trial, the prosecution presents evidence and makes their case to convict the defendant of the crimes charged. The defendant is not required to present evidence, but may do so as they see fit. The fact finder determines whether the prosecution has successfully established the defendant's guilt. The prosecution bears the **burden of proof** of each element of the crime **beyond a reasonable doubt.** If they fail to meet this burden, the accused automatically "wins" and must be found innocent of the charged offense. The defendant is considered innocent until proof of guilt beyond a reasonable doubt is demonstrated by the evidence. It is the job of the fact finder to make the decision as to whether the accused is, in fact, guilty. In California criminal jury trials, there must be 12 jurors for each case, and their finding of guilt must be unanimous. Once a determination of guilt has been made, the defendant is sentenced in a separate hearing. The criminal judicial process is complex, consisting of numerous steps; from the point of arrest through the point of acquittal, conviction, and sometimes appeal, the defendant is forced to navigate a challenging maze of difficult decisions. For this reason, the United States Supreme Court has held that even when a defendant cannot afford to pay for an attorney, the state must provide an attorney to assist in preparing his or her case for trial.

Appellate courts, or appeals courts, perform a much different function than trial courts. It is their job to resolve disputes arising out of the decisions made by trial courts and to correct misapplications of law. Appellate courts determine whether the law was applied correctly at trial, and if it wasn't, they are charged with correcting any errors and may order a reversal of the decision. If they determine on appeal that the law was followed correctly, or that any error made at trial was "harmless," the appeals court will affirm or uphold the decision of the trial court. Appellate court decisions do not have to be unanimous; a simple majority of the justices voting on appeal wins. Appellate courts write **opinions** to explain how they have reached their conclusions. There are often splintered opinions, called plurality opinions, where a majority of votes for a certain result is reached, but there is not consensus among the justices about the reasoning for that result. In these cases, a number of concurring (agreeing) or dissenting opinions may be written in addition to the opinion of the majority of the court. The decisions of appellate courts are published in **reporters.** For example, the United States Reports is the official reporter for the United States Supreme Court. When an opinion is published, it is assigned a **citation** by the reporter so that the court's opinion can be located and referenced in future cases and publications. The citation is made up of a series of letters and numbers, which represent the volume number, reporter series, and starting page number. The following example is the citation for a United States Supreme Court case:

New Jersey v. TLO, 469 U.S. 325 (1985)

The case name is written first, and is made up of the two parties to the lawsuit. Next in our example comes "469," which is the volume number of the reporter series in which the case appears. The abbreviation "U.S." represents the official United States Reports. The numbers "325" represent the page number where the case begins in the reporter, and the citation concludes with the date the case was decided set in parentheses.

The Supreme Court of the United States is the highest court in the land. It is the final arbiter of the United States Constitution and the laws of the United States. The California Supreme Court is the highest court in California and is the final arbiter of the California Constitution and issues of California law.

SOURCES OF LAW

There are four sources of American law: constitutions, codes or statutes, court opinions or cases, and administrative rules and regulations. Each of these four categories exists at both the state and federal level. Constitutions are the foundation for all American law. All three other types of law must abide by the requirements found in the state and federal constitutions. It is important to note that criminal law is traditionally left to the states to govern. The vast majority of substantive criminal law is found in state rather than federal codes, and the vast majority of criminal cases take place at the state level. According to the United States Administrative Office of the Courts, less than 500,000 federal cases are filed each year, and only 20% of those are criminal filings.[1] In stark contrast, California's Judicial Council reports that in 2009 the total number of superior court filings in California was over 9.5 million cases, and of those, over 7.7 million were criminal filings.[2]

Constitutions are governing documents that articulate the purpose, organizational structure, and assigned powers of the government. The United States Constitution is the foundation for law and government in the federal system, and each state has a constitution that serves the same purpose in the state system. **Codes or statutes** are a source of law produced by legislative bodies. At the federal level, the United States **Congress** is empowered in Article I of the United States Constitution to engage in the law-making function, and each state has a legislative counterpart responsible for producing state law through the legislative process. The California legislature consists of two houses: the **Senate** and the **Assembly.** The California State Senate is composed of 40 members and the Assembly is composed of 80 members. California's legislature operates full time in two-year legislative sessions. The members of the legislature propose new laws in the form of bills, and those bills are evaluated and debated, and if approved, become law after receiving the signature of the Governor of California.

As discussed earlier, appellate courts resolve questions relating to the application and interpretation of law and write opinions. These **cases and court opinions** serve as precedent for lower courts and for future courts. This process of developing rules of law on a case-by-case basis through judicial opinions is also referred to as **common law.** The doctrine of **stare decisis,** which is translated literally as "let the decision stand," is central to the common law development of the law of crimes and continues to be important today. This doctrine embodies the concept of **precedent,** where a court decision in a particular case will be followed by future courts when cases arise on substantially similar grounds. The foundation of this rule rests on respect for the well-reasoned decisions of prior courts, and on consistent, efficient decision-making. **Administrative rules and regulations** are very similar to statutes and codes except that rather than being produced by the legislature, they are created by administrative agencies. Administrative agencies have the power to create rules with the force of law because their grants of power come directly from the legislature itself. For example, the California Occupational Safety and Health Administration was created when the California legislature passed the California Occupational Safety and Health Act of 1973. This legislation created the agency and granted it power to act in the area of workplace safety, thus, the rules promulgated by Cal/OSHA can be enforced in the same way that legislative statutes are.

Regardless of the source, there are three types of law: substantive, procedural, and remedial. **Substantive criminal law** provides citizens with the requirements and prohibitions on conduct for which failure to adhere results in the commission of a crime. For example, the requirement that citizens refrain from killing one another is a substantive law that prohibits conduct. Conversely, substantive law also dictates that citizens provide adequate care for their children or otherwise face criminal charges for a failure to act, or a criminal omission. *Crime in California* focuses on California's substantive criminal law.

Procedural law governs the way that laws are enforced in the criminal justice and court systems. It is the practical application of the constitutional rules protecting citizens against government abuse. The law of criminal procedure ensures that the accused is protected against violations of his or her constitutional rights, such as the right to remain silent, the right to counsel, or the right to a trial by jury.

Remedial law governs the remedy offered for a successful party to a lawsuit. In civil cases, the remedy sought might be money (damages) or an injunction against the opposing party. In the law of crimes the remedy is most commonly a fine for very minor offenses (infractions or misdemeanors), jail or prison sentences for serious crimes, or, in some cases, a combination of fines and imprisonment.

---

[1] Administrative Office of the United States Courts. *Federal Judicial Caseload Statistics: March 31, 2009.* Washington, D.C. Retrieved from *http://www. uscourts.gov/caseload2009/front/IndicatorsMar09.pdf,* (2009).

[2] Administrative Office of the United States Courts. 2009 Court Statistics Report, summary pg. 3. Retrieved from http://www.courtinfo.ca.gov/reference/ documents/csr2009intro.pdf.

Crimes are also categorized into felonies, misdemeanors, and infractions by their seriousness in California.[3] A felony is the most serious type of offense and is characterized by punishment of death or imprisonment in state prison. A misdemeanor is a less serious offense and is characterized by less than one year of incarceration in a county jail. Infractions are any offenses classified as such by statute in California. The legislature has provided a list of code violations that are infractions in Cal. P.C. § 19.8. Often, the California Penal Code specifies that an offense can be charged as either a felony or a misdemeanor; these are often referred to as **wobblers** by legal professionals. Federal crimes are classified in a similar fashion, with minor exceptions. Felonies and misdemeanors are divided into lettered classes by seriousness (Class A Felony, Class B Misdemeanor). If not specifically classified by letter in the code section, the possible sentence for the offense is used to determine the category of offense.[4] These classifications impact the type of punishment available as a result of conviction as well as dictate some of the rights associated with the charge.

MODEL PENAL CODE

The Model Penal Code (MPC) is a suggested series of criminal codes, first drafted in 1962 in an effort to assist states in developing their criminal statutes. It is published by the American Law Institute, a nongovernmental organization, composed of well-respected legal practitioners and scholars. Many of the provisions of the MPC have been widely adopted, while others have not. It is important to understand that the MPC is not, by itself, the law in any American jurisdiction. Rather, it is a guide that has served as the model for many state penal code reforms taking place in the decade after its publication.

SUBSTANTIVE CRIMINAL LAW

American criminal law has its roots in early English common law. As judges decided the correct outcome of disputes, they announced the rule of law generated by those decisions in court opinions. Judicial decisions continue to play an integral role in the development of American and California substantive criminal law. The California legislature has codified many of the common law rules relating to the law of crimes, meaning that they have enacted legislation making those common law rules part of the modern California Penal Code.

A crime is composed of four **elements,** and understanding this elemental structure of criminal law is extremely important. Every true crime, one that is punishable, consists of:

1. Actus reus: the criminal act or omission
2. Mens rea: the guilty mind
   a. **Specific intent** crimes are those whose mens rea by definition requires both the intent to do the act, and the intent to achieve some future consequence. A **general intent** crime requires only that the defendant intend to commit the act, even if they do not have in mind a particular result or hope for a specific outcome. Murder is a specific intent offense, because the actor must intend to engage in the acts that produce death and must intend specifically that death or great bodily injury result.
   b. There must be **concurrence** between the criminal intent and the criminal act (Cal. PC § 20 requires "union or joint operation of act and intent or criminal negligence").
3. Causation: The criminal act must be both the legal cause and the proximate cause of the injury.
   a. Legal cause is determined by applying the "but for" test to the criminal act (e.g., but for the defendant's unlawful act, would the harm or injury have occurred? If no, the defendant is the legal cause of the harm).
   b. Proximate cause is more difficult to evaluate, but asks generally whether it is just or fair to hold the defendant responsible for the criminal act. Causation problems sometimes arise when there is an intervening act that may blur the line regarding the defendant's moral culpability.
4. Resulting harm or injury: This varies depending on the charged offense. In a homicide case, it would be the death of the victim.

---

[3] Cal. P.C. §17 (2009).

[4] Title 18 U.S.C. § 3559 (2009).

A defendant is charged formally by either an information or indictment. An **information** is the charging document used by prosecutors to inform a defendant of the charges they will be facing in court. An **indictment** is the charging document used if the charges result from the decision of a grand jury. The prosecution bears the burden of proving each of the four elements of the crime in order to obtain a conviction for the crime charged. If the fact finder believes that any of the elements has not been proven beyond a reasonable doubt, they should acquit the defendant, finding them not guilty.

English common law crimes were categorized based on their level of moral turpitude or wrongfulness. An offense is either **mala in se,** translated literally as "wrong in itself," or **mala prohibita,** translated literally as "wrong because they are prohibited." More severe crimes are categorized as mala in se because of the public's outrage at their commission. Mala prohibita offenses are criminal because the codes dictate them as such, but not because the offender has committed a moral wrong. This distinction is largely historical and does not affect the application of modern criminal statutes to modern criminal defendants.

LEARNING THE LAW

A **case brief** is a written summary of the court's opinion in a given case. The case-briefing method of study is employed in most American law schools as a way to achieve two equally important goals: (1) teaching students the law in a particular area, and (2) teaching students how to think critically and reason analytically. It is for those same reasons that undergraduate students benefit from learning the law via the case-briefing method of study. While undergraduate students may not plan to attend law school, the ability to analyze problems and make well-reasoned decisions is an indispensable skill.

Case briefs are research tools used to understand and interpret judicial opinions, and should be written in a way that most effectively and concisely summarizes the essence of individual cases for the purpose of synthesis into a general legal principle. Case briefing using the FIRAC method mirrors the way a typical judicial opinion is written. FIRAC is an acronym that refers to an analytical summary of a court opinion composed of five parts: the facts, issue, rule, analysis, and conclusion. Briefs should be written in the student's own words, but should not reflect the student's opinion of what *should have happened.* Rather, the case brief is a way to learn the rule of law relating to a particular topic based on the court's explanation of its application of the law to a specific set of facts, resulting in its decision in the case at hand.

EXERCISE 1

Case Briefing Assignment

Read and brief the following civil case. This is a case about civil battery brought during the Civil Rights Movement in the 1960s. After reading through this court opinion, complete the case briefing worksheet that follows.

OPINION BY: GREENHILL, J.

This is a suit for actual and exemplary damages growing out of an alleged assault and battery. The plaintiff Fisher was a mathematician with the Data Processing Division of the Manned Spacecraft Center, an agency of the National Aeronautics and Space Agency, commonly called NASA, near Houston. The defendants were the Carrousel Motor Hotel, Inc., located in Houston, the Brass Ring Club, which is located in the Carrousel, and Robert W. Flynn, who as an employee of the Carrousel was the manager of the Brass Ring Club. Flynn died before the trial, and the suit proceeded as to the Carrousel and the Brass Ring. Trial was to a jury which found for the plaintiff Fisher. The trial court rendered judgment for the defendants notwithstanding the verdict. The Court of Civil Appeals affirmed. 414 S.W.2d 774. The questions before this Court are whether there was evidence that an actionable battery was committed, and, if so, whether the two corporate defendants must respond in exemplary as well as actual damages for the malicious conduct of Flynn.

The plaintiff Fisher had been invited by Ampex Corporation and Defense Electronics to a one day's meeting regarding telemetry equipment at the Carrousel. The invitation included a luncheon. The guests were asked to reply by telephone whether they could attend the luncheon, and Fisher called in his acceptance. After the morning session, the group of 25 or 30 guests adjourned to the Brass Ring Club for lunch. The luncheon was buffet style, and Fisher stood in line with others and just ahead of a graduate student of Rice University who testified at the trial. As Fisher was about to be served, he was approached by Flynn, who snatched the plate from Fisher's hand and shouted that he, a Negro, could not be served in the club. Fisher testified that he was not actually touched, and did not testify that he suffered fear or apprehension of physical injury; but he did testify that he was highly embarrassed and hurt by Flynn's conduct in the presence of his associates.

The jury found that Flynn "forceably dispossessed plaintiff of his dinner plate" and "shouted in a loud and offensive manner" that Fisher could not be served there, thus subjecting Fisher to humiliation and indignity. It was

stipulated that Flynn was an employee of the Carrousel Hotel and, as such, managed the Brass Ring Club. The jury also found that Flynn acted maliciously and awarded Fisher $400 actual damages for his humiliation and indignity and $500 exemplary damages for Flynn's malicious conduct.

The Court of Civil Appeals held that there was no assault because there was no physical contact and no evidence of fear or apprehension of physical contact. However, it has long been settled that there can be a battery without an assault, and that actual physical contact is not necessary to constitute a battery, so long as there is contact with clothing or an object closely identified with the body. [1 Harper & James, The Law of Torts 216 (1956); Restatement of Torts 2d, §§ 18 and 19.] In Prosser, Law of Torts 32 (3d Ed. 1964), it is said:

"The interest in freedom from intentional and unpermitted contacts with the plaintiff's person is protected by an action for the tort commonly called battery. The protection extends to any part of the body, or to anything which is attached to it and practically identified with it. Thus contact with the plaintiff's clothing, or with a cane, a paper, or any other object held in his hand will be sufficient; . . . The plaintiff's interest in the integrity of his person includes all those things which are in contact or connected with it."

Under the facts of this case, we have no difficulty in holding that the intentional grabbing of plaintiff's plate constituted a battery. The intentional snatching of an object from one's hand is as clearly an offensive invasion of his person as would be an actual contact with the body. "To constitute an assault and battery, it is not necessary to touch the plaintiff's body or even his clothing; knocking or snatching anything from plaintiff's hand or touching anything connected with his person, when done in an offensive manner, is sufficient." (*Morgan v. Loyacomo,* 190 Miss. 656, 1 So. 2d 510 (1941).)

Such holding is not unique to the jurisprudence of this State. In *S. H. Kress & Co. v. Brashier,* 50 S.W.2d 922 (Tex. Civ. App. 1932, no writ), the defendant was held to have committed "an assault and trespass upon the person" by snatching a book from the plaintiff's hand. The jury findings in that case were that the defendant "dispossessed plaintiff of the book" and caused her to suffer "humiliation and indignity."

The rationale for holding an offensive contact with such an object to be a battery is explained in 1 Restatement of Torts 2d § 18 (Comment p. 31) as follows:

"Since the essence of the plaintiff's grievance consists in the offense to the dignity involved in the unpermitted and intentional invasion of the inviolability of his person and not in any physical harm done to his body, it is not necessary that the plaintiff's actual body be disturbed. Unpermitted and intentional contacts with anything so connected with the body as to be customarily regarded as part of the other's person and therefore as partaking of its inviolability is actionable as an offensive contact with his person. There are some things such as clothing or a cane or, indeed, anything directly grasped by the hand which are so intimately connected with one's body as to be universally regarded as part of the person."

We hold, therefore, that the forceful dispossession of plaintiff Fisher's plate in an offensive manner was sufficient to constitute a battery, and the trial court erred in granting judgment notwithstanding the verdict on the issue of actual damages.

. . . Damages for mental suffering are recoverable without the necessity for showing actual physical injury in a case of willful battery because the basis of that action is the unpermitted and intentional invasion of the plaintiff's person and not the actual harm done to the plaintiff's body. Restatement of Torts 2d § 18. Personal indignity is the essence of an action for battery; and consequently the defendant is liable not only for contacts which do actual physical harm, but also for those which are offensive and insulting. (Prosser, supra; *Wilson v. Orr,* 210 Ala. 93, 97 So. 133 (1923).) We hold, therefore, that plaintiff was entitled to actual damages for mental suffering due to the willful battery, even in the absence of any physical injury.

We now turn to the question of the liability of the corporation for exemplary damages. In this regard, the jury found that Flynn was acting within the course and scope of his employment on the occasion in question; that Flynn acted maliciously and with a wanton disregard of the rights and feelings of plaintiff on the occasion in question. There is no attack upon these jury findings. The jury further found that the defendant Carrousel did not authorize or approve the conduct of Flynn. It is argued that there is no evidence to support this finding. The jury verdict concluded with a finding that $500 would "reasonably compensate plaintiff for the malicious act and wanton disregard of plaintiff's feelings and rights . . ."

The rule in Texas is that a principal or master is liable for exemplary or punitive damages because of the acts of his agent, but only if:

(a) the principal authorized the doing and the manner of the act, or

(b) the agent was unfit and the principal was reckless in employing him, or

(c) the agent was employed in a managerial capacity and was acting in the scope of employment, or

(d) the employer or a manager of the employer ratified or approved the act.

The above test is set out in the Restatement of Torts § 909 and was adopted in *King v. McGuff,* 149 Tex. 432, 234 S.W.2d 403 (1950). At the trial of this case, the following stipulation was made in open court:

"It is further stipulated and agreed to by all parties that as an employee of the Carrousel Motor Hotel the said Robert W. Flynn was manager of the Brass Ring Club."

We think this stipulation brings the case squarely within part (c) of the rule announced in the *King* case as to Flynn's managerial capacity. It is undisputed that Flynn was acting in the scope of employment at the time of the incident; he was attempting to enforce the Club rules by depriving Fisher of service.

The rule of the Restatement of Torts adopted in the *King* case set out above has four separate and disjunctive categories as a basis of liability. They are separated by the word "or." As applicable here, there is liability if (a) the act is authorized, or (d) the act is ratified or approved, *or* (c) the agent was employed in a managerial capacity and was acting in the scope of his employment. Since it was established that the agent was employed in a managerial capacity and was in the scope of his employment, the finding of the jury that the Carrousel did not authorize or approve Flynn's conduct became immaterial.

The *King* case also cited and relied upon *Ft. Worth Elevator Co. v. Russell,* 123 Tex. 128, 70 S.W.2d 397 (1934). In that case, it was held not to be material that the employer did not authorize or ratify the particular conduct of the employee; and the right to exemplary damages was supported under what is section (b) of the Restatement or *King* rule: The agent was unfit, and the principal was reckless in employing [or retaining] him.

After the jury verdict in this case, counsel for the plaintiff moved that the trial court disregard the answer to issue number eight [no authorization or approval of Flynn's conduct on the occasion in question] and for judgment upon the verdict. The trial court erred in overruling that motion and in entering judgment for the defendants notwithstanding the verdict; and the Court of Civil Appeals erred in affirming that judgment.

The judgments of the courts below are reversed, and judgment is here rendered for the plaintiff for $900 with interest from the date of the trial court's judgment, and for costs of this suit.

CASE BRIEFING WORKSHEET

I. **Heading**—always identify the case by name and citation (including the date)—the abbreviated citation is

sufficient. _____

_____

_____

II. **Facts**—try to narrow the facts to only those that are significant to the specific legal issue being decided by

the court. _____

_____

_____

_____

_____

_____

_____

III. **Procedural History**—explain how the case made its way through the court system to this point in the ap-

pellate process. _____

_____

_____

_____

III. **Issue**—the legal question the court is faced with answering that has been raised in the case; it should be

phrased as a question or questions. _____

_____

_____

_____

IV. **Rule**—briefly describe the law the court applied in coming to their decision making. Be sure to note briefly what the specific source related to or stood for (Constitutional provisions, statutes or administrative rules or regulations, or prior cases.) _____

_____

_____

_____

_____

_____

_____

V. **Analysis**—explain how the court applied the rule(s) of law to the specific issue presented by the specific facts in the case. This section should describe in detail the court's rationale or reasoning for that application of law to the facts of the case. _____

_____

_____

_____

_____

_____

_____

_____

_____

_____

VI. **Conclusion**—did the court affirm, reverse, or remand? This should be a very short statement of the outcome.

_____

_____

_____

KEY TERMS

STUDY GUIDE CHAPTER 1

INTRODUCTION TO CRIMINAL LAW

1. Identify the four sources of law. What source of law is the California Penal Code? What source of law is *Fisher v. Carrousel Motor Hotel?*

2. What is the role of an intermediate court of appeals? Which court reviews the decision of an intermediate court of appeals?

3. Explain the key differences between trial and appellate courts.

4. What are the key elements required for any crime? Explain the two types of mens rea.

5. Read the *Fisher* case. Can there be the crime of *battery* if the victim is not actually touched? State the basic rule of law that answers that question. Cite three examples other than the snatching of a plate that may give rise to a battery charge under circumstances similar to the *Fisher* case.

CHAPTER 2

Criminal Liability and Parties to Crime

In order for an individual to be convicted of a crime under American law, the elements of the crime must each be proven beyond a reasonable doubt. The elements of each offense include the actus reus, mens rea, causation, and injury or harm.

The actus reus, or criminal act, must be voluntary. A person is not responsible for violating the law if they did not engage in the criminal act or if there was no unlawful **omission** of their own free will or volition. An omission is the failure to act. A person is only criminally liable for failing to act if the law imposes a specific or affirmative duty to do so. As a general principle, American law does not impose a legal duty to aid others in peril, considering it only a moral obligation to help others in danger. This principle is the subject of great debate, as many would argue that there should be both a moral and legal duty to do so.

The often cited case of Kitty Genovese highlights this issue. Kitty Genovese was a 28-year-old woman who was attacked three separate times during a period of over 30 minutes in 1964. She was eventually killed by her attacker as she tried to make her way the short distance from her car to her New York City apartment. Thirty-eight of Kitty's neighbors watched and listened from their windows with lights on, hearing her screams for help. One finally called the police, but it was too late. She was dead when the officers arrived just two minutes later.

A **legal duty** to intervene exists under a number of circumstances:

- When a person has a special relationship to the victim (parent/child, spouse, etc.). Similarly, when a person has supervisory responsibility or control over another (as in employer/employee relationships, parent/child relationships).

- When a statute creates the obligation to provide care (for example, statutes providing for the welfare and care of children).

- When a contract to provide care exists (such as with day-care providers or in-home caregivers).

- When a person volunteers to assist an individual in peril, they must do so with reasonable care.

- When a person creates the risk, they are responsible to intervene on behalf of someone who suffers harm at their own hand.

- Property owners are required to aid those who suffer harm as guests on their premises.

The general rule in California is that there is no legal duty to aid a person in peril. A prominent argument in favor of the current "no legal duty rule" is that people fear being held responsible if they do something wrong as they try to aid another in peril. The California legislature has encouraged citizens to aid others, by enacting a "**Good Samaritan Statute**" in Health & Safety Code §1799.102. Good Samaritan laws like California's provide legal protection for people who are willing to take the risk of helping others in need. Each state's Good Samaritan rule language is unique. California's explains that a person who acts in good faith to provide care for another in an emergency situation shall not be held liable for civil damages—so long as they do not act with **gross negligence** or willful misconduct. The rule intends to encourage people to help others in need, but to do so responsibly.

An individual possesses the requisite mens rea for criminal conviction when he or she engages in the unlawful act with a guilty mind or intent. The California criminal law defines what type of mens rea is required for a criminal offense within each statute. California does not employ the Model Penal Code categories for mens rea. The Model Penal Code divides the mens rea required for all offenses into one of four types: purpose, knowing, reckless, and negligent. While those terms are often present in California statutes, California does not utilize those categories across the board. For example, California Penal Code §187 still utilizes the complex term "malice aforethought" in defining the required mens rea for murder. The concept of mens rea, and how it affects the type of crime a person has committed, is probably best demonstrated through the study of the law of homicide. The nature of what the defendant thought and believed at the time they engaged in the act of killing determines whether a defendant should be criminally responsible for the victim's death, and if so, whether the killing is murder or manslaughter.

The actus reus and mens rea must occur in concert, or concurrently in time. This is often referred to as **concurrence** of the actus reus and mens rea. In addition to actus reus and mens rea requirements, the law also requires that there be a causal connection between those elements and the required resulting harm. **Causation** is a complex concept, and contains two components: legal causes (or **cause in fact**) and **proximate cause**. Cause in fact is demonstrated by answering "no" to the question, "but for the defendant's action, would the resulting harm have occurred?" It is the easier of the two components for most students to grasp. Proximate cause addresses questions of fairness when it comes to holding an individual responsible for an end result or harm. This typically is only an issue when there is some "intervening" act that raises questions about whether or not a person's conduct is causally connected to the harm.

There is no hard-and-fast formula for determining proximate cause, and as a result, it tends to be a murkier concept that students sometimes wrestle with understanding. The principles that have developed to help answer these complex proximate cause questions aim to determine whether the **intervening act** is the result of pure coincidence (e.g., someone or something totally unrelated to the defendant's bad act intervenes and causes the death of a victim) and the foreseeability or predictability of an intervening act (e.g., could the defendant have foreseen that the victim whom they were chasing and shouting threats at would run into traffic at a busy intersection?). Courts also often reference the "natural and probable consequences" of an individual's act. Defendants are typically responsible for harm that arises as a natural and probable consequence of their choice to act or their failure to act when they have a duty to do so.

The California Penal Code speaks to crime and punishment for individuals and groups. The Code also details specific people whom the law defines as being incapable of committing criminal acts. Section 26 of the Code explains that all people are capable of committing crime other than those specifically listed:

- Children under the age of 14, in the absence of clear proof that at the time of committing the act charged against them, they knew its wrongfulness

- Mentally incapacitated people

- People who committed the act or made the omission under a mistake of fact, which disproves any criminal intent

- People who committed the act or made the omission without being conscious of its commission

- People who committed the act or made the omission by accident

- People (unless the crime is punishable with death) who committed the act or made the omission under threats that produced a belief that their life would be in danger if they refused

These exceptions help to create many of the special defenses discussed at length in Chapter 4 of this text. For the purposes of criminal liability, it suffices to note that the code allows for broad-reaching criminal liability, carving out only very specific exceptions to that general rule for individuals whose condition or personal characteristics make them incapable of forming the required mens rea for an offense and therefore leave the elements of the crime incomplete.

Parties to crime in California are **principals** or **accessories.** Principals are defined by the code in Section 31 as "all persons concerned in the commission of a crime." This language allows for a wide range of participants to be charged as principals to a criminal act. This means that anyone "concerned" with the crime can be charged with committing the offense itself. For example, if a group of three men go to rob a bank, and one enters the bank with the gun and holds up the bank teller, another stands outside the door as a lookout, and a third acts as a "get-away" driver, all three individuals are "concerned" with the commission of the offense and can be charged with robbery. Even though the two outside the bank did not actually point a gun at the teller and demand money, they are both concerned with the commission of the offense.

Accessories are defined by Section 32 of the Code as people who "after a felony has been committed, harbors, conceals, or aids a principal in such a felony, with the intent that said principal may avoid or escape from arrest, trial, conviction, or punishment . . ." In the example of a bank robbery, if the get-away driver's mother, without prior knowledge of the robbery, learns of her son's actions and offers to hide his car in her garage so that police won't find it, she becomes an accessory. She intentionally, after the felony was committed, aided a principal in that felony in avoiding arrest, trial, conviction, or punishment. Punishment for accessories, unless otherwise prescribed for a specific offense, is a misdemeanor that can include up to a $5,000 fine or imprisonment for up to one year, or both (Cal. P.C. §33).

The current definitions for principals and accessories in California are a stark departure from the old common law definitions. In common law, there were multiple categories relating to the timing of the offender's participation in the offense. For example, a person might have been classified as a principal in the first or second degree, an accessory before the fact, or an accessory after the fact, depending upon their role in a criminal act and the timing of their involvement. California's modern penal code has done away with these classifications, and the current code allows prosecutors flexibility in charging individuals who participate in any way in a criminal offense, whether before, during, or after the criminal acts or omissions occur.

PEOPLE v. COOK

COURT OF APPEAL OF CALIFORNIA, FIFTH APPELLATE DISTRICT

61 Cal. App. 4th 1364; 72 Cal. Rptr. 2d 183

March 9, 1998

OPINION BY: VARTABEDIAN, J.

Defendant Edward L. Cook appeals his conviction for first degree murder. . . . Defendant further asserts error in the court's failure to instruct on aiding and abetting, a claim we discuss in the published portion of this opinion. . . . All of these contentions fail. We affirm the judgment.

FACTS AND PROCEDURAL HISTORY

In the evening of August 21, 1994, defendant, then 16 years old, asked his friend Adolph if he was "down for a 187." Adolph apparently thought a "187" was a robbery. The boys went out to the railroad tracks that ran behind the house where defendant was living. A frequently traveled dirt path ran alongside the tracks. The boys saw Donald Thornton, whom they did not know, walking along the path carrying a shopping bag. Defendant said, "Well you wanna get him?" Adolph said, "I don't care." The boys approached Thornton.

Defendant confronted Thornton using the command "break yourself" or "brake yourself." Adolph thought this meant "give up your stuff." Thornton began to retreat and then dropped his bag. Adolph picked up the bag, which contained three or four cans of beer. Adolph began to leave with the beer. Around seven feet away, Adolph turned and saw defendant's fist slamming into Thornton's side three or four times; he saw nothing in defendant's hand. Adolph turned away again. Seconds later, defendant caught up with Adolph. Laughing, defendant said he had stabbed the man. Adolph saw defendant was holding a pocketknife. The boys went back to defendant's house and drank the beer.

The next day, Adolph told his brother Marcus about the killing, saying "we did something stupid." Later that day, defendant told Marcus "he had stabbed some guy on the tracks late at night that night before."

Two days later, defendant told his girlfriend, Misty, about the killing. He said he and "his homies" stabbed the man for a six-pack of beer. The next day, defendant told Misty

additional details. On August 26, 1994, Misty secretly called the police. Misty obtained further details from defendant. Defendant said he had stabbed the man and that only Adolph had been with him. He also said he had taken $200 from the man, that they had worn ski masks as a disguise, and that he previously had killed people in Los Angeles, none of which apparently was true.

Three weeks later, detectives picked up Adolph for questioning. Adolph first claimed he did not know what the detectives were talking about. After they told him they knew defendant had killed Thornton and that Adolph was equally as likely as defendant to be convicted of first degree murder unless he cooperated, Adolph confessed. He described defendant's role in the robbery and murder essentially as set forth above. n1

> n1 Adolph was arrested for murder at the conclusion of the interview. Subsequently, Adolph was permitted to admit a juvenile petition alleging robbery and was committed to the California Youth Authority (hereafter Youth Authority) for up to 5 years. The plea was part of a bargain by which the murder charge was dismissed in return for Adolph's agreement to testify "truthfully" in the present case.

The detectives then questioned defendant, who stated he and Adolph had been home all evening. He persisted in this claim even when the detectives told him about Adolph's confession. "You have my story; I have my witnesses," defendant repeatedly proclaimed. The detectives arrested defendant.

After the juvenile court found defendant an unfit subject for juvenile proceedings pursuant to *Welfare and Institutions Code section 707*, the district attorney filed an information in superior court charging defendant with murder. (Count 1; Pen. Code, n2 § 187.) The information alleged as a special circumstance that defendant committed the murder during a robbery. (§ 190.2, former subd. (a)(17)(i).) . . . The information also alleged robbery as a separate count. (Count 2; § 212.5, former subd. (b). . . . As to both counts, the information alleged defendant personally used a knife in the commission of the offense. (§ 12022, subd. (b).) Defendant pleaded not guilty; he subsequently added a plea of not guilty by reason of insanity.

. . .

On April 5, 1995, a jury found defendant guilty as charged. The next day the jury found defendant was sane when he committed the crimes.

Defendant filed a motion for new trial. The court denied the motion and sent defendant to the Youth Authority for evaluation pursuant to *Welfare and Institutions Code section 707.2*. On September 1, 1995, after the arrest on a bench warrant of a subpoenaed defense witness who had failed to appear for trial, defendant renewed the new trial motion. The court again denied the motion.

At the sentencing hearing on September 19, 1995, the court found defendant was not amenable to treatment at the Youth Authority. The court declined to exercise its discretion to impose a lesser sentence pursuant to section 190.5, subdivision (b). It imposed a sentence of life in prison without possibility of parole. The court also imposed a one-year sentence on the weapon-use enhancement. The same day, defendant filed his notice of appeal.

DISCUSSION

. . .

Aiding and Abetting Instruction

Defendant contends "[t]he trial court failed to instruct . . . [on] the *mens rea* necessary to establish appellant's culpability as an aider and abettor in the robbery and robbery-murder." As the argument is further explained in defendant's reply brief: "Where the prosecution's theory of the robbery count was that a key element was performed by an accomplice, the jury must be instructed on aiding and abetting." In particular, he says, the only credible evidence concerning the robbery showed that Adolph actually took the beer.

Defendant cites no authority for the proposition that when a "key element" of a crime is performed by another person, any accomplice is merely an aider and abettor. Although we have found no California case discussing this issue in any detail, we conclude defendant is wrong and that the evidence at trial clearly showed that defendant was guilty, if at all, as a direct perpetrator of the robbery.

In some important ways, the law does not distinguish between perpetrators on the one hand and aiders and abettors on the other. The Penal Code provides: "All persons concerned in the commission of a crime . . . whether they directly commit the act constituting the offense, or aid and abet in its commission . . . are principals in any crime so committed." (§ 31; see also § 971.) As such, aiders and abettors are subject to the same range of punishment as direct perpetrators.

Despite their equal status as principals in the crime, in other instances the law does distinguish between direct perpetrators and aiders and abettors. In part, this is because the actions of a purported aider and abettor are often more peripheral and ambiguous than those of the direct perpetrator. (*People v. Beeman (1984) 35 Cal. 3d 547, 559 {199 Cal. Rptr. 60, 674 P.2d 1318}*.) Indeed, actions causally facilitating the crime may be entirely innocent. . . . Therefore, in order to ensure that the purported aider and abettor has the *mens rea* consistent with criminal liability, case law has established that such a person must "act with knowledge of the criminal purpose of the perpetrator *and* with an intent or purpose either of committing, or of encouraging or facilitating commission of, the offense." (*People v. Beeman, supra, 35 Cal. 3d* at p. 560, italics in original.) Thus, while the criminal liability of an aider and abettor is the same as that of a direct perpetrator, the required mental states differ between the two classes of principals.

. . .

In *People v. Talamantez (1985) 169 Cal. App. 3d 443 {215 Cal. Rptr. 542}*, two men kidnapped another man and beat him to death. Talamantez contended he did not inflict the fatal blow and that the trial court had given an erroneous instruction concerning the intent necessary to find him guilty of the murder on an aiding and abetting theory. The appellate court concluded the instructional error was harmless. Among its reasons, stated without a discussion of the applicable law, was that, as a participant in the beating, Talamantez was a perpetrator of the torture that culminated in the victim's death. The court stated: "The fact (if it be a fact) that Talamantez did not strike the final torturous blow that broke Heggie's voice box and caused his death does not convert him factually into an aider and abettor to torture murder. These bitter convicting facts show him violently beating, torturing Heggie up to the point of Rozzo's *coup de mort*." (*Id.* at p. 463.) Accordingly, Talamantez perpetrated the murder.

In the recent case of *People v. Rose (1997) 56 Cal. App. 4th 990 {65 Cal. Rptr. 2d 887}*, the issue was whether Rose was entitled to have his felony conviction reduced to a misdemeanor pursuant to section 659. [n11] Rose and another person entered a store to steal a purse. The other person actually left the store with the purse. She was permitted to plead guilty to petty theft with a prior, as a misdemeanor. Rose, however, had prior serious felony convictions and was charged under the three strikes law. Convicted of second degree burglary, he was sentenced to 25 years to life. In the trial court and on appeal he contended he should be convicted only of a misdemeanor since the person he aided and abetted was only convicted of a misdemeanor. The appellate court rejected this claim for a number of reasons, among them the following: "Finally, defendant was not an aider and abettor of the burglary. He personally entered the store with the intent to aid Allen in the theft of the handbag." (56 *Cal. App. 4th* at p. 994.) Again, however, there was no discussion of the applicable law.

> n11 Section 659 provides: "Whenever an act is declared a misdemeanor, and no punishment for counseling or aiding the commission of such act is expressly prescribed by law, every person who counsels or aids another in the commission of such act is guilty of a misdemeanor."

In *People v. Croy (1985) 41 Cal. 3d 1, 12 {221 Cal. Rptr. 592, 710 P.2d 392}*, footnote 5, the Supreme Court stated in dicta the following: "Like the conspirator whose liability is predicated on acts *other than and short of those constituting the elements of the charged offense*, if the acts [of the aider and abettor] are undertaken with the intent that the actual perpetrator's purpose be facilitated thereby, he is a principal and liable for the commission of the offense." Impliedly, then, one whose acts do not fall short of acts "constituting the elements of the charged offense" is not an aider and abettor, but is an "actual perpetrator."

Neither *Croy*, *Rose*, nor *Talamantez* discusses the basis for its statement concerning the distinction between direct perpetrators and aiders and abettors. Yet all three decisions readily can be explained by reference to the common law as it existed before the adoption of section 971. At common law, principals in a crime were divided into two degrees. A principal in the first degree "engages in *criminal conduct* by his own hand" or commits the crime through his constructive presence. (1 Wharton's Criminal Law (15th ed. 1993) Parties, § 30, pp. 183–184, italics added.) By contrast, "a principal in the second degree is a person who is present at the scene of a crime, but *does not engage in the criminal conduct*; he merely aids and abets the principal in

the first degree in committing the crime." (*Id.* at § 31, p. 186, italics added, fn. omitted.) An aider and abettor not present at the scene of the crime was known at common law as an accessory before the fact. (*Id.* at § 32, p. 193.)

. . .

While section 971 abolished the pleading and punishment distinctions among first degree principals, those of the second degree, and accessories, nevertheless, the former common law categories make explicit what was implicit in *Croy*, *Rose*, and *Talamantez*: one who engages in conduct that is an element of the charged crime is a perpetrator, not an aider and abettor, of the completed crime. Thus, appellant's proposed formulation of the rule, if "a key element was performed by an accomplice, the jury must be instructed on aiding and abetting," is essentially the reverse of the correct rule: If the defendant performed an element of the offense, the jury need not be instructed on aiding and abetting, even if an accomplice performed other acts that completed the crime.

In this case, the uncontradicted evidence (apart from the identity issue) was that defendant provided the "force or fear" necessary to accomplish the robbery. As such, he was one of the direct perpetrators of the offense of robbery, even if he did not physically deprive the victim of his property. No aiding and abetting instruction was necessary. In determining that defendant actually committed the robbery, the jury necessarily found he had the specific intent to deprive Thornton of the beer. There was no requirement that the jury also find that he had the specific intent or purpose to facilitate Adolph's commission of the crime.

. . .

Disposition

The judgment is affirmed.

KEY TERMS

STUDY GUIDE CHAPTER 2

CRIMINAL LIABILITY AND PARTIES TO CRIME

1. What elements are required in order to hold an individual responsible for a crime?

2. When would a person's omission or failure to act result in criminal responsibility?

3. What are the two types of cause that must be proven in order to establish causation?

4. What is the main difference between principals and accessories to a crime?

CHAPTER 3

Homicide

Homicide is the killing of a human being by another human being. Homicide is not always a crime. For example, state-sanctioned executions are characterized as **innocent homicide**. They are carried out by one human being against another, but they are not criminal in nature. Other innocent homicides are the result of justification or excuse under the law: killings in lawful self-defense or killings committed by the criminally insane.

This chapter focuses on criminal homicide, beginning with the question of whether a fetus is a human being for the purposes of homicide. According to the common law, and until the mid-1970s in California, the answer was "no." The law did not recognize fetuses as human beings for the purposes of homicide. A child must have been "born alive" in order to be legally recognized as a murder victim. The result in *Keeler v. Superior Court* (1970)[1] left people asking why a person like Keeler, who clearly intended to kill, was to go unpunished simply because the baby was delivered stillborn. Was the defendant less culpable for the baby's death because he succeeded at causing it to occur in utero rather than allowing the baby to take a breath outside the womb and then die?

The California legislature responded almost immediately to the *Keeler* decision, and the murder statute was amended to specifically include fetuses. The result is the prosecution for murder in cases like that of Scott Peterson who killed

---

[1] *Keeler v. Superior Court,* 2 Cal.3d 619 (1970).

his wife and unborn son. It is also important to note that viability of the fetus is not a requirement for fetal murder in California.[2] While the legislature solved the immediate problem raised by the result in Keeler to the satisfaction of the public, some very real ethical questions remain unanswered. If fetuses are considered human beings under the law, the conflict with American statutes legalizing abortion is one that likely cannot be ignored by the courts forever. To date, courts of appeal and even the highest courts in many states have been satisfied to acknowledge the tension in the law but rest their decision to allow both fetal homicide and legalized abortion on the grounds that the abortion statute is simply exempted from the fetal homicide statute.

KEY LEGAL PRINCIPLE:

Another general principle that is important to understand is the doctrine of **transferred intent.** Common law courts were frustrated by the question of what to do when the defendant intended to kill A, but instead missed his target and killed B. It was clear there was not intent to kill B, and if that line of reasoning were taken to its logical conclusion, the killer would be unjustly relieved of criminal responsibility for the victim's death. The doctrine of transferred intent developed to resolve this problem and ensure that a killer doesn't benefit from his or her own mistake. According to the doctrine, the killer's criminal intent "follows the bullet." In our example, the killer intended to kill A, but instead killed B, so their criminal intent to kill A is transferred to B. If both A and B were to die as a result of the defendant's intended shot at A, the same type of homicide charge should be brought in the killings of both victims.

There are two main categories of homicide: **murder** and **manslaughter.** The difference between murder and manslaughter is the presence of malice aforethought. Killings committed with malice aforethought are murder, and those without it are manslaughter. **Malice aforethought** is an archaic legal term. *Black's Law Dictionary* defines the term malice aforethought as "the intent to engage in an unlawful act without justification or excuse." This definition helps to make an important point: that not every murder requires premeditation or pre-planning, rather, every murder requires the intent to engage in the unlawful act of killing without justification or excuse. *Webster's Dictionary* defines malice as a "desire to cause pain, injury, or distress" and aforethought as "previously in mind; premeditated, deliberate." It might seem logical to simply take those two definitions together to reach a conclusion about the term, but that tactic will result in missing the mark. The legal term "malice aforethought" encompasses much of what is implicit in those plain meaning definitions, but in a sense the legal definition is more different than it might seem. In order for a person who kills to do so with malice aforethought, they must possess the specific intent to kill or the intent to kill must be implicit based on their conduct.[3]

There are sub-categories for both murder and manslaughter. The California Penal Code §187 (hereinafter "the Code") defines murder as the "killing of a human being or fetus with malice aforethought." Murder is divided into degrees: first and second. According to §189, first degree murder occurs when a murder is committed with premeditation and deliberation. The Code specifies certain murders as premeditated and deliberate based on the very nature of the killings.[4] For example, a killing committed after lying in wait for the victim is defined by the statute as a premeditated and deliberate killing, and as a result is first degree murder. The statute provides this list of premeditated and deliberate killings, and explains that they are first degree murder along with "any other premeditated and deliberate." Section 189 also outlines the first degree felony murder rule, explaining that a killing committed during the commission or attempted commission of one of the listed felonies is also first degree murder. If a killing is done with malice aforethought but the killer lacked premeditation and deliberation, the killing is second degree murder.

If a homicide lacks malice aforethought, it is manslaughter. Manslaughter is divided into three categories: voluntary, involuntary, and vehicular. The Code defines manslaughter in §192(a) as a killing committed in the heat of passion or under an unreasonable belief in the right to use deadly force in self-defense.

---

[2] *People v. Davis,* 7 Cal.4th 797 (1994).

[3] Cal. P.C. §188.

[4] Cal. P.C. §189.

These general principles are just the starting point—they don't even begin to relay the complexity of the law regarding homicide in California. This chapter provides additional background and definition, fleshing out the elements of each type of homicide, and highlights the legal rules and principles concerning homicide, which are to be gleaned by reading, analyzing, and briefing the cases provided.

KEY LEGAL PRINCIPLE:

At this point, it is useful to review the difference between specific intent and general intent in the law. Specific intent crimes are those whose mens rea by definition requires both the intent to do the act, and the intent to achieve some future consequence. A general intent crime requires only that the defendant intend to commit the act, even if they do not have in mind a particular result or hope for a specific outcome. Murder is a specific intent offense, because the actor must intend to engage in the acts that produce death and must intend specifically that death or great bodily injury result.

FIRST DEGREE MURDER

First degree murders include both intended and unintended killings. Though first degree murder is most commonly associated with premeditated murder, the felony murder doctrine also allows for first degree murder convictions in cases where the death of the victim occurs by what appears on its face to be an accident. In *People v. Perez*,[5] you will read about the killing of Victoria Mesa in a calculated and deliberate manner. In contrast, in *People v. Billa* (2003),[6] the victim was a friend and co-conspirator of the defendant. He certainly did not intend or desire for his partner in crime to die in a fire as they committed arson for the purpose of defrauding their insurance company. In fact, he was very likely distraught at the death of his cohort, but he is still guilty of murder for his death. In *People v. Chavez* (2004), the California Supreme Court explained the distinction between first degree felony murder and drive-by shootings, which are first degree murders that require intent to kill, but do not require proof of premeditation and deliberation.

First degree murders can be grouped into three categories:

- Premeditated and deliberate killings: killings where there is proof that the defendant possessed malice aforethought (intent to kill) and

    - **Premeditation:** demonstrated by balancing the three "Anderson Factors," including the defendant's planning, motive, and the manner of the killing,[7] and

    - **Deliberation:** whether the defendant weighed and considered the question of killing and the reasons for and against that choice, and, having in mind the consequences, decided to do it. A calculated decision to kill can be reached in a short amount of time.[8]

- Statutorily defined first degree murders (Cal. P.C. §189): killings committed by means of a destructive device or explosive, a weapon of mass destruction, knowing use of armor-piercing ammunition, poison, lying in wait or torture, and drive-by shootings (discharging a firearm from a motor vehicle)

- First degree **felony murder** (enumerated felonies are listed in Cal. P.C. §189): killings committed during the commission or attempted commission of arson, rape, carjacking, robbery, burglary, mayhem, kidnapping, train wrecking, torture (Cal. P.C. §206), lewd acts with children (Cal. P.C. §288 & 288(a)), or penetration with a foreign object (Cal. P.C. §289)

---

[5] *People v. Perez*, 2 Cal.4th 1117 (1992).

[6] *People v. Billa*, 31 Cal.4th 1064 (2003).

[7] *People v. Anderson*, 70 Cal. 2d 15 (1968).

[8] *People v. Perez*, 2 Cal. 4th 1117 (1992).

The **sentence,** or punishment, for first degree murder in California is death, life in prison without the possibility of parole, or 25 years to life in prison. In order to sentence a defendant to death in California, there must be a finding of **special circumstances** in connection with the killing. A judge or jury is never required to sentence a defendant to death; the option of life without the possibility of parole is always an available alternative, even when a special circumstances finding is made. There is a long list of special circumstances found in Cal. P.C. §§190.2 & 190.4. These include but are not limited to:

- Murder for financial gain

- Multiple murders in the same offense

- Murder to avoid arrest or escape from custody

- Murders where the victim was a firefighter, police officer, judge, or juror

- Murders committed because of the victim's race, color, or ethnicity

- Especially heinous, atrocious, or cruel killings manifesting exceptional depravity

The elements of *premeditated & deliberate first degree murder:*

- Actus reus—the killer engaged in the act that caused the death of another

- Mens rea—specific intent to kill, plus premeditation and deliberation

- Causation—the defendant set in motion the chain of events that led to the victim's death (a causal connection between the act of killing and the resulting death)

- Injury—death resulted

The elements of *statutorily defined first degree murders:*

- Actus reus—the killer engaged in an act of killing specifically prescribed by Cal. P.C. §189 as first degree murder

- Mens rea—specific intent to kill by engaging in the specifically prescribed act(s)

- Causation—the defendant set in motion the chain of events that led to the victim's death (a causal connection between the act of killing and the resulting death)

- Injury—death resulted

The elements of *first degree felony murder:*

- Actus reus—the killer committed or attempted to commit a felony listed in Cal. P.C. §189, and during the course of that act, a death resulted

- Mens rea—the rule creates a "legal fiction" that presumes the intent to kill, when in reality, the killer possessed the intent to engage in the "listed" felony

- Causation—while there must be a relationship between the killer's unlawful act and the death, there is no requirement that the victim's death be a foreseeable consequence of committing the underlying felony (e.g., the death may have been the result of an accident or may have been an unintended consequence of the commission of the underlying felony)

- Injury—death resulted

SECOND DEGREE MURDER

Intentional killings correctly classified as second degree murder are those in which an individual intends the death of another—but adequate proof of premeditation and deliberation cannot be demonstrated. Second degree murders can be grouped into three kinds of killings:

- Killings committed with malice aforethought, without justification or excuse, but which lack premeditation and deliberation, and which don't meet any of the statutory requirements for first degree murder.

- Killings committed with a "depraved heart," or "implied malice" murders. These are killings where the intent to kill is implied from the intentional commission of an act that is dangerous to human life. The actor deliberately performed the act with the knowledge of the danger to, and with conscious disregard for, human life. As a result, malice or intent to kill is implied from their actions.

- Killings committed during the commission or attempted commission of an **inherently dangerous felony** that is not listed in Cal. P.C. §189. Theoretically, there are hundreds of felonies that could qualify, but the California courts have demonstrated their disdain for this rule and have been extremely reluctant to apply it.

The elements of *express malice second degree murder* are:

- Actus reus—the killer engaged in the act that caused the death of another

- Mens rea—specific intent to kill

- Causation—the defendant set in motion the chain of events that led to the victim's death (a causal connection between the act of killing and the resulting death)

- Injury—death resulted

The elements of *implied malice or "depraved heart" murder* are:

- Actus reus—the killer engaged in an act from which malice can be implied because the circumstances surrounding the killing show no considerable provocation

- Mens rea—the killer showed an abandoned or malignant heart

- Causation—the defendant set in motion the chain of events that led to the victim's death (a causal connection between the act of killing and the resulting death)

- Injury—death resulted

The elements of *second degree felony murder* are:

- Actus reus—the killer committed or attempted to commit a felony NOT listed in Cal. P.C. §189 which was *inherently dangerous*, and during the course of that act, a death resulted

- Mens rea—the rule creates a "legal fiction" that presumes the intent to kill, when in reality, the killer possessed the intent to engage in the inherently dangerous felony

- Causation—while there must be a relationship between the killer's unlawful act and the death, there is no requirement that the victim's death be a foreseeable consequence of committing the underlying felony (e.g., the death may have been the result of an accident or may have been an unintended consequence of the commission of the underlying felony)

- Injury—death resulted

The second degree felony murder rule requires that the court determine, on a case-by-case basis, whether the felony itself was inherently dangerous. In order to do so, the court must analyze the felony committed in the abstract (not considering the specific facts or circumstances of the case at bar),[9] and the court must determine whether the commission of the felony created a high probability that death would result. Below are examples from California courts of felonies that are inherently dangerous, along with some that are not inherently dangerous.

Examples of some of the felonies which ARE inherently dangerous include:

- Attempted escape from prison by force or violence

- Furnishing a poisonous substance, Cal. P.C. §209(a)

- Manufacturing methamphetamine, Cal. Health & Safety Code §11379.6(a)

- Reckless possession of a bomb, Cal. P.C. §12303.2

- Shooting at an inhabited dwelling, Cal. P.C. §246

- Shooting at an occupied vehicle, Cal. P.C. §246

Some of the felonies that are NOT inherently dangerous include:

- Conspiracy to possess methamphetamine

- Driving with willful or wanton disregard for safety while fleeing a pursuing officer

- Extortion

- False imprisonment

- Felonious practice of medicine without a license

- Felony child abuse

- Felony escape from prison without force or violence

- Furnishing PCP

- Grand theft from the person of another

The punishment for second degree murder is 25 years to life in prison.[10] Exceptions to this rule exist where the defendant knowingly kills a police officer engaged in the performance of his or her duties, where the killing is by definition a hate crime, or where the defendant is a "two-time" murderer.[11] In those cases, if specific criteria are met, the punishment can be life without the possibility of parole.

---

[9] *People v. Williams,* 63 Cal.2d 452, 458 (1965).

[10] Cal. P.C. §190.

[11] Cal. P.C. §190.03 & 190.05.

VOLUNTARY MANSLAUGHTER

Manslaughter is a catchall term for killings that do not rise to the level of murder for lack of malice aforethought. There are three types of manslaughter in California: **voluntary manslaughter, involuntary manslaughter,** and **vehicular manslaughter.** In some cases, a killing is manslaughter because there is simply no intention on the part of the killer to cause the death of another but death results from a **reckless** act. In other cases, the killing is intentional but is **mitigated,** or reduced, from murder to manslaughter because of the surrounding circumstances. This is the case with **heat of passion** and **imperfect self-defense.** Lastly, killings that are the natural and probable result of the defendant's recklessness, or conscious disregard for human life or safety, are voluntary manslaughter.[13]

In the California Jury Instructions for voluntary manslaughter it is explained that: "A **natural and probable consequence** is one that a reasonable person knows is likely to happen if nothing unusual intervenes . . . there may be more than one cause of death. An act causes death only if it is a substantial factor in causing the death . . . However, it does not need to be the only factor that causes death."[14]

The California Penal Code §192(a) defines voluntary manslaughter as the "unlawful killing of a human being without malice." The Code explains that there are three types of manslaughter: voluntary, involuntary, and vehicular. According to the language in the code, voluntary manslaughter is a killing upon a sudden quarrel or heat of passion. While not specifically mentioned in §192(a), voluntary manslaughter also includes imperfect self-defense, which are killings committed under an honest but unreasonable belief in the right to use deadly force in self-defense and those that are the natural and probable result of the killer's recklessness. California courts and legal commentators have affirmed the existence of this "unreasonable belief" rule almost universally as a humane principle of law that recognizes that malice cannot co-exist with an honest belief in the need to defend oneself, even if unreasonably held. This is explained by the California Supreme Court in *People v. Flannel*[15] included in this chapter.

Heat-of-passion killings are not automatically mitigated to manslaughter. There are three key requirements that must be met in order for a defendant to succeed on such a claim. First, the killer must act in response to **legally adequate provocation;** they must experience a sudden heat of passion, and must not have an opportunity to "cool off" prior to the act of killing. The provocation must be the result of something the law recognizes as adequate, such as the murder of a family member, a sudden and violent quarrel, or the infidelity of a lover. Common examples of provocation that is not legally adequate are insulting words or gestures, the desire for revenge, or the vandalism of an automobile. Provocation alone is not enough to mitigate murder to manslaughter. The provocation must produce actual passion, a violent, intense, highly-wrought emotional response. In *People v. Breverman* (1998)[16] the court noted that the killer's reason was actually obscured as a result of a strong passion aroused by provocation sufficient to cause an "ordinary [person] of average disposition . . . to act rashly or without due deliberation."

The last requirement, that there be no "cooling off" period, does not have a rule regarding the precise amount of time within which an ordinary person must have cooled off. In some cases, it might be reasonable to expect a person to cool off in a matter of moments, while in others, a person might not cool off for months or years. The test is

---

[12] *People v. Ireland*, 70 Cal.2d 522 (1969).

[13] CALCRIM No. 572 (2010).

[14] CALCRIM No. 572 (2010).

[15] *People v. Flannel*, 25 Cal.3d 668 (1979).

[16] *People v. Breverman*, 19 Cal.4th 142 (1998).

one of reasonableness: Would a reasonable person in the same or similar circumstances have cooled off prior to the act of killing the victim? In the highly publicized 1993 killing of her son's alleged molester, Ellie Nesler pleaded guilty to voluntary manslaughter for killing Daniel Driver. Nesler fired the shots at Driver during his preliminary hearing in Jamestown, California, nearly five years after the alleged molestation of her son took place. It is reasonable to believe that Nesler was still acting in a heat of passion, even after five years had passed.

The elements of *voluntary manslaughter* are:

- Actus reus—the intentional killing of another

- Mens rea—the killer acted either:

  - under a sudden heat of passion in response to legally adequate provocation; or

  - under an honest but unreasonable belief in the right to use deadly force; or

  - the killer intentionally engaged in an act dangerous to human life or safety and consciously disregarded that risk.

- Causation—the defendant set in motion the chain of events that led to the victim's death (a causal connection between the act of killing and the resulting death)

- Injury—death resulted

The punishment for voluntary manslaughter is three, six or 11 years in state prison.[17] As noted by the court in *Flannel,* "In short, the state has no legitimate interest in obtaining a conviction for murder when, by virtue of a defendant's unreasonable belief, the jury entertains a reasonable doubt about whether the defendant harbored malice."[18]

INVOLUNTARY MANSLAUGHTER

Involuntary manslaughter results from killings committed unintentionally with criminal negligence. California Penal Code §192(b) explains that involuntary manslaughter occurs in the commission of an unlawful act not amounting to a felony, or in the commission of a lawful act that might produce death if it is committed in an unlawful manner, or without due caution and circumspection. In *People v. Penny,* the California Supreme Court held that "lack of due caution and circumspection" is the equivalent of **criminal negligence.**

The California Jury Instructions explain that "The difference between other homicide offenses and involuntary manslaughter depends on whether the person was aware of the risk to life that his or her actions created and consciously disregarded that risk. An unlawful killing caused by a willful act done with full knowledge and awareness that the person is endangering the life of another, and done in conscious disregard of that risk, is voluntary manslaughter or murder. An unlawful killing resulting from a willful act committed without intent to kill and without conscious disregard of the risk to human life is involuntary manslaughter."[19] Criminal negligence is present if the defendant's conduct is so different from the way an ordinarily careful person would act in the same situation that his or her conduct amounts to disregard for human life or indifference to the consequences of that act.[20] The punishment for involuntary manslaughter is two, three, or four years in state prison.[21]

The elements of *involuntary manslaughter* are:

- Actus reus—the defendant either:

  - committed a misdemeanor (unlawful act*) that posed a high risk of death or great bodily injury because of the way it was committed; or

---

[17] Cal P.C. §193(a).

[18] *People v. Flannel,* 25 Cal.3d 668 (1979).

[19] CALJIC No. 580.

[20] CALJIC No. 580.

[21] Cal. Pen. Code §193.

- committed a lawful act, but acted with criminal negligence; or

- had a legal duty to act and failed to perform that legal duty, and failure to do so was criminally negligent

*Note: The unlawful act need not be inherently dangerous, it must only be dangerous under the circumstances of its commission (this differs from the requirement that a felony be inherently dangerous when applying the second degree felony murder doctrine).[22]

- Mens rea—the killer intended to engage in the unlawful act or failed to adhere to the ordinary standard of care for a reasonable person under the circumstances

- Causation—the defendant set in motion the chain of events that led to the victim's death (a causal connection between the act of killing and the resulting death)

- Injury—death resulted (Note that manslaughter does not apply to the death of a fetus based on the specific wording of §192)

VEHICULAR MANSLAUGHTER

Vehicular manslaughter is defined in the California Penal Code §191.5(a) providing that:

Gross vehicular manslaughter while intoxicated is the unlawful killing of a human being without malice aforethought, in the driving of a vehicle:

- in violation of §23140 (which prohibits driving under the influence by a person under age 21), or

- §23152 (which prohibits driving under the influence of alcohol or drugs or the combined influence of both, sets the blood alcohol requirement at .08, and has provisions regarding driving commercial vehicles), or

- §23153 (which prohibits driving under the influence of drugs, alcohol, or both and concurrently committing an unlawful act or omission, which causes injury to another, and driving with a blood alcohol content of .08 or higher) of the Vehicle Code, and

- where the killing was either the proximate result of the commission of an unlawful act, not amounting to a felony, and with gross negligence, or the proximate result of the commission of a lawful act that might produce death, in an unlawful manner, and with gross negligence

The California Jury Instructions explain that gross negligence is conduct that "involves more than ordinary carelessness, inattention, or mistake in judgment. A person acts with **gross negligence** when: 1) He or she acts in a reckless way that creates a high risk of death or great bodily injury, AND 2) A reasonable person would have known that acting in that way would create such a risk . . . The combination of driving a vehicle while under the influence of an alcoholic beverage or drug is not enough by itself to establish gross negligence . . . [jurors should] consider the level of the defendant's intoxication; the way the defendant drove; and any other relevant aspects of the defendant's conduct."[23]

The elements of *gross vehicular manslaughter while intoxicated* are:

- Actus reus—a defendant drove a vehicle or vessel under the influence of alcohol, drugs, or the combination of both (with a blood alcohol level of .08 or higher for adults or .05 or higher when under 21 years of age) and while driving, committed a misdemeanor or an infraction, or otherwise lawful act that might cause death

- Mens rea—the defendant committed the act with gross negligence

---

[22] *People v. Wells,* 12 Cal.4th 979, 982 (1996).

[23] *People v. Wells,* 12 Cal.4th 979, 982 (1996).

- Causation—the defendant's grossly negligent conduct caused the death of the victim (the death must have been a natural and probable consequence of the defendant's conduct, and must have been a substantial factor in causing death, but need not have been the sole cause of death)

- Injury—death resulted[24]

California Penal Code §191.5(b) provides for the offense of vehicular manslaughter while intoxicated (without gross negligence). The key difference between this and gross vehicular manslaughter is that it requires only ordinary negligence as the mens rea. Ordinary negligence is the failure to use reasonable care to prevent reasonably foreseeable harm to oneself or someone else.[25] The same requirements apply relating to causation as well: the victim's death must be a natural and probable consequence of the defendant's conduct, and if there is more than one cause of death, the defendant's conduct need not be the sole cause, but must be a substantial factor in causing the victim's death.

In addition to vehicular manslaughter that occurs when the defendant is under the influence of drugs or alcohol, a person may be charged with gross vehicular manslaughter for causing the death of another while driving or operating a vehicle or vessel with gross negligence.[26] This offense differs from gross vehicular manslaughter while intoxicated simply because the defendant acted in a grossly negligent manner, without the influence of alcohol or drugs. Vehicular manslaughter is a wobbler, which can be charged as either a misdemeanor (punishable by up to one year in jail or prison) or a felony (punishable by two, four, six, or 10 years depending upon the specific nature of the case).[27]

The elements of *gross vehicular manslaughter* are:

- Actus reus—the defendant, while driving a vehicle or vessel, committed a misdemeanor or an infraction, or otherwise lawful act that might cause death

- Mens rea—the defendant committed the act with gross negligence

- Causation—the defendant's grossly negligent conduct caused the death of the victim (the death must have been a natural and probable consequence of the defendant's conduct, and must have been a substantial factor in causing death, but need not have been the sole cause of death)

- Injury—death resulted[28]

---

[24] CALCRIM No. 590 (2010).

[25] CALCRIM No. 591 (2010).

[26] Cal. Pen. Code §192(c)(1).

[27] Cal. Pen. Code §193(c)(1–3).

[28] CALCRIM No. 590 (2010).

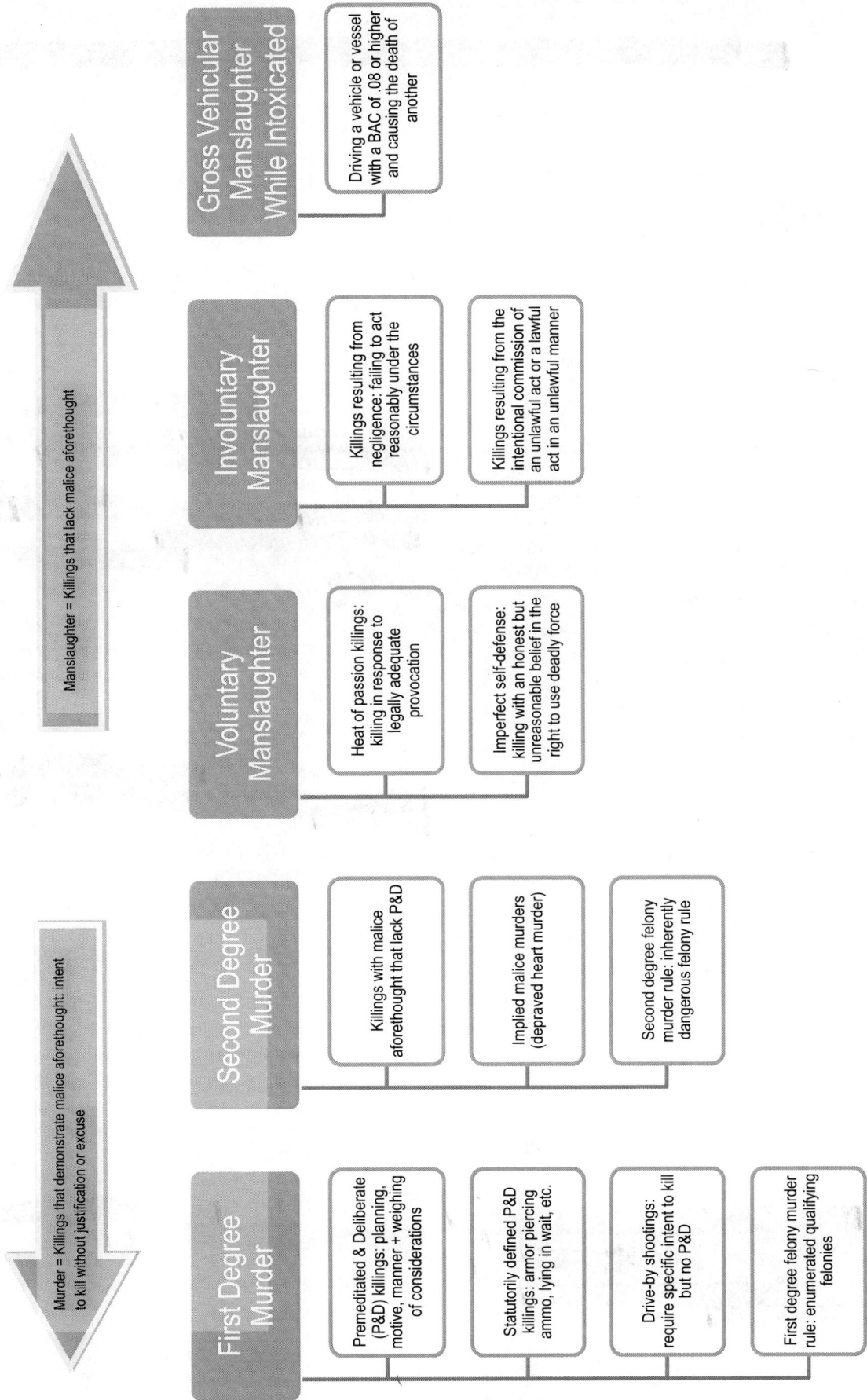

Murder = Killings that demonstrate malice aforethought: intent to kill without justification or excuse

Manslaughter = Killings that lack malice aforethought

First Degree Murder

- Premeditated & Deliberate (P&D) killings: planning, motive, manner + weighing of considerations
- Statutorily defined P&D killings: armor piercing ammo, lying in wait, etc.
- Drive-by shootings: require specific intent to kill but no P&D
- First degree felony murder rule: enumerated qualifying felonies

Second Degree Murder

- Killings with malice aforethought that lack P&D
- Implied malice murders (depraved heart murder)
- Second degree felony murder rule: inherently dangerous felony rule

Voluntary Manslaughter

- Heat of passion killings: killing in response to legally adequate provocation
- Imperfect self-defense: killing with an honest but unreasonable belief in the right to use deadly force

Involuntary Manslaughter

- Killings resulting from negligence: failing to act reasonably under the circumstances
- Killings resulting from the intentional commission of an unlawful act or a lawful act in an unlawful manner

Gross Vehicular Manslaughter While Intoxicated

- Driving a vehicle or vessel with a BAC of .08 or higher and causing the death of another

KEELER V. THE SUPERIOR COURT OF AMADOR COUNTY

SUPREME COURT OF CALIFORNIA

2 Cal. 3d 619; 470 P.2d 617; 87 Cal. Rptr. 48

June 12, 1970

OPINION BY: MOSK, J.

In this proceeding for writ of prohibition we are called upon to decide whether an unborn but viable fetus is a "human being" within the meaning of the California statute defining murder (*Pen. Code, § 187*). We conclude that the Legislature did not intend such a meaning, and that for us to construe the statute to the contrary and apply it to this petitioner would exceed our judicial power and deny petitioner due process of law.

The evidence received at the preliminary examination may be summarized as follows: Petitioner and Teresa Keeler obtained an interlocutory decree of divorce on September 27, 1968. They had been married for 16 years. Unknown to petitioner, Mrs. Keeler was then pregnant by one Ernest Vogt, whom she had met earlier that summer. She subsequently began living with Vogt in Stockton, but concealed the fact from petitioner. Petitioner was given custody of their two daughters, aged 12 and 13 years, and under the decree Mrs. Keeler had the right to take the girls on alternate weekends.

On February 23, 1969, Mrs. Keeler was driving on a narrow mountain road in Amador County after delivering the girls to their home. She met petitioner driving in the opposite direction; he blocked the road with his car, and she pulled over to the side. He walked to her vehicle and began speaking to her. He seemed calm, and she rolled down her window to hear him. He said, "I hear you're pregnant. If you are you had better stay away from the girls and from here." She did not reply, and he opened the car door; as she later testified, "He assisted me out of the car. . . . [It] wasn't roughly at this time." Petitioner then looked at her abdomen and became "extremely upset." He said, "You sure are. I'm going to stomp it out of you." He pushed her against the car, shoved his knee into her abdomen, and struck her in the face with several blows. She fainted, and when she regained consciousness petitioner had departed.

Mrs. Keeler drove back to Stockton, and the police and medical assistance were summoned. She had suffered substantial facial injuries, as well as extensive bruising of the abdominal wall. A Caesarian section was performed and the fetus was examined *in utero*. Its head was found to be severely fractured, and it was delivered stillborn. The pathologist gave as his opinion that the cause of death was skull fracture with consequent cerebral hemorrhaging, that death would have been immediate, and that the injury could have been the result of force applied to the mother's abdomen. There was no air in the fetus' lungs, and the umbilical cord was intact.

Upon delivery the fetus weighed 5 pounds and was 18 inches in length. Both Mrs. Keeler and her obstetrician testified that fetal movements had been observed prior to February 23, 1969. The evidence was in conflict as to the estimated age of the fetus; n1 the expert testimony on the point, however, concluded "with reasonable medical certainty" that the fetus had developed to the stage of viability, i.e., that in the event of premature birth on the date in question it would have had a 75 per cent to 96 per cent chance of survival.

> n1 Mrs. Keeler testified, in effect, that she had no sexual intercourse with Vogt prior to August 1968, which would have made the fetus some 28 weeks old. She stated that the pregnancy had reached the end of the seventh month and the projected delivery date was April 25, 1969. The obstetrician, however, first estimated she was at least 31 1/2 weeks pregnant, then raised the figure to 35 weeks in the light of the autopsy report of the size and weight of the fetus. Finally, on similar evidence an attending pediatrician estimated the gestation period to have been between 34 1/2 and 36 weeks. The average full-term pregnancy is 40 weeks.

An information was filed charging petitioner, in count I, with committing the crime of murder (*Pen. Code § 187*) in that he did "unlawfully kill a human being, to wit Baby Girl Vogt, with malice aforethought."

. . .

By the year 1850 this rule of the common law had long been accepted in the United States. As early as 1797, it was held that proof the child was born alive is necessary to support an indictment for murder (*State v. McKee* (Pa.) Addison 1), and the same rule was reiterated on the eve of the first session of our Legislature (*State v. Cooper* (1849) 22 N.J.L. 52). Although, the precise issue in *Cooper* was whether an attempted abortion on a woman whose fetus had not yet "quickened" was a common law crime, the opinion begins by a recital of the common law rules on abortional homicide. In its argument the State took the position that attempted abortion was an offense against the person of the child, and the court replied that "the very point of inquiry is, whether that be at all an offense or not, and whether the child be *in esse,* so that any crime can be committed against its person. In regard to offences against the person of the child, a distinction is well settled between its condition before and after its birth. Thus, it is not murder to kill a child before it be born, even though it be killed in the very process of delivery." (*Id.* at p. 54.)

. . .

We conclude that in declaring murder to be the unlawful and malicious killing of a "human being" the Legislature of 1850 intended that term to have the settled common law meaning of a person who had been born alive, and did not intend the act of feticide—as distinguished from abortion—to be an offense under the laws of California.

Nothing occurred between the years 1850 and 1872 to suggest that in adopting the new Penal Code on the latter date the Legislature entertained any different intent. The case law of our sister states, for example, remained consonant with the common law. In *Abrams v. Foshee (Cole ed. 1856) 3 Iowa 274, 278,* the court noted that Iowa's feticide statute (Iowa Rev. Stat. 1843, § 10) had been repealed by the Iowa Code of 1851; it was contended that an unborn child is nevertheless "*a human being,* within the meaning of [Iowa Code] section 2508, which provides that whoever kills any human being, with malice aforethought, either express or implied, is guilty of *murder.*" The court observed that "notwithstanding the infant in *ventre sa mere,* is treated by the law for some purposes, as born, or as a human being, yet we are not aware that it has been so treated, so far as to make the act of its miscarriage *murder,* unless so declared by statute. . . . When the child is born, however, it becomes a human being, within the meaning of the law; and if it shall then die, by reason of any potions or bruises it received in the womb, it would be murder in those who administered or gave them, with a view of causing the miscarriage." (*Ibid.*) Citing Blackstone, Coke, and other authorities, the court concluded that "an infant in *ventre sa mere,* is not a human being within the meaning of" the statute defining murder. (*Id.* at p. 279.) . . .

. . .

Settled rules of construction implement this principle. Although the Penal Code commands us to construe its provisions "according to the fair import of their terms, with a view to effect its objects and to promote justice" (*Pen. Code, § 4*), it is clear the courts cannot go so far as to create an offense by enlarging a statute, by inserting or deleting words, or by giving the terms used false or unusual meanings. (*People v. Baker* (1968) 69 Cal.2d 44, 50 {69 Cal.Rptr. 595, 442 P.2d 675}.) Penal statutes will not be made to reach beyond their plain intent; they include only those offenses coming clearly within the import of their language. (*De Mille v. American Fed. of Radio Artists* (1947) 31 Cal.2d 139, 156 {187 P.2d 769, 175 A.L.R. 382}.) Indeed, "Constructive crimes—crimes built up by courts with the aid of inference, implication, and strained interpretation—are repugnant to the spirit and letter of English and American criminal law." (*Ex parte McNulty* (1888) 77 Cal. 164, 168 {19 P. 237}.)

Applying these rules to the case at bar, we would undoubtedly act in excess of the judicial power if we were to adopt the People's proposed construction of section 187. As we have shown, the Legislature has defined the crime of murder in California to apply only to the unlawful and malicious killing of one who has been born alive. We recognize that the killing of an unborn but viable fetus may be deemed by some to be an offense of similar nature and gravity; but as Chief Justice Marshall warned long ago, "It would be dangerous, indeed, to carry the principle, that a case which is within the reason or mischief of a statute, is within its provisions, so far as to punish a crime not enumerated in the statute, because it is of equal atrocity, or of kindred character, with those which are enumerated." (*United States v. Wiltberger* (1820) 18 U.S. (5 Wheat.) 76, 96 {5 L.Ed. 37, 42}.) Whether to thus extend liability for murder in California is a determination solely within the province of the Legislature. n16 For a court to simply declare, by judicial fiat, that the time has now come to prosecute under section 187 one who kills an unborn but viable fetus would indeed be to rewrite the statute under the guise of construing it.

. . .

The second obstacle to the proposed judicial enlargement of section 187 is the guarantee of due process of law. Assuming *arguendo* that we have the power to adopt the new construction of this statute as the law of California, such a ruling, by constitutional command, could operate only prospectively, and thus could not in any event reach the conduct of petitioner on February 23, 1969.

. . .

Turning to the case law, we find no reported decision of the California courts which should have given petitioner notice that the killing of an unborn but viable fetus was prohibited by section 187. Indeed, the contrary clearly appears from *People v. Eldridge (1906) 3 Cal.App. 648, 649 {86 p. 832}*, in which the defendant challenged as uncertain an information which charged him with the murder of "a human being," to wit, the infant child "born to the said Glover H. Eldridge and said Mabel Eldridge on or about said twentieth day of February, 1905." It was urged that "such charge might include the killing before birth, and therefore it cannot be determined from the information whether murder or abortion was intended to be charged." The Court of Appeal rejected the contention, observing that "The only reasonable construction which can be given to the language employed in the information is to say that it charges that a child born to the defendant was by him unlawfully killed and murdered. That it was born is clearly stated; that it could be killed after birth of necessity implies that *it was born alive*, and we think the charge of murder was set forth with the degree of certainty required." (Italics added.)

Properly understood, the often cited case of *People v. Chavez (1947) 77 Cal.App.2d 621 {176 P.2d 92}*, does not derogate from this rule. There the defendant was charged with the murder of her newborn child, and convicted of manslaughter. She testified that the baby dropped from her womb into the toilet bowl; that she picked it up 2 or 3 minutes later, and cut but did not tie the umbilical cord; that the baby was limp and made no cry; and that after 15 minutes she wrapped it in a newspaper and concealed it, where it was found dead the next day. The autopsy surgeon testified that the baby was a full-term, 9-month child, weighing six and one-half pounds and appearing normal in every respect; that the body had very little blood in it, indicating the child had bled to death through the untied umbilical cord; that such a process would have taken about an hour; and that in his opinion "the child was born alive, based on conditions he found and the fact that the lungs contained air and the blood was extravasated or pushed back into the tissues, indicating heart action." (*Id.* at p. 623.)

On appeal, the defendant emphasized that a doctor called by the defense had suggested other tests which the autopsy surgeon could have performed to determine the matter of live birth; on this basis, it was contended that the question of whether the infant was born alive "rests entirely on pure speculation." (*Id.* at p. 624.) The Court of Appeal found only an insignificant conflict in that regard (*id.* at p. 627), and focussed its attention instead on testimony of the autopsy surgeon admitting the possibility that the evidence of heart and lung action could have resulted from the child's breathing "after presentation of the head but before the birth was completed" (*id.* at p. 624).

. . .

Chavez thus stands for the proposition—to which we adhere—that a viable fetus "in the process of being born" is a human being within the meaning of the homicide statutes. But it stands for no more; in particular it does not hold that a fetus, however viable, which is *not* "in the process of being born" is nevertheless a "human being" in the law of homicide. On the contrary, the opinion is replete with references to the common law requirement that the child be "born alive," however that term as defined, and must accordingly be deemed to reaffirm that requirement as part of the law of California. n20

> n20 In *People v. Belous (1969) 71 Cal.2d 954, 968–969 {80 Cal.Rptr. 354, 458 P.2d 194}*, a majority of this court recognized "there are major and decisive areas where the embryo and fetus are not treated as equivalent to the born child. . . . The intentional destruction of the born child is murder or manslaughter. The intentional destruction of the embryo or fetus is never treated as murder, and only rarely as manslaughter but rather as the lesser offense of abortion." . . .

Inasmuch as such rules coexisted for centuries with the common law requirement of live birth to support a conviction of homicide, they cannot reasonably be deemed to have given petitioner notice that the killing of an unborn but viable fetus would now be murder.

. . .

We conclude that the judicial enlargement of section 187 now urged upon us by the People would not have been foreseeable to this petitioner, and hence that its adoption at this time would deny him due process of law.

. . .

DISSENT:

BURKE, Acting C. J. The majority hold that "Baby Girl" Vogt, who, according to medical testimony, had reached the 35th week of development, had a 96 per cent chance of survival, and was "definitely" alive and viable at the time of her death, nevertheless was not a "human being" under California's homicide statutes. In my view, in so holding, the majority ignore significant common law precedents, frustrate the express intent of the Legislature, and defy reason, logic and common sense.

Penal Code section 187 defines murder as "the unlawful killing of a human being, with malice aforethought." *Penal Code section 192* defines manslaughter as "the unlawful killing of a human being, without malice." The majority pursue the meaning of the term "human being" down the ancient hallways of the common law, citing Coke,

Blackstone and Hale to the effect that the slaying of a "quickened" (i.e., stirring in the womb) child constituted "a great misprision," but not murder. Although, as discussed below, I strongly disagree with the premise that the words of our penal statutes must be construed as of 1648 or 1765, nevertheless, there is much common law precedent which would support the view that a viable fetus such as Baby Girl Vogt is a human being under those statutes.

. . .

Modern scholars have confirmed this aspect of common law jurisprudence. As Means observes, "The common law itself prohibited abortion after quickening and hanging a pregnant felon after quickening, *because the life of a second human being would thereby be taken,* although it did not call the offense murder or manslaughter." (Italics added; Means, *The Law of New York Concerning Abortion and the Status of the Foetus, 1664–1968: A Case of Cessation of Constitutionality (1968) 14 N.Y.L.F. 411, 504.)*

This reasoning explains why the killing of a quickened child was considered "a great misprision," although the killing of an unquickened child was no crime at all at common law (Means, *supra*, at p. 420). Moreover, although the common law did not apply the labels of "murder" or "manslaughter" to the killing of a quickened fetus, it appears that at common law this "great misprision" was severely punished.

. . .

. . . We should not presume that the Legislature ignored these common law developments and intended to punish the malicious killing of a viable fetus as the lesser offense of illegal abortion. Moreover, apart from the common law approach, our Legislature has expressly directed us to construe the homicide statutes in accordance with the fair import of their terms. There is no good reason why a fully viable fetus should not be considered a "human being" under those statutes. To so construe them would not create any new offense, and would not deny defendant fair warning or due process since the *Chavez* case anticipated that construction long ago.

The trial court's denial of defendant's motion to set aside the information was proper, and the peremptory writ of prohibition should be denied.

SUPREME COURT OF CALIFORNIA

7 Cal. 4th 797; 872 P.2d 591; 30 Cal. Rptr. 2d 50

May 16, 1994

OPINION BY: LUCAS, C. J.

Penal Code section 187, subdivision (a), provides that "Murder is the unlawful killing of a human being, or a fetus, with malice aforethought." (All further statutory references are to the Penal Code unless otherwise indicated.) In this case, we consider and reject the argument that viability of a fetus is an element of fetal murder under the statute. As will appear, however, we also conclude that this holding should not apply to defendant herein. Accordingly, we will affirm the judgment of the Court of Appeal.

FACTS

On March 1, 1991, Maria Flores, who was between 23 and 25 weeks pregnant, and her 20-month-old son, Hector, went to a check-cashing store to cash her welfare check. As Flores left the store, defendant pulled a gun from the waistband of his pants and demanded the money ($378) in her purse. When she refused to hand over the purse, defendant shot her in the chest. Flores dropped Hector as she fell to the floor and defendant fled the scene.

Flores underwent surgery to save her life. Although doctors sutured small holes in the uterine wall to prevent further bleeding, no further obstetrical surgery was undertaken because of the immaturity of the fetus. The next day, the fetus was stillborn as a direct result of its mother's blood loss, low blood pressure and state of shock. Defendant was soon apprehended and charged with assaulting and robbing Flores, as well as murdering her fetus. The prosecution charged a special circumstance of robbery-murder. (§ 190.2, subd. (a).)

At trial, the prosecution's medical experts testified the fetus' statistical chances of survival outside the womb were between 7 and 47 per cent. The defense medical expert testified it was "possible for the fetus to have survived, but its chances were only 2 or 3 per cent." None of the medical experts testified that survival of the fetus was "probable."

Although section 187, subdivision (a), does not expressly require a fetus be medically viable before the statute's provisions can be applied to a criminal defendant, the trial court followed several Court of Appeal decisions and instructed the jury that it must find the fetus was viable before it could find defendant guilty of murder under the statute. The trial court did not, however, give the standard viability instruction, *CALJIC No. 8.10;* which states that: "A viable human fetus is one who has attained such form and development of organs as to be normally capable of living outside of the uterus." The jury, however, was given an instruction that allowed it to convict defendant of murder if it found the fetus had a possibility of survival: "A fetus is viable when it has achieved the capability for independent existence; that is, when it is *possible* for it to survive the trauma of birth, although with artificial medical aid." (Italics added.)

The jury convicted defendant of murder of a fetus during the course of a robbery (§ 187, subd. (a); § 190.2, subd. (a)(17)(i)), assault with a firearm (§ 245, subd. (a)(2)) and robbery (§ 211). The jury found that, in the commission of each offense, defendant personally used a firearm. (§ 12022.5, subd. (a).) The jury found true the special circumstance allegation. Accordingly, because the prosecutor did not seek the death penalty, defendant was sentenced to life without possibility of parole, plus 5 years for the firearm use.

On appeal, defendant contended that the trial court prejudicially erred by not instructing the jury pursuant to *CALJIC No. 8.10.* He relied on United States Supreme Court decisions that have defined viability of a fetus in terms of "probabilities, not possibilities" when limiting a woman's absolute right to an abortion. (See *Roe v. Wade (1973) 410 U.S. 113, 163 {35 L.Ed.2d 147, 182–183, 93 S.Ct. 705}* [defining viability as that point in fetal development when a fetus, if born, would be capable of living normally outside the womb]; *Planned Parenthood* v. *Casey (1992)* [reaffirming Roe's viability definition].) By analogy to the abortion cases, defendant asserted that a fetus is not viable under section 187, subdivision (a), unless "there is a reasonable likelihood of [its] sustained survival outside the womb, with or without artificial support." (*Colautti v. Franklin* (1979) 439 U.S. 379, 388 {58 L.Ed.2d 596, 605, 99 S.Ct. 675}.) Thus, defendant claimed, rather than defining viability as a "reasonable possibility of survival," the trial court should have instructed the jury under the higher "probability" threshold described in *CALJIC No. 8.10*.

The People argued that no viability instruction was necessary because prosecution under section 187, subdivision (a), does not require that the fetus be viable. After reviewing the wording of section 187, subdivision (a), its legislative history, the treatment of the issue in other jurisdictions, and scholarly comment on the subject, the Court of Appeal agreed with the People that contrary to prior California decisions, fetal viability is not a required element of murder under the statute. Nonetheless, the court reversed defendant's murder conviction and set aside the special circumstance finding, on the ground that application to defendant of its unprecedented interpretation of section 187, subdivision (a), would violate due process principles.

As explained below, we agree with the People and the Court of Appeal that viability is not an element of fetal murder under section 187, subdivision (a), and conclude therefore that the statute does not require an instruction on viability as a prerequisite to a murder conviction. In addition, because every prior decision that had addressed the viability issue had determined that viability of the fetus was prerequisite to a murder conviction under section 187, subdivision (a), we also agree with the Court of Appeal that application of our construction of the statute to defendant would violate due process and *ex post facto* principles. (*People v. King* (1993) 5 Cal.4th 59, 80 {19 Cal.Rptr.2d 233, 851 P.2d 27})

. . .

Thus, we conclude we should affirm the Court of Appeal judgment in its entirety (affirming the assault and robbery counts and reversing the judgment of murder).

DISCUSSION

I. Historical Development

In 1970, section 187, subdivision (a), provided: "Murder is the unlawful killing of a human being, with malice aforethought." In *Keeler v. Superior Court* (1970) 2 Cal.3d 619 {87 Cal.Rptr. 481, 470 P.2d 617, 40 A.L.R.3d 420}, a majority of the court held that a man who had killed a fetus carried by his estranged wife could not be prosecuted for murder because the Legislature (consistent with the common law view) probably intended the phrase "human being" to mean a person who had been born alive.

The Legislature reacted to the *Keeler* decision by amending the murder statute, section 187, subdivision (a), to include within its proscription the killing of a fetus. (Stats. 1970, ch. 1311, § 1, p. 2440.) The amended statute reads: "Murder is the unlawful killing of a human being, or a fetus, with malice aforethought." (§ 187, subd. (a).) The amended statute specifically provides that it does not apply to abortions complying with the Therapeutic Abortion Act, performed by a doctor when the death of the mother was substantially certain in the absence of an abortion, or whenever the mother solicited, aided, and otherwise chose to abort the fetus. (§ 187, subd. (b).)

The legislative history of the amendment suggests the term "fetus" was deliberately left undefined after the Legislature debated whether to limit the scope of statutory application to a viable fetus. (Comment, *Is the Intentional Killing of an Unborn Child Homicide?* (1970) 2 Pacific L.J. 170, 174.) The Legislature was clearly aware that it could have limited the term "fetus" to "viable fetus," for it specifically rejected a proposed amendment that required the fetus be at least 20 weeks in gestation before the statute would apply. (Assem. Bill No. 816 (1970 Reg. Sess.).)

. . .

II. Statutory Interpretation

Defendant asserts that section 187, subdivision (a), has no application to a fetus not meeting *Roe* v. *Wade's* definition of viability. Essentially, defendant claims that because the fetus could have been legally aborted under *Roe v. Wade*, *supra*, 410 U.S. at p. 163 [35 L.Ed.2d at pp. 182–183], at the time it was killed, it did not attain the protection of section 187, subdivision (a). Defendant relies on *K.A. Smith, supra, 59 Cal.App.3d 751*, and its progeny to assert that if a fetus has not attained "independent human life" status under *Roe v. Wade, supra,* 410 U.S. at p. 163 [35 L.Ed.2d at pp. 182–183], it has not achieved "viability" under *K.A. Smith, supra, 59 Cal.App.3d at p. 759*, and he therefore cannot be prosecuted under section 187, subdivision (a), for its murder.

But *Roe v. Wade, supra, 410 U.S. 113*, does not hold that the state has no legitimate interest in protecting the fetus until viability. Indeed, contrary to the decisions in *K.A. Smith, supra, 59 Cal.App.3d 751, People v. Apodaca, supra, 76 Cal.App.3d 479, R.P. Smith, supra, 188 Cal.App.3d 1495,* and *Henderson, supra, 225 Cal.App.3d 1129, Roe v. Wade* principles are inapplicable to a statute (like section 187, subdivision (a)) that criminalizes the killing of a fetus without the mother's consent. As observed by one commentator: "By holding that the Fourteenth Amendment does not cover the unborn, the Supreme Court was left with only one constitutionally mandated right, that of the mother's privacy, to be considered along with the legitimate state interest in protecting an unborn's potential life. The Roe decision, therefore, forbids the state's protection of the unborn's interests only when these interests conflict with the constitutional rights of the prospective parent. The Court did not rule that the unborn's interests could not be recognized in situations where there was no conflict."

. . .

The Illinois and Minnesota appellate courts have rejected equal protection and due process challenges to their feticide statutes. The challenges were based on the statutes' asserted failure to distinguish between viable and nonviable fetuses. As discussed below, the arguments were rejected on the ground that protection of a woman's privacy interest in the abortion context is not applicable to a nonconsensual murder of the unborn child.

. . .

Although the Illinois and Minnesota statutes specifically state that viability is not an element to be considered for their application, both *Ford* and *Merrill* illustrate that criminalization of the killing of a fetus without regard to viability is not violative of either privacy principles, equal protection, or due process considerations. Both cases also illustrate that the Legislature is free to impose upon the killer of a fetus the same penalty as is Prescribed for the murder of a human being (although in neither state has the Legislature permitted application of the death penalty for the murder of a fetus).

Like Illinois and Minnesota, California is a "code" state, i.e., the Legislature has the exclusive province to define by statute what acts constitute a crime (§ 6), and statutory provisions must "be construed according to the fair import of their terms, with a view to effect [their] objects and to promote justice." (§ 4.) Under these principles, like Illinois and Minnesota, we find no impediment to our Legislature protecting the "potentiality of human life" from homicide.

Finally, both *Ford* and *Merrill* expressly distinguish fetal homicide from the abortion issue. Our Legislature does the same. Abortion is specifically exempted from section 187 under subdivision (b)(3), which states that section 187 shall not apply if, "The act was solicited, aided, abetted, or consented to by the mother of the fetus."

We conclude, therefore, that when the mother's privacy interests are not at stake, the Legislature may determine whether, and at what point, it should protect life inside a mother's womb from homicide. Here, the Legislature determined that the offense of murder includes the murder of a fetus with malice aforethought.

. . .

We conclude, therefore, that defendant was prejudiced by the instructional error and the conviction of fetal murder must be reversed.

CONCLUSION

We conclude that viability is not an element of fetal homicide under section 187, subdivision (a). The third party killing of a fetus with malice aforethought is murder under section 187, subdivision (a), as long as the state can show that the fetus has progressed beyond the embryonic stage of 7 to 8 weeks.

We also conclude that our holding should not apply to defendant and that the trial court committed prejudicial error by instructing the jury pursuant to a modified version of *CALJIC No. 8.10.* We therefore affirm the judgment of the Court of Appeal.

. . .

COURT OF APPEAL OF CALIFORNIA, THIRD APPELLATE DISTRICT

91 CAL. APP. 3D 1018; 154 CAL. RPTR. 628

APRIL 17, 1979

OPINION BY: EVANS, J.

Defendant, Anita Mathews, appeals from a judgment entered following her conviction of the voluntary manslaughter n1 of Donald Silva (*Pen. Code, § 192*), and discharging a firearm at a vehicle (*Veh. Code, § 23110,* subd. (b)), as charged in count two. The jury also found that the defendant used a firearm within the meaning of *Penal Code section 12022.5* during the commission of both crimes. Defendant was acquitted of the attempted murder of Darelle Ghormley, as charged in count three.

> n1 Defendant Mathews had been charged with murder (*Pen. Code, § 187*) as was codefendant Joe Waters; Waters was acquitted of all charges.

The charges against defendant arise from an incident occurring on December 13, 1976, in which defendant, while unsuccessfully attempting to kill Darelle Ghormley, fatally injured Donald Silva.

The record discloses defendant and Ghormley had dated on two or three occasions in November 1976. Their activities were mostly limited to Ghormley visiting defendant at her house where he had sexual relations with her. Ghormley testified that on the last of these dates, he took defendant to his house where he and two friends had sexual intercourse with her.

On the day of the fatal shooting Ghormley, a passenger in a car driven by decedent Donald Silva, had an occasion to stop at defendant's house. Defendant, with the assistance of Joe Waters, was in the process of moving out of the house; as defendant and Joe Waters were walking to Waters' car, she observed Ghormley in a car driven by Silva. Upon recognizing Ghormley, she momentarily froze, but quickly returned to Waters' vehicle. Ghormley had heard rumors that defendant had publicly accused him of having raped her; and when he saw defendant, he asked Silva to leave in order to avoid any possible trouble.

Defendant returned to Waters' car and declared, "[that's] him" and told Richard Grigg, a passenger in the Waters' car, to get out. Defendant and Waters then got into

Waters' car and pursued the Silva's vehicle. When Silva stopped at a red light, the Waters' vehicle drove alongside on Silva's passenger side. Ghormley testified that he noticed a shotgun extending through the vent window on the driver's side of the Waters' automobile and told Silva, "They got a gun, jump on it" and then ducked onto the floor, and heard successive gunshots and felt pieces of glass and buckshot in the back of his hair and along his neck. After the shots Ghormley looked up and observed that Silva had suffered what turned out to be fatal head injuries.

Defendant's version of the incident was somewhat different. She testified that after seeing Ghormley, she wanted to leave, but that Waters insisted on following Ghormley's car; and as Waters pulled alongside the other car, Ghormley began rolling down the car window and pointed a gun at her. Waters' testimony confirmed the existence of Ghormley's gun.

Following the shooting, defendant and Waters were apprehended in Truckee, California. After her arrest defendant gave a statement to Sacramento County Sheriff's detectives in which she admitted socializing with Ghormley, but denied she had been raped by Ghormley, or that he had stolen drugs from her, or that she had shot at anyone.

At trial defendant admitted the act of killing Silva. Her defense to the charges centered around her contention that the sexual incident in November 1976, involving Ghormley and his two friends, was not a consensual act but was instead a brutal rape, following which she suffered what was characterized as a "rape trauma syndrome." Upon this premise, she introduced psychiatric testimony tending to prove that when she saw Ghormley at her house, the "rape trauma syndrome" caused her to experience a genuine fear for her life, precipitating her subsequent actions. The psychiatric testimony also attempted to establish that as a result of the syndrome, defendant was unable to form the mental state necessary for malice aforethought.

On appeal defendant first contends the trial court should have instructed the jury *sua sponte* that a homicide is justified under the doctrine of self-defense where the act of self-defense, though directed towards the unlawful aggressor, inadvertently results in the death of an innocent bystander.

Preliminary to any analysis of whether the court has a duty so to instruct *sua sponte* is the question of whether that defense, under present circumstances, is even available. Research has disclosed no California case directly dealing with this issue. n2 However, considered decisions of other jurisdictions have uniformly held that self-defense is available to relieve one of criminal responsibility where his legitimate act of self-defense results in the inadvertent death or injury of an innocent bystander. (See e.g., Annot. (1974) 55 A.L.R.3d 620 and cases cited.)

> n2 The People's reliance upon *People v. Carson (1946) 74 Cal.App.2d 834, 841 {169 P.2d 677}*, is misplaced.

In *Carson* the defendant *intentionally* struck the victim attempting to get her out of his way so that he could defend against the assault being perpetrated upon him by the victim's sons. It is no authority for the situation where, as here, the act is directed towards the unlawful aggressor and *inadvertently* results in the injury of a nonaggressive party. Similarly distinguishable, although not cited by the People, is *People v. Martin (1910) 13 Cal.App. 96 {108 P. 1034}*.

Generally, decisions so holding rest upon the common law theory of "transferred intent" which, in its principal application, establishes that one's criminal intent follows the corresponding criminal act to its unintended consequences. As the noted cases have held, the reasoning applies equally to carry the *lack of criminal intent* to the unintended consequences and thus preclude criminal responsibility. The theory was explained in *State v. Clifton (1972) 32 Ohio App.2d 284 {61 Ohio Ops.2d 439, 290 N.E.2d 921, 923}*, as follows: "Clearly, one who kills in self-defense does so without the *mens rea* that otherwise would render him culpable of the homicide. Therefore, if the act of taking the life of an assailant is not criminal does it become so when a stray shot kills a bystander?"

"It has been long accepted that if A shoots at B, intending to kill B, but instead the bullet strikes C, then A has committed a criminal act as to C. In such instance, the 'malice follows the blow' and the criminal intent of A to harm B is transferred to C."

"However, if A had no criminal intent with respect to B, as where A is exercising a lawful right to self-defense, none could exist as to C. It follows, then, that A in shooting C has not committed a criminal act, the essential of a *mens rea* being impossible of proof. The inquiry must be whether the killing would have been justifiable if the accused had killed the person whom he intended to kill, as the unintended act derives its character from the intended."

. . .

The common law doctrine of transferred intent is recognized and followed in California. (*People v. Suesser (1904) 142 Cal. 354, 366–367 {75 P. 1093}; People v. Carlson (1974) 37 Cal.App.3d 349, 357 {112 Cal.Rptr. 321}; People v. Siplinger (1967) 252 Cal.App.2d 817, 825 {60 Cal.Rptr. 914}; People v. Clayton (1967) 248 Cal.App.2d 345, 349 {56 Cal.Rptr. 413}*; see 1 Witkin, Cal. Crimes (1963) Elements of Crime, § 61, p. 65.) We find nothing within the provisions of *Penal Code section 197*, n4 which codified in California the law of justifiable homicide, to preclude application of "transferred intent" to self-defense circumstances. Indeed, it has been held that *section 197* codifies the common law and should be construed accordingly. (*People v. Ceballos (1974) 12 Cal.3d 470, 478 {116 Cal.Rptr. 233, 526 P.2d 241}; People v. Jones (1961) 191 Cal.App.2d 478, 481 {12 Cal.Rptr. 777}*.) By reason of the foregoing cited authorities and analyses, we conclude that the doctrine of self-defense is available to insulate one from criminal responsibility where his act, justifiably in self-defense, inadvertently results in the injury of an innocent bystander.

> n4 *Penal Code section 197*, as applicable to the instant case, provides in pertinent part:

Homicide is also justifiable when committed by any person in any of the following cases:

> "1. When resisting any attempt to murder any person, . . . or to do some great bodily injury upon any person";

> ". . ."

> "3. When committed in the lawful defense of such person, . . . when there is reasonable ground to apprehend a design to commit a felony or to do some great bodily injury, and imminent danger to such design being accomplished; . . ."

. . .

If a defendant desires more specific instructions on the question of intent, he or she should request them. Furthermore, in this instance, it defies logic and common sense to assume the jury's rejection of defendant's malice and intent to kill (Ghormley) turned on consciousness of guilt. The overwhelming evidence dictates to the contrary. Defendant's reliance upon *People v. Anderson (1968) 70 Cal.2d 15, 32–33 {73 Cal.Rptr. 550, 447 P.2d 942}*, is misplaced, as that case rejected the use of consciousness of guilt as substantial evidence to uphold a finding of premeditated murder. It has no application where, as here the instruction was given as an aid for determining the threshold question of guilt or innocence.

The judgment is affirmed.

SUPREME COURT OF CALIFORNIA

28 CAL. 4TH 313; 48 P.3D 1107; 121 CAL. RPTR. 2D 546

JULY 1, 2002, DECIDED

JULY 1, 2002, FILED

OPINION BY: CHIN, J.

We granted review to resolve issues involving transferred intent and proximate causation.

In its classic form, the doctrine of transferred intent applies when the defendant intends to kill one person but mistakenly kills another. The intent to kill the intended target is deemed to transfer to the unintended victim so that the defendant is guilty of murder. (See generally *People v. Scott (1996) 14 Cal. 4th 544 {59 Cal. Rptr. 2d 178, 927 P.2d 288} (Scott)*.) Whatever its theoretical underpinnings, this result is universally accepted. But conceptual difficulties arise when applying the doctrine to other facts. Here, defendant shot at three persons, killing one and injuring, but not killing, the other two. A jury convicted him of one first degree murder and two premeditated attempted murders. We must decide whether defendant's intent to kill the murder victim transfers to an alleged attempted murder victim.

We conclude that transferred intent applies even when the person kills the intended target. Intent to kill is not limited to the specific target but extends to everyone actually killed. We also conclude, however, that the doctrine does not apply to an inchoate crime like attempted murder. A person who intends to kill only one is guilty of the attempted (or completed) murder of that one but not also of the attempted murder of others the person did not intend to kill. Thus, in this case, whether defendant is guilty of the attempted murder of the two surviving victims depends on his mental state as to those victims and not on his mental state as to the intended victim. Finally, we conclude that the trial court did not prejudicially misinstruct the jury as to these principles.

The jury also found true sentence enhancement allegations that defendant intentionally and personally discharged a firearm and proximately caused great bodily injury or death. (*Pen. Code, § 12022.53*, subd. (d); hereafter section 12022.53(d).) The trial court instructed the jury on the elements of this allegation, but did not define proximate causation. We conclude the court erred in not defining

proximate causation, but the error was harmless. A correct instruction on proximate causation could not have aided defendant.

Accordingly, we reverse the judgment of the Court of Appeal, which reversed the attempted murder convictions and enhancement findings.

I. FACTS AND PROCEDURAL HISTORY

Defendant was a member of the Insane Crips gang. Murder victim Kenneth Wilson, nicknamed Kebo, belonged to the Rolling 20's Crips. In the evening of March 6, 1999, Wilson drove through a Long Beach neighborhood with passengers Skylar Morgan and Leon Simon, who, it appears, were not gang members. Stating that he saw someone he knew, Wilson turned his car around and drove to where defendant was standing with another man. The other man pulled out a gun, and defendant asked Wilson if he was Kebo. Wilson said he was, and the man put the gun away.

The other man said he and defendant were Insane Crips. Wilson told them his passengers, Morgan and Simon, were not gang members. Invited to get out of the car and talk, Wilson instead turned his car around again. He said he would drop off his passengers and return. Defendant approached the driver's side of the car, said, "So you Kebo from 20's," and started shooting into the vehicle with a .38-calibe r handgun. Wilson managed to start driving away. As he did so, both defendant and the other man fired at the car. The car crashed into a pole. Wilson died of a gunshot wound to the chest. Simon was shot in the liver and Morgan in the shoulder, but both survived. The evidence was not clear who fired the shots that hit Morgan and Simon.

As relevant here, a jury convicted defendant of the first degree murder of Wilson and the premeditated attempted murders of Simon and Morgan. . . . The Court of Appeal reversed the two attempted murder convictions, finding the trial court erroneously instructed the jury on the doctrine of transferred intent.

We granted the Attorney General's petition for review.

II. DISCUSSION

A. Transferred Intent n1

n1 The term "transferred intent," if taken literally, is underinclusive. In his concurring opinion in *Scott*, Justice Mosk suggested that the term "transferred malice" might be more accurate (*Scott, supra, 14 Cal. 4th at* p. 554 (conc. opn. of Mosk, J.)), but even that term is too narrow. Someone who premeditates a killing but kills the wrong person is guilty of a premeditated, not just intentional, murder. (*People v. Sanchez (2001) 26 Cal. 4th 834, 850–851 {111 Cal. Rptr. 2d 129, 29 P.3d 209}.*) A more accurate designation might be "transferred mental state." However, because the term "transferred intent" is so well established in the cases, we will continue to use it on the understanding that it is not limited merely to intent but extends at least to premeditation.

. . .

B. The Law Applied to This Case

In this case, defendant's intent to kill Wilson does not transfer to Morgan or Simon. This is so, not because defendant killed his intended target, but because transferred intent does not apply to attempted murder. Whether defendant is guilty of attempted premeditated murder of Morgan or Simon depends on his mental state as to them, not on his mental state as to Wilson. We must now decide whether the court correctly instructed the jury on this law. "Once we have ascertained the relevant law, we determine the meaning of the instructions in this regard. Here the question is whether there is a 'reasonable likelihood' that the jury understood the charge as the defendant asserts." (*People v. Kelly (1992) 1 Cal. 4th 495, 525 {3 Cal. Rptr. 2d 677, 822 P.2d 385}.*)

The majority below reversed the attempted murder convictions. It concluded that the trial court, "by referring to the instruction on transferred intent in its reply [to the jury question], led the jury to believe that a finding of premeditation as to the killing of Wilson could be transferred to the wounding of Morgan and Simon." Justice Ortega dissented. He noted that *CALJIC No. 8.65* says only that when a person attempts to kill one person, "but by mistake or inadvertence *kills a different person*," the crime is the same as if the intended target had been killed. (Italics added.) He argued that this instruction "could not have been applied by the jury to transfer intent from Wilson to either Morgan or Simon." Rather its language transferred intent only to a person actually killed. "The instruction," he argued, "is not one the jury would have had any trouble understanding. It is short, to the point, and uses simple

words. I find no possibility the jury could have misapplied the instruction to nonfatal injuries. The instruction uses the words 'kill,' 'kills,' and 'killed,' and says nothing about injuries." Justice Ortega also argued that, given the strength of the evidence, a jury could not "rationally conclude that defendant did not intend to kill everyone in the car. He was at point-blank range firing at and hitting helpless people. He could not, while using such lethal force, have intended to merely 'wing' them or otherwise inflict some sort of nonfatal injury." We agree with the dissent.

CALJIC No. 8.65, as the court gave it, refers to a mistaken killing, but not to injuries. Although labeled the "transferred intent" instruction, it does not actually use that term. It merely tells the jury, correctly, that if the defendant killed the wrong person, the *killing* constituted the same crime as if the intended person had been killed. It directly related to this case and properly informed the jury it did not have to determine who, exactly, defendant intended to kill in order to find him guilty of murder. But it did not go further. It did not allow the jury to transfer intent to someone who is only injured.

In *Czahara, supra, 203 Cal. App. 3d at* p. 1472, which found prejudicial instructional error, the trial court modified *CALJIC No. 8.65*, and told the jury: "When one attempts to kill a certain person, but by mistake or inadvertence *injures* a different person, the crime, if any, so committed is the same as though the person originally intended to be killed had been *injured*." (Italics added to indicate modification.) Here, the court committed no such error. It did not modify *CALJIC No. 8.65* to extend its coverage to a person merely injured.

The district attorney's argument to the jury, unlike the later instruction, did suggest the jury could transfer intent to the attempted murder counts. But any uncertainty in this regard was dispelled when, during deliberations, the jury specifically asked whether its finding on premeditation as to Wilson would "follow over" to the attempted murder charge as to Morgan. The court responded, again correctly, that the jury had to "make a determination specifically as to each count, whether you find willful, malicious, premeditation, if you find those as to each count. You make a separate finding. . . . One does not necessarily lead and follow to the other. You have to look at each count separately." After conferring with the parties, the court additionally referred the jury to the relevant instructions, including *CALJIC No. 8.65*, and reiterated that "each count is determined separately one from another. So a finding on one does not necessarily lead to a finding on another."

The question the jury asked the court, and the foreperson's statements, showed the jury was conscientiously parsing the precise language of the instructions which, in this case, did *not* transfer intent to a person merely injured. No reason appears to believe this jury would have misread the instruction's simple language as saying what it did not say. The court also correctly answered the jury's specific question on this point. Accordingly, we see no reasonable likelihood that the jury understood the charge as permitting it to transfer intent to kill to a person merely injured. Moreover, we agree with Justice Ortega that the evidence here virtually compelled a finding that, even if defendant primarily wanted to kill Wilson, he also, concurrently, intended to kill the others in the car. At the least, he intended to create a kill zone. Contrary to the dissent, we conclude that giving instructions that correctly state the law relating to the case was not prejudicial error. n8

n8 Although we find the jury did not misunderstand the instructions in this case, in future cases involving both murder and attempted murder (or manslaughter) charges, it might be better for the court specifically to clarify that transferred intent does not apply to the attempt charges.

. . .

III. CONCLUSION

We reverse the judgment of the Court of Appeal and remand the matter for further proceedings consistent with this opinion.

GEORGE, C. J., BAXTER, J., Werdegar, J., and BROWN, J., concurred.

PEOPLE V. CHAVEZ ET AL.

COURT OF APPEAL OF CALIFORNIA, FIFTH APPELLATE DISTRICT

118 Cal. App. 4th 379; 12 Cal. Rptr. 3d 837

May 3, 2004, Filed

OPINION BY: WISEMAN, J.

This case involves the shooting, by occupants of a car, of a group of youths in another car. As a result, a young woman was killed and two others suffered gunshot wounds. The three appellants were each charged with one count of first degree murder pursuant to the first degree drive-by murder statutes (*Pen. Code, § 189, § 190.2, subd. (a)(21)*), four counts of attempted willful, deliberate, and premeditated murder, and related charges. The appellants were convicted of all the charges and sentenced to life without the possibility of parole for the first degree murder charges; they received additional sentences on the other charges. In this appeal, appellants argue, among other things, that the jury was instructed incorrectly on the drive-by murder charges.

We affirm in part and publish to clarify the proper instruction of juries regarding charges based on the first degree drive-by murder statutes. In the published portion of this opinion, we conclude that first degree drive-by murder is not felony murder, and that although premeditation is not required to establish the crime, a specific intent to kill is required. The jury was not properly instructed on these issues, but the error was harmless. In the unpublished sections, we decide that the jury was properly instructed in other respects or that instructional error was harmless; that the sentences of life without the possibility of parole imposed here were not cruel or unusual; that the jury was not required to agree on a single theory of murder; and that certain sentence enhancements were properly imposed. But we stay improper 4- and 8-month enhancements imposed on appellant Chavez and strike a fine improperly imposed on him.

PROCEDURAL HISTORY

An information was filed October 15, 1998, charging Marcos Chavez (Chavez), Jaime Guzman (Guzman), and Alejandro Prado (Prado) (appellants) with multiple felonies. In count 1, appellants were charged with the murder of Marlene Romero in violation of *Penal Code section 187*. . . . It was alleged that the murder was intentional and perpetrated by discharging a firearm from a motor vehicle with the intent to inflict death within the meaning of *section 190.2, subdivision (a)(21)*. Counts 2, 3, 4, and 5 charged appellants with the attempted premeditated and deliberate murders of Ray P., Shalisa H., Celeste M., and Joseph A. in violation of *sections 664* and *187*. Appellants were charged in count 6 with discharging a firearm from a motor vehicle in violation of *section 246*.

. . . A jury returned guilty verdicts on all counts and found all special allegations to be true. Each appellant received a sentence of life without the possibility of parole on count 1 and four consecutive sentences of life with the possibility of parole on counts 2, 3, 4, and 5. A number of sentence enhancements were also imposed on each appellant.

FACTUAL HISTORY

Marlene Romero was shot in the head about 12:45 a.m. on November 23, 1997, as she, Ray, Shalisa, and Celeste rode with Joseph in Joseph's father's Dodge Neon on Highway 65. Marlene died at a hospital the same morning. Ray and Shalisa also sustained gunshot wounds.

The shots were fired from a Honda Civic that pulled alongside the Neon on the highway. Chavez drove the Civic and Guzman and Prado were passengers. A Honda Accord, driven by Prado's cousin (also named Alejandro, and referred to in the record as Big Alex), followed behind the Neon as the shootings occurred. Police investigators found gunshot residue on Prado and on the Civic and found Prado's fingerprints on the Civic. A shell casing from one of the two guns used in the shootings was found at Prado's house. Guzman and Chavez admitted to police that they were in the Civic; Chavez admitted that he drove it and that Guzman and Prado fired shots from it at the Neon. Guzman testified at trial that he had fired a gun out the window of the Civic during the encounter with the Neon. Celeste and Shalisa identified Prado and Guzman as the passengers in the Neon.

The shootings occurred several hours after another hostile encounter between occupants of the Civic and the Neon.

As the two cars drove down a street, Big Alex, then in the Civic, had argued with Shalisa, whom he formerly had dated. Other occupants of the Civic shouted and gestured at Joseph as he drove. Chavez told police that he, Prado, and Guzman went out in the Civic to find the Neon later, shortly before the shootings occurred.

I. DISCUSSION

The First Degree Murder Instructions

Section 187 defines the crime of murder as the "unlawful killing of a human being . . . with malice aforethought." (*§ 187, subd. (a).*) Malice aforethought "may be express or implied." (*§ 188.*) "It is express when there is manifested a deliberate intention unlawfully to take away the life of a fellow creature. It is implied, when no considerable provocation appears, or when the circumstances attending the killing show an abandoned and malignant heart. (*Ibid.*)

First degree murder was presented to the jury on two theories: premeditated and deliberated murder with express malice, and "drive-by" murder, or murder "perpetrated by means of discharging a firearm from a motor vehicle, intentionally at another person outside of the vehicle with the intent to inflict death . . . ." (*§ 189.*) The jury also considered second degree murder on several theories.

On the first degree murder charges, the court gave the jury *CALJIC No. 8.21* (1998 rev.), the felony-murder instruction, modified to specify "the crime of discharging a firearm from a motor vehicle intentionally at another person outside the vehicle, when the perpetrator specifically intended to inflict death" as the predicate felony. This instruction states that a killing that occurs during the intentional commission of the predicate felony is first degree murder regardless of whether the killing is "intentional, unintentional, or accidental." The court gave a similar instruction on aider-and-abettor liability for felony murder based on *CALJIC No. 8.27* (1998 rev.).

Appellants contend that these instructions were erroneous because the drive-by-shooting component of *section 189* is not an enumerated felony under the *felony-murder rule.* They contend that *section 189* is only to be used to fix the degree of murder after malice has been established. Because drive-by shooting is not an enumerated felony, appellants argue, the jury must find malice aforethought; but the felony-murder instruction does not require such a finding.

Respondent argues that the drive-by-shooting clause in *section 189* is intended to operate as the functional equivalent of an enumerated felony under the *felony-murder rule* and that the court's instructions were correct. Alternatively, assuming the drive-by-shooting clause of *section 189* does not define an enumerated felony for purposes of the felony-murder rule, respondent contends that the jury necessarily found malice. Consequently, respondent argues, appellants suffered no prejudice from the giving of the instructions.

We answer two questions: (1) Does the drive-by-shooting clause of *section 189* define an enumerated felony within the felony-murder rule? (2) If not, did the court's felony-murder instructions constitute prejudicial error?

A. Status of the drive-by-shooting clause of section 189

In *People v. Rodriguez* (1998) 66 Cal.App.4th 157, 163–164 {77 Cal. Rptr. 2d 676}, the court explains that *section 189* establishes three categories of first degree murder: "*Section 189* . . . first establishes a category of first degree murder consisting of various types of premeditated killings, and specifies certain circumstances (use of explosives or armor-piercing ammunition, torture, etc.) which are deemed the equivalent of premeditation. *Section 189* secondly establishes a category of first degree felony murders (murders perpetrated during felonies or attempted felonies such as arson, rape, carjacking, etc.). Finally, *section 189* establishes a third category consisting of only one item, intentional murder by shooting out of a vehicle with intent to kill." Respondent contends that a killing committed in the course of a drive-by shooting really belongs in the second category and adds to the list of enumerated felonies within the felony-murder rule. We disagree.

Under the felony-murder rule, a killing, whether intentional or unintentional, is first degree murder if committed in the perpetration of, or the attempt to perpetrate, certain serious felonies. (1 Witkin & Epstein, Cal. Criminal Law (3d ed. 2000) Crimes Against the Person, *§ 134*, p. 750.) The ordinary mental-state elements of first degree murder—malice and premeditation—are eliminated by the doctrine. The only criminal intent required to be proved is the specific intent to commit the particular underlying felony. (*Id., § 135, pp. 750–751.*) Thus, the question before us is whether, in adding the drive-by-shooting clause to *section 189* in 1993, the Legislature created an offense that constitutes murder but requires no particular mental state with respect to killing.

In interpreting *section 189*, our objective is "to ascertain and effectuate legislative intent." (*People v. Woodhead* (1987) 43 Cal.3d 1002, 1007 {239 Cal. Rptr. 656, 741 P.2d 154}.) To the extent that the language in the statute may be unclear, we look to legislative history and the statutory scheme of which the statute is a part. (*People v. Bartlett* (1990) 226 Cal. App. 3d 244, 250 {276 Cal. Rptr. 460}.)

The Legislature's intent is unmistakable here. Although the drive-by-shooting clause appears immediately after the list of enumerated felonies in *section 189*, it is clear from the content of the clause that drive-by shooting is not part of that list. The drive-by-shooting clause requires an "intent to inflict death" which is never an element of felony murder. . . .

Although we have concluded that the meaning of *section 189* is clear, in the event a reader has any doubt, he or she may easily extinguish it by looking at the legislative history. Senate Bill No. 310 was enacted in 1993, amending *sections 189*, *190*, and *12022.5*. (§ *189*, as amended by Stats. 1993, ch. 609, § *1*, p. 3265.) Senator Ruben Ayala introduced the bill, stating: ". . . Existing law describes murder of the 1st degree as all murders which, among other things, are committed in the perpetration of, or attempt to perpetrate, certain enumerated felonies and specified sex crimes. This bill would add to the list of specified crimes a murder which is perpetrated by means of discharging a firearm from a motor vehicle, intentionally at another person outside of the vehicle with the intent to inflict death." (Legis. Counsel's Dig., Sen. Bill. No. 310 (1993–1994 Reg. Sess.) 5 Stats. 1993, Summary Dig., p. 236.)

When the bill was signed on September 29, 1993, Governor Pete Wilson's signature message heralded the fact that this amendment to *section 189* "adds intentional drive-by killing to the first degree murder statute . . . ." (Historical and Statutory Notes, 47A West's Ann. Pen. Code (1999 ed.) foll. § *189*, *p. 93*.) Expressly designed to curb violence, the message reiterated that the codification of "drive-by killing in the first degree murder statute allows prosecutors to convict drive-by assassins upon proof of a specific intent to kill." (*Ibid.*)

. . .   #4

In sum, we hold that the drive-by-shooting clause added to *section 189* in 1993 is not an enumerated felony for purposes of the felony-murder rule. We further conclude that although premeditation is not required to establish first degree murder under this clause, a specific intent to kill is required. And, as is well established, proof of an unlawful intent to kill is the functional equivalent of express malice. (*People v. Swain* (1996) 12 Cal.4th 593, 601 {49 Cal. Rptr. 2d 390, 909 P.2d 994}.)

Accordingly, the court erred in giving felony-murder instructions on the first degree murder charges. In stating that the jury must find that the "perpetrator specifically intended to inflict death," but also that it was irrelevant whether the killing was "intentional, unintentional, or accidental," these instructions were inconsistent on the issue of whether the jury must find that the killings were intentional.

B. Prejudical impact of giving felony-murder instructions

Because they were inconsistent on the point of intent, the instructions given could have removed the mental-state element of the offenses from the jury's consideration. Therefore, federal due process is implicated . . .

In assessing prejudice, we consider whether "it appears 'beyond a reasonable doubt that the error complained of did not contribute to the verdict obtained.'" . . . Further, "[t]o say that an error did not contribute to the verdict is . . . to find that error unimportant in relation to everything else the jury considered on the issue in question, as revealed in the record." . . . The evidence must be "'of such compelling force as to show beyond a reasonable doubt' that the erroneous instruction 'must have made no difference in reaching the verdict obtained.'" . . . Employing this standard, we conclude the error was harmless.

Significantly, the correct murder instructions were also presented to the jury. *CALJIC No. 8.10*, which defines murder, was given as modified: . . . In addition, *CALJIC No. 8.25.1* was given, which states: "Murder which is perpetrated by means of discharging a firearm from a motor vehicle intentionally and at another person outside of the vehicle when the perpetrator specifically intended to inflict death, is murder of the first degree."

Other instructions given include *CALJIC No. 3.31*, concurrence of act and specific intent, and *CALJIC No. 3.31.5*, which defines mental state. Malice aforethought was defined in *CALJIC No. 8.11*; deliberate and premeditated murder was defined in *CALJIC No. 8.20*. Also included were *CALJIC No. 3.01*, defining aiding and abetting and the requirement that the aider and abettor act with knowledge of the unlawful purpose of the perpetrator and with the intent of committing or encouraging the commission of the crime.

In addition, closing arguments to the jury are relevant in evaluating prejudice. (See *People v. Lee, supra*, 43 Cal.3d at p. 677.) Here, the prosecutor's closing argument stressed the essential requirement of an intent to kill in order to convict of first degree murder: "With respect to first degree murder, there is express malice first degree murder, things that you look for with respect to express malice first degree murder are the number of bullets that went into this particular vehicle, the location of where the bullet holes were, the hunting down of the victims. . . . The reason that the prosecution spent a significant amount of time with respect to what occurred prior to the actual shooting, is to show the intent of these three defendants, the intent to go after these victims, to hunt them down, loaded with weapons in their car, and to kill them. . . . With respect to first degree express malice, premeditation means it has to be considered beforehand. There's no timetable. The law does not say they have to think about it for 30 minutes before they do it. You have to take a look at all the factors that exist prior to the shooting, prior to this killing. Deliberations weighs—when an individual weighs the pros and cons having the consequences in mind, decides to and does kill. . . . Premeditation and deliberation, it's not a duration of time, but it's an extent of the reflection. Again, I know all of these things are coming in. You have to try to look at the instructions and it will tell you what premeditated, deliberated first degree murder is. . . . The issue as to the intent to kill can be arrived at in a short period of time. Again, going back to the facts of this case, what led up to this killing, is extremely significant. But you can also take into consideration when determining whether an individual is guilty of first degree murder the actual shooting, the actual killing itself. . . ."

The prosecutor also accurately told the jury that if it found appellants guilty of first degree murder, it had to next find the alleged special circumstances to be true. The prosecutor emphasized that three elements had to be proven beyond a reasonable doubt. These include discharging a firearm from a motor vehicle, intentionally firing at persons outside the vehicle, and doing so with the intent to inflict death. Later, as part of the same argument, the prosecutor reminded the jury that she was relying on two theories with respect to first degree murder and three with respect to second degree murder.

The prosecutor described the first degree murder theories as follows: "[T]he first theory is that the defendants intended to kill the victims. That's first degree murder. If the killing was premeditated and deliberated, express malice. . . .

"Drive-by murder is the second theory the prosecution presents to you for first degree murder. In essence, what that instruction says is murder perpetrated by means of discharging a firearm from a motor vehicle intentionally at another person outside of the vehicle when the perpetrator specifically intended to inflict death. That's murder in the first degree."

. . .

In addition, evidence of appellants' intent to kill was strong. Chavez was in the car that initially interacted with Joseph and the occupants of the Dodge Neon earlier in the evening. Big Alex, who was also in the car, testified that Chavez was upset afterward. Almost 4 hours later, Prado, Guzman, and Chavez followed Joseph, this time onto the highway. Big Alex, in a third car, followed appellants' car at their request. Big Alex witnessed "flashes" coming from appellants' car.

When Chavez spoke to an officer after his arrest, he admitted driving the car and that there were two guns inside. He also acknowledged that appellants went out to look for Joseph's car.

Daniel T., who was in custody with Guzman, testified that Guzman told him he had shot someone in a drive-by shooting and that the intended victim was "some guy." Barry M., who was also in custody, told an investigator that Guzman stated he was the shooter. He also said that Chavez did not know there were guns in the car but that they had gone to fight "some other guys."

At trial, Chavez admitted he was willing to fight Joseph and that both Guzman and Prado had guns. Although equivocal about whether he had talked about encountering Joseph's car while at Prado's house, Chavez acknowledged telling the police that he, Prado, and Guzman left the house to look for it.

This jury was told numerous times that a conviction of murder required proof of a specific intent to kill. The prosecutor consistently emphasized the requirement of finding an intent to kill. Further, the instructions accurately advised the jury that the specific intent to kill while firing intentionally at a person outside the vehicle had to be proven by the prosecution. For all these reasons, we conclude beyond a reasonable doubt that the jury believed proof of intent to kill was required to find appellants guilty of murder in the first degree. Consequently, the instructional error was harmless beyond a reasonable doubt.

. . .

A petition for rehearing was denied May 21, 2004, and appellants' petition for review by the Supreme Court was denied July 21, 2004.

SUPREME COURT OF CALIFORNIA

70 CAL. 2D 15; 447 P.2D 942; 73 CAL. RPTR. 550

DECEMBER 23, 1968

OPINION BY: TOBRINER, J.

Defendant was indicted for the murder of Victoria Hammond, a 10-year-old girl, in 1962. The jury found defendant guilty of first degree murder, found that he was sane, and fixed the penalty at death. This court, in *People v. Anderson* (1965) 63 Cal.2d 351 {46 Cal.Rptr. 763, 406 P.2d 43}, reversed the judgment both as to conviction and penalty, one of the grounds being that the introduction of defendant's extrajudicial confession violated *Escobedo v. Illinois* (1964) 378 U.S. 478 {12 L.Ed.2d 977, 84 S.Ct. 1758}.

After a second trial, the jury again found defendant guilty of first degree murder, found that he was sane, and fixed the penalty at death. This appeal is automatic. (*Pen. Code, § 1239*, subd. (b).)

We do not find it necessary to remand the case for a new penalty trial, however, because we conclude that the evidence is insufficient to support a verdict of first degree murder on the theory of either (a) premeditated and deliberate murder, or (b) murder committed during the perpetration or attempted perpetration of a violation of *Penal Code section 288.*

I. The Facts

Defendant, a San Jose cab driver, had been living for about 8 months with a Mrs. Hammond and her three children, Cynthia, aged 17, Kenneth, aged 13, and the victim, Victoria, aged 10. On the morning of the day of the murder, December 7, 1962, Mrs. Hammond left for work at 7:30 a.m., leaving only Victoria at home with the defendant. Defendant was still in bed. He had been home from work for the previous 2 days, during which time he had been drinking heavily, and apparently he did not go to work on the day of the murder.

The owner of a nearby liquor store testified that defendant purchased a quart of whiskey from him sometime between 1 and 2 p.m. on December 7, 1962. The only other witness who testified as to defendant's whereabouts that day prior to the discovery of the murder was the victim's 13-year-old brother Kenneth.

Kenneth testified that he arrived home from school at 3:30 p.m. on December 7. He found the front door locked, which was not unusual, so he went around to the back of the house and down to the basement. Kenneth stayed there while working with his microscope. In a short time he heard noise coming from upstairs in the house which sounded like boxes and other things being moved around, like someone was cleaning up. He then heard the shower water running. A police officer later verified that a person in the basement could hear water running in the shower and movement in Victoria's bedroom.

Kenneth testified further that he then came up from the basement and went to the back porch screen door. The screen door was locked, which also was not unusual, so Kenneth jerked on it so the hook would pop out. Kenneth then went from the back porch directly into his bedroom to change his clothes. He then returned through the back porch to the kitchen door which was also locked. Kenneth knocked on the door and the defendant opened it. Kenneth testified that the defendant was wearing slacks only. Kenneth went into the kitchen and asked defendant for $1.00 for a teen club dance he intended to attend that evening. Defendant obtained a dollar for him out of the pocket of another pair of slacks hanging on the knob of a bedroom door. When Kenneth noticed the blood on the kitchen floor and asked defendant about it, the defendant told Kenneth that he had cut himself. This explanation apparently satisfied Kenneth, as he finished dressing and left the house sometime before 4 p.m.

Kenneth testified that no one else was at his house when he was there between 3:30 and 4 p.m. He further testified that about 6:30 he realized that he had forgotten his wallet and returned home. As he approached the front door, his mother came out and asked to see the cut on his arm, and Kenneth explained that he had no cut. His mother than asked defendant about the blood she had noticed and defendant told her that Victoria had cut herself, but that the mother should not worry, as the cut was not serious. After defendant told her that Victoria was at a friend's for dinner, the mother wanted to take Kenneth with her to get Victoria. Kenneth went back to his room to get a jacket. Because he had a "weird" feeling, he looked into Victoria's room. He found her nude, bloody body under some boxes and blankets on the floor near her bed. Kenneth ran out of the room screaming that defendant had killed her. Mrs. Hammond, after seeing Victoria's body, went next door to phone the police.

Mrs. Hammond testified that she returned home from work at 4:45 p.m. The front door was locked she rang the doorbell, and defendant answered. Mrs. Hammond noticed blood on the couch in the living room, and when she asked defendant about it, he told her that Kenneth had cut himself playing with a knife and that he was at a teenage dance. Mrs. Hammond then went to the grocery store and returned about 5:30 p.m. She testified that at both times she arrived home defendant was drinking a highball. She also testified as to examining Kenneth's arm for a cut when he returned home for his wallet and as to defendant's subsequent explanation that Victoria had been cut, but not seriously. Mrs. Hammond discovered Victoria's body after Kenneth came out of Victoria's room.

A classmate of Victoria, who was the last person to see Victoria alive, testified that she left Victoria in front of the Hammond house about 3:45 p.m. after the two of them had walked home from school.

When the police arrived at 7 p.m. the shades were down on all the windows and the doors were locked. Defendant finally opened the front door for one of the officers who arrested and handcuffed defendant. The arresting officer testified that defendant was wearing slacks, no shirt or shoes, and that there was no blood on him.

The arresting officer found Victoria's body on the floor near her bed. He found defendant's blood-spotted shorts on a chair in the living room, and a knife and defendant's socks, with blood encrusted on the soles, in the master bedroom. The evidence established that the victim's torn and bloodstained dress had been ripped from her, that her clothes, including her panties out of which the crotch had been ripped, were found in various rooms of the house, that there were bloody footprints matching the size of the victim's leading from the master bedroom to Victoria's room, and that there was blood in almost every room including the kitchen, the floor of which appeared to have been mopped.

The TV cameraman who covered the murder story for channel 11, the officer who drove defendant to the police station, and the officer who "observed" defendant for 4 hours at the station the night of December 7, 1962, all testified that defendant did not appear intoxicated. The officers who talked to defendant testified, however, that they smelled alcohol on his breath; a blood test taken at 7:45 p.m. indicated that the alcohol content in defendant's blood was .34 per cent, which was more than necessary for an automobile driver to be classified as "under the influence."

Over 60 wounds, both severe and superficial, were found on Victoria's body. n1 The cuts extended over her entire body, including one extending from the rectum through the vagina, and the partial cutting off of her tongue. Several of the wounds, including the vaginal lacerations, were post mortem. No evidence of spermatozoa was found in the victim, on her panties, or on the bed next to which she was found.

> n1 The deputy coroner and the funeral director testified as to the condition of the body. The doctor who performed the autopsy did not testify, and the autopsy report was not introduced into evidence.

The prosecution contended that the murder was sexually motivated. The defendant, who pleaded not guilty and not guilty by reason of insanity, presented no defense whatsoever. The court instructed the jury on two theories of first degree murder, premeditated and deliberate murder, and murder committed in the perpetration or attempt to perpetrate an offense under section *288 of the Penal Code*; second degree murder; and voluntary and involuntary manslaughter. The court also instructed the jury on diminished capacity due to voluntary intoxication and its relationship to second degree murder and manslaughter. The jury found the defendant guilty of murder in the first degree.

. . .

II. The Evidence is Insufficient to Support a Verdict of First Degree Murder

We must, in the absence of substantial evidence to support the verdict of first degree murder, reduce the conviction to second degree murder . . . .

"The legislative definition of the degrees of murder leaves much to the discretion of the jury in many cases. That discretion, however must have a sound factual basis for its exercise . . . .[As] is true as to all factual issues resolved by a jury, the evidence upon which the determination is made is subject to review on the question of its legal sufficiency to support the verdict. . . .[The] jury is bound, as are we, to apply the standards fixed by law.". . .

. . .

In the instant case the court instructed the jury on two possible theories of first degree murder: (1) a willful, deliberate, and premeditated killing; (2) murder which is committed in the perpetration or attempted perpetration of an act punishable under *Penal Code section 288.*

Viewing the evidence in a light most favorable to the judgment, the first degree conviction must rest upon the following supporting proof: when Kenneth arrived home from school he found the doors locked, and when the police officers arrived to arrest defendant they found the shades in the front room down; defendant apparently had attempted to clean up the bloodstained kitchen, and had fabricated conflicting explanations of the blood that Kenneth noticed in the kitchen, the blood that Victoria's mother observed in the living room, and Victoria's absence on the evening of the killing; defendant had stabbed Victoria repeatedly and had inflicted a post mortem rectal-vaginal wound; bloodstains were found in several rooms of the house; Victoria's bloodstained and shredded dress was found under her bed next to which her nude body was discovered under a pile of boxes and blankets; Victoria's slip, with the straps torn off, was found under the bed in the master bedroom; the crotch was ripped out of Victoria's blood-soaked panties; and the only bloodstained clothes of defendant's which were discovered were his socks and his shorts, from which facts the People argue that defendant was almost nude during the attack.

We test this evidence under both of the above theories to determine whether it is sufficient to support conviction for first, rather than second, degree murder.

(a) *The evidence is insufficient to support a finding of premeditation and deliberation*

It is well established that the brutality of a killing cannot in itself support a finding that the killer acted with premeditation and deliberation. "If the evidence showed no more than the infliction of multiple acts of violence on the victim, it would not be sufficient to show that the killing was the result of careful thought and weighing of considerations." Moreover, although premeditation and deliberation may be shown by circumstantial evidence, the People bear the burden of establishing beyond a reasonable doubt that the killing was the result of premeditation and deliberation, and that therefore the killing was first, rather than second, degree murder.

Given the presumption that an unjustified killing of a human being constitutes murder of the second, rather than of the first, degree, and the clear legislative intention to differentiate between first and second degree murder, we must determine in any case of circumstantial evidence whether the proof is such as will furnish a *reasonable foundation* for an inference of premeditation and deliberation . . .

. . .

Recognizing the need to clarify the difference between the two degrees of murder and the bases upon which a reviewing court may find that the evidence is sufficient to support a verdict of first degree murder, we set forth standards, derived from the nature of premeditation and deliberation as employed by the Legislature and interpreted by this court, for the kind of evidence which is sufficient to sustain a finding of premeditation and deliberation. We then analyze representative cases, including those which the People argue require an affirmance here. In conclusion we demonstrate . . . that the kind of evidence from which a jury can reasonably infer that an accused willfully, deliberately, and with premeditation killed his victim within the meaning of *Penal Code section 189* is totally lacking here.

As we noted in *People v. Bender, supra, 27 Cal.2d 164, 183,* we find no indication that the Legislature intended to give the words "deliberate" and "premeditated" other than their ordinary dictionary meanings. Moreover, we have repeatedly pointed out that the legislative classification of murder into two degrees would be meaningless if "deliberation" and "premeditation" were construed as requiring no more reflection than may be involved in the mere formation of a specific intent to kill. (*People v. Wolff, supra, 61 Cal.2d 795,* at p. 821; *People v. Caldwell, supra, 43 Cal.2d 864,* at p. 869; *People v. Thomas (1945) 25 Cal.2d 880, 898 {156 P.2d 7}.*)

Thus we have held that in order for a killing with malice aforethought to be first rather than second degree murder, "'[the] intent to kill must be . . . formed upon a *pre-existing* reflection,' . . . [and have] been the subject of actual deliberation or *forethought.* . . ." (*People v. Thomas, supra, 25 Cal.2d* at pp. 900–901.) (Italics added.) We have therefore held that "[a] verdict of murder in the first degree . . . [on a theory of a willful, deliberate, and premeditated killing] is proper only if the slayer killed "as a result of careful thought and weighing of considerations; as a *deliberate* judgment or plan; carried on coolly and steadily, [especially] according to a *preconceived design.*"

The type of evidence which this court has found sufficient to sustain a finding of premeditation and deliberation falls into three basic categories: (1) facts about how and what defendant did *prior* to the actual killing which show that the defendant was engaged in activity directed toward, and explicable as intended to result in, the killing—what may be characterized as "planning" activity; (2) facts about the defendant's *prior* relationship and/or conduct with the victim from which the jury could reasonably infer a "motive" to kill the victim, which inference of motive, together with facts of type (1) or (3), would in turn support an inference that the killing was the result of "a pre-existing reflection" and "careful thought and weighing of considerations" rather than "mere unconsidered or rash impulse hastily executed" *(People v. Thomas, supra, 25 Cal.2d 880, at* pp. 898, 900, 901); (3) facts about the nature of the killing from which the jury could infer that the *manner* of killing was so particular and exacting that the defendant must have intentionally killed according to a "preconceived design" to take his victim's life in a particular way for a "reason" which the jury can reasonably infer from facts of type (1) or (2).

Analysis of the cases will show that this court sustains verdicts of first degree murder typically when there is evidence of all three types and otherwise requires at least extremely strong evidence of (1) or evidence of (2) in conjunction with either (1) or (3). As will become clear from the following analysis of representative cases, the present case lacks evidence of any of the three types.

. . . The Attorney General's argument that Stroble holds that premeditation and deliberation may be inferred from the condition of the body and other physical evidence at the scene of the crime, and that *therefore* there is sufficient evidence of premeditation and deliberation in the instant case is thus totally devoid of merit.

. . .

We conclude that a finding of premeditation and deliberation cannot be sustained in the absence of any evidence of (1) defendant's actions prior to the killing, (2) a "motive" or "reason" from which the jury could reasonably infer that defendant intended to kill Victoria, or (3) a manner of killing from which the jury could reasonably infer that the wounds were deliberately calculated to result in death. As in P*eople v. Granados, supra, 49 Cal.2d 490, and People v. Craig, supra, 49 Cal.2d 313*, the evidence suffices only to support a verdict of second degree murder.

. . .

The judgment is modified by reducing the degree of the crime to murder of the second degree and, as so modified, is affirmed. The cause is remanded to the trial court with directions to arraign and pronounce judgment on defendant in accordance with the foregoing ruling.

PEOPLE V. PEREZ

SUPREME COURT OF CALIFORNIA

2 Cal. 4th 1117; 831 P.2d 1159; 9 Cal. Rptr. 2d 577

July 9, 1992

OPINION BY: PANELLI, J.

OPINION:

We granted review in this case after a divided Court of Appeal reduced defendant's first degree murder conviction to second degree murder for insufficient evidence of premeditation and deliberation. As explained hereafter, we conclude that the judgment of the Court of Appeal should be reversed.

FACTS

Defendant killed Victoria Mesa in her home in Garden Grove on the morning of September 30, 1988. There is no question that he was the perpetrator. The only question is the circumstances under which the murder occurred—that is—whether it was premeditated and deliberate.

Michael Mesa, the victim's husband, testified that he left for work about 5:40 a.m. on the morning of the murder, while Victoria was still asleep. As part of their morning ritual he would leave her a note and call her before she left for work. Victoria was four months' pregnant, and Michael was concerned about her condition. This was to be their first child after years of unsuccessful attempts to have a child. In order to protect the pregnancy, Victoria's cervix had been sewn shut, and she could not have sexual relations. Michael called Victoria the morning of the murder about 7:35 a.m., before she left for work. She usually left for work around 8 a.m. He heard the sound of an automobile engine running in the background. The engine could have been his wife's car.

A neighbor who generally left for work at the same time as Victoria noticed Victoria's car in the driveway with exhaust coming from it. He also noticed that the front door to the house was open. The neighbor thought that it was about 8:05 a.m. when he drove by.

Victoria's employer called Michael about 9:45 a.m. to tell him that Victoria had not come to work. Michael called a

neighbor to ask her to check on Victoria. The neighbor enlisted the aid of a gas company meter reader who, upon approaching the house, found the front door slightly ajar; he entered, found Victoria's body, and immediately left to call the police.

Police officers arrived about 9:50 a.m. and found Victoria's fully clothed body lying face down with her arms under her head in the bathroom and her legs extending into the hallway. A broken dish and dog food were lying near the body. A six-inch blade of a serrated steak knife was found under Victoria's head. A broken piece of knife handle was near her feet. The wood appeared to be the same as the handles of knives in the kitchen drawer. There was no sign of a forced entry, and the only unlocked door was the front door.

There was a large pool of blood beneath Victoria's body and splatters all over the adjacent walls and carpet. Blood was found in every room except the nursery. There were blood drippings throughout the floor of the master bedroom. Dresser drawers were open, and drops of blood were on the clothing inside the drawers. Jewelry boxes were open and had drops of blood inside. There was blood on the sink in the master bathroom. Four Band-Aid wrappers were lying on the counter; a folded Band-Aid saturated with blood was found in the entry of the master bedroom. A guest bedroom had blood stains in the doorway of the room almost on a direct line with the light switch.

The entire kitchen was peppered with blood spots. There were drops of blood on the refrigerator and counter top and smeared blood around the handles of cupboards and drawers. Many of the cupboards and drawers were open. There were drops of blood inside some of the drawers, including one containing knives.

Victoria's purse was on top of a table in the kitchen. The contents of the purse were lying on the table. A removable car stereo was also on the table. All of the items had drops of blood on them.

The victim's husband found nothing missing from the house except for one of his dress shirts.

According to the pathologist who performed the autopsy, Victoria bled to death. She had sustained blunt force trauma to her eyes, nose and lips, probably from a fist. There were about 38 knife wounds, including 26 stab and slash wounds and 12 puncture wounds. There were deep stab and slash wounds about the head, face, and neck, in the carotid artery, around the spinal column, and on the back of the arms. There were defensive wounds on her forearms, wrists, and hands. The injuries to the front part of the body were inflicted before the injuries to the back of the body. Two different knives were used. Most of the wounds were inflicted by a single-blade knife consistent with the one found under the victim's body. Three wounds in the back were inflicted by a double-edged knife. These wounds appeared to have been inflicted after the victim was dead.

The only connection between defendant and the victim and her husband was that they had attended the same high school some 10 years earlier. Defendant had played sports with Michael Mesa. Defendant lived about two and a quarter miles away and would drive by the Mesa house about twice a week in the early evening and wave to Michael as the latter was working in the yard. Defendant's fingerprint was found on the wall in the hallway near the victim's body and on a bloody Band-Aid wrapper found in the master bathroom. Analysis of blood scrapings from the master bedroom, wall phone, kitchen floor, blood-soaked towel on the water cooler, and blood-soaked Band-Aid from the master bedroom revealed that they were consistent with 1 per cent of the population, which includes defendant. To Michael Mesa's knowledge, defendant had never been in his house before.

Defendant's sister testified that he arrived home about 9 a.m. on the day of the murder. His hand was cut, and he was sweaty and pale. Defendant told her he had cut his hand on a saw. Defendant said he was going to drive to his father's job site. His sister offered to drive him, but defendant declined.

At 9:20 a.m. the same day, defendant was treated at a hospital emergency room for severe cuts on his right hand and smaller cuts on his left hand. Defendant told the nurse that he had cut himself with a Skil Saw. Based on her experience, the nurse did not believe that defendant's injury was the result of having been cut by a Skil Saw.

As a result of information learned from the hospital, police officers went to defendant's home that night. Defendant told the officers he had injured himself at a job site at a private residence in Anaheim while using a Skil Saw. Defendant was unable to show the officers where the job

site was. Defendant's father produced for officers the shirt that Michael Mesa identified as the one missing from his house.

Defendant did not testify, and he made no statements about the offense. In argument, defense counsel challenged the sufficiency of the evidence of first degree murder and suggested that whoever killed Victoria had acted in a rage. The jury returned a verdict of guilty of first degree, premeditated and deliberate murder. As previously mentioned, a divided Court of Appeal reduced the conviction to second degree murder.

DISCUSSION

Sufficiency of Evidence of Premeditation and Deliberation

The People contend that the Court of Appeal erred in finding the evidence of premeditation and deliberation insufficient to support the judgment. Before proceeding to that question, we find it helpful to review the definition of premeditation and deliberation that was given to the jury, *CALJIC No. 8.20*, which we have found to be a correct statement of the law. *(People v. Lucero (1988) 44 Cal.3d 1006, 1021 {245 Cal.Rptr. 185, 750 P.2d 1342}.)* CALJIC No. 8.20 defines premeditated and deliberate murder as follows:

"All murder which is perpetrated by any kind of willful, deliberate and premeditated killing with express malice aforethought is murder of the first degree."

"The word 'willful' as used in this instruction, means intentional."

"The word 'deliberate' means formed or arrived at or determined upon as a result of careful thought and weighing of considerations for and against the proposed course of action. The word 'premeditated' means considered beforehand."

"If you find that the killing was preceded and accompanied by a clear, deliberate intent on the part of the defendant to kill, which was the result of deliberation and premeditation, so that it must have been formed upon pre-existing reflection and not under a sudden heat of passion or other condition precluding the idea of deliberation, it is murder of the first degree."

"The law does not undertake to measure in units of time the length of the period during which the thought must be pondered before it can ripen into an intent to kill which is truly deliberate and premeditated. The time will vary with different individuals and under varying circumstances."

"The true test is not the duration of time, but rather the extent of the reflection. A cold, calculated judgment and decision may be arrived at in a short period of time, but a mere unconsidered and rash impulse, even though it include[d] an intent to kill, is not such deliberation and premeditation as will fix an unlawful killing as murder of the first degree."

"To constitute a deliberate and premeditated killing, the slayer must weigh and consider the question of killing and the reasons for and against such a choice and, having in mind the consequences, he decides to and does kill."

. . .

In challenging the Court of Appeal's reversal of the first degree murder conviction, the People argue that there is sufficient evidence to support the jury's verdict of premeditated and deliberate murder under traditional standards of review and that the Court of Appeal majority misapplied *People v. Anderson (1968) 70 Cal.2d 15 {73 Cal.Rptr. 550, 447 P.2d 942}* in reaching a contrary determination. We agree.

In *People v. Anderson, supra, 70 Cal.2d 15,* this court surveyed a number of prior cases involving the sufficiency of the evidence to support findings of premeditation and deliberation. (at p. 26.) From the cases surveyed, the court distilled certain guidelines to aid reviewing courts in analyzing the sufficiency of the evidence to sustain findings of premeditation and deliberation. The *Anderson* analysis was intended only as a framework to aid in appellate review; it did not propose to define the elements of first degree murder or alter the substantive law of murder in any way. (*People v. Daniels (1991) 52 Cal.3d 815, 869–870 {277 Cal.Rptr. 122, 802 P.2d 906}.*) . . . The goal of *Anderson* was to aid reviewing courts in assessing whether the evidence is supportive of an inference that the killing was the result of preexisting reflection and weighing of considerations rather than mere unconsidered or rash impulse.

In identifying categories of evidence bearing on premeditation and deliberation, *Anderson* did not purport to establish an exhaustive list that would exclude all other types and combinations of evidence that could support a finding of premeditation and deliberation. From the cases surveyed, the Anderson court identified three categories of evidence pertinent to the determination of premeditation and deliberation: (1) planning activity, (2) motive, and (3) manner of killing. Regarding these categories, *Anderson* stated: "Analysis of the cases will show that this court sustains verdicts of first degree murder typically when there is evidence of all three types and otherwise requires at least extremely strong evidence of (1) or evidence of (2) in conjunction with either (1) or (3)." It is thus evident from the court's own words that it was attempting to do no more than catalog common factors that had occurred in prior cases. The *Anderson* factors, while helpful for purposes

of review, are not a *sine qua non* to finding first degree premeditated murder, nor are they exclusive.

. . . When the lead opinion finally focused on the evidence presented, it refused to credit any inference advanced in support of motive or deliberate manner of killing. In so doing, the lead opinion did not so much misapply the *Anderson* factors as it did simply disregard settled principles of appellate review. In effect, the lead opinion substituted its judgment for that of the jury. Even if we might have made contrary factual findings or drawn different inferences, we are not permitted to reverse the judgment if the circumstances reasonably justify those found by the jury. It is the jury, not the appellate court, that must be convinced beyond a reasonable doubt. Our task and responsibility is to determine whether that finding is supported by substantial evidence.

We now turn to that task. From the evidence presented, the jury reasonably could have inferred the following: Defendant surreptitiously entered the house while Victoria was warming up her car; there were no signs of forced entry or of the presence of an additional car. Defendant surprised her as she was carrying the dog food; the broken dog dish and dog food were strewn about the floor. Defendant first beat Victoria about the head and neck with his fists. Then he stabbed her with a steak knife obtained from the victim's kitchen; the handle and blade were consistent with knives in the kitchen drawer. When that knife broke, cutting him, defendant went in search of another knife; drippings of defendant's blood were found all over the kitchen, including a drawer containing knives. Regardless of defendant's motive for entering the house, once confronted by Victoria, who knew him and could identify him, he determined to kill her to avoid identification.

As so viewed, the evidence is sufficient to support the jury's findings of premeditation and deliberation. Evidence of planning activity is shown by the fact that defendant did not park his car in the victim's driveway, he surreptitiously entered the house, and he obtained a knife from the kitchen. As to motive, regardless of what inspired the initial entry and attack, it is reasonable to infer that defendant determined it was necessary to kill Victoria to prevent her from identifying him. She was acquainted with him from high school and obviously would have been able to identify him. The manner of killing is also indicative of premeditation and deliberation. The evidence of blood in the kitchen knife drawer supports an inference that defendant went to the kitchen in search of another knife after the steak knife broke. This action bears similarity to reloading a gun or using another gun when the first one has run out of ammunition.

Thus, though the evidence is admittedly not overwhelming, it is sufficient to sustain the jury's finding.

As we have stated, the relevant question on appeal is not whether *we* are convinced beyond a reasonable doubt, but whether *any* rational trier of fact could have been persuaded beyond a reasonable doubt that defendant premeditated the murder. We have previously observed that premeditation can occur in a brief period of time. "The true test is not the duration of time as much as it is the extent of the reflection. Thoughts may follow each other with great rapidity and cold, calculated judgment may be arrived at quickly. . . ."

. . .

Defendant also claims that the weight of the evidence in this case is more comparable to that in *People v. Anderson, supra, 70 Cal.2d 15* than it is to that in *People v. Wharton, supra, 53 Cal.3d 522.*

In *People v. Anderson, supra, 70 Cal.2d 15,* the defendant lived with the family of the 10-year-old victim. He killed the victim in a brutal assault involving over 60 knife wounds all over the child's body. Although there was no question that defendant was the perpetrator, there were no eyewitnesses to the crime and there was no explanation of what led up to the murder. The defendant did not testify or confess. There was, however, evidence of the defendant's subsequent efforts to conceal the crime. On this record, our court concluded that the evidence was insufficient to demonstrate that the murder was premeditated or deliberate. We therefore reduced the conviction from first to second degree murder.

In *People v. Wharton, supra, 53 Cal.3d 522*, the defendant killed the woman with whom he had been living, stuffed her body in a barrel, and left it in the apartment. The autopsy revealed that the victim had been struck three times on the head with a blunt instrument, probably a hammer. A hammer was found hidden under a mattress, and the hammer was missing from a toolbox kept in the garage. The defendant confessed, claiming that he had killed the victim in an uncontrolled rage. On appeal, we found the evidence sufficient to support the jury's finding of

premeditation and deliberation. The evidence indicated that the defendant either retrieved the hammer in advance to have it accessible in the event of an argument, or that the defendant became angry during the argument and went to the garage to obtain the hammer and kill the victim while she slept. Either version was sufficient to support planning activity. We also identified a plausible motive—the defendant was selling some of the victim's belongings. Though admitting that these were not the only inferences that could be drawn, we found the evidence of planning and motive sufficient despite the fact that the manner of killing was not in itself indicative of a preconceived design to kill. (at p. 548.)

In our view, the evidence in the present case is more comparable to that in *People v. Wharton, supra, 53 Cal.3d 522*, than it is to that in *People v. Anderson, supra, 70 Cal.2d 15*. Defendant's obtaining of the steak knife from the kitchen is indicative of planning activity. A plausible motive is evident from the fact that the victim was acquainted with defendant. After defendant initially surprised and attacked Victoria, he then decided it was necessary to silence her to prevent her from identifying him. Finally, the manner of the killing is indicative of premeditation. Defendant went searching for another knife after the first knife broke. Even if the initial knifing was spontaneous, defendant had time to reflect upon his actions when the knife broke. That he went searching for another knife is indicative of a reasoned decision to kill. Thus, the evidence here is actually stronger than that in *Wharton*.

Accordingly, we conclude that the evidence is sufficient to sustain the jury's finding of premeditation and deliberation and that the judgment of the Court of Appeal should be reversed.

. . .

CONCLUSION

The judgment of the Court of Appeal is reversed.

ATKINS V. VIRGINIA

SUPREME COURT OF THE UNITED STATES

536 U.S. 304; 122 S. Ct. 2242; 153 L. Ed. 2d 335

February 20, 2002, Argued

June 20, 2002, Decided

JUDGES

Stevens, J., delivered the opinion of the Court, in which O'Connor, Kennedy, Souter, Ginsburg, and Breyer, J. J., joined. Rehnquist, C. J., filed a dissenting opinion, in which Scalia and Thomas, J. J., joined. Scalia, J., filed a dissenting opinion, in which Rehnquist, C. J., and Thomas, J., joined.

OPINION BY: JUSTICE STEVENS delivered the opinion of the Court.

Those mentally retarded persons who meet the law's requirements for criminal responsibility should be tried and punished when they commit crimes. Because of their disabilities in areas of reasoning, judgment, and control of their impulses, however, they do not act with the level of moral culpability that characterizes the most serious adult criminal conduct. Moreover, their impairments can jeopardize the reliability and fairness of capital proceedings against mentally retarded defendants. Presumably for these reasons, in the 13 years since we decided *Penry v. Lynaugh, 492 U.S. 302, 106 L. Ed. 2d 256, 109 S. Ct. 2934 (1989),* the American public, legislators, scholars, and judges have deliberated over the question whether the death penalty should ever be imposed on a mentally retarded criminal. The consensus reflected in those deliberations informs our answer to the question presented by this case: whether such executions are "cruel and unusual punishments" prohibited by the Eighth Amendment to the Federal Constitution.

I

Petitioner, Daryl Renard Atkins, was convicted of abduction, armed robbery, and capital murder, and sentenced to death. At approximately midnight on August 16, 1996, Atkins and William Jones, armed with a semiautomatic handgun, abducted Eric Nesbitt, robbed him of the money on his person, drove him to an automated teller machine in his pickup truck where cameras recorded their withdrawal of additional cash, then took him to an isolated location where he was shot eight times and killed.

Jones and Atkins both testified in the guilt phase of Atkins' trial. n1 Each confirmed most of the details in the other's account of the incident, with the important exception that each stated that the other had actually shot and killed Nesbitt. Jones' testimony, which was both more coherent and credible than Atkins', was obviously credited by the jury and was sufficient to establish Atkins' guilt. n2 At the penalty phase of the trial, the State introduced victim impact evidence and proved two aggravating circumstances: future dangerousness and "vileness of the offense." To prove future dangerousness, the State relied on Atkins' prior felony convictions as well as the testimony of four victims of earlier robberies and assaults. To prove the second aggravator, the prosecution relied upon the trial record, including pictures of the deceased's body and the autopsy report.

> n1 Initially, both Jones and Atkins were indicted for capital murder. The prosecution ultimately permitted Jones to plead guilty to first-degree murder in exchange for his testimony against Atkins. As a result of the plea, Jones became ineligible to receive the death penalty.

> n2 Highly damaging to the credibility of Atkins' testimony was its substantial inconsistency with the statement he gave to the police upon his arrest. Jones, in contrast, had declined to make an initial statement to the authorities.

In the penalty phase, the defense relied on one witness, Dr. Evan Nelson, a forensic psychologist who had evaluated Atkins before trial and concluded that he was "mildly mentally retarded." n3 His conclusion was based on interviews with people who knew Atkins, n4 a review of school and court records, and the administration of a standard intelligence test which indicated that Atkins had a full scale IQ of 59. n5

> n3 The American Association of Mental Retardation (AAMR) defines mental retardation as follows: "*Mental*

retardation refers to substantial limitations in present functioning. It is characterized by significantly subaverage intellectual functioning, existing concurrently with related limitations in two or more of the following applicable adaptive skill areas: communication, self-care, home living, social skills, community use, self-direction, health and safety, functional academics, leisure, and work. Mental retardation manifests before age 18." Mental Retardation: Definition, Classification, and Systems of Supports 5 (9th ed. 1992).

The American Psychiatric Association's definition is similar: "The essential feature of Mental Retardation is significantly subaverage general intellectual functioning (Criterion A) that is accompanied by significant limitations in adaptive functioning in at least two of the following skill areas: communication, self-care, home living, social/interpersonal skills, use of community resources, self-direction, functional academic skills, work, leisure, health, and safety (Criterion B). The onset must occur before age 18 years (Criterion C). Mental Retardation has many different etiologies and may be seen as a final common pathway of various pathological processes that affect the functioning of the central nervous system." American Psychiatric Association, Diagnostic and Statistical Manual of Mental Disorders 41 (4th ed. 2000). "Mild" mental retardation is typically used to describe people with an IQ level of 50–55 to approximately 70. *Id.,* at pp. 42–43.

> n4 The doctor interviewed Atkins, members of his family, and deputies at the jail where he had been incarcerated for the preceding 18 months. Dr. Nelson also reviewed the statements that Atkins had given to the police and the investigative reports concerning this case.

> n5 Dr. Nelson administered the Wechsler Adult Intelligence Scales test (WAIS-III), the standard instrument in the United States for assessing intellectual functioning. AAMR, Mental Retardation, *supra.* The WAIS-III is scored by adding together the number of points earned on different subtests, and using a mathematical formula to convert this raw score into a scaled score. The test measures an intelligence range from 45 to 155. The mean score of the test is 100, which means that a person receiving a score of 100 is considered to have an average level of cognitive functioning. A. Kaufman & E. Lichtenberger, Essentials of WAIS-III Assessment 60 (1999). It is estimated that between 1 and 3 per cent of the population has an IQ between 70 and 75 or lower, which is typically considered the cutoff IQ score for the intellectual

function prong of the mental retardation definition. 2 B. Sadock & V. Sadock, Comprehensive Textbook of Psychiatry 2952 (7th ed. 2000).

At the sentencing phase, Dr. Nelson testified: "[Atkins'] full scale IQ is 59. Compared to the population at large, that means less than one percentile. . . . Mental retardation is a relatively rare thing. It's about 1 per cent of the population." App. 274. According to Dr. Nelson, Atkins' IQ score "would automatically qualify for Social Security disability income." *Id.,* at p. 280. Dr. Nelson also indicated that of the over 40 capital defendants that he had evaluated, Atkins was only the second individual who met the criteria for mental retardation. *Id.,* at p. 310. He testified that, in his opinion, Atkins' limited intellect had been a consistent feature throughout his life, and that his IQ score of 59 is not an "aberration, malingered result, or invalid test score." *Id.,* at p. 308.

The jury sentenced Atkins to death, but the Virginia Supreme Court ordered a second sentencing hearing because the trial court had used a misleading verdict form. *257 Va. 160, 510 S.E.2d 445 (1999).* At the resentencing, Dr. Nelson again testified. The State presented an expert rebuttal witness, Dr. Stanton Samenow, who expressed the opinion that Atkins was not mentally retarded, but rather was of "average intelligence, at least," and diagnosable as having antisocial personality disorder. n6 App. 476. The jury again sentenced Atkins to death.

> n6 Dr. Samenow's testimony was based upon two interviews with Atkins, a review of his school records, and interviews with correctional staff. He did not administer an intelligence test, but did ask Atkins questions taken from the 1972 version of the Wechsler Memory Scale. *Id.,* at pp. 524–525, p, 529. Dr. Samenow attributed Atkins' "academic performance [that was] by and large terrible" to the fact that he "is a person who chose to pay attention sometimes, not to pay attention others, and did poorly because he did not want to do what he was required to do." *Id.,* at pp. 480–481.

The Supreme Court of Virginia affirmed the imposition of the death penalty. *260 Va. 375, 385, 534 S.E.2d 312, 318 (2000).* Atkins did not argue before the Virginia Supreme Court that his sentence was disproportionate to penalties imposed for similar crimes in Virginia, but he did contend "that he is mentally retarded and thus cannot be sentenced to death." *Id., at* p. 386, *534 S.E.2d at 318.* The majority of the state court rejected this contention, relying on our holding in Penry. 260 Va. at 387, 534 S.E.2d at p. 319. The Court was "not willing to commute Atkins' sentence of death to life imprisonment merely because of his IQ score." *Id., at* p. 390, 534 *S.E.2d at* p. 321.

Justice Hassell and Justice Koontz dissented. They rejected Dr. Samenow's opinion that Atkins possesses average intelligence as "incredulous as a matter of law," and concluded that "the imposition of the sentence of death upon a criminal defendant who has the mental age of a child between the ages of 9 and 12 is excessive." *Id.,* at p. 394, pp. 395–396, *534 S.E.2d at* pp. 323–324. In their opinion, "it is indefensible to conclude that individuals who are mentally retarded are not to some degree less culpable for their criminal acts. By definition, such individuals have substantial limitations not shared by the general population. A moral and civilized society diminishes itself if its system of justice does not afford recognition and consideration of those limitations in a meaningful way." *Id., at* p. 397, *534 S.E.2d at* p. 325.

Because of the gravity of the concerns expressed by the dissenters, and in light of the dramatic shift in the state legislative landscape that has occurred in the past 13 years, we granted certiorari to revisit the issue that we first addressed in the *Penry case. 533 U.S. 976, 150 L. Ed. 2d 805, 122 S. Ct. 24 (2001).*

II

The Eighth Amendment succinctly prohibits "excessive" sanctions. It provides: "Excessive bail shall not be required, nor excessive fines imposed, nor cruel and unusual punishments inflicted." In *Weems v. United States, 217 U.S. 349, 54 L. Ed. 793, 30 S. Ct. 544 (1910),* we held that a punishment of 12 years jailed in irons at hard and painful labor for the crime of falsifying records was excessive. We explained "that it is a precept of justice that punishment for crime should be graduated and proportioned to the offense." (*Id., at p. 367.)* We have repeatedly applied this proportionality precept in later cases interpreting the Eighth Amendment. . . Proportionality review under those evolving standards should be informed by "'objective factors to the maximum possible extent,'" see *Harmelin, 501 U.S. at 1000* (quoting *Rummel v. Estelle, 445 U.S. 263, 274–275, 63 L. Ed. 2d 382, 100 S. Ct. 1133 (1980)).* We have pinpointed that the "clearest and most reliable objective evidence of contemporary values is the legislation enacted by the country's legislatures." *Penry, 492 U.S. at 331, 106 L. Ed. 2d 256, 109 S. Ct. 2934.* Relying in part on such legislative evidence, we have held that death is an impermissibly excessive punishment for the rape of an adult woman, *Coker v. Georgia, 433 U.S. 584, 593–596, 53 L. Ed. 2d 982, 97 S. Ct. 2861 (1977),* or for a defendant who neither took life, attempted to take life, nor intended to take life, *Enmund v. Florida, 458 U.S. 782, 789–793, 73 L. Ed. 2d 1140, 102 S. Ct. 3368 (1982). . . .*

The parties have not called our attention to any state legislative consideration of the suitability of imposing the death penalty on mentally retarded offenders prior to 1986. In that year, the public reaction to the execution of a mentally retarded murderer in Georgia n8 apparently led to the enactment of the first state statute prohibiting such executions. . . . In 1988, when Congress enacted legislation reinstating the federal death penalty, it expressly provided that a "sentence of death shall not be carried out upon a person who is mentally retarded." n10 In 1989, Maryland enacted a similar prohibition. . . . It was in that year that we decided *Penry,* and concluded that those two state enactments, "even when added to the 14 States that have rejected capital punishment completely, do not provide sufficient evidence at present of a national consensus." *492 U.S. at 334, 106 L. Ed. 2d 256, 109 S. Ct. 2934.*

> n8 Jerome Bowden, who was identified as having mental retardation when he was 14-years-old, was scheduled for imminent execution in Georgia in June of 1986. The Georgia Board of Pardons and Paroles granted a stay following public protests over his execution. A psychologist selected by the State evaluated Bowden and determined that he had an IQ of 65, which is consistent with mental retardation. Nevertheless, the board lifted the stay and Bowden was executed the following day. The board concluded that Bowden understood the nature of his crime and his punishment and therefore that execution, despite his mental deficiencies, was permissible. See Montgomery, Bowden's Execution Stirs Protest, Atlanta Journal, October 13, 1986, p. A1. . . .

> n10 The Anti-Drug Abuse Act of 1988, Pub. L. 100–690, § 7001(*l*), 102 Stat. *4390, 21 U.S.C. § 848(l).* Congress expanded the federal death penalty law in 1994. It again included a provision that prohibited any individual with mental retardation from being sentenced to death or executed. Federal Death Penalty Act of 1994, *18 U.S.C. § 3596(c).*

. . .

Much has changed since then. Responding to the national attention received by the Bowden execution and our decision in *Penry,* state legislatures across the country began to address the issue. In 1990 Kentucky and Tennessee enacted statutes similar to those in Georgia and Maryland, as did New Mexico in 1991, and Arkansas, Colorado, Washington, Indiana, and Kansas in 1993 and 1994. . . . In 1995, when New York reinstated its death penalty, it emulated the Federal Government by expressly exempting the mentally retarded. . . . Nebraska followed suit in 1998. . . . There appear to have been no similar enactments during the next 2 years, but in 2000 and 2001 six more States—South Dakota, Arizona, Connecticut, Florida, Missouri, and North Carolina—joined the procession. ... The Texas Legislature unanimously adopted a similar bill, . . . and bills have passed at least one house in other States, including Virginia and Nevada. . . .

It is not so much the number of these States that is significant, but the consistency of the direction of change. n18 Given the well-known fact that anticrime legislation is far more popular than legislation providing protections for persons guilty of violent crime, the large number of States prohibiting the execution of mentally retarded persons (and the complete absence of States passing legislation reinstating the power to conduct such executions) provides powerful evidence that today our society views mentally retarded offenders as categorically less culpable than the average criminal. The evidence carries even greater force when it is noted that the legislatures that have addressed the issue have voted overwhelmingly in favor of the prohibition. n19 Moreover, even in those States that allow the execution of mentally retarded offenders, the practice is uncommon. Some States, for example, New Hampshire and New Jersey, continue to authorize executions, but none have been carried out in decades. Thus there is little need to pursue legislation barring the execution of the mentally retarded in those States. And it appears that even among those States that regularly execute offenders and that have no prohibition with regard to the mentally retarded, only five have executed offenders possessing a known IQ less than 70 since we decided *Penry*. n20 The practice, therefore, has become truly unusual, and it is fair to say that a national consensus has developed against it. n21

> n18 A comparison to *Stanford v. Kentucky, 492 U.S. 361, 106 L. Ed. 2d 306, 109 S. Ct. 2969 (1989)*, in which we held that there was no national consensus prohibiting the execution of juvenile offenders over age 15, is telling. Although we decided *Stanford* on the same day as *Penry,* apparently only two state legislatures have raised the threshold age for imposition of the death penalty. *Mont. Code Ann. § 45-5-102* (1999); *Ind. Code § 35-50-2-3* (1998).

> n19 App. D to Brief for AAMR et al. as *Amici Curiae.*

> n20 Those States are Alabama, Texas, Louisiana, South Carolina, and Virginia. Keyes, D., Edwards, D., & Perske, R. People with Mental Retardation are Dying Legally, 35 Mental Retardation (February 1997) (updated by Death Penalty Information Center; available at http://www.advocacyone.org/deathpenalty. html) (June 18, 2002).

> n21 Additional evidence makes it clear that this legislative judgment reflects a much broader social and professional consensus. For example, several organizations with germane expertise have adopted

official positions opposing the imposition of the death penalty upon a mentally retarded offender. See Brief for American Psychological Association et al. as *Amici Curiae*; Brief for AAMR et al. as *Amici Curiae.* In addition, representatives of widely diverse religious communities in the United States, reflecting Christian, Jewish, Muslim, and Buddhist traditions, have filed an *amicus curiae* brief explaining that even though their views about the death penalty differ, they all "share a conviction that the execution of persons with mental retardation cannot be morally justified." See Brief for United States Catholic Conference et al. as *Amici Curiae* in *McCarver* v. *North Carolina,* O. T. 2001, No. 00-8727, p. 2. Moreover, within the world community, the imposition of the death penalty for crimes committed by mentally retarded offenders is overwhelmingly disapproved. Brief for The European Union as Amicus *Curiae* in *McCarver v. North Carolina,* O. T. 2001, No. 00-8727, p. 4. Finally, polling data shows a widespread consensus among Americans, even those who support the death penalty, that executing the mentally retarded is wrong. Bonner, R. & Rimer, S. Executing the Mentally Retarded Even as Laws Begin to Shift, N. Y. Times, August 7, 2000, p. A1; App. B to Brief for AAMR as *Amicus Curiae* in *McCarver* v. *North Carolina*, O. T. 2001, No. 00-8727 (appending approximately 20 state and national polls on the issue). Although these factors are by no means dispositive, their consistency with the legislative evidence lends further support to our conclusion that there is a consensus among those who have addressed the issue. See *Thompson v. Oklahoma, 487 U.S. 815, 830, 831, 101 L. Ed. 2d 702, 108 S. Ct. 2687, n. 31 (1988)* (considering the views of "respected professional organizations, by other nations that share our Anglo–American heritage, and by the leading members of the Western European community").

To the extent there is serious disagreement about the execution of mentally retarded offenders, it is in determining which offenders are in fact retarded. In this case, for instance, the Commonwealth of Virginia disputes that Atkins suffers from mental retardation. Not all people who claim to be mentally retarded will be so impaired as to fall within the range of mentally retarded offenders about whom there is a national consensus. As was our approach in *Ford v. Wainwright,* with regard to insanity, "we leave to the States the task of developing appropriate ways to enforce the constitutional restriction upon its execution of sentences." *477 U.S. 399, 405, 416–417, 91 L. Ed. 2d 335, 106 S. Ct. 2595 (1986).* n22

> n22 The statutory definitions of mental retardation are not identical, but generally conform to the clinical definitions set forth in n3, *supra.*

III

This consensus unquestionably reflects widespread judgment about the relative culpability of mentally retarded offenders, and the relationship between mental retardation and the penological purposes served by the death penalty. Additionally, it suggests that some characteristics of mental retardation undermine the strength of the procedural protections that our capital jurisprudence steadfastly guards.

. . .

In light of these deficiencies, our death penalty jurisprudence provides two reasons consistent with the legislative consensus that the mentally retarded should be categorically excluded from execution. First, there is a serious question as to whether either justification that we have recognized as a basis for the death penalty applies to mentally retarded offenders. *Gregg v. Georgia, 428 U.S. 153, 183, 49 L. Ed. 2d 859, 96 S. Ct. 2909 (1976)*, identified "retribution and deterrence of capital crimes by prospective offenders" as the social purposes served by the death penalty. Unless the imposition of the death penalty on a mentally retarded person "measurably contributes to one or both of these goals, it 'is nothing more than the purposeless and needless imposition of pain and suffering,' and hence an unconstitutional punishment." *Enmund, 458 U.S. at* p. 798.

With respect to retribution—the interest in seeing that the offender gets his "just deserts"—the severity of the appropriate punishment necessarily depends on the culpability of the offender. Since *Gregg*, our jurisprudence has consistently confined the imposition of the death penalty to a narrow category of the most serious crimes . . . . Thus, pursuant to our narrowing jurisprudence,

which seeks to ensure that only the most deserving of execution are put to death, an exclusion for the mentally retarded is appropriate.

With respect to deterrence—the interest in preventing capital crimes by prospective offenders—"it seems likely that 'capital punishment can serve as a deterrent only when murder is the result of premeditation and deliberation,'" *Enmund, 458 U.S. at* p. 799. Exempting the mentally retarded from that punishment will not affect the "cold calculus that precedes the decision" of other potential murderers. *Gregg, 428 U.S. at* p. 186. Indeed, that sort of calculus is at the opposite end of the spectrum from behavior of mentally retarded offenders.

. . .

Our independent evaluation of the issue reveals no reason to disagree with the judgment of "the legislatures that have recently addressed the matter" and concluded that death is not a suitable punishment for a mentally retarded criminal. We are not persuaded that the execution of mentally retarded criminals will measurably advance the deterrent or the retributive purpose of the death penalty. Construing and applying the Eighth Amendment in the light of our "evolving standards of decency," we therefore conclude that such punishment is excessive and that the Constitution "places a substantive restriction on the State's power to take the life" of a mentally retarded offender. *Ford, 477 U.S. 399,* at p. 405, *91 L. Ed. 2d 335, 106 S. Ct. 2595.*

The judgment of the Virginia Supreme Court is reversed and the case is remanded for further proceedings not inconsistent with this opinion.

It is so ordered.

PEOPLE V. BILLA

SUPREME COURT OF CALIFORNIA

31 C<small>AL</small>. 4<small>TH</small> 1064; 79 P.3<small>D</small> 542; 6 C<small>AL</small>. R<small>PTR</small>. 3<small>D</small> 425

N<small>OVEMBER</small> 24, 2003

OPINIONBY: CHIN, J.

Defendant conspired with two others to commit arson of his truck for purposes of insurance fraud. All three conspirators were present at the scene of the burning. While committing the arson, one of the conspirators caught fire and was burned to death. We must decide whether defendant is guilty of murdering that coconspirator under the felony-murder rule. We conclude, as did the Court of Appeal, that the felony-murder rule applies to all arsonists at the scene of the arson. . . .

I. The Facts

The prosecution presented evidence from which the jury could reasonably find the following. Defendant purchased a truck and insured it for physical damage. On August 26, 1997, defendant and two others, including Manoj Bhardwaj, drove from Yuba City towards Sacramento, with defendant and Bhardwaj in defendant's truck and the third person following in a car. They intended to burn defendant's truck and obtain the insurance proceeds. Near Wheatland, defendant drove his truck onto a gravel road and stopped about two-tenths of a mile down the road around a bend. There the three set the truck on fire, using either kerosene or diesel fuel.

During these events, Bhardwaj's clothing somehow became saturated with the fuel. It is not clear exactly what happened, but evidence suggested he might have held a leaky canister of the fuel on his lap during the drive. While the three were setting the truck on fire, Bhardwaj's clothing caught fire, and he was severely burned. He died later of his injuries.

A jury convicted defendant of the second degree murder of Bhardwaj (Pen. Code, § § 187, 189), . . . arson causing great bodily injury (§ 451, subd. (a)), and making a false or fraudulent insurance claim (§ 550, subd. (a)(4)). The trial court had instructed the jury solely on the felony-murder rule as a basis for finding defendant guilty of murder. The Court of Appeal modified the judgment and affirmed it as modified. It held that defendant was properly convicted of Bhardwaj's murder under the felony-murder rule. We granted defendant's petition for review to decide whether the felony-murder rule applies on these facts.

II. Discussion

"All murder . . . which is committed in the perpetration of, or attempt to perpetrate, [specified felonies, including arson] . . . is murder of the first degree." (§ 189.) n2 This felony-murder rule covers "a variety of unintended homicides resulting from reckless behavior, or ordinary negligence, or pure accident . . . ." (*People v. Dillon* (1983) 34 Cal.3d 441, 477 {194 Cal. Rptr. 390, 668 P.2d 697}.) We must decide whether it includes the unintended death of one of the perpetrators during the commission of arson.

> n2 Although the prosecution proceeded on a felony-murder theory with arson the underlying felony, it only sought conviction for second degree murder, possibly, as the Court of Appeal suggested, "out of a belief that a charge of first degree murder would be unduly harsh under the circumstances . . . ."

Two overarching principles guide us. First, "we are not concerned here with the wisdom of the first degree felony-murder rule itself, or with the criticisms—and defenses—directed at it by judicial and academic commentators; *section 189* is the law of California, and we are not free to ignore or alter it if we would." (*People v. Pulido* (1997) 15 Cal.4th 713, 724 {63 Cal. Rptr. 2d 625, 936 P.2d 1235}.) Second, "[n]evertheless, when the rule as ordained by the Legislature requires detailed delineation, this court properly considers policy and consistency. In particular, we have held the first degree felony-murder rule 'should not be extended beyond any rational function that it is designed to serve.'" (*Ibid.*, quoting *People v. Washington* (1965) 62 Cal.2d 777, 783 {44 Cal. Rptr. 442, 402 P.2d 130}.)

. . .

In the landmark decision of *People v. Washington, supra,* 62 Cal.2d 777, we held that the robbery felony-murder rule does not apply when someone other than a robber, such as the police or a victim, does the killing. We cited *Ferlin* for the proposition that "for a defendant to be guilty of murder under the felony-murder rule the act of killing must be committed by the defendant or by his accomplice acting in furtherance of their common design." (*People v. Washington, supra,* at p. 783.) In *People v. Antick* (1975) 15 Cal.3d 79 {123 Cal. Rptr. 475, 539 P.2d 43}, we held that one robber cannot be vicariously liable for the death of an accomplice due to the deceased robber's actions because people cannot murder themselves. We discussed *Ferlin* and said its "holding was aptly explained by the Court of Appeal in *Woodruff v. Superior Court (1965) 237 Cal. App. 2d 749 {47 Cal. Rptr. 291}*: 'We believe the rationale of that decision to be that *section 189* was inapplicable because there was no killing by the accused felon and no killing of another by one for whose conduct the accused was vicariously responsible.'" . . . [I]n *Ferlin* "the coconspirator killed himself while he alone was perpetrating the felony he conspired to commit" and "it was held in substance and effect that inasmuch as [the deceased] killed himself Ferlin could not be held criminally responsible for his death." (*Id.* at p. 751.) (*People v. Antick, supra*, at p. 89.) More recently, we cited *Ferlin* for the proposition that to be guilty of murder for a killing attributable to the act of an accomplice, "the accomplice must cause the death of another human being by an act committed in furtherance of the common design." (*People v. Caldwell (1984) 36 Cal.3d 210, 217, fn. 2 {203 Cal. Rptr. 433, 681 P.2d 274}*.)

Defendant argues primarily that *Ferlin, supra, 203 Cal. 587*, and its progeny are on point here: Bhardwaj killed himself, and his death was not in furtherance of the conspiracy but entirely opposed to it. In deciding this question, we must consider the purpose behind the felony-murder rule, for we have said the rule should not be extended beyond its purpose. (*People v. Pulido, supra*, 15 Cal.4th at p. 724.) The rule's primary purpose is "to deter felons from killing negligently or accidentally by holding them strictly responsible for killings they commit." (*People v. Washington, supra, 62 Cal.2d* at p. 781; accord, *People v. Pulido, supra, 15 Cal.4th* at p. 725; *People v. Hansen (1994) 9 Cal.4th 300, 310 {36 Cal. Rptr. 2d 609, 885 P.2d 1022}*.) In *Washington*, we found this purpose not applicable when a *third person* kills a robber. "This purpose is not served by punishing [felons] for killings committed by their victims." (*People v. Washington, supra*, at p. 781.) However, here no third person killed Bhardwaj. Making arsonists guilty of murder if anyone, including an accomplice, dies in the arson gives them an incentive to do whatever is necessary to make sure no one dies. Defendant argues that felons already have a natural incentive not to kill themselves or their accomplices while committing their crimes. To the extent this is so, making felons strictly liable for deaths maximizes this incentive, thus furthering the purpose of the felony-murder rule.

The felony-murder rule applies to the death of a cohort as much as to the death of an innocent person. (*People v. Johnson (1972) 28 Cal. App. 3d 653, 656–658 {104 Cal. Rptr. 807}* [defendant's gun discharged, apparently accidentally, killing an accomplice who was running towards one of the victims; felony-murder rule applies]; *People v. Cabaltero (1939) 31 Cal. App. 2d 52, 55–56 {87 P.2d 364}* [one accomplice shot

and killed another accomplice, apparently out of anger that that accomplice had fired his gun; felony-murder rule applies]; see also *People v. Washington, supra, 62 Cal.2d* at p. 780 [rejecting a distinction between the death of an accomplice and the death of an innocent person].) . . .

One rationale of *Ferlin* and its progeny is that the accomplice's death "was not in furtherance of the conspiracy, but entirely opposed to it." (*Ferlin, supra, 203 Cal.* at p. 597.) This reasoning is flawed. . . . The death of the accomplice in *People v. Johnson, supra, 28 Cal. App. 3d 653*, and possibly also *People v. Cabaltero, supra, 31 Cal. App. 2d 52*, was similarly not in furtherance of the conspiracy in the sense that the death harmed the conspiracy. Nevertheless, the courts found felony-murder liability in those cases. As the Attorney General argues, there is a difference between *acts* done in furtherance of the conspiracy and the *results* of those acts. We have said that the "*act of killing*" must be in furtherance of the conspiracy. . . . the "death must result from an act committed in furtherance of the robbery or the escape from such robbery" . . . In this case, all three conspirators, including Bhardwaj, were *acting* in furtherance of the conspiracy, including committing the acts that *resulted* in Bhardwaj's death. Although the unintended result— Bhardwaj's death—was opposed to the conspiracy, the acts causing that result were in furtherance of it. . . .

Another rationale of *Ferlin* is that the victim killed himself. Defendant would distinguish *People v. Johnson, supra, 28 Cal. App. 3d 653*, and *People v. Cabaltero, supra, 31 Cal. App. 2d 52*, on this basis. He argues that in those cases, an accomplice killed the victim; here Bhardwaj, like the victim in *Ferlin*, simply killed himself. We disagree. . . . he did not just kill himself. All three conspirators, including defendant, were at the crime scene and active participants in the events immediately causing his death.

. . . We agree with the Court of Appeal's assessment: "In this case, Bhardwaj did not act alone in perpetrating the arson that was the cause of his death. Defendant was present and an active participant in the crime. And his active conduct was a direct cause of Bhardwaj's death. In short, regardless of whether the death was accidental or not, defendant's act of arson killed Bhardwaj. . . . We conclude that felony-murder liability for any death in the course of arson attaches to all accomplices in the felony at least where, as here, one or more surviving accomplices were present at the scene and active participants in the crime.

. . .

III. CONCLUSION

We affirm the judgment of the Court of Appeal.
GEORGE, C.J., KENNARD, J., BAXTER, J., WERDEGAR, J., BROWN, J., and MORENO, J., concurred.

PEOPLE V. STAMP ET AL.

COURT OF APPEAL OF CALIFORNIA, SECOND APPELLATE DISTRICT, DIVISION THREE

2 Cal. App. 3d 203; 82 Cal. Rptr. 598

December 1, 1969

OPINION BY: COBEY, P. J.

These are appeals by Jonathan Earl Stamp, Michael John Koory, and Billy Dean Lehman, following jury verdicts of guilty of robbery and murder, both in the first degree. Each man was given a life sentence on the murder charge together with the time prescribed by law on the robbery count.

Defendants appeal their conviction of the murder of Carl Honeyman who, suffering from a heart disease, died between 15 and 20 minutes after Koory and Stamp held up his business, the General Amusement Company, on October 26, 1965, at 10:45 a.m. Lehman, the driver of the getaway car, was apprehended a few minutes after the robbery; several weeks later Stamp was arrested in Ohio and Koory in Nebraska.

Broadly stated, the grounds of this appeal are: (1) insufficiency of the evidence on the causation of Honeyman's death; (2) inapplicability of the felony-murder rule to this case; (3) errors in the choice of instructions given and refused; . . .

On this appeal appellants primarily rely upon their position that the felony-murder doctrine should not have been applied in this case due to the unforeseeability of Honeyman's death.

... The Facts

. . . Defendants Koory and Stamp, armed with a gun and a blackjack, entered the rear of the building housing the offices of General Amusement Company, ordered the employees they found there to go to the front of the premises, where the two secretaries were working. Stamp, the one with the gun, then went into the office of Carl Honeyman, the owner and manager. Thereupon Honeyman, looking very frightened and pale, emerged from the office in a "kind of hurry." He was apparently propelled by Stamp who had hold of him by an elbow.

The robbery victims were required to lie down on the floor while the robbers took the money and fled out of the back door. As the robbers, who had been on the premises for 10 to 15 minutes, were leaving, they told the victims to remain on the floor for 5 minutes so that no one would "get hurt."

Honeyman, who had been lying next to the counter, had to use it to steady himself in getting up off the floor. Still pale, he was short of breath, sucking air, and pounding and rubbing his chest. As he walked down the hall, in an unsteady manner, still breathing hard and rubbing his chest, he said he was having trouble "keeping the pounding down inside" and that his heart was "pumping too fast for him." A few minutes later, although still looking very upset, shaking, wiping his forehead and rubbing his chest, he was able to walk in a steady manner into an employee's office. When the police arrived, almost immediately thereafter, he told them he was not feeling very well and that he had a pain in his chest. About 2 minutes later, which was 15 or 20 minutes after the robbery had occurred, he collapsed on the floor. At 11:25 he was pronounced dead on arrival at the hospital. The coroner's report listed the immediate cause of death as heart attack.

The employees noted that during the hours before the robbery Honeyman had appeared to be in normal health and good spirits. The victim was an obese, 60-year-old man, with a history of heart disease, who was under a great deal of pressure due to the intensely competitive nature of his business. Additionally, he did not take good care of his heart.

Three doctors, including the autopsy surgeon, Honeyman's physician, and a professor of cardiology from U.C.L.A., testified that although Honeyman had an advanced case of atherosclerosis, a progressive and ultimately fatal disease, there must have been some immediate upset to his system which precipitated the attack. It was their conclusion in response to a hypothetical question that but for the robbery there would have been no fatal seizure at that time. The fright induced by the robbery was too much of a shock to Honeyman's system. There was opposing expert testimony to the effect that it could not be said with reasonable medical certainty that fright could ever be fatal.

. . .

Application of the Felony-Murder Rule

Appellant's contention that the [f]elony-murder rule is inapplicable to the facts of this case is also without merit. Under the [f]elony-murder rule of *section 189 of the Penal Code*, a killing committed in either the perpetration of or an attempt to perpetrate robbery is murder of the first degree. This is true whether the killing is willful deliberate and premeditated, or merely accidental or unintentional, and whether or not the killing is planned as a part of the commission of the robbery. *People v. Washington, 62 Cal.2d 777, 783 {44 Cal.Rptr. 442, 402 P.2d 130}*, merely limits the rule to situations where the killing was committed by the felon or his accomplice acting in furtherance of their common design. The doctrine presumes malice aforethought on the basis of the commission of a felony inherently dangerous to human life. n3 . . . This rule is a rule of substantive law in California and not merely an evidentiary shortcut to finding malice as it withdraws from the jury the requirement that they find either express malice or the implied malice which is manifested in an intent to kill. Under this rule no intentional act is necessary other than the attempt to or the actual commission of the robbery itself. When a robber enters a place with a deadly weapon with the intent to commit robbery, malice is shown by the nature of the crime. . . .

> n3 In view of the fact that the Legislature has not seen fit to change the language of *Penal Code section 189* since the decisions holding that the requisite malice aforethought is to be implied from the commission of

those felonies inherently dangerous to human life, it must be presumed that these cases accurately state the law. (*People v. Hallner, 43 Cal.2d 715, 720 {277 P.2d 393}*.)

There is no requirement that the killing occur, "while committing" or "while engaged in" the felony, or that the killing be "a part of" the felony, other than that the few acts be a part of one continuous transaction. (*People v. Chavez, 37 Cal.2d 656, 670 {234 P.2d 632}*.) Thus the homicide need not have been committed "to perpetrate" the felony. There need be no technical inquiry as to whether there has been a completion or abandonment of, or desistance from the robbery before the homicide itself was completed. (*People v. Chavez, supra, at* pp. 669–670.)

The doctrine is not limited to those deaths which are foreseeable. (See 1 Witkin, Cal. Crimes (1963) § § 78, 79, pp. 79-80; *People v. Chavez, supra, at* pp. 669–670.) Rather a felon is held strictly liable for *all* killings committed by him or his accomplices in the course of the felony. (*People v. Talbot, 64 Cal.2d 691, 704 {51 Cal.Rptr. 417, 414 P.2d 633}*.) As long as the homicide is the direct causal result of the robbery the [f]elony-murder rule applies whether or not the death was a natural or probable consequence of the robbery. So long as a victim's predisposing physical condition, regardless of its cause, is not the *only* substantial factor bringing about his death, that condition, and the robber's ignorance of it, in no way destroys the robber's criminal responsibility for the death.

. . .

CONCLUSION

The judgment is affirmed.

PEOPLE V. CONTRERAS

COURT OF APPEAL, SECOND DISTRICT, DIVISION 3, CALIFORNIA

26 CAL.APP.4TH 944; NO. B067180

JULY 12, 1994

OPINION BY: KLEIN, P. J.

Defendant and appellant Heriberto Contreras appeals the judgment entered following his conviction by jury of second-degree murder. (Pen.Code, § 187.) n1 Contreras also pleaded guilty to a violation of Vehicle Code section 14601, subdivision (a), and admitted two prior convictions for violations of the same section within five years of the instant offense. The trial court sentenced Contreras to a term of fifteen years to life in state prison.

> n1 All subsequent statutory references are to the Penal Code, unless otherwise specified.

Because the circumstances of this case support the jury's finding Contreras harbored implied malice when he caused a fatal traffic collision, and none of the remaining contentions raised by Contreras warrants reversal, the judgment is affirmed.

FACTUAL AND PROCEDURAL BACKGROUND

A child died as a result of injuries sustained in a traffic collision on February 10, 1991. The collision occurred when a tow truck driven by Contreras rear-ended the vehicle in which the child was a passenger.

The People presented evidence establishing a pattern of reckless driving by bandit tow truck drivers in general and by Contreras in particular. Contreras had received numerous citations for traffic violations, had been arrested for reckless driving, had a prior accident, and actively was racing other tow truck drivers to an accident scene at the time of the fatal collision. Further, the evidence indicated Contreras knew the brakes on his tow truck were not functioning properly on the day of the collision.

We set forth the evidence which supports the jury's finding of implied malice in accordance with the usual rule of appellate review. (*People v. Thomas* (1992) 2 Cal.4th 489, 514, 7 Cal.Rptr.2d 199, 828 P.2d 101; *People v. Johnson* (1980) 26 Cal.3d 557, 575–578, 162 Cal.Rptr. 431, 606 P.2d 738.

1. The prosecution's evidence.

a. Illegal tow truck drivers.

Los Angeles police detective Stephen Bernard testified he investigates the operation of illegal tow truck drivers in the City of Los Angeles. These drivers, referred to as "bird-doggers" or "tow bandits" illegally monitor emergency calls on police scanners and race to accident scenes. The first driver to arrive at the scene has the pick of which disabled vehicle to tow. Competition is created by the fact an automotive repair shop will pay between $500 and $1,500 for damaged high-value cars. Bird-doggers generally have poor driving records.

Admitted bird-dogger Anthony Reedburg testified Contreras was his friend and employee. At the time of the accident in issue, Reedburg controlled 33 tow trucks working out of Empire Auto Restoration. Contreras worked out of Harbor Tow which Reedburg also controlled. Reedburg testified body shops paid approximately $600 for damaged new cars but admitted he had received as much as $3,000 for a damaged vehicle.

b. Contreras's prior violations.

(1) Speeding on May 17,1990.

On May 17, 1990, Los Angeles police officer Stephen Scallon saw Contreras driving a blue Mustang at 58 miles per hour in a 35-mile-per-hour zone on Adams Boulevard. Scallon cited Contreras for speeding and for driving on a revoked or suspended license. Contreras signed the citation.

(2) Red light on June 16, 1990.

On June 16, 1990, Los Angeles police officer Billy Holland saw Contreras turn right onto Soto Street in a gray Volkswagen without stopping for the red light. Contreras was approximately 15 seconds late for the light. Holland cited Contreras for failing to stop at a red light, no driver's license in his possession, and lack of proof of insurance. Contreras signed the citation.

(3) Speeding on July 4, 1990.

On July 4,1990, California Highway Patrol officer Melanie Nava saw a Chevrolet tow truck driven by Contreras pass her on the freeway at approximately 90 miles per hour. Nava drove at 115 miles per hour to catch the truck and paced it at approximately 85 miles per hour. Contreras "was traveling in and out, using all lanes of travel." Nava stopped the truck, advised Contreras he had been driving recklessly, and told him he could be arrested for reckless driving. Nava cited Contreras for speeding because traffic conditions were light. Contreras signed the citation.

(4) Unsafe lane changes and following too closely on September 11, 1990.

On September 11, 1990, Los Angeles Police helicopter pilot Frank King noticed a tow truck speeding in a residential area at 50 to 60 miles per hour. The truck slowed down when it went through stop signs but never went less than 30 miles per hour. King thought the truck was stolen.

Los Angeles police officer Cornell Greer received a radio broadcast from King and followed a tow truck driven by Contreras on San Vicente Boulevard. Contreras made numerous unsafe lane changes and followed vehicles too closely. When the truck stopped at an accident scene, Greer cited Contreras for unsafe lane changes, following too closely, and not wearing a seat belt. Greer noted on the citation Contreras's driving had nearly caused several traffic accidents. Greer told Contreras his driving could have resulted in arrest for reckless driving.

(5) Reckless driving arrest on September 17,1990.

On September 17, 1990, at 10 a.m., Culver City police detective Maurice Vidican was stopped at a red light at Jefferson Boulevard and Overland Avenue in an unmarked police vehicle. Vidican noticed a tow truck approach from behind and enter the right-turn-only lane as if it were going to turn south. Vidican proceeded as the light changed but "the tow truck shot . . . directly in front of me." Vidican had to slam on his brakes to avoid hitting the truck. Vidican followed the truck which was traveling at speeds between 90 and 100 miles per hour on Jefferson Boulevard and weaving in and out of traffic. Vidican radioed for assistance and identified Contreras when other officers stopped the truck at an accident scene at Jefferson and La Cienega Boulevards.

Contreras was arrested for reckless driving.

(6) Unsafe U-turn on September 17, 1990.

On September 17, 1990, at 4:40 p.m. Inglewood police officer Jeffrey Steinhoff was northbound on La Cienega Boulevard at La Tijera Boulevard when he heard a report of a traffic accident. He saw a fire truck driving toward the accident followed by a tow truck "going from lane to lane" and traveling at 65 to 70 miles per hour.

At the accident scene the tow truck stopped in the southbound lanes of La Tijera, turned on its emergency lights, and made a U-turn crossing double yellow solid lines and "causing the northbound traffic to come to a sudden halt." Contreras stopped next to the accident and held up traffic. Steinhoff cited Contreras for unsafe U-turn and no driver's license in his possession. Steinhoff discussed with Contreras the near collision Contreras had caused.

(7) Traffic accident of October 6, 1990.

On October 6, 1990, Renon Baker, a private citizen, noticed a tow truck tailgating her vehicle. The truck sped past her at 55 to 60 miles per hour. Ahead of them, a passenger vehicle rolled through a stop sign in an attempt to "beat the tow truck. [¶] But the tow truck was going too fast, and . . . hit him." The passenger vehicle was pushed onto the sidewalk. Contreras told Baker, "I know I was going too fast."

(8) Speeding on January 18, 1991.

On January 18, 1991, Los Angeles police officer William Rugh saw Contreras driving a truck westbound on Slausen Avenue traveling in excess of 70 miles per hour in a 35-mile-per-hour zone and passing other vehicles. Rugh advised Contreras his driving was reckless and could kill someone. Rugh cited Contreras for speeding and Contreras signed the citation.

(9) Red light on February 7, 1991.

Los Angeles police officer Ellen Perez testified that on February 7,1991, she saw a tow truck driven by Contreras go through a red light on Manchester Boulevard. Contreras was 15 feet late for the light and was traveling at 40 to 45 miles per hour. Perez cited Contreras for failing to stop for a red light and driving with a suspended driver's license. Contreras signed the citation.

(10) Notification of suspended driving privilege on January 19, 1991.

On January 19, 1991, Los Angeles police officer Robert Di Paolo issued Contreras a Department of Motor Vehicles form formally advising Contreras his license had been suspended or revoked and he could not operate a motor vehicle in California. Contreras signed the form in Di Paolo's presence.

Roger Muro, a principal hearing officer with the Department of Motor Vehicles, testified that on February 10, 1991, Contreras's driver's license remained suspended.

c. Reedburg's trial testimony.

On February 9, 1991, Contreras drove his truck to Reedburg's house and told Reedburg, "Something [is] wrong with the brakes again on the truck. I need your truck." Contreras borrowed Reedburg's truck and left.

The next morning, February 10, 1991, Reedburg drove Contreras's truck to Empire Auto Restoration. Reedburg testified, "[Y]ou couldn't go 30 miles an hour in the truck and stop, . . . [¶] The truck didn't have no brakes. [Sic.]" The brake pedal went all the way to the floorboard.

Contreras arrived at the shop at 8 a.m. and asked about his brakes. Reedburg told him they were "no good." Contreras answered, " Yeah, that's why I brought the truck to you, so you can get it taken care of." Reedburg told Contreras the truck could be driven no more than 10 or 15 miles an hour and "if you got behind anybody, that you would have a wreck."

Contreras returned one hour later. Although Contreras's truck had been moved to an area normally reserved for repaired vehicles, Reedburg told Contreras the truck was not ready. Contreras became angry and left in Reedburg's truck. He returned at approximately 10 a.m.

At this point, Reedburg's accounts of the day's activities varied. At the preliminary hearing, Reedburg testified he was with Contreras between 9:30 a.m. and noon waiting for a mechanic to arrive to fix the brakes. When an accident report came over the police scanner, about 10 drivers, including Contreras, "took off."

At trial, Reedburg testified Contreras left Empire Auto Restoration and returned a third time at approximately 11:30 a.m. The accident call came in shortly after Contreras returned and before Reedburg had a chance to tell Contreras the brakes had not yet been fixed.

Under both accounts, Contreras had the keys to Reedburg's truck but took the keys to his own truck and left in it in response to the accident report. Reedburg was unable to stop Contreras and had not told Contreras his brakes had been fixed. Reedburg tried to call Contreras on the radio but could not reach him.

Reedburg heard about an accident at 54th Street and Denker Avenue over the radio and went to the scene. Contreras was crying and told Reedburg the brakes had failed. Contreras left the scene with another tow driver but returned when Reedburg radioed to him. In a telephone conversation two or three weeks before the trial, Contreras told Reedburg not to say Contreras knew the brakes were bad.

Reedburg further testified Contreras could not receive the radio call regarding the brakes because the radio in Contreras's truck was inoperable. However, in a statement to officer Jiminez taken April 12, 1991, which Reedburg read and signed, Reedburg said the radio was on and working in Contreras's truck before and after the accident. Reedburg told Jiminez he heard Contreras's radio receiving broadcasts at the scene of the accident.

Approximately one year before the accident, Reedburg had been a passenger in a tow truck driven by Contreras. Reedburg made Contreras pull over and Reedburg insisted on driving. He told Contreras "he was likely to kill somebody driving the way he drives."

Reedburg testified he had never driven down Denker Avenue from Empire Auto Restoration, the route to the accident, without using his brakes.

d. Facts related to the fatal collision.

At approximately noon on Sunday, February 10, 1991, Charles Mason saw two tow trucks racing side by side north on Denker Avenue at 60 to 70 miles per hour. They hit a dip at 55th Street, went airborne and made screeching sounds when they landed but did not slow down. The tow truck driven by Contreras rear-ended a car stopped at the red light at the intersection of 54th and Denker.

Margaret Ledlow heard the trucks "bottom out" at 55th Street and ran to her porch. She saw two tow trucks racing toward her "side-by-side down the street." The trucks were traveling at "freeway speed, 55 maybe 60 miles per hour, if not faster." Contreras's truck, which was on the correct side of the street, hit a car stopped for a red light at 54th and Denker. The car "went up into the air" across the intersection and into a parked car. The driver of the other tow truck refused to assist and left the scene. Contreras stayed and tried to help the victims.

The car struck by Contreras was driven by Nadine Lashley. She was on her way home from Sunday school with 9-year-old Lalisa Stewart and 13-year-old Jerry Williams. Lashley and Stewart suffered various injuries and both were hospitalized. The parties stipulated Jerry Williams died on February 10, 1991, as a result of the injuries received in the collision. The speed limit on Denker Avenue is 25 miles per hour.

2. Defense.

Los Angeles police officer Richard Haberland, an accident reconstruction expert, investigated the fatal accident and estimated the truck had been traveling at a minimum speed of 47.7 to 54 miles per hour when the front wheels locked, based on the 177.5 feet of skid marks at the scene. Haberland opined, had the truck's brakes been working properly, there was a 75 percent chance the truck would have stopped before impact.

On cross-examination, Haberland testified he had given Contreras the benefit of every doubt when estimating the coefficient of friction of the roadway and the tires and assumed the front wheels supply only 50 percent of the braking power of the vehicle. Also, Haberland assumed the rear brakes had not contributed at all to the deceleration of the truck and disregarded the energy consumed in the crush deformation of the vehicles in the crash. Each of these factors would increase the minimum speed calculation Haberland reached.

3. Rebuttal.

Roger Newsock, senior staff analysis engineer for General Motors, inspected the brakes on Contreras's 1990 Chevrolet truck. He found the front and the rear hydraulic systems and the front brakes were in good condition. However, the rear brakes were completely worn. Although average brake pedal movement is four-and-a-half inches, the brake pedal on Contreras's truck moved seven-and-a-quarter inches when depressed.

. . .

DISCUSSION

1. Contreras properly was charged with and convicted of murder.

a. The propriety of the charge.

Contreras contends an accidental homicide which does not involve a high-speed chase or drug-impaired driving cannot be classified as murder under California law. He concludes his conviction must be reversed.

This claim is meritless.

"Murder is the unlawful killing of a human being . . . with malice aforethought." (§ 187, subd. (a).) Malice is implied "when the circumstances attending the killing show an abandoned and malignant heart." (§ 188.)

Manslaughter, by contrast, is the unlawful killing of a human being without malice. (§§ 191.5, subd. (a), 192.) The required level of culpability for either gross vehicular manslaughter while intoxicated (§ 191.5) or vehicular manslaughter (§ 192, subd. (c)) is gross negligence. (*People v. Ochoa* (1993) 6 Cal.4th 1199, 1204, 26 Cal.Rptr.2d 23, 864 P.2d 103; *People v. Bennett* (1991) 54 Cal.3d 1032, 1036, 2 Cal.Rptr.2d 8, 819 P.2d 849.) Both statutes expressly provide they "shall not be construed as prohibiting or precluding a charge of murder under Section 188 upon facts exhibiting wantonness and a conscious disregard for life to support a finding of implied malice, or upon facts showing malice consistent with the holding of the California Supreme Court in *People v. Watson* [1981] 30 Cal.3d 290, 179 Cal.Rptr. 43, 637 P.2d 279." (§§ 191.5, subd. (d), 192, subd. (c)(3).)

People v. Watson (1981) 30 Cal.3d 290, 296, 179 Cal.Rptr. 43, 637 P.2d 279, distinguished gross negligence from implied malice in a drunk driving case. Gross negligence was defined as the exercise of so slight a degree of care as to raise a presumption of conscious indifference to the consequences. Implied malice requires proof the accused acted deliberately with conscious disregard for life.

"Implied malice contemplates a subjective awareness of a higher degree of risk than does gross negligence, and involves an element of wantonness which is absent in gross negligence. [Citations.] [¶] ... A finding of gross negligence is made by applying an objective test: if a reasonable person in defendant's position would have been aware of the risk involved, then defendant is presumed to have had such an awareness. [Citation.] However, a finding of implied malice depends upon a determination that the defendant actually appreciated the risk involved, ie., a subjective standard. [Citation.]" (*People v. Watson,* supra, 30 Cal.3d at pp. 296–297, 179 Cal. Rptr. 43, 637 P.2d 279.)

It is the" '"conscious disregard for human life" , " that sets implied malice apart from gross negligence. (*People v. Nieto Benitez* (1992) 4 Cal.4th 91, 109, 13 Cal.Rptr.2d 864, 840 P.2d 969; *People v. Dellinger* (1989) 49 Cal.3d 1212, 1221–1222, 264 Cal.Rptr. 841, 783 P.2d 200; *People v. Protopappas* (1988) 201 Cal.App.3d 152, 162–164, 246 Cal.Rptr. 915.) "Even if the act results in a death that is accidental, as defendant contends was the case here, the circumstances surrounding the act may evince implied malice. [Citations.]" (*People v. Nieto Benitez,* supra, 4 Cal.4th at p. 110, 13 Cal.Rptr.2d 864, 840 P.2d 969.)

Considerations such as whether the act underlying the homicide is a felony, a misdemeanor or inherently dangerous in the abstract are not dispositive in assessing whether a defendant acted with implied malice. (*People v. Nieto* Benitez, supra, 4 Cal.4th at pp. 106-108, 13 Cal.Rptr.2d 864, 840 P.2d 969.) A finding of implied malice must be based upon "consideration of the circumstances preceding the fatal act. [Citations.]" (*People v. Nieto Benitez,* supra, 4 Cal.4th at p. 107, 13 Cal.Rptr.2d 864, 840 P.2d 1. 969.)

Thus, the absence of intoxication or high-speed flight from pursuing officers does not preclude a finding of malice. These facts merely are circumstances to be considered in evaluating culpability. Where other evidence shows "a wanton disregard for life, and the facts demonstrate a subjective awareness of the risk created, malice may be implied. (§ 188.) In such cases, a murder charge is appropriate." (*People v. Watson,* supra, 30 Cal.3d at p. 298, 179 Cal.Rptr. 43, 637 P.2d 279; *People v. Young* (1992) 11 Cal.App.4th 1299, 1309, 15 Cal.Rptr.2d 30;

People v. Olivas (1985) 172 Cal.App.3d 984, 988–989, 218 Cal.Rptr. 567.)

Based on the foregoing authorities, it is clear Contreras properly may be charged with murder in this case even though he was sober and was not involved in a high-speed chase with police at the time of the fatal collision.

b. Factual sufficiency.

Contreras contends there is no evidence to support the finding he had the requisite subjective knowledge his conduct created a substantial risk of death to another. Rather, his intent was "merely to be the first on the scene to get a towing job." Contreras argues this "goal was completely contrary to a subjective knowledge of a substantial risk of death because any accident, let alone a fatal one, would be certain to frustrate it." Contreras submits the evidence establishes only negligent operation of the truck. He asserts the evidence did not conclusively establish he drove the truck knowing the brakes were defective and the fact Reedburg tried to radio Contreras shows Contreras had a reasonable basis to believe the brakes had been repaired.

Contreras further argues even if he knew or suspected the brakes were defective, the evidence did not demonstrate a conscious disregard for life because he tried to stop the truck, which skidded halfway down the block, and attempted to help the victims after the collision.

Contreras's attack upon the sufficiency of the evidence fails.

. . .

The arguments advanced by Contreras on appeal were rejected by the jury. Clearly, the evidence was sufficient to show Contreras subjectively was aware of the risk to human life posed by his driving and that he consciously and deliberately disregarded that risk. (*People v. Klvana* (1992) 11 Cal.App.4th 1679, 1703–1704,15 Cal.Rptr.2d 512; *People v. Protopappas,* supra, 201 Cal.App.3d at pp. 166–172, 246 Cal.Rptr. 915; *People v. Summers* (1983) 147 Cal.App.3d 180, 184-185, 195 Cal.Rptr. 21.)

Based on his driving record, his prior accident, and the known inadequacy of his brakes on the date in question, the issue was not whether Contreras would have a serious traffic accident, but when.

Although there was evidence from which it could be argued Contreras believed his brakes had been repaired, the jury was entitled to reject that interpretation in favor of the more credible and substantial evidence which demonstrated Contreras knew his brakes were malfunctioning and had not yet been repaired.

Moreover, even if the jury believed Contreras thought the brakes had been repaired at the time he got into the truck, the jury was entitled to conclude he knew they were damaged before he reached 54th and Denker. Reedburg testified he had never driven from Empire Auto Restoration to 54th and Denker without applying the brakes. Because the brake pedal on Contreras's truck went to the floor when depressed, Contreras knew the first time he applied them they had not been repaired.

Thus, the evidence indicates Contreras knew the truck's brakes were defective at the time of the fatal crash and that he drove recklessly, racing at high speed in a residential area, anyway. Certainly the jury rationally could conclude the evidence demonstrated conscious disregard for life.

The fact Contreras did not immediately flee the accident scene must be balanced against Reedburg's testimony Contreras did eventually flee and had to be called back by Reedburg over the radio before the police arrived.

Contreras also argues his conduct was not as aggravated as the high-speed chase in People v. Cotton (1980) 113 Cal.App.3d 294, 169 Cal.Rptr. 814, which resulted in reversal of an assault with a deadly weapon conviction for insufficiency of the evidence. However, Cotton merely held reckless driving with injury in violation of Vehicle Code section 23104 does not, per se, generate a transferable intent to commit a battery with an automobile in violation of section 245, subdivision (a). As no similar presumption was made here, Cotton is distinguishable.

For all the foregoing reasons, there is substantial evidence to support the jury's finding Contreras subjectively knew his driving created a substantial risk to human life and consciously disregarded that danger. Accordingly, this claim of error fails.

. . .

DISPOSITION

The judgment is affirmed.

CROSKEY and KITCHING, JJ., concur.

PEOPLE V. SATCHELL

SUPREME COURT OF CALIFORNIA

6 Cal. 3d 28; 489 P.2d 1361; 98 Cal. Rptr. 33

November 4, 1971

OPINION BY: SULLIVAN, J.

In a two-count indictment defendant John M. Satchell was charged respectively with murder (*Pen. Code, § 187*) and assault with a deadly weapon upon a peace officer (*Pen. Code, § 245*, subd. (b)). As amended the indictment also alleged four prior felony convictions. Defendant entered pleas of not guilty to the two substantive counts and admitted the four prior convictions. The jury acquitted him of the aggravated assault charged in the second count of the indictment but found him guilty of murder of the second degree. Defendant appeals from the judgment of conviction.

For the reasons set forth below, we have concluded that it was prejudicial error for the trial court to instruct the jury on the theory of second degree felony murder. Accordingly, we reverse the judgment.

The facts relevant to our determination can be briefly stated. On July 2, 1969, defendant and the victim Jordan became engaged in a heated argument on a public street in San Francisco. The argument progressed beyond mere harsh language when defendant shoved Jordan. The latter then withdrew to some distance down the street; defendant went to his automobile, which was parked nearby and got in. A few minutes later Jordan returned and walked over to defendant's car. The argument then resumed, but it was abruptly terminated when the defendant emerged from the car holding a sawed-off shotgun, shot Jordan once in the chest, and then drove off. Jordan died of the shotgun wound.

At trial defendant took the stand and testified that he had shot Jordan, with whom he had had no prior acquaintance, in self-defense when the latter threatened him and made movements which defendant interpreted as efforts to draw a weapon. A defense witness testified that Jordan had a gun in his hand at the time of the shooting, which gun was taken from the victim after defendant had departed. n1

n1 The charge of aggravated assault upon a police officer, of which defendant was acquitted, arose out of

circumstances surrounding defendant's arrest later in the day.

The trial court instructed the jury on the definition of murder and malice (CALJIC No. 301 (supp.) . . . and the degrees of murder (CALJIC Nos. 302 and 302-A), but it eliminated first degree murder from the consideration of the jury by indicating that none of the felonies enumerated in *section 189 of the Penal Code* was involved here and by not instructing on premeditation. (See CALJIC No. 303 (supp.)) The jury was fully instructed on second degree murder, however, and the following instruction on second degree felony murder was given: "The unlawful killing of a human being, whether intentional, unintentional, or accidental, which occurs as a direct causal result of the commission of or attempt to commit a felony inherently dangerous to human life, namely, the crime of *possession of a concealable firearm by a felon*, and where there was in the mind of the perpetrator the specific intent to commit such crime, is murder of the second degree. The specific intent to commit *the crime of possession of a concealable firearm by a felon* and the commission of or attempt to commit such crime must be proved beyond a reasonable doubt." . . .

. . .

The trial court went on to give a series of instructions . . . defining and explaining the crime of possession of a concealable firearm by a felon. (*Pen. Code, § 12021*; see *Pen. Code, § 12001*.) n5

. . .

n5 *Section 12021 of the Penal Code* at the time here pertinent provided: "Any person who is not a citizen of the United States and any person who has been convicted of a felony under the laws of the United States, of the State of California, or any other state, government, or country, or who is addicted to the use of any narcotic drug, who owns or has in his possession or under his custody or control any pistol, revolver, or other firearm capable of being concealed upon the person is guilty of a public offense, and shall be punishable by imprisonment in the state prison not exceeding 15 years, or in a county jail not exceeding one year or by a fine not exceeding five hundred dollars ($500), or by both."

. . .

Finally, the court gave instructions concerning manslaughter, heat of passion, and provocation, . . . and instructions concerning justifiable homicide and self-defense. . . . Among the manslaughter instruction given was CALJIC No. 310 (supp.), which provided in part: "If a person *while committing a felony* causes another's death, malice is implied, and the crime is murder." . . . (Italics added.)

. . .

The jury deliberated for two full days before reaching their verdict. Four times in the course of their deliberations the jury requested that the court reinstruct them on murder, manslaughter, and justifiable homicide. Questions put to the court by the jury foreman indicate that the jury's primary concern was the operation of the second degree felony-murder instruction in the context of the other homicide instructions. . . . At the end of the second day of deliberations the jury returned their verdict finding defendant guilty of second degree murder (and not guilty of the aggravated assault charged in the second count of the indictment).

. . .

Defendant moved for a new trial on the ground that the second degree felony-murder instruction should not have been given, but the motion was denied. He appeals from the judgment of conviction on the same ground among others. . . . We have concluded that his contention must be sustained.

. . .

Applying this principle to various concrete factual circumstances, we have sought to insure that the "highly artificial concept" (*People v. Phillips (1966) 64 Cal.2d 574, 582 {51 Cal. Rptr. 225, 414 P.2d 353}*) of strict criminal liability incorporate in the felony-murder doctrine be given the narrowest possible application consistent with its ostensible purpose—which is to deter those engaged in felonies from killing negligently or accidentally (see *People v. Washington, supra, 62 Cal.2d 777, 781*, and authorities there cited). Thus, for example, we have refused to apply the doctrine in cases wherein the killing is committed by persons other than the defendant or an accomplice acting in furtherance of a common felonious design (*People v. Washington, supra, 62 Cal.2d 777, pp. 781–783*); in cases wherein the operation of the doctrine depends upon "a felony which is an integral part of the homicide and which

the evidence produced by the prosecution shows to be an offense included *in fact* within the offense charged" (*People v. Ireland, supra, 70 Cal.2d 522, 539, . . .* and in cases wherein the underlying felony is not one of the six enumerated in *section 189 of the Penal Code* and is not inherently dangerous to human life.

. . .

In the instant case it is clear that the victim was killed by defendant while he was engaged in the commission of a felony . . . other than the six enumerated in *section 189 of the Penal Code*. Thus, in determining whether the felony-murder doctrine is properly applicable the threshhold inquiry is whether the felony in which defendant was engaged was a "felony inherently dangerous to human life" within the meaning of *People v. Phillips, supra, 64 Cal.2d 574*, and *People v. Williams, supra, 63 Cal.2d 452*. If the felony in question was not such an inherently dangerous felony, the felony-murder instruction given was without legal foundation and the judgment must be reversed if the giving of that instruction was prejudicial. n14

. . .

n14 Clearly the question whether the underlying felony is inherently dangerous and therefore capable of supporting a second degree felony-murder instruction logically precedes the question whether such a felony merges with the charged homicide crime and is therefore not subject to utilization as the basis of such an instruction.

At the outset it is clear that this court has unequivocally held on more than one occasion that the offense set forth in section 12021 is a felony capable of supporting a second degree felony-murder instruction. . . .

. . . in 1965 we held that, in assessing whether a felony was inherently dangerous within the meaning of *Ford*, "we look to the elements of the felony in the abstract, not the particular 'facts' of the case." (*People v. Williams (1965) supra, 63 Cal.2d 452, 458, fn. 5.*) There the victim, an illegal supplier of methedrine, was killed with a knife during an affray which resulted after defendants demanded that he pay a debt either in methedrine or in money. The jury was given a second degree felony-murder instruction based upon the crime of conspiracy to possess methedrine without a prescription. We held that the instruction was erroneous because the subject felony, viewed in the abstract "is surely not, as such, inherently dangerous." (*63 Cal.2d at p. 458.*) . . .

. . .

The teaching of *Williams* was applied and explained in *People v. Phillips (1966) supra, 64 Cal.2d 574*. There the defendant, a chiropractor, was tried for murder following the death from cancer of a patient whom he dissuaded from surgery and purported to treat through chiropractic methods. The jury was given a second degree felony-murder instruction based upon the crime of grand theft by false pretenses. (*Pen. Code, § § 484, 487.*) Holding that the crime of grand theft, viewed in the abstract, was not inherently dangerous to human life, we went on to reject the contention of the prosecution that the subject felony should be characterized in light of the defendant's actual conduct as "grand theft medical fraud," assertedly an inherently dangerous offense. "To fragmentize the 'course of conduct' of defendant so that the felony-murder rule applies if any segment of that conduct may be considered dangerous to life would widen the rule beyond calculation. It would then apply not only to the commission of specific felonies, which are themselves dangerous to life, but to the perpetration of *any* felony during which defendant may have acted in such a manner as to endanger life.

. . .

It bears emphasis that, in determining whether a felony is inherently dangerous for purposes of the felony-murder rule we assess that felony *in the abstract*. The felony here in question is possession of a concealable firearm by one who has previously been convicted of a (i.e., another) felony. n18 We do *not* look to the specific facts of the case before us in order to determine whether, in light of the nature of the particular felony of which defendant was previously convicted, his possession of a concealable firearm was inherently dangerous. Rather, we direct our attention to the genus of crimes known as felonies and determine whether the possession of a concealable firearm by one who has been convicted of *any crime within that genus* is an act inherently dangerous to human life which, as such, justifies the extreme consequence (i.e., imputed malice) which the felony-murder doctrine demands.

> n18 Unfortunately, the compound nature of the felony here considered requires that we make reference not only to that felony (possession of a concealable firearm by an ex-felon) but also to the previous felony conviction which renders such possession felonious.

It is manifest that the range of antisocial activities which are criminally punishable as felonies in this state is very wide indeed. Some of these felonies, such as certain well-known crimes against the person of another, distinctly manifest a propensity for acts dangerous to human life on the part of the perpetrator. Others, of which a random sampling is set forth in the margin, n19 just as distinctly fail to manifest such a propensity. Surely it cannot be said that a person who has committed a crime in this latter category, when he arms himself with a concealable weapon, presents a danger to human life so significantly more extreme than that presented by a non-felon similarly armed . . . as to justify the imputation of malice to him if a homicide should result. Accordingly, because we can conceive of such a vast number of situations wherein it would be grossly illogical to impute malice, we must conclude that the violation of section 12021 by one previously convicted of a felony is not itself a felony *inherently* dangerous to human life which will support a second degree felony-murder instruction.

> n19 See, for example, Corporations Code, sections 3019–3021, *25540* et seq. (fraudulent and deceptive acts relating to corporations); *Elections Code, sections 12000* et seq., *14403, 15280, 17090* et seq., *29100* et seq., 29130 et seq., 29160, 29180, 29400, *29430,* 29431 (elections offenses); *Financial Code, section 18857.1* (unauthorized sale of investment certificates); *Government Code, section 9050* et seq. (interference with the legislative process), section 9908 (crimes of legislative representatives); *Insurance Code, section 556* (false or fraudulent insurance claim), section 833 (crimes in the issuance of insurance securities); *Military and Veterans Code, section 421* (conversion of military property); *Public Resources Code, section 5190* (interest of park commissioner in park contract); *Vehicle Code, section 4463* (false evidence of registration).

. . .

The judgment is reversed.

PEOPLE V. IRELAND

SUPREME COURT OF CALIFORNIA

70 Cal. 2d 522; 450 P.2d 580; 75 Cal. Rptr. 188

February 28, 1969

OPINION BY: SULLIVAN, J.

Defendant Patrick Ireland was charged by indictment with the murder of Ann Lucille Ireland, his wife. He entered pleas of not guilty and not guilty by reason of insanity and, after a trial by jury, was found guilty of murder in the second degree. Defendant's plea of not guilty by reason of insanity was personally withdrawn by him, and he was sentenced to imprisonment for the term prescribed by law. He appeals from the judgment.

Defendant, a high school teacher, and Ann Lucille Ireland, the deceased, were married in 1957 while defendant was attending college. They had two children, born in 1958 and 1960, respectively. In 1963 they began to experience marital difficulties and Ann entered into the first of a series of secret extramarital affairs. Defendant soon began to doubt his wife's fidelity and to make accusations against her. Ann at first denied her involvement, and defendant's accusations resulted in a number of violent physical encounters between them in which Ann sustained injuries. The relationship continued in this turbulent and unhappy state for several years.

Early in 1967, Ann consulted an attorney and commenced an action for divorce. The parties continued to live together, however, and undertook several attempts to revive their marriage. Their efforts were unsuccessful, and Ann soon became involved in an extramarital relationship with the salesman for a company which had installed a swimming pool at the Ireland residence. Defendant was informed of this by a family friend, and when he accused Ann she admitted her involvement and shortly thereafter promised to sever the relationship in the interest of the family. Defendant, in order to make certain that Ann would keep her promise, hired a private detective to follow her. Apparently Ann's relationship with the salesman was terminated by the latter when he learned of the private detective, but this did not result in improved relations between the Irelands.

During this period defendant began to suffer from headaches, nervousness, and fatigue, and consulted a doctor who prescribed medication for these conditions.

On April 24, 1967, the Irelands met with a conciliation counselor attached to the county conciliation court. As a result of this meeting defendant and Ann agreed to seek the services of the Western Behavioral Institute in a last effort to save their marriage; apparently Ann's consent to this step was obtained with some reluctance on her part. n1 After the meeting defendant suggested that they have lunch together but Ann was not willing to do so and they returned to their home. Ann went out to her hairdresser that afternoon, and when she had returned and the children had been put to bed the Irelands discussed their meeting with the conciliation counselor and their future appointment at the Western Behavioral Institute. Defendant agreed to undertake certain changes in their relationship such as diminishing the influence of his parents, who lived nearby, and allowing Ann to assume a more positive role in the family. Ann again expressed to defendant a willingness to make efforts in the interest of renewed family harmony.

> n1 Apparently Ann's reluctance on this point resulted from a conviction in her own mind that no reconciliation would be effected. The prosecution produced evidence that, on April 18, without defendant's knowledge, she again consulted an attorney about obtaining a divorce, and that she had another appointment with him on April 27, 2 days after her death. It was also shown that Ann had made arrangements with a woman friend to rent an apartment together; that the two went apartment hunting on April 12 and again on April 25, the day of the murder; and that they had decided to rent the apartment in the friend's name, with the understanding that Ann was to pay the rent.

On the morning of April 25, Ann displayed a sullen and incommunicative attitude in response to defendant's attempts to engage in conversation with her. Defendant made efforts to be relieved from his teaching duties but was unsuccessful in doing so and taught five classes during the day. When he returned home between 3:30 and 4 p.m., Ann was not at home, but shortly thereafter she returned from the market where she had been shopping. During the day defendant had taken the various medications which had been prescribed for him, and prior to Ann's return from the market he drank two coffee mugs of wine. Upon her return defendant, Ann and their daughter went out to purchase chlorine for their pool and to do other errands, and on their way home defendant suggested that they have dinner at the home of a friend. Ann did not wish to do so, and they returned home where she prepared dinner for the family. Defendant at this time had another coffee mug of wine and took a rest until he was called for dinner. After dinner defendant lay down again and had another coffee mug of wine. n2

n2 The foregoing background facts are not disputed and are drawn primarily from defendant's testimony at trial.

Sometime between 7:30 and 8:30 p.m. on April 25, 1967, defendant shot and killed his wife Ann by firing into her at close range two .38 caliber bullets from a pistol which he usually kept in his bedroom. Defendant himself testified that he had no memory of the actual shooting or of certain events occurring thereafter, and the only known details of the homicide were provided at trial by the testimony n3 of his 6-year-old daughter, Terry, in whose presence the shooting took place.

n3 Terry was not actually called as a witness at trial. By stipulation of the parties a statement given by her to police officers on the night of the crime was admitted in lieu of actual testimony.

Terry testified that after she had gone to bed on the evening in question she heard her parents talking in the den where her mother had been watching television; that she asked her parents what they were talking about and they replied that they were talking about the television program; that her parents were really "talking about who was going to leave first"; that defendant shortly thereafter "got the gun in his pocket," returned to the den, and asked Ann to go outside by the swimming pool and talk; that Ann refused to go and defendant pulled her off the couch where she was lying; that Ann fell to the floor, and she, Terry, then went into the room and began crying; that defendant then sat down in a chair and Ann climbed back upon the couch; that defendant then took the gun from his pocket, and said "Now what, Ann?" and fired three shots at Ann; that the first shot went into the window and the second and third shots struck Ann in the eye and chest; that defendant then went into the front room and "was sitting and rocking and crying"; and that she, Terry, then stayed on the couch with her mother, Ann, until neighbors arrived.

. . .

Defendant also contends that it was error, in the circumstances of this case, to instruct the jury on second degree felony murder. In the alternative he contends that, if second degree felony-murder instructions were appropriate in this case, the court should have given an instruction requested by him which purported to cure any confusion which might result from the giving of such instructions. Because we agree with the former of these contentions we need not address ourselves to the latter.

The felony-murder rule operates (1) to posit the existence of malice aforethought in homicides which are the direct causal result of the perpetration or attempted perpetration of *all* felonies inherently dangerous to human life . . . Thus, "A homicide that is a direct causal result of the commission of a felony inherently dangerous to human life (other than the six felonies enumerated in *Pen. Code, § 189*) constitutes at least second degree murder." (*People v. Ford, supra, 60 Cal.2d 772, 795.*) Accordingly, the giving of a second degree felony-murder instruction in a murder prosecution has the effect of "[relieving] the jury of the necessity of finding one of the elements of the crime of murder" (*People v. Phillips, supra, 64 Cal.2d 574, 584*), to wit, malice aforethought.

The jury in this case was given an instruction based upon CALJIC No. 305 (Revised). The instruction given provided in relevant part: ". . . the unlawful killing of a human being with malice aforethought is murder of the second degree in any of the following cases: . . . Three, when the killing is a direct causal result of the perpetration or attempt to perpetrate a felony inherently dangerous to human life, such as an assault with a deadly weapon."

. . .

We have concluded that the utilization of the felony-murder rule in circumstances such as those before us extends the operation of that rule "beyond any rational function that it is designed to serve." (*People v. Washington (1965) 62 Cal.2d 777, 783 {44 Cal.Rptr. 442, 402 P.2d 130}.*) To allow such use of the felony-murder rule would effectively preclude the jury from considering the issue of malice aforethought in all cases wherein homicide has been committed as a result of a felonious assault—a category which includes the great majority of all homicides. This kind of bootstrapping finds support neither in logic nor in law. We therefore hold that a second degree felony-murder instruction may not properly be given when it is based upon a felony which is an integral part of the homicide and which the evidence produced by the prosecution shows to be an offense included *in fact* within the offense charged. n14

n14 . . . In *People v. Lewis (1960) 186 Cal.App.2d 585 {9 Cal.Rptr. 263}*, the court, discussing the effect of

Marshall upon facts there at bench, properly concluded that ". . . if the indictment in this case had charged murder with a hatchet, then assault with a deadly weapon, or with means likely to cause great bodily harm would be necessarily included offenses." *(186 Cal.App.2d at p. 600.)* The rule set forth in *Marshall* and explained in *Lewis*, which relates to whether an offense is "necessarily included" within the meaning of section 1159, is not affected by the rule which we now enunciate, the application of which is limited to the determination of whether a second degree felony-murder instruction is warranted under the evidence. *Marshall* and *Lewis* do show, however, that an offense may be included *in fact* within the offense charged even though it is not embraced within the statutory definition of the greater offense.

. . .

Although we are not at this time prepared to say that the limitation which we have above articulated, when applied to fact situations not now before us, will come to assume the exact outlines and proportions of the so-called "merger" doctrine enunciated in these other jurisdictions, n15 we believe that the reasoning underlying that doctrine is basically sound and should be applied to the extent that it is consistent with the laws and policies of this state.

n15 See generally Note: *The Doctrine of Merger in Felony-Murder and Misdemeanor-Manslaughter (1960) 35 St. John's L.Rev. 109.*

. . .

The judgment is reversed.

SUPREME COURT OF CALIFORNIA

19 Cal. 4th 142; 960 P.2d 1094; 77 Cal. Rptr. 2d 870

August 31, 1998

OPINION BY: BAXTER, J.

We granted review to consider two issues: First, does the *sua sponte* duty to instruct on lesser necessarily included offenses (*Sedeno, supra, 10 Cal. 3d 703, 715-716, 112 Cal. Rptr. 1, 518 P.2d 913*) extend to every theory of such an offense that finds rational support in the evidence? Second, what standard of appellate reversal should apply to an erroneous failure to instruct, or to instruct completely, on a lesser included offense?

We now reach the following conclusions: California law requires a trial court, *sua sponte*, to instruct fully on all lesser necessarily included offenses supported by the evidence.

Because the Court of Appeal applied the *Sedeno* standard we now overrule, and therefore reversed defendant's murder conviction without determining from the entire record whether there was a reasonable probability the error affected the outcome, the Court of Appeal's judgment must be reversed. Under the circumstances, we will remand the cause to the Court of Appeal for an evaluation of prejudice under *Watson*. If the Court of Appeal concludes the error was harmless by that standard, it should proceed to consider the numerous other claims raised by defendant on appeal.

FACTS AND PROCEDURAL BACKGROUND

Defendant was charged by information with the murder of Andreas Suryaatmadja. (§ 187, subd. (a).) n2 The information also alleged a firearm use enhancement. (§ 12022, subd. (a).)

> n2 The information alleged generally that defendant "did willfully, unlawfully, and with malice aforethought murder Andreas Suryaatmadja, a human being."

Insofar as pertinent here, the prosecution evidence was as follows:

On the evening of December 17, 1993, Yoon, Ju and Hyun, (Bill) Kim were walking in Chatsworth on their way to play pool. As they passed defendant's residence at 21747 Hiawatha Street, words were exchanged with a larger group of young people who were drinking beer in the garage and driveway area. A fight ensued. Ju and Kim were kicked and beaten, and they received minor injuries. Kim testified defendant was present at the fight but stayed in the background.

Between 8 and 10 p.m. the next evening, December 18, Kim and 6 to 10 friends, including victim Suryaatmadja, returned to defendant's neighborhood. The group was riding in two cars, a gray Nissan and a black Honda. The aim was to have an even fight with those who had beaten Kim and Ju the night before. The group parked around the corner from defendant's residence. Kim had a fishing knife, and the group was armed with other weapons, including a baseball bat and parts of a "Club" automobile security device.

Kim first approached the residence alone. When it appeared nobody was home, Kim slashed a tire of a BMW automobile parked in defendant's driveway and walked back to his waiting friends. As Kim did so, defendant came out of the house and checked the BMW. Some of Kim's friends yelled to defendant to bring out his friends for an even fight. Defendant saw the group and went back inside.

The group then drove by a back route, parked up the street on the other side of defendant's house, and began walking toward defendant's residence. Suryaatmadja and another person may have hung back at an intersection. Once the main group arrived in front of defendant's house, four or five individuals came up to the BMW and began hitting the car with the bat, the Club pieces, and a broken broomstick. The group may have been shouting epithets. Suryaatmadja was not in the group that hit the car.

The BMW's alarm went off, and moments later, shots came from the front door of defendant's residence. The shots continued as the group began to run away. During the second of two separate volleys, Kim looked back and saw defendant firing from his driveway near the public sidewalk. When the gunfire stopped, Suryaatmadja was lying in the street, unconscious and bleeding from the head. He died at a hospital several hours later. The cause of death was a bullet that entered the right rear of the victim's head and exited above his right eye.

Defendant told a responding police officer that he fired at "armed" Asians who were "beating on his car, vandalizing his car," and that he feared the people would come into his house. The officer saw two metal rods or pipes in the street.

In a tape-recorded police interview, defendant stated as follows: n3 During the fight of December 17, he was inside the house, sick and asleep. On the evening of December 18, as he entered his car to go to the market, a group of unknown men came toward him, yelling. He reactivated his car alarm, ran back inside, told his mother to call 911, but then wondered if he was being too "paranoid." Nothing happened for 5 minutes. Defendant and a friend, Kyle Beck, then peered over the back fence. They did not observe anybody in the area where the group had previously been spotted, but when defendant turned his gaze, he saw the group approaching again from the opposite direction, still yelling. Defendant ran back inside to tell his mother "they're coming." He then heard the alarm go off as they began "bashing" his car. Defendant saw at least 12 people, and they were "mobbing[,] basically." He broke the glass in the front door and fired three or four rounds "kind of . . . like downward." The intruders stopped hitting his car, but defendant came outside and shot six or seven more times as the group fled. He was not "aiming" and did not intend to hit anybody. n4 He was "trying to get them to stop" because they had "done a lot of damage to [his] car," and he wanted to "hold [them] until the cops came" so they would be "arrested or whatever." When his semiautomatic weapon, which held 13 rounds, ran out of ammunition, he ran back inside. His mother was already making an emergency call. He locked the door and waited for the police.

> n3 Defendant did not testify at trial. The tape recording of his police interview was played for the jury as part of the prosecution's case-in-chief.

> n4 At this point, according to the detective present at the interview, defendant demonstrated that he fired with his arm in a level, locked position, parallel to the ground.

Defendant also insisted that when he fired from inside, it looked like the group was "coming at me" and "rushing the door." Defendant declared that he "thought we were going to get killed."

The police recovered four shell casings from inside the house and another 10 from the driveway. There was bullet damage to the BMW, and to two vehicles parked in the street, at heights and angles that suggested level firing. One bullet passed through the third story wall of a townhome over a block away. The pool of blood where the victim fell was on Hiawatha Street, 182 feet from where the shell casings in defendant's driveway were found.

The defense case included testimony by Chad Reuser, Kyle Beck, and defendant's mother, Janet Breverman (Janet). Reuser corroborated defendant's claim that he was not present at the fight of December 17. Beck and Janet described events inside defendant's house on the night of December 18.

Beck testified as follows: He and defendant were watching television in defendant's bedroom when defendant left the room, stating he was going to the store to get lozenges for his sore throat. Defendant returned almost immediately, apparently already holding his gun. Defendant said someone should call 911 because "15 to 20 guys," armed with "bats and chains and stuff," had "rushed him" as he tried to get into his car. Beck and defendant looked out the front window, saw a white Honda pass slowly, and feared a drive-by shooting. After a few minutes, the two went outside and looked over a gate; Beck saw "four or five heads." Defendant asked Beck to guard the rear of the house while defendant ran back to the front. Beck then heard smashing sounds that caused him to think the intruders had forced their way in through a window. Within seconds thereafter, Beck heard gunfire.

Janet testified as follows: On the evening of December 18, she was watching television in her room. The chirping of defendant's car alarm indicated he had left the house, then quickly returned. Defendant reported "there were a whole group of Oriental guys" walking toward the house. Defendant, and perhaps Beck, went to check the rear of the house, while Janet went to the bathroom, which was adjacent to the driveway where defendant's car was parked. Just as she exited the bathroom, the car alarm went off, and she heard breaking glass and "blows" to the vehicle. The frequency of blows suggested at least three people were pounding the car. She "dropped to the ground," expecting "things to be coming through the window." She "absolutely" was in "fear." About that time, defendant yelled "call 911," and she crawled into the family room to the telephone. By the time she made the call, shots had been fired.

At the close of the prosecution case, the trial court ruled there was no evidence of premeditation or deliberation, and the verdict would thus be limited to second degree murder. The jury was instructed on both express and implied malice theories of that offense. The court also provided instructions, as agreed by the parties, on reasonable defense of self or others as justifiable homicide, on the permissible use of force to resist a violent domestic intruder, on voluntary manslaughter as an intentional killing arising from an honest but unreasonable belief in the need for self-defense, and on involuntary manslaughter as an unintentional killing by the reckless or grossly negligent commission of a highly dangerous act. Defendant was convicted of murder, and the firearm-use enhancement was found true. The court sentenced defendant to a term of 18 years to life.

On appeal, defendant argued, *inter alia*, that the court erred by failing, on its own motion, to instruct on a second theory of voluntary manslaughter, an unlawful intentional killing "upon a sudden quarrel or heat of passion." (§ 192(a).) In an opinion by Justice Armstrong, concurred in by Justice Grignon, the Court of Appeal, Second District, Division Five agreed. The majority reasoned, in essence, that the same evidence of threat and fear of harm which supported a claim of unreasonable self-defense also permitted a manslaughter verdict based on heat of passion. The majority concluded that the instructional error required reversal under *Sedeno, supra,* 10 Cal. 3d 703, because the jury had not necessarily resolved the heat of passion issue against defendant in another context.

In a separate concurrence, Presiding Justice Turner urged us to reconsider the scope of the rule requiring *sua sponte* instructions on lesser included offenses, as well as the circumstances under which this category of error should require reversal. We granted the People's petition for review.

DISCUSSION

Duty to Instruct on All Aupportable Theories of Lesser Included Offense.

As below, defendant urges the trial court's voluntary manslaughter instructions were defective because they did not include the heat of passion theory despite support for that theory in the evidence. The omission, defendant suggests, deprived him of his "constitutional right to have the jury determine every material issue presented by the evidence." (*People v. Modesto* (1963) 59 Cal. 2d 722, 730 {31 Cal. Rptr. 225, 382 P.2d 33} (*Modesto*); see also *People v. Wickersham* (1982) 32 Cal. 3d 307, 335 {185 Cal. Rptr. 436, 650 P.2d 311} (*Wickersham*).)

The People, on the other hand, argue that the duty to instruct *sua sponte* on a lesser included offense is satisfied when the court instructs on the theory of that offense most consistent with the evidence and the line of defense pursued at trial. The court, the People urge, need not further provide, in the absence of a defense request, instructions on additional, and perhaps conflicting, theories of the lesser offense. We find defendant's position more persuasive.

"Murder is the unlawful killing of a human being with malice aforethought. (§ 187, subd. (a).) A defendant who commits an intentional and unlawful killing but who lacks malice is guilty of . . . voluntary manslaughter. (§ 192.)" (*People v. Barton* (1995) 12 Cal. 4th 186, 199 {47 Cal. Rptr. 2d 569, 906 P.2d 531} (*Barton*).) Generally, the intent to unlawfully kill constitutes malice. (§ 188; *People v. Saille* (1991) 54 Cal. 3d 1103, 1113 {2 Cal. Rptr. 2d 364, 820 P.2d 588}; see *In re Christian S.* (1994) 7 Cal. 4th 768, 778–780 {30 Cal. Rptr. 2d 33, 872 P.2d 574} (*Christian S.*).) "But a defendant who intentionally and unlawfully kills lacks malice . . . in limited, explicitly defined circumstances: either when the defendant acts in a 'sudden quarrel or heat of passion' (§ 192, subd. (a)), or when the defendant kills in 'unreasonable self-defense'—the unreasonable but good faith belief in having to act in self-defense (see *Christian S.*[, *supra*,] 7 Cal. 4th 768; *Flannel, supra,* 25 Cal. 3d 668)." (*Barton, supra,* 12 Cal. 4th at p. 199.) Because heat of passion and unreasonable self-defense reduce an intentional, unlawful killing from murder to voluntary manslaughter by *negating the element of malice* that *otherwise inheres* in such a homicide (*ibid.*), voluntary manslaughter of these two forms is considered a lesser necessarily included offense of intentional murder (*id. at* pp. 201–202). n5

> n5 "Under California law, a lesser offense is necessarily included in a greater offense if either the statutory elements of the greater offense, or the facts actually alleged in the accusatory pleading, include all the elements of the lesser offense, such that the greater cannot be committed without also committing the lesser." (*People v. Birks* (1998) 19 Cal. 4th 108, 117 {77 Cal. Rptr. 2d 848, 960 P.2d 1073} (*Birks*).) . . .

. . .

Barton then analyzed whether heat of passion and unreasonable self-defense, insofar as they reduce a murder to voluntary manslaughter, are mere defenses which the defendant may control under *Sedeno*. *Barton* answered that question in the negative.

We acknowledged in *Barton* that because "it is [ordinarily] the defendant who offers evidence" on these theories, and because they operate to reduce murder to the lesser offense of manslaughter, they resemble traditional affirmative defenses. Mindful of *Wickersham's* holding on the issue, we also noted in particular the close conceptual similarities between unreasonable self-defense and the "actual" defense of "true" self-defense. (*Barton, supra,* 12 Cal. 4th 186, 199–200.) Nonetheless, we explained, voluntary manslaughter is itself an *offense*, i.e., an unlawful killing distinguished from murder only because it is "without malice" (§ 192). (*Barton, supra,* 12 Cal. 4th at p. 199.) Heat of passion and unreasonable self-defense, we observed, merely establish the "lack [of] malice" that distinguishes the one offense from the other. (*Ibid.*)

Hence, we concluded, *Wickersham* had not been correct in characterizing unreasonable self-defense as a mere *defense* for purposes of the *sua sponte* instructional rule of *Sedeno*. "'[U]nreasonable self-defense,'" we stated, "'is . . . not a true defense; rather, it is a shorthand description of one form of voluntary manslaughter.'" And voluntary manslaughter, *whether it arises from unreasonable self-defense or from a killing during a sudden quarrel or heat of passion*, is not a defense but a crime; more precisely, it is a lesser offense included in the crime of murder.

. . .

In deciding whether there is substantial evidence of a lesser offense, courts should not evaluate the credibility of witnesses, a task for the jury. (*Flannel, supra,* 25 Cal. 3d 668, 684; see also *Wickersham, supra,* 32 Cal. 3d 307, 324.) Moreover, as we have noted, the *sua sponte* duty to instruct on lesser included offenses, unlike the duty to instruct on mere defenses, arises even against the defendant's wishes, and regardless of the trial theories or tactics the defendant has actually pursued. Hence, substantial evidence to support instructions on a lesser included offense may exist even in the face of inconsistencies presented by the defense itself. n10

> n10 This means that substantial evidence of heat of passion and unreasonable self-defense may exist, and the duty to instruct *sua sponte* may therefore arise, even when the defendant claims that the killing was accidental, or that the states of mind on which these theories depend were absent. . . .

An intentional, unlawful homicide is "upon a sudden quarrel or heat of passion" (§ 192(a)), and is thus voluntary manslaughter (*ibid.*), if the killer's reason was actually obscured as the result of a strong passion aroused by a "provocation" sufficient to cause an "'ordinary [person] of average disposition . . . to act rashly or without due deliberation and reflection, and from this passion rather than from judgment.'" (*People v. Berry (1976)* 18 Cal. 3d 509, 515 {134 Cal. Rptr. 415, 556 P.2d 777}, quoting *People v. Valentine (1946)* 28 Cal. 2d 121, 139 {169 P.2d 1}; *People v. Borchers (1958)* 50 Cal. 2d 321, 328-329 {325 P.2d 97}.) "'[N]o specific type of provocation [is] required . . . .'" (*Wickersham, supra,* 32 Cal. 3d 307, 326, quoting *People v. Berry, supra,* 18 Cal. 3d at p. 515.) Moreover, the passion aroused need not be anger or rage, but can be any "[v]iolent, intense, high-wrought or enthusiastic emotion" (*Wickersham, supra, at p. 327,* quoting *People v. Berry, supra,* 18 Cal. 3d at p. 515) other than revenge (*People v. Valentine, supra,* 28 Cal. 2d at p. 139). "However, if sufficient time has elapsed between the provocation and the fatal blow for passion to subside and reason to return, the killing is not voluntary manslaughter . . . ." (*Wickersham, supra,* 32 Cal. 3d at p. 327.)

Here, there was evidence that a sizeable group of young men, armed with dangerous weapons and harboring a specific hostile intent, trespassed upon domestic property occupied by defendant and acted in a menacing manner. This intimidating conduct included challenges to the defendant to fight, followed by use of the weapons to batter and smash defendant's vehicle parked in the driveway of his residence, within a short distance from the front door. Defendant and the other persons in the house all indicated that the number and behavior of the intruders, which defendant characterized as a "mob," caused immediate fear and panic. Under these circumstances, a reasonable jury could infer that defendant was aroused to passion, and his reason was thus obscured, by a provocation sufficient to produce such effects in a person of average disposition. n11

> n11 The People ask us to rule as a matter of public policy that mere vandalism to an automobile is never sufficient provocation to warrant lesser included offense instructions on voluntary manslaughter. Indeed, we have so suggested. (See *Christian S., supra,* 7 Cal. 4th 768, 779, fn. 3.) However, this case presents no such isolated issue. Here the jury could infer that defendant observed an attack on his vehicle, within feet of the entrance to his home, by a large, armed, and clearly hostile group of men who, defendant had reason to suspect, were seeking revenge for the incident of the previous evening, and that defendant feared the intruders intended to force their way into the residence. Such a scenario raises grounds of provocation beyond the "mere" destruction of property.

A rational jury could also find that the intense and high-wrought emotions aroused by the initial threat had not had time to cool or subside by the time defendant fired the first few shots from inside the house, then emerged and fired the fatal second volley after the fleeing intruders. At one point in his police statement, defendant suggested that he acted in one continuous, chaotic response to the riotous events outside his door. n12 Finally, even though defendant insisted in his police statement that he did not "aim" or fire "at them," a jury could reasonably disbelieve that claim and conclude, from all the evidence, that defendant killed intentionally, but while his judgment was obscured due to passion aroused by sufficient provocation.

> n12 Thus, defendant stated that "it looks like they're rushing the door, so I break the front window with my hand . . . with the gun and I just start shooting out." Moments later, defendant continued, "[a]nd then they . . . like kept going and I shot out and they kept going and I shot out again and they like started going then I ran out and I'm like just going like this and I'm

yelling—I'm . . . trying to get em to stop and I'm just shooting, shooting, shooting and that's it."

We therefore conclude that the trial court erred in this case when it failed to instruct, even absent a defense request, on heat of passion as a theory of voluntary manslaughter. The issue remains whether the error warrants reversal of defendant's murder conviction, as the Court of Appeal concluded. While we do not finally resolve this issue, we are persuaded that the standard of reversal employed by the Court of Appeal, in accordance with existing California law, is too strict. As we explain below, that standard can and should be replaced with a rule under which actual prejudice is determined from the whole record. We will therefore remand the cause to the Court of Appeal for a determination of prejudice under correct principles.

. . . Because we here overrule the authority on which the Court of Appeal relied, we deem it appropriate to remand the matter to the Court of Appeal to permit that court to determine prejudice under the principles established herein. If the Court of Appeal concludes by correct standards that the error was harmless, it should then address the additional issues raised by defendant on appeal. (*Cahill, supra, 5 Cal. 4th 478, 510.*)

CONCLUSION

The judgment of the Court of Appeal is reversed insofar as it holds that defendant's murder conviction must be reversed because the heat of passion issue erroneously omitted from instructions on the lesser included offense of voluntary manslaughter was not necessarily resolved by the jury in another context. The cause is remanded to the Court of Appeal for further proceedings consistent with the views expressed in this opinion.

GEORGE, C. J., WERDEGAR, J., and CHIN, J., concurred.

SUPREME COURT OF CALIFORNIA

25 Cal. 3d 668; 603 P.2d 1; 160 Cal. Rptr. 84

November 13, 1979

OPINION BY: TOBRINER, J.

Defendant Charles M. Flannel appeals from a judgment of conviction entered on jury verdicts finding him guilty of second degree murder (*Pen. Code, § 187*), and finding affirmatively on a firearm use allegation (*Pen. Code, §§ 1203,* subd. (6) and *§ 12022.5*). He contends that the court erred in failing to instruct the jury *sua sponte* that defendant's honest but unreasonable belief that he must defend himself from deadly attack negates malice so that the offense is reduced from murder to manslaughter. . . . We explain our reasons for rejecting these contentions.

. . . Other decisions, including those of this court, recognize, albeit without full discussion, that one who holds an honest but unreasonable belief in the necessity to defend against imminent peril to life or great bodily injury does not harbor malice and commits no greater offense than manslaughter.

Nevertheless, a trial court's duty to instruct *sua sponte* on this defense arises only in a case in which the evidence presents issues relevant to "general principles of law." When a rule applies so seldom that courts have found no occasion to give it full, substantive discussion and California Jury Instructions, Criminal (CALJIC) has not set it out as a standard instruction, we decline to proclaim that, heretofore, the rule expressed a general principle. We conclude that the court did not err in failing to instruct of its own motion.

. . .

Therefore, we affirm defendant's conviction.

I. The Facts.

On June 28, 1976, about 4:15 in the afternoon, defendant shot and killed Charles Daniels. The two men had a history of hostile and violent relations. Daniels objected to defendant's treatment of Daniel's common law daughter, who was defendant's girlfriend, later his wife. Defendant resented Daniels' interference with his romance. Previously, both men had threatened each others' lives. In January 1976 defendant attacked Daniels at a friend's home, kicking Daniels in the chest and head and hitting him with a glass. Rather than prosecute defendant, the district attorney's office held a citation hearing and warned the two men to avoid one another.

On the morning of the killing defendant consumed some four tall cans of beer and a shot or two of whiskey, took his girlfriend shopping, and ate lunch. He joined friends in front of a building in Oakland about 2:30 that afternoon. As he talked with friends, defendant shared some beer and whiskey.

About 4 p.m. defendant, observing Daniels approach from nearby, retrieved his gun from the trunk of his car. One friend reassured him that there was no need for a gun, that everybody was "his friend"; when Daniels came close a second time at 4:15 p.m. another friend urged defendant to leave in order to prevent trouble. Defendant walked about 12 or 14 feet away but changed his mind and returned to watch Daniels arrive.

Daniels and the group exchanged greetings. Defendant walked up to Daniels and, standing directly in front of him with his hand on the gun in his right front pocket, asked him what was "happening." Daniels graphically told defendant to "stop messing" with him, that they were not supposed to be around each other, and asked him to "get goin'."

Daniels began backing away from the car upon which he had been leaning, waving defendant away with his left hand while his right hand remained near his back pocket where he was known to have kept his knife. Defendant followed, saying "Was you going to stick me in the side with a knife?" "Come on pull your knife." He then drew the gun from his pocket, extended his arm full length and fired one shot into Daniels' temple from a distance of approximately 2 feet. As Daniels fell, his switchblade knife flew into the air, landing on the ground where it spun around and popped open. No one observed the knife in Daniels' hand.

Defendant immediately told his friends not to touch Daniels but to "leave him right there." He said, "He pulled a knife on me," adding that Daniels "deserved to be dead, nobody cares." Defendant dropped his weapon and waited until the police arrived.

At trial defendant relied on a theory of self-defense. He testified that Daniels came toward him, grabbed his chest to stabilize him, that Daniels then drew his knife from his back pocket. Defendant was "surprised and scared." Seeing the knife, he pulled his gun out of his front pocket, then jerked away from Daniels and, as Daniels came at him again, he fired. Defendant also testified that he thought he was drunk at the time of the killing.

The trial court instructed the jury on first and second degree murder, the nature and role of malice in murder and manslaughter, the effect of sudden quarrel and heat of passion, and the effect of intoxication on the intent to commit murder (*CALJIC No. 4.21*).

. . .

II. An Honest but Unreasonable Belief That It Is Necessary to Defend Oneself From Imminent Peril to Life or Great Bodily Injury Negates Malice Aforethought, the Mental Element Necessary for Murder, so That the Chargeable Offense Is Reduced to Manslaughter.

To be exculpated on a theory of self-defense one must have an honest *and* reasonable belief in the need to defend. (*Pen. Code, § 197; Jackson v. Superior Court (1965) 62 Cal. 2d 521, 529 {42 Cal. Rptr. 838, 399 P.2d 374}; People v. Moore (1954) 43 Cal. 2d 517, 526–529 {275 P.2d 485}; People v. Holt (1944) 25 Cal. 2d 59, 65 {153 P.2d 21}.*) A bare fear is not enough; "the circumstances must be sufficient to excite the fears of a reasonable person, and the party killing must have acted under the influence of such fears alone." (*Pen. Code, § 198.*)

This rule is not questioned here. Rather, the issue is whether a defender has committed murder or manslaughter when his belief, although honestly held, fails to meet the standard of a "reasonable person."

In *People v. Wells (1949) 33 Cal. 2d 330 {202 P.2d 53}*, a prison inmate charged with assault on an officer, a capital offense requiring malice aforethought, sought to introduce evidence of an abnormal mental condition, not amounting to insanity, which caused him to fear for his personal safety. We stated that if defendant "acted only under the influence of fear of bodily harm, in the belief, *honest though unreasonable,* that he was defending himself from such harm by the use of a necessary amount of force, then defendant, although he would not be guiltless of crime, would not have committed that particular aggravated offense with

which he is charged, for the essential element of '*malice aforethought*' would be lacking." (Italics added.) (*33 Cal. 2d at* p. 345.) *Wells,* then, stands for the proposition that as a mental state, malice cannot coexist with such an unreasonable belief; in finding no prejudicial error, we stated that the jury could find malice motivated the action rather than the "influence of honest, mistaken fear," (*id., at* p. 358) which could have negated malice aforethought.

. . .

Most recently in *People v. Sedeno (1974) 10 Cal. 3d 703 {112 Cal. Rptr. 1, 518 P.2d 913},* this court in dicta affirmed the existence of the unreasonable belief rule. We observed "No instructions were requested and none was given on voluntary manslaughter as an intentional killing committed 'upon a sudden quarrel or heat of passion,' on involuntary manslaughter, on unconsciousness, or on self-defense, or the effect of an unreasonable belief that deadly force was necessary in defense of self." (*10 Cal. 3d at* p. 715.) We went on to emphasize the close relationship between a defendant's claim of self-defense and the unreasonable belief doctrine. "Since there was no evidence that defendant believed he was acting in self-defense, there was likewise no basis for an instruction on the effect of an unreasonable belief that deadly force was necessary in defense of self." (*Id. at* p. 718.)

. . .

The nature of malice is central here for "[murder] is the unlawful killing of a human being . . . with malice aforethought" (*Pen. Code, § 187*); "[manslaughter] is the unlawful killing . . ., without malice." (*Pen. Code, § 192.*) In *Conley* we examined the meaning of that mental state. We observed that a person who carefully weighs a course of action, and chooses to kill after considering reasons for and against, is normally capable of comprehending his societal duty to act within the law. "If, *despite such awareness,* he does an act that is likely to cause serious injury or death to another, he exhibits that wanton disregard for human life or antisocial motivation that constitutes malice aforethought." (Italics added.) (*Id.,* p. 322.)

Given this understanding of malice aforethought, we cannot accept the People's claim that an honest belief, if unreasonably held, can be consistent with malice.

. . .

This approach to unreasonable belief expresses the rule at common law. As one scholar notes, "Since manslaughter is a 'catch-all' concept, covering all homicides which are neither murder nor innocent, it logically includes some killings involving other types of mitigation, and such is the rule of the common law. For example, if one man kills another intentionally, under circumstances beyond the scope of innocent homicide, the facts may come so close to justification or excuse that the killing will be classed as voluntary manslaughter rather than murder." (Perkins on Criminal Law (2d ed. 1969) pp. 69–70.) n6 Perkins goes on to add that "some legislative enactments have spoken of voluntary manslaughter in terms only of a killing in 'a sudden heat of passion caused by a provocation' and so forth. Such restriction is probably unintentional, being attributable to the fact that this is by far the most common type of mitigation; but it is very unfortunate." (*Id.*, at p. 70.) n7

n6 A few commentators would hold that *any* honestly held but mistaken belief exculpates rather than mitigates. (See e.g., Williams, Criminal Law, The General Part (2d ed. 1961) p. 204; Keedy, *Ignorance and Mistake in the Criminal Law (1908) 22 Harv. L. Rev. 75, 84–85.*)

n7 In some jurisdictions, such as California, the courts have given effect to the "lack of malice" requirement of otherwise restrictive manslaughter statutes to uphold the unreasonable belief principle. (See, e.g., *Allison v. State (1904) 74 Ark. 444, 453–454 {86 S.W. 409}; Hartfield v. State (1936) 176 Miss. 776, 784 {170 So. 531}; Wood v. State (Okla. 1971) 486 P.2d 750, 752; Commonwealth v. Thompson (1957) 389 Pa. 382 {133 A.2d 207}.*) In still other states, legislators have passed statutes specifically providing for manslaughter when an individual holds an unreasonable but honest belief in the need to defend against deadly attack. (See, e.g., *Colo. Rev. Stat., § 18–3–105(1)(b)* (1978); Ill. Rev. Stat. Ann. ch. 38, *§ 9–2*(b) (1972); *Wis. Stat. Ann., § 940.05(2)* (1958).)

California's rule on the effect of an unreasonably held belief in the need to defend is almost universally supported by those legal commentators who have given it consideration. In the words of two scholars it is "the more humane view that, while [the defender] is not innocent of crime, he is nevertheless not guilty of murder; rather, he is guilty of the in-between crime of manslaughter." (LaFave & Scott, Handbook on Criminal Law (1972) p. 397; see also Model Pen. Code, *§ 201.3*, coms. at pp. 40–46 (Tent. Draft No. 9, 1959); Model Pen. Code, *§ 3.09*, coms. at p. 78 (Tent. Draft No. 8, 1958).) In short, the state has no legitimate interest in obtaining a conviction of murder when, by virtue of defendant's unreasonable belief, the jury entertains a reasonable doubt whether defendant harbored malice. Likewise, a defendant has no legitimate interest in complete exculpation when acting outside the range of reasonable behavior. (Cf. *People v. St. Martin (1970) 1 Cal. 3d 524 {83 Cal. Rptr. 166, 463 P.2d 390}.*) The vice is the element of malice; in its absence the level of guilt must decline.

. . .

The judgment is affirmed.

PEOPLE V. PENNY

SUPREME COURT OF CALIFORNIA

44 CAL. 2D 861; 285 P.2D 926

JULY 8, 1955

OPINION BY: CARTER, J.

Appeal by defendant Mary Penny from a judgment of conviction of involuntary manslaughter.

Defendant was charged with a violation of section 192, subdivision 2, of the Penal Code. That section provides that manslaughter is the unlawful killing of a human being, without malice. "2. Involuntary—in the commission of an unlawful act, not amounting to felony; or in the commission of a lawful act which might produce death, in an unlawful manner, or without due caution and circumspection; provided that this subdivision shall not apply to acts committed in the driving of a vehicle."

For 7 years defendant had been engaged in "face rejuvenation" in the city of Los Angeles. It is conceded that she had no license from either the Cosmetology Board or the Medical Board of this state; she did have a business license from the city of Los Angeles for the business of "Face Rejuvenation."

Defendant had a year's training with a Madame Bergeron (now deceased) in Los Angeles and approximately 3 months' training with one Geraldine Gorman in New York. In New York, she received the formula which she used in her work. The formula consisted of one ounce of water, a heaping tablespoon of resorcinol (of the same chemical group) and 16 drops of phenol (carbolic acid).

Kay Stanley, the victim, had consulted with defendant some 7 months earlier about having her face treated to remove wrinkles and pock marks, but did not have the money to do it at that time. Around Easter time of 1953, she again asked defendant to treat her face, but defendant was to be away and could not do it then. On the morning of May 4, 1953, Kay Stanley arrived at about 10 in the morning at defendant's home where she was to stay during the treatment. Kay's face was first washed with warm water and soda; the formula was then applied with a cotton wrapped wooden applicator to Kay's cheeks, a square inch at a time. After each application, the area was pressed with sterile gauze to remove excess moisture. The entire

forehead was covered as well as the eyelids, the process taking about 2 hours. The treated area was then covered with gauze and taped with small pieces of tape which overlapped and covered the area; regular waterproof adhesive tape was then put on over the other tape; this formed a mask over the upper portion of the patient's face. After the taping had been completed, Kay walked to an adjoining room where she had lunch, listened to the radio and looked at magazines. At approximately 6 in the evening, defendant proceeded to treat the lower half of Kay's face in the same manner as she had treated the upper portion which took about three quarters of an hour. When the treatment was completed, Kay asked defendant if she could sit up for awhile before the taping was started; she sounded sleepy. The defendant told her she could and said she would get her a glass of water. When defendant returned with the water, Kay said, "I feel a little bit faint" and lay back as though in a faint. Defendant asked her how she felt but received no answer. When defendant tried to lift her she found she was dead weight and felt that she had fainted. Defendant tried unsuccessfully to call a Dr. Wallace and left a message for him; she then called a nurse-anesthetist who arrived at the house about 10 or 15 minutes later. Mrs. Jevne, the nurse, tried to take the patient's pulse without success; there was no respiration. She then administered Coramine, a heart stimulant by hypodermic needle, in the arm; she then gave a hypodermic injection of Metrazol, another stimulant; she then tried artificial respiration and caffeine benzoate. She told defendant to call the doctor again. Dr. Wallace arrived about an hour after Mrs. Jevne did and examined the lady whom he found lying on the treatment table. He was able to feel no pulse and there was no respiration. He noticed signs indicating death had existed for some period of time.

Defendant called her attorney who called the police.

The finding, after an autopsy had been had, was that the immediate cause of death was phenol (carbolic acid) poisoning and edema of the glottis due to "application of phenol-containing mixture to the face and neck." Other findings were that 5.1 milligrams of phenol per 100 grams were found in the liver and 2.9 milligrams of phenol per 100 grams were found in the blood of the victim. It was the opinion of Dr. Newbarr, prosecution witness and chief autopsy surgeon for the Los Angeles coroner's office, that these findings were the result of the application of a solution containing more than 10 per cent phenol to the face and neck of the victim. It was the opinion of Mr. Abernathy, the toxicologist, that the reddish-brown discoloration of the victim's face was a third degree burn caused by phenol, and that the normal finding of phenol in a normal human being would be practically zero.

There was evidence in the record which showed that the victim had been taking reducing pills prescribed by a Texas doctor; that in order to obtain replacement of the pills, it was necessary for her to have her heart examined and blood pressure taken by a local doctor; that prior to going to the defendant's home for the face rejuvenation treatment she had had her heart and pulse examined and her blood pressure taken and that all findings were normal.

The defendant testified that when she first received the formula for face rejuvenation she had it analyzed and that it contained only 3.1 per cent phenol. The defense also took the position that the victim may have had an allergy to phenol which was the cause of death. Dr. Newbarr testified for the prosecution and gave, as his opinion, that the solution contained over 10 per cent phenol and that the findings were not consistent with the theory of allergy. Dr. Johnstone testified for the defense and it was his opinion that the solution contained approximately 3 per cent phenol; that when applied to the skin it would not cause death; that all autopsy findings were consistent with the theory that the victim was allergic to phenol. Without going into great detail, it seems sufficient to note that the medical testimony was in direct conflict. Defendant's argument that the evidence is insufficient to support the judgment insofar as the cause of death is concerned is without merit. The testimony is ample to show that the victim died of phenol poisoning.

Defendant's argument that Dr. Newbarr was "allowed" to give an "unsupported and incompetent opinion" that the solution contained more than 10 per cent phenol is also without merit. Dr. Newbarr was found to be qualified by the trial court; his opinion was based on his reading on the subject, his own observation of the victim, and his own previous experiences.

. . .

INSTRUCTIONS

Defendant contends that the following instruction was without basis in the evidence. "Any *licensed* cosmetologist who applies to any human being a solution of phenol greater than 10 per cent is guilty of a misdemeanor."

"This is an unlawful act not amounting to a felony. *Business & Professions Code, Section 7415*." (Emphasis added.).

As heretofore pointed out, it is admitted that defendant was not licensed as a cosmetologist.

It is contended that the just quoted instruction was calculated to mislead and confuse the jury when considered with the following instruction: "Every person who engages in, or attempts to engage in, the practice of cosmetology or any branch thereof without a license therefore issued by the State Board of Cosmetology or in an establishment other than one licensed by the State Board of Cosmetology is guilty of a misdemeanor.

"The art of cosmetology includes the beautifying of the face, neck, arms, bust or upper part of the human body, by the use of cosmetic preparations, antiseptics, tonics, lotions or creams."

"A violation of this law is an unlawful act not amounting to a felony."

"*Business & Professions Code, Section 7325.*"

"*Business & Professions Code, Section 7321(b)* [sic] [c]."

It is argued that under these two instructions defendant could have been convicted (1) if the jury believed she used a solution containing more than 10 per cent phenol and had a license; or (2) that she was guilty because she was required to have a license and had none.

There can be no doubt but that the instruction concerning a "licensed" cosmetologist was erroneous and that it had no foundation in the evidence. On the issue of defendant's guilt, the jury could well have inferred that she was guilty of the crime by reasoning that *even* a licensed cosmetologist could not use a solution containing more than 10 per cent phenol. So far as the second instruction is concerned, it is supported by the evidence and correctly stated by the law as it relates to those practicing cosmetology and the persons considered engaged in that practice. It appears to us that as a matter of law, defendant was engaged in the practice of cosmetology and the jury should have been so instructed.

. . .

The next question which presents itself is whether defendant's lack of a license (and the fact that she was, therefore, guilty of a misdemeanor) was the cause of Mrs. Stanley's death. Section 192.2 of the Penal Code provides that a person is guilty of involuntary manslaughter if a human being is unlawfully killed "in the commission of an unlawful act, not amounting to a felony; . . ." The jury was instructed that defendant's conduct must have been the proximate cause of the death. The People argue that the law requiring licensing of those practicing cosmetology was designed to prevent injury to others and that one who violates such a law may be guilty of manslaughter if death is caused thereby. . .

It is extremely dubious that defendant's lack of a license had any causal connection with Mrs. Stanley's death and yet it should be noted that the statute (*Bus. & Prof. Code, § 7415*) provides that if a *licensed* cosmetologist uses a solution of phenol greater than 10 per cent on any human being, he, or she, is guilty of a misdemeanor. *Had* defendant been a licensed cosmetologist, under the evidence she would have been guilty of a misdemeanor, and, as a result, the first clause of *section 192.2* of the Penal Code would have been directly applicable.

Another question which presents itself is whether defendant was guilty of an unlawful act in applying a solution containing phenol and resorcinol to the human face and neck with the knowledge that both chemicals were poisonous. The statute providing that a licensed cosmetologist may not use a solution containing greater than 10 per cent phenol without being guilty of a misdemeanor sets the standard for licensed persons in that profession or occupation. . . . Is defendant, who was as a matter of law, practicing cosmetology, to be judged by the same standards as a *licensed* cosmetologist? The record shows that face rejuvenation, as practiced by defendant, was done to make the face look younger and fresher. The "art of cosmetology" is defined as that which beautifies the face, or neck, by the use of "cosmetic preparations, antiseptics, tonics, lotions or creams." It would appear that the legislative standard set for licensed cosmetologists in the interest of the public health and safety, could, conceivably, be considered applicable to defendant had the jury been so instructed.

DUE CAUTION AND CIRCUMSPECTION

The second clause of *section 192*, subdivision 2, of the Penal Code provides that one is guilty of manslaughter if a human being is killed in the commission of a "lawful act which might produce death, in an unlawful manner, or without due caution and circumspection. . . ." It has been held that without "due caution and circumspection" is the equivalent of "criminal negligence" (*People v. Driggs, 111 Cal.App. 42 {295 P. 51}; People v. Hurley, supra, 13 Cal.App.2d 208*) and the jury was so instructed. . . .

If we assume that a treatment aimed at removing wrinkles from the human face is a "lawful act," it must next be determined whether such act was one which "might cause death." Defendant admitted she knew the substances used were poisons; that they were dangerous substances; that their indiscriminate use could be dangerous. Inasmuch as

defendant was knowingly using poison in her treatment solution, the jury could have concluded that her treatment was one which could have caused death.

The jury was also instructed that "The doing of an act ordinarily lawful which results in the death of a human being may be manslaughter where the act, being one which might cause death, is performed in an unlawful manner or without due caution and circumspection. When a person is doing anything dangerous in itself or has charge of anything dangerous in its use and acts with reference thereto without taking those proper precautions which a person of ordinary prudence would have used under the circumstances and the death of another results there from, his act or neglect is a criminal act against the person so killed."

. . .

Defendant relies on the rules set forth in *People v. Driggs, supra, 111 Cal.App. 42,* and *People v. Hurley, supra, 13 Cal.App.2d 208,* wherein the rule was said to be: "In order to constitute criminal negligence, there must enter into the act some measure of wantonness or flagrant or reckless disregard of the safety of others, or willful indifference. If no one of these elements enters into the act, the person charged cannot be held guilty of criminal negligence." (*People* v. *Driggs*, at page 47.) As we read the Pociask case which approved the instruction given in *People v. Wilson, supra, 193 Cal. 512,* which was almost the same as that here given, wherein it is said (p. 84), "Anything in the Driggs and Hurley cases inconsistent therewith must be deemed to be disapproved," it appears that the requirement of wantonness, flagrant or reckless disregard of the safety of others, or willful indifference, was deleted from the definition of criminal negligence or lack of due care and circumspection.

. . .

The law in California as to what constitutes "criminal negligence" or a lack of "due caution and circumspection" is confused.

. . .

The court in the Pociask case, *supra,* comments on the opinion of the Supreme Court in denying a hearing in the case of *People v. Seiler, 57 Cal.App. 195 {207 P. 396},* wherein it was said: "The statute (*Pen. Code, § 192,* subd. 2) defines involuntary manslaughter of this specific character as the unlawful killing of a human being, involuntarily, but 'in the commission of a lawful act which might produce death . . . without due caution and circumspection.' In order to constitute this kind of manslaughter the act may be lawful but it must be one which might produce death, and which does produce death, and it must be committed without due caution and circumspection. The lack of due caution and circumspection *need not go to the extent of being wanton or reckless, although it might possibly be such as would be defined as culpable.*" (Emphasis added.) In 1941, the negligent homicide statute (*Veh. Code, § 500*) was amended by deleting the words "in a negligent manner or in the commission of an unlawful act not amounting to a felony" and substituting therefore "with reckless disregard of, or willful indifference to, the safety of others." In *People v. Young, 20 Cal.2d 832 {129 P.2d 353},* the court concluded that in amending the statute the Legislature intended that something more than ordinary negligence was to be required as a basis for criminal liability thereunder and that the phrase used in the amendment must be considered as being similar in meaning to willful misconduct. . . .

In *People v. Sidwell, 29 Cal.App. 12 {154 P. 290},* defendant was charged with involuntary manslaughter; the death occurred through the medium of a revolver. It was there held (p. 17) that "it will be observed that, while involuntary manslaughter may be committed in two different ways, the legislature has not recognized, as between those two ways [192, subd. 2], any distinction in the degree of turpitude characterizing that crime. In other words, the crime is that of involuntary manslaughter, whether the killing be committed in the execution of an unlawful act, etc., or in the execution of a lawful act, etc., or where death, not willfully or intentionally produced, is, nevertheless, caused by the *gross or culpable negligence* of the defendant—negligence which, in degree, goes so far beyond that negligence merely which suffices to impose a civil liability for damages as to constitute it as criminal negligence for which the party guilty of it may be held criminally liable." (Emphasis added.)

. . .

In *People v. Montecino, 66 Cal.App.2d 85, 102 {152 P.2d 5},* which involved the death of an elderly, bedridden woman by reason of the brutal treatment and lack of care on the part of defendant, the court held that "it is established in the State of California that involuntary manslaughter may result even though the conduct of the offender is not wanton or reckless. See comment by the Supreme Court in denying a hearing in *People v. Seiler (1922), 57 Cal.App. 195 {207 P. 396}, . . .*" The Seiler case, as heretofore noted, was a negligent driving case.

. . .

Defendant here was charged with a violation of *section 192*, subdivision 2, of the Penal Code. The jury should have been instructed according to the rule which generally prevails in this country as to what constitutes criminal negligence, or lack of due caution and circumspection so that her guilt or innocence might be determined in accord therewith.

Because of the errors heretofore noted, the judgment is reversed.

PEOPLE V. RODRIGUEZ

COURT OF APPEAL OF CALIFORNIA, SECOND APPELLATE DISTRICT, DIVISION THREE

186 CAL. APP. 2D 433; 8 CAL. RPTR. 863

NOVEMBER 16, 1960

OPINION BY: VALLEE, J.

By information defendant was accused of manslaughter in that on November 8, 1959, she did willfully, unlawfully, feloniously, and without malice kill Carlos Quinones. In a nonjury trial she was found guilty of involuntary manslaughter. A new trial was denied. She appeals from the judgment and the order denying a new trial.

In November 1959 defendant was living with her four children in a single-family residence at 130 South Clarence Street, Los Angeles. The oldest child was 6 years of age. Carlos Quinones was the youngest, either 2 or 3 years of age.

Olive Faison lived across the street from defendant. About 10:45 p.m. on November 8, 1959, Miss Faison heard some children calling, "Mommy, mommy." For about 15 or 20 minutes she did not "pay too much attention." She noticed the cries became more shrill. She went to the front window and saw smoke coming from defendant's house. She "ran across the street and commenced to knock the door in and started pulling the children out." There was a screen door on the outside and a wooden door inside the screen door. The screen door was padlocked on the outside. The other door was open. She broke the screen door and with the help of neighbors pulled three of the children out of the house. She tried to get into the house through the front door but could not because of the flames. A neighbor entered through the back door but could not go far because of the flames. Miss Faison took the three children to her apartment and shortly thereafter returned to the scene of the fire. She remained "until after the little boy was brought out and revived and sent to the hospital." Miss Faison did not see defendant around the house or the neighborhood at the time of the fire.

Firemen arrived at the scene some time after 10 p.m. The front door was open; there was no obstruction. Fireman Hansen went inside and found a baby boy in the back bedroom near the bed. The fire was about 3 feet away from the boy. Hansen took the boy out of the house. "He appeared to be dead at the time." The child was Carlos Quinones.

Around 4 or 4:30 p.m. on November 8, 1959, defendant was in "Johnny's Place." She was at the bar drinking "coke." She stayed about an hour. As John Powers, one of the bartenders, was closing the place about 2:30 a.m. on the morning of November 9, he saw defendant outside the building. He had not seen her inside before that time.

Maria Lucero, defendant's sister, went to defendant's home about 12 p.m. on November 8, 1959. She went looking for defendant. She found her about 2 or 2:30 a.m. in the same block as "Johnny's Place." Defendant was nervous and frightened, said she knew about the fire and that she went over to tell Johnny Powers about it. Defendant had not been drinking.

Carlos Quinones died from "thermal burns, second and third degree involving 50 to 60 per cent of the body surface." Defendant did not testify.

It is first contended the evidence fails to establish a *corpus delicti* of the offense charged. In a homicide case the *corpus delicti* consists of two elements: the death of a human being, and the existence of a criminal agency as the cause. (*People v. Amaya, 40 Cal.2d 70, 75 {251 P.2d 324}.*) The argument is that there was no proof of the existence of a criminal agency as the cause of the death of Carlos.

"Manslaughter is the unlawful killing of a human being, without malice. It is of three kinds: . . . Involuntary—in the commission of an unlawful act, not amounting to felony; or in the commission of a lawful act which might produce death, in an unlawful manner, or without due caution and circumspection . . . ." (*Pen. Code, § 192.*) "In every crime or public offense there must exist a union, or joint operation of act and intent, or criminal negligence." (*Pen. Code, § 20.*) *Section 20 of the Penal Code* makes the union of act and wrongful intent or criminal negligence an invariable element of every crime unless it is excluded expressly or by necessary implication. (*People v. Stuart, 47*

Cal.2d 167,171{302 P.2d 5, 55 A.L.R.2d 705}.) Section 26 of the Penal Code lists, among the persons incapable of committing crimes, "Persons who committed the act or made the omission charged through misfortune or by accident, when it appears that there was no evil design, intention, or culpable negligence." Thus the question is: Was there any evidence of criminal intent or criminal negligence?

The attorney general contends that even if defendant had no criminal intent and was not criminally negligent, she violated *section 273a of the Penal Code* and therefore committed an unlawful act within the meaning of *section 192 of the Penal Code.*

Penal Code, section 273a, reads: "Any person who willfully causes or permits any child to suffer, or who inflicts thereon unjustifiable physical pain or mental suffering, and whoever, having the care or custody of any child, causes or permits the life or limb of such child to be endangered, or the health of such child to be injured, and any person who willfully causes or permits such child to be placed in such situation that its life or limb may be endangered, or its health likely to be injured, is guilty of a misdemeanor."

It does not follow, however, that such acts, committed without criminal intent or criminal negligence, are unlawful acts within the meaning of *section 192 of the Penal Code*, for it is settled that this section is governed by *section 20 of the Penal Code.* Thus, in *People v. Penny, 44 Cal.2d 861, 877–880 {285 P.2d 926}*, we held that "there was nothing to show that the Legislature intended to except *section 192 of the Penal Code* from the operation of section 20 of the same code" and that the phrase "without due caution and circumspection" in section 192 was therefore the equivalent of criminal negligence. Since section 20 also applies to the phrase "unlawful act," the act in question must be committed with criminal intent or criminal negligence to be an unlawful act within the meaning of section 192. By virtue of its application to both phrases, section 20 precludes the incongruity of imposing on the morally innocent the same penalty (*Pen. Code, § 193*) appropriate only for the culpable. Words such as "unlawful act, not amounting to felony" have been included in most definitions of manslaughter since the time of Blackstone and even since the time of Lord Hale, "unlawful act" as it pertains to manslaughter has been interpreted as meaning an act that aside from its unlawfulness was of such a dangerous nature as to justify a conviction of manslaughter if done intentionally or without due caution. To be an unlawful act within the meaning of section 192, therefore, the act in question must be dangerous to human life or safety and meet the conditions of section 20. (*People v. Stuart, 47 Cal.2d 167, 173 {302 P.2d 5, 55 A.L.R.2d 705}.)*

It appears from the record that guilt was predicated on the alleged "commission of a lawful act which might produce death, in an unlawful manner, or without due caution and circumspection." (*Pen. Code, § 192.)*

In *People v. Penny, 44 Cal.2d 861 {285 P.2d 926}*, the defendant was convicted of involuntary manslaughter. While engaged in the practice of "face rejuvenation" she applied a formula containing phenol to the skin. Death was caused by phenol poisoning. The trial court charged the jury that ordinary negligence was sufficient to constitute lack of "due caution and circumspection" under *Penal Code, section 192.* The court said (p. 869): "It has been held that without 'due caution and circumspection' is the equivalent of 'criminal negligence.'" After reviewing numerous California authorities, the court continued (p. 876):

"So far as the latest cases are concerned, it appears that mere negligence is sufficient to constitute a lack of due caution and circumspection under the manslaughter statute (*Pen. Code, § 192*, subd. 2). This does not appear to be a correct rule. Something more, in our opinion, is needed to constitute the criminal negligence required for a conviction of manslaughter."

"[P. 879.] The statute (*Pen. Code, § 192*, subd. 2) provides (in part) that in order to convict a person of involuntary manslaughter, there shall be an unlawful killing of a human being in the commission of a lawful act which might produce death without due caution and circumspection. The words lack of 'due caution and circumspection' have been heretofore held to be the equivalent of 'criminal negligence' (*Pen. Code, § 20*). The general rule is set forth in *26 American Jurisprudence, Homicide, section 210, page 299*, as follows: 'The authorities are agreed, in the absence of statutory regulations denouncing certain acts as criminal, that in order to impose criminal liability for a homicide caused by negligence, there must be a higher degree of negligence than is required to establish negligent default on a mere civil issue. The negligence must be aggravated, culpable, gross, or reckless, that is, the conduct of the accused must be such a departure from what would be the conduct of an ordinarily prudent or careful man under the same circumstances as to be incompatible with a proper regard for human life, or in other words, a disregard of human life or an indifference to consequences.' The article continues thus: 'Aside from the facts that a more culpable degree of negligence is required in order to establish a criminal homicide than is required in a civil action for damages and that contributory negligence is not a defense, criminal responsibility for a negligent homicide is ordinarily to be determined pursuant to the general principles of negligence, the fundamental of which is knowledge, actual or imputed, that the act of the slayer tended to endanger life. The facts must be such that the fatal consequence of the negligent act could reasonably have been foreseen. It must appear that the death was not the result of misadventure, but the natural and probable result of a reckless or culpably negligent act.'"

"We hold, therefore, that the general rule just quoted, sets forth the standard to be used in California for negligent homicide (*Pen. Code, § 192*, subd. 2) in other than vehicle cases. Defendant here was charged with a violation of section 192, subdivision 2, of the Penal Code."

. . .

It is generally held that an act is criminally negligent when a man of ordinary prudence would foresee that the act would cause a high degree of risk of death or great bodily harm. The risk of death or great bodily harm must be great. (See cases collected *161 A.L.R. 10.*) Whether the conduct of defendant was wanton or reckless so as to warrant conviction of manslaughter must be determined from the conduct itself and not from the resultant harm. (*Commonwealth v. Bouvier, 316 Mass. 489 {55 N.E.2d 913}.*) Criminal liability cannot be predicated on every careless act merely because its carelessness results in injury to another. (*People v. Sikes, 328 Ill. 64 {159 N.E. 293, 297}.*) The act must be one which has knowable and apparent potentialities for resulting in death. Mere inattention or mistake in judgment resulting even in death of another is not criminal unless the quality of the act makes it so. The fundamental requirement fixing criminal responsibility is knowledge, actual or imputed, that the act of the accused tended to endanger life. (*State v. Studebaker, 334 Mo. 471 {66 S.W.2d 877, 881}.*)

In a case of involuntary manslaughter the criminal negligence of the accused must be the proximate cause of the death. (25 Cal.Jur.2d 667, § 53; *Cain v. State, 55 Ga.App. 376 {190 S.E. 371, 375}; State v. Darchuck 117 Mont15 {156 P.2d 173, 175}; State v. Ramser, 17 Wn.2d 581 {136 P.2d 1013, 1015–1016}.*)

It clearly appears from the definition of criminal negligence stated in *People v. Penny, supra, 44 Cal.2d 861*, that knowledge, actual or imputed, that the act of the slayer tended to endanger life and that the fatal consequences of the negligent act could reasonably have been foreseen are necessary for negligence to be criminal at all. Must a parent never leave a young child alone in the house on risk of being adjudged guilty of manslaughter if some unforeseeable occurrence causes the death of the child? The only reasonable view of the evidence is that the death of Carlos was the result of misadventure and not the natural and probable result of a criminally negligent act. There was no evidence from which it can be inferred that defendant realized her conduct would in all probability produce death. There was no evidence as to the cause of the fire, as to how or where it started. There was no evidence connecting defendant in any way with the fire. There was no evidence that defendant could reasonably have foreseen there was a probability that fire would ignite in the house and that Carlos would be burned to death. The most that can be said is that defendant may have been negligent; but mere negligence is not sufficient to authorize a conviction of involuntary manslaughter. (*Cf. Williams v. State, 88 Ga.App. 761 {77 S.E.2d 770}; Turner v. State, 65 Ga.App. 292 {16 S.E.2d 160}; Jabron v. State, 172 Miss. 135 {159 So. 406}.*)

The judgment and order denying a new trial are reversed.

COURT OF APPEAL OF CALIFORNIA, SIXTH APPELLATE DISTRICT

79 Cal. App. 4th 40; 93 Cal. Rptr. 2d 803

March 16, 2000

NOTICE: Opinion certified for partial publication.

OPINION BY: WUNDERLICH, J.

I. STATEMENT OF THE CASE

Defendant Deborah Lynette Thompson appeals from a judgment entered after a jury convicted her of gross vehicular manslaughter while intoxicated (GVMI) and found that she previously served a prison term and had two prior convictions for driving under the influence (DUI), one of which involved bodily injury to another person (*Pen. Code, § 191.5*, subds. (a) and (d) and 667.5, subd. (b).)

On appeal, defendant claims that the court erred in giving incorrect instructions on GVMI and the required predicate acts, duplicative instructions concerning GVMI and a lesser included offense, and an inadequate cautionary instruction concerning the evidence necessary to establish gross negligence. She claims the court further erred in making improper comments on the evidence; admitting autopsy pictures of the victim and evidence of her mental state; and excluding evidence of the victim's prior DUI arrest, her prior inconsistent statements, and the fact that she did not make certain statements to a police officer. Last, defendant claims the prosecutor was guilty of misconduct.

We affirm.

II. FACTS

On March 18, 1997, around 5:30 p.m., defendant and Ed Traster, the victim, were driving in his blue Thunderbird on Summit Road, a two-lane mountain road in Santa Cruz County east of Highway 17. It was still daylight, visibility was good, and there were no obstructions in the road. Both defendant and Traster had been drinking and taking drugs.

While traveling on a straight stretch of the road where the posted speed is 40 mph (25 mph when children are present), defendant, the driver, accelerated to at least 55 mph. She veered across the double line into the oncoming lane, jerked back into her own lane, and then lost control of the car. It spun around, jumped the curb, went up an embankment, careened along a cyclone fence, hit a tree, plowed back down the embankment, rolled over onto its side, and finally came to rest.

Traster had not been wearing a seat belt and was partially ejected. His head was crushed, and he died instantly. Defendant, who was also not wearing a seat belt, survived and managed to climb out of the car through the sun roof. She suffered a laceration on the bridge of her nose and various bruises.

Kelly Raftery-Piunit, an assistant district attorney for Santa Clara County, witnessed the accident. She called "911" and then stopped at the scene. Traster was in the passenger seat. Raftery-Piunit testified that defendant kept saying "'Poor,' and then a man's name. It was a male name, but I don't remember what name it was, but it was just— she was pretty hysterical. 'Poor,' let's just say, 'Dave,' or something. 'Poor Dave, poor Dave. I can't believe I did this to poor Dave,' and kind of hysterical. I don't know—two, three, four times."

Joshua Doak also witnessed the accident. He saw two people inside the car immediately before the accident and identified defendant as the driver and Traster as the passenger. After the accident, he saw Traster hanging out of the passenger seat.

Richard Mason, a forensic pathologist and Officer Dane Lobb of the California Highway Patrol, an expert in accident reconstruction, opined that defendant was the driver and Traster the passenger at the time of the accident and that neither was wearing a seat belt. They based their opinions on numerous factors, including the separate seat-position settings that corresponded to defendant's and Traster's physical size, the impact marks on the driver's side that corresponded to defendant's injuries, and Traster's position after the crash and the injuries he suffered.

Blood tests revealed that at the time of the accident defendant and Traster had blood-alcohol levels of .20 and methamphetamine in their systems. Defendant also had valium and its metabolite in her system.

The Defense

Defendant attempted to show that Traster was driving the car at the time of the accident. To this end, Gary Fairchild testified that he saw defendant in the passenger seat of the Thunderbird parked in front of a liquor store sometime between 3:00 and 4:00 p.m. He did not see Traster at all.

Whitaker Deiniger testified that around 4:00 p.m., Traster drove up to his house with defendant as a passenger. He and Traster spoke for a few minutes, and then Traster drove away.

Michael Tabler testified that around 5:00 p.m., Traster and defendant picked him up at his residence, and they all went to a liquor store. Traster then drove back to Tabler's house. According to Tabler, Traster was drunk and drove fast and made quick turns. He said he tried to take Traster's flask before they left, but he could not find it.

III. INSTRUCTIONAL CLAIMS CONCERNING GVMI

A. The Statute and Instruction

Penal Code section 191.5, subdivision (a), provides, "Gross vehicular manslaughter while intoxicated is the unlawful killing of a human being without malice aforethought, in the driving of a vehicle, where the driving was in violation of *Section 23140, 23152, or 23153 of the Vehicle Code,* and the killing was either the proximate result of the commission of an unlawful act, not amounting to a felony, and with gross negligence, or the proximate result of the commission of a lawful act which might produce death, in an unlawful manner, and with gross negligence." n1

> n1 *Vehicle Code section 23140* proscribes driving under the influence of alcohol by a person under 21 years of age.

Vehicle Code section 23152, subdivisions (a) through (d), proscribe driving under the influence of alcohol or drug or the combined influence of both (subd. (a)); driving with a blood-alcohol content of .08 or more (subd. (b)); driving by a person addicted to the use of any drug (subd. (c)); and driving a commercial vehicle with a blood-alcohol content of .04 or more (subd. (d)).

Vehicle Code section 23153, subdivisions (a) and (b), proscribe driving under the influence of alcohol or a drug or the combined influence of both and concurrently committing an unlawful act or omission, which, in turn, causes injury to another person (subd. (a)) and driving with a blood-alcohol content of .08 per cent and concurrently

committing an unlawful act or omission, which, in turn, causes injury to another person (subd. (b)).

Unless otherwise specified, all further statutory references are to the Penal Code.

The court instructed the jury as follows: "Every person who drives a vehicle in a grossly negligent manner, and in violation of [section] 23152, i.e. driving under the influence of alcohol and/or drugs, and/or [section] 23153, which is driving under the influence causing injury . . . . [a]nd unintentionally, but unlawfully, kills another human being, is guilty of the crime of Gross vehicular manslaughter while intoxicated, in violation of Penal Code Section 191.5(a). A killing is unlawful when a person commits an unlawful act, not amounting to a felony, dangerous to human life under the circumstances of its commission, or commits an act ordinarily lawful, which might produce death, which unlawful act is a cause of the death of another human being. The commission of an unlawful act with gross negligence would necessarily be an unlawful act dangerous to human life, under the circumstances of its commission. In order to prove this crime, each of the following elements must be proved: One, the driver of the vehicle violated *Vehicle Code Section 23152* or *23153*, who's driving under the influence or driving while under the influence and causing injury; Two, in addition to that violation, the driver of the vehicle committed, with gross negligence, an unlawful act not amounting to a felony, namely, a violation of . . . *Vehicle Code Sections 22107* [failure to make safe lane change], 21662 [unsafe driving on mountain roads], 21650 [failure to drive on right side of road], 27315 [failure to ensure passengers wearing seat belts], 22350 [failure to drive at safe speed under the circumstances] or 22351 [failure to comply with posted speed] . . . dangerous to human life under the circumstances of its commission or committed with gross negligence, or an act ordinarily lawful which might cause death; And three, that unlawful act was a cause—that the unlawful act was a cause of the death of a human being." n2

> n2 *CALJIC No. 8.93* is the standard instruction on GVMI. It reads, in pertinent part, "Every person who drives a vehicle [in a grossly negligent manner and] in violation of section [23140,] [23152,] [or] [23153] of the Vehicle Code, and unintentionally but unlawfully kills another human being, is guilty of the crime of [Gross] Vehicular Manslaughter While Intoxicated. . . . ."

. . .

B. The Definition of "Unlawful" Killing

Defendant notes that the court's instruction defined an "unlawful" killing in terms of the commission of the underlying acts: "A killing is unlawful when a person commits an unlawful act, not amounting to a felony, dangerous to human life under the circumstances of its commission, or commits an act ordinarily lawful, which might produce death, which unlawful act is a cause of the death of another human being." Citing *People v. Frye* (1992) 7 Cal. App. 4th 1148 {10 Cal. Rptr. 2d 217}, defendant claims the true meaning of "unlawful" is a killing without excuse or justification. Defendant claims the court erred in failing to instruct on this meaning. We disagree.

. . .

In rejecting this claim, the court stated that "in connection with the use of violence against another person in a homicide case, the word 'unlawful' is a term of art" and refers to the absence of excuse or justification. (*People v. Frye, supra,* 7 Cal. App. 4th at p. 1155.) The court explained that where the evidence shows a killing by force or violence and no more, the killing is by definition unlawful, and the defendant must raise a reasonable doubt by presenting some evidence of excuse or justification. If he or she does, then the prosecutor must disprove the defense beyond a reasonable doubt. (*People v. Frye, supra,* 7 Cal. App. 4th at pp. 1154–1155; see *section 189.5.* . . .)

. . .

With these principles in mind, the court further explained that where there is no evidence of excuse or justification, such concepts are irrelevant, and the court need not instruct the jury on them.

. . .

There are material differences between a prosecution for murder and a prosecution for GVMI and the defenses available to both. Even if we assume that the phrase "unlawful killing" in section 191.5 ("Gross vehicular manslaughter while intoxicated is the unlawful killing of a human being without malice aforethought . . . .") includes the concept that a killing without excuse or justification is unlawful, that concept was not an issue in this case. As in *Frye*, there was no evidence of excuse or justification, defendant did not rely on either defense, n4 and she did not object to the court's instruction. Moreover, here the court's instruction did not tell the jury that defendant's acts were unlawful acts. Under the circumstances, we find no deficiency in the court's instruction.

> n4 The primary defense was that Traster was the driver. The alternative partial defense to GVMI was that defendant's conduct was not grossly negligent.

C. Committing a Lawful Act in an Unlawful Manner

As set forth above, GVMI occurs where a killing results from the commission of either an unlawful act, not amounting to a felony, (i.e., a misdemeanor or infraction) with gross negligence, or "a lawful act which might produce death, *in an unlawful manner,* and with gross negligence." (*section 191.5*, subd. (a), italics added.) Defendant contends the court misinstructed the jury on the second alternative because the instruction eliminated the requirement that the lawful act be performed "in an unlawful manner."

The trial court instructed the jury that a killing is unlawful when a person commits an unlawful act, not amounting to a felony, dangerous to human life under the circumstances of its commission, "*or commits an act ordinarily lawful, which might produce death, which unlawful act is a cause of the death of another . . . human being.*" Then, in enumerating the elements of the offense, the court stated that "in addition to [violating sections 23152 or 23153], the driver of the vehicle committed, with gross negligence . . . an act ordinarily lawful which might cause death." Thus, as defendant correctly points out, the court did not describe the second alternate as a lawful act performed in *an unlawful manner*. Nevertheless, we find no error.

. . .

In *People v. DeSpenza* (1962) 203 Cal. App. 2d 283, 291 {21 Cal. Rptr. 275}, the court cited *Wilson* for the "prevailing rule" that ordinary negligent driving "is in itself an unlawful act" under the manslaughter statute. (Accord, *In re Dennis B.* (1976) 18 Cal. 3d 687, 697 {135 Cal. Rptr. 82, 557 P.2d 514}.) In *People v. Ross* (1956) 139 Cal. App. 2d 706 {294 P.2d 174}, the court considered speeding through an intersection evidence of either a total lack of attention or a disregard for the consequences of his speed. Citing *Wilson*, the court opined, "This evidence justifies an inference of negligence on the part of the operator of the vehicle. Thus defendant was doing a lawful act which might, and actually did, produce death, in an unlawful manner, . . ." (*Id.* at pp. 710–711.)

From these cases we glean the following: committing a lawful act in an unlawful manner simply means to commit a lawful act with negligence, that is, without reasonable caution and care. It follows, then, that in the context of vehicular manslaughter, a killing is unlawful either when one commits a misdemeanor or infraction (an unlawful act, not amounting to a felony) or when one commits a negligent act (a lawful act in an unlawful manner). Indeed, *CALJIC No. 8.93* uses the phrase "negligently commits an ordinarily lawful act," instead of "commits a lawful act in an unlawful manner," to define "unlawful killing."

In light of our discussion, it is clear why the phrase "in an unlawful manner" and the word "negligently" are absent from the enumeration of elements in the court's instruction and *CALJIC No. 8.93*. Both instructions require the jury to find that the lawful act was committed with *gross* negligence. Such a finding would necessarily include a finding of simple negligence. Accordingly, the Supreme Court in *People v. Wells (1996) 12 Cal. 4th 979 {50 Cal. Rptr. 2d 699, 911 P.2d 1374},* stated, albeit in dicta, that even if the prosecution fails to prove that the defendant committed a Vehicle Code violation (i.e., unlawful act), the jury may still convict the defendant of gross vehicular manslaughter "if it finds that the defendant drove in a grossly negligent manner and, that this conduct was the proximate cause of a death." (*Id. at p. 990, fn. 9.*)

Under the circumstances, the failure to include the phrase "unlawful manner" or the word "negligently" in enumerating the elements of the offense was not error. And although the court should have included one or the other in defining an "unlawful killing," the error was harmless under any standard of review.

D. The Dangerousness Requirement

As defined by section 191.5, subdivision (a), one alternative element of GVMI is that the killing be the result of "an unlawful act, not amounting to a felony" committed with gross negligence. In *Wells,* the court held that the identical element in section 192, subdivision (c)(1) [gross vehicular manslaughter] requires that the unlawful act be "dangerous under the circumstances of its commission." (*People v. Wells, supra, 12 Cal. 4th* at p. 982.)

Defendant argues that "[a]lthough there does not appear to be any specific case deciding the point, it is logical that this same dangerous requirement to human life be applicable to the second alternative (i.e., a lawful act done in an unlawful manner)." Thus, she contends that in defining the "lawful act/unlawful manner" alternative element, the court erred in failing to say that the lawful act must be dangerous to human life under the circumstances of its commission. Again we find no error.

. . .

Gross negligence involves aggravated, reckless, or flagrant disregard for human life, or indifference to the consequences of one's conduct. (See *People v. Alonzo (1993) 13 Cal. App. 4th 535, 539–540 {16 Cal. Rptr. 2d 656}.*) The court here specifically instructed the jury to consider the circumstances surrounding the commission of defendant's conduct in determining whether death was reasonably foreseeable.

. . .

E. Lawful Act and Proximate Cause

Defendant contends that in connection with the lawful act/unlawful manner alternative element, the court erred in failing to instruct the jury that such conduct had to be a cause of Traster's death. The record supports defendant's claim.

The court defined an unlawful killing as follows: "when a person commits an *unlawful act*, not amounting to a felony dangerous to human life under the circumstances of its commission, or commits an act ordinarily lawful, which might produce death, which *unlawful* act is a cause of the death of another . . . human being." As defendant correctly points out, the last clause refers only to an unlawful act being a cause of death and does not expressly state, or make explicitly clear, that, alternatively, the commission of a lawful act in an unlawful manner must be a cause of death. The court reiterated the mistake by telling the jury that the prosecution had to prove the following: that (1) while defendant was driving under the influence, (2) she committed either an unlawful act or a lawful act with gross negligence, and (3) "the *unlawful* act was a cause of the death of a human being." . . . Thus, in the abstract, a jury could convict without finding that negligent driving (lawful act/unlawful manner) was a cause of death. Returning to the real world, we find the instructional omission harmless. (See *Chapman v. California (1967) 386 U.S. 18, 24 {87 S. Ct. 824, 828, 17 L. Ed. 2d 705, 24 A.L.R.3d 1065}.*)

. . .

Stated differently, we are satisfied beyond a reasonable doubt that the omission here did not contribute in any way to the verdict.

. . .

XIV. LE DISPOSITION

The judgment is affirmed.

BAMATTRE-MANOUKIAN, Acting P. J., and MIHARA, J., concurred.

A petition for a rehearing was denied April 14, 2000, and the opinion was modified to read as printed above. Appellant's petition for review by the Supreme Court was denied July 12, 2000.

KEY TERMS

STUDY GUIDE CHAPTER 3

FETAL MURDER

1. What is the statutory law at issue in the Keeler and Davis cases?

2. Does the definition of *murder* as set forth in the California Penal Code affect whether a defendant can be convicted of killing a fetus? Explain.

3. In the Keeler case, the statute defined *murder* as the killing of a "human being." Can the defendant be convicted of murder if the baby was stillborn? State the basic rule of law from Keeler that explains when a defendant may be charged with *murder* under the circumstances of the case.

4. How did the definition of *murder* change from the Keeler case to the Davis case?

5. What is the rule of law for *murder* of a fetus after the Davis case? Does the prosecutor need to prove that the fetus was viable to obtain a *murder* conviction? Explain.

MURDER AND MANSLAUGHTER

1. What are the elements necessary to establish a first degree *murder?*

2. How do you prove premeditation and deliberation? Identify precedent that factually demonstrates each such way to prove premeditation and deliberation. State any rules of law relevant to the requisite decision making and time to establish premeditation and deliberation.

3. What is the doctrine of transferred intent? How does the doctrine help prove a murder charge? Explain how the doctrine may be used in an *attempted murder* case. Does the doctrine permit elements, other than intent to kill, to transfer in a prosecution for first degree murder? Explain.

4. What are the elements for the *felony-murder rule?* How does this rule make it easier to establish the crime of *murder?* Discuss the types of felonies that can be the predicate felony. What is the rationale for the *felony-murder rule?* Cite examples of the use of this rule.

5. Explain the key difference between first and second degree *murder.* What is common to both?

6. Why does *imperfect self-defense* result in the reduction of the charge from murder to manslaughter? What is the key difference between *murder* and *manslaughter* in general?

CHAPTER 4

Special Defenses

The law recognizes that sometimes conduct that could be deemed criminal is done for a rational or legitimate purpose—this would be referred to as a legal justification. Self-defense is a classic **justification** defense. In other circumstances, an actor engages in a criminal act, but because of the circumstances surrounding the actor or his/her circumstances, they have a legal **excuse** for their actions. Insanity is a classic excuse. This chapter discusses the California rules relating to these and a number of other special defenses. These defenses can typically apply to the commission of any criminal act, but some are most easily understood when considered in the context of homicide. Many of the cases in this chapter involve defendants in homicide cases and illustrate how the defenses operated (or in some cases, did not operate) to alleviate the defendant of criminal responsibility.

JUSTIFIABLE HOMICIDE

The Code requires more than bare fear to justify killing another person in self-defense. The killer must experience fear that is sufficient to "excite the fears of a reasonable person, and the party killing must have acted under the influence of such fears alone."[1] In order to successfully prove a claim that the use of deadly force was lawful in self-defense, or defense of another, the defendant must have reasonably believed that he/she or a third party was in imminent (immediate) danger of death or suffering great bodily injury and the defendant must have reasonably believed that immediate use of **deadly force** was necessary to defend against that danger.[2] Deadly force is an amount of force likely to cause death or great bodily injury. For example, the use of a gun is always a threat of deadly force. Belief in future harm is not enough to warrant the use of deadly force, even if that belief is reasonable.

The amount of force used must be reasonable under the circumstances. It is also important to note that the standard is one of **objective reasonableness.** The question to ask is "whether a reasonable person in the same or similar circumstances would have believed that he or she faced an imminent, unlawful, and deadly threat?" The defendant does not have to be correct in their assessment of the danger; the danger may not have in fact really existed, but their belief must be reasonable. The law doesn't take into account the unique characteristics of the defendant or his or her mental capacity when determining whether he has acted as the reasonable person would act.[3] In California, there is *no duty to retreat* from an imminent, unlawful, and deadly threat.[4] Some other states require that a killer first attempt to retreat or find a safe place before resorting to the use of deadly force to protect himself, but California law does not require it.

According to California Penal Code §197 a homicide is justifiable when committed by any person under the following circumstances.

- **Self-defense:** resisting an imminent, unlawful, and deadly threat to oneself

- **Defense of habitation:** when committed in defense of one's home

- **Defense of another:** resisting an imminent, unlawful, and deadly threat to another person

- **Peace officers:** when carrying out the death penalty or when apprehending or arresting certain dangerous felons

- **Citizen's arrests:** when attempting, by lawful means, to apprehend any person for any felony committed, or in lawfully suppressing a riot, or in lawfully keeping and preserving the peace

The use of deadly force on behalf of oneself or another will only be justified when the defendant reasonably believed that he or she was facing an imminent, unlawful, and deadly threat and used no more force than was necessary.

The defendant claiming self-defense may not invoke the doctrine if he or she was the initial aggressor in a confrontation. A person who was the initial aggressor may "regain" the right to use deadly force in self-defense, but in order to do so, must have communicated and affected a withdrawal from the original confrontation. If the victim and the defendant were engaged in mutual combat, and the victim responded with a sudden escalation of force, the defendant may legally defend against the higher level of force. The use of force is only justified if it is proportional to the force threatened.

When a defendant, claiming self-defense, fails to demonstrate the reasonableness of his or her belief, the resulting conviction should be for voluntary manslaughter based on "imperfect" self-defense. It is the reasonableness of the defendant's belief in an imminent, unlawful deadly threat that "perfects" her belief and in turn, gives her the right to use deadly force. The result if a defendant successfully proves that he or she acted in lawful self-defense is to be fully acquitted and discharged.[5]

---

[1] Cal. Pen. Code §198.

[2] CALCRIM No. 505 (2010).

[3] CALCRIM No. 505 (2010) citing Prosser, W.L., Keeton, W.P., Dobbs D.B., Keeton, R.E. & Owen D.G. (Eds.) (1984). *Prossen & Keeton on Torts* (5th ed.) (§ 32 p. 177). West Group.

[4] *People v. Hughes,* 107 Cal.App.2d 487 (1951).

[5] Cal. Pen. Code §199.

In California, the courts have concluded that evidence of **battered women's syndrome** can be considered by the jury when assessing the reasonableness of the defendant's belief in her right to use deadly force in self-defense. In *People v. Humphrey* (1996),[6] the court held that evidence of battered women's syndrome could be considered by the jury to help determine the defendant's actual belief in the need for deadly force—but specifically noted that this does not create a "battered women's standard" of reasonableness, rather that it requires juries to consider all relevant circumstances when determining the reasonableness of the defendant's belief.

Defense of habitation involves the right of a person to protect herself inside of her home or residence. The law justifies a killing committed when a person fears for the life and safety of himself or herself, or the family members or people within the residence, against a person who "violently, riotously, or tumultuously tried to enter their home intending to commit an act of violence."[7] If the requirements are met, the killer is not guilty of a crime because the killing is a justifiable homicide. There is a presumption under California law in favor of a person who uses deadly force in self-defense inside his or her residence.[8] If a person uses deadly force against an intruder, the person inside is presumed to have acted with reasonable fear of imminent peril of death or great bodily injury to himself or herself, his or her family, or a member of the household when the intruder has entered unlawfully and forcibly.

The use of deadly force in defense of habitation will only be justified when the defendant possessed reasonable belief that he or she was defending a home against an intruder who imminently intended or tried to commit a forcible and atrocious crime or who violently, riotously, or tumultuously tried to enter that home intending to commit an act of violence against someone inside.

According to California Penal Code §196, homicide committed by peace officers and those acting by their command in their aid and assistance is justified when it is ordered by a competent court (as in state-sanctioned executions that are carrying out a death sentence), when it is necessary to overcome actual resistance to the execution of some legal process or in the discharge of any other legal duty, or when re-taking felons who have been rescued or escaped, or when arresting persons charged with a felony, and who are fleeing from justice or resisting such arrest. These rules permitting police officers to use deadly force are narrowly defined. In the case of *Tennessee v. Garner* (1985), the United States Supreme Court held that it is unlawful for officers to use deadly force to apprehend a fleeing felon who is unarmed and poses no imminent threat to public or officer safety.[9] Police officers must act reasonably in exercising deadly force.

The law of justifiable homicide protects a private citizen against prosecution for homicide in cases where they kill another person while trying to effect a citizen's arrest. The killer must possess a reasonable belief that the person they are attempting to arrest is committing a crime that poses a deadly threat. The test is one of objective reasonableness, and the prosecution has the burden of proving that the killing was not justified.

Homicide committed during a citizen's arrest is justified when:

- The defendant committed the killing while lawfully trying to arrest or detain a person for committing a forcible and atrocious crime or felony that threatened death or great bodily harm; or

- The decedent actually committed the crime alleged; or

- The defendant had reason to believe that the decedent posed a threat of serious physical harm, either to the defendant or to others or knew that the decedent had committed the crime alleged; *and*

- The killing (or attempted killing) was necessary to prevent the decedent's escape.

---

[6] *People v. Humphrey*, 13 Cal.4th 1073 (1996).

[7] CALCRIM No. 506 (2010).

[8] Cal. Pen. Code §198.5.

[9] *Tennessee v. Garner*, 471 U.S. 1 (1985).

Self-defense in non-homicide cases is explained in California Penal Code §692–964. The code explains that lawful resistance to a public offense can be made by both the party injured and by third parties on their behalf. If made by the party injured, a person may prevent an offense against his person, his family, or some member thereof or prevent an illegal attempt by force to take or injure property in his lawful possession. If lawful resistance is committed by a third party in the aid of another, force may be sufficient to prevent the offense. Whenever non-deadly force is used in self-defense or defense of another, it must be reasonable and proportional. Deadly force is *never* justified to defend property alone.

INSANITY

There is no uniform rule or test for determining whether a defendant is legally insane. American states differ in how they treat the issue. California's rule for proof of insanity is that in **M'Naghten's case.** In 1843, Daniel M'Naghten attempted to kill the British Prime Minister, and in the process successfully killed his aid. British courts found M'Naghten not guilty by reason of insanity. As a result of this case, British Parliament set about creating a rule that would govern cases where a defendant pled not guilty by reason of insanity. The rule focuses on the defendant's ability to comprehend the nature and/or wrongfulness of his or her conduct. It has been criticized over the years and in many American states is not employed.

Throughout American legal history, a number of alternatives to the **M'Naghten Rule** have been utilized, many of which focus on the defendant's ability to control his or her actions—even if the wrongfulness of the act can be comprehended. Insanity at the time of the actus reus negates criminal responsibility and entitles the defendant to an acquittal. In California, the people voted to approve Proposition 8 in 1982, which abolished the defense of diminished capacity and set the standard for proof of insanity in criminal and juvenile court proceedings. This was in response to public outcry over the "loophole" that California's old diminished-capacity rule had created, which had allowed President Reagan's would-be assassin, John Hinckley, Jr. to successfully plead insanity, and returned California to the M'Naghten Rule:

In order for a plea of not guilty by reason of insanity to be successful, the defendant must prove by a preponderance of the evidence that he or she was incapable of knowing or understanding the nature and quality of his or her act or of distinguishing right from wrong at the time of commission of the offense.[10]

Evidence of diminished capacity or of a mental disorder may only be considered at the time of sentencing or other disposition or commitment. In California, a personality or adjustment disorder, a seizure disorder, or an addiction to or abuse of intoxicating substances cannot, alone, be the basis of a successful claim of insanity.[11] The trial for a defendant who pleads not guilty by reason of insanity can be **bifurcated,** or have two parts. First, if both insanity and another type of plea or pleas were entered, the case is treated as if only those other plea or pleas were entered, and a determination of guilt or innocence is made by a jury. If the jury finds the defendant guilty, or if the defendant plead only not guilty by reason of insanity, a separate trial is then held to determine whether the defendant was sane or insane at the time of the offense. If the defendant is found to have been sane, then he or she is sentenced appropriately. If the defendant is found to have been insane, then a determination is made regarding whether he or she has fully recovered.

KEY LEGAL PRINCIPLE:

If the defendant has fully recovered, they are released. See *People v. Skinner* (1985)[12] in this chapter; **temporary insanity** can be as good a defense as insanity itself.

---

[10] Cal. Pen. Code §25.

[11] Cal. Pen. Code §25.5.

[12] *People v. Skinner,* 39 Cal. App. 3d 765 (1985).

If the defendant has not fully recovered, the defendant is committed to a facility for care and treatment of the mentally disordered. The process of commitment for treatment involves an evaluation and report back to the court by mental health professionals.[13] The term of commitment under normal circumstances may not be longer than the longest term of imprisonment that could have been imposed for offense(s) for which the defendant was convicted (including upper terms and sentencing enhancements). The Board of Prison Terms has some flexibility to extend a person's commitment beyond that time, and is responsible for evaluating and making decisions regarding the length of commitment.[14]

INTOXICATION

Intoxication is either **voluntary intoxication** or **involuntary intoxication.** In the majority of circumstances, a person is voluntarily intoxicated, or has come under the influence of alcohol or drugs of their own choice. In rare circumstances, a person is intoxicated involuntarily. This might occur because of coercion to ingest the intoxicating substance, because of a mistake as to ingestion or a mistake as to the character of the substance, or because of pathological intoxication. **Pathological intoxication** results when a person has an extraordinary reaction or disproportionate response to the ingestion of a substance, and had no prior knowledge of their propensity for the response. This might also result from the ingestion of a prescription drug which causes an unexpected reaction. Involuntary intoxication is typically a defense to criminal conduct.[15] Involuntary intoxication is a defense when it leaves the defendant temporarily insane (according to the M'Naghten Rule), when it causes the defendant to lack the requisite mens rea for the offense, or when intoxication is an element of the offense charged (e.g., public drunkenness).

In contrast, a person's conduct is no less criminal as the result of their voluntary intoxication.[16] A defendant is not even permitted to introduce evidence of their voluntary intoxication in an effort to prove that he or she lacked the capacity to commit the offense. A defendant cannot claim that a person in their intoxicated condition "could never have done X, Y, or Z." Rather, it is admissible only for the narrow purpose of demonstrating that they did not *in fact* form the requisite *specific intent* for the offense, or that they did not premeditate, deliberate, or harbor express malice in a murder case.[17] Evidence of their voluntary intoxication is irrelevant against charges that the defendant committed a general intent offense.

MISTAKE

There are two types of mistakes: **mistake of fact** and **mistake of law.** A mistake of fact *may* be an excuse for criminal conduct if the person committed the act or made the omission in a way that demonstrates a lack of criminal intent (because of the mistake, they did not possess the necessary mens rea and as a result, are not guilty of the crime).[18] A mistake of law is no defense to criminal conduct. A long-standing principle of American jurisprudence is that individuals are required to know what the rules of law are and abide by them. A claim that a person didn't know at the time they committed a criminal act that they were breaking the law is not a defense to the charge. The test for a mistake of fact is one of objective reasonableness. The court in *People v. Lucero* (1988) cited *Matter of Application of Ahart,* noting that "at common law an honest and reasonable belief in the existence of circumstances, which, if true, would make the act for which the person is indicted an innocent act, has always been held to be a good defense."[19]

---

[13] Cal. Pen. Code §1026.

[14] Cal. Pen. Code §1026.5.

[15] Cal. Pen. Code §26(3).

[16] Cal. Pen. Code §28(b).

[17] Cal. Pen. Code §22(a)(c).

[18] Cal. Pen. Code §26.

[19] *People v. Lucero,* 203 Cal. App. 3d 1011, (1988) citing *Ahart,* 172 Cal.762, 765 (1916).

PEOPLE V. HUMPHREY

SUPREME COURT OF CALIFORNIA

13 CAL. 4TH 1073; 921 P.2D 1; 56 CAL. RPTR. 2D 142

AUGUST 29, 1996

OPINION BY : CHIN, J.

The Legislature has decreed that, when relevant, expert testimony regarding "battered women's syndrome" is generally admissible in a criminal action. (*Evid. Code, § 1107*.) We must determine the purposes for which a jury may consider this evidence when offered to support a claim of self-defense to a murder charge.

The trial court instructed that the jury could consider the evidence in deciding whether the defendant actually believed it was necessary to kill in self-defense, but not in deciding whether that belief was reasonable. The instruction was erroneous. Because evidence of battered women's syndrome may help the jury understand the circumstances in which the defendant found herself at the time of the killing, it is relevant to the reasonableness of her belief. Moreover, because defendant testified, the evidence was relevant to her credibility. The trial court should have allowed the jury to consider this testimony in deciding the reasonableness as well as the existence of defendant's belief that killing was necessary.

Finding the error prejudicial, we reverse the judgment of the Court of Appeal.

I. THE FACTS

A. Prosecution Evidence

During the evening of March 28, 1992, defendant shot and killed Albert Hampton in their Fresno home. Officer Reagan was the first on the scene. A neighbor told Reagan that the couple in the house had been arguing all day. Defendant soon came outside appearing upset and with her hands raised as if surrendering. She told Officer Reagan, "I shot him. That's right, I shot him. I just couldn't take him beating on me no more." She led the officer into the house, showed him a .357 magnum revolver on a table, and said, "There's the gun." Hampton was on the kitchen floor, wounded but alive.

A short time later, defendant told Officer Reagan, "He deserved it. I just couldn't take it anymore. I told him to stop beating on me." "He was beating on me, so I shot him. I told him I'd shoot him if he ever beat on me again." A paramedic heard her say that she wanted to teach Hampton "a lesson." Defendant told another officer at the scene, Officer Terry, "I'm fed up. Yeah, I shot him. I'm just tired of him hitting me. He said, 'You're not going to do nothing about it.' I showed him, didn't I? I shot him good. He won't hit anybody else again. Hit me again; I shoot him again. I don't care if I go to jail. Push come to shove, I guess people gave it to him, and, kept hitting me. I warned him. I warned him not to hit me. He wouldn't listen."

Officer Terry took defendant to the police station, where she told the following story. The day before the shooting, Hampton had been drinking. He hit defendant while they were driving home in their truck and continued hitting her when they arrived. He told her, "I'll kill you," and shot at her. The bullet went through a bedroom window and struck a tree outside. The day of the shooting, Hampton "got drunk," swore at her, and started hitting her again. He walked into the kitchen. Defendant saw the gun in the living room and picked it up. Her jaw hurt, and she was in pain. She pointed the gun at Hampton and said, "You're not going to hit me anymore." Hampton said, "What are you doing?" Believing that Hampton was about to pick something up to hit her with, she shot him. She then put the gun down and went outside to wait for the police.

Hampton later died of a gunshot wound to the chest. The neighbor who spoke with Officer Reagan testified that shortly before the shooting, she heard defendant, but not Hampton, shouting. The evening before, the neighbor had heard a gunshot. Defendant's blood contained no drugs but had a blood-alcohol level of .17 percent. Hampton's blood contained no drugs or alcohol.

B. Defense Evidence

Defendant claimed she shot Hampton in self-defense. To support the claim, the defense presented first expert testimony and then non-expert testimony, including that of defendant herself.

Dr. Lee Bowker testified as an expert on battered women's syndrome. The syndrome, he testified, "is not just a psychological construction, but it's a term for a wide variety of controlling mechanisms that the man or it can be a woman, but in general for this syndrome it's a man, uses against the woman, and for the effect that those control mechanisms have."

Dr. Bowker had studied about 1,000 battered women and found them often inaccurately portrayed "as cardboard figures, paper-thin punching bags who merely absorb the violence but didn't do anything about it." He found that battered women often employ strategies to stop the beatings, including hiding, running away, counter-violence, seeking the help of friends and family, going to a shelter, and contacting police. Nevertheless, many battered women remain in the relationship because of lack of money, social isolation, lack of self-confidence, inadequate police response, and a fear (often justified) of reprisals by the batterer. "The battering man will make the battered woman depend on him and generally succeed at least for a time." A battered woman often feels responsible for the abusive relationship, and "she just can't figure out a way to please him better so he'll stop beating her." In sum, "It really is the physical control of the woman through economics and through relative social isolation combined with the psychological techniques that make her so dependent."

Many battered women go from one abusive relationship to another and seek a strong man to protect them from the previous abuser. "[W]ith each successful victimization, the person becomes less able to avoid the next one." The violence can gradually escalate, as the batterer keeps control using ever more severe actions, including rape, torture, violence against the woman's loved ones or pets, and death threats. Battered women sense this escalation. In Dr. Bowker's "experience with battered women who kill in self-defense their abusers, it's always related to their perceived change of what's going on in a relationship. They become very sensitive to what sets off batterers. They watch for this stuff very carefully. . . . Anybody who is abused over a period of time becomes sensitive to the abuser's behavior and when she sees a change acceleration begin in that behavior, it tells them something is going to happen."

Dr. Bowker interviewed defendant for a full day. He believed she suffered not only from battered women's syndrome, but also from being the child of an alcoholic and an incest victim. He testified that all three of defendant's partners before Hampton were abusive and significantly older than she.

Dr. Bowker described defendant's relationship with Hampton. Hampton was a 49-year-old man who weighed almost twice as much as defendant. The two had a

battering relationship that Dr. Bowker characterized as a "traditional cycle of violence." The cycle included phases of tension building, violence, and then forgiveness-seeking in which Hampton would promise not to batter defendant any more and she would believe him. During this period, there would be occasional good times. For example, defendant told Dr. Bowker that Hampton would give her a rose. "That's one of the things that hooks people in. Intermittent reinforcement is the key." But after a while, the violence would begin again. The violence would recur because "basically . . . the woman doesn't perfectly obey. That's the bottom line." For example, defendant would talk to another man, or fail to clean house "just so."

The situation worsened over time, especially when Hampton got off parole shortly before his death. He became more physically and emotionally abusive, repeatedly threatened defendant's life, and even shot at her the night before his death. Hampton often allowed defendant to go out, but she was afraid to flee because she felt he would find her as he had in the past. "He enforced her belief that she can never escape him." Dr. Bowker testified that unless her injuries were so severe that "something absolutely had to be treated," he would not expect her to seek medical treatment. "That's the pattern of her life . . ."

Dr. Bowker believed defendant's description of her experiences. In his opinion, she suffered from battered women's syndrome in "about as extreme a pattern as you could find."

2. Non-expert Testimony   Defendant confirmed many of the details of her life and relationship with Hampton underlying Dr. Bowker's opinion. She testified that her father forcefully molested her from the time she was 7 years old until she was 15. She described her relationship with another abusive man as being like "Nightmare on Elm Street." Regarding Hampton, she testified that they often argued and that he beat her regularly. Both were heavy drinkers. Hampton once threw a can of beer at her face, breaking her nose. Her dental plates hurt because Hampton hit her so often. He often kicked her, but usually hit her in the back of the head because, he told her, it "won't leave bruises." Hampton sometimes threatened to kill her, and often said she "would live to regret it." Matters got worse towards the end.

The evening before the shooting, March 27, 1992, Hampton arrived home "very drunk." He yelled at her and called her names. At one point when she was standing by the bedroom window, he fired his .357 magnum revolver at her. She testified, "He didn't miss me by much either." She was "real scared."

The next day, the two drove into the mountains. They argued, and Hampton continually hit her. While returning, he said that their location would be a good place to kill her because "they wouldn't find [her] for a while." She took it as a joke, although she feared him. When they returned, the arguing continued. He hit her again, then entered the kitchen. He threatened, "This time, bitch, when I shoot at you, I won't miss." He came from the kitchen and reached for the gun on the living room table. She grabbed it first, pointed it at him, and told him "that he wasn't going to hit [her]." She backed Hampton into the kitchen. He was saying something, but she did not know what. He reached for her hand and she shot him. She believed he was reaching for the gun and was going to shoot her.

Several other witnesses testified about defendant's relationship with Hampton, his abusive conduct in general, and his physical abuse of, and threats to, defendant in particular. This testimony generally corroborated defendant's. A neighbor testified that the night before the shooting, she heard a gunshot. The next morning, defendant told the neighbor that Hampton had shot at her, and that she was afraid of him. After the shooting, investigators found a bullet hole through the frame of the bedroom window and a bullet embedded in a tree in line with the window. Another neighbor testified that shortly before hearing the shot that killed Hampton, she heard defendant say, "Stop it, Albert. Stop it."

C. Procedural History

Defendant was charged with murder with personal use of a firearm. At the end of the prosecution's case-in-chief, the court granted defendant's motion under *Penal Code section 1118.1* for acquittal of first degree murder.

The court instructed the jury on second degree murder and both voluntary and involuntary manslaughter. It also instructed on self-defense, explaining that an actual and reasonable belief that the killing was necessary was a complete defense; an actual but unreasonable belief was a defense to murder, but not to voluntary manslaughter. In determining reasonableness, the jury was to consider what "would appear to be necessary to a reasonable person in a similar situation and with similar knowledge."

The court also instructed:

"Evidence regarding battered women's syndrome has been introduced in this case. Such evidence, if believed, may be considered by you only for the purpose of determining whether or not the defendant held the necessary subjective honest [belief] which is a requirement for both perfect and imperfect self-defense. However, that same evidence regarding battered women's syndrome may not be considered or used by you in evaluating the objective reasonableness requirement for perfect self-defense."

"Battered women's syndrome seeks to describe and explain common reactions of women to that experience. Thus, you

may consider the evidence concerning the syndrome and its effects only for the limited purpose of showing, if it does show, that the defendant's reactions, as demonstrated by the evidence, are not inconsistent with her having been physically abused or the beliefs, perceptions, or behavior of victims of domestic violence."

During deliberations, the jury asked for and received clarification of the terms "subjectively honest and objectively unreasonable." It found defendant guilty of voluntary manslaughter with personal use of a firearm. The court sentenced defendant to prison for eight years, consisting of the lower term of 3 years for manslaughter, plus the upper term of 5 years for firearm use. The Court of Appeal remanded for re-sentencing on the use enhancement, but otherwise affirmed the judgment.

We granted defendant's petition for review.

II. DISCUSSION

A. Background

With an exception not relevant here, *Evidence Code section 1107*, subdivision (a), makes admissible in a criminal action expert testimony regarding "battered women's syndrome, including the physical, emotional, or mental effects upon the beliefs, perceptions, or behavior of victims of domestic violence." Under subdivision (b) of that section, the foundation for admission is sufficient "if the proponent of the evidence establishes its relevancy and the proper qualifications of the expert witness." n1 Defendant presented the evidence to support her claim of self-defense. It is undisputed that she established the proper qualifications of the expert witness. The only issue is to what extent defendant established its "relevancy." To resolve this question we must examine California law regarding self-defense.

> n1 *Evidence Code section 1107* was adopted in 1991, effective January 1, 1992. (Stats. 1991, ch. 812, § 1.) It currently provides: "(a) In a criminal action, expert testimony is admissible by either the prosecution or the defense regarding battered women's syndrome, including the physical, emotional, or mental effects upon the beliefs, perceptions, or behavior of victims of domestic violence, except when offered against a criminal defendant to prove the occurrence of the act or acts of abuse which form the basis of the criminal charge.
>
> "(b) The foundation shall be sufficient for admission of this expert testimony if the proponent of the evidence establishes its relevancy and the proper qualifications of the expert witness. Expert opinion testimony on battered women's syndrome shall not be considered a new scientific technique whose reliability is unproven.

"(c) For purposes of this section, 'abuse' is defined in *Section 6203 of the Family Code* and 'domestic violence' is defined in *Section 6211 of the Family Code.*

"(d) This section is intended as a rule of evidence only and no substantive change affecting the Penal Code is intended."

For killing to be in self-defense, the defendant must actually and reasonably believe in the need to defend. (*People v. Flannel (1979) 25 Cal. 3d 668, 674 {160 Cal. Rptr. 84, 603 P.2d 1}.*) If the belief subjectively exists but is objectively unreasonable, there is "imperfect self-defense," i.e., "the defendant is deemed to have acted without malice and cannot be convicted of murder," but can be convicted of manslaughter. . . . To constitute "perfect self-defense," i.e., to exonerate the person completely, the belief must also be objectively reasonable. . . . As the Legislature has stated, " [T]he circumstances must be sufficient to excite the fears of a reasonable person.". . . Moreover, for either perfect or imperfect self-defense, the fear must be of imminent harm. "Fear of future harm—no matter how great the fear and no matter how great the likelihood of the harm—will not suffice. The defendant's fear must be of *imminent* danger to life or great bodily injury."

. . .

Although the belief in the need to defend must be objectively reasonable, a jury must consider what "would appear to be necessary to a reasonable person in a similar situation and with similar knowledge . . ." (*CALJIC No. 5.50.*) It judges reasonableness "from the point of view of a reasonable person in the position of defendant . . . . . . To do this, it must consider all the 'facts and circumstances . . . in determining whether the defendant acted in a manner in which *a reasonable man* would act in protecting his own life or bodily safety 1 . . . As we stated long ago, ". . . a defendant is entitled to have a jury take into consideration all the elements in the case which might be expected to operate on his mind . . ."

. . .

We recently discussed this question in a different context. In *People v. Ochoa (1993) 6 Cal. 4th 1199 {26 Cal. Rptr. 2d 23, 864 P.2d 103}*, the defendant was convicted of gross vehicular manslaughter while intoxicated. The offense requires "gross negligence," the test for which is "objective: whether a reasonable person in the defendant's position would have been aware of the risk involved." (*Id.* at p. 1204, quoting *People v. Bennett (1991) 54 Cal. 3d 1032, 1036 {2 Cal. Rptr. 2d 8, 819 P.2d 849}.*) The defendant argued that, "because the test of gross negligence is an *objective* one . . ., evidence of his own subjective state of mind was irrelevant and unduly

prejudicial." (*People v. Ochoa, supra, at p. 1205,* italics in original.) We disagreed. "In determining whether a reasonable person *in defendant's position* would have been aware of the risks, the jury should be given relevant facts as to what defendant knew, including his actual awareness of those risks." (*Ibid.*, italics in original.) "[A]lthough the test for gross negligence was an objective one, '[t]he jury should therefore consider all relevant circumstances . . . . [Citations.]'." (*Ibid.*, quoting *People v. Bennett, supra, 54 Cal. 3d* at p. 1038.)

What we said in *Ochoa* about the defendant's actual awareness applies to this case. Although the ultimate test of reasonableness is objective, in determining whether a reasonable person in defendant's position would have believed in the need to defend, the jury must consider all of the relevant circumstances in which defendant found herself.

With these principles in mind, we now consider the relevance of evidence of battered women's syndrome to the elements of self-defense.

B. Battered Women's Syndrome n3

n3 We use the term "battered women's syndrome" because *Evidence Code section 1107* and the cases use that term. We note, however, that according to *amici curiae* California Alliance Against Domestic Violence et al., ". . . the preferred term among many experts today is "expert testimony on battering and its effects" or "expert testimony on battered women's experiences." Domestic violence experts have critiqued the phrase "battered women's syndrome" because (1) it implies that there is one syndrome which all battered women develop, (2) it has pathological connotations which suggest that battered women suffer from some sort of sickness, (3) expert testimony on domestic violence refers to more than women's psychological reactions to violence, (4) it focuses attention on the battered woman rather than on the batterer's coercive and controlling behavior, and (5) it creates an image of battered women as suffering victims rather than as active survivors." (Fns. omitted.)

Battered women's syndrome "has been defined as 'a series of common characteristics that appear in women who are abused physically and psychologically over an extended period of time by the dominant male figure in their lives.' . . .

The trial court allowed the jury to consider the battered women's syndrome evidence in deciding whether defendant actually believed she needed to kill in self-defense. The question here is whether the evidence was also relevant on the reasonableness of that belief. Two Court of Appeal decisions have considered the relevance of battered women's syndrome evidence to a claim of self-defense.

. . .

The Attorney General concedes that Hampton's behavior towards defendant, including prior threats and violence, was relevant to reasonableness (see *People v. Minifie (1996) 13 Cal. 4th 1055, 1065 {56 Cal. Rptr. 2d 133, 920 P.2d 1337}*), but distinguishes between evidence of this *behavior*—which the trial court fully *admitted*—and *expert testimony* about its effects on defendant. The distinction is untenable. "To effectively present the situation as perceived by the defendant, and the reasonableness of her fear, the defense has the option to explain her feelings to enable the jury to overcome stereotyped impressions about women who remain in abusive relationships. It is appropriate that the jury be given a professional explanation of the battering syndrome and its effects on the woman through the use of expert testimony. . . ."

The Attorney General also argues that allowing consideration of this testimony would result in an undesirable "battle of the experts" and raises the specter of other battles of experts regarding other syndromes. The Legislature, however, has decided that, if relevant, expert evidence on battered women's syndrome is admissible. (*Evid. Code, § 1107.*) We have found it relevant; it is therefore admissible. We express no opinion on the admissibility of expert testimony regarding other possible syndromes in support of a claim of self-defense, but we rest today's holding on *Evidence Code section 1107*.

Contrary to the Attorney General's argument, we are not changing the standard from objective to subjective, or replacing the reasonable "person" standard with a reasonable "battered woman" standard. Our decision would not, in another context, compel adoption of a "'reasonable gang member' standard." *Evidence Code § 1107* states "a rule of evidence only" and makes "no substantive change." (*Evid. Code, § 1107*, subd. (d).) The jury must consider defendant's situation and knowledge, which makes the evidence relevant, but the ultimate question is whether a reasonable *person*, not a reasonable battered woman, would believe in the need to kill to prevent imminent harm. Moreover, it is the *jury*, not the expert that determines whether defendant's belief and, ultimately, her actions, were objectively reasonable.

Battered women's syndrome evidence was also relevant to defendant's credibility. It "would have assisted the jury in objectively analyzing [defendant's] claim of self-defense by dispelling many of the commonly held misconceptions about battered women." (*People v. Day, supra, 2 Cal. App. 4th* at p. 416.) For example, in urging the jury not to believe defendant's testimony that Hampton shot at her

the night before the killing, the prosecutor argued that "if this defendant truly believed that [Hampton] had shot at her, on that night, I mean she would have left. . . . If she really believed that he had tried to shoot her, she would not have stayed." Dr. Bowker's testimony "would help dispel the ordinary lay person's perception that a woman in a battering relationship is free to leave at any time. The expert evidence would counter any 'common sense' conclusions by the jury that if the beatings were really that bad the woman would have left her husband much earlier. Popular misconceptions about battered women would be put to rest . . . . ." (*People v. Day, supra, 2 Cal. App. 4th* at p. 417, *quoting State v. Hodges (1986) 239 Kan. 63 {716 P.2d 563,* 567}.) "[I]f the jury had understood [defendant's] conduct in light of [battered women's syndrome] evidence, then the jury may well have concluded her version of the events was sufficiently credible to warrant an acquittal on the facts as she related them." (*People v. Day, supra, 2 Cal. App.* 4th at p. 415.)

. . .

We also emphasize that, as with any evidence, the jury may give this testimony whatever weight it deems appropriate in light of the evidence as a whole. The ultimate judgment of reasonableness is solely for the jury. We simply hold that evidence of battered women's syndrome is generally *relevant* to the reasonableness, as well as the subjective existence, of defendant's belief in the need to defend, and, to the extent it is relevant, the jury may *consider* it in deciding both questions. The court's contrary instruction was erroneous. We disapprove of *People v. Aris, supra, 215 Cal. App. 3d 1178*, and *People v. Day, supra, 2 Cal. App. 4th 405*, to the extent they are inconsistent with this conclusion.

C. Prejudice

. . . we conclude the error was prejudicial. The jury found defendant guilty of voluntary manslaughter, not murder. Although the verdict may have been based on a finding of provocation, the arguments to the jury and the jury's request for clarification of the terms "subjectively honest and objectively unreasonable" suggest the question of unreasonable self-defense was critical. The jury likely concluded that defendant actually believed in the need to defend, but her belief was unreasonable. If so, guilt or innocence hinged on the precise issue—objective reasonableness—on which the court told the jury not to consider the battered women's syndrome evidence. As stated above, the prosecutor argued that defendant's actions were unreasonable because the last "threat that she says he made was like so many threats before. There was no reason for her to react that way." The testimony the court told the jury not to consider was directly responsive to this argument.

Although we do not know what weight the jury would have given the expert testimony in determining reasonableness, the testimony "was not only relevant, but critical in permitting the jury to evaluate [defendant's] testimony free of the misperceptions regarding battered women." (*People v. Day, supra,* 2 *Cal. App. 4th* at p. 419.) Overall, the evidence, including defendant's corroborated testimony about the shooting the night before, presented a plausible case for perfect self-defense. The actual verdict was reasonable, but so too would have been a different one. Under all of these circumstances, it is reasonably probable the error affected the verdict adversely to defendant.

III. DISPOSITION

The judgment of the Court of Appeal is reversed.

PEOPLE V. BANKS

COURT OF APPEAL OF CALIFORNIA, SECOND APPELLATE DISTRICT, DIVISION TWO

67 Cal. App. 3d 379; 137 Cal. Rptr. 652

December 16, 1976

OPINION BY: COMPTON, J.

Defendant appeals from the judgment entered following a jury trial that resulted in his conviction of involuntary manslaughter (*Pen. Code, § 192*, subd. 2) . . . He contends:

"The trial court's extemporaneous jury instruction that the defendant has the burden of proof to show justifiable homicide once the prosecution has proved a homicide committed by defendant was error and clearly prejudicial. . . ."

On October 29, 1975 at approximately 10:15 p.m., Stephen Kaufman had engaged in a quarrel with his ex-wife, Karen McGee, outside her family's residence concerning his right to see his child. After Kaufman departed, Karen and her two brothers, Lucius and Merlin, being angered at Kaufman's conduct, determined to seek him out and "beat him up." Some 45 minutes to an hour later they observed him driving his car with appellant, with whom they were unacquainted, as a passenger. When Kaufman stopped his vehicle and exited he was set upon by Lucius McGee and a fistfight followed.

Though varying slightly as to details the testimony of the parties concerning the ensuing events was remarkably consistent, with the exception of the version given by Karen. Her hostility and enmity toward her ex-husband and appellant was manifest and a substantial portion of her testimony was refuted by her brother Lucius, Stephen Kaufman, also a People's witness, as well as appellant. A fair reading of the record indicates that initially appellant had remained seated within Kaufman's car. At some point, however, all parties exited their respective vehicles. Each witness agreed that appellant was armed with a pistol and fired several shots into the air, apparently as a warning.

Lucius McGee and Stephen Kaufman, who were struggling on the driver's side of Kaufman's car, did not see the fatal confrontation between appellant and Merlin McGee. Karen McGee testified, contrary to all other witnesses as indicated, that appellant and Stephen Kaufman had been handing the subject gun back and forth to each other and that each of them in turn shot at her or Lucius. She asserted that when her brother Merlin stepped out of his car Kaufman passed the gun back to appellant who proceeded to shoot and kill Merlin without provocation. n1

> n1 Although Karen McGee denied her brother Merlin had advanced on appellant she acknowledged that his body had fallen between the two cars, i.e., in front of the McGee car and to the rear of Kaufman's car that was parked ahead of it.

Stephen Kaufman, called as a witness by the People, and appellant in his own defense, each testified that after Kaufman's original encounter with Karen at the McGee residence appellant and Kaufman, who were acquaintances, met at a liquor store and Kaufman agreed to drive appellant to the home of appellant's cousin. Appellant did not know Kaufman's ex-wife Karen, or her brothers, and was unaware of the extreme hostility that had developed between them and Kaufman earlier that night. Appellant testified that he had borrowed the gun earlier from his cousin to use on a projected hunting trip which had been canceled. He was, therefore, carrying the gun and a clip of bullets in a paper bag with the intention of returning them.

Kaufman testified that while he was fighting with Lucius McGee he saw other persons exiting from the McGee car and heard one of them state, "This is the mother fucker, you're dead now." Appellant, too, averred that he saw others exiting from the McGee's car and "The one who come from the back driver's side on the left was going straight to the trunk of the car, and that was as the person got out of the car and made the statements, 'We going to kill you mother fuckers.'" He asserted that he then stepped from his car, loaded the gun and fired three shots into the air, saying, "Hey, we don't have to do this. . . ."

Appellant further testified that he then tripped on the curb and as he was getting up he saw a person, later shown to be Merlin McGee, "coming from behind a pole." Merlin "had black gloves on and . . . a gun in his hand." n2

Appellant fired "trying to disable him . . . [to] keep [him] from shooting me . . . I didn't mean to kill him." After Merlin fell appellant and Kaufman reentered their car and while doing so appellant fired more shots at the McGee vehicle itself to guard their retreat because, he alleged, Lucius McGee had reentered his car and was "digging under the bucket seat" for what appellant feared might be another gun.

> n2 Karen McGee confirmed the fact her deceased brother was wearing gloves.

Appellant steadfastly maintained his version of the encounter upon cross-examination. When asked to explain what had become of the gun allegedly held by the deceased, appellant replied, "Ask his brother and sister; they've been up here lying; ask them. I have no reason to go out in the street and look for any trouble. I got a home and kids and going into the maintenance business. I have no reason to be going out and getting into something that should have never been."

During the jury's second day of deliberation the foreman sent a written note to the judge stating "a member of the jury would like to know if it is the burden of proof of the defendant to prove self-defense." The following exchange took place: "The Court: All right. Well, ladies and gentlemen, there is a reasonably short answer to this particular point. n3 You understand that it is the burden of proof of the People to prove, beyond a reasonable doubt, the elements charged or lesser included within the charge; that is, the fact that there is a wrongful homicide committed. *If so, at that point, the defense has the burden of proof or it does shift to the defense to prove whether or not the homicide was committed by way of self-defense.* Is that clear to all of you? The Foreman: No, Your Honor. The Court: All right. Let's see, Juror No.—that's Mr. Moore. Juror Moore: I think I have it basically in my mind, what you are saying. You are saying, if the prosecution does not prove the charge as such—The Court: Prove what? Juror Moore: If they don't present enough evidence to prove the charge of murder, then—The Court: Well, the point is, they must prove the fact that the homicide occurred; when the homicide occurs, then you have to determine whether or not it was a wrongful or a rightful homicide. Juror Moore: Now, I understand. The Court: And a rightful homicide would be in self-defense. Juror Moore: Thank you, Your Honor. The Court: But it is, up to that time, the question of whether or not the homicide has been connected with the defendant, you see; and if you reach the conclusion, beyond a reasonable doubt, because that is the burden of the prosecution, that the homicide was committed, then you begin considering whether or not it was one of the privileged-type of homicides under the law, including self-defense. Is that clear to everybody? (The jury answers in

the affirmative.) The Court: All right. The Foreman: Wait a minute, Your Honor. The Court: Yes, Mr. Klein? The Foreman: I want to amplify upon this, I think it might not be fully clear. The Court: Now, let's not get into the debate you have in the jury room. The Foreman: Can you—maybe the court reporter could read the statement you made when Mr. Moore asked you the question just before that; that's the statement I want to make sure that everybody understands. The Court: Well, I'll state it again if it means anything more. I state that the burden of proof with respect to the homicide itself falls on the State, beyond a reasonable doubt; at that time, the question of defense comes in. If you believe that the State has carried its burden thus far, that is, *in proving the homicide committed by the defendant*, then you may consider the evidence for the purpose of determining if the homicide was justifiable; that is, *was it done in self-defense, and then the burden carrier there is the defendant*. I can't state it any plainer than that. Does anybody feel it is still obscure? (The jury answers in the negative.)" (Italics added.)

> n3 The "short answer," and the only correct answer to the juror's question, was: "No."

It was error for the trial court to give the jury an extemporaneous instruction which shifted to the defendant the burden of proof that the homicide had been committed in self-defense. "In a criminal case, of course, the defendant is presumed to be innocent and the prosecution has the burden of proving his guilt beyond a reasonable doubt (*Pen. Code, § 1096*). Error occurs if a trial court tells a jury that any burden of persuasion rests on the defense as to the general issue of guilt." (*People v. Loggins, 23 Cal. App.3d 597, 600–601 {100 Cal. Rptr. 528}.*)

The court in *Loggins* even held to be erroneous, though not necessarily prejudicial, the giving of *CALJIC No. 5.15* relating to a defendant's procedural burden of coming forward with evidence sufficient "to raise a reasonable doubt as to his guilt of the charge of murder." The court's extemporaneous instruction in the instant case did not purport to simply place a procedural burden on the accused, or require him merely to "raise a reasonable doubt" as to his guilt. Here the court repeatedly advised the jury that the defense was required "*to prove* whether or not the homicide was committed by way of self defense." (Italics added.)

In *Mullaney v. Wilbur, 421 U.S. 684 {44 L.Ed.2d 508, 95 S.Ct. 1881},* the United States Supreme Court found to be unconstitutional a state law which affirmatively shifted the burden of proof of justification for a homicide to the defendant. The court held (*Mullaney, supra,* at p. 701 {44 L.Ed.2d at pp. 520–521}), "The result, in a case such as this one where the defendant is required to prove the critical fact in dispute, is to increase further the likelihood of an erroneous murder conviction. Such a result directly contravenes the principle articulated in *Speiser v. Randall, 357 U.S. 513, 525–526 . . .*

"'[Where] one party has at stake an interest of transcending value—as a criminal defendant his liberty—[the] margin of error is reduced as to him by the process of placing on the [prosecution] the burden . . . of persuading the factfinder at the conclusion of the trial. . . .'"

The court in *Mullaney* concluded "that the Due Process Clause requires the prosecution to prove beyond a reasonable doubt the absence of the heat of passion on sudden provocation when the issue is properly presented in a homicide case." (*Mullaney, supra,* at p. 704 [*44 L.Ed.2d* at p. 522].) Similarly we conclude that the prosecution must prove beyond a reasonable doubt the absence of justification, herein self-defense, when the issue is properly presented in a homicide case. The contrary instruction here given to an obviously confused jury in the midst of deliberation was prejudicial.

The judgment of conviction must be reversed and the cause remanded for a new trial. In so doing we note that appellant may now be retried only for manslaughter, a charge to which *Penal Code section 12022.5* is inapplicable. (See *People v. Strickland, 11 Cal.3d 946, 961 {114 Cal.Rptr. 632, 523 P.2d 672}.*) Whether or not the provisions of Penal Code sections 3024 and *12022* would be applicable in the event that appellant is convicted upon retrial of manslaughter will depend upon the underlying theory and basis for such conviction.

The judgment is reversed.

OPINION BY: GAROUTTE, J.

The appellant was charged with the crime of murder and convicted of manslaughter. He now appeals from the judgment and order denying his motion for a new trial.

For a perfect understanding of the principle of law involved in this appeal it becomes necessary to state in a general way the facts leading up to the homicide. As to the facts thus summarized there is no material contradiction. The deceased, the defendant, and several other parties were camped in the mountains. They had been drinking, and, except a boy, were all under the influence of liquor more or less, the defendant to some extent, the deceased to a great extent. The deceased was lying on the ground with his head resting upon a rock, when a dispute arose between him and the defendant, and the defendant thereupon kicked or stamped him in the face. The assault was a vicious one, and the injuries of deceased occasioned thereby most serious. One eye was probably destroyed, and some bones of the face broken. An expert testified that these injuries were so serious as likely to produce in the injured man a dazed condition of mind, impairing the reasoning faculties, judgment, and powers of perception. Immediately subsequent to this assault the defendant went some distance from the camp, secured his horse, returned and saddled it, with the avowed intention of leaving the camp to avoid further trouble. The time thus occupied in securing his horse and preparing for departure may be estimated at from 5 to 15 minutes. The deceased's conduct and situation during the absence of defendant is not made plain by the evidence, but he was probably still lying where assaulted. At this period of time, the deceased advanced upon defendant with a knife, which was taken from him by a bystander, whereupon he seized his gun, and attempted to shoot the defendant, and then was himself shot by the defendant and immediately died.

. . .

Upon this state of facts the court charged the jury as to the law of the case, and declared to them in various forms the principle of law which is fairly embodied in the following instruction: "One who has sought a combat for the purpose of taking advantage of another, may afterward endeavor to decline any further struggle, and, if he really and in good faith does so before killing the person with whom he sought the combat for such purpose, he may justify the killing on the same ground as he might if he had not originally sought such combat for such purpose, provided that you also believe that his endeavor was of such a character, so indicated as to have reasonably assured a reasonable man, that he was endeavoring in good faith to decline further combat, *unless* you further believe that in the same combat in which the fatal shot was fired, and prior to the defendant endeavoring to cease further attack or quarrel, the deceased received at the hands of the defendant such injuries as deprived him of his reason or his capacity to receive impressions regarding defendant's design and endeavor to cease further combat."

It is to that portion of the foregoing instruction relating to the capacity of the deceased to receive impressions caused by the defendant's attack upon him that appellant's counsel has directed his assault; and our attention will be addressed to its consideration. The recital of facts indicates, to some extent at least, that the assault upon deceased was no part of the combat subsequently arising in which he lost his life; yet the events were so closely connected in point of time that the court was justified in submitting to the jury the question of fact as to whether or not the entire trouble was but one affray or combat. *Section 197 of the Penal Code*, wherein it says, in effect, that the assailant must really and in good faith endeavor to decline any further struggle before he is justified in taking life, is simply declarative of the common law. It is but the reiteration of a well-settled principle, and in no wise broadens and enlarges the right of self-defense as declared by courts and text-writers ever since the days of Lord Hale. It follows that the declaration of the code above cited gives us no light upon the matter at hand, and, from an examination of many books and cases, we are unable to find a single authority directly in point upon the principle of law here involved. It is thus apparent that the question is both interesting and novel.

The point at issue may be made fairly plain by the following illustrations: If a party should so violently assault another by a blow or stroke upon the head as to render that party incapable of understanding or appreciating the conditions surrounding him, and the party assailed should thereupon pursue the retreating assailant for many hours and miles with a deadly weapon and with deadly intent, and upon overtaking him should proceed to kill him, would the first assailant, the party retreating, be justified in taking the then aggressor's life in order to save his own? In other words, did the first assault, producing the effect that it did, debar defendant (after retreating under the circumstances above depicted) from taking his opponent's life, even though that opponent at the time held a knife at his throat with deadly intent; or, putting it more concisely, did the aggressor by his first assault forfeit his life to the party assaulted? Or, viewing the case from the other side, should a man be held guiltless who without right assaults another so viciously as to take away his capacity to reason, to deprive him of his mind, and then kill him, because, when so assaulted, his assailant is unable to understand that the attacking party is retreating, and has withdrawn from the combat in good faith? In other words, may a defendant so assault another as to deprive him of his mind, and then kill him in self-defense when he is in such a condition that he is unable to understand that his assailant has withdrawn in good faith from the combat?

In order for an assailant to justify the killing of his adversary he must not only endeavor to really and in good faith withdraw from the combat, but he must make known his intentions to his adversary. His secret intentions to withdraw amount to nothing. They furnish no guide for his antagonist's future conduct. They indicate in no way that the assault may not be repeated, and afford no assurance to the party assailed that the need of defense is gone. This principle is fairly illustrated in Hale's Pleas of the Crown, page 482, where the author says: "But if A assaults B first, and upon that assault B re-assaults A, and that so fiercely, that A cannot retreat to the wall or other *non ultra* without danger of his life, nay, though A falls upon the ground upon the assault of B and then kills B this shall not be interpreted to be *se defendendo*." The foregoing principle is declared sound for the reason that, though A was upon the ground and in great danger of his life at the time he killed B, still he was the assailant, and at the time of the killing had done nothing to indicate to the mind of B that he had in good faith withdrawn from the combat, and that B was no longer in danger. In *Stoffer v. State, 15 Ohio St. 47, 86 Am. Dec. 470,* in speaking to this question, the court said: "There is every reason for saying that the conduct of the accused relied upon to sustain such a defense must have been so marked in the matter of time,

place, and circumstance as not only clearly to evince the withdrawal of the accused in good faith from the combat, but also such as fairly to advise his adversary that his danger had passed, and to make his conduct thereafter the pursuit of vengeance, rather than measures taken to repel the original assault." It is also said in *State v. Smith, 10 Nev. 106,* citing the Ohio case: "A man who assails another with a deadly weapon cannot kill his adversary in self-defense until he has fairly notified him by his conduct that he has abandoned the contest; and, if the circumstances are such that he cannot so notify him, it is his fault, and he must take the consequences."

It is, therefore, made plain that knowledge of the withdrawal of the assailant in good faith from the combat must be brought home to the assailed. He must be notified in some way that danger no longer threatens him, and that all fear of further harm is groundless. Yet, in considering this question, the assailed must be deemed a man of ordinary understanding; he must be gauged and tested by the common rule—a reasonable man; his acts and conduct must be weighed and measured in the light of that test, for such is the test applied wherever the right of self-defense is made an issue. His naturally demented condition will not excuse him from seeing that his assailant has withdrawn from the attack in good faith. Neither his passion nor his cowardice will be allowed to blind him to the fact that his assailant is running away, and all danger is over. If the subsequent acts of the attacking party be such as to indicate to a reasonable man that he in good faith has withdrawn from the combat, they must be held to so indicate to the party attacked. Again, the party attacked must also act in good faith. He must act in good faith toward the law, and allow the law to punish the offender. He must not continue the combat for the purpose of wreaking vengeance, for then he is no better than his adversary. The law will not allow him to say, "I was not aware that my assailant had withdrawn from the combat in good faith," if a reasonable man so placed would have been aware of such withdrawal. If the party assailed has eyes to see he must see; and, if he has ears to hear he must hear. He has no right to close his eyes or deaden his ears.

This brings us directly to the consideration of the point in the case raised by the charge of the court to the jury. While the deceased had eyes to see and ears to hear he had no mind to comprehend, for his mind was taken from him by the defendant at the first assault. Throughout this whole affray it must be conceded that the deceased was guilty of no wrong, no violation of the law. When he attempted to kill the defendant he thought he was acting in self-defense, and according to his lights he was acting in self-defense. To be sure, those lights, supplied by a vacant mind, were dim and unsatisfactory, yet they were all the deceased had at the time, and not only were furnished by the defendant himself, but the defendant in furnishing them forcibly and unlawfully deprived the deceased of others which were perfect and complete. But where does the defendant stand? It cannot be said that he was guilty of no wrong, no violation of the law. It was he who made the vicious attack. It was he who was guilty of an unprovoked and murderous assault. It was he who unlawfully brought upon himself the necessity for killing the deceased. It cannot be possible that in a combat of this character no crime has been committed against the law. Yet the deceased has committed no offense. Neither can the defendant be prosecuted for an assault to commit murder, for the assault resulted in the commission of a homicide as a part of the affray. For these reasons we consider that the defendant cannot be held guiltless.

Some of the earlier writers hold that one who gives the first blow cannot be permitted to kill the other, even after retreating to the wall, for the reason that the necessity to kill was brought upon himself. (1 Hawkins' Pleas of the Crown, 87.) While the humane doctrine, and especially the modern doctrine, is more liberal to the assailant, and allows him an opportunity to withdraw from the combat, if it is done in good faith, yet it would seem that under the circumstances here presented the more rigid doctrine should be applied. The defendant not only brought upon himself the necessity for the killing, but, in addition thereto, brought upon himself the necessity of killing a man wholly innocent in the eyes of the law; not only wholly innocent as being a person naturally *non compos*, but wholly innocent by being placed in this unfortunate condition of mind by the act of the defendant himself. We conclude, therefore, that the instruction contains a sound principle of law. The defendant was the first wrongdoer; he was the only wrongdoer; he brought on the necessity for the killing, and cannot be allowed to plead that necessity against the deceased, who at the time was *non compos* by reason of defendant's assault. The citations we have taken from Hale, the Ohio case, and the Nevada case, all declare that the assailant must notify the assailed of his withdrawal from the combat in good faith, before he will be justified in taking life. Here the defendant did not so notify the deceased. He could not notify him, for by his own unlawful act he had placed it out of his power to give the deceased such notice. Under these circumstances he left no room in his case for the plea of self-defense.

2. The court gave the following instruction to the jury as to the law bearing upon the facts of the case: "And no man,

by his own lawless acts, can create a necessity for acting in self-defense, and then, upon killing the person with whom he seeks the difficulty, interpose the plea of self-defense, subject to the qualification next hereinafter set out." The plea of necessity is a shield for those only who are without fault in occasioning it and acting under it. The court instructs the jury that "if you are satisfied that there was a quarrel between the defendant and deceased, in which the defendant was the aggressor and first assaulted the deceased by means or force likely to produce and actually producing great bodily injury to the deceased, and that the defendant thereafter in the same quarrel fatally shot the deceased, then you must find the defendant guilty, subject to this qualification."

This instruction appears to have been given subject to some qualification, and as to the extent and character of the qualification the record is not plain. But, whatever it may have been, the vice of the instruction could not be taken away. The instruction is bad law, and no explanation or qualification could validate it. It is not true that the plea of necessity is a shield for those only who are without fault in occasioning it and acting under it. As we have already seen, this is the rigid doctrine declared by Sergeant Hawkins, but not the humane doctrine of Lord Hale and modern authority. The latter portion of the instruction is in direct conflict with the Stoffer case, already cited, where the declaration of the same principle in a somewhat different form caused a reversal of the judgment. It was there said: "If this is a sound view of the matter the condition of the accused would not have been bettered if he had fled for miles, and had finally fallen down with exhaustion, provided Webb was continuous in his efforts to overtake him. But this view is consistent with neither the letter nor the spirit of the legal principle." The instruction assumes that, if the defendant was the aggressor, the quarrel could subsequently assume no form or condition whereby the defendant would be justified in taking the life of the party assailed. The law of self-defense is to the contrary, and is clearly recognized to the contrary by the provision of the Penal Code to which we have already referred.

. . .

We think the questions we have discussed dispose of all material matters raised upon the appeal.

For the foregoing reasons the judgment and order are reversed and the cause remanded for a new trial.

PEOPLE V. MYERS

COURT OF APPEAL OF CALIFORNIA, FIFTH APPELLATE DISTRICT

61 CAL. APP. 4TH 328; 71 CAL. RPTR. 2D 518

FEBRUARY 4, 1998

OPINION BY: BUCKLEY, J.

This case arose under unusual and tragic circumstances. During a relatively minor confrontation between Thomas Myers, Jr., and George Staley, Staley fell to the ground and struck his head on the concrete pavement. The impact fractured his skull and left him with serious and permanent neurological injuries. There was conflicting testimony about what caused Staley to fall. On the theory that Myers attacked Staley without provocation and knocked him unconscious with a punch in the nose, Myers was charged with assault by means of force likely to produce great bodily injury (*Pen. Code, § 245*, subd. (a)(1)) n1 and with battery resulting in serious bodily injury (§ 243, subd. (d)). Myers, on the other hand, maintained Staley was the aggressor and suddenly began yelling and poking him in the chest; when Myers pushed Staley away defensively, Staley accidentally slipped and fell on the wet pavement.

n1 Except as noted, all future statutory references are to the Penal Code.

The jury evidently accepted Myers's version of events. It found him guilty of aggravated battery, but only of simple assault. (§ 240.) On appeal, Myers argues the court gave an inadequate self-defense instruction. Specifically, he contends that the standard instruction on self-defense against an assault (*CALJIC No. 5.30*) should have been modified to say that a person may, in appropriate circumstances, use reasonable force to resist a battery even when he has no reason to believe he is about to suffer bodily injury. We agree and will reverse. n2

n2 We find it peculiar that an incident such as alleged here has not been the subject of previous case authority discussing this issue. However, we have found no such case.

FACTS

Thomas Myers, Jr., lived with Debra Lystad and their 12-year-old son Brandon in one of the 242 units at the Merit Manor apartments in Clovis. George "Bud" Staley,

age 64, and his wife, Betty, managed the complex. Myers and Staley did not get along. Staley often confronted Myers over alleged violations of apartment rules, which Myers felt were being applied unfairly to him and his family. Staley denied, however, that he harbored any prejudice against Myers because Myers was a Black man living with a White woman.

Tension between the two men eventually developed to the point that Staley's supervisor instructed him to have no further contact with Myers, and to leave all future dealings with him to Betty. But this arrangement was not entirely successful. Staley and Myers still encountered each other occasionally at the apartment complex. And, according to Betty Staley, Myers told her, "'If you don't keep that old man away from [me], . . . I can have him killed. . . .'"

About 6:30 in the evening of October 25, 1994, Staley was talking with another tenant in the parking lot of the complex when he saw Myers "burning rubber" in his car. Myers drove out of the complex and across the street to a self-service carwash, where he pulled into one of the bays and prepared to wash his car. Debra and Brandon walked across the street and met him there after stopping to get change at a nearby convenience store. Staley was annoyed by what he viewed as Myers's repeated violation of apartment rules and, notwithstanding his supervisor's no-contact order, he decided to go over and talk to Myers about it. Staley had, by his own admission, "a little bit of an attitude." He crossed the street and went through some bushes at the edge of the carwash to a paved area about 25 feet from Myers's car. Myers walked "swiftly" up to him and then, without saying a word, "he apparently hit me and knocked me totally out because I don't remember a thing after that." Staley asserted he did not do or say anything to provoke the attack.

. . .

Staley was taken by ambulance to the hospital, where he remained for the next several days. He was found to have suffered a traumatic brain injury consisting of a skull fracture along his left forehead, a hemorrhagic contusion (bruising) around his left temple, and "a small amount of pneumocephalus" (air in his skull). The injury left him with "some cognitive and to a degree some behavioral deficits and problems" manifested particularly by "extremely poor memory, [and] poor concentration." Betty Staley described her husband since his injury as "cranky" and "very nervous" AND SHE EXPLAINED: "He didn't remember a lot of things, didn't remember a lot of our family. He was just kind of flat. He has no feelings toward me. He still doesn't. Has no feelings toward me at all."

Staley was subsequently treated by Dr. John Edwards, a specialist in physical medicine and rehabilitation. According to Dr. Edwards, Staley could have sustained his neurological injuries (but probably not his bloody nose) by falling backwards and hitting his head. The doctor noted, however, that someone who is falling will ordinarily react reflexively to protect his head. Therefore, given the extent of the injuries in this case, he expressed the opinion that Staley "had altered consciousness or loss of consciousness before his head hit the ground." Such loss of consciousness, he concluded, might have been caused by having been "frontally assaulted with a fist."

Defense

Myers, along with Debra and Brandon, gave a very different account of events. According to them, Myers's tires "squeaked" a little bit but he did not break traction in his car. Over at the carwash, he had the hood of the car up and was washing the engine when Staley came up suddenly behind him and started yelling angrily that "'You people . . . [are] always causing trouble. . . .'" Myers turned and yelled back at Staley, telling him to go away. But Staley came closer and began poking Myers in the chest with his finger. With that, Myers pushed Staley away. He explained: "I wanted him to stop putting his hands on me. You know, I wanted him to get out of my face. I really wanted him just to go back across the street." The pavement in the carwash bay was wet and Staley was wearing leather-soled shoes. He slipped and fell backwards to the ground. Myers denied punching Staley or intending to injure him.

. . .

Dr. Richard Goka, a specialist in the same field as Dr. Edwards, generally discounted the theory that Staley was struck in the nose and rendered unconscious before he hit the ground. n4 He testified that, in his opinion, there was simply no way to tell whether Staley was punched or pushed.

> n4 According to Dr. Goka, a punch to the nose hard enough to knock someone unconscious would be expected to cause obvious facial bruising and swelling (and possibly "raccoon eyes") within a few hours, a

condition worth noting in the victim's medical records. Staley's records indicated only that he had some blood in his left nostril. The punch probably would also cause noticeable damage to the assailant's hand. There is no evidence Myers suffered any such injury.

DISCUSSION

. . .

n5 The court gave the following instruction based on *CALJIC No. 9.11*: "No words of abuse, insult or reproach addressed to or uttered concerning a person, however insulting or objectionable the words may be, if unaccompanied by any threat or apparent threat of bodily injury[,] or any assault upon the person[,] will justify an assault by any means of force likely to produce bodily injury. The provocation of such words alone does not constitute a defense to a charge of having committed such an assault." The instruction in this form omitted the term "great" immediately preceding the two references to "bodily injury."

. . .

CALJIC No. 5.30 as read to the jury stated: "It is lawful for a person who is being assaulted to defend himself from attack if [,] as a reasonable person, he has grounds for believing and does believe that bodily injury is about to be inflicted upon him. In doing so, such person may use all force and means which he believes to be reasonably necessary and which would appear to a reasonable person in the same or similar circumstances to be necessary to prevent the injury which appears to be imminent."

Myers's objection to this instruction, which he renews on appeal, was that it did not adequately cover his theory of the case under which he claimed the right to defend himself against a battery, i.e., the right to resist Staley's poking by pushing him away. The right to resist a battery, he maintains, is not necessarily dependent upon whether or not the battery poses an imminent danger of bodily injury.

. . .

It has long been established, both in tort and criminal law, that "the least touching" may constitute battery. In other words, *force* against the person is enough, it need not be violent or severe, it need not cause bodily harm or even pain, and it need not leave any mark. The "violent injury" here mentioned is not synonymous with "bodily harm," but includes any wrongful act committed by means of physical force against the person of another, even although only the feelings of such person are injured by the act. (*People v. Rocha* (1971) 3 Cal. 3d 893, 899–900, fn. 12 {92 Cal. Rptr. 172, 479 P.2d 372}.)

It follows that an offensive touching, although it inflicts no bodily harm, may nonetheless constitute a battery, which the victim is privileged to resist with such force as is reasonable under the circumstances. The same may be said of an assault insofar as it is an attempt to commit such a battery. n8 To hold otherwise would lead to the ludicrous result of a person not being able to lawfully resist or defend against a continuing assault or battery, such as the act defendant alleged here. n9

> n8 "An assault is an unlawful attempt, coupled with a present ability, to commit a violent injury on the person of another." (§ 240; see also People v. Colantuono (1994) 7 Cal. 4th 206, 215–217 {26 Cal. Rptr. 2d 908, 865 P.2d 704}; 1 Witkin & Epstein, Cal. Criminal Law (2d ed. 1988) Crimes Against the Person, § 398, pp. 461–462.)

> n9 In so holding we, of course, do not imply that we believe or disbelieve defendant's "version"; we merely say that the jury should have been given that opportunity.

Here, the jury found Myers guilty in count 1 of simple assault rather than the charged offense of assault by means of force likely to produce great bodily injury. It thus evidently concluded that Myers had pushed rather than punched Staley. It is also reasonable to suppose that the jury credited Myers's account of events leading up to the confrontation, i.e., that Staley was poking him in the chest with his finger. As to count 2, the jury found Myers guilty as charged of battery resulting in serious bodily injury. Since there is no question Myers's use of force caused Staley to suffer serious bodily injury, his right, if any, to defend himself against Staley's poking was central to the jury's verdict.

We conclude the trial court erred in refusing to give a modified self-defense instruction, and that the error was prejudicial under the peculiar circumstances of this case.

DISPOSITION

The judgment is reversed.

PEOPLE V. CURTIS

COURT OF APPEAL OF CALIFORNIA, FOURTH APPELLATE DISTRICT, DIVISION TWO

30 Cal. App. 4th 1337; 37 Cal. Rptr. 2d 304

December 14, 1994

OPINION BY: RAMIREZ, P. J.

Defendant David Scott Curtis (defendant) had an affair with a married woman, Abigail Camacho Medina (Abby). n1 This brought him into conflict, sometimes violent conflict, with Abby's husband, brother, and other members of her family.

> n1 The dramatis personae will include various family members who share the same last names. For the sake of clarity, we refer to such persons by their first names.

Defendant's relationship with Abby herself was not free from conflict. They broke up and got back together many times. Abby gave birth to a child, Nicole. At one point, she told defendant he was Nicole's father; later, however, she denied this. Defendant filed suit for visitation rights.

One day, defendant stole Abby's car. According to him, he hoped that in exchange for the return of her car, she would help him to prove that it was her husband who had committed a previous theft of his truck. At defendant's request, Abby came to his apartment; her brother and her uncle came with her, but they waited outside. Abby also brought a tape recorder, concealed in her purse, in case defendant confessed to stealing her car.

They argued at length. Abby's brother became concerned because she was taking so long; he knocked on defendant's door. Moments later, defendant shot Abby and killed her. Both the argument and the shooting were tape-recorded.

Defendant claimed to have thought that Abby's brother, and perhaps others, were about to break down his door and attack him. He got out his rifle to defend himself, he claimed, but it went off and struck Abby by accident.

Defendant was convicted of second degree murder. On appeal, he contends:

. . . The trial court's refusal to instruct on self-defense and defense of habitation was error because the fact that defendant was acting in either self-defense or defense of habitation tended to disprove implied malice.

. . .

We find no error, and we affirm.

. . .

Defense of Habitation

Defense of habitation applies where the defendant uses reasonable force to exclude someone he or she reasonably believes is trespassing in, or about to trespass in, his or her home. However, the intentional use of deadly force merely to protect property is never reasonable. Accordingly, a homicide involving the *intentional* use of deadly force can never be justified by defense of habitation alone. The defendant must also show either self-defense or defense of others, i.e., that he or she reasonably believed the intruder intended to kill or inflict serious injury on someone in the home. (*People v. Smith* (1967) 249 Cal. App. 2d 395, 402 {57 Cal. Rptr. 508}; *People v. Hubbard* (1923) 64 Cal. App. 27, 35 {220 P. 315}; *Pen. Code, § 197*, subd. 2, 198; see also *People v. Ceballos* (1974) 12 Cal. 3d 470, 477–483 {116 Cal. Rptr. 233, 526 P.2d 241}.)

A few older cases suggest, however, that a homicide involving the *unintentional* and accidental use of deadly force may be justified on the ground that it occurred while the defendant was exercising the right of defense of habitation. If so, defense of habitation, unlike self-defense, is not inconsistent with an accidental shooting. For example, in *People v. Hubbard, supra,* the defendant got into an argument with a visitor to his house, one Dennis Cope. The defendant told Cope to get out; Cope refused. The defendant picked up a gun, showed it to Cope, and again told him to get out. Cope again refused. Cope shoved the defendant; when the defendant shoved back, the gun went off and Cope was fatally shot. The defendant testified that he had just been bluffing. He denied firing the gun intentionally. He was convicted of second degree murder. (*64 Cal. App.* at pp. 29–31.)

. . .

Like traditional self-defense, however, defense of habitation applies only if the defendant's belief that a trespass is occurring or about to occur is reasonable. (*People v. Corlett, supra,* 67 Cal. App. 2d at pp. 51–53; see also *CALJIC Nos. 5.42, 5.43* (5th ed. 1988).) As we held in part IV.B., *ante*, the trial court correctly found no substantial evidence that defendant's belief that Bernardo was about to break in was reasonable. As the trial court put it, "No one was coming in. No one was breaking in the door." *Penal Code section 198.5*, entitled the "Home Protection Bill of Rights," "creates a rebuttable presumption that a residential occupant has a reasonable fear of death or great bodily injury when he or she uses deadly force against an unlawful and forcible intruder into the residence. For section 198.5 to apply, four elements must be met. There must be an unlawful and forcible entry into a residence; the entry must be by someone who is not a member of the family or the household; the residential occupant must have used 'deadly' force (as defined in § 198.5) against the victim within the residence; and finally, the residential occupant must have had knowledge of the unlawful and forcible entry." (*People v. Brown* (1992) 6 Cal. App. 4th 1489, 1494–1495 {8 Cal. Rptr. 2d 513} . . . Defendant, however, is not entitled to the benefit of this presumption because there was no actual entry. Because there was no evidence that a reasonable person in defendant's position would have believed Bernardo was about to break in, the trial court had no duty to instruct on defense of habitation.

. . .

The judgment is affirmed.

PEOPLE V. SKINNER

SUPREME COURT OF CALIFORNIA

39 Cal. 3d 765; 704 P.2d 752; 217 Cal. Rptr. 685

September 16, 1985

OPINION BY: GRODIN, J.

For over a century prior to the decision in *People v. Drew* (1978) 22 Cal.3d 333 {149 Cal. Rptr. 275, 583 P.2d 1318}, California courts framed this state's definition of insanity, as a defense in criminal cases, upon the two-pronged test adopted by the House of Lords in *M'Naghten's Case (1843) 10 Clark & Fin. 200, 210 {8 Eng. Rep. 718, 722}:* "[To] establish a defence on the ground of insanity, it must be clearly proved that, at the time of the committing the act, the party accused was laboring under such a defect of reason, from disease of the mind, as not to know the nature and quality of the act he was doing; *or*, if he did know it, that he did not know he was doing what was wrong." (Italics added; see *People v. Coffman (1864) 24 Cal. 230, 235.)*

Over the years the M'Naghten test became subject to considerable criticism and was abandoned in a number of jurisdictions. In *Drew* this court followed suit, adopting the test for mental incapacity proposed by the American Law Institute: "'A person is not responsible for criminal conduct if at the time of such conduct as a result of mental disease or defect he lacks substantial capacity either to appreciate the criminality [wrongfulness] of his conduct or to conform his conduct to the requirements of law.'" (*Drew, supra, 22 Cal.3d at p. 345.)*

In June 1982 the California electorate adopted an initiative measure, popularly known as Proposition 8, which (among other things) for the first time in this state established a statutory definition of insanity: "In any criminal proceeding . . . in which a plea of not guilty by reason of insanity is entered, this defense shall be found by the trier of fact only when the accused person proves by a preponderance of the evidence that he or she was incapable of knowing or understanding the nature and quality of his or her act *and* of distinguishing right from wrong at the time of the commission of the offense." (Pen. Code, § 25, subd. (b) [hereafter section 25(b)], italics added.) n1

> n1 Unless otherwise indicated all future statutory references are to the Penal Code.

It is apparent from the language of section 25(b) that it was designed to eliminate the *Drew* test and to reinstate the prongs of the M'Naghten test. However, the section uses the conjunctive "and" instead of the disjunctive "or" to connect the two prongs. Read literally, therefore, section 25(b) would do more than reinstate the M'Naghten test. It would strip the insanity defense from an accused who, by reason of mental disease, is incapable of knowing that the act he was doing was wrong. That is, in fact, the interpretation adopted by the trial court in this case.

Defendant claims that the purpose of the electorate in adopting section 25(b) was to restore the M'Naghten test as it existed in California prior to this court's decision in *People v. Drew, supra, 22 Cal.3d 333.* If read literally, he argues, section 25(b) would violate both the state and federal Constitutions by imposing criminal responsibility and sanctions on persons who lack the *mens rea* essential to criminal culpability.

The People do not dispute the proposition that the intent of the electorate was to reinstate the pre-*Drew* test of legal insanity. They argue, however, that section 25(b), "amplifies" and "clarifies" the M'Naghten test. Amicus curiae, the Criminal Justice Legal Foundation, agrees that the intent was not to adopt a stricter test than that applicable prior to *Drew*, but suggest that in fact there is no difference between the two prongs of the M'Naghten test—ability to distinguish between right and wrong, and knowledge of the nature and quality of the particular criminal act.

Mindful of the serious constitutional questions that might arise: were we to accept a literal construction of the statutory language, and of our obligation wherever possible both to carry out the intent of the electorate and to construe statutes so as to preserve their constitutionality (*Amador Valley Joint Union High Sch. Dist. v. State Bd. of Equalization (1978) 22 Cal.3d 208, 245 {149 Cal. Rptr. 239, 583 P.2d 1281}; Associated Home Builders etc., Inc. v. City of Livermore (1976) 18 Cal.3d 582, 598 {135 Cal. Rptr. 41, 557 P.2d 473, 92 A.L.R.3d 1038}; People v. Amor (1974) 12 Cal.3d 20, 30 {114 Cal. Rptr. 765, 523 P.2d*

1173}), we shall conclude that section 25(b) was intended to, and does, restore the M'Naghten test as it existed in this state before *Drew*. We shall also conclude that under that test there exist two distinct and independent bases upon which a verdict of not guilty by reason of insanity might be returned.

I

. . . In finding the defendant sane, the judge acknowledged that it was more likely than not that defendant suffered from a mental disease, paranoid schizophrenia, which played a significant part in the killing. The judge stated that under the *Drew* test of legal insanity defendant would qualify as insane, and also found that "under the right–wrong prong of section 25(b), the defendant would qualify as legally insane; but under the other prong, he clearly does not." Concluding that by the use of the conjunctive "and" in section 25(b), the electorate demonstrated an intent to establish a stricter test of legal insanity than the M'Naghten test, and to "virtually eliminate" insanity as a defense, the judge found that defendant had not established that he was legally insane.

Probation was denied and defendant was sentenced to a term of 15 years to life in the state prison.

Defendant strangled his wife while he was on a day pass from the Camarillo State Hospital at which he was a patient. Evidence offered at the trial on his plea of not guilty by reason of insanity included the opinion of a clinical and forensic psychologist that defendant suffered from either classical paranoic schizophrenia, or schizoaffective illness with significant paranoid features. A delusional product of this illness was a belief held by defendant that the marriage vow "till death do us part" bestows on a marital partner a God-given right to kill the other partner who has violated or was inclined to violate the marital vows, and that because the vows reflect the direct wishes of God, the killing is with complete moral and criminal impunity. The act is not wrongful because it is sanctified by the will and desire of God.

Although there was also evidence that would have supported a finding that defendant was sane, it was apparently the evidence summarized above upon which the trial judge based his finding that defendant met one, but not both, prongs of the M'Naghten test. Defendant knew the nature and quality of his act. He knew that his act was homicidal. He was unable to distinguish right and wrong, however, in that he did not know that this particular killing was wrongful or criminal.

In this context we must determine whether the trial court's conclusion that section 25(b), requires that a defendant meet both prongs of the M'Naghten test to establish legal insanity was correct, and if not, whether the court's finding

that defendant met the "right-wrong" aspect of the test requires reversal with directions to enter a judgment of not guilty by reason of insanity.

II

The Insanity Defense in California

. . . This rule is one aspect of the equally well established and no less fundamental principle that wrongful intent is an essential element of crime, a principle reflected in the first statutory criminal law scheme adopted by our Legislature in 1850. The Act Concerning Crimes and Punishments (Stats. 1850, ch. 99, p. 229) set forth this principle and its applicability to the insane as the first three sections of the law:

"§ 1. In every crime or public offence there must be a union or joint operation of act and intention, or criminal negligence."

"§ 2. Intention is manifested by the circumstances connected with the perpetration of the offence, and the sound mind and discretion of the person accused."

"§ 3. A person shall be considered of sound mind who is neither an idiot, nor lunatic, nor affected with insanity, and who hath arrived at the age of 14 years; or before that age, if such person knew the distinction between good and evil."

. . .

The principle that wrongful intent or criminal *mens rea* is an essential element of crime was carried over into the Penal Code of 1872 which incorporated section 1 of the Act Concerning Crimes and Punishments as section 20 of the code, and expanded the classes of persons deemed incapable of committing crime. Section 26, as adopted in 1872, provided that [all] persons are capable of committing crimes, except those belonging to the following classes:

"1. Children under the age of 14 years, in the absence of clear proof that at the time of committing the act charged against them, they knew of its wrongfulness";

"2. Idiots";

"3. Lunatics and insane persons";

"4. Persons who committed the act or made the omission charged, under an ignorance or mistake of fact which disproves any criminal intent";

"5. Persons who committed the act charged, without being conscious thereof";

"6. Persons who committed the act or made the omission charged, through misfortune or by accident, when it appears that there was no evil design, intention, or culpable negligence";

"7. Married women (unless the crime be punishable with death) acting under the threats, command, or coercion of their husbands";

"8. Persons (unless the crime be punishable with death) who committed the act or made the omission charged, under threats or menaces sufficient to show that they had reasonable cause to and did believe their lives would be endangered if they refused."

. . .

The test of legal insanity when the Penal Code of 1872 was adopted by the Legislature was the two-prong M'Naghten test recognized by this court in *People v. Coffman, supra, 24 Cal. 230, 235:* "The unsoundness of mind, or insanity, that will constitute a defense in a criminal action is well described by Tindal, C. J., in answer to questions propounded by the House of Lords to the Judges. He says, 'that to establish a defense on the ground of insanity, it must be clearly proved that, at the *time* of committing the act, the party accused was laboring under such a defect of reason, from disease of the mind, as not to know *the nature or quality of the act*, or if he did know it, that he did not know he was doing *what was wrong*.'" (Original italics.) *Coffman's* exposition of the M'Naghten test was set out in the commissioners' note to section 1016, confirming the legislative understanding of the applicable definition of legal insanity.

For more than a century after *Coffman* recognized the M'Naghten test as applicable in this state it continued to be used, and although sometimes stated in the conjunctive, was in fact applied so as to permit a finding of insanity if either prong of the test was satisfied.

. . .

Because *mens rea* or wrongful intent is a fundamental aspect of criminal law, the suggestion that a defendant whose mental illness results in inability to appreciate that his act is wrongful could be punished by death or imprisonment raises serious questions of constitutional dimension under both the due process and cruel and unusual punishment provisions of the Constitution.

. . .

We need not face these difficult constitutional questions, however, if section 25(b) does no more than return to the pre-*Drew* California version of the M'Naghten test.

III

Post-Proposition 8 Return to M'Naghten

If the use of the conjunctive "and" in section 25(b) is not a draftsman's error, a defendant must now establish both that he "was incapable of knowing or understanding the nature and quality of his or her act *and* of distinguishing right

from wrong." We recognize the basic principle of statutory and constitutional construction which mandates that courts, in construing a measure, not undertake to rewrite its unambiguous language. . . . That rule is not applied, however, when it appears clear that a word has been erroneously used, and a judicial correction will best carry out the intent of the adopting body. . . . The inadvertent use of "and" where the purpose or intent of a statute seems clearly to require "or" is a familiar example of a drafting error which may properly be rectified by judicial construction. . . . Whether the use of "and" in section 25(b) is, in fact, a drafting error can only be determined by reference to the purpose of the section and the intent of the electorate in adopting it.

The ballot summaries and arguments are not helpful. The Attorney General's summary of Proposition 8 advises only that the measure included a provision "regarding . . . proof of insanity." (Official title and summary, Prop. 8, Ballot Pamp., Proposed Amends. to Cal. Const. with arguments to voters, Primary Elec. (June 8, 1982 p. 32.) The analysis of the Legislative Analyst quotes the conjunctive language and states only that the provision "could increase the difficulty of proving that a person is not guilty by reason of insanity." (*Id.*, at p. 55.) No reference to the insanity provision appears in the arguments for or against Proposition 8. (*Id.*, at pp. 34–35.) . . . Since 1850 the disjunctive M'Naghten test of insanity has been accepted as the rule by which the minimum cognitive function which constitutes wrongful intent will be measured in this state. As such it is itself among the fundamental principles of our criminal law. Had it been the intent of the drafters of Proposition 8 or of the electorate which adopted it both to abrogate the more expansive ALI-*Drew* test and to abandon that prior fundamental principle of culpability for crime, we would anticipate that this intent would be expressed in some more obvious manner than the substitution of a single conjunctive in a lengthy initiative provision.

. . .

Applying section 25(b) as a conjunctive test of insanity . . . would return the law to that which preceded M'Naghten, a test known variously as the "wild beast test" and as the "good and evil test" under which an accused could be found insane only if he was "totally deprived of his understanding and memory, and doth not know what he is doing, no more than an infant, than a brute, or a wild beast. . . ." (*Rex* v. *Arnold* (1724) 16 Howell St. Tr. 695, 765.) We find nothing in the language of Proposition 8, or in any other source from which the intent of the electorate may be divined which indicates that such a fundamental, far-reaching change in the law of insanity as that was intended. n8

. . .

n8 A test of insanity requiring that a defendant meet both prongs of the M'Naghten test would not, of course, carry out the intent that was express in Proposition 8 and in the materials supplied to the voters. That intent, insofar as the criminal justice system is concerned, is deterrence of criminal behavior. (See *People v. Smith* (1983) 34 Cal.3d 251, 258 {193 Cal. Rptr. 692, 667 P.2d 149}.) A person who does not know his act is wrong is not likely to be deterred by the prospect of punishment for wrongful conduct. Nor is there a prospect that one who does not know the nature of his act will be deterred.

In *People v. Horn* (1984) 158 Cal. App. 3d 1014, 1029–1031 {205 Cal. Rptr. 119}, the Court of Appeal considered the absence of any indicia of intent to accomplish more than restoration of the California version of the M'Naghten test and found the use of the traditional, century old phraseology of M'Naghten persuasive evidence of an intent to return to that test, notwithstanding the apparently inadvertent use of the conjunctive "and."

We conclude, as did the Court of Appeal in *Horn* that section 25(b) reinstated the M'Naghten test as it was applied in California prior to *Drew* as the test of legal insanity in criminal prosecutions in this state.

. . .

IV

Although the People agree that the purpose of section 25(b) was to return the test of legal insanity in California to the pre-ALI-*Drew* version of the M'Naghten test, they argue that reversal of this judgment is not required because both prongs of that test are actually the same. The findings of the trial judge in this case illustrate the fallacy inherent in this argument. It is true that a person who is unaware of the nature and quality of his act by definition cannot know that the act is wrong. In this circumstance the "nature and quality" prong subsumes the "right and wrong" prong.

. . .

The expert testimony in this case supported the findings of the trial court that this defendant was aware of the nature and quality of his homicidal act. He knew that he was committing an act of strangulation that would, and was intended to, kill a human being. He was not able to comprehend that the act was wrong because his mental illness caused him to believe that the act was not only morally justified but was expected of him. He believed that the homicide was "right."

The People argue further that section 25(b) was intended to "clarify" the meaning of the right/wrong prong of the California M'Naghten test by establishing that the "wrong" which the defendant must comprehend is a legal, rather than a moral wrong. Under this formulation this defendant, who was able to recognize that his act was unlawful, would not escape criminal responsibility even though he believed his act was commanded by God. We fail to see the manner in which section 25(b) conveys this clarification of the M'Naghten test. Moreover, even assuming the validity of this argument, reversal here would be necessary. The trial court did not find that appellant was able to comprehend that his act was considered unlawful or "wrong" even though it was commanded by God. That theory does not appear to have been put forth by the People at trial. . . . Neither appellant, nor the trial court addressed the question of ability to comprehend legal right or wrong.

. . .

In any event, past decisions do not support the People's argument that under the California version of the M'Naghten test a defendant who could comprehend that his act was unlawful could not be legally insane. That was certainly not the understanding at the time of the adoption of the Penal Code of 1872. The notes accompanying section 26 of that enactment refer to *People v. Coffman, supra, 24 Cal. 230,* which, as we have observed, is the case in which the M'Naghten test was recognized as being applicable in this state. The *Coffman* opinion, in addition to stating the test, considered the standard of proof, quoting as it did so: "Mansfield, Chief Justice, in Billingham's case, 1 Collinson on Lunacy, 636 . . .: 'To support such a defense, (insanity,) it ought to be proved . . . that the person was incapable of judging between right and wrong; . . . that at the time he committed the act he did not consider that murder was a crime *against the laws of God and nature.* . . .'" (*24 Cal.* at p. 236, italics added.)

. . .

The trial court found, on clearly sufficient evidence, that defendant could not distinguish right and wrong with regard to his act. No further hearing on the issue of sanity at the time of the act is required. The judgment is reversed and the superior court is directed to enter a judgment of not guilty by reason of insanity and to proceed thereafter pursuant to section 1026.

PEOPLE V. KELLY

SUPREME COURT OF CALIFORNIA

10 CAL. 3D 565; 516 P.2D 875; 111 CAL. RPTR. 171

DECEMBER 26, 1973

OPINION BY: SULLIVAN, J.

Defendant Valerie Dawn Kelly was charged in count one of an information with assault with a deadly weapon with intent to commit murder (*Pen. Code, § 217*), . . . in count two thereof with attempted murder (§ § 187, 664) and in count three with assault with a deadly weapon and by means of force likely to produce great bodily injury (§ 245, subd. (a)). Defendant pleaded not guilty and not guilty by reason of insanity to all counts. Trial by jury was waived, counts one and two were dismissed by the court on the People's motion on the ground of insufficiency of evidence, and the court found defendant guilty of assault with a deadly weapon in violation of section 245, subdivision (a). The court thereafter found that defendant was legally sane at the time the offense was committed. Imposition of sentence was suspended and defendant was granted probation for a period of 5 years under specified terms and conditions. She appeals from the judgment of conviction. (§ 1237.)

. . .

Defendant has used drugs ever since she was 15 years old. n2 In the fall of 1970, when she was 18 years old, she began taking mescaline and LSD, using those drugs 50 to 100 times in the months leading up to the offense. On December 6, 1970, her parents received a telephone call that defendant was being held at the police substation located at the Los Angeles International Airport after being found wandering about the airport under the influence of drugs. In response to the call, her parents picked up defendant at the airport and drove her back to their home in San Diego. Although they recognized that she was not acting normally, at defendant's request they drove her to her own apartment where she spent the night.

> n2 In 1968, following a call by her parents to the police, defendant, then just 16 years old, was taken into custody for being under the influence of drugs. She spent 3 weeks in a ward of the county mental health clinic for abuse of habit-forming drugs and was released on 2 years' probation. In December 1968, she

voluntarily entered Patton State Hospital, after again being found under the influence of drugs. Two months later, she ran away from the hospital but refrained from using drugs until the period preceding the instant offense. In November 1970, about a month before the offense here involved, defendant was again taken into custody for drug abuse and spent several days in the county mental health clinic after which she was released.

On the next morning, December 7, defendant telephoned her mother and asked to be driven to her parents' home. Mrs. Kelly did so but noticed that defendant "wasn't there"; she seemed to be "[just] wandering" and told her mother that she heard "a lot of noises, and a lot of people talking. . . ." n3 Mrs. Kelly made defendant change into pajamas and lie down, and then went into the kitchen to prepare defendant's breakfast. Shortly thereafter, defendant entered the kitchen and, while Mrs. Kelly was turned toward the stove, repeatedly stabbed her mother with an array of kitchen knives. The police were called, defendant was arrested, and eventually charged as already indicated.

> n3 In a psychiatric report made after the attack and introduced into evidence, defendant described her hallucinations at this time. She thought that her parents "were with the devils." She would talk to her parents "but not out loud." Her mother "told" her that "they had devils," and defendant "realized that something was going to die—that they were going to kill me."

On December 14, 1971, the case proceeded to trial before the court sitting without a jury. n4 The parties waived their right to a bifurcated trial on the separate issues of guilt and insanity (Pen. Code, § 1026), and agreed that the court upon receiving evidence at a single trial, could separately decide the two issues after allowing counsel to argue as to each. (*People v. Dessauer (1952) 38 Cal.2d 547, 554 {241 P.2d 238};* see generally Witkin, Cal. Criminal Procedure (1963) § 502, p. 508.)

> n4 Before defendant could be tried, the trial court, doubting her competency, ordered a hearing to

determine whether she was presently sane. (*Pen. Code, §§ 1367, 1368.*) The court found that defendant was insane and ordered her committed to Patton State Hospital. (*Pen. Code, § 1370.*) She remained there for 9 months and was released in September 1971, after being certified as sane and able to stand trial. (*Pen. Code, § 1372.*)

Much of the evidence presented at the trial consisted of the reports and testimony of seven psychiatrists. Since there was substantial agreement among them, we briefly summarize their testimony, referring to illustrative examples of it in the footnotes.

Defendant suffered from personality problems—according to one witness an underlying schizophrenia—but was normally a sane person.. . . However, her voluntary and repeated ingestion of drugs over a 2-month period had triggered a legitimate psychosis . . . so that on the day of the attack, defendant was unable to distinguish right from wrong. . . . Nevertheless, defendant was conscious in that she could perceive the events that were taking place. . . .

. . .

The trial court heard considerable testimony that defendant was not acting simply as a person who, after ingesting drugs or alcohol is unable to perceive reality and reason properly. Rather, the drug abuse was deemed the indirect cause of a legitimate, temporary psychosis that would remain even when defendant was temporarily off drugs. n9 Finally, there was general agreement that defendant, although still a "brittle" person with latent schizophrenic tendencies, was sane at the time of trial.

> n9 It is important to note that defendant's psychosis was not merely temporarily related to the period in which she was under the influence of drugs. The testimony of Dr. Strauss made this clear, when he characterized defendant's insanity as "A temporary psychosis or temporary insanity brought about by an extended drug abuse with hallucinogens and not recovering very quickly . . . taking, I would estimate, until she was released from Patton State Hospital, a period of some 9 or 10 months." Similarly, Dr. Carl Lengyel testified that defendant's psychosis, although drug-induced, would continue even after she went off the drug. Dr. Alfred Larson testified that her psychosis, which was due to an organic disturbance of the brain cells, could last anywhere from 2 weeks to 2 years' time.

At the conclusion of all the evidence, the prosecutor and defense counsel presented their arguments to the court on the guilt phase of the case. The court then in essence found that defendant did the acts constituting an assault with a deadly weapon, that at such time she was not in a state of unconsciousness, n10 and that defendant was "guilty as charged."

n10 The court stated in pertinent part: "The state of mind existing at that time was certainly not a state of unconsciousness, as it has been defined here in a medical sense; that is, the defendant was not in a coma, or incapable of locomotion or manual action."

. . .

After a recess, counsel for both parties then presented their arguments on the sanity phase of the case. At the conclusion of the arguments the court found that while defendant was indeed psychotic both before and after the attack, and "was not capable of understanding that her act was wrong," her insanity was no defense because it "was not of a settled and permanent nature, and, in addition, was produced by the voluntary ingestion of hallucinatory drugs." . . . Accordingly the court found that defendant was legally sane at the time the offense was committed. As already stated, the court eventually suspended imposition of sentence and granted probation.

. . .

Defendant contends (1) that the evidence before the court established a defense of unconsciousness and (2) that insanity, however caused, was a defense to section 245, subdivision (a), a general intent crime.

In support of her first contention, defendant argues that the evidence showed her to be psychotic at the time of her actions. She relies on the court's findings that there was no evidence she was fully aware of what she was doing on the day of the assault but was shown to have been intermittently aware of her actions.

. . .

It follows, therefore, that unconsciousness caused by voluntary intoxication is no defense to a general intent crime—by definition a crime in which no specific intent is required. Assault with a deadly weapon is such a crime, and we have held that the requisite general intent therefore may not be negated through a showing of voluntary intoxication. Thus, if there was substantial evidence to support the trial court's conclusion, defendant's argument that she was not guilty because of unconsciousness must fail.

. . .

We turn to defendant's second contention which relates to the sanity phase of her trial. She claims that the court erred in finding her legally sane at the time of the offense on the basis that, although she did not know that what she was doing was wrong, her insanity was drug-induced and not of a settled and permanent nature. (See fn. 11, *ante*.) She argues that insanity, however caused, is a defense to a criminal charge.

It is fundamental to our system of jurisprudence that a person cannot be convicted for acts performed while insane. (*People v. Nash (1959) 52 Cal.2d 36, 50-51 {338 P.2d 416}; Pen. Code, § 26,* subd. Three.) Insanity, under the California M'Naghten test, denotes a mental condition which renders a person incapable of knowing or understanding the nature and quality of his act, or incapable of distinguishing right from wrong in relation to that act. (*People v. Wolff (1964) 61 Cal.2d 795, 801 {40 Cal.Rptr. 271, 394 P.2d 959}*.) This is a factual question to be decided by the trier of fact. (*Id.* at p. 804.)

In this case the trial court found that defendant "was not capable of understanding that her act was wrong." We can only construe this finding to mean that defendant was insane under the aforementioned test. Despite this finding, the trial court adjudged defendant legally sane because her psychosis was "not of a settled and permanent nature, and, in addition, was produced by the voluntary ingestion of hallucinatory drugs." In so ruling, the trial court misinterpreted the rules regarding the defense of insanity and committed prejudicial error.

As we have already stated, voluntary intoxication by itself is no defense to a crime of general intent such as assault with a deadly weapon. . . . However, we have repeatedly held that "when insanity is the result of long continued intoxication, it affects responsibility in the same way as insanity which has been produced by any other cause." . . .

Policy considerations support this distinction in treatment between voluntary intoxication resulting in unconsciousness and voluntary intoxication which causes insanity. The former encompasses those situations in which mental impairment does not extend beyond the period of intoxication.

. . .

When long-continued intoxication results in insanity, however, the mental disorder remains even after the effects of the drug or alcohol have worn off. The actor is "legally insane," and the traditional justifications for criminal punishment are inapplicable because of his inability to conform, intoxicated or not, to accepted social behavior. (See La Fave & Scott, *op. cit. supra,* at pp. 271–272.) He is, of course, subject to commitment in a mental institution. In the instant case, the trial court appears to have confused these separate rules. The proper rule of law was early established in *People v. Travers, supra,* 88 *Cal.* at pp. 239–240: "[Settled] insanity produced by a long-continued intoxication affects responsibility in the same way as insanity produced by any other cause. *But it must be*

settled insanity and not merely a temporary mental condition produced by recent use of intoxicating liquor." (Italics added.) Thus it is immaterial that voluntary intoxication may have caused the insanity, as long as the insanity was of a settled nature and qualifies under the M'Naghten test as a defense.

The trial court carried this distinction too far, however, for it required proof that defendant's insanity was both settled and *permanent.* . . . Such a requirement violates the rule that "[temporary] insanity as a defense to crime is as fully recognized by law as is permanent insanity." (*People v. Ford (1902) 138 Cal. 140, 141-142 {70 P. 1075}.*) Thus, if defendant at the time of the offense was insane under the California M'Naghten test, it makes no difference whether the period of insanity lasted several months, as in this case, or merely a period of hours. (See *People v. Donegan (1939) 32 Cal.App.2d 716, 719 {90 P.2d 856}.*) n16

. . .

n16 Of course, the burden is on the defendant to establish by a preponderance of the evidence that the offense occurred during a period of insanity. (See *People v. Baker (1954) 42 Cal.2d 550, 564 {268 P.2d 705},* and cases cited therein.)

We have reviewed the record in the instant case and we find substantial evidence to support the trial court's finding that defendant was psychotic at the time of the offense. This finding is amply supported by the testimony of psychiatrists. Substantial evidence also supports the finding that the psychosis was a product of voluntary ingestion of drugs. Finally, the trial court found that defendant "was not capable of understanding that her act was wrong," a finding supported by considerable psychiatric testimony that defendant could not distinguish right from wrong at the time of her offense. . . .

. . . The trial court also found that defendant suffered from a "temporary psychosis" that "was operating on this defendant from some time in November, at least through December and beyond the date of December 7." We hold that such a temporary psychosis which was not limited merely to periods of intoxication (see fn. 9, *ante*) and which rendered defendant insane under the M'Naghten test constitutes a settled insanity that is a complete defense to the offense here charged.

The judgment is reversed and the cause is remanded to the trial court with directions to enter a judgment of not guilty by reason of insanity and to take such further proceedings as are required by law. . . .

PEOPLE V. SAILLE

SUPREME COURT OF CALIFORNIA

54 Cal. 3d 1103; 820 P.2d 588; 2 Cal. Rptr. 2d 364

December 12, 1991

OPINION BY: PANELLI, J.

We granted review in this case to resolve a conflict among the Courts of Appeal regarding the impact of legislation abolishing diminished capacity on the crime of voluntary manslaughter. Specifically, the issue is whether the law of this state still permits a reduction of what would otherwise be murder to nonstatutory voluntary manslaughter due to voluntary intoxication and/or mental disorder. n1 In this case, the Court of Appeal held that it does not. After careful examination of the relevant statutes and legislative history, we agree.

> n1 Another type of nonstatutory voluntary manslaughter—the so-called "imperfect self-defense" doctrine—has been recognized in California. That doctrine applies to reduce an intentional killing from murder to manslaughter when a person kills under an honest but unreasonable belief in the necessity to defend against imminent peril to life or great bodily injury. (*People v. Flannel* (1979) 25 Cal.3d 668, 674–680 {160 Cal.Rptr. 84, 603 P.2d 1}; *People v. Van Ronk* (1985) 171 Cal.App.3d 818, 823 {217 Cal.Rptr. 581}.) This doctrine has no application to the facts before us, and we do not decide whether it has been affected by Proposition 8 and the 1981 legislation.

Following a retrial, defendant was convicted of the first degree murder of Guadalupe Borba (*Pen. Code, § 187*) . . . and the attempted murder of David Ballagh (§ § 664/187).

. . .

Facts

On November 30, 1985, defendant started drinking at a friend's house shortly before noon. He had drunk 15 to 18 beers by about 6 o'clock that evening; he then went to a bar and drank about three or four more beers. He was noticeably drunk when he went to Eva's Cafe about 9 p.m. The bartender signaled the security guard, David Ballagh, to ask defendant to leave. Ballagh told defendant he could not drink there because he appeared intoxicated and asked

defendant to leave; defendant did so. Defendant returned about an hour later, but was reminded by Ballagh that he could not come in. Defendant left but returned again around 11 p.m. and was rebuffed once again by Ballagh. As he left he said to Ballagh, "I'm going to get a gun and kill you."

Defendant went home around 1 a.m., got his rifle (a semiautomatic assault rifle), and returned to the bar. As he entered the bar, defendant said to Ballagh, "I told you I would be back." Ballagh tried to grab the rifle; it discharged and killed a patron. Defendant was eventually subdued outside the bar; both he and Ballagh were shot during the struggle.

A blood sample taken from defendant about 2 hours later showed a blood-alcohol level of .14 per cent. Expert testimony at trial established that the level would have been about .19 per cent at the time of the shooting.

Contentions

Defendant contends the court's instructions on the effect of voluntary intoxication were inadequate. The court gave *CALJIC No. 4.21*, stating that voluntary intoxication could be considered in determining whether defendant *had the specific intent to kill.* The court instructed on first and second degree murder and voluntary and involuntary manslaughter. It did not, however, relate voluntary intoxication to anything other than the specific intent to kill. Defendant contends the instructions were insufficient because they did not tell the jury that voluntary intoxication, like heat of passion upon adequate provocation, could negate express malice and reduce what would otherwise be murder to voluntary manslaughter. Defendant also contends that the court should have instructed *sua sponte* that the jury could consider his voluntary intoxication in determining whether he had premeditated and deliberated the murder. Defendant further contends that the instructions on involuntary manslaughter improperly required a showing of unconsciousness.

In rejecting these contentions, the Court of Appeal based its reasoning on the legislative enactments that (1) abolished diminished capacity and (2) clarified the definition of malice aforethought. . . .

In response to our request, the Joint Committee for Revision of the Penal Code held two public hearings on the subject of psychiatric evidence and the defenses of diminished capacity and insanity. These hearings led to the introduction of Senate Bill No. 54, 1981–1982 Regular Session, to abolish the defense of diminished capacity. (Comment, *Admissibility of Psychiatric Testimony in the Guilt Phase of Bifurcated Trials: What's Left After the Reforms of the Diminished Capacity Defense? (1984) 16 Pacific L.J. 305, 316-318.*) After substantial amendment, Senate Bill No. 54 was enacted into law in September 1981. (Stats. 1981, ch. 404, pp. 1591–1592.) n4

> n4 The original version of Senate Bill No. 54 was far more sweeping in effect. It would have repealed the plea of not guilty by reason of insanity, abolished diminished capacity, and made mental illness and voluntary intoxication matters to be considered only in mitigation of punishment. The scope of the bill was narrowed as it went through the Legislature. The last amendments made by the Assembly on August 11, 1981, resulted in the language we must interpret in sections 22, 28, and 29. (Sen. Bill No. 54, as amended August 11, 1981.)

Senate Bill No. 54 added to the *Penal Code sections 28 and 29,* which abolished diminished capacity and limited psychiatric testimony. It amended section 22 on the admissibility of evidence of voluntary intoxication, section 188 on the definition of malice aforethought, and section 189 on the definition of premeditation and deliberation. n5 Other sections not relevant here were also amended.

> n5 Subsequent minor amendments have been made to these statutes. We quote the current version of the statutes.

Section 28, subdivision (a) provides in pertinent part that evidence of mental illness "shall not be admitted to show or negate the *capacity* to form any mental state," but is "admissible solely on the issue of whether or not the accused *actually formed* a required specific intent, premeditated, deliberated, or harbored malice aforethought, when a specific intent crime is charged." (Italics added.) Subdivision (b) of section 28 abolishes the defenses of diminished capacity, diminished responsibility, and irresistible impulse "as a matter of public policy."

Section 29 provides that any expert testifying in the guilt phase of a criminal action "shall not testify as to whether the defendant had or did not have the required mental states, which include, but are not limited to, purpose, intent, knowledge, or malice aforethought, for the crimes

charged. The question as to whether the defendant had or did not have the required mental states shall be decided by the trier of fact."

Section 22 was amended to reflect the abolition of diminished capacity. It provides that evidence of voluntary intoxication is not admissible to negate the capacity to form any mental state, but it is admissible "solely on the issue of whether or not the defendant actually formed a required specific intent, premeditated, deliberated, or harbored malice aforethought, when a specific intent crime is charged."

. . .

Scope of Voluntary Manslaughter

. . .

We still must reconcile the narrowed definition of malice aforethought in section 188 with the language of sections 22, subdivision (b) and 28, subdivision (a). These latter sections make evidence of voluntary intoxication and mental illness admissible solely on the issue of whether the accused "actually formed a required specific intent, premeditated, deliberated, or harbored malice aforethought, when a specific intent crime is charged."

Molina had relied on the reference to malice aforethought in section 28, subdivision (a) to conclude that the Legislature had not foreclosed the possibility of a reduction of murder to voluntary manslaughter where malice is lacking due to mental illness or intoxication. (*People v. Molina, supra, 202 Cal.App.3d* at p. 1174.) As previously stated, however, the *Molina* analysis did not consider the effect of the Legislature's amendment of the definition of malice in section 188.

As the Court of Appeal noted in *People v. Bobo, supra, 229 Cal.App.3d* at p. 1442, "section 28, subdivision (a), is a general statute covering all specific intent crimes. Leeway in the language is needed to ensure such coverage. Moreover, malice aforethought can be either express or implied. Nothing is generalized about the definition of express malice in section 188 and no leeway in the language is needed for that precise definition. Furthermore, evidence of mental disease, disorder, or defect is still admissible on the issue of whether the accused actually formed an intent unlawfully to kill, i.e., whether the accused actually formed express malice."

Sections 22 and 28 state that voluntary intoxication or mental condition may be considered in deciding whether the defendant actually had the required mental state, including malice. These sections relate to *any* crime, and make no attempt to define what mental state is required. Section 188, on the other hand, defines malice for purposes of murder. In combination, the statutes provide that voluntary intoxication or mental condition may be considered in deciding whether there was malice as defined in section 188. Contrary to defendant's contention, we see no conflict in these provisions.

Defendant further argues that the Legislature's narrowing of the definition of express malice and the resulting restriction of the scope of voluntary manslaughter presents a due process problem. We disagree. The Legislature can limit the mental elements included in the statutory definition of a crime and thereby curtail use of *mens rea* defenses.

. . . even if there were a duty on the trial court to instruct *sua sponte* on voluntary intoxication when the defense of diminished capacity existed, we do not believe that it is reasonable for such a duty to continue after abolition of the diminished capacity defense.

In our view, under the law relating to mental capacity as it exists today, it makes more sense to place on the defendant the duty to request an instruction which relates the evidence of his intoxication to an element of a crime, such as premeditation and deliberation. This is so because the defendant's evidence of intoxication can no longer be proffered as a defense to a crime but rather is proffered in an attempt to raise a doubt on an element of a crime which the prosecution must prove beyond a reasonable doubt. In such a case the defendant is attempting to relate his evidence of intoxication to an element of the crime. Accordingly, he may seek a "pinpoint" instruction that must be requested by him (See 5 Witkin & Epstein, Cal. Criminal Law (2d ed. 1989) Trial, § 2925, pp. 3586–3587), but such a pinpoint instruction does not involve a "general principle of law" as that term is used in the cases that have imposed a *sua sponte* duty of instruction on the trial court. The court did not err, therefore, in failing to instruct *sua sponte*.

. . .

Conclusion

The judgment of the Court of Appeal is affirmed.

COURT OF APPEAL OF CALIFORNIA, THIRD APPELLATE DISTRICT

175 CAL. APP. 3D 785; 221 CAL. RPTR. 631

DECEMBER 16, 1985

OPINION BY: SIMS, J.

In this case, defendant Alfredo Eddie Velez voluntarily smoked a marijuana cigarette furnished by others at a social gathering. The cigarette contained phencyclidine (PCP) which caused defendant to become legally unconscious. While thus unconscious, defendant brutally assaulted the victim and was ultimately convicted by a jury of assault with a deadly weapon (*Pen. Code, § 245*, subd. (a)), n1 with the special finding that his victim was over 60 years old at the time of the crime. (§ 1203.09.) n2 Defendant testified he did not know the cigarette contained PCP.

> n1 All further statutory references are to the Penal Code unless indicated otherwise.

> n2 The jury found defendant did not intentionally inflict great bodily injury within the meaning of section 12022.7. The jury also made the following special findings:

"1. Do you find beyond a reasonable doubt the defendant was conscious, as that term is described in the instructions, at the time of the attack? . . . No"

"2. Do you find by a preponderance of the evidence that the defendant consumed a powerful and unpredictable drug involuntarily? . . . No"

Sentenced to state prison for the upper term, defendant appeals. In the published portion of this opinion, . . . we conclude, among other things, that defendant was voluntarily intoxicated as a matter of law (§ 22) and was not entitled to jury instructions on the absolute defense of unconsciousness due to involuntary intoxication. Since we reject all of defendant's contentions of error, we affirm the judgment.

. . .

FACTUAL AND PROCEDURAL BACKGROUND

On November 4, 1983, the victim, a 64-year-old man, was sitting in the living room of his home watching television with his wife. Defendant, who was unknown to the victim, suddenly crashed into the house by kicking open a locked wooden door. According to the victim, defendant was angry and looked like an animal.

Defendant attacked the victim with a screwdriver, stabbing him all over his body, including his eyes. Defendant also stomped on him. The victim's wife ran outside and begged her neighbor to call the police.

Stockton Police Officers Smallie and Manley arrived at the victim's house shortly after midnight. Smallie saw defendant trying to stab his bloodied victim as he and his wife struggled in defense. Smallie pointed his gun at defendant and told him to drop his weapon. Defendant apparently ignored Smallie and continued to try to stab the victim. The officers started hitting defendant with their clubs, pulled him away from the victim, and handcuffed him while he jumped on the victim's legs. Defendant then became limp and the officers dragged him outside. Both officers thought defendant was under the influence of PCP.

A neighbor saw defendant before the stabbing and thought defendant acted as if drunk. Defendant had been walking in the middle of the street in a zigzag fashion without regard for traffic. As the police dragged defendant from the victim's house, the neighbor stated that defendant still acted drunk and insulted the police.

Two defense witnesses familiar with the use and influence of PCP, a psychologist and a psychiatrist, testified defendant's behavior on the night of the assault was consistent with PCP ingestion.

Defendant testified that on the night in question, he was going around with some people who were new acquaintances, i.e., people defendant had seen but did not really know. The group went to the house of the brother-in-law of one of the group. Defendant sat down, had a beer, and began to watch television.

Some of the other members of the group were in the kitchen, smoking marijuana. They called defendant into the kitchen and offered him a marijuana cigarette. Defendant smoked marijuana "maybe three times a month" and knew what it looked like. Defendant took a puff on the cigarette and passed it back. Defendant then took a second puff on the cigarette.

The people in the room began to look like devils. After that, defendant remembered only running and crawling. Nobody mentioned to defendant that the cigarette might contain PCP. Defendant had never before experienced such an effect when he smoked marijuana.

Jose Hernandez was with defendant on the evening of the assault. Hernandez testified he saw defendant smoke a marijuana "joint" that was being passed around. Hernandez knew it was a "K.J." (a cigarette containing PCP) judging from the behavior of others who had also smoked the same marijuana cigarette. Hernandez claimed no one told him or any of the others it was a "K.J."

Others who were with defendant in the house before the assault testified defendant appeared to be under the influence of PCP though none of them had any that night. They testified they smoked marijuana but were unaware of any PCP in the house.

As a result of defendant's attack, the victim is partially blind, his hearing is impaired, his legs are stiff, and he has no feeling in his left palm.

DISCUSSION

I

Defendant contends the trial court erred in instructing the jury to the effect that unconsciousness caused by voluntary intoxication is not a defense to a charge of assault with a deadly weapon. Defendant asserts that unconsciousness, however caused, is a complete defense even to a general intent crime. We must disagree.

. . .

Assault with a deadly weapon is a general intent crime. (*People v. Rocha* (1971) 3 Cal.3d 893, 898–899 {92 Cal.Rptr. 172}.) In ordinary circumstances, in order to commit the crime of assault with a deadly weapon a defendant must have the general intent willfully to commit an act, the direct, natural, and probable consequences of which, if successfully completed, would be injury to another. (*Id., at* p. 899.)

Section 26 provides in pertinent part: "All persons are capable of committing crimes except those belonging to the following classes:

"Four persons who committed the act charged without being conscious thereof."

This statute obviously suggests that one who is unconscious for any reason is incapable of committing a crime.

. . .

The answer to this dilemma was provided nearly 20 years ago by Chief Justice Traynor: "Unconsciousness is ordinarily a complete defense to a criminal charge. (Pen. Code, § 26, subd. 5.) . . . If the state of unconsciousness is caused by voluntary intoxication, however, it is not a complete defense. Intoxication can so diminish a person's mental capacity that he is unable to achieve a specific state of mind requisite to a crime, but, even if it is sufficient to destroy volition, it cannot excuse homicide. *Unconsciousness caused by voluntary intoxication is governed by Penal Code section 22, rather than section 26, and it is not a defense when a crime requires only a general intent.*

. . .

Section 22 provides that unconsciousness caused by voluntary intoxication is available only as a partial defense to an offense requiring a specific intent; it is not a defense to a general intent crime such as assault with a deadly weapon. (*People v. Kelly, supra,* 10 Cal.3d at pp. 572–573; *People v. Corson* (1963) 221 Cal.App.2d 579, 582 {34 Cal.Rptr. 584}; *People v. Lim Dum Dong* (1938) 26 Cal.App. 2d 135, 138 {78 P.2d 1026}.)

. . .

The trial court did not err in giving the subject instructions.

II

Defendant contends the trial court erroneously instructed the jury that defendant had the burden of proving by a preponderance of the evidence that he involuntarily consumed a drug that caused his unconsciousness. He asserts he was lawfully required only to produce sufficient evidence to create a reasonable doubt (a) that he was unconscious and (b) that any condition of unconsciousness was due to voluntary (as opposed to involuntary) intoxication. (See *People v. Tewksbury* (1976) 15 Cal.3d 953, 962–964 {127 Cal.Rptr. 135, 544 P.2d 1335}; *People v. Hardy* (1948) 33 Cal.2d 52, 65–66 {198 P.2d 865}.) We need not resolve this contention because we conclude defendant was not entitled to instructions on the defense of unconsciousness due to involuntary intoxication, so that any error in such instructions did not prejudice him.

Section 22 operates as a limitation on the absolute defense of unconsciousness otherwise provided by section 26. (*People v. Conley, supra,* 64 Cal.2d at p. 323.) Section 22 applies only where unconsciousness is caused by voluntary intoxication. (*Ibid.*) Consequently, if unconsciousness is caused by involuntary intoxication, that unconsciousness is a complete defense, and a defendant is wholly excused from criminal responsibility for his conduct.

Defendant's contention that he was entitled to instructions wholly excusing him from criminal responsibility in this case is premised on his previously recounted testimony that he was offered and smoked a marijuana cigarette which, unbeknownst to him, contained PCP. However, if this conduct falls within the definition of voluntary intoxication under section 22 as a matter of law, then defendant was not entitled to instructions on unconsciousness caused by involuntary intoxication. We therefore examine whether defendant's intoxication was voluntary as a matter of law.

We begin by noting that the drug defendant admitted he knowingly consumed—marijuana—is a controlled substance classified as a hallucinogen in California. (*Health & Saf. Code, § 11054*, subd. (d)(13).) Except possibly in circumstances not here relevant, it is unlawful in this state to possess, transport, sell, furnish, administer, or give away marijuana. (*Health & Saf. Code, § § 11357, 11360*.) n9 Consequently, when defendant possessed the marijuana he consumed, and when he gave or furnished it to others, he broke the law.

> n9 When we refer to marijuana as an "unlawful drug," we refer to these prohibitions.

. . .

Section 22 codified the common law rule that voluntary intoxication does not excuse the commission of a crime. (*People v. Haskins (1960) 177 Cal.App.2d 84, 88 {2 Cal.Rptr. 34}.*) It is therefore appropriate to construe the statute in "the spirit of the common law". . .

. . .

Clearly, then, one who becomes voluntarily intoxicated to the point of unconsciousness can have no actual intent to commit a crime; rather, criminal responsibility is justified on the theory that having chosen to breach one's duty to others of acting with reason and conscience, one may not entirely avoid criminal harm caused by one's breach of duty. It is therefore apparent the imposition of criminal responsibility for acts committed while voluntarily intoxicated is predicated on a theory of criminal negligence. (See, e.g., § 20; Model Penal Code (1985) com. to § 2.08, p. 354.) In California, whether one is criminally negligent is ascertained by applying an objective test: whether *a reasonable person* in defendant's circumstances has engaged in criminally negligent behavior. (See *People v. Watson (1981) 30 Cal.3d 290, 296 {179 Cal.Rptr. 43, 637 P.2d 279}*) We shall apply such a test here to ascertain whether defendant was voluntarily intoxicated as a matter of law.

Boiled down to its essentials, defendant's defense was that he smoked marijuana given to him at a social gathering by others, but he did not in fact know it contained PCP,

which produced an unexpected intoxicating effect. This defense depends on the validity of defendant's assumptions that the cigarette did not contain PCP and would produce a predictable intoxicating effect. However, for reasons previously discussed, these assumptions are tested not by defendant's subjective belief but rather by the standard of a reasonable person. In this regard, it is common knowledge that unlawful street drugs do not come with warranties of purity or quality associated with lawfully acquired drugs such as alcohol. Thus, unlike alcohol, unlawful street drugs are frequently not the substance they purport to be or are contaminated with other substances not apparent to the naked eye. (See, e.g., Brecher, Licit and Illicit Drugs (1972) 376, 525.) In particular, marijuana is frequently contaminated with PCP or other psychoactive drugs. (Coles, Brenner, Meagher, Drugs, and Youth (1970) 27–28.) Indeed, the reported decisions of the California appellate courts provide a ready compilation of cases involving "lacing" or "dusting" of marijuana with PCP. . . .

The instant case simply reflects this well-established knowledge. Marijuana cigarettes laced with PCP were sufficiently common among defendant's acquaintances that they were given a nickname: "K.J.'s" Indeed, one of defendant's own experts, psychologist Dr. Steven Edwin Lerner, testified that PCP was commonly concealed in hand-rolled cigarettes containing various leaf materials including marijuana, and that the most common method of PCP intoxication involved smoking "joints."

Putting aside the question whether a defendant may be precluded in all circumstances from invoking the absolute defense of involuntary intoxication where he has consumed an unlawful drug, we hold a reasonable person has no right to assume that a marijuana cigarette furnished to him by others at a social gathering will not contain PCP; nor may such a person assume such a marijuana cigarette will produce any predictable intoxicating effect. Absent these assumptions, defendant cannot contend he was involuntarily intoxicated, because he had no right to expect the substance he consumed was other than it was nor that it would produce an intoxicating effect different from the one it did. We therefore conclude defendant was voluntarily intoxicated as a matter of law within the meaning of section 22.

. . .

The result we reach is consistent with the law of other American jurisdictions. Thus, involuntary intoxication is sometimes referred to as "innocent" intoxication. (Perkins & Boyce, *op. cit. supra*, at p. 1001.) The defense is allowed where the defendant has been without fault. "Involuntary intoxication, it appears, was first recognized as that caused by the unskillfulness of a physician or by the contrivance of one's enemies. Today, where the intoxication is induced through the fault of another *and without any fault on the part of the accused*, it is generally treated as involuntary. Intoxication caused by the force, duress, fraud, or contrivance of another, for whatever purpose, without any fault on the part of the accused, is uniformly recognized as involuntary intoxication." (Annot., *op. cit. supra*, 73 A.L.R.3d *at* pp. 199–200, fns. omitted, italics added; see also Annot., Effect of Voluntary Drug Intoxication Upon Criminal Responsibility *(1976) 73 A.L.R.3d 98.)*

In accordance with this view, courts have allowed the defense of involuntary intoxication based on the ingestion of an unlawful drug where the defendant reasonably believed he was consuming a lawful substance or where the unlawful drug was placed without defendant's knowledge *in a lawful substance.* (See *People v. Scott, supra,* 146 Cal.App.3d *at* pp. 826–827 [PCP surreptitiously placed in punch at family reunion-type party]; *People v. Carlo (1974) 46 App.Div.2d 764 {361 N.Y.S.2d 168}* [defendant took hallucinogenic pill in reasonable belief it was aspirin or lawful tranquilizer]; *Commonwealth v. McAlister (1974) 365 Mass. 454 {313 N.E.2d 113},* cert. den. *419 U.S. 1115 {42 L.Ed.2d 814, 95 S.Ct. 794}*

[coffee spiked with drug that produced reaction consistent with LSD]; *People v. White (1970) 131 Ill.App.2d 652 {264 N.E. 2d 228}* [drug put in defendant's beer without his knowledge]; *People v. Penman (1915) 271 Ill. 894 {110 N.E. 894}* [intoxicating pills reasonably believed to be breath perfume].)

. . .

Since we have concluded defendant's own evidence showed he was voluntarily intoxicated as a matter of law, he was not entitled to instructions on the absolute defense of unconsciousness. . . . (§ 22, subds. (a), (b); *People v. Kelly, supra,* 10 Cal.3d *at* p. 574.) And, since the defense instructions at issue were erroneously given in the first place, any error in those instructions did not prejudice defendant and was necessarily harmless.

. . .

Iii [Text Omitted.] Not Certified For Publication.

The judgment is affirmed.

PEOPLE V. LUCERO

COURT OF APPEAL OF CALIFORNIA, FIRST APPELLATE DISTRICT, DIVISION TWO

203 CAL. APP. 3D 1011; 250 CAL. RPTR. 354

AUGUST 15, 1988

OPINION BY: KLINE, P.J.

On September 19, 1985, appellant Daniel Lucero was found guilty of conspiring to smuggle narcotics into a county jail facility (*Pen. Code, § § 182, 4573*), transporting a controlled substance (*Health & Saf. Code, § 11352*), and extortion (*Pen. Code, § 520*). Appellant alleges the convictions must be reversed because the trial court refused to instruct on his mistake of fact defense. We agree. n1

n1 Since we are reversing the convictions for failure to instruct on appellant's defense, we do not reach the prosecutorial misconduct claim and sentencing error alleged by appellant.

FACTS

In the evening hours of January 11, 1985, appellant visited a friend, Michael Cummer. Appellant left Cummer's home to purchase drugs. He bought some cocaine, then sold a portion to, and was arrested by, Al Delacerda, an undercover officer with the San Francisco Police Department. From jail he telephoned Cummer to advise him that he was in custody and had left Cummer's car on the street. The following day Cummer went to see appellant in jail to learn where appellant had left his car, which he claimed was taken without permission. Appellant said he was unaware of the exact location and suspected that a friend who was with him at the time of his arrest might have it.

The day after his arrest appellant was also visited by Officer Delacerda. Appellant told Delacerda he was willing to act as an informant in exchange for leniency on the charges facing him. At the time of his arrest, appellant was on formal probation and other charges were pending against him. Delacerda told appellant he wanted information leading to arrests involving narcotics, and that the general police policy was to require evidence leading to three arrests as a condition of assistance.

Appellant testified that he and Delacerda maintained almost daily contact for several weeks. As a result of information relayed, and telephonic arrangements set up by appellant, two persons were arrested for the sale of a controlled substance; one on January 15, 1985, and another on January 31, 1985. Both arrests resulted in convictions. In return for the information, Officer Delacerda wrote a letter to the district attorney's office on appellant's behalf. The letter, dated February 4, 1985, related that appellant had provided information resulting in two felony arrests, that Delacerda wanted appellant to continue working with him, and that he hoped appellant's work would be taken into consideration by the district attorney. Although Delacerda wanted more information from appellant, they had made no further arrangements. Appellant testified that he believed Delacerda expected information resulting in at least one more arrest in order to meet the condition that he provided evidence leading to at least three arrests.

While in custody appellant learned that a person employed at the jail was willing to smuggle drugs into the facility. He thought this would be an important case, and that he would obtain Delacerda's help if he could put it together. Appellant testified that he informed Officer Delacerda of his idea and Delacerda told him it would be a good case, and to inform him when it was worked out. Delacerda admitted appellant mentioned the idea, but claimed he referred appellant to the sheriffs responsible for running the county jail.

Meanwhile, Michael Cummer had notified the police that appellant had stolen his car. Cummer testified that appellant would call him demanding money or drugs in exchange for the return of his car. Appellant testified that he did not know the location of Cummer's car, but that Cummer had offered him a reward to find it, and he was calling friends and relatives in order to do so.

On February 7, 1985, appellant spoke with a Northern California Service League volunteer, Donna Marcinowsky, who had a pass to enter the jail facility. According to appellant, she agreed to bring him contraband in exchange for some marijuana. Appellant telephoned Cummer and asked him to provide Marcinowsky the contraband; in return he promised to reveal the location of Cummer's car.

Cummer testified that he informed San Francisco Police Officer Kemmitt that appellant wanted him to assist in bringing drugs into the jail. On February 8, 1985, Officer Kemmitt accompanied Cummer to the Oakland location specified by appellant, where he purchased heroin and marijuana. They then delivered the contraband to Donna Marcinowsky at the Hall of Justice. She was arrested while heading for the jail elevator.

Appellant testified that he tried to reach Delacerda all day on February 8, 1985, to notify him that he had arranged for a third arrest. Delacerda was testifying in the Hall of Justice in an unrelated matter that day, and was not expected at the station until 7 p.m. Appellant claimed to have left several messages at the police department. Appellant explained that it was difficult to get in touch with Delacerda because he could not receive calls while in jail. Appellant also stated that he could not leave specific messages at the police department because other inmates would have overheard him and that he would be in great danger if they discovered he was an informant.

At approximately 5 p.m. on February 8, appellant was arrested at a jail telephone; he testified he was at that very moment still trying to contact Delacerda.

DISCUSSION

Appellant's defense to the charges was that he held an honest and reasonable belief that he was immune from prosecution because his actions were in furtherance of his work with officer Delacerda. He relies upon *Health and Safety Code section 11367*, which provides: "All duly authorized peace officers, while investigating violations of this division in performance of their official duties, and any person working under their immediate direction, supervision or instruction, are immune from prosecution under this division." n2

n2 Further statutory references will be to the Health and Safety Code unless otherwise noted.

The trial court denied appellant's request for the following jury instruction: "The prosecution has the burden of proof beyond a reasonable doubt as to the element of intent for every allegation in the information. When a mistake of fact disproves any criminal intent which is a requisite element of any crime, the mistake is a defense to the crime. When a person commits an act based on a mistake of fact, his guilt or innocence is determined as if the facts were as he perceived them. Thus a person is not guilty of a crime if he commits an act under an honest and reasonable

belief in the existence of certain facts and circumstances which, if true, would make such act lawful. Thus if you find that the defendant had an honest mistake of fact with regard to his acting and working for Officer [Delacerda] as a credible reliable informant, and that such mistake of fact negated the required intent under my instructions, you must find him not guilty of any allegation where such intent has been negated."

The question before us is, in effect, whether appellant's claim that he honestly and reasonably believed he was immune from prosecution pursuant to section 11367 constitutes a valid defense to the action.

"'At common law an honest and reasonable belief in the existence of circumstances, which, if true, would make the act for which the person is indicted an innocent act, has always been held to be a good defense. . . .'" (*Matter of Application of Ahart (1916) 172 Cal. 762, 765 {159 P. 160}.*) "The primordial concept of *mens rea*, the guilty mind, expresses the principle that it is not conduct alone but conduct accompanied by certain specific mental states which concerns, or should concern, the law. In a broad sense the concept may be said to relate to such important doctrines as justification, excuse, mistake, necessity, and mental capacity, but in the final analysis it means simply that there must be a 'joint operation of act and intent,' as expressed in *section 20 of the Penal Code*." . . .

Judicial application of this doctrine has most often occurred in relation to statutes defining offenses in part by the age of the victim. In *People v. Hernandez, supra, 61 Cal.2d 529,* the Supreme Court held that a reasonable and good faith belief that the complaining witness was over 18 years of age is a defense to statutory rape. (*Pen. Code, § 261.5.*) . . . n3

n3 In *People v. Olsen (1984) 36 Cal.3d 638 {205 Cal.Rptr. 492, 685 P.2d 52},* however, the Supreme Court held that the mistake of age defense was *not* applicable to the charge of lewd and lascivious conduct with a minor under 14 years of age. (*Pen. Code, § 288,* subd. (a).) The court distinguished *Hernandez* and its progeny by reasoning that the considerations that justified the defense were outweighed by the strong public policy of protecting children of tender years. (*Id.* at p. 649.)

Mistake of fact has also been asserted in connection with factors other than the age of the victim. (*Pen. Code, § 281.*) In *People v. Vogel (1956) 46 Cal.2d 798 {299 P.2d 850},* the Supreme Court held that a good faith belief in the termination of prior marriage was defense to bigamy. In *People v. Navarro (1979) 99 Cal.App.3d Supp. 1 {160 Cal. Rptr. 692},* it was held that a good faith belief in the legal right to the subject property was a defense to the charge of theft. (*Pen. Code, § 487*, subd. 1.) Finally, in *People v. Mayberry (1975) 15 Cal.3d 143 {125 Cal. Rptr. 745, 542 P.2d 1337}*, the Supreme Court held that a reasonable, good faith belief that the complaining witness had voluntarily consented to accompany the defendant, and to engage in sexual intercourse with him, is a defense to the charges of forcible rape (*Pen. Code, § 261*, subds. (2) & (3)) and kidnapping (*Pen. Code, § 207*). (*Id.*, at p. 155; see also the resulting *CALJIC instruction, No. 10.23.*)

We have found only one case addressing the issue of mistake of fact in relation to immunity pursuant to section 11367. In *People v. Jones (1962) 200 Cal. App.2d 805 {19 Cal. Rptr. 787}*, the defendant was arrested in November 1960 for selling a substance in lieu of heroin to an undercover officer. Though there was no evidence the evidence the defendant acted as an informant during the 5 months prior to his arrest, there was evidence he had worked as a police informant in 1958–1959, and once in June of 1960. The trial court refused a requested instruction that defendant was immune from prosecution if he reasonably believed he was working under the immediate direction of a police officer. The Court of Appeal affirmed, reasoning that the defendant's personal belief was not relevant since the "deranged mind of a narcotic addict" could not be trusted as the standard for reasonableness. (*Id.*, at p. 813.) We find the analysis in *Jones* unpersuasive because the question of reasonableness must be resolved on the basis of an objective standard. The issue is not whether it was reasonable for a narcotic addict with a "deranged mind" to believe he or she was immune from prosecution; but rather whether in the context presented an ordinary person could have a *bona fide* and reasonable belief in his or her immunity from prosecution. In addition, *Jones* is factually distinguishable. Here, appellant's claim was corroborated to a large extent by Officer Delacerda, whereas in *Jones* the defendant offered no evidence supporting his belief in immunity.

We find that if appellant harbored a reasonable and good faith belief that his actions shielded him from prosecution pursuant to section 11367, such belief constituted a valid defense to the charge against him. We emphasize that appellant would need to convince the jury both that he honestly acted as an informant, and that his belief immunity was reasonable under the circumstances.

It is well settled that "a defendant has a constitutional right to have the jury determine every material issue presented by the evidence. . . ."

. . . Though the jury was not required to believe it, the defense in this case presented substantial evidence supporting defendant's claim that he had a reasonable and good faith belief he was immune from prosecution: the defendant testified that he had been working as an informant at the time of the arrest, that he believed he was immune from prosecution, and that he was not arranging for the drugs to be brought into the jail for his personal use, but in order to facilitate the arrest of Donna Marcinowsky and thereby obtain Officer Delacerda's assistance in connection with charges pending against him. In addition, Officer Delacerda corroborated much of appellant's story, including the fact that Delacerda generally required an informant's assistance in three arrests—one more than defendant had then provided— before providing assistance with the district attorney. Considering this evidence, we find that it was error for the trial court to refuse the requested instruction.

Such error cannot be cured by weighing the evidence and finding it reasonably probable that a correctly instructed jury nevertheless would have convicted the defendant of the charge.

. . .

Because the jury was not instructed that appellant's claim was a defense to the charge, the error was prejudicial.

Accordingly, the judgment is reversed.

KEY TERMS

Justification, 103

Excuse, 103

Deadly force, 104

Objective reasonableness, 104

Self-defense, 104

Defense of habitation, 104

Defense of another, 104

Peace officers, 104

Citizen's arrests, 104

Battered women's syndrome, 105

M'Naghten's Rule, 106

Bifurcated, 106

Temporary insanity, 106

Voluntary intoxication, 107

Involuntary intoxication, 107

Pathological intoxication, 107

Mistake of fact, 107

Mistake of law, 107

STUDY GUIDE CHAPTER 4

SPECIAL DEFENSES

1. State the basic rule of law for *self-defense.* Does the belief in the need to defend need to be **both** honest and reasonable? Explain.

2. What is necessary to use deadly or lethal *self-defense?* What happens if a defendant kills another with an honest but **unreasonable** belief in the need to defend? What is this type of *self-defense* called?

3. Can an aggressor or mutual combatant ever claim the right of *self-defense?* Explain. State the applicable rule of law.

4. What is the test for *insanity* used in California? Explain that test. Who has the burden of proving *insanity?*

5. When can *voluntary intoxication* be used as a defense? Does it matter if the crime requires general or specific intent? Explain. Why did the Velez court refuse to allow intoxication as a defense?

CHAPTER 5

Crimes Against the Person

This chapter discusses the most serious crimes against the person other than homicide (which was discussed earlier in Chapter 3). These very serious crimes, often violent, are the subject of media reports and have lasting repercussions for the victims left behind. Cases relating to offenses such as rape, kidnapping, and stalking may be difficult to read and study. Their facts can evoke strong emotions, particularly for past victims of violent crime or their family members. It is critical for you, as students of criminal justice, to understand that the law doesn't operate in a vacuum. People's lives are impacted from moment to moment as crime takes place. It is helpful to work on striking a balance, as you study criminal law, between having an awareness of the human elements of crime and acquiring the ability to analyze and solve legal problems.

ASSAULT AND BATTERY

Assault is an unlawful attempt, coupled with the present ability, to commit a violent injury upon the person of another.[1] The California statute requires both the attempt to batter and the present ability to complete the battery. This imposes a requirement that in order for the assault to take place, battery must have been a realistic possibility.

---

[1] Cal. Pen. Code §240.

Battery is the willful and unlawful use of force of violence upon the person of another.[2] It might be helpful to think of an assault as an "incomplete" or failed battery. For example, the assault is the "swing" and the battery takes place when the fist connects with the victim's face. The touching necessary to establish a battery can be slight; the key is that it is unlawful or non-consensual. Assault is a specific intent offense, because in addition to intending to do the physical act associated with the crime (the swing), the defendant must also intend a future consequence (causing injury to the victim). Unlike assault, battery is a general intent offense. The mens rea for battery is simply the intent to engage in the unlawful touching.

The offenses of assault and battery are often discussed as though they are one and the same, when in fact they are separate offenses. This is probably because they are intricately connected: an assault is always present when a completed battery has taken place, but the reverse is not true. An assault can take place without a battery at all. Assault with a deadly weapon is an offense that is often talked about by laypeople. In California, it is a wobbler that can be charged as a misdemeanor or a felony under Cal. Pen. Code §245. If charged as a felony, it is punishable by two, three, or four years in state prison.

In California, there are a wide range of very specific types of assault and battery. These are laid out in the Penal Code from §241 through §246. Examples include assault against a highway worker, school employee, or member of the armed forces. These sections also outline specific offenses targeted at children and the elderly. The elements of assault change only from the standpoint that a particular type of victim is required, or that the assault take place in a specific location. These unique characteristics are **attendant circumstances** for the particular offense.

The elements of *assault* are as follows:

- Actus reus—an attempted or threatened battery coupled with the present ability to complete it

- Mens rea—specific intent to injure or intent to place in fear of injury

- Causation—the defendant set in motion the chain of events that led to the resulting harm

- Injury—fear of injury

The elements of *battery* are as follows:

- Actus reus—harmful or offensive touching (non-consensual)

- Mens rea—intent to unlawfully touch another (general intent); criminal negligence is not enough

  - Caveat—a person who commits an act that is inherently dangerous to others with a conscious disregard for human life or safety (e.g., driving in the dark with no lights) is presumed to have the intent to commit battery because the person acted willfully

- Causation—the defendant set in motion the chain of events that led to the injury

- Injury—pain or injury

MAYHEM AND TORTURE

Mayhem is the unlawful and malicious deprivation of a human being of a member of their body; disabling, disfiguring, or rendering useless any member of the body; cutting or disabling the tongue; putting out an eye; or slitting the nose, ear, or lip.[3] For the purpose of defining mayhem, the term "malicious" refers to the intent to commit a wrongful act or to annoy or injure someone else.[4] Mayhem is a felony punishable by two, four, or eight years in state prison and is an **enumerated felony** for the purposes of the first degree felony murder rule in California. If the defendant acted with extreme indifference to the physical or psychological well-being of the victim, even if the

---

[2] Cal. Pen. Code §242.

[3] Cal. Pen. Code §203.

[4] CALCRIM No. 800 (2010).

defendant did not intend to kill the victim, the crime is aggravated mayhem and punishment is life with the possibility of parole.[5]

The elements of *mayhem* are as follows:

- Actus reus—deprivation of the victim of a member of their body (gouging out the eye, cutting the tongue, slitting the nose, ear ,or lip)

- Mens rea—intent to "vex, annoy, or injure;" mayhem is a general intent crime

- Causation—the defendant set in motion the chain of events that led to the resulting harm

- Injury—physical injury and disability

Torture takes place when the defendant inflicts great bodily injury on someone else with the intent to cause cruel or extreme pain and suffering for the purpose of revenge, extortion, persuasion, or for any sadistic purpose.[6] The victim is not actually required to suffer pain; the offense is focused on the mindset of the perpetrator, not the actual pain inflicted.[7] Torture is a felony punishable by life in prison and is also an offense to which the first degree felony murder rule applies.[8]

SEXUAL ASSAULT AND CRIMES AGAINST PUBLIC DECENCY AND GOOD MORALS

This section covers sexual assaults against adults and children, as well as related offenses, such as prostitution, pimping, and public conduct. The type of sexual assault a defendant can be charged with depends upon the specific act(s) and in some cases, the age of the victim. Rape, sodomy, oral copulation, sexual penetration, and lewd and lascivious acts are all offenses that can be charged regardless of the victim's age.

Rape is a general intent offense. The mens rea requirement is simply the intent to engage in the act of sexual intercourse; there is no requirement that the perpetrator intend some future or additional consequence. The term **duress** in this section means a direct or implied threat of force, violence, danger, or retribution sufficient to coerce a reasonable person of ordinary susceptibilities to perform an act or acquiesce to submit to an act to which they otherwise would not have.[9] Section 262 details spousal rape in a very similar way, with a list of specific circumstances under which sexual intercourse with the spouse of the perpetrator is rape. According to the code, sexual intercourse means any penetration, no matter how slight, of the vagina or genitalia by the penis, and lack of consent means that the act was not free and voluntary.[10] A woman who initially consents can change her mind if she communicates her objection to the act to the defendant in words or in actions that would be understood by a reasonable person to show her lack of consent. It is important to note that the statute and CALCRIM use gender-specific language when defining rape and in the instructions provided to juries—referring to the victim as a woman and the perpetrator as a man. This is done to provide clear, concrete instructions. Under the common law, rape was defined as "carnal knowledge of a woman without her consent" and was limited to female victims; under modern law, men can be victims of rape and women can be perpetrators, even though it is statistically far less common. Rape is also an enumerated felony for the purposes of first degree felony murder.

According to Cal. Pen. Code §260, **rape** is an act of sexual intercourse with a person who is not the spouse of the perpetrator (there is a separate spousal rape statute in California) under certain specific circumstances:

- When the victim is incapable of consenting to sex because of a mental or developmental disorder and that disorder is known or reasonably should be known by the perpetrator

---

[5] Cal. Pen. Code §205.

[6] Cal. Pen. Code §206.

[7] CALCRIM No. 810 (2010).

[8] Cal. Pen. Code §206.1.

[9] Cal. Pen. Code §260.

[10] CALCRIM No. 1000 (2010).

- When it is accomplished against the victim's will by force, violence, duress, menace, or fear of immediate and unlawful bodily injury (in this context, force simply refers to the amount of force necessary to overcome the victim's will—the victim is *not* required to resist in order to prove force)

- When the victim is intoxicated and this condition is known or reasonably should be known by the perpetrator

- When the victim is unconscious due to sleep, doesn't realize the act has occurred, or is unaware of the nature of the act because of the perpetrator's fraud, or where the perpetrator engages in fraud as to a professional purpose for the act

- When the victim submits under the belief that the perpetrator is their spouse due to the perpetrator's trickery

- When the victim submits in light of future threats of harm to the victim or any other person and there is a reasonable possibility that the perpetrator could execute the threat

- When the victim is threatened by the use of public authority, even if the perpetrator is not a public official

Oral copulation by force, fear, or threats is a violation of Cal. Pen. Code §288(a). It is any contact, no matter how slight, between the mouth of one person and the sexual organ or anus of another (without penetration).[11] **Sodomy** is any penetration, no matter how slight, of the anus of one person by the penis of another person (ejaculation is not required).[12] **Sexual penetration** against a person's will by a foreign object is a violation of Cal. Pen. Code §289(a)(1).

Like rape, the force necessary to accomplish the crimes of oral copulation, sodomy, or sexual penetration is simply that amount of force necessary to overcome the victim's will. *People v. Iniguez* (1994)[13] discusses the legal rules relating to force and resistance by a victim of rape. A perpetrator can be charged with separate individual counts of any of these sex offenses arising out of one encounter, even when each act of touching or penetration follows another in quick uninterrupted fashion. Each individual violation of the victim is a separate and distinct offense.

The punishment for rape, oral copulation, and sodomy when the victim is an adult and the act is accomplished by force, fraud, future threats of harm, or the use of public authority against the victim, or when the victim is unconscious, intoxicated, or developmentally disabled is three, six or eight years in state prison.[14] If rape is committed in concert with others (this offense is called "gang rape"), the punishment is five, seven, or nine years in state prison.[15] When the victim of rape, sodomy, oral copulation, or any of those offenses in concert with others is under the age of 14 and where the perpetrator is seven or more years older than the victim, the crime is **aggravated sexual assault of a child,** and the punishment is 15 years to life in prison.[16] Other sexual assaults against children are defined and punished according to Section 288 as **lewd and lascivious acts involving children.** Section 288 and its many subdivisions include a wide range of specific provisions that detail sentencing for various sex offenses against minors, and it also prohibits the use of technology (e.g., telephones, e-mail, the Internet) to send harmful matter to or to contact minors with the intent to commit a sexual offense.[17]

A defendant's claim of mistake about the age of a victim under the age of 14 is no defense to a charge that the defendant committed lewd and lascivious acts with the minior.[18] In *People v. Hernandez* (1964), the court held that if a defendant reasonably and actually believed that the other person was over 18 years old, he is not guilty of the crime.[19]

---

[11] CALCRIM No. 1015 (2010).

[12] Cal. Pen. Code §286(c)(2).

[13] *People v. Iniguez,* 7 Cal. 4th 847 (1994).

[14] Cal. Pen. Code §264.

[15] Cal. Pen Code §264.1.

[16] Cal. Pen. Code §269.

[17] Note that consent on the part of the minor child is no defense to charges under §288

[18] CALCRIM No. 1080 (2010) citing *People v. Olsen,* 36 Cal.3d 638, 649 (1984).

[19] *People v. Hernandez,* 61 Cal.2d 529 (1964).

Continuous sexual abuse of a child under 14 occurs when a perpetrator who lives in the same home with the child or has recurring access to the child engages in three or more acts of substantial sexual conduct or lewd and lascivious acts with them, where three or more months pass between the first and the last acts. If the perpetrator is convicted of continuous child sexual abuse of a child under 14, the punishment is six, 12, or 16 years in state prison.[20]

Consensual sexual intercourse with a minor is unlawful in California under Section 261.5. Often referred to as **statutory rape**, unlawful sexual intercourse with a minor to whom the perpetrator is not married is a wobbler in California, being charged as either a felony or a misdemeanor depending upon the ages of the victim and perpetrator and the difference between the two. The younger the victim and the older the perpetrator is, the more serious the charge (and the higher the likelihood that it will be charged as a felony). The key difference between rape and statutory rape is consent. In statutory rape cases, the victim and the perpetrator engage in the act of sexual intercourse willingly. The statute is intended to protect minor children in situations where they lack the ability to make well-reasoned decisions or to account for the serious life-changing implications of engaging in sexual intercourse.

In addition to jail or prison sentences, Section 261.5 provides for possible civil fines of up to $25,000, depending on the seriousness of the offense. These fines are paid into the State of California's Underage Pregnancy Prevention Fund. Statutory rape is also an offense for which a judge can require the defendant to register as a sex offender under Section 290. In re T.A.J. explains that minors have no constitutional right to engage in sexual intercourse, and that even though the statute is written to protect them, when two minors engage in sexual intercourse they too can be charged in juvenile court for a violation of the statute.[21]

KEY LEGAL PRINCIPLE:

> California's Sex Offender Registration Act, or **"Megan's Law,"** requires registration with the chief of police or the sheriff in the county where a convicted sex offender chooses to live. It is a lifetime requirement.[22] The Act contains lengthy provisions in the code outlining the registration requirements, supervision of registered sex offenders, notice to victims, restrictions on where registered offenders can live, restrictions on certain types of employment, and public distribution of information in the Megan's Law database. Access to information regarding Megan's Law and a searchable database of registered offenders are located at *www.meganslaw.ca.gov.*

Pimping, pandering, and prostitution are offenses that relate to the exchange of sexual acts for money or other compensation.[23] **Pimping** is where a perpetrator knowingly derives a financial benefit as a keeper or manager of a prostitute. **Pandering** is the procurement of another person for the purpose of prostitution. Both pimping and pandering are felonies punishable by three, four, or six years in state prison. If the prostitute is a minor, the punishments can range from three to eight years in state prison. A person is guilty of prostitution when they willfully engage in sexual intercourse or a lewd act with someone else in exchange for money.[24] Probably most common is the charge of solicitation for the purposes of prostitution. Solicitation will be discussed at length in Chapter 8 of this text.

Indecent public exposure occurs when a defendant willfully exposes his or her genitals to another in either a public place or an inhabited dwelling, where the others might be offended or annoyed, intending to bring public attention to himself or herself.[25] There is no requirement that someone was actually offended, nor is there a requirement that the other person actually see the exposed genitals. Indecent exposure is a misdemeanor, so long as the defendant has no prior qualifying convictions (prior indecent exposure convictions, or convictions under Section 288).

[20] Cal. Pen. Code §288.5.

[21] In re T.A.J., 62 Cal.App.4th 1350 (1998).

[22] Cal. Pen. Code §290.

[23] Cal. Pen. Code §266h.

[24] CALCRIM No. 1153 (2010) citing Cal. Pen. Code §647(b).

[25] Cal. Pen. Code §314.

FALSE IMPRISONMENT AND KIDNAPPING

False imprisonment is the unlawful violation of the personal liberty of another.[26] False imprisonment is a general intent crime; the perpetrator need not intend any future consequence beyond the intent to restrict the victim's liberty (movement). False imprisonment charges can result when a person unreasonably tries to make a citizen's arrest. If false imprisonment involves restraint by violence or menace, it is a felony punishable by two, three, or four years in state prison.[27] "Violence" has a specific meaning in the context of false imprisonment. It refers to an amount of force that is greater than the force reasonably necessary to restrain someone, and "menace" refers to verbal or physical threats of harm, which can be either express or implied.[28]

The elements of *false imprisonment* are:

- Actus reus—unlawful restraint (using force or threats of force, but not necessarily physical barriers)

- Mens rea—intent to restrain or confine (general intent)

- Causation—the defendant set in motion the chain of events that led to the resulting harm

- Injury—loss of liberty, fear, anguish

KEY LEGAL PRINCIPLE:

Human trafficking is an offense closely related to false imprisonment and kidnapping. While often portrayed by the media as a problem that only occurs in Third World or developing countries, recently the reality of human trafficking in the United States has garnered attention as well. Under Cal. Pen. Code § 236.1(a), (c) human trafficking occurs when a person deprives or violates the personal liberty of another with intent to obtain from the victim forced labor, to engage in pimping or forced prostitution of adults or minors, to abduct minors for the purpose of prostitution, to exploit minors in the production of obscene materials, or to engage in extortion. When the victim of human trafficking is an adult, the punishment is three, four, or five years in state prison; when the victim is a minor, the punishment is four, six, or eight years in state prison.[29]

A person who "forcibly, or by any other means of instilling fear, steals or takes, or holds, or detains, or arrests any person in this state and carries the person into another country, state, or county, or into another part of the same county is guilty of **kidnapping**."[30] Simple kidnapping is a general intent crime.[31] According to People v. Moya, kidnapping can be accomplished by the application of force or threats of force, or by any other method used to instill fear.[32] Kidnapping is an enumerated felony for the purposes of first degree felony murder. Kidnapping is a felony punishable by three, five, or eight years in state prison.

The elements of *kidnapping* include:

- Actus reus—unlawful restraint and transportation of the victim to another location

- Mens rea—intent to restrain (general intent)

- Causation—the defendant set in motion the chain of events that led to the resulting harm

- Injury—loss of liberty, fear, anguish

---

[26] Cal. Pen. Code §236.

[27] Cal. Pen. Code §268f.

[28] Cal. Pen. Code §236–237.

[29] Cal. Pen. Code §236.1(c), (d).

[30] Cal. Pen. Code §207.

[31] *People v. Moya,* 4 Cal. App. 4th 912 (1992).

[32] *People v. Moya,* 4 Cal. App.4th 912 (1992).

CRIMINAL THREATS AND STALKING

A person who willfully threatens to commit a crime that will result in death or great bodily injury to another, with the specific intent that the statement is to be taken as a threat (regardless of whether the perpetrator intends to carry out the threat), causing the victim to experience a reasonable fear for their safety, or the safety of their immediate family, is guilty of a **criminal threat.** The perpetrator can communicate the threat in a variety of ways (orally, in writing, or by an electronic communication device, such as a cell phone, pager, or computer) and need not possess the ability to carry out the threat immediately.[33]

Prompted by the 1989 murder of 21-year-old actress Rebecca Schaeffer by Robert Bardo, the California legislature passed the first anti-stalking statute in the United States. Bardo had stalked Schaeffer for three years prior to killing her. Bardo confessed to murdering Schaeffer and was sentenced to life without the possibility of parole for her murder. Like criminal threats, a stalking charge punishes conduct that gives rise to fear in the victim because of the threat of future harm. **Stalking** is the willful, malicious, and repeated harassment of another coupled with a credible threat, with the intent to place the victim in fear for his or her safety, or the safety of their immediate family.[34] Stalking is a wobbler that can be charged as either a felony or a misdemeanor at the discretion of the prosecutor. Section 646.9(c)(1) provides for a two, three, or five year sentence for repeat stalking offenders. Regarding stalking, the code defines a course of conduct as two or more acts that take place over a period of time (regardless of the length of time) that demonstrate a "continuity of purpose." The legislature defines a credible threat as one that is verbal or written (regardless of the method of communication), or a threat implied by a pattern of conduct—or a combination of both—intended to create reasonable fear in the victim. In 1994, the Driver's Privacy Protection Act[35] was also passed, protecting the residential addresses of victims of stalking.

ROBBERY AND CARJACKING

California Penal Code §211 defines **robbery** as the "felonious taking of personal property in the possession of another, from his person or immediate presence, and against his will, accomplished by means of force or fear." The taking of the property requires asportation, or movement, but the distance can be slight.[36] Robbery in California is divided into first and second degree, with first degree robberies being those where the victim is a mass transit provider, those taking place in an inhabited dwelling, and those where the victim is using or is in the immediate vicinity of an automated teller machine (ATM).[37] All other robberies are second degree. Depending upon the degree and circumstances of the robbery, the punishment ranges from two to nine years in state prison. Robbery is an enumerated felony for the purposes of first degree felony murder.

The elements of *robbery* are as follows:

- Actus reus—taking the property of another, from their person or immediate presence, by imminent threats of force or fear

- Mens rea—specific intent to permanently deprive the owner of the property in possession (felonious intent to take the property)

- Causation—the defendant's act set in motion the chain of events that led to the resulting injury

- Injury—fear and loss of property

Carjacking is very similar to robbery, but requires slightly different attendant circumstances. To be guilty of carjacking, the perpetrator must take the motor vehicle of another, from their possession or immediate presence, by imminent threats of force or fear.[38] In contrast to robbery, the felonious intent to take the vehicle can be to either permanently or *temporarily* deprive the owner of possession.

---

[33] *People v. Lopez,* 74 Cal. App. 4th 675, 679 (1999).

[34] Cal. Pen. Code § 646.9(a).

[35] 18 U.S.C. §123.

[36] *People v. Lopez,* 31 Cal. 4th 1051, 1061 (2003).

[37] Cal. Pen. Code §212.5.

[38] Cal. Pen. Code §215.

PEOPLE v. MYERS

COURT OF APPEAL OF CALIFORNIA, FIFTH APPELLATE DISTRICT

61 Cal. App. 4th 328; 71 Cal. Rptr. 2d 518

February 4, 1998

OPINION BY: BUCKLEY, J.

This case arose under unusual and tragic circumstances. During a relatively minor confrontation between Thomas Myers, Jr., and George Staley, Staley fell to the ground and struck his head on the concrete pavement. The impact fractured his skull and left him with serious and permanent neurological injuries. There was conflicting testimony about what caused Staley to fall. On the theory that Myers attacked Staley without provocation and knocked him unconscious with a punch in the nose, Myers was charged with assault by means of force likely to produce great bodily injury (Pen. Code, § 245, subd. (a)(1)) . . . and with battery resulting in serious bodily injury (§ 243, subd. (d)). Myers, on the other hand, maintained Staley was the aggressor and suddenly began yelling and poking him in the chest; when Myers pushed Staley away defensively, Staley accidentally slipped and fell on the wet pavement.

. . .

During his cross-examination, the prosecutor asked Myers whether, at the moment he pushed Staley away, he feared Staley was about to do him bodily harm. The defense offered to stipulate that Myers had no such fear, but the prosecutor refused to accept the stipulation. Myers's subsequent responses to the prosecutor's persistent questioning on this subject can best be described as equivocal and somewhat confusing, although at one time he did say he thought Staley might hit him.

"Resistance sufficient to prevent the [commission of a public] offense may be made by the party about to be injured . . . [t]o prevent an offense against his person. . . ." (§ 693.) n7 "A battery is any willful and unlawful use of force or violence upon the person of another." (§ 242.)

> n7 Similarly, *section 50 of the Civil Code* provides in part: "Any necessary force may be used to protect from wrongful injury the person or property of oneself. . . ."

"It has long been established, both in tort and criminal law, that 'the least touching' may constitute battery. In other words, *force* against the person is enough, it need not be violent or severe, it need not cause bodily harm or even pain, and it need not leave any mark." "The 'violent injury' here mentioned is not synonymous with 'bodily harm,' but includes any wrongful act committed by means of physical force against the person of another, even although only the feelings of such person are injured by the act." (*People v. Rocha (1971) 3 Cal. 3d 893, 899–900, fn. 12 {92 Cal. Rptr. 172, 479 P.2d 372}.)*

It follows that an offensive touching, although it inflicts no bodily harm, may nonetheless constitute a battery, which the victim is privileged to resist with such force as is reasonable under the circumstances. The same may be said of an assault insofar as it is an attempt to commit such a battery. n8 To hold otherwise would lead to the ludicrous result of a person not being able to lawfully resist or defend against a continuing assault or battery, such as the act defendant alleged here. n9

> n8 "An assault is an unlawful attempt, coupled with a present ability, to commit a violent injury on the person of another." (§ 240; see also *People v. Colantuono (1994) 7 Cal. 4th 206, 215–217 {26 Cal. Rptr. 2d 908, 865 P.2d 704}; 1 Witkin & Epstein, Cal. Criminal Law (2d ed. 1988) Crimes Against the Person, § 398, pp. 461–462.)*

> n9 In so holding we, of course, do not imply that we believe or disbelieve defendant's "version"; we merely say that the jury should have been given that opportunity.

Here, the jury found Myers guilty in count 1 of simple assault rather than the charged offense of assault by means of force likely to produce great bodily injury. It thus evidently concluded that Myers had pushed rather than punched Staley. It is also reasonable to suppose that the jury credited Myers's account of events leading up to the confrontation, i.e., that Staley was poking him in the chest with his finger. As to count 2, the jury found Myers guilty as charged of battery resulting in serious bodily injury. Since there is no question Myers's use of force caused Staley to suffer serious bodily injury, his right, if any, to defend himself against Staley's poking was central to the jury's verdict.

We conclude the trial court erred [Incorrect] in refusing to give a modified self-defense instruction, and that the error was prejudicial [hurtful] under the peculiar circumstances of this case.

to the guy charged w/ assault & battery therefore

DISPOSITION

The judgment is reversed.

PEOPLE v. LARA

COURT OF APPEAL OF CALIFORNIA, SECOND APPELLATE DISTRICT, DIVISION SIX

44 Cal. App. 4th 102; 51 Cal. Rptr. 2d 402

April 2, 1996

OPINION BY: YEGAN, J.

No reported California case has ever said that a battery can be committed with "criminal negligence." We shall not be the first to so hold. With commendable candor, the Attorney General has conceded error at oral argument. We reverse because the trial court instructed the jury that appellant could be convicted of battery if he acted with "criminal negligence." It is unnecessary to reach appellant's remaining contentions. → *careless*

Pete Lara, Jr., was convicted by jury of battery with serious bodily injury. (*Pen. Code, § 242 and 243*, subd. (d).) n1 In a bifurcated proceeding, the jury found that appellant had suffered two "strikes" within the meaning of section 667, subdivisions (d) and (e). The trial court sentenced appellant to state prison for an indeterminate term of 25 years to life pursuant to the "three strikes" law. (§ 667, subd. (e)(2)(A).)

> n1 All statutory references are to this code unless otherwise stated.

FACTS

Appellant spent the weekend at the home of his girlfriend, Michelle M. On Sunday afternoon Michelle returned home from work to find appellant watching a video and drinking beer. While Michelle straightened up the house, appellant stood on the front porch watching two teenage girls walking in front of the house. Michelle became angry and an argument ensued.

Michelle told appellant to leave. They argued while appellant gathered his belongings. Appellant removed $60 from Michelle's purse. When he was a few steps from the front door, Michelle stood behind him, asked him to stay, and asked for the return of her money. Appellant swung around to face her and the side of his right hand struck Michelle, breaking the bone in her nose. Appellant looked shocked and said: "Your nose," or "I broke your nose."

Michelle picked up the telephone to dial 911. When appellant attempted to take it from her, she hit him on the hand with the receiver. Appellant left the house and dropped Michelle's money outside. Michelle retrieved her money and called 911, requesting that appellant be arrested. She then drove herself to the hospital.

At the hospital, Michelle gave a tape-recorded statement to a Ventura police officer. During the interview, Michelle stated that she did not touch appellant before he hit her. When asked whether appellant had been "physical" with her before, Michelle answered: "Actually, . . . he has never hit me. OK, the guy he pushed me . . . It's always when I tell him to leave, you know I tell him to leave, and he'll, you know, be getting ready to leave but I start running off at the mouth . . . I don't shut up so he flips out on me, you know."

In a subsequent interview with an investigator with the district attorney's office, Michelle stated this was the first time appellant struck her and that she had mixed feelings about the prosecution. Toward the end of the interview, Michelle claimed, for the first time, that appellant might have hit her by accident.

At trial, Michelle testified that, before appellant hit her, she grabbed the back of his Pendleton shirt with such force that most of the buttons popped off the front of the shirt. Appellant turned around to free himself from her grasp and hit her in the nose by accident.

INSTRUCTIONS

At the People's request the trial court also instructed the jury with a modified version of *CALJIC No. 3.35*: "You may find the defendant guilty of [the] crime charged or the lesser crimes if there exists a union or joint operation of act or conduct and criminal negligence." The "use note" indicates: "This instruction is limited to those few offenses where criminal negligence and not intent is involved." (*CALJIC No. 3.35* (5th ed. 1988 bound vol.) p. 131.)

The reporter's transcript affirmatively shows that the genesis of the erroneous instruction was with the prosecutor. The prosecutor believed he could obtain conviction on both a general criminal intent theory and on a "criminal negligence". . .

GENERAL INTENT V. CRIMINAL NEGLIGENCE

Our Supreme Court has recently reiterated the long-standing rule that battery is a general intent crime. . . . This necessarily excludes criminal liability when the force or violence is accomplished with a "lesser" state of mind, i.e., "criminal negligence." As with all general intent crimes, "the required mental state entails only an intent to do the act that causes the harm. . . ." (*People v. Davis (1995) 10 Cal. 4th 463, 519, fn. 15 {41 Cal. Rptr. 2d 826, 896 P.2d 119}.*) Thus, the crime of battery requires that the defendant actually intend to commit a "willful and unlawful use of force or violence upon the person of another." (§ 242; *People v. Colantuono, supra, 7 Cal. 4th* at p. 217.) In this context, the term "willful" means "simply a purpose or willingness to commit the act. . . ." (§ 7, subd. 1.)

"Reckless conduct alone does not constitute a sufficient basis for . . . battery. . . ."

(*People v. Lathus (1973) 35 Cal. App. 3d 466, 469–470 {110 Cal. Rptr. 921}.*) However, if an act "'inherently dangerous to others' . . . [is] done 'with conscious disregard of human life and safety,' the perpetrator must be aware of the nature of the conduct and choose to ignore its potential for injury, i.e., act willfully. If these predicates are proven to the satisfaction of the trier of fact, the requisite intent is . . . established by the evidence.

. . .

Acting with "conscious disregard" . . . is not the equivalent of "criminal negligence." The former requires proof that the defendant subjectively intended to engage in the conduct at issue. General criminal intent may be inferred

by the conduct of the defendant if he or she acts with a "conscious disregard." On the other hand, "criminal negligence" requires jurors to apply an objective standard and to ask whether a reasonable person in the defendant's position would have appreciated the risk his or her conduct posed to human life.

. . .

"Criminal negligence" requires proof of "aggravated, culpable, gross, or reckless conduct, which is such a departure from the conduct of an ordinarily prudent person under the same circumstances as to demonstrate an indifference to consequences or a disregard of human life."

. . .

Here, appellant was charged with battery with serious bodily injury, a general intent crime. Accordingly, the jury should only have been instructed with *CALJIC No. 3.30.* As indicated, the jury was also instructed that it could convict appellant if it found that he acted with the "lesser" mental state of "criminal negligence." This was error.

. . .

REVERSAL REQUIRED

Appellant's state of mind, i.e., whether he acted with general intent or not, was the key issue in the case. . . . We have no way of determining whether the jury found that appellant acted with general criminal intent or with "criminal negligence." We cannot say that this misinstruction was harmless beyond a reasonable doubt. Appellant is entitled to a trial without reference to "criminal negligence."

The judgment is reversed.

STONE S. J., P. J., and GILBERT, J., concurred.

PEOPLE v. MARTINEZ

COURT OF APPEAL OF CALIFORNIA, SECOND APPELLATE DISTRICT, DIVISION FIVE

3 Cal. App. 3d 886; 83 Cal. Rptr. 914

January 27, 1970

OPINION BY: STEPHENS, J.

This is an appeal by the People, pursuant to *Penal Code section 1238,* subdivision 1, from an order setting aside count I of an information on a defense motion pursuant to *Penal Code section 995.* Defendant was charged by information with violation of *Penal Code section 242* (battery on a peace officer) in count I . . .

On July 7, 1968, at approximately 3:30 in the afternoon, Officer Erland E. Polson, a uniformed police officer for the City of Manhattan Beach, in the company of six other policemen, was attempting to shut down a loud party at 1618 Tenth Street in Manhattan Beach. While Officer Polson was standing next to a police vehicle helping a fellow officer arrest another person, defendant, who lived at that address, came to within two feet of the officers and shouted in a very loud tone of voice, "Who do you think you are? You can't do this. Where are you taking him?" Defendant kept repeating these statements and Officer Polson advised him to go back to the sidewalk and stop interrupting the officers. Finally defendant backed up onto the sidewalk, continuing "to yell at [Officer Polson], abuses at [Officer Polson]." The officer, who was wearing motorcycle boots, said, "Now, what are you going to do about it?" At the time he made the statement, Officer Polson "might have touched [defendant's] property. [He could not] say. [Officer Polson and defendant] were standing on the west side of the property. [The officer didn't] know if it was [defendant's] property or the property of the other resident." Defendant, who was barefooted, kicked him twice in the shin. Officer Polson did not suffer any injury. "The most I would say it smarted due to the fact I was wearing motorcycle boots."

Penal Code section 243 provides that battery is punishable by a fine of not exceeding one thousand dollars, or by imprisonment in the county jail not exceeding 6 months, or both, unless the battery is committed against the person of a peace officer engaged in the performance of his duties. In that case the battery shall be punished by imprisonment in the county jail not exceeding 1 year, or by imprisonment in the state prison for not less than one nor more than 10 years. Defendant argues that when a barefooted young man kicks a police officer's booted leg after the officer has asked "What are you going to do about it?" and the officer suffers no injury, there has not been a battery on a police officer within the provisions of section 243. n1 However, section 243 does not change the definition of battery, it only provides for a greater penalty when acts otherwise constituting a battery are committed upon a peace officer engaged in the performance of his duties. To paraphrase Gertude Stein, "A battery is a battery is a battery." As the court in *People v. Williams, 264 Cal. App.2d 885, 888 {70 Cal. Rptr. 882}*, added: "A battery is a battery whoever may be the victim. It is simply that *section 243 of the Penal Code* increases the punishment if the victim is a peace officer and certain other requirements are satisfied."

n1 The court below apparently accepted this argument. At the hearing on defendant's 995 motion on September 6, 1968, the court stated:

"It certainly doesn't seem to me to be a felony. This defendant's conduct is not approved by the Court; but at the same time it hasn't reached the felony grade, where the officer has on boots and the defendant kicked him in the leg barefooted. . . .

"My Code, as I have the 1967 cumulative part . . . This section provides there is no alternative sentence here. The punishment is in State Prison 1 to 10 years. I don't believe it is the intention of the Legislature to have a defendant sentenced to State Prison 1 to 10 years when he is barefoot and kicks a police officer with boots on. I think it would have to be something more than that. You can't even make this a misdemeanor."

On November 13, 1968, the amendment providing for alternative punishment went into effect. This amendment applies to all cases in which a judgment has not become final prior to its effective date. *(People v. Francis, 71 Cal.2d 66, 75 {75 Cal. Rptr. 199, 450 P.2d 591}.)*

The definition of battery in Penal Code section 242, any willful and unlawful use of force or violence upon the person of another, remains the same. Any harmful or offensive touching constitutes an unlawful use of force or violence. *(People v. Bradbury, 151 Cal. 675, 676–677 {91 P. 497}.)* We are not prepared to say that a barefooted kick is unoffensive. Given the appropriate circumstances and the appropriate barefoot, it may be more than ordinarily offensive.

Defendant could not argue that the officer's words justified the battery. No conduct or words, no matter how offensive or exasperating, are sufficient to justify a battery. *(People v. Mayes, 262 Cal. App.2d 195, 197 {68 Cal.Rptr. 476}.)* . . .

The judgment is reversed.

PEOPLE v. LOPEZ

COURT OF APPEAL OF CALIFORNIA, FIFTH APPELLATE DISTRICT

176 CAL. APP. 3D 545; 222 CAL. RPTR. 101

JANUARY 10, 1986

OPINION BY: CASTELLUCCI, J.

Defendant, Bernie Lopez, was convicted by jury trial of mayhem *(Pen. Code, § 203)* with the additional finding that he used a deadly and dangerous weapon within the meaning of *Penal Code section 12022,* subdivision (b). n1 He appeals claiming instructional error. We affirm.

> n1 All code section references shall be to the Penal Code unless otherwise noted.

STATEMENT OF THE CASE

An information was filed against the defendant charging him with two crimes arising from the same incident. Count one alleged a violation of section 203, mayhem, with the additional allegation that he used a deadly weapon during the commission of the offense. (§ 12022, subd. (b).) . . .

Jury trial commenced on May 7, 1984. Prior to its deliberations the jury was instructed on the law. These instructions included *CALJIC No. 9.30* (1979 revision), mayhem defined. The jury returned its verdict finding defendant guilty of count one as charged . . .

On June 12, 1984, defendant was sentenced to state prison for the lower term of 2 years with a 1 year enhancement for the section 12022, subdivision (b) violation, for a total of 3 years.

STATEMENT OF FACTS

On the evening of February 9, 1984, Jesus Ramos, Raul Morales, Esther Gomez and Sylvia Flores got together to play cards, and later left to get a pizza. Esther was driving the car; Raul was in the front seat on the passenger side; Jesus was in the back seat on the passenger side; and Sylvia was in the back seat on the driver's side. They drove up to the pizza parlor and parked the car under the balcony area of an apartment. There were several individuals on the balcony including the defendant and two of his brothers.

Sylvia got out of the car and went inside to order the pizza. She returned to the car to wait for the pizza. The defendant's brother, Victor, spat on the car from the balcony. Defendant and his brother George came down from the balcony and approached the car. The defendant was carrying two beer bottles. George asked Raul and Jesus if they "had any shit with their boy Steve." The window of the car was partially down and George attempted to punch Jesus through the opening. The defendant stated to his brother "Let's jam" because there were ladies in the car. George and the defendant started to walk away, George returned and opened the car door and defendant threw a beer bottle into the car striking Raul in the left eye. Another bottle was thrown from the balcony area which struck and broke the windshield of the car. Sylvia, Jesus, Esther, and Raul then drove off as George continued to try to attack Jesus.

The trauma to Raul's left eye from the blow resulted in his being legally blind in that eye. The chance for improvement in his vision is "very slight."

DEFENSE

George Lopez and the defendant testified similarly to the prosecution witnesses with the exception that George testified that the defendant did not have a beer bottle in his hands and George and defendant both testified that when the defendant said to "back off" they walked away from the car. As they were walking away they heard beer bottles being thrown. Defendant testified he did not throw a beer bottle.

Does the 1979 Revision of *CALJIC No. 9.30* Impermissibly broaden the statutory definition of mayhem by stating that a malicious intent can be an intent to vex or annoy?

Section 203 defines mayhem as follows: "Every person who unlawfully and maliciously deprives a human being of a member of his body, or disables, disfigures, or renders it useless, or cuts or disables the tongue, or puts out an eye, or slits the nose, ear, or lip, is guilty of mayhem."

The jury was instructed pursuant to *CALJIC No. 9.30* (1979 revision) as follows: "Every person who unlawfully and maliciously deprives a human being of a member of his body, or disables, disfigures, or renders it useless, or who cuts or disables the tongue, or puts out an eye, or slits the nose, ear, or lip, is guilty of the crime of mayhem."

In order to find defendant guilty of the crime of mayhem, each of the following elements must be proved:

"1. That defendant unlawfully and by means of physical force put out the eye of another person," and

"2. That defendant did so maliciously, that is, with an unlawful intent to vex, annoy, or injure another person."

Defendant asks this court to undertake a fresh examination of the *mens rea* aspect of this standardized **CALJIC** instruction. While recognizing that the Legislature did not incorporate a specific intent requirement as one of the elements of mayhem, defendant contends that the intent to vex and annoy impermissibly broadens the type of conduct which is statutorily proscribed by section 203 and is therefore not "statutorily authorized." Furthermore, defendant asserts that the instruction may also be viewed as violative of the doctrine of *stare decisis.* His final attack on the instruction is that the verbs "vex and annoy" are so vague and uncertain that sufficient notice as required by the federal and state Constitutions is not provided to people accused of violating section 203. Defendant asserts that the instructional error should be held reversible per se, and if not reversible *per se,* requires reversal in any event based upon the particular facts of this case.

Respondent contends that the instruction is proper. Respondent bases this assertion on section 7 which defines malice and maliciously as including a wish to vex or annoy. Therefore, *CALJIC No. 9.30* "contains the precise statutory language defining the crime of mayhem." Respondent does not address defendant's other attacks upon the terms vex or annoy.

It is necessary to undertake a somewhat detailed analysis of the inclusion of "vex or annoy" in the jury instruction since it appears that this is a theory which the jury considered seriously when reaching its verdict. During its deliberations the jury sent out two notes. The first note requested a rereading of Sylvia's testimony, in particular where the defendant was when the bottle was thrown and whether "it was aimed or just thrown at the car." The other note requested Raul's testimony concerning whether the defendant "took aim with the bottle or if he merely saw a blur and turned and saw the bottle coming toward him."

A. IS THE INCLUSION OF VEX OR ANNOY IN CALJIC NO. 9.30 STATUTORILY UNAUTHORIZED?

Defendant's argument that the inclusion of the terms to vex or annoy in the standard mayhem instruction is not statutorily authorized must fail. Section 7 provides in pertinent part: The following words have in this code the signification attached to them in this section, unless otherwise apparent from the context:

". . . ."

"4. The words 'malice' and 'maliciously' import a wish to vex, annoy, or injure another person, or an intent to do a wrongful act, established either by proof or presumption of law; . . ."

Section 203 requires that the defendant must act maliciously. Section 7, subdivision 4 defines "maliciously" and includes within that definition the wish to vex or annoy. Thus, the expansion of *CALJIC No. 9.30* to include vex or annoy as a part of the intent requirement is expressly authorized by statute.

. . .

B. ARE THE TERMS VEX OR ANNOY SO VAGUE AND UNCERTAIN THAT THEY VIOLATE CONSTITUTIONAL PRINCIPLES OF DUE PROCESS?

Defendant's final attack on *CALJIC No. 9.30* is that the terms vex or annoy are so vague and uncertain that sufficient notice, as required by the federal and state Constitutions, is not provided to people accused of violating section 203. This contention is also unsound.

"'[A] statute which either forbids or requires the doing of an act in terms so vague that men of common intelligence must necessarily guess at its meaning and differ as to its application violates the first essential of due process of law.'" *(People v. McCaughan (1957) 49 Cal.2d 409, 414 {317 P.2d 974}.)* ""'. . . The dividing line between what is lawful and unlawful can not be left to conjecture. The citizens can not be held to answer charges based upon penal statutes whose mandates are so uncertain that they will reasonably admit of different constructions. A criminal statute cannot rest upon an uncertain foundation. The crime, and the elements constituting it, must be so clearly expressed that the ordinary person can intelligently choose, in advance, what course it is lawful for him to pursue. *Penal statutes prohibiting the doing of certain things, and providing a punishment for their violation, should not admit of such a double meaning that the citizen may act upon the one conception of its requirements and the courts upon another!'"'* (Drucker v. State Bd. of Med. Examiners (1956) 143 Cal.App.2d 702, 709–710 {300 P.2d 197}, italics in original.)

The void-for-vagueness doctrine rests upon the lack of fair notice of proscribed conduct. But when this conduct is already criminal in nature the essential element of lack of notice of proscribed conduct is missing. *(People v. Barksdale (1972) 8 Cal.3d 320 {105 Cal. Rptr. 1, 503 P.2d 257}.)* "The fundamental test is whether a reasonable person in the position of the defendant would be apprised with reasonable certainty that his conduct is proscribed." *(People v. Williams (1976) 59 Cal.App.3d 225, 231 {130 Cal.Rptr. 460}, disapproved on other grounds in Pryor v. Municipal Court (1979) 25 Cal.3d 238, 257 {158 Cal.Rptr. 330, 599 P.2d 636}.)*

In the instant case, common sense would tell one that it is unlawful to hurl a beer bottle into an occupied vehicle. Such conduct foreseeably may result in injury to an occupant or damage to the vehicle. Thus, the defendant clearly had notice that his conduct was proscribed, whether it be under section 203 (mayhem) or other criminal statutes (e.g., § 240, assault, § 242, battery, and § 594, vandalism).

Furthermore, the terms vex or annoy were used in *CALJIC No. 9.30* not as separate intent but as a further definition of the term maliciously. The definition of maliciously as set forth in section 7, which includes an intent to vex or annoy, has been used since 1872. The Legislature deliberately acted in defining maliciously in section 7, subdivision 4, and stated that the words defined in the Penal Code have the signification attached to them in this section. "'All (7) presumptions and intendments favor the validity of a statute and mere doubt does not afford sufficient reason for a judicial declaration of invalidity. Statutes must be upheld unless their unconstitutionality clearly, positively and unmistakably appears.'" *(In re Dennis M. (1969) 70 Cal.2d 444, 453 {75 Cal.Rptr. 1, 450 P.2d 296}.)*

The judgment is affirmed.

PEOPLE v. INIGUEZ

SUPREME COURT OF CALIFORNIA

7 Cal. 4th 847; 872 P.2d 1183; 30 Cal. Rptr. 2d 258

May 23, 1994

OPINION BY: ARABIAN, J.

Defendant Hector Guillermo Iniguez admitted that on the night before Mercy P.'s wedding, he approached her as she slept on the living room floor, removed her pants, fondled her buttocks, and had sexual intercourse with her. He further conceded that he had met Mercy for the first time that night, and that Mercy did not consent to any sexual contact or intercourse. The Court of Appeal reversed defendant's conviction for rape on the grounds that the evidence of force or fear of immediate and unlawful bodily injury was insufficient. We granted review to determine whether there was sufficient evidence to support the verdict, and to delineate the relationship between evidence of fear and the requirement under *Penal Code section 261*, subdivision (a)(2), that the sexual intercourse be "accomplished against a person's will," in a case where lack of consent is not disputed. We reverse the Court of Appeal.

I. FACTS AND PROCEDURAL BACKGROUND

On June 15, 1990, the eve of her wedding, at approximately 8:30 p.m., 22-year-old Mercy, P. arrived at the home of Sandra, S., a close family friend whom Mercy had known for at least 12 years and considered an aunt. Sandra had sewn Mercy's wedding dress, and was to stand in at the wedding the next day for Mercy's mother who was unable to attend. Mercy was planning to spend the night at her home.

Mercy met defendant, Sandra's fiance, for the first time that evening. Defendant was scheduled to stand in for Mercy's father during the wedding.

Mercy noticed that defendant was somewhat "tipsy" when he arrived. He had consumed a couple of beers and a pint of Southern Comfort before arriving at Sandra's. Mercy, Sandra, and defendant celebrated Mercy's impending wedding by having dinner and drinking some wine. There was no flirtation or any remarks of a sexual nature between defendant and Mercy at any time during the evening.

Around 11:30 p.m., Mercy went to bed in the living room. She slept on top of her sleeping bag. She was wearing pants with an attached skirt, and a shirt. She fell asleep at approximately midnight.

Mercy was awakened between 1:00 and 2:00 a.m. when she heard some movements behind her. She was lying on her stomach, and saw defendant, who was naked, approach her from behind. Without saying anything, defendant pulled down her pants, fondled her buttocks, and inserted his penis inside her. Mercy weighed 105 pounds. Defendant weighed approximately 205 pounds. Mercy "was afraid, so I just laid there." "You didn't try to resist or escape or anything of that nature because of your fear?" "Right." Mercy further explained that she "didn't know how it was at first, and just want[ed] to get on with my wedding plans the next day." Less than a minute later, defendant ejaculated, got off her, and walked back to the bedroom. Mercy had not consented to any sexual contact.

Officer Fragoso, who interviewed Mercy several days after the attack, testified that she told him she had not resisted defendant's sexual assault because, "She said she knew that the man had been drinking. She hadn't met him before; he was a complete stranger to her. When she realized what was going on, she said she panicked, she froze. She was afraid that if she said or did anything, his reaction could be of a violent nature. So she decided just to lay still, wait until it was over with and then get out of the house as quickly as she could and get to her fiancee {sic} and tell him what happened."

Mercy immediately telephoned her fiance Gary and left a message for him. She then telephoned her best friend Pam, who testified that Mercy was so distraught she was barely comprehensible. Mercy asked Pam to pick her up, grabbed her purse and shoes, and ran out of the apartment. Mercy hid in the bushes outside the house for approximately half an hour while waiting for Pam because she was terrified defendant would look for her.

Pam arrived about 30 minutes later, and drove Mercy to Pam's house. Mercy sat on Pam's kitchen floor, her back to the wall, and asked Pam, "do I look like the word 'rape' [is] written on [my] face?" Mercy wanted to take a shower because she felt dirty, but was dissuaded by Pam. Pam telephoned Gary, who called the police.

Gary and his best man then drove Mercy to the hospital, where a "rape examination" was performed. Patricia Aiko Lawson, a blood typing and serology expert, testified that there was a large amount of semen present in Mercy's vagina and on the crotch area of her underpants. A deep vaginal swab revealed that many sperm were whole, indicating intercourse had occurred within a few hours prior to the rape examination.

. . .

The following day, Mercy and Gary married. Gary picked up the wedding dress from Sandra while Mercy waited in the car. Neither Sandra nor defendant participated in the wedding.

Defendant was arrested the same day. When asked by the arresting officer if he had had sexual intercourse with Mercy, defendant replied, "I guess I did, yes."

Dr. Charles Nelson, a psychologist, testified as an expert on "rape trauma syndrome." He stated that victims respond in a variety of ways to the trauma of being raped. Some try to flee, and others are paralyzed by fear. This latter response he termed "frozen fright."

. . . defense counsel argued that the element of force or fear was absent. "So if he was doing anything, it wasn't force or fear . . . It's a situation where it looks to him like he can get away with it and a situation where his judgment is flown out the window . . . He keeps doing it, probably without giving much thought to it, but certainly there is nothing there to indicate using fear ever entered his mind. What he was doing was taking advantage, in a drunken way, of a situation where somebody appeared to be out of it."

The jury was instructed on both rape pursuant to then Penal Code n1 section 261, subdivision (2), and sexual battery. n2 Upon the jury's request for further instruction on the definition of fear of immediate and unlawful bodily injury, the court instructed in relevant part, "'fear' means, a feeling of alarm or disquiet caused by the expectation of danger, pain, disaster, or the like." . . . Verbal threats are not critical to a finding of fear of unlawful injury, threats can be implied from the circumstances or inferred from the assailant's conduct. A victim may entertain a reasonable fear even where the assailant does not threaten by words or deed."

n1 All statutory references contained herein are to the California Penal Code unless otherwise indicated.

n2 Sexual battery is defined in section 243.4, which at the time of the crime provided in relevant part:

"(a) Any person who touches an intimate part of another person while that person is unlawfully restrained by the accused or an accomplice, and if the touching is against the will of the person touched and is for the purpose of sexual arousal, sexual gratification, or sexual abuse, is guilty of sexual battery. . . ."

"(f)(2) 'Sexual battery' does not include the crimes defined in Section 261. . . ."

The jury found defendant guilty of rape. He was sentenced to state prison for the midterm of 6 years.

The Court of Appeal reversed, concluding that there was insufficient evidence that the act of sexual intercourse was accomplished by means of force or fear of immediate and unlawful bodily injury. On the issue of fear, the court stated: "While the [defendant] was admittedly much larger than the small victim, he did nothing to suggest that he intended to injure her. No coarse or sexually suggestive conversation had taken place. Nothing of an abusive or threatening nature had occurred. The victim was sleeping in her aunt's house, in which screams presumably would have raised the aunt and interrupted the intercourse. Although the assailant was a stranger to the victim, she knew nothing about him which would suggest that he was violent. [The] event of intercourse is singularly unusual in terms of its ease of facilitation, causing no struggle, no injury, no abrasions or other marks, and lasting, as the victim testified, '"maybe a minute."' The court modified the judgment, reducing defendant's conviction of rape under section 261, former subdivision 2, to the offense of sexual battery under section 243.4, subdivision (a), and remanded for resentencing.

We granted the Attorney General's petition for review.

II. DISCUSSION

The test on appeal for determining if substantial evidence supports a conviction is whether "'a reasonable trier of fact could have found the prosecution sustained its burden of proving the defendant guilty beyond a reasonable doubt.'" (*People v. Johnson* (1980) 26 Cal.3d 557, 576 {162 Cal.Rptr. 431, 606 P.2d 738, 16 A.L.R.4th 1255}.) In making this determination, we "'must view the evidence in a light most favorable to respondent and presume in support of the judgment the existence of every fact the trier could reasonably deduce from the evidence.'" (*Ibid.*)

Prior to 1980, section 261, subdivisions 2 and 3 "defined rape as an act of sexual intercourse under circumstances where the person resists, but where 'resistance is overcome by force or violence' or where 'a person is prevented from resisting by threats of great and immediate bodily harm, accompanied by apparent power of execution. . . .'"

. . .

Section 261 was amended in 1980 to eliminate both the resistance requirement and the requirement that the threat of immediate bodily harm be accompanied by an apparent power to inflict the harm. . . . As the legislative history explains, "threat is eliminated and the victim need only fear harm. The standard for injury is reduced from great and immediate bodily harm to immediate and unlawful bodily injury."

. . .

In discussing the significance of the 1980 amendments in *Barnes,* we noted that "studies have demonstrated that while some women respond to sexual assault with active resistance, others 'freeze,' and 'become helpless from panic and numbing fear.'" (*Barnes, supra, 42 Cal.3d* at p. 299.) In response to this information, "For the first time, the Legislature has assigned the decision as to whether a sexual assault should be resisted to the realm of personal choice." (at p. 301.) "By removing resistance as a prerequisite to a rape conviction, the Legislature has brought the law of rape into conformity with other crimes such as robbery, kidnapping, and assault, which require force, fear, and nonconsent to convict. In these crimes, the law does not expect falsity from the complainant who alleges their commission and thus demand resistance as a corroboration and predicate to conviction." (at p. 302.)

. . .

The deletion of the resistance language from section 261 by the 1980 amendments thus effected a change in the purpose of evidence of fear of immediate and unlawful injury. Prior to 1980, evidence of fear was directly linked to resistance; the prosecution was required to demonstrate that a person's *resistance* had been overcome by force, or that a person was prevented from resisting by threats of great and immediate bodily harm. . . . As a result of the amendments, evidence of fear is now directly linked to the overbearing of a victim's will; the prosecution is required to demonstrate that the act of sexual intercourse was accomplished against the person's *will* by means of force, violence, or fear of immediate and unlawful bodily injury.

. . .

"[T]he trier of fact 'should be permitted to measure consent by weighing both the acts of the alleged attacker and the response of the alleged victim, rather than being required to focus on one or the other.'"

. . .

Thus, the element of fear of immediate and unlawful bodily injury has two components, one subjective and one objective. The subjective component asks whether a victim genuinely entertained a fear of immediate and unlawful bodily injury sufficient to induce her to submit to sexual intercourse against her will. In order to satisfy this component, the extent or seriousness of the injury feared is immaterial. . . .

In addition, the prosecution must satisfy the objective component, which asks whether the victim's fear was reasonable under the circumstances, or, if unreasonable, whether the perpetrator knew of the victim's subjective fear and took advantage of it. . . .

Applying these principles, we conclude that the evidence that the sexual intercourse was accomplished against Mercy's will by means of fear of immediate and unlawful bodily injury was sufficient to support the verdict in this case. First, there was substantial evidence that Mercy genuinely feared immediate and unlawful bodily injury. Mercy testified that she froze because she was afraid, and the investigating police officer testified that she told him she did not move because she feared defendant would do something violent.

. . .

Moreover, even absent the officer's testimony, the prosecution was not required to elicit from Mercy's testimony regarding what precisely she feared. "Fear" may be inferred from the circumstances despite even superficially contrary testimony of the victim.

. . .

In addition, immediately after the attack, Mercy was so distraught her friend Pam could barely understand her. Mercy hid in the bushes outside the house waiting for Pam to pick her up because she was terrified defendant would find her; she subsequently asked Pam if the word "rape" was written on her forehead, and had to be dissuaded from bathing prior to going to the hospital.

. . .

Second, there was substantial evidence that Mercy's fear of immediate and unlawful bodily injury was reasonable. The Court of Appeal's statements that defendant "did nothing to suggest that he intended to injure" Mercy, and that '[a]lthough the assailant was a stranger to the victim, she knew nothing about him which would suggest that he was violent'" ignores the import of the undisputed facts. Defendant, who weighed twice as much as Mercy, accosted her while she slept in the home of a close friend, thus violating the victim's enhanced level of security and privacy.

. . .

Defendant, who was naked, then removed Mercy's pants, fondled her buttocks, and inserted his penis into her vagina for approximately 1 minute, without warning, without her consent, and without a reasonable belief of consent. Any man or woman awakening to find himself or herself in this situation could reasonably react with fear of immediate and unlawful bodily injury. Sudden, unconsented-to groping, disrobing, and ensuing sexual intercourse while one appears to lie sleeping is an appalling and intolerable invasion of one's personal autonomy that, in and of itself, would reasonably cause one to react with fear.

. . .

The Court of Appeal's suggestion that Mercy could have stopped the sexual assault by screaming and thus eliciting Sandra, S.'s help, disregards both the Legislature's 1980 elimination of the resistance requirement and our express language in *Barnes* upholding that amendment. (*Barnes,*

supra, 42 Cal.3d at p. 302.) It effectively guarantees an attacker freedom to intimidate his victim and exploit any resulting reasonable fear so long as she neither struggles nor cries out.

. . .

The jury could reasonably have concluded that under the totality of the circumstances, this scenario, instigated and choreographed by defendant, created a situation in which Mercy genuinely and reasonably responded with fear of immediate and unlawful bodily injury, and that such fear allowed him to accomplish sexual intercourse with Mercy against her will.

CONCLUSION

The judgment of the Court of Appeal is reversed, and the case is remanded to that court for further proceedings consistent with this opinion.

IN RE T.A.J.

COURT OF APPEAL OF CALIFORNIA, FIRST APPELLATE DISTRICT, DIVISION TWO

62 CAL. APP. 4TH 1350; 73 CAL. RPTR. 2D 331

APRIL 9, 1998

OPINION BY: RUVOLO, J.

I.

Penal Code section 261.5, subdivision (b), makes it a misdemeanor for "any person" to have sexual intercourse with a minor who is no more than 3 years older or younger than the perpetrator. Does this statute infringe a constitutional privacy right of minors to engage in consensual sexual intercourse? Is the statute unconstitutional as applied to appellant who was a minor himself at the time of the alleged offense, and therefore, an individual within the class of persons protected by the statute? In affirming the finding of the trial court determining appellant to be a ward of the court, we answer both questions in the negative.

II.

A juvenile petition pursuant to *Welfare and Institutions Code section 602* was filed on April 22, 1996, charging appellant T.A.J. with misdemeanor statutory rape in violation of *Penal Code section 261.5,* subdivision (b). The petition alleged that 16-year-old T.A.J. engaged in an act of unlawful sexual intercourse with another minor no more than 3 years older or younger than himself on February 9, 1996. . . . A jurisdictional hearing was held on September 30 and October 2, 1996, at the conclusion of which the court found true the statutory rape allegation . . . This timely appeal was filed on November 19, 1996.

. . .

The incident out of which this case arises was an admitted act of sexual intercourse which occurred at the home of the 14-year-old female victim, T.P. The evidence need not be recounted in detail here. The disputed factual issue before the court at the jurisdictional hearing was simply whether that act was consensual. If consensual, appellant was at worst guilty of misdemeanor statutory rape (count 1,

violation of § 261.5, subd. (b)). If nonconsensual, appellant faced a true finding on the forcible rape charge (count 2, violation of § 261, subd. (a)(2)). As noted, the court found only count one true, and therefore concluded the admitted act was consensual. Appellant does not contest this factual finding on appeal.

Instead, appellant contends that section 261.5 n2 is unconstitutional both facially and as applied to him. His constitutional challenge to the statute rests on two arguments: first, that the statute violates his right to privacy guaranteed by the California Constitution, article I, section 1, and second, that the statute may not be constitutionally applied to him since he is a member of the "protected class" as defined by the statute. *(Cf. In re Meagan R. (1996) 42 Cal. App. 4th 17 {49 Cal. Rptr. 2d 325}.)* As a "victim," he may not also be prosecuted under the statute as a "perpetrator." For reasons set forth below, we reject both contentions.

n2 Section 261.5 states as follows:

"(a) Unlawful sexual intercourse is an act of sexual intercourse accomplished with a person who is not the spouse of the perpetrator, if the person is a minor. For the purposes of this section, a 'minor' is a person under the age of 18 years and an 'adult' is a person who is at least 18 years of age.

"(b) Any person who engages in an act of unlawful sexual intercourse with a minor who is not more than 3 years older or 3 years younger than the perpetrator, is guilty of a misdemeanor.

"(c) Any person who engages in an act of unlawful sexual intercourse with a minor who is more than 3 years younger than the perpetrator is guilty of either a misdemeanor or a felony, and shall be punished by imprisonment in a county jail not exceeding 1 year, or by imprisonment in the state prison."

. . .

III.

A.

We begin with an area of agreement between the parties. Both agree that minors, as well as adults, enjoy a right of privacy protected by the California Constitution in article I, section 1. That provision, which was amended significantly by the voters of California in 1972, states simply: "All people are by nature free and independent and have inalienable rights. Among these are enjoying and defending life and liberty, acquiring, possessing, and protecting property, and pursuing and obtaining safety, happiness, and privacy."

The parties diverge, however, in their respective views as to whether the right of privacy for minors is as extensive as it is for adults, and in particular whether minors' privacy rights include the right to engage in consensual sexual intercourse. n3 Appellant claims consensual sexual conduct is a core right of personal "autonomy" which attaches to all persons and which may be infringed by the Legislature only in the presence of a compelling state interest. Under the applicable test of "strict scrutiny," appellant urges no such compelling state interest exists sufficient to deprive him of his right to engage freely in consensual sexual conduct. Respondent retorts that the right of privacy enjoyed by minors has not been defined as broadly as it has for adults, and in many instances has specifically been limited. Therefore, respondent argues that the right of privacy applicable to minors does not encompass the right of minors to engage in consensual sexual intercourse with each other. Alternatively, respondent asserts that even if a right to engage in sex falls within a minor's right of privacy, there are indeed state interests which outweigh the limitation on that right imposed by section 261.5, subdivision (b).

> n3 Neither side disputes that adults have such a right under the California Constitution.

Undoubtedly, the most comprehensive analysis governing constitutional challenges under the state right of privacy is last year's Supreme Court opinion in *American Academy of Pediatrics v. Lungren* (1997) 16 Cal. 4th 307 {66 Cal. Rptr. 2d 210, 940 P.2d 797} (*American Academy*).

> n4 The majority recited its view as to the proper methodology to be employed when evaluating claims of the type asserted in this appeal, citing from *Hill v. National Collegiate Athletic Assn.* (1994) 7 Cal. 4th 1 {26 Cal. Rptr. 2d 834, 865 P.2d 633} (Hill): "'[A] plaintiff alleging an invasion of privacy in violation of the state constitutional right to privacy must establish each of the following: (1) a legally protected privacy interest; (2) a reasonable expectation of privacy in the circumstances; and (3) conduct by defendant constituting a serious invasion of privacy.' . . . 'A defendant may prevail in a state constitutional privacy case by negating any of the three elements just discussed or by pleading and proving, as an affirmative defense, that the invasion of privacy is justified because it substantively furthers one or more countervailing interests.'" . . .

B.

The plurality opinion in *American Academy* clearly enunciated that the precise issue before us today was not directly involved in that case: "The issue presented by this case, of course, does not concern any claim that a minor enjoys a constitutional right to engage in sexual activity, but rather concerns whether a minor who already has become pregnant has a constitutional right to determine whether she will continue or terminate her pregnancy." (*American Academy, supra,* 16 Cal. 4th at p. 335, fn. 19.)

Conversely, the question presented in this appeal does not visit issues of minors' rights to abortion, contraception, or parental permission relating to reproductive rights which were germane to the Supreme Court's analysis in American Academy. Nor is the issue here articulated as an unlawful restriction on procreation rights. (See *American Academy, supra,* 16 Cal. 4th at pp. 327–328.) To be sure, we need not, and do not, take any position with regard to these matters in this opinion. Instead, our devoir is limited to the question of the Legislature's prerogative to enact a law making it a crime for minors closely related in age to engage in sexual intercourse with each other.

. . .

The primary defense to appellant's constitutional attack on section 261.5 is that the rights of adults and minors are not "coterminous." Thus, respondent argues there are freedoms adults enjoy which are beyond those afforded minors, primarily because of age and maturity. We agree.

A long line of cases since 1972 have explained that California Constitution, article I's umbrella of individual freedoms provides less protection to minors from perceived inclement governmental intrusion than it does for adults. As noted by Justice Kennard in her concurring opinion in *American Academy:* "[T]he . . . concept of legal minority, or nonage, embodies an assumption of incompetence to exercise the full panoply of rights and privileges available to adults. Our laws have established various age restrictions for voting, driving motor vehicles, purchasing alcoholic beverages, and the like. Because individuals mature at different rates, these age limits are a necessarily inexact and therefore arbitrary measure of maturity, but they have nonetheless been accepted as constitutionally valid for most purposes. But not for all." (*American Academy, supra,* 16 Cal. 4th at pp. 372–373 (conc. opn. of Kennard, J.).)

Justice Brown in that same opinion embellished this theme of disparate constitutional entitlements for adults and children: "'[I]t has been of profound importance in all legal inquiries involving children that minors are presumed by all phases of the law (and by the culture reflected by our law) not to have the same basic capacities as adults.' . . . [M]inors are treated differently from adults in our laws, which reflects the simple truth derived from communal experience, that juveniles as a class have not the level of maturation and responsibility that we presume in adults and consider desirable for full participation in the rights and duties of modern life. ". . . The fact there may be exceptions only serves to validate this truism." (*American Academy, supra, 16 Cal. 4th* at pp. 429–430 (dis. opn. of Brown, J.).)

. . .

Although minors have privacy rights under article I, section 1, of the California Constitution, they do not have a constitutionally protected interest in engaging in sexual intercourse. While we do not ignore the reality that many California teenagers are sexually active, that fact alone does not establish that minors have a right of privacy to engage in sexual intercourse. We accept the premise that due to age and immaturity, minors often lack the ability to make fully informed choices that take account of both immediate and long-range consequences. While they may have the ability to respond to nature's call to exercise the gift of physical love, juveniles may yet be unable to accept the attendant obligations and responsibilities. For all of these reasons we conclude there is no privacy right among minors to engage in consensual sexual intercourse.

. . .

After considering the factors deemed important in *American Academy,* we conclude the reasonable expectation of privacy that was found to exist for minors to obtain an abortion cannot be imputed to their decision to engage in consensual sexual intercourse. Considering all the circumstances, we hold that a minor does not have a legitimate expectation of privacy to engage in consensual sexual activity with another minor. . . .

. . .

IV.

For the reasons stated in this opinion, the finding on the petition is affirmed.

KLINE, P. J., and HAERLE, J., concurred.

PEOPLE v. HERNANDEZ,

SUPREME COURT OF CALIFORNIA

61 Cal.2d 529, Crim. No. 7386,

July 9, 1964

OPINION BY: PEEK, J.

By information defendant was charged with statutory rape. (*Pen. Code, § 261*, subd. 1.) Following his plea of not guilty he was convicted as charged by the court sitting without a jury and the offense determined to be a misdemeanor.

Section 261 of the Penal Code provides in part as follows: "Rape is an act of sexual intercourse, accomplished with a female not the wife of the perpetrator, under either of the following circumstances: 1. Where the female is under the age of eighteen years: . . ."

The sole contention raised on appeal is that the trial court erred in refusing to permit defendant to present evidence going to his guilt for the purpose of showing that he had in good faith a reasonable belief that the prosecutrix was 18 years or more of age.

The undisputed facts show that the defendant and the prosecuting witness were not married and had been companions for several months prior to January 3, 1961–the date of the commission of the alleged offense. Upon that date the prosecutrix was 17 years and 9 months of age and voluntarily engaged in an act of sexual intercourse with defendant.

In support of his contention defendant relies upon *Penal Code, section 20*, which provides that "there must exist a union, or joint operation of act and intent, or criminal negligence" to constitute the commission of a crime. He further relies upon section 26 of that code which provides that one is not capable of committing a crime who commits an act under an ignorance or mistake of fact which disproves any criminal intent.

Thus the sole issue relates to the question of intent and knowledge entertained by the defendant at the time of the commission of the crime charged.

Consent of the female is often an unrealistic and unfortunate standard for branding sexual intercourse a crime as serious as forcible rape. Yet the consent standard has been deemed to be required by important policy goals. We are dealing here, of course, with statutory rape where, in one sense, the lack of consent of the female is not an element of the offense. In a broader sense, however, the lack of consent is deemed to remain an element but the law makes a conclusive presumption of the lack thereof because she is presumed too innocent and naive to understand the implications and nature of her act. (*People v. Griffin,* 117 Cal. 583, 585 [49 P. 711, 59 Am.St.Rep. 216]; *Golden v. Commonwealth,* 289 Ky. 379 [158 S.W.2d 967].) The law's concern with her capacity or lack thereof to so understand is explained in part by a popular conception of the social, moral and personal values which are preserved by the abstinence from sexual indulgence on the part of a young woman. An unwise disposition of her sexual favor is deemed to do harm both to herself and the social mores by which the community's conduct patterns are established. Hence the law of statutory rape intervenes in an effort to avoid such a disposition. This goal, moreover, is not accomplished by penalizing the naive female but by imposing criminal sanctions against the male, who is conclusively presumed to be responsible for the occurrence. (See *Elkins v. State,* 167 Tenn. 546 [72 S.W.2d 550].)

The assumption that age alone will bring an understanding of the sexual act to a young woman is of doubtful validity. Both learning from the cultural group to which she is a member and her actual sexual experiences will determine her level of comprehension. The sexually experienced 15-year-old may be far more acutely aware of the implications of sexual intercourse than her sheltered cousin who is beyond the age of consent. A girl who belongs to a group whose members indulge in sexual intercourse at an early age is likely to rapidly acquire an insight into the rewards and penalties of sexual indulgence. Nevertheless, even in circumstances where a girl's actual comprehension contradicts the law's presumption, the male is deemed criminally responsible for the act, although himself young and naive and responding to advances which may have been made to him.[FN1]

n1 The inequitable consequences to which we may be led are graphically illustrated by the following excerpt from

State v. Snow (Mo. 1923) 252 S.W. 629 at page 632: "We have in this case a condition and not a theory. This wretched girl was young in years but old in sin and shame. A number of callow youths, of otherwise blameless lives . . . fell under her seductive influence. They flocked about her, . . . like moths about the flame of a lighted candle and probably with the same result. The girl was a common prostitute. . . . The boys were immature and doubtless more sinned against than sinning. They did not defile the girl. She was a mere 'cistern for foul toads to knot and gender in.' Why should the boys, misled by her, be sacrificed? What sound public policy can be subserved by branding them as felons? Might it not be wise to ingraft an exception in the statute?"

The law as presently constituted does not concern itself with the relative culpability of the male and female participants in the prohibited sexual act. Even where the young woman is knowledgeable it does not impose sanctions upon her. The knowledgeable young man, on the other hand, is penalized and there are none who would claim that under any construction of the law this should be otherwise. However, the issue raised by the rejected offer of proof in the instant case goes to the culpability of the young man who acts *without* knowledge that an essential factual element exists and has, on the other hand, a positive, reasonable belief that it does not exist.

The primordial concept of *mens rea*, the guilty mind, expresses the principle that it is not conduct alone but conduct accompanied by certain specific mental states which concerns, or should concern, the law. In a broad sense the concept may be said to relate to such important doctrines as justification, excuse, mistake, necessity and mental capacity, but in the final analysis it means simply that there must be a "joint operation of act and intent," as expressed in *section 20 of the Penal Code,* to constitute the commission of a criminal offense. The statutory law, however, furnishes no assistance to the courts beyond that, and the casebooks are filled to overflowing with the courts' struggles to determine just what state of mind should be considered relevant in particular contexts. In numerous instances culpability has been completely eliminated as a necessary element of criminal conduct in spite of the admonition of *section 20* to the contrary. (See *In re Marley, 29 Cal.2d 525 {175 P.2d 832}* (shortweight); *People v. McClennegen, 195 Cal. 445 {234 P. 91}* (membership in organizations advocating criminal syndicalism); *People v. McCalla 63 Cal.App. 783 {220 P. 436}* (violation of Corporate Securities Act); *People v. Bickerstaff, 46 Cal.App. 764 {190 P. 656}* (sale of liquor).) More recently, however, this court has moved away from the imposition of criminal sanctions in the absence of culpability where the governing statute, by implication or otherwise, expresses no legislative intent or policy to be served by imposing strict liability. (*People v.*

Stuart, 47 Cal.2d 167 {302 P.2d 5, 55 A.L.R.2d 705}; People v. Vogel, 46 Cal.2d 798 {299 P.2d 850}; People v. Winston, 46 Cal.2d 151 {293 P.2d 40}.)

Statutory rape has long furnished a fertile battleground upon which to argue that the lack of knowledgeable conduct is a proper defense. The law in this state now rests, as it did in 1896, with this court's decision in *People v. Ratz, 115 Cal. 132,* where it is stated at pages 134 and 135 {46 P. 915}: "The claim here made is not a new one. It has frequently been pressed upon the attention of courts, but in no case, so far as our examination goes, has it met with favor. The object and purpose of the law are too plain to need comment, the crime too infamous to bear discussion. The protection of society, of the family, and of the infant, demand that one who has carnal intercourse under such circumstances shall do so in peril of the fact, and he will not be heard against the evidence to urge his belief that the victim of his outrage had passed the period which would make his act a crime." The age of consent at the time of the *Ratz* decision was 14 years, and it is noteworthy that the purpose of the rule, as there announced, was to afford protection to young females therein described as "infants." The decision on which the court in *Ratz* relied was *The Queen v. Prince,* L.R. 1 Crown Cas. 154. However England has now, by statute, departed from the strict rule, and excludes as a crime an act of sexual intercourse with a female between the ages of 13 and 16 years if the perpetrator is under the age of 24 years, has not previously been charged with a like offense, and believes the female "to be of the age of sixteen or over and has reasonable cause for the belief." (Halsburg's Statutes of England (2d ed.) vol. 36, Continuation Volume 1956, at p. 219.)[n2]

> [n2] The American Law Institute in its Model Penal Code (1962) provides in part as follows at pages 149 and 150: "Section 213.6. Provisions Generally Applicable (Article 213 [Sexual Offenses].)"(1) *Mistake as to Age.* Whenever in this Article the criminality of conduct depends upon a child's being below the age of 10, it is no defense that the actor did not know the child's age, or reasonably believed the child to be older than 10. When criminality depends upon the child's being below a critical age other than 10, it is a defense for the actor to prove that he reasonably believed the child to be above the critical age."

The rationale of the *Ratz* decision, rather than purporting to eliminate intent as an element of the crime, holds that the wrongdoer must assume the risk; that, subjectively, when the act is committed, he consciously intends to proceed regardless of the age of the female and the consequences of his act, and that the circumstances involving the female, whether she be a day or a decade less than the statutory age, are irrelevant.[n3] There can be no dispute that a criminal intent exists when the perpetrator proceeds with utter disregard of, or in the lack of grounds for, a belief that the female has reached the age of consent. But if he participates in a mutual act of sexual intercourse, believing his partner to be beyond the age of consent, with reasonable grounds for such belief, where is his criminal intent? In such circumstances he has not consciously taken any risk. Instead he has subjectively eliminated the risk by satisfying himself on reasonable evidence that the crime cannot be committed. If it occurs that he has been misled, we cannot realistically conclude that for such reason alone the intent with which he undertook the act suddenly becomes more heinous.

> n3 "When the law declares that sexual intercourse with a girl under the age of ten years is rape, it is not illogical to refuse to give any credence to the defense, 'I thought she was older, and I therefore did not believe that I was committing a crime when I had sexual intercourse with her.' . . . But when age limits are raised to sixteen, eighteen, and twenty-one, when the young girl becomes a young woman, when adolescent boys as well as young men are attracted to her, the sexual act begins to lose its quality of abnormality and physical danger to the victim. Bona fide mistakes in the age of girls can be made by men and boys who are no more dangerous than others of their social, economic and educational level. . . . Even if the girl looks to be much older than the age of consent fixed by the statute, even if she lies to the man concerning her age, if she is a day below the statutory age sexual intercourse with her is rape. The man or boy who has intercourse with such girl still acts at his peril. *The statute is interpreted as if it were protecting children under the age of ten.*" (Italics added.) (Plascowe, Sex and Law (1951) at pp. 184 and 185.)

While the specific contentions herein made have been dealt with and rejected both within and without this state, the courts have uniformly failed to satisfactorily explain the nature of the criminal intent present in the mind of one who in good faith believes he has obtained a lawful consent before engaging in the prohibited act. As in the *Ratz* case the courts often justify convictions on policy reasons which, in effect, eliminate the element of intent. The Legislature, of course, by making intent an element of the crime, has established the prevailing policy from which it alone can properly advise us to depart.

We have recently given recognition to the legislative declarations in *section 20* and *26 of the Penal Code,* and departed from prior decisional law which had failed to accord full effect to those sections as applied to charges of bigamy. (*People v. Vogel, supra, 46 Cal.2d 798.*) We held there that a good faith belief that a former wife had obtained a divorce was a valid defense to a charge of bigamy arising out of a second marriage when the first marriage had not in fact been terminated. Pertinent to the instant contention that defendant's intent did not suddenly become more criminal because it later developed that he had been misled by the prosecutrix, are the following

comments appearing in *Vogel* at page 804: "Nor would it be reasonable to hold that a person is guilty of bigamy who remarries in good faith in reliance on a judgment of divorce or annulment that is subsequently found not to be the 'judgment of a competent court.' . . . Since it is often difficult for laymen to know when a judgment is not that of a competent court, we cannot reasonably expect them always to have such knowledge and make them criminals if their bona fide belief proves to be erroneous." Certainly it cannot be a greater wrong to entertain a bona fide but erroneous belief that a valid consent to an act of sexual intercourse has been obtained.

Equally applicable to the instant case are the following remarks, also appearing at page 804 of the *Vogel* decision: "The severe penalty imposed for bigamy, the serious loss of reputation conviction entails, . . . and the fact that it has been regarded for centuries as a crime involving moral turpitude, make it extremely unlikely that the Legislature meant to include the morally innocent to make sure the guilty did not escape."

We are persuaded that the reluctance to accord to a charge of statutory rape the defense of a lack of criminal intent has no greater justification than in the case of other statutory crimes, where the Legislature has made identical provision with respect to intent. "'At common law an honest and reasonable belief in the existence of circumstances, which, if true, would make the act for which the person is indicted an innocent act, has always been held to be a good defense. . . . So far as I am aware it has never been suggested that these exceptions do not equally apply to the case of statutory offenses unless they are excluded expressly or by necessary implication.'" (*Matter of Application of Ahart, 172 Cal. 762, 764-765 {159 P. 160},* quoting from *Regina v. Tolson, {1889} 23 Q.B.D. 168, s.c., 40 Alb.L.J. 250.*) Our departure from the views expressed in *Ratz* is in no manner indicative of a withdrawal from the sound policy that it is in the public interest to protect the sexually naive female from exploitation. No responsible person would hesitate to condemn as untenable a claimed good faith belief in the age of consent of an "infant" female whose obviously tender years preclude the existence of reasonable grounds for that belief. However, the prosecutrix in the instant case was but three months short of 18 years of age and there is nothing in the record to indicate that the purposes of the law as stated in *Ratz* can be better served by foreclosing the defense of a lack of intent. This is not to say that the granting of consent by even a sexually sophisticated girl known to be less than the statutory age is a defense.n4 We hold only that, in the absence of a legislative direction otherwise, a charge of statutory rape is defensible wherein a criminal intent is lacking.

> n4 See an article on forcible and statutory rape in *62 Yale Law Journal* (1952) which concludes at page 82 as follows: "The crime of statutory rape is unsupportable in its present form. Neither the policies underlying the law nor public

sentiment warrants the imposition of rape penalties solely because of the girl's youth. By making the presumption of the underage girl's incapacity rebuttal, [rebuttable] the law would continue to protect the 'naive.' But although legally underage, the girl who is past puberty and sexually sophisticated would be capable of granting operative consent to sexual intercourse."

For the foregoing reasons *People v. Ratz, supra, 115 Cal. 132,* and *People v. Griffin, supra, 117 Cal. 583* are overruled, and *People v. Sheffield, 9 Cal.App. 130 {98 P. 67}* is disapproved to the extent that such decisions are inconsistent with the views expressed herein.

Some question has been raised that the offer of proof of defendant's reasonable belief in the age of the prosecutrix was insufficient to justify the pleading of such belief as a defense to the act. It is not our purpose here to make a determination that the defendant entertained a reasonable belief. Suffice to state that the offer demonstrated a sufficient basis upon which, when fully developed, the trier of fact might have found in defendant's favor. We conclude that it was reversible error to reject the offer.

The judgment is reversed.

GIBSON, C. J., TRAYNOR, J., SCHAUER, J., MCCOMB, J., PETERS, J., and TOBRINER, J., concurred.

PEOPLE v. HILL

COURT OF APPEAL OF CALIFORNIA, SECOND APPELLATE DISTRICT, DIVISION FOUR

103 CAL. APP. 3D 525; 163 CAL. RPTR. 99

MARCH 19, 1980

OPINION BY: JEFFERSON, J.

In count I of an information, defendant was charged with the felony offense of pimping, committed on January 27, 1978, in violation of Penal Code section 266h. It was alleged that the pimping offense had been committed by defendant in knowing that Eugene Griswald was a prostitute and then willfully and unlawfully living and deriving support and maintenance in whole and in part from the earnings and proceeds of Griswald's prostitution. In count II of the information, defendant was charged with the felony offense of pandering, committed on the same date in violation of section 266i of the Penal Code. It was alleged that the offense of pandering was committed by the defendant willfully and unlawfully procuring Eugene Griswald, a male person, for purposes of prostitution.

Defendant entered a plea of not guilty and was tried by a jury. The jury found defendant guilty as charged in both counts of the information. Proceedings were suspended and defendant was granted probation for 3 years subject to certain specified terms and conditions including spending the first 90 days in county jail. Defendant has appealed from this judgment of conviction.

Defendant primarily advances two contentions with respect to errors committed below. One contention is that the jury instructions given by the court were inadequate and erroneous and that the trial court had a duty, *sua sponte,* to give adequate instructions. The second contention advanced by defendant is to the effect that he received inadequate assistance of counsel by reason of the failure of defense counsel to request any instructions at all or to object to the erroneous and inadequate instructions given.

I. THE FACTUAL BACKGROUND

On the date in question, Peter Waack was a member of the Los Angeles Police Department and was working as an undercover vice officer. Upon receiving certain information from Police Officer Samprone, Waack looked at an advertisement in the Advocate newspaper, a publication sold in newspaper vending machines, adult book stores and adult theaters. The advertisement started off with the phrase, "warm, wet and wild," and stated the name "Don" with a phone number listed for a nude photograph. About 7:30 p.m., Waack called the phone number indicated in the advertisement. The phone was answered and Waack stated he wanted to speak to Don. The individual answering the phone said that he was Don. Waack indicated that his name was Peter; Don's response was "[oh], yes, Tim had told me you were going to call."

Don then asked Waack if he was interested in obtaining a young 15-year-old boy. Waack said he was interested. Don indicated that it was expensive and would cost $300. Waack replied that the price was satisfactory. Waack advised Don that he was staying at the Marriott hotel at the airport and gave Don his room number and telephone number. Don indicated that he had a friend that he would bring to Waack's hotel room that evening.

Around 9 p.m., the phone rang in Waack's room at the Marriott hotel. Waack answered and the caller identified himself as Don. Waack recognized the voice as being the same as the voice in the earlier telephone call to the number contained in the advertisement. Don indicated that he would have to drive to the valley to pick up his friend who was named Gene. Don said that he would bring Gene to Waack's room, but it would be at approximately 11 p.m. About 11 p.m., the phone rang in Waack's room and the voice on the other end of the phone again identified himself as Don and said that he would be there in about 30 minutes.

Shortly thereafter there was a knock on Waack's door. Waack opened the door and the individual at the door stated that he was Don. Waack identified Don as Donald Hill, the defendant. Defendant entered the room and requested the $300. Waack indicated that he would not pay the money until he saw the individual who was to be brought to him, fearing otherwise that it would be a rip-off. Defendant told Waack that his friend Gene knew what he would be required to do and that he knew what to do sexually, but that he did not care for S & M n1 and beatings.

n1 Officer Waack testified that the term "S and M" referred to sadism and masochism.

Defendant then left and returned shortly with a young man who was introduced as Gene, whose true name was Eugene Griswald. It was established that Griswald was 17 years of age at the time. Griswald sat in a chair while defendant and Waack went into the bathroom. Waack testified that he again stated his qualms to defendant about being ripped off and that defendant told him not to worry, that Gene knew what to do sexually but simply didn't care for S & M and the beatings. Waack and defendant then returned to the room and, in the presence of Griswald, Waack handed $300 to defendant. Defendant then left, stating that he would be back after 1 hour to pick up Gene.

After defendant left, Waack asked Griswald what he would do, and Griswald replied that he would engage in an act of oral copulation and an act of sodomy. Griswald then started to get undressed. By prearranged signals, other officers who were in the hotel came forth and arrested defendant in the hallway, and then came into Waack's room and placed Griswald under arrest.

Defendant's defense was to the effect that he had received a telephone call from Tim Stiller before Waack's call, indicating that Stiller had a friend named Peter who was staying at the Marriott hotel and that defendant should send over someone young-looking that would be used as a model for a photo session and nothing else. Defendant then called Griswald for the purpose of having him be a nude model for photographs to be taken by Peter. Defendant denied telling Waack that Gene knew what to do sexually. Defendant stated that he told Griswald over the phone that he was wanted for a nude photo session and would receive $40 for his services as a model.

Griswald was called as a witness by the prosecutor and testified that defendant had called him to be a model for photographs to be taken in the nude. Officer Samprone testified that, after his arrest, Griswald waived his *Miranda* rights and stated that, when defendant called him and said he had a job for him, it meant that he was to have sex with someone in the hotel room. Officer Samprone also testified that Griswald stated that he was to receive $40 for his services that evening.

II. THE QUESTION OF WHETHER THE INSTRUCTIONS WERE ERRONEOUS AND INADEQUATE

A. THE INSTRUCTIONS RELATING TO THE OFFENSE OF PIMPING

The trial judge gave the following instruction defining the offense of pimping: "Every person who, knowing another person is a prostitute, lives, or derives support or maintenance in whole or in part from the earnings or proceeds of such person's prostitution, or who solicits or receives compensation for soliciting for such person, is guilty of pimping." This instruction was substantially in the language of Penal Code section 266h. n2

n2 Penal Code section 266h provides: "Any person who, knowing another person is a prostitute, lives or derives support or maintenance in whole or in part from the earnings or proceeds of such person's prostitution, or from money loaned or advanced to or charged against such person by any keeper or manager or inmate of a house or other place where prostitution is practiced or allowed, or who solicits or receives compensation for soliciting for such person, is guilty of pimping, a felony, and is punishable by imprisonment in the state prison for 2, 3, or 4 years."

In addition, the court gave an instruction defining the term "prostitution"—used in Penal Code section 266h without explanation—as including "sexual intercourse, sodomy, oral copulation, *or other lewd or dissolute acts between persons* in return for money or other consideration." (Italics added.) The trial court also gave instructions defining oral copulation and sodomy. However, no instruction was given defining "other lewd or dissolute acts"—the terms used in the instruction defining "prostitution."

Defendant advances the argument that the instruction defining pimping was misleading. Defendant asserts that the instruction defining the offense of pimping was so ambiguous that the jury may well have considered that the offense of pimping had been committed if the only act committed by defendant was that of soliciting a customer for Griswald without receiving any compensation for such solicitation or attempting to receive any compensation therefore.

Defendant makes reference to the phrase in the instruction that one commits the offense of pimping "who solicits or receives compensation for soliciting for such person" (a prostitute). In *People v. Smith (1955) 44 Cal.2d 77, 79,* the court points out that this phrase is properly interpreted to limit commission of the offense of pimping through solicitation to a "soliciting compensation for soliciting for a prostitute, and not by merely soliciting a customer." Undoubtedly, the jury in the case at bench might well have interpreted the pimping instruction given by the trial court as creating an offense for merely soliciting a customer for Griswald without receiving or expecting compensation.

It was thus error for the trial court not to expand upon the pimping instruction by pointing out that, for soliciting a customer for a prostitute to constitute the offense of pimping, a defendant had to solicit compensation for his service of solicitation. But in the instant case, as in the

Smith case, the evidence clearly established that defendant received compensation for any solicitation of the customer Waack for Griswald as a prostitute. Hence, the failure of the trial court to further define the offense of pimping constituted a nonprejudicial error.

There was little danger in the case at bench that the jury would consider that the prosecution had established the first alternative of the pimping offense against defendant—that defendant was a person who, with knowledge that Griswald was a prostitute, lived, or derived support from the earnings of Griswald's prostitution. Defendant urges us to accept the view that the trial judge's instruction on this aspect of pimping should have set forth the following specifics: to constitute the offense it had to be established (1) that Griswald was a prostitute; (2) that defendant knew Griswald was a prostitute; (3) that Griswald made some earnings from prostitution; (4) that defendant derived some financial benefit from Griswald's prostitution; and (5) that defendant knew that the money he received from Waack constituted proceeds from Griswald's earnings from prostitution. This view urged by defendant presents unacceptable reasoning, even though *People v. Tipton (1954) 124 Cal.App.2d 213, 217–218 {268 P.2d 196},* set forth these five elements as constituting the first alternative of the pimping statute. The prosecution's evidence in the case at bench obviously was geared to the solicitation alternative of the offense, rather than the deriving-of-earnings alternative.

. . .

Although no instruction was given by the trial court with respect to the meaning of "prostitution" other than that it included sexual intercourse, sodomy, oral copulation, or "other lewd or dissolute acts between persons in return for money or other consideration," the issue remains of whether the failure of the trial court to give any such instruction constituted prejudicial error, an issue we shall discuss subsequently herein.

. . .

III. WAS THERE A DUTY ON THE PART OF THE COURT, SUA SPONTE, TO INSTRUCT ON THE DEFENSE THEORY OF THE CASE?

Defendant advances the contention that the trial court had a duty, *sua sponte,* to give an instruction to the jury on the defense theory of the case, and that it was error for the trial court not to give such an instruction. The defense presented by defendant was that he had procured Griswald for Officer Waack—not for the purpose of prostitution—but for the purpose of nude modeling for photographs. As we have pointed out herein, nude modeling for photographic purposes, which involves no bodily contact between model and photographer, does not fall within the concept of prostitution. Such conduct by the model cannot be deemed a "lewd" act between persons for money in light of the views of the California Supreme Court set forth in the Pryor case.

Defendant relies upon *People v. Sedeno (1974) 10 Cal.3d 703 {112 Cal. Rptr. 1, 518 P.2d 913},* in which the court set forth the principles for determining when the trial court has a duty to instruct, sua sponte, on a theory raised by the defense.

. . .

The trial court should have instructed the jury that nude modeling does not constitute an act of prostitution and that an act of procuring a person solely for the purpose of nude modeling does not violate either the pimping or pandering statute. In the absence of such an instruction, the jury might well consider defendant's evidence—even though different from the prosecution's evidence—as itself amounting to the commission of the crimes charged. We hold, therefore, that defendant's defense evidence required the trial court, sua sponte, to give such an instruction. Such an instruction was "necessary for the jury's understanding of the case." (*People v. St. Martin (1970) 1 Cal.3d 524, 531 {83 Cal. Rptr. 166, 463 P.2d 390}.)*

Since the errors we have discussed herein are such that it is reasonably probable that a result more favorable to defendant would have been reached had not such errors been made . . .

. . .

The judgment is reversed.

COURT OF APPEAL, FIRST DISTRICT, DIVISION 3, CALIFORNIA.

58 CAL. APP. 4TH 1113, NO. A073612.

OCTOBER 29, 1997

OPINION BY: PARRILLI, J.

In the published portion of this case, we hold that *Penal Code section 236* is neither unconstitutionally vague nor overbroad.

A jury convicted appellant Frank Greg Bamba of one count of assault with a deadly weapon (a van) (*Pen. Code, § 245, subd. (a)(1)),n1* one count of felony false imprisonment (§§ 236/237), and one count of possessing methamphetamine (*Health & Saf. Code, § 11377, subd. (a)*). The jury further found appellant had personally used a deadly weapon in committing the assault.

> n1 Subsequent statutory references are to the Penal Code, unless otherwise noted. In a bifurcated trial, the court found appellant had suffered two prior robbery convictions which constituted strikes under the "Three Strikes" law. (*§ 1170.12,* subd. (c)(2).) At sentencing, the court reduced the assault with a deadly weapon and methamphetamine possession charges to misdemeanors. Nevertheless, the court sentenced appellant to 25 years to life under the Three Strikes law based on the current felony false imprisonment conviction and appellant's 2 prior robbery convictions (*§ 1170.12,* subd. (c)(2). This timely appeal followed.

Appellant raises numerous arguments on appeal. His chief contentions are: . . . (2) the evidence does not support his conviction for *felony* false imprisonment (which requires evidence he effected the false imprisonment by "violence, menace, fraud or deceit" (*§ 237*)); . . . and (4) we must remand for resentencing under *People v. Superior Court (Romero) (1996) 13 Cal.4th 497 {53 Cal.Rptr.2d 789, 917 P.2d 628} (Romero)*. We remand to permit the trial court to exercise its authority to strike one or more of the prior convictions pursuant to *Romero*, but otherwise affirm the judgment.

I. FACTS

On Friday, May 26, 1995, appellant and the victim, Elizabeth Albertini, ended their five-month romantic relationship. Although they fought during the breakup, Albertini spent the night with appellant at his father's Belmont apartment. Appellant stayed up all night smoking methamphetamine.

The next morning, Saturday, May 27, appellant was angry and paranoid. He hallucinated his parole officer was outside the apartment. Appellant would not let Albertini leave the apartment.

About noon, however, appellant and Albertini left in his van. The van contained all of Albertini's possessions. They stopped at a convenience store where appellant returned some rental videos and Albertini bought cigarettes.

When Albertini returned to the van, appellant began backing it directly toward her. Albertini grabbed onto the spare tire attached to the back of the van because she "didn't want to get run over." She yelled at appellant to stop and he yelled back at her. Appellant did not stop; instead, he drove out of the parking lot and headed down Ralston Road toward Highway 101. Albertini, who was on the back of the van, continued to yell at appellant to stop, but he continued driving. Appellant shouted at Albertini: "I am going to kill you, Liz."

Appellant entered southbound Highway 101 at Ralston Avenue. Albertini estimated he reached speeds of 55 to 80 miles per hour on the freeway. After appellant got onto the freeway, Albertini managed to climb onto the roof of the van to a skylight which she had opened earlier when she was inside the vehicle. She tore off the skylight cover because she thought she could enter the van through that opening, but a metal bar blocked it. Albertini grabbed onto the metal bar to keep from falling off the roof. As appellant drove down the freeway, Albertini lay facedown on the top of the van, with her arms stretched above her head and her feet dangling off the back of the van.

At some point appellant slowed down. He yelled at Albertini through the skylight to get off the van. Albertini said she would if he stopped the van. Appellant exited the freeway and drove into a parking lot off Woodside Road in

Redwood City. In the parking lot, appellant repeatedly swerved under some low trees which scratched Albertini. Appellant then briefly stopped in the parking lot and threw most of Albertini's belongings (including her identification) out of the van.

According to Albertini, she tried to get off the van while appellant was unloading it in the parking lot. However, appellant left the engine running and every time Albertini attempted to get off the roof, appellant jumped back in and moved the van. After he unloaded Albertini's belongings, appellant raced out of the parking lot and reentered Highway 101, this time going the opposite direction (northbound).

Eventually, appellant stopped on the shoulder of Highway 101 near Holly Street. Albertini did not get off the van, however, because she was afraid if she tried appellant would take off and slam on the brakes. She again asked appellant to turn off the van.

Shortly thereafter, a Highway Patrol vehicle pulled behind the van as it was parked by the side of Highway 101. Albertini got off the van when she saw the officers. According to the responding officers, Albertini was shaking, her face was streaked with tears, she was disheveled, and she had numerous scratches and bruises. The police arrested appellant. During his booking search, the police discovered a plastic bag containing methamphetamine and a small glass pipe hidden on appellant's person.

Before trial, appellant contacted Albertini and tried to dissuade her from testifying. Albertini was, in fact, reluctant to testify at trial and the district attorney had her arrested the day before trial to ensure she would appear in court.

DEFENSE

Appellant testified in his own behalf. He claimed he thought he left Albertini in the convenience store parking lot when he first drove off. He did not know she was on his vehicle until he pulled over on the freeway near Woodside Road. He claimed Albertini got off of the van when he stopped in the parking lot in Redwood City. He did not realize she had climbed back onto the van until he returned to the freeway. He then pulled over to the side of the freeway and the Highway Patrol arrived about an hour later.

Appellant said he had been trying to leave Albertini for several weeks unsuccessfully. He denied trying to dislodge Albertini from the top of his vehicle. He claimed he drove the vehicle safely until he could find an area where Albertini could get down safely.

Based on this evidence, the jury convicted appellant of felony false imprisonment, assault with a deadly weapon, and possession of methamphetamine.

. . .

Section 236 provides: "False imprisonment is the unlawful violation of the personal liberty of another."

. . .

B. SUBSTANTIAL EVIDENCE SUPPORTS THE FELONY FALSE IMPRISONMENT CONVICTION.

(7a) Appellant next contends the evidence is insufficient to support his conviction for felony false imprisonment because there is no evidence he effected the false imprisonment by "violence" or "menace." *(§ 237.)* We disagree.

Again, the essential element of false imprisonment is restraint of the person. Any exercise of express or implied force which compels another person to remain where he does not wish to remain, or to go where he does not wish to go, is false imprisonment. *(People v. Fernandez (1994) 26 Cal.App.4th 710, 717 {31 Cal.Rptr.2d 677}.)* False imprisonment is a felony if it is effected by violence or menace. *(§ 237.)*

Here, there is no question the evidence is sufficient to show appellant forced Albertini to remain where she did not wish to remain, or to go where she did not wish to go. The evidence established appellant knew Albertini was on the roof of the van but refused to stop to let her off, despite her pleas to do so. The remaining question is whether there is substantial evidence of violence or menace. We conclude there is.

. . .

In the context of *section 237,* "violence" means " 'the exercise of physical force used to restrain over and above the force reasonably necessary to effect such restraint.'" *(People v. Babich (1993) 14 Cal.App.4th 801, 806 {18 Cal.Rptr.2d 60},* quoting CALJIC No. 9.60, italics omitted.) In this context, "menace" means " 'a threat of harm express or implied by word or by act.'" *(People v. Babich, supra, 14 Cal.App.4th 801, 806,* quoting CALJIC No. 9.60.) Here, there was substantial evidence of both violence and menace. With respect to violence, the "physical force" appellant used to effect the false imprisonment—the driving of the vehicle—was greater than the force necessary to effect the restraint. Albertini stayed on the van primarily because she was afraid to get off while it was moving. It is likely appellant could have caused Albertini to remain on the vehicle if he had obeyed the speed limit and driven safely. However, there was evidence appellant drove as fast as 80 miles per hour on the freeway and purposefully swerved his vehicle, thus increasing the danger to Albertini. Thus, the "force" appellant used to keep appellant on top of the van was greater than that reasonably necessary to effect her restraint, and increased the danger to her.

There is also substantial evidence of menace—that is, a threat of harm express or implied. Here, appellant expressly told Albertini he intended to kill her. In addition, Albertini claimed she first got on the van in order to prevent appellant from running her over. Thus, the clear implication of this verbal threat and assault was that, if Albertini did try to get down, appellant might again try to hit her with the van. Consequently, a reasonable trier of fact could conclude this was part of the reason Albertini was afraid to get off the van even when it came to a standstill. It follows there is substantial evidence appellant effected the false imprisonment at least in part through an implied or express threat of harm.

Substantial evidence supports the felony false imprisonment conviction.

. . .

III. DISPOSITION

The judgment is vacated and this matter is remanded to the trial court for the limited purpose of allowing the trial court to exercise its discretion pursuant to *Romero*. "If, on remand, the trial court . . . decides to exercise its discretion to strike [one or both of] the prior felony conviction allegations in furtherance of justice ..., the court must set forth the reasons for that decision in strict compliance with *section 1385(a)*. Any such decision will be reviewable for abuse of discretion according to the procedures generally applicable to such decisions." (*Romero, supra, 13 Cal.4th* at p. 532.) In all other respects, the judgment is affirmed.

CORRIGAN, Acting P. J., and WALKER, J. concurred.

PEOPLE v. AISPURO

COURT OF APPEAL, FIFTH DISTRICT, CALIFORNIA

157 CAL.APP.4TH 1509, No. F052506

DECEMBER 18, 2007
REVIEW DENIED MARCH 26, 2008

OPINION BY: KANE, J.

A jury found defendant not guilty of kidnapping (*Pen.Code, § 207*, subd. (a)), as alleged in counts 1 and 2 of an amended information, and found him guilty of false imprisonment by violence or menace *(Pen.Code, § 236)* as alleged in counts 3 and 4 of the amended information. He was sentenced to the middle term of two years' imprisonment for count 3 to run consecutively to eight months' imprisonment for count 4. Time credits were awarded, and fines and fees were imposed.

The sole ground of appeal is defendant's contention that there was insufficient evidence of menace and violence to support the convictions for felony false imprisonment. Defendant urges this court to modify the judgment to reflect convictions for misdemeanor false imprisonment and requests that the court remand the matter to the trial court for resentencing.n1

> n1. The jury was instructed on misdemeanor false imprisonment as a lesser offense.

. . .

The jury found defendant guilty of two counts of false imprisonment by violence or menace within the meaning of *Penal Code section 236.* The jury was instructed that in order for defendant to be guilty of the crime of false imprisonment by violence or menace, the People must prove that defendant "intentionally restrained or confined or detained someone or caused that person to be restrained or confined or detained by violence or menace" and "defendant made the other person stay or go somewhere against that person's will." They were told that "Violence means using physical force that is greater than the force reasonably necessary to restrain someone" and that "Menace means a verbal or physical threat of harm. The threat of harm may be express or implied." The jury was further instructed that an act is done against a person's will if that person does not consent to the act. In order to consent, a person must act freely and voluntarily and know the nature of the act. *(CALCRIM No. 1240.)*

Defendant does not contest the propriety or accuracy of the instructions given to the jury. Defendant's sole contention is that the evidence was insufficient to justify the jury's finding that defendant falsely imprisoned the victims by menace or violence.

On March 10, 2006, G., age 13, and her sister, A., age 9, walked to school. They became aware of defendant when they saw him knocking on the front door of a house. He then asked the girls if they knew the time. As the girls approached a street corner, G. heard defendant ask her where she was going. G. then heard rapid footsteps and felt defendant grab the hood of her jacket, which covered her head. The girls stopped walking and defendant held the hood of her jacket. G. began to cry and asked him to let go and not to hurt her. He did not respond to her request that he not hurt her. Defendant then told the girls he wanted them to sit in the middle of the road. When G. told him no, he said "If you don't, then I will do something." Both girls were crying at that time. He continued to hold onto G.'s hood.

A. testified as they walked he placed his hands behind each of the girls and A. felt his hand on her back. They walked across the road, but did not stop in the middle of the street as he had requested. When he and the girls reached the other side of the street, A. said she wanted her mother. Defendant held her in both arms and said, "It's okay." G. still felt threatened. A. testified that she did not feel better and remained frightened. Defendant asked G. to take off her jacket and she complied. G. said several times, "Please let us go." G. tried to pull A. away from defendant. Defendant then said, "Just leave." The girls ran away and he did not pursue them.

Defendant contends that the conviction for felony false imprisonment cannot stand because the evidence is insufficient to support a finding that he used menace or violence. He concedes there is sufficient evidence that he committed two counts of misdemeanor false imprisonment and requests the court to modify the judgment to reflect convictions for the lesser offenses. *(People v. Matian (1995)*

35 Cal.App.4th 480, 488, 41 Cal.Rptr.2d 459 (Matian); People v. Castro (2006) 138 Cal.App.4th 137, 144, 41 Cal.Rptr.3d 190.) It is unnecessary to address the question of whether the evidence supports a finding that these crimes were carried out with violence because the record sufficiently justifies a finding of menace.

Menace is defined as "a verbal or physical threat of harm. The threat of harm may be express or implied." *(CALCRIM No. 1240.)* In reviewing the whole record in the light most favorable to the judgment *(People v. Johnson, supra, 26 Cal.3d at p. 562, 162 Cal.Rptr. 431, 606 P.2d 738),* substantial evidence exists from which a reasonable trier of fact could have found defendant falsely imprisoned these victims with an express or implied threat of harm based on words or conduct.

Defendant accosted these two young girls, laid his hands on them, caused them to cry, did not respond to their requests that he not hurt them, ordered them to sit in the middle of the street and when they initially resisted, told them "If you don't, then I will do something." These words alone, in context, constituted evidence of an implied, if not express, threat to harm them. The fact that he did not respond to them when they asked him not to hurt them is additional evidence that his words constituted a threat. There was ample evidence of menace to support the convictions for felony false imprisonment.

Defendant cites *Matian, supra, 35 Cal.App.4th 480, 41 Cal.Rptr.2d 459,* in support of his contention that at most these facts support misdemeanor false imprisonment. In *Matian,* the defendant sexually assaulted the victim and thereafter grabbed her arm and yelled at her not to leave. She sat in a chair while the defendant went into a nearby office where he could see the victim. Each time she rose from her chair, he glared at her and got out of his chair to approach her. The appellate court held that this evidence was inadequate to establish an express or implied threat of harm because there were no verbal threats of additional physical harm nor was there evidence to suggest that the defendant raised his fist or otherwise made any threatening movements suggesting harm each time the victim got out of her chair to leave.

We disagree with the *Matian* court's conclusion that such facts were inadequate to establish an express or implied threat of harm. In our view, the *Matian* court erroneously required evidence of a deadly weapon or an express verbal threat of additional physical harm before menace could be found. (See also *People v. Castro, supra, 138 Cal.App.4th at p. 143, 41 Cal.Rptr.3d 190* [disagreeing with the result in *Matian*].) An express or implied threat of harm does not require the use of a deadly weapon or an express verbal threat to do additional harm. Threats can be exhibited in a myriad number of ways, verbally and by conduct. There can be no doubt that Matian's conduct constituted a threat of harm to his victim, even though he did not specifically say to the victim, "If you leave I'm going to physically harm you," and even though he did not raise his fist or display a deadly weapon.

Our case is also factually distinguishable from *Matian* in that defendant herein verbally threatened the girls ("If you don't, then I will do something"). He had his hand on one of the girls' hoods at the time. He was an adult. They were young girls. They were crying. When asked not to hurt them, he did not reply giving them assurance that he would not. Clearly on this record, the evidence supports a finding that he falsely imprisoned the girls by menace.

DISPOSITION

The judgment is affirmed.

We concur: LEVY, Acting P.J., and HILL, J.

PEOPLE v. MOYA et al.

COURT OF APPEAL OF CALIFORNIA, FOURTH APPELLATE DISTRICT, DIVISION TWO

4 Cal. App. 4th 912; 6 Cal. Rptr. 2d 323

March 17, 1992

OPINION BY: HOLLENHORST, ACTING P. J.

After a jury trial, all three defendants, Rigoberto Salazar Angulo (Rigo), Jose Manuel Moya (Moya) and Blanca Angulo-Rodriguez (Blanca), were found guilty of kidnapping for ransom (*Pen. Code, § 209,* subd. (a) . . . and conspiracy to commit kidnapping for ransom. (*§ 182, 209.*) Blanca was also convicted of one count of burglary. (*§ 459.*) . . . Defendants were each sentenced to life with possibility of parole for the conspiracy and kidnapping counts. With respect to Rigo and Moya the court ordered the life sentences for the kidnapping and conspiracy counts to run concurrently. The court, acting pursuant to section 654, stayed the life sentence on the conspiracy charge in sentencing Blanca but imposed an upper term of 6 years for the burglary charge to run concurrently with her life sentence on the kidnapping charge.

. . .

On appeal, defendants raised the following issues: . . . the court failed to instruct on all of the elements of simple kidnapping . . .We affirm the judgments of convictions, reject their contentions of cruel and unusual punishment. . . . Accordingly we will direct the trial court to prepare amended abstracts of judgment.

FACTS

On March 30, 1989, Aurora Imelda Corrales (Imelda) lived in Riverside with her husband and children, including her four-and-one-half-year-old daughter, Adriana. Around noon that day, Imelda's sister, Blanca, came to the house with her children. Shortly after arriving, Blanca and/or her daughter Vanessa went back down to the car to get a diaper bag. Imelda's children, including Adriana, went outside also. Approximately 15 minutes later, Imelda noticed that Adriana was missing. Imelda was extremely upset and eventually called the police. Blanca appeared unconcerned.

Sometime around 3 p.m. the same day, Imelda received a telephone call from a man stating that he had the child and would return her in exchange for $5,000. The man said he

would call back around 6 p.m. Imelda thought the man sounded like either Moya or Rigo trying to disguise his voice.

Imelda told the police about a dispute she had with Blanca and Moya about some missing money. Blanca and Moya had accused Imelda of taking the money and Imelda had denied it. Blanca told Imelda that she would do "whatever it takes" to find out if Imelda had the money.

The police eventually brought the defendants in for questioning. After questioning Blanca's daughter Vanessa, the police questioned Blanca. Blanca initially denied any involvement in the kidnapping of Adriana but eventually admitted that she knew where Adriana was and took the police to Rosemarie Diaz's house in El Monte where the police recovered Adriana at approximately 2:30 a.m.

During police interrogation, Blanca and Moya admitted there had been a dispute with Imelda about missing money. All three defendants eventually admitted their involvement in the incident but gave varying explanations for taking Adriana. Blanca said they wanted to scare Imelda, wanted her to know what it felt like and took Adriana because she was not being taken care of properly. Moya told police that they took the child to try to get the money back and that Blanca had told Rigo to demand a certain sum but to get whatever he could. Rigo told the police that the whole purpose was to find out if Imelda had the money.

. . .

CALJIC NO. 9.50—KIDNAPPING INSTRUCTION

Blanca contends that because simple kidnapping is a lesser included crime of kidnapping for ransom and the court failed to properly instruct the jury on all of the elements of simple kidnapping, the conviction must be reversed. Not so.

Blanca's contention the court did not fully instruct on all of the elements of simple kidnapping is premised on an incorrect reading of *section 207,* subdivision (a) as amended in 1990. Prior to 1990, *section 207,* subdivision (a) provided: "Every person who forcibly steals, takes, or arrests any person in this state, and carries the person into another country, state, or county, or into another part of the same county, is guilty of kidnapping." As amended in 1990, this section now provides: "Every person who forcibly, *or by any other means of instilling fear,* steals *or* takes, or *holds, detains, or* arrests any person in this state, and carries the person into another country, state, or county, or into another part of the same county, is guilty of kidnapping." (Italics added.)

Blanca contends: "[T]he phrase 'or by any other means of instilling fear,' in reference to the term 'forcibly,' defines the word 'forcibly' and suggests an intent that any force necessary to constitute kidnapping must instill fear in the victim." She subsequently states: "The interpretation of amended *section 207* subdivision (a), most favorable to appellant is that the amended clause suggest an the [*sic*] intent which must accompany the force used in a forcible kidnap. Without the further instruction, the jury was unable to determine whether she possessed the required intent in the kidnap of Adriana." Whether Blanca is suggesting the amended *section 207,* subdivision (a) requires a specific intent to instill fear or whether she is contending that the use of force must actually instill fear is unclear. We reject either such contention.

Nothing on the face of the section as amended supports Blanca's contention that a defendant must intend to instill fear when he or she uses force to kidnap a victim. Simple kidnapping traditionally has been a general intent crime. . . . Absent express language requiring a specific intent, we will not presume the Legislature intended to change simple kidnapping from a general intent crime to a specific intent crime by adding the phrase "by any other means of instilling fear."

Nor do we interpret the statute as now requiring an additional element before a conviction for kidnapping can be sustained. Prior to the amendment, kidnapping could only be sustained upon a finding that the person was taken, stolen or arrested by the use or threat of force. . . . If a person's free will was not overborne by the use of force or the threat of force, there was no kidnapping.

. . .

As we read the amended version of *section 207,* kidnapping can now be accomplished not only by the application of force or threats of force but also by other methods which instill fear. Rather than modifying and defining (and thereby limiting) the word "forcibly" as contended by Blanca, the phrase "by any other means of instilling fear" expands the types of methods by which a person can overcome the free will of his or her victim. Thus, rather than being an additional element for the crime of kidnapping, the new language provides an alternative basis for finding a defendant guilty of kidnapping. Whether the court should have given this alternative definition of kidnapping or not, defendants cannot establish any prejudice in the failure to do so.

. . .

DISPOSITION

. . . In all other respects the judgments are affirmed.

COURT OF APPEAL, SECOND DISTRICT

180 Cal. App. 4th 1342, No. B209030

January 11, 2010

APPEAL from a judgment of the Superior Court of Los Angeles County. Judith Champagne, Judge. Affirmed.

OPINION BY: MOHR, J.

Appellant Alejandro Fierro appeals from his conviction of making criminal threats and giving false information to a police officer. He contends that the verdicts are not supported by substantial evidence. We disagree and affirm the judgment.

STATEMENT OF THE CASE

In a three-count information, appellant was charged in count 1 with making criminal threats in violation of *Penal Code section 422.* n1 He was charged in count 2 with attempted criminal threats *(§§ 664/422),* and in count 3, giving false information to a police officer. *(§ 148.9,* subd. (a).) It was further alleged as to counts 1 and 2 that appellant had suffered a prior conviction and had not remained free of custody for five years before committing the current felonies. *(§ 667.5,* subd. (b).) Appellant pleaded not guilty. The jury convicted him on all three counts. After waiving a jury trial on the prior conviction, appellant admitted the allegation. He was sentenced on May 13, 2008, to a total of five years in state prison plus various fines and assessments. Appellant filed a timely notice of appeal.

> n1 Unless otherwise noted, all statutory references are to the Penal Code.

STATEMENT OF THE FACTS

1. THE INCIDENT AT THE GAS STATION

This case stems from what should have been a non-event between two motorists: appellant and Michael Ibarra. Ibarra's 14-year-old son, A.I., was a passenger in Ibarra's car.

The Ibarra's and appellant never knew each other until August 8, 2007, when they met at an ARCO gas station.n2 Both arrived, in their respective cars, at about the same time. Ibarra believed that appellant was blocking access to the pumps. (A.I. actually believed appellant had cut them off as they approached a pump.) Ibarra asked appellant to move his car. In a sarcastic tone of voice, appellant told Ibarra to make that request in Spanish. Even though Ibarra speaks Spanish, he repeated his request in English. Again appellant told him to ask, politely, in Spanish. Appellant then went into the store to pay for his gas.

> n2 Much of what transpired was captured on a surveillance video, which the prosecution played for the jury while Ibarra narrated.

Perturbed, Ibarra followed appellant into the store and asked him again to move his car. And once more appellant said—in Spanish—to make the request politely in Spanish. When it became clear appellant was not going to cooperate, Ibarra said, "Well, fuck you, then," and returned to his car, where he waited by the driver's side for appellant to finish fueling.

Once he finished, appellant got back in his car, opened a beer bottle, and gestured as if offering some to Ibarra. Ibarra "gave him the bird as he did that," and appellant smiled at Ibarra. Appellant drove forward, slowly, until he was even with Ibarra. Again he picked up the bottle and gestured as if offering Ibarra a drink. And again, Ibarra gave appellant "the middle finger." Finally, appellant drove away.

Ibarra repositioned his car so he could fill his gas tank. As he started to use his debit card at the paypoint kiosk next to the pump, he noticed that appellant had not left after all. Instead, he had circled and was driving back toward Ibarra. Ibarra canceled his purchase and attempted to leave in order to avoid a second confrontation. Since another car was in front of his, Ibarra backed up, turned, and started forward. That is when appellant got out of his car and walked toward Ibarra.

Appellant called a nearby patron to interpret and, in an aggressive tone of voice, told this person several times to ask Ibarra, "Do you want to fuck with me now?" The interpreter said in Spanish to appellant, "I think he understands you," and the interpreter left.

But appellant did not leave. He stood about seven feet from Ibarra on the passenger side of Ibarra's car, and he lifted his shirt to display what Ibarra and A.I. believed was a weapon tucked into a waistband. Although father and son described it differently, they both said the weapon was in a holster and believed it was either a handgun or pistol. This got A.I.'s "heart pumping. I got a little scared. . . . Like he might pull the gun out of the holster and shoot us or something." Ibarra wanted to drive away but still could not; other vehicles were blocking his car. He said that during the minute or so that appellant displayed his weapon, ". . . the game changed. I was in fear for my life. I was in fear for my son's life. . . . The only thing that kept me there was I was completely backed in. . . . I was afraid for my son and my life. I was afraid. . . . I was have [sic] afraid of losing my life that day."

While Ibarra looked for an escape route, appellant harangued him. In Spanish, appellant uttered profanities, asked appellant if he was "a faggot," said words to the effect that he should have more respect for people from Jalisco (a state in Mexico).

Then—still in Spanish—appellant said, "I should kill you. I will kill you." Appellant also said, "I ought to kill you and"—pointing to A.I.—"the stupid mother fucker too." Worse yet, appellant said he ought to kill them "ahorita," which means "right now." Finally, appellant said, "Now get the fuck out of here." Ibarra obeyed him.

A.I. saw appellant hold up the beer bottle as he was leaving the station. A.I. speaks no Spanish and could not understand what appellant was saying. After appellant lifted up his jacket to display it, A.I. saw what he thought was a silver gun in a black holster. Seeing the weapon made A.I. feel uncomfortable.

Ibarra tried to get a grip on his emotions as he drove away. He had been "scared to death during the whole ordeal." Within about 15 minutes—once he was on the freeway and "out of harm's way"—he called 9-1-1 and told the operator that he was "scared shitless."

The operator told Ibarra to return to the gas station and wait across the street; the police would be approaching in "silent mode." Police Officer William Robinson and his partner interviewed the Ibarras, viewed the surveillance tape, and then searched the area and found appellant within walking distance of the gas station. They detained him until Ibarra identified him. Appellant was not carrying a gun; instead, he had a folding knife with a black handle. The weapon was in a black nylon holster with a Smith & Wesson logo on it.

. . .

DISCUSSION

1. SUBSTANTIAL EVIDENCE SUPPORTS THE CONVICTION UNDER COUNT 1

Appellant contends there was insufficient evidence to support his conviction of making a criminal threat against Ibarra (count 1). Appellant's contention lacks merit.

The standard for appellate review of the sufficiency of the evidence to support a criminal conviction is well established. "Claims challenging the sufficiency of the evidence to uphold a judgment are generally reviewed under the substantial evidence standard. Under that standard, an appellate court reviews the entire record in the light most favorable to the prosecution to determine whether it contains evidence that is reasonable, credible, and of solid value, from which a rational trier of fact could find [the elements of the crime] beyond a reasonable doubt." [Citations.] "'If the circumstances reasonably justify the trier of fact's findings, the opinion of the reviewing court that the circumstances might also be reasonably reconciled with a contrary finding does not warrant a reversal of the judgment.' [Citations.]" (In re George T. (2004) 33 Cal.4th 620, 630-631, 16 Cal.Rptr.3d 61, 93 P.3d 1007 (George T.).) Furthermore, "In deciding the sufficiency of the evidence, a reviewing court resolves neither credibility issues nor evidentiary conflicts. [Citation.] Resolution of conflicts and inconsistencies in the testimony is the exclusive province of the trier of fact. [Citation.] Moreover, unless the testimony is physically impossible or inherently improbable, testimony of a single witness is sufficient to support a conviction. [Citation.]" (People v. Young (2005) 34 Cal.4th 1149, 1181, 24 Cal.Rptr.3d 112, 105 P.3d 487.)

In George T., supra, 33 Cal.4th at page 630, 16 Cal.Rptr.3d 61, 93 P.3d 1007, the Supreme Court enumerated the elements of a criminal threat under section 422: "The prosecution must prove '(1) that the defendant "willfully threaten[ed] to commit a crime which will result in death or great bodily injury to another person," (2) that the defendant made the threat "with the specific intent that the statement . . . is to be taken as a threat, even if there is no intent of actually carrying it out," (3) that the threat—which may be "made verbally, . . ." was "on its face and under the circumstances in which it [was] made, . . . so unequivocal, unconditional, immediate, and specific as to convey to the person threatened, a gravity of purpose and an immediate prospect of execution of the threat," (4) that the threat actually caused the person threatened "to be in sustained fear for his or her own safety or for his or her immediate family's safety," and (5) that the threatened person's fear was "reasonabl[e]" under the circumstances.' [Citations.]" *(Ibid.; see also § 422.)*

We list the above-quoted elements below, followed by the reasons why more than substantial evidence supports each such element here:

First element—willful threat to commit a crime that will result in death or great bodily injury: There was solid, competent evidence that appellant displayed a weapon and said, "I will kill you."

Second element—specific intent: The evidence shows that for up to one minute appellant was close to Ibarra's car, displaying the weapon, making pejorative statements about appellant and his son, and saying words to the effect that he could and would kill them. There is no reason for appellant to do what he did and say what he said if he had not had the specific intent that the Ibarras interpret his actions as a threat.

Third element—unequivocal, unconditional, immediate threat: Mr. Ibarra testified that appellant not only said, "I will kill you," but said (in Spanish) that he was going to do so "right now." As if to stress the immediacy of his intentions, appellant did not say "ahora," which means "now." He said "ahorita," which means "right now."[n4] Appellant's proximity to the victim and his threatening gesture added weight to his words.

n4 http://www.spanishdict.com/translation (as of January 11, 2010).

Fourth element—the threat actually caused sustained, reasonable fear: Mr. Ibarra testified clearly and more than once that he was horribly scared, and his fright was not fleeting. Regardless of who was at fault during the first confrontation, it had ended. Appellant had driven away. But then appellant circled and returned with the obvious intent of confronting Ibarra again and, this time, frightening him. In light of the (albeit recent) history between these people, appellant amply succeeded. Facing what he thought was a gun and hearing words to the effect that he and his son were about to be killed, Mr. Ibarra was in sustained fear for his and his son's life. The fear lasted not only through the minute or so that appellant stood there exposing his weapon, but for up to fifteen minutes after Ibarra drove away. It is entirely reasonable that he would react as he did for as long as he did. That is exactly what appellant wanted to accomplish.

Appellant claims we should not consider the victims' time on the freeway—fifteen minutes—in calculating the last element—"sustained fear." He argues that as shown on the security videotape, the threat itself did not exceed 40 seconds.[n5] This argument ignores human nature. "Sustained fear" refers to a state of mind. As one court put it, "[d]efining the word 'sustained' [in section 433] by its opposites, we find that it means a period of time that extends beyond what is momentary, fleeting or transitory." *(People v. Allen (1995) 33 Cal.App.4th 1149, 1151, 1153, 40 Cal.Rptr.2d 7* (Allen).) n6 The word fear, of course, describes the emotion the victim experiences.

n5 Testimony established that appellant's display of the knife lasted a minute or so.

n6 When we consider the totality of the time the victims were in fear, this case is similar to what happened in Allen, which held that 15 minutes is more than fleeting. In Allen, the defendant used profanity. Then he declared: "I'm gonna kill you. I'm gonna kill you and your daughter." *(Id. at p. 1153, 40 Cal.Rptr.2d 7.)* As he spoke he pointed a gun at the victim. Then defendant left the scene. *(Ibid.)* The victim called the police, who arrested the defendant about 15 minutes later. *(Id. at pp. 1153, 1155-1156, 40 Cal.Rptr.2d 7.)* Thus, as in this case, the threat did not last fifteen minutes, but the fear continued for that period after the defendant had fled.

In light of the facts and circumstances we have noted, the jury reasonably could have found that appellant's actions created a sustained fear, a state of mind that was certainly more than momentary, fleeting, or transitory. We submit that a person who hears someone say, "I will kill you . . . right now," coupled with seeing a weapon, is quite justified in remaining "scared shitless"—as Mr. Ibarra put it—for 15 minutes. "Fifteen minutes of fear of a defendant who is armed, mobile, and at-large, and who has threatened to kill the victim and [his son], is more than sufficient to constitute 'sustained' fear for purposes of this element of section 422." *(Allen, supra, 33 Cal.App.4th at p. 1156, 40 Cal.Rptr.2d 7.)* But even if we accept appellant's argument, we believe that the minute during which Ibarra heard the threat and saw appellant's weapon qualifies as "sustained" under the statute. When one believes he is about to die, a minute is longer than "momentary, fleeting, or transitory." *(Ibid.)*

The facts in this case differ sharply from a good example of momentary fear that is found in In re Ricky T. *(2001) 87 Cal.App.4th 1132, 105 Cal.Rptr.2d 165,* in which a student threatened to "get" a teacher, but made no physical movements or gestures. The teacher responded by sending the student to the school office; the teacher did not call the police until the next day; and there had been no prior history between defendant and victim. (*Id.* at pp. 1135-1136, *105 Cal.Rptr.2d 165.*) The court found the teacher's fear to be fleeting. (*Id.* at p. 1140, *105 Cal.Rptr.2d 165.*) As discussed above, the facts here are quite different and constitute substantial evidence to support the guilty verdict on count 1.

Substantial Evidence Supports the Conviction under Count 3.

DISPOSITION

The judgment is affirmed.

We concur: RUBIN, Acting P.J., and FLIER, J.

PEOPLE v. FRANZ

COURT OF APPEAL, THIRD DISTRICT, CALIFORNIA

88 CAL. APP. 4TH 1426, NO. C034462

MAY 10, 2001

OPINION BY: SIMS, ACTING P. J.

Defendant Anthony Ronald Franz appeals from a judgment following conviction on one count of spousal battery (*Pen. Code, § 243,* subd. (e)), two counts of making terrorist threats (§ 422),n1 two counts of dissuading a witness from reporting a crime (§ 136.1, subd. (b)(1)), one count of battery (§ 243, subd. (e)(1), and one count of assault and battery (§ 242). The trial court found true and imposed a one-year enhancement for a prior prison term. (§ 667.5, subd. (b).)

> n1 Undesignated statutory references are to the *Penal Code. Section 422* provides in part: "Any person who willfully threatens to commit a crime which will result in death or great bodily injury to another person, with the specific intent that the statement, made verbally, in writing, or by means of an electronic communication device, is to be taken as a threat, even if there is no intent of actually carrying it out, which, on its face and under the circumstances in which it is made, is so unequivocal, unconditional, immediate, and specific as to convey to the person threatened, a gravity of purpose and an immediate prospect of execution of the threat, and thereby causes that person reasonably to be in sustained fear for his or her own safety or for his or her immediate family's safety, shall be punished by imprisonment in the county jail not to exceed one year, or by imprisonment in the state prison."

In the published portion of the opinion, we consider and reject defendant's contention that there is no substantial evidence he made a verbal "statement" to support the terrorist threat convictions. However, we agree with defendant that the trial court erroneously found true the prior prison term enhancement, which was founded on a federal conviction for possession of counterfeit United States currency.

Defendant also raises other contentions of insufficient evidence, evidentiary error, instructional error, and

sentencing error, all of which we reject in the unpublished portion of the opinion.

We shall reverse the trial court's finding that the *section* 667.5 enhancement was true and remand to the trial court for a retrial of the enhancement. We shall also order correction of the abstract of judgment to stay the sentences on the section 422 counts (counts 3 and 4) and strike the prior prison term enhancement. We shall otherwise affirm the judgment.

FACTUAL AND PROCEDURAL BACKGROUND

By an information filed in September 1999, defendant was charged with: (1) inflicting corporal injury on cohabitant Erika Schmidt between June 15, 1999, and July 4, 1999 (§ 273.5); (2) making a terrorist threat to Erika Schmidt on July 31, 1999 (§ 422); (3) making a terrorist threat to Matthew Zook on July 31, 1999 (§ 422); (4) making a terrorist threat to Jordan Immer on July 31, 1999 (§ 422); (5) attempting on July 31, 1999, to dissuade Erika Schmidt from reporting a crime to law enforcement officers (§ 136.1, subd. (b)(1)); (6) attempting on July 31, 1999, to dissuade Matthew Zook from reporting a crime (§ 136.1, subd. (b)(1)); (7) attempting on July 31, 1999, to dissuade Jordan Immer from reporting a crime (§ 136.1, subd. (b)(1)); (8) using force and violence on July 31, 1999, upon Erika Schmidt, a person with whom defendant had a previous dating relationship (§ 243, subd. (e)(1)); (9) using force and violence on July 29, 1999, upon Erika Schmidt, a person with whom defendant had a previous dating relationship (§ 243, subd. (e)(1)); and (10) using force and violence on July 31, 1999, upon Matthew Zook (§ 242).

The following evidence was adduced at trial:

Erika Schmidt (age 20) testified that defendant (age 28) was a former boyfriend who lived with her briefly. They fought often. In mid-June 1999, defendant hit her and tried to choke her at Benham Park after expressing anger that Schmidt received a telephone call from a male friend.

Around the end of June 1999, Schmidt and defendant broke up (though he continued to drive her home from work), and defendant moved in with neighbor Judy Pena.

On the evening of July 29, 1999, while Schmidt was a passenger in defendant's car, defendant asked to borrow money from Schmidt. They stopped for gasoline at an AM/PM store, where some "kids" approached and asked defendant to buy beer for them. He agreed to do so (testimony that was admitted over defense objection). While defendant was in the store, Schmidt saw in defendant's car a photograph of two of her sister's friends, ages 12 and 13, with their legs spread open. She told him it was disgusting. He said it was not his, and he hit her several times, bruising her eye and cutting the back of her ear. Schmidt was afraid of defendant because he previously told her she would be sorry if she called the police on him. Schmidt's mother reported the incident to the police.

On the afternoon of July 31, 1999, Schmidt was on the street near her workplace, waiting for a taxi to take her home, conversing with her sister's 17-year-old boyfriend, Matthew Zook, and Zook's 17-year-old friend, Jordan Immer. Schmidt saw defendant's car and ducked into a nearby pizza restaurant and went into the restroom to avoid him. When she emerged, Zook said defendant "got in his face."

Schmidt, Zook and Immer took a taxi to Schmidt's home, where she shut all the curtains and locked all the doors, because she was afraid of defendant. The phone rang repeatedly, but she did not answer. Defendant came knocking on her door, but she did not answer. Schmidt, Zook and Immer stayed in a bedroom, which was "movie theater dark" with the blackout curtains closed, but with some daylight coming in through the open hallway door. When defendant tried to gain access to the house through a window, Schmidt agreed to go outside to speak with him. When she opened the door, he pushed his way inside. He asked who was with her; she said no one. Defendant found Zook and Immer in the bedroom, called Schmidt a liar and slapped her face as she stood in the living room. Defendant then turned on the bedroom light and hit Zook on the face several times with a closed fist, yelling that he (defendant) wanted Zook to telephone and apologize to Zook's aunt (Judy Pena) for calling her a whore. Schmidt grabbed a cordless phone, ran out of the house, and called the police. She hung up when she saw defendant coming after her. He took the phone and punched her several times, causing her nose to bleed. He pulled her back inside the house, told her "I'm going to fucking kill you," and resumed yelling at Zook in the bedroom.

The police arrived. Schmidt ran outside, crying. She heard defendant tell the officers that she had fallen down the stairs. At first, Schmidt did not tell the officers what happened, because she was afraid of defendant, but she spoke to the police after being taken to the hospital.

Schmidt admitted she was jealous of defendant's new girlfriend, Judy Pena, and admitted she made telephone calls to Pena's house, but said the calls she made were to return defendant's calls to her.

A tape recording of Schmidt's 911 call was played for the jury; on it was heard the yelling of a male voice, which Schmidt identified as defendant's voice. A transcription of the 911 tape reads as follows:

"911 Operator: 911 emergency.

"[Schmidt]: Please help me! Help me! Help me!

"911 Operator: What's going on?

"[Schmidt]: 5635 Canal Street.

"911 Operator: What's happening?

"[Schmidt]: Hurry! Hurry! Hurry! Please! No! Please help me!

"911 Operator: What's happening to you?

"End of Call [¶] . . . [¶]

"[Defendant]: Fucker!n2

    n2 It would appear the 911 operator then called back.

"911 Operator: Hello! Hello! This is 911.

"[Defendant]: Want to fucking talk (unintelligible) me of being drunk, huh? You'd better fucking watch your mouth!

"911 Operator: Hello!

"[Defendant]: I'm not no fucking little kid. I'll fucking kill you, boy! . . . (unintelligible) . . . You (unintelligible) you mother fucking . . . (unintelligible)

"911 Operator: I can hear males arguing.

"[Defendant]: (unintelligible) . . . shit! I'll fuck you up! I don't give a fuck about going back to the pen! I got connections, bro! My family is Mafia! Mafia! (unintelligible)

"911 Operator: Hello, this is 911.

"[Defendant]: . . . give a fuck! You'd better leave your mother-fucking aunt alone! And . . . Apologize to her! If you don[']t . . .

"911 Operator: (unintelligible)

"[Defendant]: . . . play it cool for you. (unintelligible) from here. I got a fucking calling card.

"Unknown voice: (unintelligible)

"[Defendant]: Don't worry about it. You're going to apologize. I'm going to call her right now.

"(unintelligible)

"End of Call."n3

> n3 The transcription contained in the augmented clerk's transcript on appeal bears a notation that it was not admitted into evidence, but other notations in the record indicate it was admitted into evidence. Because both sides on appeal cite to the transcription, we assume the parties agree it was admitted in evidence.

Matthew Zook testified. He witnessed the incident in which defendant hit Schmidt in the park. Regarding the July 31, 1999, incident at Schmidt's home, Zook was afraid of defendant because a couple of days earlier, defendant threatened Zook, saying he was going to kill Zook, Zook's girlfriend (Schmidt's sister), and his girlfriend's family. Zook did not know why defendant was mad at him, other than the fact he associated with the Schmidts. At the pizza restaurant, defendant threatened to kill Zook. At Schmidt's house, Zook hid in the bedroom with Immer and heard Schmidt at the front door screaming "no, Tony," and hitting sounds. Defendant came into the bedroom and hit Zook three times with a closed fist, blurring Zook's vision. Defendant demanded that Zook call his aunt and apologize for calling her a whore. Zook made the call.

Zook said that when the police arrived, he "wasn't scared then because they were there because I felt threatened still [sic] . . . [b]y [defendant]." Officer Jacobs came into the bedroom where Zook and Immer were sitting on the bed. Zook saw defendant standing behind the officer; defendant "did a gesture like this, like shush. And then ran his finger across his throat." The record reflected Zook showed an index finger in front of the lips and then held up a thumb and ran it across his throat. Zook said defendant looked right at Zook's eyes as he did this. Immer was also sitting on the bed. The officer was between the bed and the door with his back to the door. Zook understood defendant was threatening to "cut my throat" if Zook said anything to the officer. Zook took the threat seriously. Later that evening, Zook and Immer were walking home when Officer Santos pulled over and said he knew what had happened at the Schmidt house. Because defendant was not present, Zook told "what defendant had done." Zook did not recall if he told the officer about defendant's "silence motion and the cutting-the-throat motion."

Jordan Immer testified he was in the bedroom and heard hitting sounds at the front door and Schmidt crying.

Defendant came into the bedroom and hit Zook. Immer was scared. When the police arrived, Officer Jacobs came into the bedroom and stood by the bed where the boys were sitting. Immer did not answer the officer's questions, because defendant was in the bedroom, behind the officer, and defendant "swiped his hand across his throat" perhaps twice, shook his head and put his finger to his lips, which Immer understood to mean defendant would slice his throat if he said anything to the police. Immer testified he did not recall if defendant said anything at that point. After the police left, defendant told them not to say anything. Later, Immer saw the police as he was walking home and told them what happened because he no longer felt threatened. Immer testified at trial that he never saw defendant hit Schmidt and denied having told the police he saw it.

Officer John Jacobs testified that when he arrived at Schmidt's home, she ran past him, and he did not see her injuries until later. Defendant said he and Schmidt got into an argument about her "harboring juveniles" in her home. Officer Jacobs went into the bedroom to speak with the two juveniles, but they would not answer his questions. The officer did not see any injuries on Zook, but the room was semi-dark. During the several minutes the officer spent in the bedroom with his back to the door, the officer was not aware of anyone coming into the room. The officer left the bedroom, saw defendant in the living room, told him to go home, and escorted him out of the house. It was not until after defendant left that Officer Jacobs saw that Schmidt had a bloody nose and other fresh injuries. She said nothing happened, but she wanted a restraining order against defendant.

On cross-examination, Officer Jacobs testified his instincts were developed with 20 years' experience, and no one could have "snuck up behind [him] in that bedroom."

Officer Frank Santos testified he spoke to Schmidt at the hospital, and she told him what happened. Later that evening, he came into contact with Zook and Immer, told them he had already learned from Schmidt what happened and knew they were scared. Officer Santos spoke with Zook and Immer separately; each gave a similar account of the incident corresponding with Schmidt's account. Each boy said he came out of the bedroom and saw defendant hitting Schmidt. Zook indicated defendant made a verbal statement and physical gesture not to talk to the police. Officer Santos testified "[t]he verbal statement was noise coming out. . . . What I understood was that shush and a swipe across the throat. I don't mean the actual say this or say that [sic]. I mean a noise that they [sic] made and it was interpreted to them don't talk to the police. . . . Some sort of noise, shushing noise. I believe one said he actually heard the noise and there was a finger to the mouth."

The defense presented evidence that Schmidt falsely claimed to be pregnant with defendant's child, and that Schmidt would provoke defendant to anger by calling him names and "pushing his buttons."

During a break in the presentation of defendant's case, the trial court granted the prosecutor's request to dismiss counts 2 and 5, terrorist threat with respect to Schmidt and attempting to dissuade a witness with respect to Schmidt.

The jury returned verdicts finding defendant guilty on the following counts: spousal battery in violation of section 243, subdivision (e), as a lesser included offense to the charge of corporal injury to spouse alleged in count 1; terrorist threat against Matthew Zook in violation of section 422 (count 3); terrorist threat against Jordan Immer in violation of section 422 (count 4); dissuading witness Matthew Zook from reporting a crime in violation of section 136.1, subdivision (b)(1) (count 6); dissuading witness Jordan Immer from reporting a crime in violation of section 136.1 (count 7); battery on Erika Schmidt in violation of section 243, subdivision (e)(1) (count 8); and assault and battery on Zook (count 10).

The jury also returned verdicts finding defendant not guilty on the following counts: Corporal injury to spouse (count 1); and battery (count 9).

The court allowed amendment of the pleading to allege a prior prison term enhancement under section 667.5, subdivision (b). In a bifurcated proceeding, the trial court found the enhancement allegation true, based on a prior federal conviction for possession of counterfeit United States currency with intent to defraud in violation of 18 United States Code section 472.

The trial court denied probation and sentenced defendant to a total term of four years and eight months as follows: the upper term of three years on count 6 as the principal term (dissuading Zook from reporting a crime); concurrent three-year upper terms on counts 3 and 4 (terrorist threats); a consecutive eight months (one-third the middle term) on count 7 (dissuading Immer from reporting a crime); a one-year enhancement under section 667.5 to run consecutive to count 6; two one-year jail terms on counts 1 and 8 (spousal battery and battery) to run concurrently with count 6; a six-month jail term on count 10 (battery) to run concurrently with count 6.n4

> n4 The concurrent sentences on the misdemeanors in counts 1, 8, and 10 are not mentioned in the abstract of judgment.

DISCUSSION

. . .

SUFFICIENCY OF THE EVIDENCE

Defendant contends the evidence is insufficient to support his convictions for terrorist threats or dissuading a witness. We disagree.

. . .

A. TERRORIST THREATS, SECTION 422

Defendant contends the evidence is insufficient to support his conviction of terrorist threats (§ 422) with respect to Zook and Immer (counts 3 and 4), because (1) there is no substantial evidence he made a verbal, written, or electronic statement, as required by section 422 (see fn. 1, ante); (2) the throat-slashing gesture was not an unequivocal statement; and (3) the throat-slashing gesture was made under circumstances in which no immediate threat existed. We disagree.

1. SECTION 422 REQUIRES A VERBAL STATEMENT, NOT MERE CONDUCT

Section 422 (see n1, ante) refers to a person who willfully threatens to commit a crime which will result in death or great bodily injury, with the specific intent that "the statement, made verbally, in writing, or by means of an electronic communication device," is to be taken as a threat.

. . .

Defendant contends that section 422 requires a verbal, written, or electronic "statement," and the only possibility in this case is a verbal statement. According to defendant, defendant's gestures, unaccompanied by verbal sound, do not qualify as verbal statements under section 422. We agree with defendant's view of the statute, but we find substantial evidence in the record that defendant made a verbal statement.

. . .

We conclude section 422 required in this case proof that defendant's threat to be quiet was "made verbally," i.e., that defendant orally made some noise or sound that was capable of conveying meaning.

2. THE RECORD CONTAINS SUBSTANTIAL EVIDENCE THAT DEFENDANT MADE A VERBAL STATEMENT

We turn to the question whether substantial evidence supports defendant's conviction for violating section 422. The prosecutor argued to the jury that the section 422 offenses with respect to Zook and Immer occurred when Officer Jacobs was in the bedroom, with his back to the door, questioning Zook and Immer, and defendant appeared behind the officer.

Defendant argues the only substantial evidence concerning this incident was of conduct, not a statement, i.e., that defendant put his finger to his lips in a "shushing gesture" and slid his finger across his throat.

Thus, Zook testified at trial that defendant stood behind the officer, "did a gesture like this, like shush [witness demonstrated by placing his index finger in front of his lips]. And then ran his finger across his throat."

Immer testified at trial as follows:

"Q And was there some reason why you didn't say anything [to Officer Jacobs] with [defendant] in the bedroom [behind the officer]?

"A Yes.

"Q Why is that?

"A Because he swiped his hand across his throat.

"Q When you say he swiped his hand, could you show us what he did? (Witness demonstrating.)

"Q You're waving your hand across the throat. Did he do it several times?

"A Yes.

"Q Did he do anything else?

"A He told—said not to say anything.

"Q Did he actually say that?

"A After Officer Jacobs left.n8

> n8 Officer Jacobs testified that after his contact with the minors, he told defendant to leave and escorted defendant out of the house and halfway down the street.

"Q What about while Officer Jacobs was there, did [defendant] say anything while Officer Jacobs was standing in front of you?

"A Yes.

"Q What did he say?

"A I'm not sure.

"Q Did he actually speak while Officer Jacobs was there?

"A He was speaking to Officer Jacobs.

"Q Was that before Officer Jacobs spoke to you?

"A No, it was after.

"Q After Officer Jacobs spoke to you?

"A Yes.

"Q Was that when Officer Jacobs was done talking to you?

"A No."

On cross-examination, Immer testified:

"Q And what did [defendant] say to you after he did [the swiping motion across the throat]?

"A Not to say anything.

"Q And he said that by speaking; is that right?

"A He nodded his head and did that. (Witness demonstrating.)

"Q Did he say anything?

"A I don't recall.

"Q But he nodded his head and put his finger to his lips?

"A Yes.

"Q That was after the motion across the neck?

"A Yes."

Assuming that the foregoing testimony does not describe a verbal statement, that description is nonetheless found in the testimony of Officer Santos. Thus, Officer Santos, who contacted Zook and Immer in the street later in the evening, testified during cross-examination by defendant's counsel that the minors did report that defendant made a verbal noise. Thus, Officer Santos testified:

"Q . . . [D]id Mr. Immer tell you that [defendant] stated to them that they should not talk to the police?

"A He made a statement similar to that.

"Q Did you ask them [sic] to go into detail about that statement?

"A Yes. I wrote down the statement they told me.

"Q And what was the statement that [defendant] allegedly gave to tell these guys not to go to the police—to tell them not to go to [the] police?

"A If you would like the exact statement, I could refer to my report.

"Q Thank you.

"A If I have that page. Mr. Zook's statement was something about not talking to the police.

"Q He said [defendant] stated that to him?

"A [Defendant] made a statement generally about not talking to the police.

"Q [H]e made a statement. Did you take that to mean a verbal or oral statement?

"A He made a verbal statement and a physical gesture.

"Q He made a verbal statement. Did Mr. Zook show you the physical gesture?

"A Yes; he told me the gesture and the verbal statement together.

"Q And did Mr. Immer show you a verbal statement or did Mr. Immer show you a gesture?

"A Yes, he did."

Officer Santos further testified upon cross-examination by defendant's counsel:

"Q Okay. Just so we're clear by verbal statement does that mean he said anything?

"A The verbal statement was noise coming out. If you would like me to demonstrate?

"Q Sure.

"A What I understood was that shush and a swipe across the throat. I don't mean the actual say this or say that. I mean a noise that they made and it was interpreted to them don't talk to the police.

"Q So he said shush and he actually made the—

"A Some sort of noise, shushing noise. I believe one said he actually heard the noise and there was a finger to the mouth."

Thus, Officer Santos testified that at least one of the victims reported defendant made a verbal noise.

In this case, we do not have to decide whether section 422 requires that a defendant use a word in order to fulfill the requirement of a "statement made verbally." Even upon the assumption that the statute requires the use of a word, defendant cannot prevail. According to the testimony of Officer Santos, defendant uttered a sound that was either "shush" or "sh." Both "shush" and "sh" are defined as words by Webster's Third New International Dictionary (1961) pages 2108, 2082. Thus, "shush" means, "to urge quiet upon (as by making the sound 'sh' and holding an index finger before the lips). . . ." Likewise, Webster's defines "sh" as, "often used in prolonged or reduplicated form to enjoin silence or urge moderation of sound." We therefore conclude that the "shush" or "sh" sound made by defendant constituted a "statement made verbally" for purposes of section 422.

. . .

Consequently, the testimony of Officer Santos that at least one victim heard defendant make a "shushing" noise constitutes substantial evidence of a verbal "statement," the import of which was amplified by the throat-slashing gesture to constitute a threat to kill if the victim talked to the police. (7) "[T]he determination whether a defendant intended his words to be taken as a threat, and whether the words were sufficiently unequivocal, unconditional, immediate and specific they conveyed to the victim an immediacy of purpose and immediate prospect of execution of the threat can be based on all the surrounding circumstances and not just on the words alone." (*People v. Mendoza, supra,* 59 Cal.App.4th at p. 1340, followed in *People v. Butler* (2000) 85 Cal.App.4th 745, 754 {102 Cal.Rptr.2d 269}.)

Defendant argues he "could not have made" a shushing sound or statement, because Officer Jacobs, who was standing between the defendant and the minors at the time in question, testified he did not hear any noise behind him and he would have heard if someone "snuck up behind him." However, the testimony of Officer Jacobs does not make it impossible for defendant to have made a sound. . . .

While it may have been foolish for defendant to make a shushing noise in the officer's presence, it was not impossible or inherently improbable for him to have done so. . . .

We conclude there was substantial evidence of a statement "made verbally" within the meaning of section 422.

3. UNEQUIVOCAL STATEMENT

Defendant argues the evidence was insufficient to convict him of terrorist threats because the throat-slashing gesture was not an "unequivocal statement" for section 422 purposes. We disagree.

Section 422 (see n1, ante) requires that the threat "on its face and under the circumstances in which it is made, is so unequivocal, unconditional, immediate, and specific as to convey to the person threatened, a gravity of purpose and an immediate prospect of execution of the threat. . . ."

Defendant says the record was unclear which gesture defendant made first—the finger to the lips or the finger across the throat. Defendant proffers no rational explanation why this should make a difference. Defendant says a finger slashed across the throat also means "cut" or "quiet." Defendant claims the context in which the gesture was made did not clarify whether the gesture meant "quiet" or "quiet or I'll cut your throat." Defendant cites authority that wordless conduct is particularly susceptible to misconstruction. Defendant argues a gesture to be quiet, absent words to clarify the meaning of the gesture, may not form the basis for a section 422 conviction. However, we have seen there was evidence of a verbal statement.

In rejecting an argument that a threat was not unconditional as required by section 422, *People v. Bolin* (1988) 18 Cal.4th 297 {75 Cal.Rptr.2d 412, 956 P.2d 374}, observed the statute did not require an absolutely unconditional threat, but that the threat be "so" unconditional as to convey gravity of purpose and immediate prospect of execution. (*Id.* at pp. 339-340.) Bolin said, " '[t]he use of the word "so" indicates that unequivocality, unconditionality, immediacy and specificity are not absolutely mandated, but must be sufficiently present in the threat and surrounding circumstances to convey gravity of purpose and immediate prospect of execution to the victim.' [Citation.]" (*Id.* at p. 340.)

Here, defendant's shushing noise, accompanied by the throat-slashing gesture, was "so" unequivocal that it conveyed to Zook and Immer a sufficient gravity of purpose and immediate prospect of execution of the threat.

4. IMMEDIACY

Defendant contends the throat-slashing gesture was made under circumstances in which there was no immediacy of the threat, as required by section 422. We disagree.

Section 422 (see fn. 1, ante) requires that the threat be "so . . . immediate . . . as to convey to the person threatened, a gravity of purpose and an immediate prospect of execution of the threat. . . ."

Defendant suggests there is no substantial evidence of immediacy because the police officer was present during the threat and thereafter escorted defendant away from the scene, and neither juvenile saw defendant again until prosecution of this matter. However, defendant fails to cite any evidence as to when the minors next saw defendant. In any event, at the time of the threat the minors did not know when they would next see defendant. The immediacy

factor was present in the surrounding circumstances that defendant was in a rage. He had already hit Schmidt, punched Zook, and said he was going to kill Zook, as documented by the 911 call. Although the officer was present when defendant made the threat, the threat and surrounding circumstances were a reminder that the officer would not always be there to protect the minors.

Defendant argues there was insufficient evidence to support the terrorist threat conviction as to Immer, because there was evidence defendant looked at Zook when he made the threat, but there was no evidence defendant looked into Immer's eyes. We disagree. Zook and Immer were in close proximity; they were both sitting on the same bed. Obviously, defendant attempted to dissuade both witnesses. On appeal, defendant does not contend that separate acts must be present for the separate victims.

We conclude substantial evidence supports the section 422 convictions (counts 3 and 4).

. . .

DISPOSITION

The trial court's finding that the section 667.5, subdivision (b) enhancement was true is reversed, and the cause is remanded to the trial court for a retrial of the enhancement in accordance with the views set forth in this opinion. The abstract of judgment is ordered modified to stay the sentences on the section 422 counts (counts 3 and 4) and to strike the prior prison term enhancement. The judgment is otherwise affirmed.

DAVIS, J., and MORRISON, J., concurred.

PEOPLE v. GAUT

COURT OF APPEAL, SECOND DISTRICT, DIVISION 5, CALIFORNIA

95 Cal. App. 4th 1425; No. B149066

February 7, 2002

OPINION BY: TURNER, P.J.

Defendant, William Prince Gaut, appeals from his convictions for two counts of making terrorist threats. (*Pen. Code,* n1 *§ 422.*) . . . Defendant argues there was insufficient evidence to support his conviction for violating *section 422* as a matter of law because he was incarcerated when the threats were made. We disagree and affirm the judgment.

> n1 All further statutory references are to the *Penal Code* unless otherwise indicated.

. . . Collette Blizzard met defendant at church in September 1999. They began dating shortly thereafter. Defendant began arguing with Ms. Blizzard, questioning where she was going and with whom she spoke. In November, defendant began grabbing Ms. Blizzard's clothing and pushing her against the wall during arguments. The arguments escalated during December. On New Year's Eve, defendant and Ms. Blizzard had plans to go out on a date. Defendant left in Ms. Blizzard's car and returned at 11:00 p.m. Defendant threw Ms. Blizzard against the wall and "snatche[d her] hair off." Ms. Blizzard knew they must separate.

Defendant convinced Ms. Blizzard he would not repeat this violence toward her. However, by mid-January the arguments began to reoccur. Defendant slapped Ms. Blizzard in the face with his open hand. The slapping incident occurred while Ms. Blizzard spoke with a tow truck driver. On February 1, 2000, defendant went out with Ms. Blizzard and his sister. Defendant left in Ms. Blizzard's car and did not return. Ms. Blizzard later learned that defendant had been arrested. Defendant remained in custody until April 23, 2000. Defendant telephoned Ms. Blizzard daily from jail. He assured Ms. Blizzard that he would attend anger management classes and change his behavior. Defendant returned to Ms. Blizzard's home. Shortly thereafter the arguments began anew. Defendant took Ms. Blizzard's car. He disappeared for a few days without explanation. On

Memorial Day, defendant took her car. He claimed that it had been stolen. However, defendant returned the car a few days later, indicating he found it. Although Ms. Blizzard wanted to break off her relationship with defendant, she knew it would be "vicious." Defendant told her he had "pistol-whipped" his former girlfriend. Defendant also told Ms. Blizzard he would have shot his former girlfriend if others had not intervened.

On June 2, 2000, Ms. Blizzard told defendant he must leave her home. Defendant had a key to the security gate on her front door. But he did not have a key to her home. Defendant refused to leave. However, defendant left the following day. On June 4, 2000, Ms. Blizzard took defendant's belongings to his mother's home. Later that evening defendant attempted to contact Ms. Blizzard by telephone and pager. Ms. Blizzard did not respond. When she returned home, her home appeared to have been burglarized. Someone had broken the security grill on the bedroom window. Ms. Blizzard's gun and rings were missing. Several of her belongings had been slashed. Although she thought defendant had burglarized her home, she reported the burglary to the police.

Ms. Blizzard was frightened. She did not return home that evening. Ms. Blizzard owned a transportation company. She worked the following morning transporting children. Ms. Blizzard stopped at her home to check on her dog. When she approached her door, she saw defendant's shoes and she ran. Defendant followed despite her pleas to leave her alone because she had children in her van. Defendant smashed his hand through the driver's side window of the van. Ms. Blizzard drove away, dragging defendant with the van. Later that day, defendant telephoned Ms. Blizzard from her home. Defendant told Ms. Blizzard she could have all of her things back for $1,200. Ms. Blizzard told him to get out and leave her alone. She was worried something would happen while her gun was in defendant's possession. Ms. Blizzard gave defendant $800 and told him to get out of her life.

On June 8, 2000, defendant told Ms. Blizzard they needed to talk. He said he would take care of her Jacuzzi, which he had torn up. Defendant had also taken the wires from the car in her driveway. Defendant offered to replace the items he destroyed. Ms. Blizzard told him to just leave her alone. Defendant continued to contact Ms. Blizzard by telephone on a daily basis thereafter. On June 19, 2000, defendant hid in a van in Ms. Blizzard's driveway. He jumped out at Ms. Blizzard as she approached her car. Defendant pushed Ms. Blizzard back into the house. Defendant told Ms. Blizzard she could not break up with him. Ms. Blizzard contacted the police the following day. She obtained a temporary restraining order against defendant. On July 11, 2000, a permanent restraining order was issued. Both were served on defendant while he was in custody.

Defendant made threatening telephone calls to Ms. Blizzard on June 19, 2000, and for three months thereafter. Ms. Blizzard recorded many of those calls. She had also recorded threatening calls made by defendant prior to June 19, 2000, which were saved on her voicemail. The tapes were played at trial for the jury. Defendant made numerous telephone calls to Ms. Blizzard on a daily basis. In one such call, defendant stated: "I'm gone [*sic*] do some real ugly shit to you. . . ." In a subsequent message defendant told Ms. Blizzard: "[Y]ou know I'm livid and I'm ready to fuck you show [*sic*] enough up. I'm going to make it my business to fuck your life up starting today. . . ." In other messages, defendant told Ms. Blizzard: "I'm gone [*sic*] cross your ass out of the game. . . . [¶] . . . [¶] And you say that I have done some evil shit. Girl you ain't seen nothing yet. . . . [¶] . . . [¶] I'll make your life miserable . . . for disrespecting me." On June 26, 2000, Ms. Blizzard received a call from defendant on her cell phone. She believed the number defendant called from was near her office. Ms. Blizzard telephoned the police. Defendant was arrested at a nearby pay telephone. Ms. Blizzard was frightened by defendant's telephone calls. She believed defendant would carry out his threats.

Defendant continued to call Ms. Blizzard from jail following his arrest. Most of the calls were collect calls, which she did not accept. However, once the operator indicated it was a collect call, there was a brief period for defendant to say who was calling. During those brief messages, defendant often made threats. Ms. Blizzard testified defendant left messages like: "'Yeah, you [*sic*] going to die,'" or "'You put it on your mama. You [*sic*] going to die. I'm going to make sure your life, you going to wish you never met me. . . . [¶] . . . [¶] Face it, you gone [*sic*] die you taking that risk.'" Ms. Blizzard called the jail in an attempt to get defendant's phone privileges terminated. Ms. Blizzard felt she could not take it any longer: she could not sleep or eat; her work was affected; and she felt as though she would have a nervous breakdown. She was very

frightened by defendant's threats. She felt he would kill her. Ms. Blizzard also feared defendant would arrange for someone else to harm or kill her.

Ms. Blizzard attended defendant's parole hearing on August 2, 2000. Ms. Blizzard feared defendant would: be released; come after her; or have someone else come after her. Ms. Blizzard spoke to the police on August 2, 2000. Inglewood Police Officer Ray Wunno interviewed her. Ms. Blizzard gave him a cassette tape of the recorded threats. Officer Wunno believed Ms. Blizzard was frightened because her life had been threatened. Defendant continued to make threatening telephone calls from the jail to Ms. Blizzard. On August 4, 2001, Ms. Blizzard spoke with Inglewood Police Officer Sherry Rumsey. Ms. Blizzard brought additional cassette tapes, to which Officer Rumsey listened. Ms. Blizzard appeared to be frightened. Ms. Blizzard feared defendant would have a friend come to her home and harm her.

Defendant argues there was insufficient evidence to support his convictions for making terrorist threats.

. . .

Section 422 provides in relevant part: "Any person who willfully threatens to commit a crime which will result in death or great bodily injury to another person, with the specific intent that the statement, made verbally, in writing, or by means of an electronic communication device, is to be taken as a threat, even if there is no intent of actually carrying it out, which, on its face and under the circumstances in which it is made, is so unequivocal, unconditional, immediate, and specific as to convey to the person threatened, a gravity of purpose and an immediate prospect of execution of the threat, and thereby causes that person reasonably to be in sustained fear for his or her own safety or for his or her immediate family's safety, shall be punished by imprisonment in the county jail not to exceed one year, or by imprisonment in the state prison." (See also *People v. Toledo (2000) 26 Cal.4th 221, 227-228 {109 Cal.Rptr.2d 315, 26 P.3d 1051}.*)

Defendant argues the prosecution failed to prove the threats he made were so unequivocal and immediate as to convey an immediate prospect of execution. Defendant explains that because he was incarcerated and unable to carry out the threats there was no immediate prospect of execution. We disagree. In *People v. Mendoza (1997) 59 Cal.App.4th 1333, 1340-1341 {69 Cal.Rptr.2d 728},* our colleagues in Division Seven of this appellate district held: "[T]he determination whether a defendant intended his words to be taken as a threat, and whether the words were sufficiently unequivocal, unconditional, immediate and specific they conveyed to the victim an immediacy of purpose and immediate prospect of execution of the threat can be based on all the surrounding circumstances and not just on the words alone. The parties' history can also be considered as one of the relevant circumstances. (See, e.g., *People v. Martinez (1997) 53 Cal.App.4th 1212, 1218 {62 Cal.Rptr.2d 303}* [the meaning of the defendant's threat must be gleaned from the words and all of the surrounding circumstances]; *People v. Gudger (1994) 29 Cal.App.4th 310, 321 {34 Cal.Rptr.2d 510}* [it is necessary to review the language and context of the threat to determine if the speaker had the specific intent the statement was to be taken as a threat]; *People v. Stanfield {(1995)} 32 Cal.App.4th 1152, 1159 {38 Cal.Rptr.2d 328}* [the statute does not concentrate on the precise words of the threat but whether the threat communicated a gravity of purpose and immediate prospect of execution of the threat].)" (See also *People v. Solis (2001) 90 Cal.App.4th 1002, 1011-1017 {109 Cal.Rptr.2d 464}*.)

In this case, defendant had a lengthy history of not only threatening but also physically assaulting Ms. Blizzard. Between November 1999 and June 2000, defendant: pushed Ms. Blizzard against the wall on several occasions; pulled her clothing and hair; broke into her apartment; tore up her belongings; disabled her car; smashed his fist through her car window; and verbally abused her. In addition, defendant said he had pistol-whipped his former girlfriend and intended to shoot her. It was reasonable for Ms. Blizzard to fear that defendant would also follow through on the threats he made from jail based on the totality of the circumstances. (*People v. Franz (2001) 88 Cal.App.4th 1426, 1448-1449 {106 Cal.Rptr.2d 773}* [although the defendant's threat was made as he was being arrested, the victims' fear of immediate harm was reasonable because of his prior assault]; *People v. Mendoza, supra, 59 Cal.App.4th at pp. 1340-1341; People v. Martinez, supra, 53 Cal.App.4th at p. 1218.*) In addition, the first series of threats preceded defendant's parole violation hearing. Not only did Ms. Blizzard fear defendant would

be released following the hearing, but also his threats made reference to the fact that she had only a few days until he would be released: "Just three more days"; "You got [*sic*] three more days to apologize for your disrespect"; and "Hey tramp. I'm gone [*sic*] spare you one more day." Moreover, both before and after his parole hearing, defendant made reference to the fact that he would send someone to get her: "Somebody gone [*sic*] come see you. . . ." There was evidence of defendant's past domestic abuse of both Ms. Blizzard and his former girlfriend. This further supported Ms. Blizzard's fears his threats were specific, unequivocal, and immediate. (See *People v. Franz, supra, 88 Cal.App.4th at pp. 1448-1449; People v. McCray (1997) 58 Cal.App.4th 159, 172 {67 Cal.Rptr.2d 872}; People v. Allen (1995) 33 Cal.App.4th 1149, 1156 {40 Cal.Rptr.2d 7};* [history of stormy relationship between the defendant and victim relevant in establishing victim's fear].) As our colleagues in the Fifth District Court of Appeals have held: "A threat is sufficiently specific where it threatens death or great bodily injury. A threat is not insufficient simply because it does 'not communicate a time or precise manner of execution, section 422 does not require those details to be expressed.'" (*People v. Butler (2000) 85 Cal.App.4th 745, 752 {102 Cal.Rptr.2d 269},* quoting *In re David L. (1991) 234 Cal.App.3d 1655, 1660 {286 Cal.Rptr. 398};* see also *People v. Lopez (1999) 74 Cal.App.4th 675, 679-680 {88 Cal.Rptr.2d 252}* [§ 422 does not require an immediate ability to carry out the threat]; *People v. Melhado (1998) 60 Cal.App.4th 1529, 1538 {70 Cal.Rptr.2d 878}* ["[W]e understand the word 'immediate' to mean that degree of seriousness and imminence which is understood by the victim to be attached to the *future prospect* of the threat being carried out, should the conditions not be met."].) Substantial evidence supports the judgment.

The judgment is affirmed.

ARMSTRONG, J., and MOSK, J., concurred.

COURT OF APPEAL, THIRD DISTRICT, CALIFORNIA

No. C058061

MARCH 24, 2009
REVIEW DENIED JULY 15, 2009

OPINION BY: ROBIE, J.

A jury found defendant Danny Greg Uecker guilty of stalking two women. The trial court found he had four strike priors and sentenced him to 50 years to life in prison.

Defendant appeals, raising the following five contentions: (1) there was insufficient evidence to support both stalking convictions; (2) the trial court prejudicially erred in admitting certain evidence of defendant's prior bad acts; (3) the court prejudicially erred in admitting evidence defendant was a registered sex offender; (4) the court erred in refusing to dismiss some or all of his strike priors; and (5) defendant's sentence is cruel and/or unusual punishment.

Disagreeing with these contentions, we affirm the judgment.

FACTUAL AND PROCEDURAL BACKGROUND

A

COUNT 1—STALKING OF M.

M. is a service representative at the Social Security Administration in Shasta County. Her first encounter with defendant was at her work parking lot around the end of May or beginning of June 2006 when she noticed him sitting by her white Mustang between noon and 1:00 p.m. Defendant was on his bicycle, parked three to four feet from her car. M. commented that bicycling was good exercise. Thereafter, defendant would be beside M.'s car every day when she would go to lunch, even when her lunch hour varied. They would exchange greetings, and defendant sometimes would try to engage M. in further conversation. On occasion M. would oblige, but she always would say she had to get back to work because she was running late. She was polite to defendant because her job taught her to treat human beings with kindness and respond to their conversation. This pattern continued week after week, month after month.

About the same time defendant starting hanging around M.'s car, he started leaving notes for her on her car. The first note included his telephone number and read as follows: "'If you want to go riding bicycles, give me a call.'" M. ripped up the note and threw it away because she "wasn't interested."

In September, M. started parking on the street because she no longer needed the shade the original parking spot provided and somebody else had started parking in her spot. Defendant approached her at her new spot and asked whether she was trying to "'get away from [him].'" She said "'[n]o.'" He continued showing up at her new parking spot, leaving her notes and trying to engage her in conversation. One of these notes read as follows: "'I'm not a homeless guy. I have a job. I have a roof over my head. I want to go out with you.'" She threw it away and did not talk to him about the note. His behavior was beginning to concern M., and she decided she needed to "prepare for stuff" "if he got crazy or something." She bought mace and started taking "evasive" actions by moving her car.

But defendant persisted. His next note was a Christmas card that read as follows: "[M.], [¶] I hope you have a nice holiday season! I know how we met is a little rare, and I look like a transient on the side of the road but I can assure you I do have a full time job and a roof over my head. [Smiley face.] Listen, no strings attached, if ever you want to call sometime just to talk, I'm open for it, if you haven't lost my number? Its [sic] really nice talking to you as an attractive, mature lady! I'm not looking for anything super serious but I wouldn't mind the companionship on a cold, rainy day, sipping hot chocolate. [Smiley face.] [¶] Danny [¶] P.S. Nice car. [Smiley face.] I like it better than the Mustang." (Capitalization omitted.)

M., who had bought a Toyota Camry a week before, was concerned and terrified defendant knew her every move. She went inside her workplace and talked with the administrative secretary for management, Nancy Patterson, and told her the following: "'Something's not right. This man just doesn't go away. And I don't know what to do anymore. I thought I could handle it on my own.'" M. had now become so fearful of defendant she stopped going out in the evenings and shopping and had her girlfriend stay with her a few times.

The next day, M. was so scared she parked in another location that was 10 feet from her work's exit. As she was walking out of work, defendant approached her on his bicycle and asked if she got his Christmas card. She thanked him but "[f]irm[ly]" said she was "not interested" because she was "seeing someone" and asked whether his statement about her being a mature woman implied she was old. Defendant said "no," "got mad," and asked why she had been flirting with him. She said she had not been and was simply responding to his conversation. She then announced she had to go pick up her son, and defendant left.

The following day, M. took a much later than normal lunch because her son was very ill. She did not see defendant but received the following note: "[M.], [¶] I'm not on my bike anymore. The weather is too cold, wet or unpredictable. [¶] I'm in a small brown truck w/ a camper shell. I still spend my lunch hour here because its [sic] quiet. I don't like to keep leaving notes on your car. Would much rather talk to you. [Smiley face.] [¶] Ok so you're not mature! You're an immature trouble making brat! Now what? [Smiley face.] [¶] What's a guy gotta do to get a call from a beautiful woman? I'll be here tomorrow if you want to see me. You sure have some funny lunch hours. [Smiley face.] [¶] Dan."

When M. read this note, she "really freaked out." She "started to realize that this is more than just someone interested in dating, that this guy is just watching [her] every move." She "started parking way down the road" so defendant would not be able to see her car, had people walk her to her car, and alerted the guard at her workplace. As with the last note, M. gave it to Patterson. M. did not call the police herself because office protocol required her to go through management.

Patterson spoke to her manager, Linde Ballentine, about the situation, and Ballentine called M. into her office. M. told Ballentine defendant had been leaving notes on her car, "he was now scaring her with some of the things in the notes, [and] that she didn't know how to interpret them." M. was crying on and off, was shaky, and had to sit down several times.

The following day, December 19, Ballentine saw defendant in his truck eating lunch. He was positioned "with a good view of the entry to the parking lot where the cars come in" and of the "employee entrance." Management then contacted law enforcement.

B

COUNT 2—STALKING OF J.

J. is a part-time real estate agent in Shasta County who began her career in November 2006. To generate business, she posted real estate advertisements with her photograph and phone number in local newspapers and magazines.

At the end of November or early December 2006, J. received a phone message from "Danny" saying he was looking for a "livable shack in the boonies for less than 60,000 dollars." J. returned his call, and when she had found a couple of houses that might work, she asked for his last name so she could mail the information to him. Defendant said it was "Eucker."

Defendant then began calling J. a couple of times a day both on her cellular phone and her office line. She thought his messages were "a little too comfortable and playful." He joked about his friends coming over and "rid[ing her] horses" after she mentioned she liked the country and had horses. He told her she had a "really cool voice" and he could "'[p]robably talk to [her] all day.'" That message left her with a "haunting and violating feeling." In reference to a listing of property she had found him in "[n]ot the greatest area," he asked if she ever went to check the places out and hinted she should take him there. She had no intention of doing so because she "wanted to make sure [she] was coming back." She pressed him for information to help him qualify for a loan, but he never provided any and simply wanted more listings.

During the second week of phone calls, defendant left a message stating he had something to tell J. He then laughed and said, "'Oh, no, never mind. If you're curious enough, you'll call back.'" When J. did not call back, defendant called her a couple of days later and asked if she had received his message. When she said she had, defendant asked her, "'Do you like surprises?'" J. responded that she was "'[n]ot particularly fond of them.'"

By now, J. was questioning defendant's credibility. He had said a friend had referred him to her, which she knew was a lie because defendant was her first client. J. decided to check Megan's Law database to see if defendant was listed. When she tried Danny "Eucker" nothing came up. When she tried Danny "Uecker" she saw defendant's picture with his residence address listed as a hotel. J. drove by the hotel several times to look at the trucks parked there, since defendant had told her he drove a truck. She "wanted to get a visual of every truck in there, so in case he pulled up behind [her, she] would know" and "wouldn't get caught off guard."

At some point after she learned defendant was a "sex offender," defendant left a message for her saying he wanted to come by the office. J. responded by parking her car "far out in the parking lot backwards, so it wouldn't look like a real estate car," putting her hair in a knot, wearing sweats, and "frump[ing] on in." She asked coworkers to let her know if anybody came to the door looking for her.

A couple of days after their last phone contact, defendant left the following "irate" message: "'I guess that's what you realtors do, you just drop us.'" J. responded with the following message: "'I'm a little offended that, you know, you would speak to me that way because I had been trying to help. Every step of the way. And didn't really appreciate that.'" She falsely told him she was quitting the residential real estate business to focus on commercial real estate and she would send him to someone who could help him. Thereafter, J. decided not to host open houses and asked her manager whether she could put someone else's photograph in the advertisements.

Defendant called J. back about three times after her last message. The first two messages were lengthy and extremely apologetic. In one, defendant said the following: "'I started this with you, [J.], because you didn't treat me like everybody else—some other realtors. So, with all due respect, I'd like to finish this with you. But I want to handle this with you—I want you to handle this or at least handle my issues, anyway.'" The message scared her. In another, defendant said the following: "'I'm sorry. I shouldn't have yelled at you like that. I had some words with a buddy at work. It wasn't your fault, but I want you to finish what you've started here with me. I know you're doing the commercial thing, but I want you to finish what you started with me.'" J.'s reaction to the second message was, "this guy is like talking to a girlfriend or something . . . [i]t . . . just . . . didn't s[i]t well, either." The third said, "'Hey, I just want, you know, out of dodge and by now, you probably know why.'"

J. reported defendant's conduct to law enforcement on December 13, 2006. She was afraid of defendant and felt trapped by him.

In all, defendant called her about 30 times over a three-week period, and of those calls, 6 to 10 were direct conversations.

Defendant was arrested on December 21, 2006.

DISCUSSION

I

SUFFICIENT EVIDENCE SUPPORTED BOTH STALKING CONVICTIONS

Defendant contends there was insufficient evidence he stalked either M. or J. As we will explain, he is incorrect.

A

STATUTORY DEFINITIONS

The Legislature has defined the crime of stalking as follows: "Any person who willfully, maliciously, and repeatedly follows or willfully and maliciously harasses another person and who makes a credible threat with the intent to place that person in reasonable fear for his or her safety, or the safety of his or her immediate family." (*Pen.Code,*n7 § 646.9, subd. (a).)

> n7 All further statutory references are to the Penal Code unless otherwise indicated.

"'[H]arasses' means engages in a knowing and willful course of conduct directed at a specific person that seriously alarms, annoys, torments, or terrorizes the person, and that serves no legitimate purpose." (§ 646.9, subd. (e).)

"'[C]ourse of conduct' means two or more acts occurring over a period of time, however short, evidencing a continuity of purpose. Constitutionally protected activity is not included within the meaning of 'course of conduct.'" (§ 646.9, subd. (f).)

"'[C]redible threat' means a verbal or written threat, including that performed through the use of an electronic communication device, or a threat implied by a pattern of conduct or a combination of verbal, written, or electronically communicated statements and conduct, made with the intent to place the person that is the target of the threat in reasonable fear for his or her safety or the safety of his or her family, and made with the apparent ability to carry out the threat so as to cause the person who is the target of the threat to reasonably fear for his or her safety or the safety of his or her family. It is not necessary to prove that the defendant had the intent to actually carry out the threat. The present incarceration of a person making the threat shall not be a bar to prosecution under this section. Constitutionally protected activity is not included within the meaning of 'credible threat.'" (§ 646.9, subd. (g).)

C

THERE WAS SUFFICIENT EVIDENCE DEFENDANT STALKED M.

Defendant argues there was insufficient evidence of all three elements of stalking, namely: (1) following or harassing another person; (2) making a credible threat; and (3) intending to place the victim in reasonable fear for her safety. We take each element in turn, finding sufficient evidence supported all three.

The first element of stalking is "willfully, maliciously, and repeatedly follow[ing] or willfully and maliciously harass[ing] another person." (§ 646.9, subd. (a).) Here, there was sufficient evidence to support this element. After M. told defendant firmly she was not interested in him, he got mad. The next day, after she had taken a much later lunch hour than normal, defendant left a note calling her derogatory names. The day after this note, defendant positioned himself in his car with a good view of the employee entrance. From this evidence, a reasonable jury could have found defendant purposefully (i.e., willfully) followed M. on more than one occasion (i.e., repeatedly) with the intent to disturb or annoy her (maliciously) after she told him she was not interested in him and refused to acquiesce in his requests to go out with him.n8

> n8 The jury was instructed that "willfully" means doing an act "willingly or on purpose." "[M]aliciously" means "intentionally" doing "a wrongful act" or "act[ing] with the unlawful intent to disturb, annoy or injure someone else." And "[r]epeatedly means more than once."

The second element is "mak[ing] a credible threat," which includes a threat implied by a pattern of conduct or a combination of verbal and written communicated statements and conduct. (§ 646.9, subd. (g).) Here, defendant's pattern of conduct, his written notes, and verbal statements implied he was going to do whatever it took to get M. to go out with him, reasonably causing M. to fear for her safety. Almost every work day for approximately seven months, defendant followed M. and/or placed notes on her car. He would always find her or her car no matter what time she had taken her lunch hour or what location she had parked her car. When she told him firmly she was not interested in him, he got mad. The next day, defendant tracked her car down yet again, left her a note stating he did not like to keep leaving notes on her car, she was an "immature trouble making brat" and asking, "Now what" and what he had to do to get a call from a beautiful woman. When M. read this note, she "really freaked out," "starting parking way down the road" so defendant would not see her car and had people walk her to her car. The next day, he returned again and positioned himself with a good view of the employee entrance. From this evidence, a reasonable jury could have found that defendant made an implied threat to her safety in that he was going to do whatever he needed to get M. to go out with him and that she reasonably feared for her safety. His persistence lasted seven months with no signs of abating, his last conversation with M. and his last note to her evidenced hostility toward her, and his final action of positioning himself where he could see her comings and goings at work signaled he was not going to take no for an answer.

The third element of stalking is intending to place the victim in reasonable fear for safety. Here, defendant's intent was evidenced by comments in two notes he left for M.

explicitly alerting her he had been tracking her. The first was when he mentioned her new car within the first week she purchased it. The second was when he mentioned she had "funny lunch hours." From these comments, a reasonable jury could conclude defendant wanted M. to know he had been watching her while she was parked at work and keeping track of her schedule to place her in fear of her safety.

Taken as a whole, therefore, there was sufficient evidence to support the jury's verdict that defendant stalked M. within the meaning of section 646.9.

D

THERE WAS SUFFICIENT EVIDENCE DEFENDANT STALKED J.

Defendant makes a similar sufficiency-of-the-evidence argument with respect to J., challenging all three elements of the crime. Again, we find sufficient evidence to support the stalking conviction.

As to the first element, there was no evidence defendant followed J., so we focus on the evidence he harassed her within the meaning of the statute. Defendant called J. under the guise of searching for a "livable shack in the boonies for less than 60,000 dollars." It was apparent defendant's contact with J. was not directed toward the legitimate purpose of buying real estate, as he refused her request to provide her information to help him qualify for a loan, would not give her the correct spelling of his name, and would not tell her the truth about how he got her contact information. When she tried to cut off contact with him, defendant kept calling her, leaving her one irate message about realtors dropping customers and another message that he wanted to "finish this with [her]" and wanted her to "handle [his] issues." Defendant left her feeling afraid and trapped. This evidence was sufficient to support the element of harassment.

The second element is making a credible threat. Here, defendant's pattern of conduct in calling J. over 30 times in three weeks despite her desire to cut off contact with him and his verbal statements in those calls implied a threat that caused her to reasonably fear for her safety. He left messages for J. that were "a little too comfortable and playful," ones that left her with a "haunting and violating feeling," and ones that scared her. He told her he wanted a house in the boonies and then hinted she should take him out in her car to look at the properties. He told J. that she had a "really cool voice" and he could "'[p]robably talk to [her] all day.'" He left a message saying he had something to tell her, laughed, and then told her if she was curious enough, she would call back. When she did not, he asked her if she liked surprises. He left a message saying he wanted to come by the office. She changed her parking habits and dress to hide from defendant and would not hold open houses. When she did not return this call, he left her an irate message about realtors dropping their clients. When she told him that she was quitting the residential real estate market, he still persisted calling her. In his last messages, he cryptically told her he wanted to "finish this with [her]," wanted her to "handle [his] issues," and he wanted "out of dodge and by now, [she] probably kn[e]w why." It was after this series of calls that J. contacted law enforcement.

Taken as a whole, this conduct implied a threat to J.'s safety. She knew defendant is a sex offender and defendant's last comment to J. indicated he knew that she knew.n9 He intimated he wanted to be alone with her, made suggestive comments about her voice, asked if she liked surprises, told her he wanted to come by the office, was irate when she tried to get rid of him, and left cryptic messages on her answering machine. Simply put, this pattern of unrelenting conduct over the course of three weeks that toward the end became hostile and demanding perpetrated by someone who is a sex offender and had no legitimate interest in real estate was sufficient to satisfy this element.

n9 The evidence supports this inference because of defendant's comment to J. that she probably knew why he wanted "out of dodge."

The third element is intending to place the victim in reasonable fear for safety. Here, it can be inferred defendant intended to place J. in reasonable fear for her safety from his persistent phone contacts with her despite her attempts to end them, his apparent knowledge that she knew he is a registered sex offender, and his hostile and demanding tone in one of his last messages. This evidence supported not only the conclusion J. reasonably feared defendant and had reason to fear him but also that he acted with the intent to induce that fear. *(People v. Falck, (1997) 52 Cal.App.4th 287, 299, 60 Cal.Rptr.2d 624.)*

DISPOSITION

The judgment is affirmed.

We concur: NICHOLSON, Acting P.J., and RAYE, J.

PEOPLE v. ALVARADO

COURT OF APPEAL OF CALIFORNIA, FIRST APPELLATE DISTRICT, DIVISION THREE

224 Cal. App. 3d 1165; 274 Cal. Rptr. 452

October 26, 1990

OPINION BY: STRANKMAN, J.

John Anthony Alvarado appeals from the judgment after a jury convicted him of two counts of first degree robbery (*Pen. Code, § § 211, 212.5,* subd. (a)), . . . and found true an allegation that he had used a firearm in the commission of the offenses. (*§ 12022.5,* subd. (a).) He contends that evidence that he had robbed two victims in his motel room was insufficient to support convictions of first degree robbery. We find that appellant was properly convicted of first degree robbery, and affirm.

DISCUSSION

I. ROBBERY

Appellant's principal argument on appeal presents a narrow question of law. For the purposes of appeal, the parties do not dispute the facts that raise that issue. We therefore do not provide a detailed summary of facts. Instead, we recite the facts as they are relevant to our discussion.

With respect to appellant's claim that he was improperly convicted of first degree robbery, it is enough to say that appellant lured two itinerant stereo salesmen to a motel room in which he was living, where he robbed them at gunpoint. Appellant argues that he should not have been convicted of first degree robbery. His theory is that although the robbery took place in "an inhabited dwelling house" (§ 212.5, subd. (a) [defining circumstances in which robbery is of the first degree]; and see *People v. Fleetwood (1985) 171 Cal. App.3d 982, 987–988 {217 Cal. Rptr. 612}* [hotel room is "inhabited dwelling house" for purposes of robbery statute]), because it was *his* dwelling house, the first degree robbery statute should not apply. Appellant relies on *People v. Gauze (1975) 15 Cal.3d 709, 714 {125 Cal. Rptr. 773, 542 P.2d 1365}* (defendant may not be convicted of burglarizing his or her own residence). For the reasons set out below, we disagree and decline to reduce the degree of appellant's robbery convictions.

We begin with the statute. Section 212.5 provides in part that ". . . every robbery which is perpetrated in an inhabited dwelling house, . . . or the inhabited portion of any other building, is robbery of the first degree." (§ 212.5, subd. (a).) . . . By comparing this history and the language of the statutes to the burglary provisions of the Penal Code, it is clear that the Legislature intended to create an enhanced robbery offense equivalent to first degree burglary. (Compare § 212.5 with § 460 [providing that "burglary of an inhabited dwelling house, . . . or the inhabited portion of any other building, is burglary of the first degree."].) Based on this connection between the robbery and burglary statutes, appellant argues that the "inhabited dwelling house" provisions of the robbery statutes should be limited by the holding of *People v. Gauze, supra,* 15 Cal.3d at pp. 715–716 (defendant may not commit burglary of own residence). However, it does not follow either from the statutory language or from the Legislature's evident intent to enhance the penalty for residential robbery that the Legislature also intended to import into the robbery statutes the limitations imposed by Gauze.

In Gauze, the defendant, intending to shoot one of his roommates, entered his own apartment. (*People v. Gauze, supra, 15 Cal.3d at p. 711.*) He was convicted of first degree burglary on the theory that he had entered an inhabited dwelling with felonious intent. (*Ibid.*) The Gauze court held that the burglary statute "retained two important aspects of [the common law] crime. A burglary remains an entry which invades a possessory right in a building. And it still must be committed by a person who has no right to be in the building." (*Id.,* at p. 714.) Thus, the defendant in Gauze could not be guilty of burglary, as he had entered his own home. (*Ibid.*) The court emphasized that the danger the burglary laws were intended to meet was that created by the intrusion of a wrongdoer without permission, and noted that no such danger exists where there is no intrusion. (*Id.,* at pp. 715–716.) In the burglary context, the court's reasoning has great force. As the court pointed out, it would be absurd to find a burglary where a forger, intent upon creating a false document, peacefully enters his or her own house to accomplish the deed. (*Id.,* at p. 716.)

However, the same reasoning does not carry over into robbery. Robbery, unlike burglary, is not a crime which threatens property rights in a particular place. A robbery occurs whenever there is a taking from the person of the victim by force or fear, regardless of the location of the event. (§ 211; and see 2 *Witkin & Epstein, Cal. Criminal Law (2d ed. 1988) Crimes Against Property, § 635 et seq.,* pp. 715–726.) For that reason, none of the concerns of the Gauze court have any application in a robbery case. First, there is no common law requirement that a robbery occur in any particular place; the Legislature could not have had such a rule in mind when it drafted the robbery statute. Second, the evil to be prevented by robbery statutes is theft by violence, not a trespass with intent to commit some other crime. Third, the absurd result that would follow from a rule which would allow a resident to be convicted of burglarizing his or her own residence is not present. Finally, the penalty enhancement we discuss here is fundamentally different from the issue in *Gauze,* which was whether the defendant could have committed any burglary at all. Here, the question is whether the penalty for the crime should be increased, not whether the defendant's acts satisfy the basic elements of the offense. The determination of an appropriate penalty does not implicate the social theories on which particular conduct is made criminal. Thus, unlike the *Gauze* court, we need not decide whether the Legislature intended to make residential robbery

criminal. Rather, we need only decide whether it intended to punish that crime more severely than other robberies, a much more limited inquiry. We therefore decline to apply the reasoning of *Gauze* to the residential robbery statute.

. . .

There is no absurdity in increasing the penalty for a robbery committed in one's own home as opposed to one committed in a public street, and no common law rule restricting the variation of penalties for robbery based on the place where the robbery occurs.

. . .

There is nothing in the language of the statute which would limit its effect where the dwelling house or building in question is the robber's own residence, nor have we discovered anything in the legislative history of the statute which compels the conclusion that the Legislature intended such a limitation. The Legislature evidently thought that a robbery occurring in an inhabited building was a more serious offense than an ordinary robbery, just as it found a robbery committed against a trolley car operator more serious than one committed against an ordinary motorist. (See § 212.5.) Here, it has enacted increased penalties for robbery committed in an inhabited building and has not expressly exempted the robber's residence from that category. It is not our function to judge the wisdom of the statute, but only to apply it. Unlike the *Gauze* court, we find no compelling reason to read an exemption into the statute which the Legislature omitted to provide.

The judgment is affirmed.

COURT OF APPEAL OF CALIFORNIA, FOURTH APPELLATE DISTRICT, DIVISION TWO

103 CAL. APP. 4TH 599; 126 CAL. RPTR. 2D 855

NOVEMBER 7, 2002

OPINION BY: GAUT, J.

INTRODUCTION

After confining two female employees to a back room, defendant robbed a Temecula jewelry store of $40,000 worth of jewelry and escaped in the car of one of the employees. A jury convicted defendant of armed robbery, aggravated kidnapping, carjacking, and various related special allegations. In addition, the court found defendant had incurred three previous strike convictions. The court sentenced defendant to a total indeterminate sentence of 45 years to life.

Defendant appeals, challenging the two convictions for kidnapping to commit robbery and the conviction for carjacking for insufficiency of evidence. We hold that defendant's movement of the victims was merely incidental to the robbery and did not increase the risk of harm to them. We reverse the convictions for aggravated kidnapping but affirm the conviction for carjacking even though it differs somewhat from the more typical carjacking scenario where a victim is accosted in or near her car.

FACTS

Joy Salem and Sarah Gibeson were employed by the Jewelry Mart. The owner, Roukan Hatter, had twice purchased jewelry from defendant.

Defendant entered the store shortly after it opened one Sunday afternoon. He displayed a gun and ordered the women to give him the key to the jewelry cases. He also demanded the keys to Gibeson's car. He directed the women into the office at the back, tied their ankles and wrists with duct tape, and taped their mouths. Then he began taking jewelry from the cases. When customers entered the store, he told them it was closed for maintenance or performing inventory.

Gibeson tried to call 911 on her cellular phone but she dropped the phone. Defendant returned to the office, threatened the women, and pulled the office phone out of

the wall. After that, he left. After some other customers helped release the women, Gibeson saw her car had been taken.

. . .

CARJACKING

"'Carjacking' is the felonious taking of a motor vehicle in the possession of another, from his or her person or immediate presence . . . against his or her will and with the intent to either permanently or temporarily deprive the person in possession of the motor vehicle of his or her possession, accomplished by means of force or fear." Defendant asserts a carjacking was not proved because defendant did not take Gibeson's car from "her person or immediate presence," an area defined for the jury as being within her "reach, observation or control, so that he or she could, if not overcome by violence or prevented by fear, retain possession of the subject property." Instead, defendant took Gibeson's keys from her while her car was parked outside the store in a parking lot.

. . .

Defendant relies on *People v. Medina,* in which the court found there was a carjacking when the victim "was inside a motel room when his keys were forcibly taken and his nearby car was driven away." The court sidestepped the issue of what constitutes "immediate presence" in the context of a carjacking because the victim had been lured away from his car by a trick. But *Medina* offers no support to defendant here. Instead, it held: "The statute requires force or fear to be applied to the driver . . . clearly a confrontation must occur. . . . [But] the victim need not actually be physically present in the vehicle when the confrontation occurs."

. . .

In a subsequent case, the appellate court concluded the crime of carjacking, like the crime of robbery, "may be established not only when the defendant has taken property out of physical presence of the victim, but also when the defendant exercises dominion and control over the victim's property through force or fear."

. . .

Additionally, the People cite a number of federal cases, originating with *United States v. Burns,* in which the courts have found that carjackings occurred when the owner was forced to give up his car keys at an inside location and the car was taken from an outside location.

. . .

In the present case, the elements of carjacking were established. Defendant took possession of Gibeson's car by threatening her and demanding her car keys. Although she was not physically present in the parking lot when he drove the car away, she had been forced to relinquish her car keys. Otherwise, she could have kept possession and control of the keys and her car. Although not the "classic" carjacking scenario, it was a carjacking all the same.

DISPOSITION

We reverse the convictions for aggravated kidnapping but affirm the carjacking and armed robbery convictions.

KEY TERMS

Assault, 145

Battery, 146

Attendant circumstances, 146

Mayhem, 146

Enumerated felony, 146

Torture, 147

Duress, 147

Rape, 147

Oral copulation, 148

Sodomy, 148

Sexual penetration, 148

Aggravated sexual assault of a child, 148

Lewd and lascivious acts involving children, 148

Statutory rape, 149

Megan's Law, 149

Pimping, 149

Pandering, 149

Indecent public exposure, 149

False imprisonment, 150

Human trafficking, 150

Kidnapping, 150

Criminal threat, 151

Stalking, 151

Robbery, 151

Carjacking, 151

STUDY GUIDE CHAPTER 5

CRIMES AGAINST THE PERSON

1. Is *battery* a general intent crime? Read *People v. Lara.* Is an accident or criminal negligence sufficient to prove the criminal intent necessary for the crime of *battery?* Explain. What facts would the prosecutor argue to prove that the defendant in Lara is guilty of a *battery?*

2. Does consent matter in the crime of *statutory rape?* Explain.

3. Does a rape victim need to resist or cry out to prove the crime of *rape?* Explain the *Iniguez* ruling.

4. How is the crime of *false imprisonment* different from a *battery?* Explain.

5. How is the crime of *false imprisonment* different from a *kidnapping?* Explain.

6. What makes the crime of *aggravated mayhem* more serious than a *battery?* What is the difference between the crime of *mayhem* and a *battery?* Explain.

7. How is the crime of *carjacking* different from a *false imprisonment?* Explain.

8. Read *People v. Hoard.* Can a defendant be convicted of *carjacking* when the victim was not physically present when the car was taken? Explain.

9. What are the elements for the crime of *robbery?*

10. What are the elements for the crime of *stalking?*

CHAPTER 6

Crimes Against Habitation

Burglary and arson are crimes against property. The common law requirements for both offenses have been modified in important ways by the modern California Penal Code. Common law burglary was the breaking and entering into the dwelling house of another, at nighttime, with the intent to commit a felony inside. Section 459 requires simply the unlawful entry into any structure, with the intent to commit grand or petty theft or any other felony inside; it does away with the requirements that the entry be by 'breaking,' that the property be a dwelling or owned by another, or that the entry be at night. The modern statute allows for the prosecution of shoplifters and those who break into locked vehicles for burglary.

Burglary is divided into degrees in California: **first degree burglary** takes place when the entry is to an inhabited dwelling, and **second degree burglary** when the entry is into any other structure.[1] The punishment for burglary in the first degree is always a felony, punishable by two, four, or six years in state prison. In contrast, second degree burglary is a wobbler, which the prosecutor can charge as either a misdemeanor or a felony with a possible sentence of a year in state prison or up to a year in county jail.[2] First degree (residential) burglary can sometimes present a challenge in deciding what areas are considered part of an inhabited dwelling. In *People v. Thorn* the court explained that where breaking into a car in a car port was first degree burglary because the car port was closely connected to

---

[1] Cal. Pen. Code §460.

[2] Cal. Pen. Code §461.

the apartments and where the tenants had a reasonable expectation of privacy when parking in the spaces. The court held that the inquiry for determining whether a space is part of an inhabited dwelling is whether it is: "'functionally interconnected with and immediately contiguous to other portions of the house.' …'Functionally interconnected' means used in related or complementary ways. 'Contiguous' means adjacent, adjoining, nearby or close." In order to be considered a structure for the purposes of burglary, a building must have walls—which were missing from the barn at issue in *In re Amber S.*[5]

The elements of *burglary* are as follows:

- Actus reus—unlawful entry into any structure (must have walls and a door)
- Mens rea—intent to commit grand or petty theft, or any other felony inside (specific intent offense)
- Causation—the defendant's act set in motion the chain of events that led to the resulting injury
- Injury—fear and loss of or damage to property

Receiving stolen property takes place when a person buys or receives any property that has been stolen or that has been obtained in any manner constituting theft or extortion, while knowing about the character of the property.[6] It is a general intent crime. A person who is a principal to the theft can be charged with receipt of stolen property, but cannot be charged with both theft and receipt of the same stolen property. Receiving stolen property is a misdemeanor. California has also criminalized **looting** during a state of emergency or a local emergency.[7] The elements of the crime of looting are the same as that of second degree burglary, but require specific attendant circumstances: a natural or man-made disaster, riot, etc. Looting is a wobbler, which a prosecutor may choose to charge as either a felony or a misdemeanor.

Arson is the willful and malicious setting of fire to or burning of [or aiding others in burning, counseling others to burn, or procuring the burning of] any structures, forest land, or property.[8] Arson is a felony in California, and the punishment for it varies widely depending upon the circumstances surrounding the offense. Section 451.1 outlines sentencing enhancements for defendants convicted of arson when

- they have been convicted of a prior arson,
- great bodily injury to a firefighter, peace officer, or other emergency personnel has occurred,
- more than one victim was injured,
- multiple structures were burned in the fire, or
- a device designed to accelerate or delay ignition was used to start the fire.

Aggravated arson (punishable by 10 years to life in prison) takes place when the defendant willfully, maliciously, deliberately, and with premeditation set the fire with the intent to cause injury to one or more persons, or to cause damage to property under circumstances likely to produce injury to one or more persons, and when one of the following is true:

- The defendant has had another arson conviction in the previous 10 years.
- The fire caused damage or loss in excess of $5,650,000.
- The fire caused damage to five or more inhabited structures.

The elements of *arson* are as follows:

- Actus reus—setting fire to or burning any structure, forest land, or property
- Mens rea—willful and malicious (specific intent to burn)
- Causation—the defendant's actions set in motion the chain of events that led to the injury
- Injury—loss or damage to lands or property

Burglary and arson are enumerated felonies for the purposes of first degree felony murder in California.

---

[3] (2009) 176 Cal. App. 4th 255.

[4] Id at 261.

[5] In re Amber S., 33 Cal.App.4th 185 (1995).

[6] Cal. Pen. Code §496.

[7] Cal. Pen. Code §463.

[8] Cal. Pen. Code §451.

IN RE AMBER S.

COURT OF APPEAL OF CALIFORNIA, FIRST APPELLATE DISTRICT, DIVISION FIVE

33 Cal. App. 4th 185; 39 Cal. Rptr. 2d 672

March 16, 1995

OPINION BY: KING, J.

In this case we hold that an "open pole barn" without walls is not a building within the scope of California's burglary statute.

Amber S. and an accomplice were caught in the act of stealing some 30 bales of hay from a structure described by the owner as an "open pole barn." The structure was open on all sides, consisting of a roof and overhang held up by poles. Amber was charged with burglary (*Pen. Code, § 459*), and a referee found the allegation to be true. The referee adjudged Amber a ward of the court and placed her on probation.

Amber correctly contends the structure at issue is not within the scope of *Penal Code section 459,* which applies to "any house, room, apartment, tenement, shop, warehouse, store, mill, barn, stable, outhouse, or other building" and certain enumerated non-buildings not relevant here. It has long been the rule that a "building" within the meaning of California's burglary statute "is any structure which has walls on all sides and is covered by a roof.". . . but they must "act as a significant barrier to entrance without cutting or breaking." (*Id.* at p. 206.) "The proper question is whether the nature of a structure's composition is such that a reasonable person would expect some protection from unauthorized intrusions." . . . The open pole barn described by

the owner in the present case does not meet this test, for lack of any walls whatsoever. There was no significant barrier to entrance, no protection from unauthorized intrusions.

The Attorney General argues *Penal Code section 459* encompasses this structure because it is a "barn," which is specifically enumerated in the statute. But the list of structures in which "barn" appears ends with the phrase "or *other* building." (*Pen. Code, § 459,* italics added.) Thus, the statute treats a barn as a type of building, making it subject to the requirement of walls.

Everyday knowledge is consistent with the applicable law here. We have all heard that it is pointless to close the barn door after the horse has gotten out. But if there are no walls, there is no barn door, and the horse is free to leave anytime. This venerable aphorism is not just a metaphor, but tells us something practical about barns: they must have walls and a door to keep the horse in. If there are no walls, there is no barn.

We conclude this structure is not within the scope of the burglary statute. Amber might have committed a theft or trespass offense, but she did not commit burglary. She was charged with the wrong offense.

The judgment is reversed.

PETERSON, P. J., and HANING, J., concurred.

PEOPLE v. THORN

COURT OF APPEAL, FIRST DISTRICT

176 CAL. APP. 4TH 255. NO. A121336

JULY 31, 2009

OPINION BY: JENKINS, J.

Defendant and appellant Richard Thorn (Thorn) appeals his jury-trial conviction for first-degree burglary in violation of *Penal Code, section 460,* subdivision (a).n1 Thorn contends his conviction should be reversed because the carport area where he committed the offense does not fall within the ambit of the burglary statutes. Thorn also contends the conviction should be reversed because the trial court directed a verdict of guilty on the first degree burglary charge by the manner in which it instructed the jury on the charge. As explained more fully below, we find these contentions unpersuasive, and therefore affirm.

   n1 Further statutory references are to the Penal Code unless otherwise noted.

PROCEDURAL BACKGROUND

On December 24, 2007, the San Mateo County District Attorney filed an information charging defendant with the following offenses: count 1—commercial burglary, a felony (§ 460, subd. (b)); count 2—automobile burglary, a felony (§ 460, subd. (b)); count 3—first-degree burglary of an inhabited dwelling house, a felony (§ 460, subd. (a)); count 4—being under the influence of a controlled substance, a misdemeanor (*Health & Saf.Code, § 11550,* subd. (a)); count 5—possession of drug paraphernalia, a misdemeanor (*Health & Saf.Code, § 11364);* and count 6-possession of a burglary tool, a misdemeanor (§ 466).

During trial on February 21, 2008, the *People* filed an amended information to change the name of the defendant from Ray Glass to Richard Thorn and to insert the correct date for certain prior convictions. The *People* also dismissed count 1 (commercial burglary) in the interests of justice.

As amended, the information alleged that Thorn suffered two prior serious felony convictions for first-degree burglary in June 1994, pursuant to section 667, subdivision (a). The information alleged the same two convictions for first-degree burglary were strike convictions within the meaning of section 1170.12, subdivision (c)(1).

Additionally, the information alleged Thorn had ten prior felony convictions between May 1986 and June 2000 for purposes of section 1203, subdivision (e)(4). Further, the information alleged six prior felonies for purposes of section 667.5, subdivision (b).

On February 22, 2008, the jury returned a verdict of not guilty on count 2 (automobile burglary)n2 and a verdict of guilty on the lesser charge of vehicle tampering, in violation of *Vehicle Code, section 10852.* The jury also found defendant not guilty on count 6 (possession of a burglary tool). The jury returned guilty verdicts on count 3 (first-degree residential burglary), count 4 (under the influence of a controlled substance), and count 5 (possession of drug paraphernalia).

   n2 For auto burglary, the prosecution must prove defendant made a forced entry into a locked vehicle. (In *re Young K.* (1996) 49 Cal.App.4th 861, 863, 57 Cal.Rptr.2d 12.)

After the jury was dismissed the court held a bench trial on the alleged prior convictions. The trial court found all the prior conviction allegations true beyond a reasonable doubt. Furthermore, pursuant to section 667.5, subdivision (b), the trial court found that defendant had not remained free of prison custody for a five-year period between any of the priors alleged. The prosecution dismissed one of Thorn's prior two strike convictions for first-degree burglary in the interests of justice.

. . .

FACTS

The facts are adduced from the witness testimony and photographic evidence submitted at trial. In October 2007, Jose Hernandez and his wife lived at the apartment building at 50 Hillcrest Drive in Daly City where the burglary took place. On the evening in question, Hernandez parked his vehicle in his parking stall underneath the apartments on the ground floor of the building. On the way to his apartment on the level above the carport area, Hernandez met the "lady in Apartment 4." The lady pointed out an African-American man and told Hernandez she'd seen the man looking into the cars parked in the carports below. Hernandez saw the man walking around a red car parked in one of the carports. After Hernandez saw the man get into the red car, he went to his apartment and dialed 911. As he was talking to the 911 operator, Hernandez went back to observe the man's activities in the carport. Hernandez watched as the man got in and out of the driver's side, front passenger side, and back seat of the red car. One time the man got out of the car with a screwdriver in his hand. Hernandez stayed on the phone with the 911 dispatcher until the police arrived. Hernandez watched as the man got out of the red car for the last time and saw the police contact him as he tried to walk away.

Luis Arias also lived at the apartment building in October 2007. At that time, Arias was driving a red Volkswagen Jetta belonging to his cousin. Arias parked the vehicle at the apartment building in his designated parking stall between 5:00 and 6:00 p.m. on the evening in question. Arias recalled he locked the car when he parked it. The police contacted Arias about his car around 11:00 p.m. When Arias went to view the car the police asked him if anything was missing. Arias noticed the stereo was missing from the dashboard. The stereo had been placed in his daughter's backpack, which was lying on the driver's seat. An amplifier had been removed from underneath the passenger seat and placed inside his daughter's backpack. Beside his daughter's backpack was a "plastic bag with beers in it" that did not belong to Arias. When Arias parked the car earlier that evening, his daughter's backpack had been in the back seat.

A police officer apprehended Thorn on the public sidewalk adjacent to the apartment building between the building's courtyard and the street. When stopped by the officer, Thorn removed an object from his waist band and dropped it. A screwdriver was later recovered underneath an adjacent parked car. In the subject vehicle, police found a stereo, an amplifier inside a backpack, and two white plastic Safeway bags containing beers and items of clothing. An officer who was dispatched to the apartment building regarding the reported burglary in progress arrived to find a suspect (Thorn) already in custody. The officer realized he had seen Thorn about 20–30 minutes before he received the dispatch. The officer recalled that Thorn crossed the street in front of his patrol car two blocks from the apartment building while carrying two white plastic bags.

50 Hillcrest Drive, where the burglary occurred, is a V-shaped building. Five carports comprise the ground floor of the four-story residential apartment complex (the upper three floors are residential units). Each carport contains up to three parking stalls. The carports (not the individual parking stalls) are enclosed by solid brick walls on three sides with the front completely open to the paved courtyard in front of the building. To park, a tenant turns his or her vehicle from the street into the courtyard and drives directly into a parking stall. There are three stairwells leading from the courtyard to the apartments above. There is a walkway on each floor that provides access for entry into the respective apartment units. The parking spaces in the carports are numbered but the numbers do not correlate to the numbers of the apartment units. Parking spaces are limited and are assigned by building management according to availability. Each carport has a sign above it saying "Tenant Parking Only."

DISCUSSION

A. THE CARPORT IS PROTECTED BY THE BURGLARY STATUTES

Section 459 provides in pertinent part that "[e]very person who enters any house, room, apartment, tenement . . . with intent to commit grand or petit larceny or any felony is guilty of burglary. As used in this chapter, 'inhabited' means currently being used for dwelling purposes, whether occupied or not." (§ 459.) Section 460 provides in pertinent part that "[e]very burglary of an inhabited dwelling house . . . is burglary of the first degree. [¶] All other kinds of burglary are of the second degree." (§ 460, subds. (a)–(b).) A conviction for first degree burglary thus requires "entry" of an "inhabited dwelling house" with the intent to commit a felony. (§§ 459, 460.)

"[T]he term 'inhabited dwelling house' means a 'structure where people ordinarily live and which is currently being used for dwelling purposes. [Citation.] A place is an inhabited dwelling if a person with possessory rights uses the place as sleeping quarters intending to continue doing so in the future.' (Citations.)" (*People v. Cruz (1996) 13 Cal.4th 764, 776, 55 Cal.Rptr.2d 117, 919 P.2d 731 (Cruz).*) Courts have broadly interpreted the term "inhabited dwelling house" to include a variety of structures and places (see *id.* at p. 777, 55 Cal.Rptr.2d 117, 919 P.2d 731 [inhabited vessel qualifies as inhabited dwelling house]; *People v. Wilson (1992) 11 Cal.App.4th 1483, 1488, 15 Cal.Rptr.2d 77* [tent qualifies as inhabited dwelling house]) in order to effect the legislative purpose of the burglary statutes—"to protect the peaceful occupation of one's residence" against intrusion and violence. (*Cruz, supra, 13 Cal.4th at p. 775, 55 Cal.Rptr.2d 117, 919 P.2d 731.*)

Thorn contends on two grounds that the carport is not part of an inhabited building under the burglary statutes. First, he contends the carport areas in question are not "part of" the inhabited dwelling house, due to the manner in which they are configured in relation to the apartment building as a whole. Second, Thorn contends the carport falls outside the ambit of the burglary statutes because it did not carry a reasonable expectation of protection from intrusion. We address each of these arguments in turn.

"In determining whether a structure is part of an inhabited dwelling, the essential inquiry is whether the structure is 'functionally interconnected with and immediately contiguous to other portions of the house.' (Citation.)" (*People v. Rodriguez* (2000) 77 *Cal.App.4th* 1101, 1107, 92 *Cal.Rptr.2d* 236 (*Rodriguez*).) "'Functionally interconnected' means used in related or complementary ways. 'Contiguous means adjacent, adjoining, nearby or close. (Citations.)" (Ibid.)

Thorn presents no argument on the "immediately contiguous" requirement. However, the immediately contiguous requirement is easily met because here the carports are situated close to and directly underneath the occupied apartments themselves.

On the second requirement, Thorn argues there is no functional interconnection between the apartments and the carports because they are separated by common areas—the stairwells and the walkways—open to members of the public, not just to residents of the apartments. According to Thorn, this demarcates the apartments as "the place[s] used for residential activities" from the parking areas which are not used for residential activities. This argument misses the point.

The question is not whether the carports are used for "residential activities," but whether they are "functionally interconnected to and immediately contiguous to" the apartments used for "residential activities." (See *Rodriguez, supra,* 77 *Cal.App.4th* at p. 1110, 92 *Cal.Rptr.2d* 236 [defendant's contention that a home office attached to a residence "was not part of the family living space" missed the point because "[t]he question is not whether the specific area is used for sleeping or everyday living, but whether the area is functionally interconnected to and immediately contiguous to the residence, which is used for sleeping or everyday living"].) Indeed, courts have concluded in several cases that garage or carport type structures not normally considered part of the living space are nevertheless functionally connected to the dwelling for purposes of the burglary statutes. (See, e.g., *In re Edwardo V.* (1999) 70 *Cal.App.4th* 591, 594-595, 82 *Cal.Rptr.2d* 765 [attached garage at rear of duplex shared by tenants, not accessible from either duplex and entered only through an exterior door, was functionally interconnected to duplex]; *People v. Ingram* (1995) 40 *Cal.App.4th* 1397, 1402, 1404, 48 *Cal.Rptr.2d* 256, overruled on other grounds in *People v. Dotson* (1997) 16 *Cal.4th* 547, 560, 66

Cal.Rptr.2d 423, 941 *P.2d* 56 [garage was functionally connected to residence where it was used for storing garden tools and equipment, and shared roof with residence but was not directly connected to it]; *People v. Zelaya* (1987) 194 *Cal.App.3d* 73, 75-76, 239 *Cal.Rptr.* 289 [storage rooms in basement area under apartment house were functionally connected to the building's living quarters].)

Moreover, and contrary to Thorn's suggestion, a structure may be functionally interconnected to an inhabited dwelling even where access to the structure is from a common area. (See *People v. Woods* (1998) 65 *Cal.App.4th* 345, 347, 75 *Cal.Rptr.2d* 917 [defendant convicted of first degree burglary of a laundry room on the ground floor of a two-story, U-shaped apartment block, where entry to the individual apartments was via an unlocked open-air courtyard in the middle of the building].) The record here shows that the carports are located directly underneath the apartments and provide parking facilities for designated residents of the apartment complex only. These parking facilities allow the designated residents to drive their vehicles off the street and park in a covered location with convenient access to their living space in the apartments above via the communal stairways adjacent to the carports. In short, the use of the carports by the designated residents is inextricably related or complementary to their living space in the apartments above. Thus, the carports are functionally interconnected with the inhabited dwelling.

. . .

(*Rodriguez, supra* 77 *Cal.App.4th* at p. 1107, 92 *Cal.Rptr.2d* 236 ["'Functionally interconnected' means used in related or complementary ways."].)

We conclude, based upon our review of the record, that the carports are contiguous to and functionally interconnected with the inhabited apartment building. Accordingly, Thorn's first contention, that the carport falls outside the burglary statutes on the grounds it is not "part of" the inhabited dwelling house due to the manner in which it is situated in relation to the apartment building as a whole, must fail.

The second ground upon which Thorn contends the carports are not part of the inhabited building under the burglary statutes is that they do not carry a reasonable expectation of protection from intrusion. In this regard, Thorn asserts that the purpose of the burglary statutes is "to criminalize entry into places in which people have a reasonable expectation of protection from intrusion," and the carports are not that type of place because "[t]he car was no more protected than it would have been on the street." Thorn relies on *People v. Valencia* (2002) 28 *Cal.4th* 1, 120 *Cal.Rptr.2d* 131, 46 *P.3d* 920 (*Valencia*). While we agree with the premise of Thorn's argument, we arrive at a different conclusion based on the Supreme Court's teachings in Valencia.

In Valencia, the Supreme Court granted review "to determine whether penetration into the area behind a window screen amounts to an entry of a building within the meaning of the burglary statute when the window itself is closed and is not penetrated."n4 (*Valencia, supra, 28 Cal.4th at pp. 3–4, 120 Cal.Rptr.2d 131, 46 P.3d 920.*) As its starting point, the court noted that California has "greatly expanded" the common law definition of burglary as the breaking and entering of a dwelling in the nighttime. (*Id.* at p. 7, *120 Cal.Rptr.2d 131, 46 P.3d 920.*) Under California's more expansive burglary law, "'[t]here is no requirement of a breaking; an entry alone is sufficient. The crime is not limited to dwellings, but includes entry into a wide variety of structures. The crime need not be committed at night.'" (*Ibid.,* citing *People v. Davis (1998) 18 Cal.4th 712, 720-721, 76 Cal.Rptr.2d 770, 958 P.2d 1083.*) Further, the court noted "'burglary remains an entry which invades a possessory interest in a building.' [Citation.] . . . Burglary laws are based primarily upon a recognition of the dangers to personal safety created by the usual burglary situation—the danger that the intruder will harm the occupants in attempting to perpetrate the intended crime or to escape and the danger that the occupants will in anger or panic react violently to the invasion, thereby inviting more violence. The laws are primarily designed, then, not to deter the trespass and the intended crime, which are prohibited by other laws, so much as to forestall the germination of a situation dangerous to personal safety. [The burglary statute], in short, is aimed at the danger caused by the unauthorized entry itself." (*Ibid.*)

> n4 The defendant in Valencia "removed a window screen from a bathroom window of the [ ] house and tried unsuccessfully to open the window itself." (*28 Cal.4th at p. 4, 120 Cal.Rptr.2d 131, 46 P.3d 920.*)

With that in mind, the Supreme Court turned to the question of whether penetration into an area behind a window screen "amounts to an entry of a building." (*Valencia, supra, 28 Cal.4th at p. 8, 120 Cal.Rptr.2d 131, 46 P.3d 920.*) The court stated that where "the outer boundary of a building for purposes of burglary is not self-evident, . . . a reasonable belief test generally may be useful in defining the building's outer boundary. Under such a test, in dealing with items such as a window screen, a building's outer boundary includes any element that encloses an area into which a reasonable person would believe that a member of the general public could not pass without authorization. . . . The test reflects and furthers the occupant's possessory interest in the building and his or her personal interest in freedom from violence that might

ensue from unauthorized intrusion." (*Id.* at p. 11, *120 Cal.Rptr.2d 131, 46 P.3d 920.*)

Applying the reasonable belief test, the Supreme Court concluded "that a window screen is clearly part of the outer boundary of a building for purposes of burglary. A reasonable person certainly would believe that a window screen enclosed an area into which a member of the general public could not pass without authorization." (*Valencia, supra, 28 Cal.4th at p. 12, 120 Cal.Rptr.2d 131, 46 P.3d 920.*) On this point, the court noted that "even the minimal entry effected by penetration into the area behind a window screen—without penetration of the window itself—is 'the type of entry the burglary statute was intended to prevent' (citations) [because] [s]uch an entry 'violates the occupant's possessory interest in the building [and] also threatens the "germination of a situation dangerous to personal safety."'" (*Ibid.*)

Under the reasonable belief test as described in Valencia, the question here is whether Thorn's penetration into the open carport was an entry of the building for purposes of the burglary statute. Applying the reasonable belief test, we conclude that the open entrance to the carport marked the outer boundary of the apartment building for purposes of burglary. The open carport here is directly analogous to the area behind the window screen in Valencia in that a reasonable person certainly would believe that the carport "enclosed an area into which a member of the general public could not pass without authorization." (*Valencia, supra, 28 Cal.4th at p. 12, 120 Cal.Rptr.2d 131, 46 P.3d 920.*) Indeed, a member of the general public such as Thorn had no business entering the carport at issue here. It is enclosed on three sides. It is not open at either end or in such other way that it could be reasonably viewed as a throughway or a short-cut to some point beyond. It constitutes a private, individually designated parking space in which its occupant has a possessory interest for the purpose of parking his or her vehicle as well as storing personal possessions. Indeed, that the carport at issue here was recognized as "an area into which a member of the general public could not pass without authorization" (ibid) is further evidenced by the reaction of the residents when they saw Thorn lurking therein—they concluded he was up to no good and immediately called the police. Thorn's entry into the carport, therefore, violated both "the occupant's possessory interest" and his or her "personal interest in freedom from violence that might ensue from unauthorized intrusion." (*Id.* at p. 13, *120 Cal.Rptr.2d 131, 46 P.3d 920.*) Thus, as in Valencia, Thorn's entry into the carport amounts to "an entry of the building within the meaning of the burglary statute." (*Ibid.*)

Nor is our analysis on this point swayed by the fact that there was no physical barrier to Thorn's entry of the

#4

carport. In Valencia, the Supreme Court commented on language in an appellate court case "that might be understood to cast the reasonable belief test in terms of 'whether a reasonable person would believe' that any given element of a building 'provides some [physical] protection against unauthorized intrusions.' (Citation.)" The court stated the "latter quoted language might be appropriate if the offense of burglary continued to require unlawful breaking as well as entering. In that event, an element of a building would have to be something that could protect against breach. But, as we have stated most recently in Davis, burglary now entails only unlawful entry. (Citation.)" (*Valencia, supra, 28 Cal.4th at p. 12, 120 Cal.Rptr.2d 131, 46 P.3d 920.*) Accordingly, the court reiterated that the reasonable belief test "properly is phrased in terms of whether a reasonable person would believe that the element of the building in question enclosed an area into which a member of the general public could not pass without authorization." (Ibid.)n5

n5 Nor does our analysis run afoul of the Supreme Court's admonition in Valencia that "in defining the outer boundary of a building for purposes of burglary, the reasonable belief test necessarily refers only to an element of a building that reasonably can be viewed as part of the building's outer boundary. The test does not encompass any feature that is not such an element, such as a lawn, courtyard, unenclosed patio, or unenclosed balcony that may be located in front of or behind a building; nor does the test purport to define any such feature as part of a building's outer boundary." (*Valencia,*

supra, 28 Cal.4th at p. 11, fn. 5, 120 Cal.Rptr.2d 131, 46 P.3d 920.) The carport area is not located in front of or behind the apartment building. Rather, it is an integral part of the apartment building because it comprises the entire ground floor of the apartment building, is roofed by the apartments above, shares common walls with the apartments above, structurally supports the apartments built above it, and lies entirely within the plane of the apartment building structure.

In sum, a reasonable person would view the carport as an "enclosed [ ] area into which a member of the general public could not pass without authorization." (*Valencia, supra, 28 Cal.4th at p. 12, 120 Cal.Rptr.2d 131, 46 P.3d 920.*) Accordingly, under the reasonable belief test, Thorn's entry of the carport with felonious intent constitutes first degree burglary.

. . .

DISPOSITION

We have concluded that the carport area at issue here is protected by the burglary statutes under both the "functionally-interconnected-with-and-immediately-contiguous-to" test and the "reasonable belief" test. In addition, we discern no error in the jury instructions. Accordingly, the judgment is affirmed.

We concur: McGUINESS, P.J., and SIGGINS, J.

PEOPLE v. RODRIGUEZ

COURT OF APPEAL OF CALIFORNIA, FIFTH APPELLATE DISTRICT

77 Cal. App. 4th 1101; 92 Cal. Rptr. 2d 236

January 28, 2000

OPINION BY: VARTABEDIAN, J.

A jury convicted defendant David Michael Rodriguez of first degree burglary. The issues on appeal are: whether a burglary of a home office that, among its features, shares a roof and a common wall with the residence constitutes first degree burglary, and whether the court adequately instructed the jury. We affirm.

PROCEDURAL BACKGROUND

On June 16, 1998, the District Attorney for Madera County filed a third amended information charging defendant with residential burglary in violation of *Penal Code section 459*. In addition, the information contained three special allegations. First, defendant had suffered three prior serious felony convictions within the meaning of section 667, subdivisions (b) through (i). Second, defendant had been convicted of first degree burglary on November 28, 1989, within the meaning of section 667, subdivision (a)(1). Third, defendant had been convicted of first degree burglary on August 12, 1991, had served a prior prison term within the meaning of section 667.5 for that crime, and had committed another felony offense within five years of that prior prison term within the meaning of section 667.5, subdivision (b). Defendant pled not guilty and denied the special allegations.

. . .

A jury found defendant guilty of burglary, with a special finding that the burglary was of the first degree. The court found true defendant's three prior conviction allegations. After denying defendant's motion to dismiss two of his prior strikes pursuant to section 1385, the court sentenced defendant to 30 years to life.

Defendant timely appeals.

FACTUAL BACKGROUND

Bill Moss operated Bill Moss Electric out of his home office in Madera. The office provided clerical functions for Moss's work as an electrician. His residence and office were under the same roof and shared a common wall. The office was not used as living quarters and there was no interior door connecting the office to the residence. The office and the dwelling had exterior doors leading to the same driveway. The door to the office was four to five feet away from the door to the residence. The home and the home office were partially surrounded by the same chain link fence.

On the morning of January 28, 1997, Bill Moss and his wife, Denise, left their home office. Denise left later than Bill, just before noon. She had prepared some invoices, which she was taking to the post office for mailing. The office door was closed, but unlocked. When Bill returned around noon, he found parked in his driveway an unfamiliar car. He pulled in behind it and then saw defendant standing on the side of his house looking at a ladder that was leaning against the outside wall, on the office side of the house, inside the chain link fence. Bill accosted a nervous defendant who claimed he was looking for some girl and that he was at the wrong house.

Noticing that the door to the office was ajar about 10 inches, Bill said to defendant, "I hope you haven't been in my house." Defendant replied, "No, I haven't." Defendant then left quickly on foot, saying "I'll be back for my car. . . ."

After defendant departed, Bill went into the office to see if anything was missing. He noticed that the fax machine, a television (which Denise had been watching before she left), and a cordless screwdriver had been moved away from their original locations to a table near the door. The wires from the fax machine and the television were broken, indicating that they had been torn from the wall.

Bill called the police, who later apprehended the defendant. Keys found on defendant after his arrest fit the vehicle parked in the Mosses' driveway . . .

DISCUSSION

I. SUFFICIENCY OF THE EVIDENCE OF RESIDENTIAL BURGLARY

When reviewing the sufficiency of evidence on appeal, as long as circumstances reasonably justify the fact finder's determination, we must accept it, even though another fact finder may have reasonably determined the opposite. . . .

Before reviewing the specific arguments and evidence, we note the longstanding reasoning for treating residential burglaries more seriously than other burglaries. Common law burglary sought to protect the peace of mind and security of residents so that they could enjoy their home without intrusion because, at common law, "a person's home was truly his castle." (*People v. Gauze (1975) 15 Cal. 3d 709, 712 {125 Cal. Rptr. 773, 542 P.2d 1365}*.)n2 By maintaining the distinction between an inhabited and an uninhabited dwelling, current burglary statutes continue to provide increased protection for the privacy and enjoyment of one's home. (See *ibid.*)

> n2 At common law, burglary was generally defined as "'the breaking and entering of the dwelling of *another* in the nighttime with intent to commit a felony.'" (*15 Cal. 3d at* p. 711.)

As the Supreme Court explained: In general, "Cases interpreting the term 'inhabited dwelling house' in section 460 . . . ha[ve] made it clear that this term should be construed to effectuate the legislative purposes underlying the statute, namely, to protect the peaceful occupation of one's residence." Thus, the courts [have] recognized that our burglary law stems from the common law policy of providing heightened protection to the residence. The occupied dwelling continued to receive heightened protection under our statutes in order to avoid the increased danger of personal violence attendant upon an entry into a "building currently used as sleeping and living quarters." As [one court has] explained, "a person is more likely to react violently to burglary of his living quarters than to burglary of other places because in the former case persons close to him are more likely to be present, because the property threatened is more likely to belong to him, and because the home is usually regarded as a particularly private sanctuary, even as an extension of the person." Courts specifically have recognized that the distinction between first and second degree burglary is founded upon the perceived danger of violence and personal injury that is involved when a residence is invaded.

. . .

Defendant contends the evidence was insufficient to show that he committed first degree burglary. Specifically, he asserts the home office he burglarized was not a functional part of the residence, even though the office and residence shared the same roof, because the office was neither used as living space nor connected to the dwelling by an interior door. According to defendant, breaking into such a home office constitutes merely a second degree burglary.

By statute, "[e]very burglary of an inhabited dwelling house, . . . or the inhabited portion of any other building, is burglary of the first degree." (§ 460, subd. (a).) "All other kinds of burglary are of the second degree." (*Id.*, subd. (b).) The term "inhabited" is statutorily defined as "currently being used for dwelling purposes, whether occupied or not." (§ 459.) Courts have construed the terms "residence" and "inhabited dwelling house" to have equivalent meanings.

. . .

In determining whether a structure is part of an inhabited dwelling, the essential inquiry is whether the structure is "functionally interconnected with and immediately contiguous to other portions of the house." . . . "Functionally interconnected" means used in related or complementary ways. "Contiguous" means adjacent, adjoining, nearby or close. . . .

The immediately contiguous requirement is easily met here because this home office adjoined the residence and shared the same roof and a common wall. The closer issue is functional interconnection.

. . .

Functionally, the home office permitted the residents to have a flexible work schedule and to travel back and forth between the home and the office frequently and easily in order to eat, to rest and the like. Moreover, the office allowed the residents to spend more time with family, including children.n4 A family member could be expected to enter the home office, not necessarily to work, but to ask a question, seek advice, or simply to "check in" or "touch base." A child coming home from school might go into the office looking for a parent, even before going into the residence.

> n4 The Mosses lived at the house along with their two sons.

The common walkway and driveway increased the functionality of the setup, as did the chain link fence. The office also provided income in order to maintain the home. Thus, the multifarious purposes of a home office reveal its integral relationship with the main house.

The conduct of the parties reflects this integration. Upon seeing the door to the home office ajar and observing defendant, Bill Moss remarked, "I hope you haven't been in my house." This suggests that Moss considered the home office an extension of his home and his person. In short, defendant's invasion of the Mosses' home office involved a significant intrusion into the Mosses' personal privacy. . . .

. . .

Defendant also claims that just because the same driveway serviced both the home and the business does not mean that the business area was used for dwelling purposes. This is true, but misses the point. The question is not whether the specific area is used for sleeping or everyday living, but whether the area is functionally interconnected to and immediately contiguous to the residence, which is used for sleeping or everyday living. . . .

The area in question must be integrally related to and immediately contiguous to the living area—not necessarily part of it. (*People v. Ingram, supra, 40 Cal. App. 4th at* p. 1404.) Defendant's argument that the office was not part of the family living space thus misses this important distinction spelled out in *Ingram.*

. . .

People v. Moreno (1984) 158 Cal. App. 3d 109 {204 Cal. Rptr. 17}, likewise held that a garage under the same roof as the living quarters, contiguous to and functionally interconnected with other parts of the home, was part of an inhabited dwelling, even though there was no door connecting the garage to the interior of the house. (*Id. at* p. 112.)

. . .

Accordingly, under sections 459 and 460, we find significant similarities between a garage, a storeroom, a laundry room, and a home office. Entry into a structure that is functionally related to and immediately contiguous to a dwelling qualifies for first degree burglary. This is so even though there is no connecting door to the residence and the structure serves as a storehouse, workshop, or office or serves some other need of the residents. The use of the area need not be limited to the storage or use of property ordinarily related to dwelling places. Whereas, a garage or storage area next to a residence typically contains items related to the home and its maintenance (e.g., food, bicycles and other athletic equipment, gardening equipment, a washer and dryer, an extra refrigerator, or furniture) and a home office generally contains office-related items (e.g., a computer, fax, phone, printer, desk, files, and bookshelves), we are satisfied the contents of the structure are not determinative.

Thus, many of the reasons that make traditional inhabited dwelling burglaries dangerous are present when a home office attached to a main house is burglarized, even though the office is not connected to the home by an interior door. The common law origins of burglary and the justifications for distinguishing between inhabited and uninhabited buildings further support our broad interpretation of the term inhabited dwelling house.

We conclude that a reasonable jury could conclude from the evidence that the home office was functionally related to and immediately contiguous to the home. Sufficient evidence supports the verdict of first degree burglary.

. . .

DISPOSITION

The judgment is affirmed.

PEOPLE v. LABAER

COURT OF APPEAL OF CALIFORNIA, FOURTH APPELLATE DISTRICT, DIVISION ONE

88 CAL. APP. 4TH 289; 105 CAL. RPTR. 2D 629

APRIL 5, 2001

OPINION BY: HALLER, J.

A jury convicted Gary Lawrence Labaer of arson of a structure, arson of the property of another, . . . The court sentenced Labaer to prison for 4 years on the arson of a structure count, Labaer appeals. . . .

In the published portion of the opinion, we conclude substantial evidence supported the jury's implied finding that the subject matter of the fire, a stripped-down mobilehome, was a "structure" within the meaning of section 451, subdivision (c).

. . .

FACTS

Labaer owned a double-wide mobilehome that he kept at RV World, a storage facility. Although the storage contract did not allow him to do so, he frequently stayed in the mobilehome. After Labaer repeatedly failed to pay monthly storage fees, a court declared the mobilehome abandoned and permitted sale of the home and its contents.

Immediately before the public auction began, the auctioneer saw Labaer and several other men disassemble parts of the mobilehome. The men removed trusses from the roof, aluminum siding panels, and sliding glass doors, and loaded the parts on a truck. The auctioneer called the sheriff's department, and sheriff's deputies arrested Labaer on unrelated misdemeanor warrants. While waiting in court, Labaer referred to the mobilehome and said, "I should just burn the damn thing down." Labaer was later released from custody.

At the auction held later that day, RV World, the only bidder, purchased Labaer's mobilehome for $100. The next day, Jeffrey Funk, manager of a nearby nursery, noticed the mobilehome on fire and saw Labaer backing away from the southeast portion. When Deputy Sheriff Roderick MacDonald arrived, Funk identified Labaer as the person who was near the mobilehome when the fire started. Labaer interfered with Deputy MacDonald's investigation of the fire by being hostile and slapping Deputy MacDonald's hand when the deputy reached for Labaer's jacket. When Deputy Sheriff Jonda Hammons directed Labaer to the patrol car, Labaer began pushing and hitting her. After witnessing this and receiving punches from Labaer, Deputy MacDonald placed Labaer in a carotid restraint hold and handcuffed him.

The jury found Labaer guilty of arson of a structure (§ 451, subd. (c)), arson of property of another (§ 451, subd. (d)) . . .

DISCUSSION

I. THE MOBILEHOME WAS A STRUCTURE WITHIN THE MEANING OF SECTION 451, SUBDIVISION (C)

Labaer contends the prosecution failed to introduce sufficient evidence that the mobilehome was a "structure" within the meaning of section 451, subdivision (c).

"A person is guilty of arson when he or she willfully and maliciously sets fire to or burns or causes to be burned . . . any structure, forest land or property . . . ." (§ 451.) The arson statutes provide different levels of punishment, depending on the subject matter of the arson. (§ 451.) These statutory categories, in descending level of punishment, are: (1) arson resulting in great bodily injury (5, 7, or 9 years); (2) arson to "an inhabited structure or inhabited property" (3, 5, or 8 years); (3) arson of a "structure or forest land" (2, 4, or 6 years); and (4) arson to other types of property (16 months, 2, or 3 years). (§ 451, subds. (a), (b), (c), & (d).) By creating these different levels of punishment, the Legislature intended to impose punishment "'in proportion to the seriousness of the offense,'" and, in particular, "according to the injury or potential injury to human life involved . . . ." (*People v. Green (1983) 146 Cal. App. 3d 369, 378 {194 Cal. Rptr. 128}.)

In this case, Labaer was charged and found guilty of the third type of arson: the burning of a "structure or forest land." (§ 451, subd. (c).) Section 450, subdivision (a) states that for purposes of the arson statutes, 'Structure' means any building, or commercial or public tent, bridge, tunnel, or powerplant." The trial court instructed the jury on this definition. The prosecutor's theory was that the mobilehome was a "structure" because it was a "building." The Penal Code does not define "building" for purposes of arson; we therefore apply the plain meaning of the word. (*People v. Jasso* (1994) 25 Cal. App. 4th 591, 595 {30 Cal. Rptr. 2d 572}.)

Labaer does not dispute that the mobilehome —as it existed during the months before the fire—constituted a "building" under the arson statutes. The evidence established the home was fixed to a particular location, could not be readily moved, and had been used as Labaer's residence for several months. Labaer argues instead that the dilapidated condition of the home on the day of the fire— caused primarily by his illegal dismantling activities the previous day—converted the mobilehome from a "structure" under section 451, subdivision (c) to generic "property" subject to lesser punishment under section 451, subdivision (d).

The easy answer to this contention is that the Legislature could not have intended that a criminal defendant benefit from his or her unlawful activities to obtain a lesser punishment merely by attempting to take apart a building shortly before setting it on fire. The more lengthy but equally correct—response to Labaer's contention is that despite his dismantling activities, the mobilehome remained a "building" within the meaning of the arson statute because the dismantling was never completed. Although the mobilehome was in a substantially substandard condition, there was ample evidence showing it remained a standing and constructed structure that had four sides and a partial roof.

In this respect, Labaer's argument that the home no longer had walls or a roof does not accurately reflect the record. Four witnesses testified concerning the nature of the mobilehome's exterior. Although each witness had a slightly different opinion on the subject, the evidence showed that the mobilehome did have some form of exterior walls and at least a portion of a roof.

The auctioneer testified that after Labaer's dismantling activities there "absolutely" were walls on the mobilehome: "the front was still there. The front door, the sides, [and] the roof to the front [portion] of the mobile home [were] still there . . . ." He stated that someone could walk into the home and be shielded from the sun, rain, and wind. He explained that the roof fully covered one of the two parts that composed the double-wide mobilehome.

The storage park manager testified that after the sale she viewed the outside of the mobilehome and walked through the inside of the home. She said, "the outside of the mobile home mostly looked pink because of insulation, and it had been out in the weather and the insulation was kind of drooping off of it, and there were studs, and there was no siding on the double-wide. There were windows, doors. In places, there was plastic or visqueen over the outside. . . . There were some stairs in the north side . . . leading into a doorway, or a door, that was on the north side. There were windows along the east side. I think on the south side there was plywood . . . instead of just insulation, there was plywood on there as well."

Jeffrey Funk, the neighboring commercial nursery manager, testified, "there were no walls on it, really. It was an open mobilehome. Looked unfinished, actually." In response to the court's question as to what he meant by "open," Funk stated, "two-by-four framing. No plastic, no outside wall." Funk later clarified that there was two-by-four wood framing around the entire mobilehome, and that at least two sides were covered by "plastic sheeting." Funk testified that a roof covered the entire home, but admitted he could only see two sides of the mobilehome.

The arson investigator, who viewed the mobilehome only after the fire, testified that the structure did not appear to "have any walls to it [before the fire]. What was used on it was a plastic visqueen that looked like it was used to shield or give some sort of shielding from the weather, which is a little unusual. It looked like it was either under construction or being torn down . . . ." He also confirmed that the mobilehome had only one-half of a roof before the fire.

Viewing this evidence in the light most favorable to the prosecution (*People v. Hatch* (2000) 22 Cal. 4th 260, 272 {92 Cal. Rptr. 2d 80, 991 P.2d 165}), the jury could have reached certain reasonable conclusions regarding the mobilehome. First, it appears reasonably clear that although the mobilehome did not have four solid walls, it had four "sides," and each of these sides was enclosed by some material-two-by-four open wood framing and/or plastic visqueen sheeting with studs and insulation. Second, it was essentially undisputed that although the home did not have a full roof, an aluminum or light metal roof covered at least one-half of the mobilehome, the front section that contained the bedroom. Third, despite this unfinished-looking exterior, the mobilehome's interior was largely intact. A solid middle wall divided the double-wide mobilehome lengthwise. Stairs led to the front door, and the mobilehome had a particleboard floor. The home contained furniture and other accessories, including a bed, desk, dresser, lounge, and fish aquarium.

On this factual record, there was sufficient evidence for the jury to conclude this partly disassembled mobilehome was a "structure" within the meaning of section 451, subdivision (c).

. . .

Further, even assuming we apply the definition of "building" applicable to the burglary statutes, the mobilehome here would satisfy this requirement.

A person commits burglary when he or she "enters any house, room, apartment, tenement, shop, warehouse, store, mill, barn, stable, outhouse *or other building*, tent, vessel . . . trailer coach . . . any house car . . . inhabited camper . . . ." (§ 459, italics added.) Under this statute, a building is generally defined to mean a place that has walls on all sides and is covered by a roof. (*In re Amber S. (1995) 33 Cal. App. 4th 185, 187 {39 Cal. Rptr. 2d 672}; People v. Brooks, supra, 133 Cal. App. 3d* at p. 204.) . . .

As discussed, Labaer's mobilehome had four sides, as well as a middle wall. In addition, a roof covered at least one-half of the home. The law of burglary treats Labaer's mobilehome, made of two-by-four framing, plastic and insulation, the same as if it were made of different material, such as brick or plaster. Because chicken wire and a chain link fence have satisfied the requirement of walls, two-by-four wood studs and/or plastic and insulation similarly satisfy the requirement in this case. (*People v. Brooks, supra, 133 Cal. App. 3d* at p. 205.) Therefore, even if we applied the definition of a building under the burglary statutes, Labaer's mobilehome would qualify under section 450.

. . .

DISPOSITION

. . . In all other respects, the judgment is affirmed.

KEY TERMS

First degree burglary, 209

Second degree burglary, 209

Receiving stolen property, 210

Looting, 210

Arson, 210

STUDY GUIDE CHAPTER 6

CRIMES AGAINST HABITATION

1. What are the elements for the crime of *burglary?*

2. What is the legal significance of a charge of a first or second degree *burglary?* What is necessary to prove a first degree *burglary?*

3. How is the crime of *burglary* different from a *robbery?* Explain.

4. What are the elements for the crime of *arson?*

CHAPTER 7

Property Crimes

Property crimes like theft, forgery, and extortion involve taking the property of others with the intent to permanently deprive the rightful owners of that property. These offenses might be as minor as stealing a bicycle or as serious as extortion of money by a public official.

THEFT

The common law relating to larceny has been consolidated in California's modern theft statute. The application of the English common law definition of **larceny** was wrought with gaps and holes that developed over the years. This somewhat disjointed body of law was brought to America as part of our English legal heritage. Common law larceny was the taking and carrying away (asportation or movement) of the personal property of another, with the intent to permanently deprive the holder of possession. Each individual phrase in this definition—"taking," "carrying away," "property of another"—was challenged over the years by defendants who claimed that their act of stealing someone else's property didn't meet the requirements. A classic example of such a challenge is a horse thief who "borrowed" a horse from a neighbor, rode off to a neighboring town, and never returned the horse. When apprehended, he claimed that he didn't possess the felonious intent to permanently deprive the owner of his horse at the time of the "taking," therefore an element of the crime of larceny was missing.

As courts were faced with questions like this, which, if answered in a strict sense, led to illogical results, they developed "fixes" to help fill in these gaps. The **Doctrine of Continuing Trespass** was developed to deal with the example above. It states that even if at the time of the taking, the felonious intent is lacking, and the thief develops the felonious intent to convert the property permanently to his own use even after acquiring possession lawfully (he changes his mind as he is riding to the next town on the borrowed horse, deciding to keep it or sell it and keep the money) that felonious intent to take is rolled back to the time of the original taking for the purposes of larceny. This legal fiction allowed for the right result: conviction of the defendant for stealing his neighbor's horse.

- the goods are severed from the possession or custody of the owner,

- he goods are in complete possession of the thief or thieves, and

- the property is moved, even if only slightly.

KEY LEGAL PRINCIPLE:

Modern theft still requires **asportation** of the property of another in order to convict the defendant of theft by larceny. Asportation refers to the carrying away of the goods described in the common law definition of larceny. Asportation includes three elements: [1]

Another example is seen in the problem that led to the development of the crime of **embezzlement**. If treated as larceny, the taking involved in embezzlement would not be unlawful because the rightful owner entrusted the property to the thief, so there was no "wrongful taking" involved. The classic example of this problem can be illustrated by a bank teller's theft of a patron's cash deposit. The patron enters the bank, handing the teller his cash, intending for it to be deposited into his own account. Instead of doing so, the teller keeps the money for his own use. Under the common law definition of larceny, there was no wrongful taking of the patron's money, and as a result, no larceny. Courts developed the law of embezzlement to deal with just this type of problem. Embezzlement was defined as the wrongful conversion of property with which the holder was entrusted. This solved the problem illustrated when the bank teller "pocketed" the patron's cash deposit.

The crime of **false pretenses** developed for a similar reason. Takings by false pretenses are achieved through trickery. Because the victim hands over their property willingly, the law of larceny was not met—there was not an unlawful taking by the thief. Courts developed the offense of false pretenses in the same manner as they did embezzlement, defining the taking as one achieved through false or fraudulent representation or pretense.

As a result of this case-by-case development, the law of larceny was not a clear, coherent body of law. In response, California and many other American states have crafted consolidated theft statutes. California's statute is located in Penal Code §484. California's theft statute is broad and encompasses larceny, embezzlement,[2] **theft (larceny) by trick,** and **false pretenses,** all under the umbrella of "theft." The offenses are charged as theft, but the prosecutor must plead and prove the elements of the specific type of taking (e.g. embezzlment, larceny or false pretenses).

The elements of theft by *larceny* are:[3]

- Actus reus—taking possession of property owned by someone else, without the owner's consent, moving the property—even a small distance—and keeping it for a period of time, even if brief

- Mens rea—intent to permanently deprive the owner of the property, or to keep it for such an extended period of time that the owner would be deprived of a major portion of the value or enjoyment of the property

- Causation—the defendant set in motion the chain of events that led to the taking

- Injury—loss or destruction of property or loss of use of property

---

[1] CALCRIM No. 1800 (2010) citing *People v. Shannon,* 66 Cal.App.4th 649, 654 (1998).

[2] §503 of the Code includes a separate discussion of embezzlement, including definitions and specific rules that relate to theft by embezzlement. Remember to note that even though the elements and specific rules that apply to embezzlement are used, the taking is charged as theft under §484.

[3] CALCRIM No. 1800 (2010).

The elements of theft by *false pretenses* are:[4]

- Actus reus—taking ownership and possession of the property of another, obtained by false or fraudulent misrepresentations or pretenses that led the rightful owner to let the thief take ownership and possession of the property

- Mens rea—knowingly and intentionally engaging in the making of the false or fraudulent misrepresentations, with the intent to permanently deprive the owner of ownership and possession of their property

- Causation—the defendant set in motion the chain of events that led to the taking

- Injury—loss or destruction of property or loss of use of property

The elements of *theft by trick* are:[5]

- Actus reus—taking *possession* of the property of another, obtained by false or fraudulent misrepresentations or pretenses that led the rightful owner to let the thief take *possession* of the property, and keeping the property for any length of time (when the rightful owner did NOT intend to part with ownership of the property)

- Mens rea—knowingly and intentionally engaging in the making of the false or fraudulent misrepresentations, with the intent to permanently deprive the owner of *possession* of their property

- Causation—the defendant set in motion the chain of events that led to the taking

- Injury—loss or destruction of property or loss of use of property

The elements of theft by *embezzlement* are:[6]

- Actus reus—the thief fraudulently converted (used) the property of another for his own benefit, which was entrusted to him by the owner or the owner's agent; the taking is fraudulent when the thief breaches a duty, trust, or confidence

- Mens rea—the intent to deprive the owner of the property and/or its use (intent to deprive the owner, even temporarily, is enough)

- Causation—the defendant set in motion the chain of events that led to the taking

- Injury—loss or destruction of property or loss of use of property

Theft in California is now a very broad term that encompasses three key types of *felonious* takings: the stealing, taking, carrying away, leading away, or driving away of the personal property of another—this is what would have been categorized as larceny under the common law rules. It also includes the fraudulent appropriation of property which has been entrusted to the taker—this is what would have been categorized as embezzlement under the common law rules. Lastly, it includes the knowing use of false or fraudulent representations or pretenses to induce another person to hand over their property to the taker—this is what would have been categorized as false pretenses under the common law rules. It is important to note that the modern definition maintains that the nature of the taking must be felonious: meaning it is done with the intent to permanently deprive the holder of possession. The Code notes that if any statute uses the words larceny, embezzlement, or stealing in any other sections, it should be interpreted as if the word "theft" were in place of those words. The California statutes include specific types of theft too numerous to detail in this chapter, ranging from the use of counterfeit access cards to the theft of a fire hydrant and from theft of utility services to grand theft of a dog.

---

[4] CALCRIM No. 1804 (2010).

[5] CALCRIM No. 1805 (2010).

[6] CALCRIM No. 1806 (2010).

[7] Cal. Pen. Code §486.

[8] Cal. Pen. Code §490.

[9] Cal. Pen. Code §489.

Theft is divided into degrees: **grand theft** and **petty theft**. Petty theft involves property valued at under $950, and is always a misdemeanor. Grand theft involves the taking of property valued at $950 or more, and unless the property taken is a firearm, is a wobbler. There are a few exceptions to the $950 division between petty and grand theft. The Code specifies that over $250 in certain produce, shellfish or aquacultural products is grand theft. Grand theft also takes place when the item taken is an automobile, firearm, livestock animal, or when the property is taken from the person of another. Grand theft of a firearm is a felony, grand theft of any other type is a "wobbler", and petty theft is a misdemeanor.

KEY LEGAL PRINCIPLE:

"Petty Theft with a Prior"[10] is an offense that has gained significant attention in recent years. The families of Kimber Reynolds and Polly Klass, both of whom were murdered by repeat offenders, helped to bring about the passage of California's **"Three Strikes and You're Out Law"** in 1994. It remains one of the harshest sentencing statutes in the country. The statute provides for increased sentences for repeat offenders. It requires that the first two strikes (convictions) be for offenses categorized as "serious and violent felonies" in §667.5 and §1192.7 of the Code, but that the third can be any felony, including petty theft with a prior theft offense (which is a wobbler). This application of the law has raised significant debate as media reports feature stories of offenders whose third offense is a minor theft or non-violent felony and who are sentenced to 25-to-life in prison. The United States Supreme Court took up the issue of whether a 25-to-life sentence handed down in this context was unconstitutionally disproportionate to the crime charged, and thus cruel and unusual punishment. The answer, according to their opinion in *Ewing v. California,* (2003),[11] is "no." California voters rejected an opportunity to change the Three Strikes statute by voting down Proposition 66 in 2004, showing their continued support for the harsh sentencing measure.

Of significance relating to theft in California is a 2010 change to Cal. Pen. Code §666: Petty Theft with a Prior Theft Conviction. The Legislature increased the number of prior petty theft offenses to three before a defendant can be charged with a felony for a petty theft offense. This change affects the application of the Three Strikes and You're Out Law.

Receiving stolen property takes place when a person buys or receives any property that has been stolen or that has been obtained in any manner constituting theft or extortion, while knowing about the character of the property.[12] Receiving stolen property is a general intent crime. A person who is a principal to the theft can be charged with receipt of stolen property, but cannot be charged with both theft and receipt of the same stolen property. Receiving stolen property is a misdemeanor.

EXTORTION

Extortion is the obtaining of property from another, with his or her consent, or the obtaining of an official act of a public officer, induced by a wrongful use of force or fear, or under color of official right.[13] For the purposes of extortion, the Code defines threats very specifically as threats:[14]

- to do an unlawful injury to the person or property of the individual threatened or of a third person,

- to accuse the individual threatened, or any relative of him or her, or member of his or her family, of a crime,

- to expose, or to impute to him or her any deformity, disgrace, or crime, or

- to expose any secret affecting him or her

Extortion is forcing people to consent to handing over their property in the face of a threat. It is often confused with robbery, for good reason. Robbery and extortion both involve takings by threats of force or fear. The difference between

---

[10] Cal. Pen. Code §489–490.

[11] *Ewing v. California*, 58 U.S. 11 (2003).

[12] Cal. Pen. Code §496.

[13] Cal. Pen. Code §518.

[14] Cal. Pen. Code §519.

the two is the timing of the threat. Robbery involves imminent (immediate) threats while extortion involves a threat of future harm. Future threats are not sufficiently imminent to satisfy the requirements for robbery.

Extortion is often associated with public officials who can be both perpetrator or victim. A threat may be made against them because of their public position in exchange for an official act, or they may abuse their public authority and power in order to extort property from others.

The elements of *extortion* are:

- Actus reus—the defendant threatened the victim or a third party

- Mens rea—specific intent to use the threats against the victim to secure their consent to give them money or property

- Causation—the defendant's actions caused the victim to hand over the property or do the official act

- Injury—fear of injury and loss of property

KEY LEGAL PRINCIPLE:

Even if a person has a good faith belief that the property belongs to them, they cannot resort to threats of force or fear to recover it, and debts cannot be collected by extortion.[15]

FORGERY

Forgery may involve either a false signature or a forged or counterfeit document of legal significance, such as a will or contract. Section 470(d) lists the documents that the legislature has identified are the proper subject of a forgery, but other documents may qualify as well. The document must "affect an identifiable legal, monetary or property right."[16] Forgery requires the specific intent to defraud. Passing or attempting to use a forged instrument is also a crime. This common law rule crime was called "uttering a forged instrument." A defendant is guilty of **passing a forged document** if she presents a forged instrument as true, with the specific intent to defraud the victim, causing loss of money, goods, or services—or damage to a legal, financial, or property right.[17] As with forgery, it is not necessary that anyone actually lose property as a result; the crime is complete at the time the defendant passes the instrument as true with the intent to defraud. It is also criminal to possess a forged document, a blank check, or a completed check with the intent to defraud under §475(a)–(c).

Other offenses related to forgery are the writing of "bad checks," counterfeiting money, and the production of false identification. Each of these is covered in a separate section of the Code and the elements are specific to the type of fraud or deceit involved.

The elements of *forgery* are:[18]

- Actus reus—the making of a false writing or signature (or signing without permission) on a document of legal significance. It is not necessary that any property actually be taken or lost—only that the writing is made with the requisite mens rea

- Mens rea—the specific intent to defraud

- Causation—the defendant's act of signing or falsifying the writing set in motion the chain of events that led to the harm or injury

- Injury—loss of property, money, or something of value, or causing damage to a legal, financial, or property right

---

[15] CALCRIM No. 1830 (2010) citing *People v. Serrano,* 11 Cal.App.4th 1672, 1677–1678 (1992).

[16] *Lewis v. Superior Court,* 217 Cal.App.3d 379 (1990).

[17] Cal. Pen. Code §470(d).

[18] CALCRIM No. 1900, 1903 (2010).

MALICIOUS MISCHIEF

Vandalism is often committed by juvenile offenders. The California Penal Code states that a person is guilty of vandalism when they maliciously deface with graffiti, damage, or destroy real or personal property that belongs to another person.[19] The damage done to the property of the victim doesn't have to be permanent—it might just be marking on a glass window with markers, which could be cleaned up.[20] Vandalism is typically a misdemeanor, and juveniles who are caught may simply be required to do community service, pay a fine, or pay restitution to the property owner. It may seem to be a benign crime, but it can be an indicator of much more serious criminal conduct to come, or can be the work of more sophisticated offenders. Defacing property with graffiti or "tagging" is often the work of gang members. Entire policing units are committed in urban areas to photographing and cataloging the graphics left on walls, highway overpasses, fences, and the like by gang members. This information can be critical in identifying and proving membership in a criminal street gang. When juvenile offenders act on behalf of a criminal street gang in committing serious and violent crimes, the minor can be charged as an adult in criminal court.

In addition to vandalism, cruelty to animals is also criminalized as malicious mischief in the Code. It may seem strange that cruelty to animals would be codified in the same section as vandalism and trespass, but it is a property crime as well.[21] The crime involves the malicious and intentional harming of a living animal, or the intentional killing of an animal, and is a wobbler for which a fine of up to $20,000 can be levied in addition to prison or jail time.[22] The law views animals as personal property, and as such, they do not possess rights in the same way people do. The people who own them are protected against damage, theft, or destruction of their livestock and pets. Owners are also at risk of being charged with a crime for failing to adequately care for their animals, and the 2007 conviction of NFL superstar Michael Vick for engaging in a dog-fighting operation has brought to light the seriousness with which prosecutors will pursue these cases.

Trespass on the property of others can range from a very minor offense to one coupled with serious threats. The Code creates a variety of types of criminal trespass: trespass into a dwelling, trespass for the purpose of interfering with a business, and trespass coupled with a credible threat to do serious bodily injury. Trespass is the intentional and unlawful entry onto the property of another. It is a general intent crime. The mens rea requires only the intent to enter; there is no proof of intent to achieve a further consequence required. Some examples of minor trespasses include carrying away wood or timber from another person's lot, entering other's lands for the purpose of injuring the property, refusing or failing to leave lands immediately upon the request of the owner, and maliciously tearing down a posted sign or notice indicating ownership of a property by another party.[23] Minor trespass is a misdemeanor, while trespass with threats of serious bodily injury is a wobbler that can be charged as either a felony or a misdemeanor at the prosecutor's discretion.[24]

The California legislature added §502, titled **"Computer Crime,"** to the Code in 1987, and has continued to update it and the related sections over the years as technology rapidly advances. Computer crimes as defined in this section are specifically those offenses relating to the knowing destruction of information, data, or software, or the knowing access without permission of another person's computer, computer system, or network. The offenses can be punished by a wide range of fines, and depending upon the nature of the loss to the victim, can be charged as misdemeanors or felonies at the prosecutor's discretion. It is important to note that computers and other devices that access the Internet can be used to facilitate the commission of a wide range of other offenses which are not covered in Section 502. In recent years, the use of the Internet to lure minors into sexual encounters has been widely covered in the media, and is just one example of thousands of offenses that might involve the use of a computer or the Internet in its commission.

---

[19] Cal. Pen. Code §594.

[20] In re Nicholas Y., 85 Cal.App.4th 941, 944 (2000).

[21] Cal. Pen. Code §597.

[22] Cal. Pen. Code §597.

[23] Cal. Pen. Code §602.

[24] Cal. Pen. Code §602.

PEOPLE v. WILLIAMS

COURT OF APPEAL OF CALIFORNIA, SECOND APPELLATE DISTRICT, DIVISION TWO

73 CAL. APP. 2D 154; 166 P.2D 63

FEBRUARY 19, 1946

OPINION BY: MOORE, P. J.

. . . Appellant was convicted of petty theft with prior convictions of felonies. He appeals from the judgment and from the order denying his motion for a new trial. Pursuant to stipulation of counsel the case was tried to the court without a jury. The only attack made upon the judgment is the insufficiency of the evidence to support it.

The facts given in evidence by the People's witnesses and adopted by the court are substantially these: On January 7, 1945, at the request of David Harris appellant was at the Harris home in Los Angeles for the purpose of assisting in the moving of some furniture. While there appellant was seated in the Harris living room for about 30 minutes on a divan at the end of which was a small table. While he was so seated Mrs. Harris was occupied in the kitchen and for 15 minutes or more Mr. Harris was intermittently in and out of the living room. Mrs. Harris had left her purse on the table where it lay during the forenoon. She last saw it about 11 o'clock. Her husband also observed it there both before he left the house about 12:30 p.m. and after his return with appellant. The two men departed from the house for the furniture in a truck driven by Williams. As they approached the intersection of Main and Almira Streets appellant observed his brother-in-law, Lucian Haddocks, and stated that he desired to talk to him about a drink. Haddocks was there engaged in conversation with one Stokes. Appellant jumped from the truck and walked back to meet Haddocks. Leaving Stokes where he stood, Haddocks approached appellant and when they met the latter took from his pocket a coin purse impliedly found to have been the property of Mrs. Harris, gave it to Haddocks and asked him to keep it until appellant returned. He resumed his journey with Harris while Haddocks, without showing the purse to Stokes, took it to his home. About 4 o'clock in the afternoon he first examined the pocketbook and inspected its contents but removed nothing therefrom. He saw that it contained $21 in currency, three pennies and three tokens; also a white gold watch and a lady's silver

ring. About an hour later appellant called at the Haddocks' home, asked for the purse and received it, stating that he had found it. At the same time he repaid Haddocks $1.75 borrowed a few days prior thereto. Mrs. Harris established the value of the jewelry and testified that she had never given appellant permission to remove it from her home.

. . .

Larceny is one of the varieties of theft. (*Pen. Code, § 484; People v. Cook, 10 Cal. App.2d 54, 57 {51 P.2d 169}*.) The essential elements of larceny are all present in the crime of appellant: (1) The articles stolen were the property of Mrs. Harris; (2) he took them from her possession without her consent; (3) he asported them; (4) he had the intent without claim of right wholly to deprive the owner thereof.

. . .

In addition to the testimony showing that the property was removed by human agency with intent permanently to deprive Mrs. Harris thereof, appellant stated to Harris on the day set for the trial that the lost property would be returned if Harris did not appear against him. Also, Harris testified that directly after the preliminary trial defendant admitted to him that he had taken the purse away. Appellant did not deny that he was at the Harris home on January 7 or that he sat on the divan during his visit or that Mrs. Harris was in the kitchen and that Mr. Harris intermittently left the living room during the 30 minutes. These facts and the proof that no other person visited the Harris home on the afternoon of January 7 and that the purse and its contents were last seen on the end table about the time of appellant's visit make proof of the *corpus delicti* complete and establish appellant's opportunity to commit the crime.

. . .

Evidence of the attempt of appellant to return the property and to suppress the testimony of the prosecuting witness indicates a consciousness of guilt and was properly received for that purpose.

. . .

We can find no relief for appellant unless we first usurp the powers of the trial judge and thereafter derive a different conclusion. We are impotent legally to do the first and we cannot say that we would do the latter.

The judgment and the order denying appellant's motion for a new trial are affirmed.

PEOPLE v. SHANNON

COURT OF APPEAL OF CALIFORNIA, SECOND APPELLATE DISTRICT, DIVISION ONE

66 CAL. APP. 4TH 649; 78 CAL. RPTR. 2D 177

SEPTEMBER 4, 1998

OPINION BY: ORTEGA, J.

Defendant Jeffrey Antwan Shannon appeals from the judgment entered after his conviction by jury of petty theft with a prior. (*Pen. Code, § 666.*)n1 The trial court found Shannon had three prior felony convictions under the "Three Strikes" law (§ 667, subds. (b)-(i)), for one of which he served a prison term. (§ 667.5, subd. (b).) Shannon received a 25-year-to-life prison sentence.

n1 All further section references are to the Penal Code.

The case arose when Shannon went into a department store, took clothes from a rack, hid them in a bag, and took them to a cashier. Falsely claiming ownership of the clothes, Shannon asked to exchange them for a cash refund. Store personnel had seen Shannon hide the clothes and knew he had stolen them from the rack. Nonetheless, the cashier completed the exchange as part of the store's plan to catch Shannon. Security agents arrested Shannon after he left the store with the money.

In the published portion of the opinion (pt. I), we hold that Shannon completed theft by larceny when he dropped the clothes in his bag intending to defraud the store of their value.

We affirm the judgment.

FACTS

On July 11, 1996, Roger Jara, a loss prevention agent at the J. C. Penney store at the Stonewood Mall in Downey, watched Shannon walking around the store. Shannon was carrying a bag which appeared to have two items in it. Jara followed Shannon to the dress department. Jara saw Shannon hold up two skirts and a sweater, undo the clips holding these items to their hangers, and allow the items to fall to the ground, out of Jara's sight. Shannon bent down, picked up the bag, and walked over to the cashier. The bag was now noticeably fuller. Jara checked the area where Shannon had been standing and found three empty hangers.

Lisa Lugo, another loss prevention agent who was monitoring the store's surveillance cameras, also watched Shannon's actions. She agreed the bag Shannon was carrying was noticeably fuller after he stood up and walked to the cashier.

When Shannon reached the cashier, he placed the items in his bag on the counter. Jara telephoned the cashier, Maria Mikhailides. In response to Jara's question, Mikhailides confirmed Shannon asked for a cash refund for the items. Jara told her to give him the refund.

When Mikhailides tried to process the refund, a code appeared on the cash register, indicating Shannon had exceeded the refund limit for that time period. She telephoned store security and was authorized to complete the refund. She gave Shannon a $102.83 cash refund. Shannon then left the store. After he did so, Jara placed him under arrest.

In defense, Yamileth Santos, Shannon's fiancee, said that on July 11, 1996, she asked him to return some items for her at the store. Santos had bought these items, including two skirts and a sweater, earlier. Edmundo Santos, Yamileth's father, lent Shannon his automobile that day so defendant could return the items for her.

Shannon urges us to reduce his conviction to attempted petty theft, a misdemeanor (§ 1181, subd. 6), or grant him a new trial. . . .

DISCUSSION

I

Shannon makes two related arguments why, as a matter of law, he committed only attempted, not completed, theft. First, Shannon argues he could not be convicted of completed theft of the skirts and sweater which he put into his bag and subsequently returned for a cash refund, because he did not remove the clothes from the store. Second, Shannon argues the theft was not completed at that point because he did not intend to permanently deprive the store of the clothes. We reject both arguments.

Theft, of which Shannon was convicted, is the unlawful taking of another's property. . . . The crime includes larceny, embezzlement, larceny by trick, and theft by false pretenses. . . .Larceny, larceny by trick, and embezzlement involve taking another's personal property from the owner's possession, without the owner's consent, with the intent to deprive the owner permanently of the property. . . . Theft by false pretenses does not require that the defendant take the property; it requires that the defendant use false pretenses to induce the other to give the property to him.

. . .

The jury here was instructed only on larceny. (*CALJIC No. 14.41.*) The jury was not instructed on larceny by trick, theft by false pretenses, or embezzlement.

"'The completed crime of larceny—as distinguished from an attempt—requires *asportation* or carrying away, in addition to the taking' . . . . The element of asportation is not satisfied unless it is shown that 'the goods were severed from the possession or custody of the owner, and in the possession of the thief, though it be but for a moment." . . . However, one need not remove property from the store to be convicted of theft of the property from the store. . . . One need only take possession of the property, detaching it from the store shelves or other location, and move it slightly with the intent to deprive the owner of it permanently. (*People v. Khoury, supra, 108 Cal. App. 3d at pp. Supp. 4–5* [affirming completed theft conviction, and rejecting claim that it was only at attempt, where Khoury hid $900 worth of merchandise in a chandelier box, took it to the check stand, and tried to pay only the much lower price marked on the box, but the salesclerk became suspicious and refused the sale, whereupon Khoury abandoned the box and its contents, walked away from the counter, and was arrested inside the store].) Indeed, the standard jury instruction defining theft by larceny states: "To constitute a 'carrying away,' the property need not be actually removed from the [place] [or] premises where it was kept . . . ." (*CALJIC No. 14.02.*) Thus, Shannon's claim that he could not be guilty of completed theft unless he took the clothes outside the store is wrong.

. . .

Likewise, in our case, the theft was complete when Shannon put the clothes in his bag with the intent to fraudulently obtain money for them by falsely exchanging them for their monetary value. This conclusion alone compels affirmance.

Shannon then makes a related point: The theft was not complete when he took the clothes because he did not intend to permanently deprive the store *of the clothes*, but

only intended to take *the money* he would receive from the false refund. . . . As the jury was instructed, theft requires the specific intent to permanently deprive the owner of its property. (*CALJIC No. 14.41*; accord, *Callan v. Superior Court, supra, 204 Cal. App. 2d* at p. 667.) However, the intent to later restore or make restitution for the property is no defense. (*People v. Costello (1951) 107 Cal. App. 2d 514, 518 {237 P.2d 281}.*) Likewise, "the property need not . . . be retained by the perpetrator." (*CALJIC No. 14.02.*) "Asportation of the property with the intention to appropriate it is sufficient to constitute larceny even though the property may subsequently be returned to the owner. . . . The fact that a thief is prevented by an officer from getting away with the property, or that he may change his mind and return the property to escape prosecution for the crime, does not relieve him from the consequences of the theft. . . . [T]heft may be committed when the accused persons, with a preconceived design to obtain and appropriate property by means of fraud or trickery, thereby gain possession of the property, even though they do not retain or use it for their own benefit." (*People v. Post (1946) 76 Cal. App. 2d 511, 514 {173 P.2d 48}.*) Moreover, the prosecution need not show the defendant took the property for his own use; the intent to destroy it and thus deprive the owner of its use is sufficient. (*2 Witkin & Epstein, Cal. Criminal Law (2d ed. 1988) Crimes Against Property, § 587*, p. 663.)

Thus, the fact that Shannon apparently did not intend to keep the clothes, but to steal its monetary value by exchanging the clothes while falsely claiming to own them, does not alter our conclusion that the theft was complete when he put the clothes in his bag with the described intent. Shannon unquestionably intended to permanently deprive the store of money equal to the clothes' value, and thus to "use [them] for [his] own benefit." (*People v. Post, supra, 76 Cal. App. 2d* at p. 514.) There is no evidence that had Shannon been unable to complete the fraudulent refund, he would have abandoned the stolen clothes rather than leaving the store with them.

In any event, even if Shannon intended to abandon the clothes if his scheme failed, the theft was complete when he dropped the clothes into his bag intending to defraud the store of their monetary value. The fact that Shannon planned to get the money from the store, rather than taking the clothes and selling them to a fence or an innocent buyer, or trading them for drugs, or any of the other myriad ways in which he could have appropriated their value other than by wearing them, is irrelevant. Unlike a joyrider, who plans to use the car temporarily and then return it, Shannon intended not to *unconditionally* return the clothes, but to *appropriate* them for his purpose of *selling* them back. "One who takes another's property intending at the time he takes it to use it temporarily and then to return it *unconditionally* within a reasonable time—and having a substantial ability to do so—lacks the intent to steal required for larceny." (2 LaFave & Scott, Substantive Criminal Law (1986) Crimes Relating to Property, § 8.5(b), p. 359, italics added, fn. omitted.) Put another way, "[t]he intent to steal is an intent to deprive the possessor permanently. One who takes another's property for temporary use or concealment, with the intention of returning it, is liable in tort for damages but is not guilty of larceny." (2 Witkin & Epstein, Cal. Criminal Law, *supra*, Crimes Against Property, § 585, p. 661.)

In support, both texts cite *People v. Brown (1894) 105 Cal. 66 {38 P. 518}*, which reversed a burglary conviction based on incorrect jury instructions. Brown admitted entering, intending to take his landlord's son's bicycle "to get even with the boy" for an earlier quarrel. (*Id.* at p. 68.) Brown intended to return the bicycle unconditionally within a day. However, by mistake Brown took another's bicycle. Brown was caught before he could return the bicycle. The court ordered a new trial because the jury instruction stated the taking did not have to be with the intent to permanently deprive.

Shannon, of course, did not intend to return the store's property unconditionally. Instead, he intended to sell the store's own property, which he took with wrongful intent, back to it, falsely claiming to be the rightful owner. Thus, Shannon neither lacked wrongful intent nor intended to return the clothes unconditionally and cannot benefit from this defense.

In *People v. Stay (1971) 19 Cal. App. 3d 166 {96 Cal. Rptr. 651}*, the defendant's employees picked up retail store shopping carts, each marked with the owning store's identification, which patrons used to take their purchases home and then left on the streets surrounding the stores. Stay then contacted the stores and offered to return each store's carts for $2.50 each, although other legitimate companies returned the carts for 25 cents each. A few of the stores complied with Stay's ransom demands, while most did not. Stay removed the names and numbers from the carts he could not sell back to their owners' stores and then sold the relabeled carts to other stores. Stay was convicted of five counts of completed grand theft, some from stores that paid him for their returned carts, some from stores that refused to pay and whose carts he resold after altering them. We affirmed.

First, we rejected Stay's claim that, like the legitimate companies described above, he was acting under a statute which entitled those who returned shopping carts to their owners "'without compensation'" to receive "'a reasonable charge for saving and taking care of the property[,]'" and thus was not guilty of theft or attempted theft. (*People v. Stay, supra*, 19 Cal. App. 3d at p. 171, *fn. 3; id.* at pp. 171–175.) Second, and dispositive of this issue, we rejected Stay's argument that he did not commit theft because he did not intend to deprive the stores of their carts permanently. In doing so, we did not distinguish between those stores that paid the ransom and got their carts back, and those that refused and never got them back because Stay sold them to others. Thus, although Stay never intended to keep the carts, but stole them intending to ransom them back to their owners or, failing that, sell them to others, we affirmed his completed theft convictions. (*Id.* at pp. 175–176.)

Although the scheme here is different, the result is the same. In neither case does it matter that the thief intends to sell the victim's property back to the victim after wrongfully stealing the property and claiming to be the rightful owner, thus ultimately stealing the victim's money rather than the property. Shannon completed the theft when he moved the clothes, thus appropriating them and intending to fraudulently resell them to the store. On this basis, the evidence supports Shannon's larceny conviction.

. . .

DISPOSITION

We affirm the judgment.

PEOPLE v. WOOTEN

COURT OF APPEAL OF CALIFORNIA, SECOND APPELLATE DISTRICT DIVISION SIX

44 CAL. APP. 4TH 1834; 52 CAL. RPTR. 2D 765

MAY 7, 1996

OPINION BY: YEGAN, J.

Michael Wooten appeals from the judgment entered on a jury verdict convicting him of one count of felony grand theft. (*Pen. Code, § 487.*)n1 The jury determined that appellant obtained $10,000 from a construction lender by misrepresenting to the lender that the money would be used to pay a specified licensed general contractor for supervising a construction project. In fact, appellant, who was not a licensed contractor, personally supervised the construction and kept the money for himself and his partner. This is grand theft.

> n1 At the probation and sentencing hearing, the trial court reduced the conviction to a misdemeanor and granted probation.

Appellant contends: (1) the trial court erroneously restricted the presentation of defense evidence; (2) the prosecution could not, as a matter of law, establish theft on a false pretense theory; and (3) the jury was erroneously instructed. We affirm.

FACTS

Appellant and his partner, Frank Marasco (Marasco), were the principals of Darrik-Marten Company (Darrik-Marten), a firm engaged in real estate development. They obtained a $550,000 loan from Community Group Funding, Inc. (CGF) to construct a subdivision in Santa Paula. The two-page loan agreement states, "[t]he loan will consist of the following disbursements:" (1) $110,000 to Darrik-Marten; (2) $172,000 for loan fees, a payment to Darrik-Marten and interest reserves; and (3) $268,000 for construction costs and interest reserves.

The loan agreement does not establish a procedure to be used in requesting disbursements under the loan or state whether CGF could deny such requests. Although Darrik-Marten used letters to request the first two disbursements, it used a voucher to request funds for construction costs, including the payment at issue here. The voucher certified that the payee, Gary Johnson Construction, "actually

performed work or labor, . . . in connection with, or upon the above described construction project . . . and that the sum set forth above [$10,000] actually has been paid or will be paid by the undersigned to the person or firms named."

Before the loan agreement was signed, Darrik-Marten did not discuss with CGF whether it would hire a general contractor for the project. After the agreement was signed, however, appellant and Marasco told CGF that Gary Johnson (Johnson) had been hired as the general contractor and would be paid $16,000. In February 1992, appellant submitted a construction budget to CGF which listed Johnson as the general contractor. Johnson also signed the building permit and subcontracts. In fact, appellant and Johnson agreed that CGF would pay the fee to Johnson, that Johnson would return the fee to Darrik-Marten and that appellant would supervise the project himself.

On March 9, 1992, appellant's partner mailed to CGF a voucher for a $10,000 payment to Johnson. The voucher was accompanied by an invoice from Johnson for "[s]upervision of tract 4753 which includes building of roads [and] cul-de-sac [and] all underground utilities." Marasco also sent a letter falsely stating: "I've included the next draw for our contractor, Gary Johnson, in yesterday's mailing. He won't receive another payment until after all the work is complete, and the City has signed it off. Normally we pay him monthly, but this job shouldn't take more than 6 weeks. Gary will want to begin right away."

Ten days later, CGF wrote a check to Johnson for $10,000. Appellant gave the check to Johnson and Johnson gave appellant his own check for the same amount. Appellant deposited Johnson's check into the Darrik-Marten account and immediately paid himself $5,000. It is undisputed that $10,000 was a reasonable supervision fee and was $6,000 less than the amount budgeted.

Don Lukens, the owner of CGF, was responsible for approving disbursements under the loan. It was his understanding that the loan agreement did not expressly require Darrik-Marten to use a general contractor or give CGF the right to reject a contractor retained by Darrik-Marten. Nevertheless, Lukens thought it was important to have a general contractor working on the project, and he believed appellant and Marasco when they told him that Johnson would perform as the licensed contractor. He also believed in and relied upon the information contained in Marasco's correspondence.

Lukens acknowledged that the loan agreement did not expressly allow CGF to withhold loan disbursements so long as the funds requested were actually used on the project. He testified, however, that he approved the disbursement to Johnson based upon his understanding that Johnson was the licensed general contractor working on the project. Lukens unequivocally testified that he would not have paid Johnson if he had known the truth.

When Darrik-Marten lost the project in foreclosure, appellant got a job managing a small cardroom in Oxnard. He and Marasco then applied for a permit to build their own cardroom. While the application was pending, the Ventura County District Attorney began to investigate appellant. By late spring 1993, appellant knew he was under investigation for making illegal campaign contributions.

The $10,000 payment to Johnson was discovered during the course of that investigation. In early August 1993, Johnson and Lukens agreed that an investigator could tape-record their telephone conversations with appellant. During the first conversation, appellant told Lukens and CGF's attorney that he did not know why Johnson had returned the $10,000 to Darrik-Marten. Appellant also assured Lukens that Johnson actually performed work on the project.

During the second conversation, appellant asked Johnson to exaggerate his involvement in the project: "[H]ere's how I want to couch that, okay? And see, see if you can live with this. [Y]ou helped me get the thing put together on the front end. . . . You know, you just walked it with me and told me what we needed to do. That kind of stuff. And . . . I want to take the position that we were gonna use you and that, uh, you know, we just decided not to. Um, and that we had already paid you the first installment and when we decided not to use you, you gave us the money back. . . . [JOHNSON]: Jesus, I don't know. Um, because, you know, technically, you know, we lied about this thing. [APPELLANT]: You know I know that." When Johnson expressed concerns about lying, appellant told him nothing would happen if they both told the same story because, "nobody, nobody can prove it one way or the other, the two of us saying that."

. . .

THEFT BY FALSE PRETENSES

A theft conviction on the theory of false pretenses requires proof that (1) the defendant made a false pretense or representation to the owner of property; (2) with the intent to defraud the owner of that property; and (3) the owner transferred the property to the defendant in reliance on the representation. (*Perry v. Superior Court (1962) 57 Cal. 2d 276, 282–283 {19 Cal. Rptr. 1, 368 P.2d 529}; People v. Whight (1995) 36 Cal. Cal. App. 4th 1143, 1151 {43 Cal. Rptr. 2d 163}.*) In this context, reliance means that the false representation "materially influenced" the owner's decision to part with his property; it need not be the sole factor motivating the transfer. (*People v. Ashley (1954) 42 Cal. 2d 246, 259 {267 P.2d 271}.*) A victim does not rely on a false representation if "there is no causal connection shown between the [representations] alleged to be false" and the transfer of property. (*People v. Bliss (1920) 47 Cal. App. 503, 506 {190 P. 1046}; see also People v. Canfield (1915) 28 Cal. App. 792, 795 {154 P. 33}; People v. Emmons (1910) 13 Cal. App. 487, 495–95 {110 P. 151}.*) Thus, if the defendant makes both true and false statements to the owner, but the false statements are irrelevant to the owner's decision to transfer the property, theft on the theory of false pretense has not been committed. (*People v. Bliss, supra, 47 Cal. App. at p. 506.*) Reliance may be inferred from all the circumstances. (*People v. Randono (1973) 32 Cal. App. 3d 164, 174 {108 Cal. Rptr. 326}.*)

Appellant argues his conviction must be reversed because the jury was instructed on an erroneous theory of grand theft and it is impossible to determine whether the verdict was based in whole or in part on that theory. (*People v. Green (1980) 27 Cal. 3d 1, 69 {164 Cal. Rptr. 1, 609 P.2d 468}.*) According to appellant, false pretense does not apply as a matter of law because appellant did not procure the loan agreement through fraud and once that agreement was signed, CGF had no choice but to approve every request for disbursement submitted by Darrik-Marten. Thus, when Lukens approved the March 9, 1992, request for payment, he relied solely upon a preexisting contractual obligation and not upon any representation concerning Johnson's involvement in the project.

Appellant's argument fails. There is no express term requiring CGF to "rubber-stamp" every disbursement request submitted by Darrik-Marten, no matter how false or inaccurate.

. . .

Moreover, there is evidence that the parties established a course of dealing which allowed CGF to refuse loan disbursements under these circumstances. Lukens believed that he had the ability to deny or delay disbursements based on irregularities in a voucher or other problems with the project. Lukens also testified that he in fact relied on the statements included in the March 9, 1992, voucher and invoice. He expressly testified that he would not have approved the payment to Johnson had he known Johnson would not perform any work on the project. Appellant and his partner shared that understanding. They chose to use a voucher form which specifically declared that the person named in the voucher had done the work described and would be paid for it. Marasco falsified the request for payment because he was afraid CGF would not approve, or would delay the disbursement if it knew the truth.

In sum, the evidence concerning the loan agreement and the parties' course of dealing did not establish, as a matter of law, that CGF had no alternative but to approve the March 9 voucher. Accordingly, it was legally permissible for CGF to rely on the representations and the trial court did not err in presenting the theft by false pretense theory to the jury.

. . .

JURY INSTRUCTIONS—EMBEZZLEMENT

The trial court gave two instructions on embezzlement. The first quoted *Penal Code section 484c* which provides: "Any person who submits a false voucher to obtain construction loan funds and does not use the funds for the purpose for which the claim was submitted is guilty of embezzlement." The second was the standard instruction on the elements of embezzlement. (*CALJIC No. 14.07.*) This instruction was intended by the trial court to "define" the term embezzlement as it is used in section 484c. It informed the jury that embezzlement occurs only where: "1. A relation of trust and confidence existed between two persons, 2. Pursuant to such relationship one of those persons accepted property entrusted to [him] by the other person, and 3. With the specific intent to deprive the person of [his] property, the person appropriated or converted it to [his] own use or purpose."

Appellant contends the trial court erred in giving this instruction because Darrik-Marten and CGF did not have the required relationship of trust and confidence. We agree. The crime of embezzlement requires the existence of a "relation of trust and confidence," similar to a fiduciary relationship, between the victim and the perpetrator. "'If the relation is that of creditor and debtor merely, an appropriation by the latter does not constitute embezzlement.'" (*People v. Petrin (1954) 122 Cal. App. 2d 578, 581 {265 P.2d 149}*.) There is no fiduciary or "special" relationship between a real estate developer and its construction lender . . . There was no evidence indicating the relationship between appellant and CGF was anything other than a standard debtor-creditor relationship. Accordingly, the general embezzlement instruction ought not to have been presented to the jury.

The error was, however, harmless because its only effect was to force the prosecution to carry a heightened burden of proof.

. . .

Moreover, in California, the various common law theories of theft, including embezzlement, have been consolidated. "[U]nder section 484, there is simply one consolidated crime of theft, which the jury may find upon either theory, if there is an 'unlawful [taking]' . . . ." . . . Here, the evidence was sufficient to support a conviction under a false pretenses theory or, as discussed below, under *Penal Code section 484c*. Any error in instructing the jury on an additional embezzlement theory requiring a "relation of trust and confidence" was harmless beyond a reasonable doubt. (*People v. Swain (1996) 12 Cal. 4th 593, 607 {49 Cal. Rptr. 2d 390, 909 P.2d 994}*.)

. . .

CONCLUSION

In appellant's petition for rehearing, he claims that our ". . . contempt for appellant's lack of candor appears to be the linchpin of the opinion." This advocatorial "spin" misses the mark. In circumstances such as those here presented, the Legislature has declared that "lack of candor" directed to a construction lender is a crime. No matter how one characterizes appellant's actions, he lied to get the $10,000 and knew that he would not receive the money if he had told the truth. That is grand theft.

The judgment is affirmed.

PEOPLE v. HIDALGO

COURT OF APPEAL OF CALIFORNIA, SECOND APPELLATE DISTRICT, DIVISION ONE

128 Cal. App. 703; 18 P.2d 391

January 16, 1933

OPINION BY: HOUSER, J.

On each of six separate counts of an information filed against him defendant was convicted of the crime of forgery. From the ensuing judgment, as well as from an order by which his motion for a new trial was denied, defendant appeals to this court.

In each count of the information the instrument alleged to have been forged and "passed" was a check on Seaboard National Bank of Los Angeles, purportedly drawn by "Baker Ice Machine Company, L. Baker, H. Spencer." The only variations that distinguished any one of such checks from either of the others were its serial number, its date, the amount for which, and the person in whose favor, it was drawn. The following is a copy of one of such checks:

> "Baker Ice Machine Co., Inc.
>
> Los Angeles Factory No. 33292
>
> Los Angeles, April 14, 1932.
>
> Pay to the order of Antonio Gomez $18.54 Eighteen Dollars Fifty Four Cents only Dollars
>
> Baker Ice Machine Co.
>
> L. Baker,
>
> H. Spencer.
>
> To Seaboard National Bank
>
> Los Angeles, California."

In effect, it is contended by appellant that each of the several verdicts returned by the jury was "contrary to law . . . and to the evidence"; that is to say, that neither the verdict nor the judgment was supported by the evidence.

On the part of the prosecution it was shown that a large number of blank checks had been stolen from Baker Ice Machine Company; that defendant admitted having had such blank checks in his possession; and that in each instance a stolen blank check was made use of in uttering a so-called forged check; also that defendant "passed" each of the checks in question. As to three of such checks only,

testimony was received in substance that defendant indorsed each of them; but as to the three remaining checks, no evidence was offered which tended to show that defendant had indorsed either of them. The evidence disclosed the facts that Baker Ice Machine Company was a foreign corporation; that it had a branch office in the city of Los Angeles; that one J. M. McKenzie was its local manager; and that the said corporation had a banking account with Seaboard National Bank. By reference to "signature cards" and other records of Seaboard National Bank, the assistant cashier thereof testified that the bank was "authorized" to honor Baker Ice Machine Company checks on the signature of "J. L. Baker, President; F. J. Bette, Secretary; J. M. McKenzie, Manager of the Corporation, *or any other* by said J. M. McKenzie, and there are two other signatures, Charles E. Hollingsworth, and Laurel K. Brink."

Another witness, who was "head of the bookkeeping department of the Seaboard National Bank," testified that the bank was not "authorized" to honor any checks drawn by H. Spencer or L. Baker, or "by the joint signatures of those two names"; and that the "authority" to honor checks came from J. M. McKenzie, who was the local manager of Baker Ice Machine Company. A man who called himself the "office manager" of the branch office of Baker Ice Machine Company testified that he did not know defendant; that to his knowledge defendant was not "connected" with Baker Ice Machine Company; that none of the officers of that company was in Los Angeles; that "Mr. Baker's" name is J. L. Baker, and that the signature "L. Baker" on each of the questioned checks was not the signature of J. L. Baker; that he did not know L. Baker or H. Spencer; nor was he acquainted with the person in whose favor either of the questioned checks was drawn.

Section 470 of the Penal Code is the statute under the provisions of which defendant was prosecuted. As far as concerns the particular offense which defendant was alleged to have committed, the statute requires that "with intent to defraud," defendant sign either the name of another person or the name of a fictitious person to the questioned check; or that he utter or pass such check "as true and genuine . . . knowing the same to be . . . forged . . . with intent to prejudice, damage, or defraud any person . . ."

Reverting to the evidence introduced on the trial of the action, and applying to it the statutory requirements, it will be noticed that the evidence is lacking in sufficiency to support either of the several verdicts returned therein in at least the following particulars: Other than the mere passing of the check (not shown to have been forged), there was no specific, or even general, evidence of "intent to defraud" (see *People v. Mitchell, 92 Cal. 590 {28 P. 597, 788}; People v. Ball, 102 Cal. App. 353 {282 P. 971}*); no evidence that defendant either signed the name of another person or persons to the check, or that either of such names was fictitious; or that, if fictitious, it was signed by defendant. By no evidence did it appear that the handwriting of either of the signatures on the check was identical with the indorsed signature of the payee thereof. Nor was any direct evidence introduced from which it might be inferred that defendant passed either of such checks "knowing the same to be *forged.*" The prior theft from the corporation of the blank checks, and the subsequent admission by defendant that they had been in his possession, had no tendency to prove that a forgery had been committed either in the issuance, or in the utterance, of checks which purportedly were authorized to be drawn and issued by the corporation. The fact that defendant "passed" the checks in question merely tended to show that *if* a forgery had been committed, defendant might have been the person who committed the offense. No evidence that the check, or any checks, had been forged was placed before the jury. The most that appeared was that Baker Ice Machine Company had a banking account with Seaboard National Bank, and that *as far only as the bank was concerned,* it would honor checks drawn against said account which were signed by certain designated individuals. Neither by the minutes, nor by the records, of Baker Ice Machine Company was it shown that no other person or persons (possibly including L. Baker and H. Spencer) was or were respectively authorized by the corporation to draw checks

on the said banking account. In part to the contrary, according to the records of the bank, it was "authorized" to honor a signature by "J. M. McKenzie, Manager of the Corporation, *or any other* by said J. M. McKenzie". No showing was made that J. M. McKenzie did not authorize L. Baker and H. Spencer to draw the checks which were the subject of the forgery. It is probable that even within the city of Los Angeles there are many different persons whose names would be properly represented by that of "L. Baker"; and the same situation would apply to the name "H. Spencer". Assuming that neither "L. Baker" nor "H. Spencer" was a fictitious name, it was necessary for the prosecution to show that neither of those persons was authorized to sign the check, and if authorized, that neither of them had either signed the check or authorized his name to be signed by defendant thereto. (*People v. Elliott, 90 Cal. 586 {27 P. 433}; People v. Mitchell, supra; People v. Whiteman, 114 Cal. 338 {46 P. 99}; People v. Lundin, 117 Cal. 124 {48 P. 1024}; People v. McWilliams, 117 Cal. App. 732 {4 P.2d 601}; 12 Cal. Jur. 666*, and authorities there cited.) No attempt was made by the prosecution so to do. In fact, neither J. M. McKenzie nor any other officer of the corporation was called as a witness. If the checks were not forged, manifestly in that regard no crime was committed.

By no evidence did it appear that the payee of either of the checks was a fictitious person; nor that defendant indorsed either of three of such checks; nor as to the three checks that he did indorse, that he was unauthorized by the payee thereof so to do—which latter fact was one of the essential elements of the crime to be proved by the prosecution. (*People v. Lundin, supra; People v. Mitchell, supra.*)

It follows that on each of the six counts of the information on which defendant was convicted, the evidence was insufficient to support the verdict returned by the jury.

It is ordered that the judgment and the order by which defendant's motion for a new trial was denied be and they are reversed.

CONREY, P. J., concurred.

PEOPLE v. PUGH

COURT OF APPEAL OF CALIFORNIA, FOURTH APPELLATE DISTRICT, DIVISION ONE

104 CAL. APP. 4TH 66; 127 CAL. RPTR. 2D 770

DECEMBER 6, 2002

OPINION BY: BENKE, J.

Darrell Reginald Pugh was convicted of forgery and the fraudulent uttering of a check. Pugh was granted probation. He appeals, arguing the evidence was insufficient to support his convictions . . .

FACTS

A. PROSECUTION CASE

In February 2001, Connie Sagredo placed an advertisement in the newspaper offering to sell her 50-foot cabin cruiser. On Monday, February 26, appellant called Sagredo expressing an interest in buying the boat. The two discovered they attended the same church. Based on that connection Sagredo trusted appellant. Later, on February 26, Sagredo's son Derek Morris showed appellant the boat. Appellant wanted to buy it. He gave Morris two checks, one for $500, the other for $10,000, both dated February 28. Appellant also gave Morris a note for Sagredo. The note asked that she wait until Wednesday, i.e., February 28, to deposit the $500 check and until March 10 to deposit the $10,000 check. Appellant agreed to pay the balance of the purchase price before March 25. The note ended with appellant's statement that if Sagredo needed an additional $2,000 to $4,000 in light of his inability to pay cash, he would pay it.

On February 28 appellant went to Sagredo's home. He gave her $500 in cash, took back the check in that amount and told her she could deposit the $10,000 check on March 10. Sagredo did not give appellant the keys to the boat, or its title or registration. She told appellant he could not live on the boat.

On March 10 Sagredo called appellant's bank and discovered the funds in his account were insufficient to cover the check. Sagredo called appellant. He stated he would need a few more days. Sagredo called the bank over the next several days and was told each time that appellant's funds were insufficient to cover the check. She called appellant. He stated he would make it "right." After

appellant failed to keep an earlier appointment, the pair met at a restaurant. Appellant did not have the money. Citing problems with the boat, he asked Sagredo to lower the purchase price. Desperate for money, she agreed to do so. Sagredo wrote out and signed a document stating the new price. When Sagredo asked for the money, appellant stated he would need a few more days. Sagredo agreed.

The pair arranged to meet again at the restaurant in several days. Appellant did not appear. The two made repeated arrangements to meet. Appellant did not keep the appointments. On April 4 Sagredo received a call from a friend that someone was on her boat. Sagredo called the police.

On April 4 Harbor Patrol Officer Richard Jordan picked up Sagredo and the two went to her boat. Robert Peterson was on the vessel making repairs. He explained that appellant had purchased the boat. Sagredo told the officer the boat was hers. Unsure who owned the vessel, Jordan gave his card to Sagredo and Peterson and asked that they provide him with documents supporting their claims of ownership.

On April 6 appellant contacted Jordan. Appellant told the officer he was the new owner of Sagredo's boat. Appellant showed Jordan a sales agreement for the boat dated February 2 indicating Sagredo as the owner and appellant as the buyer. Both appellant's and Sagredro's signatures were on the document. Appellant also showed the officer a copy of a small claims suit filed by him against Sagredo. It alleged Pugh gave $10,500 for the boat and that Sagredo was unwilling to abide by the contract or return appellant's money. Based on the documents, the officer concluded appellant was the owner of the boat.

That evening Sagredo appeared at the police station with the title to the boat. When Jordan showed her a copy of the sales agreement provided by appellant, she stated she had never seen the agreement before and had not signed it.

Appellant later explained to investigators from the district attorney's office that he prepared the purchase agreement without Sagredo's knowledge and that he cut and pasted her signature onto it.

B. DEFENSE CASE

Appellant testified in his own defense. He stated he planned to buy Sagredo's boat to live on. Sagredo suggested as early as February 28 that he move onto the boat and after a meeting on March 22, appellant understood he could do so. Appellant testified the purchase price of the boat was $17,500. It was agreed that if repairs to the engine were more than $2,000, the repair amount would be deducted from the price. By March 12 the cost of repairs had not been determined and appellant asked Sagredo not to cash the $10,000 check for a few days.

On March 31 appellant informed Sagredo that the boat needed a new engine and other repairs that would cost $18,500. Sagredo refused to allow him to deduct the cost of replacing the engine from the sale price and told him he could not live on the boat. On April 2 appellant sued Sagredo.

Appellant testified he prepared the documents he gave Officer Jordan to convince his mechanic that he could go on the boat without being accused of trespass. He admitted he cut and pasted Sagredo's signature on the document. He stated he was not trying to trick the police.

DISCUSSION

A. FORGERY

Appellant notes he was convicted of forgery based on his preparation of a document that reflected the terms of his purchase of Sagredo's boat and having placed her signature on that document. He states there was insufficient evidence to support that conviction since there was no evidence appellant prepared the document with the intent to defraud. More specifically, he argues that there could be no intent to defraud since although he prepared a false document, it nonetheless did nothing more than reflect the verbal contract he had with Sagredo. He also argues that the document was on its face so defective that it was incapable of defrauding anyone.

In determining whether the evidence is sufficient to support the verdict, we review the entire record, viewing the evidence in the light most favorable to the judgment, and presuming in support of the verdict the existence of every fact the jury could reasonably deduce from the evidence. The issue is whether the record so viewed discloses evidence that is reasonable, credible and of solid value such that a rational trier of fact could find the elements of the crime beyond a reasonable doubt. (*People v. Brown* (1995) 35 *Cal. App.4th* 1585, 1598 {42 *Cal. Rptr.* 2d 155}.)

Among other elements, a conviction of forgery requires the person utter, publish or pass, in this case, the purchase agreement with the specific intent to defraud another person. (*Pen. Code, 470*, subd. (d); *CALJIC No. 15.01.*) An intent to defraud is an intent to deceive another person for the purpose of gaining a material advantage over that person or to induce that person to part with property or alter that person's position by some false statement or false representation of fact, wrongful concealment or suppression of the truth or by any artifice or act designed to deceive. (*People v. Booth* (1996) 48 *Cal.App.4th* 1247, 1253 {56 *Cal. Rptr. 2d 202*}.)

We agree with the Attorney General's position. While it is true that appellant and Sagredo had an agreement for the sale of the boat, the evidence indicates part of the agreement was that appellant not take possession of the craft until the full purchase price was paid. When a disagreement arose concerning appellant's right to possession, he presented to Officer Jordan the sales agreement he had manufactured along with other documents to prove his right to be on the boat. The purchase agreement was an artifice designed to deceive the officer into believing appellant had the right to possession of the boat.

Neither do we accept appellant's argument that the forgery was so defective on its face that it was as a matter of law incapable of defrauding anyone. The document may not have had a formal appearance and may have appeared incomplete. Nonetheless, appellant uttered it, along with other documents, and it was accepted by the officer as evidence of appellant's rights to possession of the boat. The purchase agreement was not so defective that as a matter of law it was incapable of supporting a fraud.

B. UTTERING A CHECK WITH INTENT TO DEFRAUD

Appellant argues there was insufficient evidence to support his conviction of issuing a check with the intent to defraud. Specifically, he argues it was undisputed that when he uttered the $10,000 check, he informed Sagredo there were insufficient funds in the account to cover it and that he had a reasonable expectation that the check would be paid on the date he told her to present it. He notes both are defenses to the crime.

Conviction for a violation of *Penal Code section 476a*, subdivision (a), requires a person with the intent to defraud, make, draw, utter or deliver, in this case, a check, knowing at that time there are insufficient funds for its payment. There is, however, no fraudulent intent if the maker informs the payee at the time the check is uttered that there are insufficient funds to pay the check. (*People v. Poyet* (1972) 6 *Cal.3d* 530, 536 {99 *Cal. Rptr.*

758, 492 P.2d 1150}.) Neither is there fraudulent intent if the person uttering the check, while aware there are insufficient funds to cover it, believes sufficient funds will be in the account when the check is presented for payment. (*People v. Griffith (1953) 120 Cal. App. 2d 873, 880 {262 P.2d 355}*.)

There is no dispute that when appellant uttered the $10,000 check to Sagredo on February 26 he told her not to cash it until March 10, stating he was expecting a deal to close before that date. As to the uttering of the check on February 26, therefore, appellant could not be convicted of uttering a check to defraud since he told Sagredo there were insufficient funds at that time to cover it.

A dispute does exist, however, concerning events after March 10. Appellant's position was that he communicated with Sagredo and told her for various reasons not to cash the check. Sagredo on the other hand testified appellant sometime not long after March 10 told her to resubmit the check for payment. At that time appellant did not tell Sagredo there were insufficient funds to cover the check. By that time appellant by his own admission knew that his expected windfall was not forthcoming at least in the immediate future. In any event, his claim of expected funds was based solely on his own impeachable testimony and could be reasonably rejected by the jury.

"Utter" means to "use or *attempt to use* an instrument, whereby or in connection with which a person asserts or represents to another, directly or indirectly, expressly or impliedly, by words or conduct, that the instrument is genuine." (*People v. Jackson (1979) 92 Cal. App. 3d 556, 561 {155 Cal. Rptr. 89}*.) After March 10 when appellant told Sagredo to resubmit the check, he uttered it. The evidence was sufficient to convict him of fraudulently uttering a check.

. . .

The judgment is affirmed.

KREMER, P. J., and MCCONNELL, J., concurred.

PEOPLE v. HESSLINK

COURT OF APPEAL OF CALIFORNIA, FOURTH APPELLATE DISTRICT, DIVISION TWO

167 Cal. App. 3d 781; 213 Cal. Rptr. 465

May 1, 1985

OPINION BY: KAUFMAN, J.

. . . Charles W. Hesslink (defendant) was found guilty by a jury of forcible oral copulation (*Pen. Code, § 288a*, subd. (c), count 1); extortion (*Pen. Code § 146a* count 3). . . .

Defendant appeals contending: The conviction of extortion must be reversed because (1) it is not supported by the evidence and (2) the court erred in failing to deliver, *sua sponte*, an instruction on specific intent; . . .

FACTS

The victim, a prostitute, was in the area of Chestnut and Seventh Streets in Riverside about 11 a.m. on November 30, 1982. Sometime between 12 and 1 p.m., defendant, driving a blue Chevrolet Malibu, stopped his car on Seventh Street. The victim walked over to defendant's car and talked to him because she thought he might be a customer. . . . A price of $20 for the act of oral copulation was agreed to. The two then drove for about 5 minutes to a secluded road under the freeway near Fairmont Park in Riverside. When the car stopped, defendant and the victim engaged in conversation during which the victim told defendant that she had a 6-year-old daughter and was separated from her husband.

Defendant displayed a badge and handcuffs and told the victim he was a police officer and would have to arrest her. Defendant then proceeded to pat the victim down in a nonsexual manner. He asked her if she had ever before been arrested and she replied she had not. The victim was fearful she was going to go to jail. Defendant then initiated a discussion about working out a deal with her since she would not have anyone to look after her daughter while she was in jail. Defendant insinuated that the victim's daughter would be taken away from her. The victim interpreted defendant's statement to mean that her daughter might be placed in a foster home.

Defendant asked the victim if she had $2,500 to post bail. When the victim replied that she did not, defendant stated that he could possibly get the bail reduced. The victim believed at that time that defendant was interested in money and that if she gave him some he would not take her to jail. She then reached into her back pocket and handed defendant $50. Defendant accepted the money.

Defendant then unzipped his pants, exposed himself and asked the victim if she could do him another favor. Defendant placed his hand on the victim's head and pushed her face down toward his penis. The victim then orally copulated defendant. She did so to avoid being taken to jail.

After the victim finished orally copulating him, defendant gave the victim a lecture on vice officers. He intimated to her that some other vice officers would be interested in working out a deal with her, but warned her that one particular officer would arrest her for soliciting. Defendant then drove her back to Chestnut and University. Before dropping her off at that location, he told her that his name was Rick Thomas and gave her a phone number where he could be reached. He also told her that she would see him around and that if she did not have a date when he came by she should come over to his car and they would take a ride. As defendant drove away, the victim memorized all but one digit of his license plate number and wrote it down immediately thereafter.

The victim called the police later that day but did not reveal all of the facts for fear she would get herself into trouble. The victim later reported the entire incident to Officer Ken Fouse. She gave Fouse a physical description of defendant, including the fact that defendant had a dark scar on his lower left abdomen, a description of defendant's car and the license plate number. Based on this information, defendant's car was located on December 6, 1982. Defendant was arrested and taken to Riverside, as was his car. Officer Fouse later searched defendant's car in the rear parking lot of the Riverside police station and found a badge and a holder and a pair of handcuffs under a floor mat on the driver's side. The handcuffs were marked with the initials "CWH."

DISCUSSION

I THE EXTORTION CONVICTION

Sufficiency of the Evidence   As we shall explain, we agree with defendant's contention that extortion is a specific intent crime and that his conviction of that charge must be reversed because the trial court failed to instruct the jury on the required specific intent. However, because of the nature of several of defendant's arguments concerning the sufficiency of the evidence and the possibility of retrial on that charge, it is appropriate that we address preliminarily his contention that the extortion conviction is not supported by substantial evidence.

Citing a long list of cases in which the accused demanded from the victim a specific sum of money, defendant points out that he did not and argues that evidence of a request or demand for a specific sum is required to support a conviction for extortion. We do not agree. *Penal Code section 518* which defines the crime of extortion contains no such requirement. It reads: "Extortion is the obtaining of *property* from another, with his consent, . . . induced by a wrongful use of force or fear, or under color of official right." (Italics added.)

It is true that in many cases a specific sum of money was requested or demanded, but so far as we are informed no appellate decision has held or stated that evidence of a demand or request for a specific sum is a prerequisite to a conviction of extortion.

Next, defendant asserts that he had a legal right to make a citizen's arrest of the victim for the misdemeanor of soliciting an act of prostitution (*Pen. Code, § 647*, subd. (b)), and argues that since he had the right to make such an arrest, his threat to arrest the victim could not be "a wrongful use of . . . fear" under the statute. Not so. First, even if defendant had the right to arrest the victim, he was not at liberty to threaten to arrest her for the purpose of extorting money or property from her. (*People v. Powell (1920) 50 Cal. App. 436, 441 {195 P. 456}*; cf. *People* v. *Beggs (1918) 178 Cal.79, 84–85 {179 P. 152}*.) As stated by the court in *Powell*: "But we do not think that, merely because of the conceded guilt of the complaining witness, defendant is thereby relieved of the pains and penalties of the offense charged—extortion. . . . Under section 518, . . . obtaining the payment of money from a violator of the ordinance referred to by a threat of arrest and detention if the payment be not made, is extortion, and this without regard to the exercise of good faith in threatening to make the arrest." (*50 Cal. App. 436, 441.*)

. . .

Failure to Instruct on Specific Intent   As noted preliminarily, we agree with defendant that extortion is a specific intent crime and that the trial court was required *sua sponte* to so instruct the jury. It is well settled, of course, that the trial court has a duty in criminal cases, even in the absence of a request, to instruct the jury on the general principles of law relevant to the issues raised by the evidence . . . Thus, in a case in which specific intent is a required element, the court must instruct the jury as to that requirement even in the absence of a request. (*People v. Ford, supra, 60 Cal.2d 772, 793,* and cases there cited.)

The dispositive question therefore is whether the crime of extortion requires proof of a specific intent. Urging it does not, the Attorney General relies on the generally accepted approach to the problem set forth in *People* v. *Hood (1969) I Cal.3d 444, 456–457 {82 Cal. Rptr. 618, 462 P.2d 370}*: "Specific and general intent have been notoriously difficult terms to define and apply, and a number of text writers recommend that they be abandoned altogether. Too often the characterization of a particular crime as one of specific or general intent is determined solely by the presence or absence of words describing psychological phenomena— 'intent' or 'malice' for example—in the statutory language defining the crime. *When the definition of a crime consists of only the description of a particular act, without reference to intent to do a further act or achieve a future consequence,* we ask whether the defendant intended to do the proscribed act. This intention is deemed to be a *general criminal intent. When the definition refers to defendant's intent to do some further act or achieve some additional consequence,* the crime is deemed to be one of *specific intent.*" (Italics added; accord *People v. Daniels (1975) 14 Cal.3d 857, 860 {122 Cal. Rptr. 872, 537 P.2d 1232}.*)

As previously quoted, *Penal Code section 518* reads in relevant part: "Extortion is the obtaining of property from another, with his consent . . . induced by a wrongful use of force or fear, or under color of official right." Applying the *Hood* formulation to this language, the Attorney General argues that the act proscribed is "the obtaining of property," that until the property is obtained the crime is not complete and that after the property is obtained there is no further act to be done or no further consequence to be achieved and that, therefore, the crime must be one of general intent rather than specific intent.

While we cannot fault the logic in the argument, we are unable to agree with it. We think the problem stems from the way in which the statute is worded. *In substance,* what is proscribed is the successful wrongful use of force or fear to obtain property from another with his or her consent. Viewed from that standpoint, the elements of the offense are: (1) A wrongful use of force or fear, (2) with the specific intent of inducing the victim to consent to the defendant's obtaining his or her property, (3) which does in fact induce such consent and results in the defendant's obtaining property from the victim. Applying the *Hood* formulation to the elements thus stated, the intent required is seen to be a specific one. The crime requires an unlawful use of force or fear with the intent of achieving a further consequence, the inducement of another person to consent to the actor's obtaining the other's property. (See *31 Am.Jur.2d, Extortion, Blackmail, etc., § 9,* pp. 906–907; cf. *People v. Francisco (1931) 112 Cal. App. 442, 444 {297 P. 34}.*)

The crime of extortion is related to and sometimes difficult to distinguish from the crime of robbery. (See, e.g., Perkins on Criminal Law (2d ed. 1969) pp. 372–373; 1 Witkin, Cal. Crimes (1963) § 443, p. 409; see also *In re Stanley E. (1978) 81 Cal. App.3d 415 {146 Cal. Rptr. 232}.*) It is instructive to observe that the statutory definition of robbery found in *Penal Code section 211* is very similar in structure to the definition of extortion found in *Penal Code section 518*, and that although the statutory language in section 211 does not require a specific intent,n1 the decisions have nevertheless determined that a prerequisite to conviction of robbery is proof of a specific intent, the intent to steal. (E.g., *People v. Ford, supra, 60 Cal.2d 772, 793,* and cases there cited.)

> n1 *Penal Code section 211* reads: "Robbery is the felonious taking of personal property in the possession of another, from his person or immediate presence, and against his will, accomplished by means of force or fear."

Nor can we conclude the failure to instruct on specific intent was not prejudicial. There appears to have been no instruction whatever on intent in connection with the charge of extortion, and it appears therefore that, in effect, the essential element of intent as to that offense was removed from the jury's consideration. If that is true, the error must be deemed prejudicial under the decision in *People v. Garcia (1984) 36 Cal.3d 539, 549–550 {205 Cal. Rptr. 265, 684 P.2d 826}.*

Even if it were otherwise, however, under the evidence adduced in the instant case we could not conclude the error was harmless. Defendant never made any express request or demand for money. The victim testified that without prior discussion of her paying defendant any money, she reached into her pocket, pulled out the $50 and handed it to defendant in the hope that would cause him not to arrest her or take her to jail. One inference to be drawn from the evidence was that defendant intended by his conduct to obtain oral copulation without payment and that the $50 given him by the victim was an unexpected windfall.

We conclude the conviction for extortion must be reversed.

. . .

Defendant's conviction of extortion (*Pen. Code, § 518*) is reversed and the sentence imposed thereon is vacated. Defendant must be resentenced only if he is again tried and convicted of the extortion charge. If he is not retried or not again convicted of the extortion charge, the abstract of judgment must be amended to eliminate the extortion conviction and the sentence imposed thereon. In all other respects the judgment is affirmed.

IN RE NICHOLAS Y.

COURT OF APPEAL OF CALIFORNIA, SECOND APPELLATE DISTRICT, DIVISION FOUR

85 Cal. App. 4th 941; 102 Cal. Rptr. 2d 511

December 21, 2000

OPINION BY: EPSTEIN, ACTING P. J.

Appellant Nicholas Y. appeals from orders of the juvenile court finding that he vandalized property belonging to the AMC theater, declaring him a ward of the court pursuant to *Welfare and Institutions Code section 602*, and placing him a home on probation. He contends the evidence was insufficient to prove he violated *Penal Code section 594* (vandalism). In the published part of this opinion we hold that writing on the glass window of a projection booth of a motion picture theater constituted defacing, and hence vandalism within the meaning of the statute. . . . we find no error and affirm the juvenile court's orders.

FACTUAL SUMMARY

The evidence, briefly stated in the light most favorable to the judgment, proved that in the early morning hours of February 11, 2000, appellant wrote on a glass window of a projection booth at an AMC theater with a Sharpie marker. After his arrest, appellant admitted to police that he had written "RTK" on the window. Police saw "approximately 30 incidents" in red magic marker throughout the theater, including the one on the glass. Appellant said the initials stood for "The Right to Crime."

At the close of the prosecution's case, appellant's counsel argued that no defacing of or damage to property had been proved, stating: "[i]t's a piece of glass with a marker on it. You take a rag and wipe it off. End of case. It's ridiculous." The prosecutor countered that appellant trespassed and left fresh marks on the window, thus defacing the window with graffiti. The court found that appellant violated *Penal Code section 594*, subdivision (a), a misdemeanor.

DISCUSSION

I

Penal Code section 594 provides, in relevant part: "(a) Every person who maliciously commits any of the following acts with respect to any real or personal property not his or her own, in cases other than those specified by state law, is guilty of vandalism: (1) Defaces with graffiti or other inscribed material. (2) Damages. (3) Destroys. . . . (4)(A) If the amount of defacement, damage, or destruction is less than four hundred dollars ($400), vandalism is punishable by imprisonment in a county jail for not more than 6 months, or by a fine of not more than one thousand dollars ($1,000) or by both that fine and imprisonment. . . . (e) As used in this section the term 'graffiti or other inscribed material' includes any unauthorized inscription, word, figure, mark, or design that is written, marked, etched, scratched, drawn, or painted on real or personal property."

Appellant contends he did not violate the statute because the word "deface" contemplates a "permanent alteration" of the surface of an object rather than the easily removed marking he placed on the window. He compares the facts of this case to chalk writing on a sidewalk held not to constitute vandalism in violation of *Penal Code section 594* in *MacKinney v. Nielsen (9th Cir. 1995) 69 F.3d 1002*. As appellant acknowledges, however, the statutory language interpreted in that case was different, making it "illegal to (1) *deface* 'with paint or any other liquid,' (2) damage or (3) destroy any real or personal property that is not one's own." (*Id. at p. 1005,* italics added.) The Ninth Circuit Court of Appeals reasoned that chalk is not a liquid and did not damage the sidewalk. Therefore, it found the defendant did not violate the statute. (*Ibid.*) The Legislature subsequently amended the statute to delete the phrase "defaces with paint or any other liquid" and substitute in its place the phrase "defaces with graffiti or other inscribed material." Accordingly, the *MacKinney* case is of no assistance to appellant's cause.

Appellant also seeks support in the holding of *People v. Brumley (1966) 242 Cal. App. 2d 124 {51 Cal. Rptr. 131}*, in which the defendant contended the evidence was insufficient to prove he altered or defaced a brand on an animal because the original brand could still be seen. The court rejected this contention, explaining: "To deface does not necessarily mean to obliterate . . . nor does 'alter' mean to change beyond recognition. There is no doubt from the evidence that although the [victims] were able to identify their brands on the cattle, defendant's brand was superimposed upon a part of each brand and materially altered the same." (*Id.* at p. 128.) *Brumley* is factually and legally distinguishable. It did not involve defacement with graffiti, but instead interpreted a statute criminalizing the alteration or defacement of a brand or mark on an animal with the intent to prevent identification by the true owner. But even in that context the court did not require obliteration. Certainly the case does not support appellant's contention that there is no defacement unless the act makes a material alteration or permanent change to the surface of the defaced object.

Graffiti may be, and regularly is, created with marker pens. (See *Sherwin-Williams Co. v. City of Los Angeles (1993) 4 Cal. 4th 893, 901 {16 Cal. Rptr. 2d 215, 844 P.2d 534}*.) It would be irrational to hold that use of a marker pen on, for example, a painted or stucco surface constitutes vandalism in violation of *Penal Code section 594*, subdivision (a)(1) while use of a marker pen on glass is not. Each mars the surface with graffiti which must be removed in order to restore the original condition. This pragmatic fact is consistent with the primary meaning of the word deface as defined in the Oxford English Dictionary: "To mar the

face, features, or appearance of; to spoil or ruin the figure, form, or beauty of; to disfigure."n1 This definition does not incorporate an element of permanence. Thus, it appears that a marring of the surface is no less a defacement because it is more easily removed. It follows that appellant was properly found to have violated *Penal Code section 594*, subdivision (a)(1).

n1 The entry for the word "deface" in the *Oxford English Dictionary* reads: "1. *trans.* To mar the face, features, or appearance of; to spoil or ruin the figure, form, or beauty of; to disfigure. b. *fig.* (of things immaterial). 2. To destroy, demolish, lay waste. *Obs.*
3. To blot out, obliterate, efface (writing, marks). B. *fig.* To blot out of existence, memory, thought, etc.; to extinguish. 4. To destroy the reputation or credit of; to discredit, defame. *Obs.* 5. To put out of countenance; to outface, abash. *Obs.* 6. To outshine by contrast, cast in the shade." (Oxford English Dict. (2d ed. CD-ROM 1994).)

. . .

DISPOSITION

For the foregoing reasons, the judgment is affirmed.

KEY TERMS

Larceny, 227

Doctrine of Continuing Trespass, 228

Asportation, 228

Embezzlement, 228

False pretenses, 228

Theft (larceny) by trick, 228

Grand theft, 230

Petty theft, 230

Three Strikes and You're Out Law, 230

Receiving stolen property, 230

Extortion, 230

Forgery, 231

Passing a forged document, 231

Vandalism, 232

Trespass, 232

Computer crime, 232

STUDY GUIDE CHAPTER 7

PROPERTY CRIMES

1. What are the elements for the crime of *theft?*

2. Read *People v. Shannon.* State the general rule of law that explains the point at which a *theft* has been committed.

3. What is the difference between petty and grand *theft?*

4. When can a misdemeanor petty *theft* be charged as a felony? Explain.

5. How is the crime of *theft by false pretenses* different from an *embezzlement* offense? Explain.

6. What is the key aspect of an *embezzlement* offense?

7. What is the key aspect of a *forgery?*

8. How is the crime of *theft by false pretenses* different from an *extortion* offense? Explain.

CHAPTER 8

Incomplete Crimes: Attempt, Conspiracy, and Solicitation

Inchoate or incomplete crimes are charged against those offenders who are caught before they are able to complete their intended crime, those who try but fail to complete their target offense, those who encourage others to commit crimes, or those who take steps toward executing a criminal plan.

ATTEMPT

Attempt requires more than just mere preparation; it requires some action toward commission of the intended crime. Determining how much action is enough can be challenging. Attempt is always a specific intent offense, because the offender must intend a future consequence (the one he or she did not achieve). California requires that a person who attempts any crime but fails or is intercepted in its perpetration should be punished by one-half of the sentence of the target offense; the exceptions to this rule are murder or other crimes which carry a punishment of life imprisonment. There are specific guidelines for determining the sentence for those more serious attempts and for dealing with offenses divided into degrees.[1] (A defendant cannot be guilty of an attempt to commit a crime in addition to the crime itself because attempts "merge" with their target offense once the crime is completed.)

---

[1] Cal. Pen. Code §664(a).

The analysis to determine when an attempt has occurred can be difficult. It may be helpful to think of a crime as taking place along a spectrum in terms of time. At one end, there is preparation, which is not criminal conduct. At the other end, the completed offense. The criminal attempt takes place somewhere in between, and in most cases, determining precisely when enough action has taken place to demonstrate an act in furtherance is not clear-cut. One question to ask when trying to pinpoint this moment is "did the defendant commence with consummation of the offense?" In other words, did the defendant start to complete the crime? Commencement may take place at any point on that spectrum, but when it does, the attempt is complete and punishable; the defendant can no longer abandon the plan and avoid criminal responsibility.

Mere Preparation...........................Commencement: Act in Furtherance...............................Completed Crime

(not punishable)   (attempt = 1/2 punishment)   (full punishment)

The law of attempt is divided between homicide and non-homicide cases. The Code explains the mens reus and actus rea required for attempts: the specific intent to commit the crime and a direct but ineffectual act done toward its commission.[2] This "direct act" must go beyond merely preparing to commit the offense, thinking about it, or making plans. It must show that the defendant unambiguously moved toward commission of the offense. Attempted murder requires that the defendant took at least one direct but ineffective step toward killing a person or fetus, and that the defendant possessed the specific intent to kill. In addition to deciding whether a defendant possessed the specific intent to kill, a jury must decide whether the defendant premeditated and deliberated their intent to commit the murder. Intent is determined in the same way as it would be in the context of a successful homicide by looking for evidence of pre-planning and a motive to kill, and examining the manner of the killing to determine premeditation; and looking to whether the defendant "weighed the considerations for and against his/her choice, knowing the consequence, and still decided to kill"[3] to determine deliberation. An accomplice or co-defendant can also be charged with premeditated and deliberate attempted murder, even when they did not engage in the premeditation personally.[4]

If found guilty of attempted premeditated and deliberate murder, the defendant is sentenced to life in prison with the possibility of parole, and if the intended victim is a peace officer, fire fighter, or prison guard, the term is 15 years to life in prison without the opportunity for release prior to the minimum 15-year term.[5] A defendant can be charged with attempted voluntary manslaughter based on either a heat of passion or imperfect self-defense theory if he acted with specific intent to kill, but there can be no charge or conviction for attempted involuntary manslaughter.[6] Also, as noted in *People v. Saephanh* (2000), attempted solicitation of murder is a crime.[7] The crime of solicitation will be discussed later in this chapter.

KEY LEGAL PRINCIPLE:

Abandonment and impossibility are defenses often raised in the context of attempt. Abandonment of a criminal attempt does not "undo" the attempt itself. Because the elements of the crime are complete at the point of a direct act in combination with intent to commit the target offense, abandonment at some point prior to completion does not relieve the defendant of criminal responsibility (but a good decision to stop before succeeding will provide for a much less significant punishment for the defendant at trial). In order for abandonment to relieve the defendant of criminal liability, it must take place during the "mere preparation" phase of the criminal plan—before a direct act toward commission of the offense is done. **Legal impossibility** is conduct where the goal of the actor is not criminal, although he believes it to be. It is a valid defense. **Factual impossibility** is conduct where the objective is illegal, but a circumstance unknown to the actor prevents him from

---

[2] Cal. Pen. Code §21(a).

[3] CALCRIM No. 601 (2010).

[4] *People v. Lee*, 31 Cal.4th 613, 622–623 (2003).

[5] Cal. Pen. Code §664(a),(e) & (f)

[6] *People v. Johnson*, 51 Cal.App.4th 1329, 1332 (1996).

[7] *People v. Saephanh*, 80 Cal.App.4th 451, 460 (2000).

bringing it about. Factual impossibility is *not* a defense to a charge of attempt. For example, if a defendant held a gun to the head of an intended victim and fired, intending to kill them, but the gun jammed, preventing the victim's death, the defendant is guilty of attempted murder even though he or she may argue that he or she in fact, could never have killed the victim.

CONSPIRACY

If two or more people agree to commit any crime, and commit some overt act in furtherance of the crime, a **conspiracy** has been committed. The agreement need not be formal; it doesn't have to be in writing or even be the result of a face-to-face meeting. Jurors are allowed to infer the agreement based on the conduct of the conspirators. Members of a conspiracy do not even have to personally know all of their coconspirators, but if they are merely acquaintances or associates who don't intend to commit the crime, they are not guilty of conspiracy.[8] Each member of a conspiracy is responsible for the acts of the others, so long as their act furthers the common criminal plan and is a natural and probable consequence of the common plan—even if the act was not part of the original agreement.[9] An exception to the **hearsay rule** (which forbids the admission of out-of-court statements being offered in court to prove the truth of the matter asserted) permits a coconspirator's statements made during the commission of the conspiracy to be heard at trial.[10] In order to admit these statements, "It must be proved by a **preponderance of the evidence** that

- some evidence other than the statement itself establishes that a conspiracy to commit a crime existed when the statement was made;

- the defendant was a member and participating in the conspiracy when the statement was made;

- the statement was made in furtherance of the goal of the conspiracy; *and*

- the statement was made *before* or during the time the defendant was participating in the conspiracy."[11] (Out-of-court statements made after the goal of the conspiracy was accomplished cannot be considered.)

KEY LEGAL PRINCIPLE:

A preponderance of the evidence is an evidentiary standard that is different than proof beyond a reasonable doubt. Proof beyond a reasonable doubt is the standard required to find a defendant guilty of a crime. A preponderance of the evidence requires proof that it is "more likely than not" that the event or fact in question is true. It is a significantly less stringent standard than proof beyond a reasonable doubt. In addition to its use for some matters of evidence like the one relating to conspiracy discussed above, a preponderance of the evidence is the standard of proof required in civil trials.

The mens rea required for conspiracy has two components: 1.) the specific intent to agree or conspire, and 2.) the specific intent to commit the offense that is the objective of the agreement. The actus reus of conspiracy is an overt act in furtherance of the common criminal plan. The overt act need not be criminal by itself, it can be any step in furtherance of a criminal plan or scheme.[12] Conspiracy is a "stand alone" offense that is complete at the time of an agreement on a criminal plan and an overt act in furtherance. Unlike attempts, which "merge" with their target offense when completed, a conspiracy can be charged alongside the completed offense(s) that the actors conspired to commit.

---

[8] CALCRIM No. 415 (2010).

[9] CALCRIM No. 417 (2010).

[10] Cal. Evidence Code §1223.

[11] CALCRIM No. 418 (2010).

[12] *People v. Saugstad,* 203 Cal.App.2d 536 (1962).

Punishment for a conspiracy, if it is a felony, is the same as for the completed offense.[13] If the conspiracy includes plans for more than one felony to be committed, the punishment is to be for whichever has the greater maximum term.[14] If the conspiracy is to commit an act against the president of the United States or other high-ranking government officials, the punishment is five, seven, or nine years in state prison.[15] Section 182.5 makes these same sentencing provisions that are applicable to coconspirators are also applicable to knowing members of criminal street gangs, according to Section 182.5. As with attempt, factual impossibility is not a defense to conspiracy.

A coconspirator may make an effort to leave the group or conspiracy. If he or she withdraws from the alleged conspiracy before any overt act is committed, and affirmatively rejects the conspiracy by clearly communicating his or her intentions in word or deed to the other members of the conspiracy, he or she is not guilty. Failure to act is not enough on its own to effectively withdraw a coconspirator from the conspiracy. The burden of proof in this situation is on the prosecution to show that the defendant did not withdraw from the conspiracy.[16]

SOLICITATION

Every person who, with the intent that the crime be committed, solicits another to commit the crime, is guilty of **solicitation.**[17] A defendant solicits someone else when they request or ask that person to commit the crime. A very common example of the crime of solicitation is solicitation of prostitution. In the context of prostitution, a john or potential customer approaches the prostitute asking for the price for sex or sexual acts, and he does so with the intent that the prostitute provide sex acts in exchange for money (he requests the unlawful act with the intent that the other person commit the offense). Law enforcement agencies often utilize undercover officers posing as prostitutes in order to catch offenders in the act of solicitation. In *People v. Saephanh* (2000), the court held that the requesting communication must be received by the target of the solicitation.[18] Section 653(f) lists the crimes that are the target offenses for solicitation and explains the punishments for each type of target offense. Solicitation, like conspiracy, can be charged independently even when the target offense is completed; it does not merge with the target offense. The Code also requires that proof of solicitation be made by the testimony of two witnesses, or one witness in combination with some corroborating evidence; this helps to avoid wrongful prosecution in cases where it is one person's word against another's.[19]

---

[13] Cal. Pen. Code §182(a)(6).

[14] Cal. Pen. Code §182(a)(6).

[15] Cal. Pen. Code §182(a)(6).

[16] CALCRIM No. 420 (2010).

[17] Cal. Pen. Code §653f(a–c).

[18] *People v. Saephanh,* 80 Cal.App.4th 451 (2000).

[19] Cal. Pen. Code §653f(f).

PEOPLE v. STAPLES

COURT OF APPEAL, SECOND DISTRICT, DIVISION 5, CALIFORNIA

6 CAL. APP. 3D 61; CRIM. NO. 15693

MARCH 27, 1970

OPINION BY: REPPY, J.

Defendant was charged in an information with attempted burglary (*Pen. Code, §§ 664, 459*). Trial by jury was waived, and the matter submitted on the testimony contained in the transcript of the preliminary hearing together with exhibits. Defendant was found guilty. Proceedings were suspended before pronouncement of sentence, and an order was made granting defendant probation. The appeal is from the order which is deemed a final judgment. (*Pen. Code, § 1237.*)

I. THE FACTS

In October 1967, while his wife was away on a trip, defendant, a mathematician, under an assumed name, rented an office on the second floor of a building in Hollywood which was over the mezzanine of a bank. Directly below the mezzanine was the vault of the bank. Defendant was aware of the layout of the building, specifically of the relation of the office he rented to the bank vault. Defendant paid rent for the period from October 23 to November 23. The landlord had 10 days before commencement of the rental period within which to finish some interior repairs and painting. During this prerental period defendant brought into the office certain equipment. This included drilling tools, two acetylene gas tanks, a blow torch, a blanket, and a linoleum rug. The landlord observed these items when he came in from time to time to see how the repair work was progressing. Defendant learned from a custodian that no one was in the building on Saturdays. On Saturday, October 14, defendant drilled two groups of holes into the floor of the office above the mezzanine room. He stopped drilling before the holes went through the floor. He came back to the office several times thinking he might slowly drill down, covering the holes with the linoleum rug.n1 At some point in time he installed a hasp lock on a closet, and planned to, or did, place his tools in it. However, he left the closet keys on the premises. Around the end of November, apparently after November 23, the landlord notified the police and turned the tools and equipment over to them. Defendant did not

pay any more rent. It is not clear when he last entered the office, but it could have been after November 23, and even after the landlord had removed the equipment. On February 22, 1968, the police arrested defendant. After receiving advice as to his constitutional rights, defendant voluntarily made an oral statement which he reduced to writing.

> n1 This is defendant's characterization of what occurred after his initial drilling session. (See partial text of confession, post.)

Among other things which defendant wrote down were these:

"Saturday, the 14th . . . I drilled some small holes in the floor of the room. Because of tiredness, fear, and the implications of what I was doing, I stopped and went to sleep.

"At this point I think my motives began to change. The actual [*sic*] commencement of my plan made me begin to realize that even if I were to succeed a fugitive life of living off of stolen money would not give the enjoyment of the life of a mathematician however humble a job I might have.

"I still had not given up my plan however. I felt I had made a certain investment of time, money, effort and a certain pschological [*sic*] commitment to the concept.

"I came back several times thinking I might store the tools in the closet and slowly drill down (covering the hole with a rug of linoleum square. As time went on (after two weeks or so). My wife came back and my life as bank robber seemed more and more absurd."

II. DISCUSSION OF DEFENDANT'S CONTENTIONS

Defendant's position in this appeal is that, as a matter of law, there was insufficient evidence upon which to convict him of a criminal attempt under *Penal Code section 664*. Defendant claims that his actions were all preparatory in nature and never reached a stage of advancement in relation to the substantive crime which he concededly intended to commit (burglary of the bank vault) so that criminal responsibility might attach.

In order for the prosecution to prove that defendant committed an attempt to burglarize as proscribed by *Penal Code section 664,* it was required to establish that he had the specific intent to commit a burglary of the bank and that his acts toward that goal went beyond mere preparation. (*People v. Buffum,* 40 Cal.2d 709, 718 {256 P.2d 317}; *People v. Miller,* 2 Cal.2d 527, 530 {42 P.2d 308}; *People v. Anderson,* 1 Cal.2d 687, 689-690 {37 P.2d 67}; *People v. Gibson,* 94 Cal.App.2d 468, 470 {210 P.2d 747}.)

The required specific intent was clearly established in the instant case. Defendant admitted in his written confession that he rented the office fully intending to burglarize the bank, that he brought in tools and equipment to accomplish this purpose, and that he began drilling into the floor with the intent of making an entry into the bank.

The question of whether defendant's conduct went beyond "mere preparation" raises some provocative problems. The briefs and the oral argument of counsel in this case point up a degree of ambiguity and uncertainty that permeates the law of attempts in this state. Each side has cited us to a different so-called "test" to determine whether this defendant's conduct went beyond the preparatory stage. Predictably each respective test in the eyes of its proponents yielded an opposite result.

Defendant relies heavily on the following language: "Preparation alone is not enough [to convict for an attempt], there must be some appreciable fragment of the crime committed, *it must be in such progress that it will be consummated unless interrupted by circumstances independent of the will of the attempter,* and the act must not be equivocal in nature." (Italics added.) (*People v. Buffum, supra,* 40 Cal.2d 709, 718.) Defendant argues that while the facts show that he did do a series of acts directed at the commission of a burglary—renting the office, bringing in elaborate equipment and actually starting drilling—the facts do not show that he was interrupted by any outside circumstances. Without such interruption and a voluntary desistence on his part, defendant concludes that under the above stated test, he has not legally committed an attempt. The Attorney General has replied that even if the above test is appropriate, the trial judge, obviously drawing reasonable inferences, found that defendant was interrupted by outside circumstances—the landlord's acts of discovering the burglary equipment, resuming control over the premises, and calling the police.

However, the Attorney General suggests that another test, as set out in *People v. Anderson, supra,* 1 Cal.2d 687, 690, is

more appropriate: "Whenever the design of a person to commit crime is clearly shown, slight acts in furtherance of the design will constitute an attempt." (Note absence of reference to interruption.) The *People* argue that defendant's felonious intent was clearly set out in his written confession; that the proven overt acts in furtherance of the design, although only needing to be slight, were, in fact, substantial; that this combination warrants the affirmance of the attempt conviction.

We suggest that the confusion in this area is a result of the broad statutory language of *section 664,* which reads in part: "Any person who attempts to commit any crime, but fails, or is prevented or intercepted in the perpetration thereof, is punishable. . . ." This is a very general proscription against all attempts not specifically made a crime (see e.g., *Pen. Code, § 217).* The statute does not differentiate between the various types of attempts which may be considered culpable. Reference must be made to case law in order to determine precisely what conduct constitutes an attempt. However, the statute does point out by the words "fails," "prevented," and "intercepted," those *conditions* which separate an attempt from the substantive crime.

An examination of the decisional law reveals *at least two* general categories of attempts, both of which have been held to fall within the ambit of the statute.

In the first category are those situations where the actor does all acts necessary (including the last proximate act) to commit the substantive crime, but nonetheless he somehow is unsuccessful. This lack of success is either a "failure" or a "prevention" brought about because of some extraneous circumstances, e.g., a malfunction of equipment, a miscalculation of operations by the actor or a situation wherein circumstances were at variance with what the actor believe them to be.n2 Certain convictions for attempted murder illustrate the first category. Some turn on situations wherein the actor fires a weapon at a person but misses (*People v. Glick,* 107 Cal.App.2d 78, 79 {236 P.2d 586}); takes aim at an intended victim and pulls the trigger, but the firing mechanism malfunctions (*People v. Van Buskirk,* 113 Cal.App.2d 789, 793 {249 P.2d 49}); plants on an aircraft a homemade bomb which sputters but does not explode (*People v. Grant,* 105 Cal.App.2d 347, 356-357 {233 P.2d 660}). Another first category example is highlighted in *People v. Fulton,* 188 Cal.App.2d 105 {10 Cal.Rptr. 319}. The factual setting and legal reasoning in *Fulton* is well characterized by Justice Kingsley in *People v. Orndorff,* 261 Cal.App.2d 212, 215 {67 Cal.Rptr. 824}: "*Fulton* . . . involved an alleged Jamaica Switch, practiced on two alleged intended victims. The schemes failed, in one instance because a bank officer told the intended victim that it was a bunco scheme. . . . [T]he court unanimously held that . . . [this] instance was a punishable attempt . . . All three judges lay stress on the element of the procuring cause of failure, saying that it must be 'by extraneous circumstances,' or 'by circumstances independent of any actions of their [defendants'] part.'" The defendants in *Fulton* did every act in their preconceived plan. It was only the extraneous circumstance of the intended victim acquiring knowledge that the defendants' proposal to his was a bunco scheme which resulted in the defendants not obtaining the money.

> n2 The "classic" case, often used as a law school hypothetical example, occurs when the pickpocket thrusts his hand into an empty pocket (*Commonwealth* v. *Cline* (1913) 213 Mass. 225 {100 N.E. 358}; compare with *People v. Fiegelman, 33 Cal.App.2d 100 {91 P.2d 156}*).

In the above situations application of the rule stated in *People v. Buffum, supra, 40 Cal.2d 709, 718,* which defendant herein seeks to have applied, would appear to be quite appropriate. After a defendant has done all acts necessary under normal conditions to commit crime, he is culpable for an attempt if he is unsuccessful *because* of an extraneous or fortuitous circumstance.n3

> n3 It is interesting to note how the rule enunciated in *Buffum* entered California law. It first appeared in *People* v. *Miller, 2 Cal.2d 527, 530 {42 P.2d 308},* as quoted material from volume one of Wharton's Criminal Law. The source revealed in Wharton is *Sipple v. State (1883) 46 N.J.L. 197.* While the report of the decision is quite brief, the factual setting of *Sipple* looks remarkably like that presented in *Fulton*, above, i.e., a larcenous scheme wherein the defendant did all acts he had planned but the intended victim balked. The court in *Sipple* goes on to state: "At the trial the court ruled and charged that an attempt to steal, accompanied by an overt act or acts towards its commission, contituted an attempt to commit larceny under the law, and further, that the act or acts done towards the commission of an offense, in order to constitute an attempt, must be such as will apparently result, in the usual and natural course of events, if not hindered by extraneous causes, in the commission of the crime itself. . . ."

However, it is quite clear that under California law overt act, which, when added to the requisite intent, is sufficient to bring about a criminal attempt, need not be the last proximate or ultimate step towards commission of the substantive crime. "It is not necessary that the overt act proved should have been the ultimate step toward the consummation of the design. It is sufficient if it was 'the first or some subsequent step in a direct movement towards the commission of the offense after the preparations are

made.' [Citation.]" (*People* v. *Gibson, 94 Cal.App.2d 468, 470 {210 P.2d 747};* see also *People v. Seach, 215 Cal.App.2d 779, 783 {30 Cal.Rptr. 499}; People v. Parrish, 87 Cal.App.2d 853, 856 {197 P.2d 804}*.) Police officers need not wait until a suspect, who aims a gun at his intended victim, actually pulls the trigger before they arrest him; nor do these officers need to wait until a suspect, who is forcing the lock of a bank door, actually breaks in before they arrest him for attempted burglary.

This rule makes for a second category of "attempts." The recognition of this separate category is well articulated by Mr. Chief Judge Learned Hand in *United States* v. *Coplon (2d Cir. 1950) 185 F.2d 629, 633 {28 A.L.R.2d 1041},* as follows: "A neat doctrine by which to test when a person, intending to commit a crime which he fails to carry out, has 'attempted' to commit it, would be that he has done all that it is within his power to do, but has been prevented by intervention from outside; in short that he has passed beyond any *locus poenitentiae.* Apparently that was the original notion, and may still be law in England; but it is certainly not now generally the law in the United States, for there are many decisions which hold that the accused has passed beyond 'preparation,' although he has been interrupted before he has taken the last of his intended steps."

Applying criminal culpability to acts directly moving toward commission of crime (but short of the last proximate act necessary to consummate the criminal design) under *section 664* is an obvious safeguard to society because it makes it unnecessary for police to wait before intervening until the actor has done the substantive evil sought to be prevented. It allows such criminal conduct to be stopped or intercepted when it becomes clear what the actor's intention is and when the acts done show that the perpetrator is acually putting his plan into action. *Discovering precisely what conduct falls within this latter category, however, often becomes a difficult problem.* Because of the lack of specificity of *section 664,* police, trial judges, jurors, and in the last analysis, appellate courts, face the dilemma of trying to identify that point beyond which conduct passes from innocent to criminal absent a specific event such as the commission of a prohibited substantive crime.

Our courts have come up with a variety of "tests" which try to distinguish acts of preparation from completed attempts. "The preparation consists in devising or arranging the means or measures necessary for the commission of the offense; the attempt is the direct movement toward the commission after the preparations are made." (*People v. Murray, 14 Cal. 159;* see also, *People v. Franquelin, 109 Cal.App.2d 777, 784 {241 P.2d 651}*.) "'[T]he act must reach far enough towards the accomplishment of the desired result to amount to the commencement of the consummation.'" (*People v. Miller, supra, 2 Cal.2d 527, 530.*) "[W]here the intent to commit the substantive offense is . . . clearly established . . . [,] acts done toward the commission of the crime may constitute an attempt, where the same acts would be held insufficient to constitute an attempt if the intent with which they were done is equivocal and not clearly proved." (*People v. Berger, 131 Cal.App.2d 127, 130 {280 P.2d 136}.*)

None of the above statements of the law applicable to this category of attempts provide a litmus-like test, and perhaps no such test is achievable. Such precision is not required in this case, however. There was definitely substantial evidence entitling the trial judge to find that defendant's acts had gone beyond the preparation stage. Without specifically deciding where defendant's preparations left off and where his activities became a completed criminal attempt,n4 we can say that his "drilling" activity clearly was an unequivocal and direct step toward the completion of the burglary. (*Cf. People v. Burton, 184 Cal.App.2d 299 {8 Cal.Rptr. 153}; People v. Cloninger, 165 Cal.App.2d 86 {331 P.2d 441}; People v. Davis, 24 Cal.App.2d 408 {75 P.2d 80}.*) It was a fragment of the substantive crime contemplated (*People v. Gallardo, 41 Cal.2d 57, 66 {257 P.2d 29}*) i.e., the beginning of the "breaking" element. Further, defendant himself characterized his activity as the *actual commencement of his plan*. The drilling by defendant was obviously one of a series of acts which logic and ordinary experience indicate would result in the proscribed act of burglary. (See *People v. Berger, supra, 131 Cal.App.2d 127, 132.*)

> n4 Commentator Bernard Witkin points out the difficulty of pinpointing in any given case the dividing line between acts of preparation and those acts which constitute the completed attempt. He suggests that courts review the entire factual pattern in what might be termed a "common sense approach" rather than trying to extrapolate from precisely drawn lines. (See *1 Witkin, Cal. Crimes (1963) Elements of Crime, § 96,* p. 92.) Compare the approach taken by the drafters of the Model Penal Code, discussed in Wechsler, Jones and Korn, *The Treatment of Inchoate Crimes in the Model Penal Code (1961) 61 Colum. L.Rev. 571, 592-607.*)

The instant case provides an out-of-the-ordinary factual situation within the second category. Usually the actors in cases falling within that category of attempts are intercepted or caught in the act (see e.g., *Burton, Cloninger and Davis, supra*). Here, there was no direct proof of any actual interception. But it was clearly inferable by the trial judge that defendant became aware that the landlord had resumed control over the office and had turned defendant's equipment and tools over to the police. This was the equivalent of interception.

The inference of this nonvoluntary character of defendant's abandonment was a proper one for the trial judge to draw. (*People v. Burton, supra, 184 Cal.App.2d 299, 301; People v. Von Hecht, 133 Cal.App.2d 25, 37 {283 P.2d 764}.*) However, it would seem that the character of the abandonment in situations of this type, whether it be voluntary (prompted by pangs of conscience or a change of heart) or nonvoluntary (established by inference in the instant case), is not controlling. The relevant factor is the determination of whether the acts of the perpetrator have reached such a stage of advancement that they can be classified as an attempt. Once that attempt is found there can be no exculpatory abandonment. (*People v. Claborn, 224 Cal.App.2d 38, 41 {36 Cal.Rptr. 132}; People v. Robinson, 180 Cal.App.2d 745, 750-751 {4 Cal.Rptr. 679}, and cases cited therein; but see People v. Montgomery, 47 Cal.App.2d 1, 13 {117 P.2d 437}.*)

"One of the purposes of the criminal law is to protect society from those who intend to injure it. When it is established that the defendant intended to commit a specific crime and that in carrying out this intention he committed an act that caused harm n5 or sufficient danger of harm, it is immaterial that for some collateral reason he could not complete the intended crime." (*People v. Camodeca, 52 Cal.2d 142, 147 {338 P.2d 903}.*)

> n5 In the instant case defendant's drilling was done without permission and did cause property damage.

The order is affirmed.

STEPHENS, Acting P. J., and AISO, J., concurred.

PEOPLE v. FIELDS

COURT OF APPEAL, SECOND DISTRICT, DIVISION 2, CALIFORNIA

56 CAL. APP. 3D 954; CRIM. NO. 27528

APRIL 1, 1976

OPINION BY: FLEMING, ACTING P. J.

Defendant appeals the judgment in a nonjury trial that resulted in his conviction for attempted kidnapping. *(Pen. Code, §§ 207, 664.)* He contends, (1) the evidence was insufficient to establish intent to kidnap and the commission of any act beyond mere preparation, and (2) the attempted asportation was purely incidental to the commission of an associated crime.

The evidence, viewed in the light most favorable to the judgment, shows that about 5 p.m. on September 4, 1974 during daylight hours defendant stopped his automobile beside a 13-year-old girl walking alone on a residential street in Bellflower and asked for directions. As she was responding, he grabbed her with both hands by her hair and head and told her to get into his vehicle, saying that if she complied she would not get hurt. When she refused, he threatened to hit her between the eyes. When she said she knew everybody up and down the street and was going to scream, he let her go and drove off. The motor of his vehicle was probably running throughout the incident. Defendant was later traced through his vehicle's license number, which the girl memorized as he was driving away.

At trial defendant testified that he had just quarreled with his girlfriend at home and that when he spoke to the girl on the street he was planning to go to Knott's Berry Farm, but he admitted he had no money at the time and insufficient gasoline to get there.

We think this evidence, together with the reasonable inferences derived therefrom, sustains defendant's conviction of the crime charged. Where, as here, a strange man seizes the person of a young girl on a residential street and orders her to get into a vehicle whose motor is running, the specific intent and the affirmative act required to constitute the crime of attempted kidnapping are adequately manifested. Defendant's contention that as a matter of law his action amounted to no more than battery

lacks merit, for his statements to the girl, interpreted in the light of their setting, strongly suggest an intent to kidnap. The cause is comparable to *People v. Loignon*, 160 Cal.App.2d 412, 416, 421 {325 P.2d 541}, where the defendant asked the victim to enter his vehicle, and when his invitation was rejected, pulled the victim inside and started up the motor, whereupon the victim escaped. In upholding a conviction for attempted kidnapping this court said, "Defendant's act in opening the door of his car and pulling Ricky into it against his will and then, after quieting him, starting the motor, clearly shows an attempt to kidnap the child and amply sustains his conviction on that count." Since the decision in *Loignon*, it has been judicially determined that kidnapping requires a forcible movement of the victim for more than a slight or trivial distance. *(People v. Stanworth*, 11 Cal.3d 588, 601 {114 Cal.Rptr. 250, 522 P.2d 1058}, and cases there cited.) Nevertheless, under the circumstances at bench the trier of fact could reasonably find that defendant not only intended to force the girl into his vehicle but intended to carry her away some appreciable distance. In a completed kidnapping where asportation has been accomplished, the requisite movement for more than a slight distance can be measured with some precision. But in an unsuccessful kidnapping which has been aborted, to require the prosecution to show more than a forcible attempt to move the victim into a motor vehicle in order to prove intent to move the victim a substantial distance, would be to read the crime of attempted kidnapping out of the law. In the absence of any evidence to suggest that defendant contemplated no more than a trivial movement of his victim, the requisite intent to kidnap may be inferred.

. . .

The judgment is affirmed.

COMPTON, J., and BEACH, J., concurred.

PEOPLE v. VIZCARRA

COURT OF APPEAL, SECOND DISTRICT, DIVISION 4, CALIFORNIA

110 CAL. APP. 3D 858; CRIM. NO. 36272

OCTOBER 2, 1980

OPINION BY: WOODS, J.

By virtue of joinder of informations, the appellant has been charged with five counts of robbery, in violation of *Penal Code section 211* (counts I, II, IV, V and VI), and one count of attempted robbery, in violation of Penal Code sections 664/211 (count III). In each count, except count VI, it was alleged that, in the commission and attempted commission of the offenses, appellant personally used a firearm, to wit, a rifle, within the meaning of *Penal Code sections 12022.5* and *1203.06,* subdivision (a)(1). Counts IV, V and VI alleged an armed allegation pursuant to *Penal Code section 12022,* subdivision (a). Appellant pleaded not guilty to all counts and denied the armed use allegations.

Appellant's motion pursuant to *Penal Code section 1538.5* was denied. A jury trial was held. Appellant's motion pursuant to *Penal Code section 1118.1* for judgment of acquittal as to count VI was denied. The People's motion to strike the armed allegations as to counts IV and V was granted. Appellant was found guilty on all counts, the jury also sustained the use allegations in counts I through V and the armed allegation in count VI.

Probation was denied and appellant was sentenced to state prison for a term of 14 years.

. . .

I

Appellant contends that there is insufficient evidence to support his conviction of attempted robbery as there was no overt act proved. We disagree.

Appellant's statement of the law is correct. In order to establish attempted robbery, the People must prove specific intent to commit robbery and a direct unequivocal overt act toward its commission. This act must go beyond mere preparation.

The thrust of appellant's argument is twofold. He appears to argue that since Mr. Vizcarra did not enter the liquor store, his conduct could not constitute more than mere

preparation; relying on *People v. Davis (1966) 241 Cal.App.2d 51 {50 Cal.Rptr. 215},* he contends that the potential victim was therefore never subjected to force or fear.

The record in the instant case reflects that the appellant went to the Red Vest Liquor Store at night wearing a poncho and carrying a rifle. He was standing on a small walkway approximately four feet wide in front of the liquor store door when a customer, Mr. Craddock, came onto the walkway. The appellant immediately turned away from Mr. Craddock, so that his nose was right up against the block wall, and Mr. Craddock observed his peculiar behavior and the butt of a rifle protruding from his poncho. Appellant, who had parked across the street from the liquor store, returned to his car. Later he again drove past the liquor store.

Approaching the liquor store with a rifle and attempting to hide on the pathway immediately adjacent to the liquor store when observed by a customer, is in the opinion of this court a sufficient direct act toward the accomplishment of the robbery. As stated in *People v. Miles (1969) 272 Cal.App.2d 212, 218 {77 Cal.Rptr. 89},* the acts of proximity need not include the last proximate act for the completion of the crime. It is sufficient that the overt acts reach far enough for the accomplishment of the offense to amount to the "*commencement* of its consummation." (*People v. Lanzit (1925) 70 Cal.App. 498, 505 {233 P. 816}; People v. Gibson (1949) 94 Cal.App.2d 468 {210 P.2d 747}; People v. Parrish (1948) 87 Cal.App.2d 853 {197 P.2d 804}.*) Climbing up on a second story balcony and approaching the doors which led therefrom to the intended victim's bedroom and then making his escape without ever entering the bedroom, was held to be a sufficient act to constitute an attempted burglary in *People v. Gilbert (1927) 86 Cal.App. 8 {260 P. 558},* and in *People v. Machen (1935) 3 Cal.App.2d 499 {39 P.2d 893},* a defendant, who at the time of his arrest had his hands raised up against the screen of an apartment house, was found guilty of attempted burglary, and this conviction was upheld on appeal. In *People v. Parrish, supra.*, 87 *Cal.App.2d 853,* going to the home of his wife with a loaded gun and listening outside to be sure that she was alone, was held a sufficient overt act to sustain a conviction of attempted murder.

It should further be noted that in none of the cases cited above was there an element of force or fear against the intended victim. It is true that an element of force or fear must be proved in order to establish a conviction for robbery under *Penal Code section 211.* It is not necessary, however, for this element to be reflected in the overt act of an attempted robbery if the crime has not progressed to that point. We agree with the analysis in the respondent's brief, that the language relied upon in *People v. Davis, supra., 241 Cal.App.2d 51,* was part of the discussion that established that the assault, in that case, was in furtherance of the robbery and could not be charged as a separate offense under *Penal Code section 654.* Since a completed robbery would have required a force-and-fear element, an attempted robbery *may* also include this element of the offense, but it is erroneous to say that the crime *must* have progressed this far in order to constitute an attempt.

In determining whether a person has been guilty of attempted robbery, the courts are guided by the facts of each case as to when the defendant has gone further than mere preparation. In reported cases which have not discussed whether or not an element of force or fear is required in attempted robbery, convictions of attempted robbery have been upheld without this element having been proved. In *People v. Moran (1912) 18 Cal.App. 209* [122 P. 969] a defendant, with intent to rob, pushed open the door of a saloon and fled because there was a large crowd within. He and his codefendant were later found with a scarf mask and a gun. The court held that the pushing open of the door constituted a sufficient overt act for attempted robbery. There was no element of force or fear proved against the intended victim. The federal court held, in *United States v. Stallworth (2d Cir. 1976) 543 F.2d 1038 {37 A.L.R.Fed. 268}* that defendants were properly convicted of attempted bank robbery where they had carried out a number of preparatory activities, including the securing of weapons, driving to the bank and making a move to enter the bank. There was no element of force or fear established. The court emphasized the importance of early intervention by the police. An attempt to commit the crime of robbery does not of itself necessarily amount to an assault and does not require assault as an essential element.

Knowing that an attempt to steal may be proved by inference from all of the circumstances of the case, appellant has not attempted to argue a lack of intent to commit robbery.

Applying the criteria of *Jackson v. Virginia (1979) 443 U.S. 307 {61 L.Ed.2d 560, 99 S.Ct. 2781},* the rational trier of fact was justified in finding that the essential elements of attempted robbery were proved beyond a reasonable doubt in the case before us. The conviction under count III is sustained.

. . .

Appellant's convictions on counts I through VI are affirmed. Appellant's sentence on count I to the upper base term is affirmed. The order providing for consecutive sentences on counts II through VI is affirmed, and the enhancements imposed on counts II, IV, V and VI are stricken from this sentence.

As modified, the judgment is affirmed.

KINGSLEY, Acting P. J., and MCCLOSKY, J., concurred.

PEOPLE v. UGALINO

COURT OF APPEAL, THIRD DISTRICT, CALIFORNIA

174 Cal. App. 4th 1060; No. C055469

June 9, 2009

OPINION BY: DAVIS, J.

A jury found defendant Del Jay Ugalino guilty of the following crimes: (1) first degree residential burglary *(Pen.Code, § 459)*; (2) attempted robbery of Joshua Johnson *(Pen.Code, §§ 664/211)*; (3) attempted robbery of Jessie Rider *(Pen.Code, §§ 664/211)*; (4) possession of a controlled substance for sale *(Health & Saf.Code, § 11378)*; (5) possession of ammunition by a felon *(Pen.Code, § 12316, subd. (b)(1))*; (6) robbery of Bendon Lee *(Pen.Code, § 211)*; (7) battery of Charles Maroosis *(Pen.Code, § 242)*; and (8) making a criminal threat to Mickey Lathum *(Pen.Code, § 422)*. The jury also found true the allegation that defendant personally used a handgun during the commission of the crimes set forth in (1) to (3), above. Defendant was sentenced to an aggregate term of 14 years six months in state prison. He appeals his conviction, claiming prosecutorial misconduct, ineffectiveness of counsel, and insufficiency of the evidence. We will reverse defendant's conviction for attempted robbery of Jessie Rider and otherwise affirm the conviction.

I

FACTS RELATING TO AUGUST 28, 2005, INCIDENT

In August 2005, Joshua Johnson was living in a two-bedroom apartment with his girlfriend, Denise Galindo, their infant daughter, and two roommates: Jessie Rider and Devon McDermott. For income, Johnson sold marijuana from the apartment.

On August 28, 2005, defendant called Johnson on Johnson's cell phone, telling Johnson he wanted to buy three ounces of marijuana. Having sold to defendant 10–15 times before, Johnson told him to come over. So, driving a pickup truck, Aorn Saechow drove defendant and a third man to Johnson's apartment, where Johnson met them at the curb. Defendant and the third man then followed Johnson to his apartment.

When the three men got to Johnson's apartment, Rider was in the front room looking through CDs, Galindo was on the front porch, and McDermott was sleeping in one of the bedrooms. Once inside the apartment, defendant began counting out his money and Johnson went to his bedroom to get the marijuana out of a locked safe.

Johnson went into the kitchen area with the marijuana and defendant asked to use the restroom. Defendant walked down the hall toward the restroom and then turned around, aimed a gun at Johnson, and said, "you're getting jacked." The man who came with defendant had his own gun and he pointed it at Rider, telling Rider to lie face down on the ground.

Johnson initially "froze" but quickly grabbed the marijuana and stuffed it in his underwear, covering it with his shirt. Defendant then turned to his cohort and said, "give me your nine," and started walking toward Johnson. While defendant was looking the other way, Johnson ran out of the apartment, down the stairs, out to the parking lot, and past the truck in which defendant had arrived.

Approximately 30 seconds later, defendant and his cohort ran out of the apartment, down the stairs, and out to the parking lot, where they jumped into the waiting truck. As the truck pulled away, it hit a pole; the bumper fell off and was left behind, with the license plate attached. The police were called and shortly thereafter, Galindo and Johnson identified defendant as the man who had attempted to rob them.n1

> n1 The roommates initially lied to the police, telling them defendant simply kicked in the front door and started waving a gun around, leaving out the fact that Johnson was selling drugs from the apartment. They later amended their story and explained that defendant was there to buy drugs from Johnson. Johnson was given immunity for his testimony.

Defendant was arrested and a search of defendant's person revealed a .380-caliber round and a nine-millimeter caliber round of ammunition in defendant's left pocket. Both cartridges bore magazine marks indicating they had been loaded into a handgun. The search also revealed 20 Ecstasy pills and a cell phone in defendant's right pocket.

Defendant admitted stealing from Johnson, but told the police they "couldn't arrest him for ripping off a drug dealer." He also claimed the Ecstasy was for personal use and not for sale. Defendant was subsequently charged with one count of first degree residential burglary *(Pen.Code, § 459*—count one), two counts of attempted robbery (Johnson and Rider, respectively; *Pen.Code, §§ 664/211*—counts two-three), possession of a controlled substance (Health & *Saf.Code, § 11378*—count five), and being a felon in possession of ammunition *(Pen.Code, § 12316,* subd. (b)(1)-count six). It was further alleged that defendant used a handgun in the commission of counts one through three.

A jury found defendant guilty on counts one through three, five, and six. The jury also found true the allegation that defendant had used a handgun during the commission of counts one through three. Defendant appeals, arguing prosecutorial misconduct, ineffective assistance of counsel, and insufficiency of the evidence. We find only one of defendant's claims has merit.

. . .

ATTEMPTED ROBBERY OF JESSIE RIDER

Defendant contends he cannot be convicted of attempting to rob Rider because the marijuana he was trying to steal belonged to Johnson. We agree.

"Robbery is the felonious taking of personal property in the possession of another, from his person or immediate presence, and against his will, accomplished by means of force or fear." *(Pen. Code § 211.)* California follows "the traditional approach that limits victims of robbery to those persons in either actual or constructive possession of the property taken." *(People v. Nguyen (2000) 24 Cal.4th 756, 764, 102 Cal.Rptr.2d 548, 14 P.3d 221.)* "'Robbery' is an offense against the person[.]" *(People v. Miller (1977) 18 Cal.3d 873, 880, 135 Cal.Rptr. 654, 558 P.2d 552.)* Accordingly, a victim can be any person who shares "some type of 'special relationship' with the owner of the property sufficient to demonstrate that the victim had authority or responsibility to protect the stolen property on behalf of the owner." *(People v. Scott (2009) 45 Cal.4th 743, 753, 89 Cal.Rptr.3d 213, 200 P.3d 837.)* Persons with just such a special relationship include business employees and parents living with their adult children. *(Scott, supra, 45 Cal.4th at pp. 752, 753-754, 89 Cal.Rptr.3d 213, 200 P.3d 837; see People v. Jones (2000) 82 Cal.App.4th 485, 491, 98 Cal.Rptr.2d 329.)*

In *People v. Gordon (1982) 136 Cal.App.3d 519, 186 Cal.Rptr. 373,* the defendants entered a residence by ruse, threatened a couple with a firearm, and took drugs and money belonging to the couple's absent adult son. *(Id.* at pp. 523-524, *186 Cal.Rptr. 373.)* The appellate court noted neither parent physically possessed the items taken nor did either know about the marijuana or money, and the only evidence to support a finding of possession was the couple's ownership and residence in the home where the crime occurred. *(Id.* at p. 529, *186 Cal.Rptr. 373.)* The court upheld the jury's determination that the parents were robbery victims who possessed their son's items for purposes of the robbery statute. *(Ibid.)* The court noted various individuals have been designated as victims in a robbery, such as a purchasing agent in charge of payroll, store clerks, barmaids, janitors in sole occupation of premises, watchmen, and gas station attendants. *(Ibid.)* "Clearly, if those individuals . . . were responsible for the protection and preservation of the property entrusted to them, parents have at least the same responsibility to protect goods belonging to their son who resides with them in their home." *(Ibid.)*

The evidence at trial established defendant attempted to steal marijuana from Johnson, saying, "you're getting jacked[.]" "Give [me] the weed." It was undisputed that Rider did not have actual possession of the marijuana, and Johnson stored the marijuana locked in a safe in his bedroom. There was no evidence Rider, who had been living with defendant for only three to four months, had access to the safe. In fact, Rider did not even have a key to the apartment, most of the time coming and going only when someone else was home.

Unlike the victims in Gordon, there is no parent-child relationship between Johnson and Rider, nor was Rider an employee of Johnson's. Rider and Johnson were simply roommates. Thus, Rider had no obligation to protect Johnson's belongings. Furthermore, at the time of the robbery, Johnson was present to protect his own belongings and there was no evidence he expected Rider to assist him in that regard.

Lacking any evidence that Rider owned, had access to, control over, or an obligation to protect the marijuana defendant attempted to steal, defendant's conviction for attempted robbery of Jessie Rider cannot be sustained and we reverse the conviction.

. . .

DISPOSITION

Defendant's conviction for the attempted robbery of Jessie Rider (count three of the information) is reversed. The judgment is otherwise affirmed and the matter is remanded for the limited purpose of recalculating defendant's sentence in light of this court's decision to reverse the conviction on count three. After resentencing, the trial court is directed to send a certified copy of the amended abstract of judgment to the Department of Corrections and Rehabilitation.

We concur: SIMS, Acting P.J., and HULL, J.

PEOPLE v. LUNA

COURT OF APPEAL, FIRST DISTRICT, DIVISION 4, CALIFORNIA

170 Cal. App. 4th 535; No. A119768

January 15, 2009

OPINION BY: RUVOLO, P. J.

INTRODUCTION

Appellant Manuel Christopher Luna was convicted by jury of attempting to manufacture a controlled substance (*Health & Saf.Code, § 11379.6,* subd. (a); *Pen.Code § 664*). Appellant claims his conviction must be reversed because "there is no evidence whatsoever that appellant ever advanced beyond mere planning or preparation." We agree with appellant that there was insufficient evidence to support his conviction. Consequently, we reverse.

FACTS AND PROCEDURAL HISTORY

Around midnight on March 6, 2005, Mendocino County Deputy Sheriff Jason Lucas stopped appellant, who was driving a pickup truck with a camper shell, for a traffic violation. When appellant stepped out of his pickup truck, he appeared to be under the influence of alcohol, although he passed a field sobriety test.

During a consensual search of the pickup truck, Lucas found equipment used to manufacture hashish. These items included PVC pipe, PVC glue, couplings, fittings, adapters, Teflon tape, Pyrex bowls, a butane burner, rubbing alcohol, activated carbon filters, and a metal spigot with an open/close valve. Lucas also found 299 bottles of butane, and a sales receipt indicating that the pipe fittings and a metal nozzle had just been purchased several hours earlier. Appellant was found to be in possession of a small quantity of marijuana and $1,200 in cash. When Lucas asked appellant if he had a hashish lab, appellant "half-heartedly" indicated that he did not.

California Department of Justice Senior Criminalist Matthew Kirsten, who qualified as an expert in manufacturing hashish, testified about all of the items that were found in appellant's truck and how they contribute to the manufacturing of concentrated cannabis, or as laymen call it, hashish. He testified that in order to manufacture hashish using the "butane extraction method," PCV pipes are connected with fittings at one end to accommodate a butane canister, and at the other end to attach a spigot. All parts of the marijuana plant are placed inside the pipe and are held in place by a screen or mesh. The butane is then injected into the pipe, dissolving the marijuana plant resin that contains tetrahydrocannabinol (THC) and allowing it to be collected in its concentrated form. Kirsten believed that the equipment in appellant's possession had previously been utilized in the manufacture of hashish as evidenced by hash oil residue and part of a marijuana leaf found on some of the seized equipment. With respect to whether everything necessary to manufacture hashish was present in appellant's truck, he testified that "all one needed would be . . . the marijuana to continue that process." Kirsten testified that in order for appellant to actually begin manufacturing hashish, appellant would have had to obtain "grocery bags full of marijuana."

Appellant testified at trial. He testified that he was homeless and having trouble getting a job when he purchased the equipment to make hashish from homeless persons in Golden Gate Park in San Francisco. The sellers explained the process of making hashish to appellant. Appellant acknowledged that he bought the equipment with the intention of making hashish. "I bought this stuff because it was presented to me for a low price and at the time I made a poor decision and I considered making hash." Appellant claimed, however, that he did not try to purchase marijuana after acquiring the remainder of the necessary equipment.

On September 27, 2007, a jury found appellant not guilty of manufacturing a controlled substance, but guilty of the lesser-included offense of attempting to manufacture a controlled substance (*Health & Saf.Code, § 11379.6,* subd. (a); *Pen.Code § 664*). On November 9, 2007, the court suspended imposition of sentence and placed appellant on probation. This appeal followed.

DISCUSSION

In this case, the sole issue is whether the evidence is sufficient to sustain appellant's conviction for attempting to manufacture a controlled substance. (*Health & Saf.Code, § 11379.6,* subd. (a); *Pen.Code § 664.*)

. . .

Health and Safety Code section 11379.6, subdivision (a) punishes "every person who manufactures, compounds, converts, produces, derives, processes, or prepares, either directly or indirectly by chemical extraction or independently by means of chemical synthesis, any controlled substance. . . ." The elements of a criminal attempt are "[(1)] a specific intent to commit the crime, and [(2)] a direct but ineffectual act done toward its commission." (*Pen.Code, § 21a; People v. Toledo (2001) 26 Cal.4th 221, 229, 109 Cal.Rptr.2d 315, 26 P.3d 1051.*)

First, on the issue of intent, appellant himself testified that at the time he purchased the equipment, it was his intention to manufacture hashish by using "the butane extraction process." Appellant's counsel conceded at oral argument that appellant's intent to manufacture hashish was established by his own testimony. In this case, the key dispute is the second component of an attempt crime. That is, whether appellant's actions had progressed to the point where they could be considered "a direct but ineffectual act done towards [the crime's] commission, i.e., an overt ineffectual act which is beyond mere preparation yet short of actual commission of the crime. [Citations.]" (*People v. Ross (1988) 205 Cal.App.3d 1548, 1554-1555, 253 Cal.Rptr. 178.*)

Appellant argues that his actions were not extensive enough to be considered an attempt because, when he was arrested, the manufacturing activity "had not advanced beyond planning or preparation." He emphasizes that he had not taken steps to begin the manufacturing process. In making this argument, appellant focuses on the absence of evidence that he "ever obtained or arranged to obtain THE essential ingredient necessary for manufacturing hashish, the starting material, marijuana. . . ." (Original capitalization.)

In considering appellant's argument, we first note that in a case such as this one "[w]here the intent to commit the crime is clearly shown, an act done toward the commission of the crime may be sufficient for an attempt even though that same act would be insufficient if the intent is not as clearly shown. [Citation.]" (*People v. Bonner (2000) 80 Cal.App.4th 759, 764, 95 Cal.Rptr.2d 642; People v. Anzalone (2006) 141 Cal.App.4th 380, 387, 45 Cal.Rptr.3d*

876.) "[T]he plainer the intent to commit the offense, the more likely that steps in the early stages of the commission of the crime will satisfy the overt act requirement. [Citations.]" (*People v. Dillon (1983) 34 Cal.3d 441, 455, 194 Cal.Rptr. 390, 668 P.2d 697.*) Thus, even "'slight acts done in furtherance of that design will constitute an attempt, and the courts should not destroy the practical and common-sense administration of the law with subtleties as to what constitutes preparation and what constitutes an act done toward the commission of a crime.' [Citations.]" (*People v. Memro (1985) 38 Cal.3d 658, 698, 214 Cal.Rptr. 832, 700 P.2d 446 (Memro); People v. Superior Court (Decker) (2007) 41 Cal.4th 1, 8-9, 58 Cal.Rptr.3d 421, 157 P.3d 1017 (Decker).*)

As our Supreme Court recently emphasized, "Whether acts done in contemplation of the commission of a crime are merely preparatory or whether they are instead sufficiently close to the consummation of the crime is a question of degree and depends upon the facts and circumstances of a particular case." (*Decker, supra, 41 Cal.4th at p. 14, 58 Cal.Rptr.3d 421, 157 P.3d 1017.*) Although the distinction between preparation and attempt may be difficult to gauge in some instances, our Supreme Court has given us this important guideline: "'[T]here is a material difference between the preparation antecedent to an offense and the actual attempt to commit it. The preparation consists of devising or arranging the means or measures necessary for the commission of the offense, while the attempt is the direct movement toward its commission after the preparations are made. In other words, to constitute an attempt the acts of the defendant must go so far that they would result in the accomplishment of the crime unless frustrated by extraneous circumstances. [Citations.]' [Citations.]"n1 (*Memro, supra, 38 Cal.3d at p. 698, 214 Cal.Rptr. 832, 700 P.2d 446,* italics added.)

> n1 In discussing the quantum of conduct considered sufficient to establish a criminal attempt, the Model Penal Code sets out the example of "possess[ing] materials to be employed in the commission of the crime. . . ." (*Model Pen.Code § 501(2)(e).*) This type of evidence is sufficient if it is "strongly corroborative of the actor's criminal purpose." (*Model Pen.Code, § 501(2).*) There is no doubt that this approach has influenced the law of attempt in other jurisdictions; and if we followed it here, appellant's arguments would have no legal merit. (See, e.g., *United States v. Rahman (2d Cir.1999) 189 F.3d 88, 128-129; People v. Lehnert (Colo.2007) 163 P.3d 1111, 1115; State v. Sheikh (Kan.App.2001) 30 Kan.App.2d 188, 191, 41 P.3d 290.*) However, as our Supreme Court pointed out in *Dillon, supra, 34 Cal.3d at pages 453–454, footnote 1, 194*

Cal.Rptr. 390, 668 P.2d 697, the evidence that the Model Penal Code finds to be legally sufficient to support an attempt conviction does not conform to California law because under the Model Penal Code standard "acts normally considered only preparatory could be sufficient to establish liability. [Citation.]"

In evaluating appellant's conduct, respondent argues that appellant took direct, but ineffectual steps toward the commission of the crime—beyond the mere noncriminal planning or preparation stages—and that those steps constitute " 'slight acts done in furtherance' " of his intent to commit the crime. (Memro, supra, 38 Cal.3d at p. 698, 214 Cal.Rptr. 832, 700 P.2d 446.) Respondent relies on evidence from which the jury could reasonably infer that appellant knew how to manufacture hashish and that he had purchased the butane and equipment intending to make hashish. Some of the equipment in appellant's possession contained the indicia of previous manufacturing activity. Just hours before his arrest, appellant had purchased the last two legally obtainable items associated with manufacturing hashish from a hardware store. Appellant was also in the possession of $1,270 in cash, which would be more than enough to purchase marijuana, the only missing ingredient for the manufacture of hashish.

As we have indicated, the critical issue is whether, at the time of his arrest, appellant had proceeded far enough down the path toward manufacturing hashish that a reasonable jury could find that he committed the crime of attempted manufacture. In analyzing the evidence supporting appellant's attempt conviction, we have not discovered any published California case addressing what constitutes "a direct but ineffectual act" toward manufacturing. (Pen.Code, § 21a.) However, there are numerous cases discussing the evidence necessary to support a conviction under Health and Safety Code section 11379.6, subdivision (a), which subjects to liability not only one who "manufactures" a controlled substance, but also one who "compounds, converts, produces, derives, processes, or prepares" such a substance.

Respondent points out that the conduct proscribed by Health and Safety Code section 11379.6, subdivision (a), the crime which appellant purportedly attempted, has been found to "criminalize all acts which are part of the manufacturing process, whether or not those acts directly result in completion of the final product." (People v. Heath (1998) 66 Cal.App.4th 697, 705, 78 Cal.Rptr.2d 240 (Heath).) In assessing how close appellant's conduct came to committing the actual offense, respondent claims "the fact that appellant was missing an ingredient for the extraction process does not invalidate the jury's determination of attempted manufacture of a controlled substance."

The case which is at the centerpiece of respondent's argument is People v. Lancellotti (1993) 19 Cal.App.4th 809, 23 Cal.Rptr.2d 640. The defendant in Lancellotti stored most of the equipment and chemicals needed to manufacture methamphetamine at a commercial storage facility. (Id. at p. 812, 23 Cal.Rptr.2d 640.) The locker was opened after storage facility personnel noticed an unusual odor, and it was found to contain chloropseudoephedrine "'an immediate precursor of methamphetamine.' " (Id. at pp. 810–813, 23 Cal.Rptr.2d 640.)

On appeal from his conviction for manufacturing methamphetamine (Health & Saf.Code, § 11379.6, subd. (a)), the Lancellotti court rejected defendant's argument that the evidence was insufficient to support his conviction because the storage unit lacked a certain piece of equipment and a reducing agent that were necessary to complete the methamphetamine manufacturing process. (Lancellotti, supra, 19 Cal.App.4th at p. 811, 23 Cal.Rptr.2d 640.) The court noted that the manufacture of methamphetamine is an incremental, as opposed to an instantaneous process, and is often conducted in a piecemeal fashion and moved from place-to-place to avoid detection. (Ibid.) The court reasoned, "The cumulative nature of the evidence in appellant's case, including the contents of the locker which all taken together are only used in the manufacture of methamphetamine, the presence of chloropseudoephedrine, a substance which cannot be purchased and is used only in the manufacture of methamphetamine, and the odor emanating from the locker, provide substantial evidence that the manufacture of methamphetamine, an incremental and not instantaneous process, was in progress." (Id. at p. 813, 23 Cal.Rptr.2d 640.)

Relying on the Lancellotti decision, respondent asserts that "appellant took unequivocal intermediate steps towards making hashish with the avowed purpose of doing so" and therefore, "[s]ubstantial evidence supports [his] conviction." However, respondent misses the key point made in the Lancellotti decision. The Lancellotti court did not find that the defendant was guilty of the crime of manufacturing methamphetamine because he possessed certain pieces of equipment associated with the drug's manufacture. Rather, the defendant's conviction was upheld because there was evidence he had engaged in an intermediate step in the methamphetamine manufacturing process. This point was emphasized by our Supreme Court in People v. Coria (1999) 21 Cal.4th 868, 89 Cal.Rptr.2d 650, 985 P.2d 970, when it cited Lancellotti for the proposition that Health and Safety Code section 11379.6, subdivision (a) "makes it unlawful to engage in the chemical synthesis of a substance as one part of the process of manufacturing a controlled substance." (People v. Coria, supra, at p. 874, 89 Cal.Rptr.2d 650, 985 P.2d 970.)

Numerous cases illustrate the point that *Health and Safety Code section 11379.6,* subdivision (a) is aimed at ongoing manufacturing operations. Thus, while the manufacturing process need not be complete, it must at least be started. (See, e.g. *People v. Jackson (1990) 218 Cal.App.3d 1493, 1503-1504, 267 Cal.Rptr. 841; People v. Stone (1999) 75 Cal.App.4th 707, 713-714, 89 Cal.Rptr.2d 401 (Stone); Heath, supra, 66 Cal.App.4th at p. 705, 78 Cal.Rptr.2d 240; People v. Combs (1985) 165 Cal.App.3d 422, 427, 211 Cal.Rptr. 617; People v. Hard (2003) 112 Cal.App.4th 272, 279, 5 Cal.Rptr.3d 107.)* These decisions illustrate that *Health and Safety Code section 11379.6,* subdivision (a), criminalizes participation in each and every stage of the manufacturing process, "from inception through completion." *(Stone, supra, 75 Cal.App.4th at p. 715, 89 Cal.Rptr.2d 401.)*

In reviewing the record in this case, we find no act—not even a slight act—on the part of appellant that goes beyond preparation and can be regarded as an "unequivocal overt act which can be said to be a commencement of the commission of the intended crime. [Citation.]" *(People v. Adami (1973) 36 Cal.App.3d 452, 458, 111 Cal.Rptr. 544,* disapproved on other grounds in *Decker, supra, 41 Cal.4th at pp. 10-13, 58 Cal.Rptr.3d 421, 157 P.3d 1017.)* At the time appellant was arrested, he had no ability to begin manufacturing hashish, which expert opinion established is an instantaneous as opposed to an incremental process. In order to begin manufacturing hashish, appellant still had numerous steps to accomplish, including assembling the components of the manufacturing device, which were found unassembled and in pieces in appellant's truck. He also had to obtain the key ingredient, "grocery bags full of marijuana."

We acknowledge that the line between preparation and an attempt is often indistinct. However, we conclude that this line has not been crossed where the prosecution's evidence shows that a defendant is still engaged in preparatory acts and that there is a complete inability to take even initial steps toward producing the finished product. After all, "planning the offense" and "devising, obtaining or arranging the means for its commission" are merely aspects of preparation. *(Dillon, supra, 34 Cal.3d at p. 452, 194 Cal.Rptr. 390, 668 P.2d 697.)* Moreover, "'[p]reparation alone is not enough [to establish an attempt], there must be some appreciable fragment of the crime committed [and] it must be in such progress that it will be consummated unless interrupted by circumstances independent of the will of the attempter. . . .' [Citation.]" *(Id. at p. 454, 194 Cal.Rptr. 390, 668 P.2d 697; Memro, supra, 38 Cal.3d at p. 698, 214 Cal.Rptr. 832, 700 P.2d 446.)* We believe the acts undertaken by appellant were too preliminary to indicate with any certainty that "a crime [was] about to be consummated absent an intervening force. . . ." *(Dillon, supra, 34 Cal.3d at pp. 454-455, 194 Cal.Rptr. 390, 668 P.2d 697.)* Consequently, we conclude that the evidence is insufficient to sustain appellant's conviction for attempting to manufacture a controlled substance. *(Health & Saf.Code, § 11379.6,* subd. (a); *Pen.Code § 664.)*

DISPOSITION

The judgment is reversed.

We concur: SEPULVEDA and RIVERA, JJ.

OPINION BY: BAXTER, J.

Defendants Jamal K. Swain and David Chatman were each convicted of conspiracy to commit murder and other crimes, stemming from the drive-by shooting death of a 15-year-old boy. As we shall explain, we hold that intent to kill is a required element of the crime of conspiracy to commit murder. In light of the jury instructions given, and general verdicts returned, we cannot determine beyond a reasonable doubt whether the jury found that the defendants conspired with an intent to kill. That conclusion requires us to reverse defendants' conspiracy convictions.

FACTS AND PROCEDURAL BACKGROUND

The question before us is one of law; the facts found by the Court of Appeal, summarized below, are not disputed.

Prosecution evidence established that a brown van passed through the Hunter's Point neighborhood of San Francisco about 2 a.m. on January 13, 1991. It slowed down near the spot where the young victim, who was of Samoan descent, and his friends were listening to music on the street.

A young Black male who appeared to have no hair was driving the van. Suddenly several shots were fired from the front of the van. Defendant Chatman and another young man also fired guns from the rear of the van. One of the intended victims had yelled out "drive-by" as a warning of the impending shooting, so most of the people on the street ducked down. The 15-year-old victim, Hagbom Saileele, who was holding the radio from which music was playing, was shot twice from behind. He later died in surgery.

Afterward, defendant Swain was in jail and boasted to jail mates about what good aim he had with a gun: "He was talking about what a good shot he was. . . . He was saying he had shot that Samoan kid when they were in the van going about 30 miles an hour up a hill." The area where the shooting occurred is hilly; the van would have had to

have been traveling uphill as it passed by the scene of the shooting.

Evidence also established that defendant Swain had used his jailhouse visiting privileges to threaten and intimidate witnesses into changing their stories, so that he would not be identified as involved in the crime.

The abandoned brown van was recovered by police; in the van and nearby were found surgical gloves, expended cartridges, a hooded ski mask, and two handguns—a .380-caliber semiautomatic and a .25-caliber automatic. Defendant Swain's fingerprint was on the inside of the driver's side window. The forensic evidence established that whoever had used the .380-caliber semiautomatic handgun, from which the fatal shots were fired, had been sitting in the driver's side front seat of the van.

The .380-caliber gun was traced, through a series of owners and transactions involving narcotics, to defendant Chatman. Chatman was interrogated by police; he denied any knowledge of the van and claimed he had not purchased the gun. When this story proved false, Chatman admitted he had bought the gun, but claimed it had been stolen from him. Still later, he claimed he had sold it to someone else.

A warrant was obtained for Chatman's arrest. After waiving his rights, Chatman told police he and two other people, not including Swain, had driven the van to the crime scene in order to get revenge for a car theft by a rival gang. Chatman insisted, to the police and at trial, that Swain had not been in the van. He could not, however, explain Swain's fingerprint inside the van.

The owner of the van testified Swain had never been inside his van prior to the incident, but that Swain had intimidated him into telling police he (Swain) had previously been inside the vehicle, since otherwise "he was going to have something done to him."

At trial, Chatman admitted he had been in the van, which was driven to Hunter's Point to retaliate for a car theft attributed to a neighborhood youth who was not the victim of the shooting. The original plan was allegedly to steal the car of the thief. Chatman admitted he had fired shots, but claimed he fired wildly and only in self-defense. In support of this self-defense theory, he testified he heard an initial shot and thought it was fired by someone outside the van shooting at him, so he returned the fire. As noted, Chatman claimed Swain was not in the van.

Swain testified he was not in the van during the shooting and did not do any shooting. He claimed he had entered the van earlier in the evening, but had left because "the smell of marijuana bothered him." He claimed he took BART (Bay Area Rapid Transit) to Berkeley, where he spent the evening at a relative's home. He denied boasting about shooting the victim and denied having threatened any witnesses.

The jury first returned a verdict finding defendant Chatman guilty of second degree murder and conspiracy. As instructed, the jury also made a finding that the target offense of the conspiracy was murder in the second degree. Several days later, the jury returned verdicts against defendant Swain, finding him not guilty of murder or its lesser included offenses, but guilty of conspiracy and of attempting to dissuade a witness from testifying by threats. Once again, the jury made a finding under the conspiracy count that the target offense of the conspiracy was murder in the second degree.

At the sentencing hearing, the parties disputed the proper sentence for the crime of conspiracy to commit murder, where the target offense is found by the jury to be murder in the second degree. The trial court ultimately ruled that the proper sentence was an indeterminate term of 15 years to life, that prescribed for murder in the second degree, not 25 years to life that prescribed for murder in the first degree, as the People had argued.

Chatman was sentenced to 15 years to life for second degree murder, with a consecutive 4-year enhancement for personal firearm use. A sentence of 15 years to life for the conspiracy count was imposed but stayed pursuant to *Penal Code section 654*.

Swain was sentenced to 15 years to life for conspiracy, and an additional 3 years for the conviction of attempting to dissuade a witness from testifying by threats.

Both defendants appealed on several grounds, including the question of whether intent to kill is a required element of the crime of conspiracy to commit murder. More particularly, where, as here, the target offense is determined to be murder *in the second degree*, does conviction of conspiracy to commit murder necessarily require proof of express malice—the functional equivalent of intent to

kill—or can one conspire to commit implied malice murder? The *People* also appealed, contending the trial court improperly sentenced defendants to indeterminate terms of 15 years to life on the conspiracy counts because, assertedly under *Penal Code section 182*, every "conspiracy to commit murder" must be punished as a first degree murder, with a sentence of 25 years to life. The Court of Appeal affirmed the convictions and judgments imposing sentence in their entirety.

Defendants and the People each petitioned for review. We granted the petitions, limiting review to two issues: (1) is intent to kill a required element of conspiracy to commit murder and (2) what is the punishment for conspiracy to commit murder, given the prescripts of *Penal Code section 182*?

DISCUSSION

I

Defendants contend the jury should have been instructed that proof of intent to kill is required to support a conviction of conspiracy to commit murder, whether the target offense of the conspiracy—murder—is determined to be in the first or second degree. More particularly, defendants assert it was error to instruct the jury on the principles of *implied malice* second degree murder in connection with the determination of whether they could be found guilty of conspiracy to commit murder, since *implied malice* does not require a finding of intent to kill. As we shall explain, we agree.

We commence our analysis with a brief review of the elements of the crime of conspiracy, and of murder, the target offense of the conspiracy here in issue.

Conspiracy is an inchoate crime. (See *United States v. Feola (1975) 420 U.S. 671, 694 {43 L. Ed. 2d 541, 558, 95 S. Ct. 1255}*.) It does not require the commission of the substantive offense that is the object of the conspiracy. (*People v. Manson (1977) 71 Cal. App. 3d 1, 47 {139 Cal. Rptr. 275}*.) "As an inchoate crime, conspiracy fixes the point of legal intervention at [the time of] agreement to commit a crime," and "thus reaches further back into preparatory conduct than attempt. . . ." (Model Pen. Code & Commentaries (1985) com. 1 to § 5.03, pp. 387–388.)

The crime of conspiracy is defined in the Penal Code as "two or more persons conspir[ing] . . . [t]o commit any crime," together with proof of the commission of an overt act "by one or more of the parties to such agreement" in furtherance thereof. (*Pen. Code, § 182*, subd. (a)(1), 184.) "Conspiracy is a 'specific intent' crime. . . . The specific intent required divides logically into two elements: (a) the intent to agree, or conspire, and (b) the intent to commit the offense which is the object of the conspiracy. . . . To sustain a conviction for conspiracy to commit a particular offense, the prosecution must show not only that the conspirators intended to agree *but also that they intended to commit the elements of that offense.*" (*People v. Horn (1974) 12 Cal. 3d 290, 296 {115 Cal. Rptr. 516, 524 P.2d 1300}* (*Horn*), citations omitted, italics added.) In some instances, the object of the conspiracy "is defined in terms of proscribed conduct." (*Model Pen. Code & Commentaries, supra, com. 2(c) to § 5.03,* p. 402.) (See fn.1.) In other instances, it "is defined in terms of . . . a proscribed result under specified attendant circumstances." (*Ibid.*)n1

> n1 As Witkin summarizes it: "[t]he elements [of conspiracy] are (a) agreement . . .; (b) specific intent . . .; (c) two or more persons . . .; (d) unlawful object or means . . .; and (e) overt act. . . ." (1 Witkin & Epstein, Cal. Criminal Law (2d ed. 1988) Elements of Crime, § 156, p. 174.)

Another provision of the *Penal Code, section 182,* the current version of which was enacted in 1955, prescribes the punishment for the crime of conspiracy. "If the felony is one for which different punishments are prescribed for different degrees, the jury or court which finds the defendant guilty thereof shall determine the degree of the felony defendant conspired to commit. If the degree is not so determined, the punishment for conspiracy to commit such felony shall be that prescribed for the lesser degree, except in the case of conspiracy to commit murder, in which case the punishment shall be that prescribed for murder in the first degree."

Turning next to the elements of the target offense of the conspiracy here in issue, *Penal Code section 187* defines the crime of murder as the "unlawful killing of a human being . . . with malice aforethought." (*Pen. Code, § 187,* subd. (a).) Malice aforethought "may be express or implied." (*Pen. Code, § 188.*) "It is express when there is manifested a deliberate intention unlawfully to take away the life of a fellow creature. It is implied, when no considerable provocation appears, or when the circumstances attending the killing show an abandoned and malignant heart." (*Ibid.*)

This court has observed that proof of unlawful "intent to kill" is the functional equivalent of express malice. (See *People v. Saille (1991) 54 Cal. 3d 1103, 1114 {2 Cal. Rptr. 2d 364, 820 P.2d 588}* ["Pursuant to the language of [*Penal Code} section 188,* when an intentional killing is shown, malice aforethought is established."].)n2

> n2 Of course unreasonable self-defense or a heat of passion defense can further reduce an intentional killing to voluntary manslaughter.

Penal Code section 189 distinguishes between murders in the first degree and murders in the second degree. "All murder which is perpetrated by means of a destructive device or explosive . . . , poison, lying in wait, torture, *or by any other kind of willful, deliberate, and premeditated killing*, or which is committed in the perpetration of, or attempt to perpetrate, [certain enumerated felonies], or any murder which is perpetrated by means of discharging a firearm from a motor vehicle, intentionally at another person outside of the vehicle with the intent to inflict death, is *murder of the first degree*. All other kinds of murders are of the second degree." (Italics added.)n3

> n3 The provision of *Penal Code section 189*, making all murders "perpetrated by means of discharging a firearm from a motor vehicle, intentionally at another person outside of the vehicle with the intent to inflict death" murders of the first degree, was added after commission of the crimes in this case (see Stats. 1993, ch. 611, § 4.5, eff. Oct. 1, 1993, operative Jan. 1, 1994) and thus does not apply herein.

California law, in turn, recognizes three theories of *second degree* murder.

The first is unpremeditated murder with express malice. (See *CALJIC No. 8.30* ["Murder of the second degree is [also] the unlawful killing of a human being with malice aforethought when there is manifested an intention unlawfully to kill a human being but the evidence is insufficient to establish deliberation and premeditation."].)

The second, of particular concern here, is implied malice murder. (See *CALJIC No. 8.31* ["Murder of the second degree is [also] the unlawful killing of a human being when: 1. The killing resulted from an intentional act, 2. The natural consequences of the act are dangerous to human life, and 3. The act was deliberately performed with knowledge of the danger to, and with conscious disregard for, human life. When the killing is the direct result of such an act, it is not necessary to establish that the defendant intended that his act would result in the death of a human being."].)

The third theory is second degree felony murder. (See *CALJIC No. 8.32* ["The unlawful killing of a human being, whether intentional, unintentional or accidental, which occurs [during] [as the direct causal result of] the commission or attempted commission of [certain crimes] is murder of the second degree when the perpetrator had the specific intent to commit such crime."] [Third bracket added].)

As noted, the jury in this case was instructed on the elements of murder, including principles of *implied malice* second degree murder. Under the instructions given, the jury could have based its verdicts finding defendants guilty of conspiracy to commit murder in the second degree on a theory of implied malice murder. The Court of Appeal below concluded it could find no authority supportive of the proposition that the crime of conspiracy to commit murder in the second degree must be accompanied by an intent to kill (i.e., express malice).

. . .

We have noted that conspiracy is a specific intent crime requiring an intent to agree or conspire, and a further intent to commit the target crime, here murder, the object of the conspiracy. Since murder committed with intent to kill is the functional equivalent of *express malice* murder, conceptually speaking, no conflict arises between the specific intent element of conspiracy and the specific intent requirement for such category of murders. Simply put, where the conspirators agree or conspire with specific intent to kill and commit an overt act in furtherance of such agreement, they are guilty of conspiracy to commit express malice murder. The conceptual difficulty arises when the target offense of murder is founded on a theory of implied malice, which requires no intent to kill.

Implied malice murder, in contrast to express malice, requires instead an intent to do some act, the natural consequences of which are dangerous to human life. *"When the killing is the direct result of such an act,"* the requisite mental state for murder—malice aforethought—is implied. (*CALJIC No. 8.31*, italics added.) In such circumstances, ". . . it is not necessary to establish that the defendant intended that his act would result in the death of a human being." (*Ibid*.) Hence, under an *implied malice* theory of second degree murder, the requisite mental state for murder—malice aforethought—is by definition "implied," as a matter of law, from the specific intent to do some act dangerous to human life *together with the circumstance that a killing has resulted from the doing of such act.*

. . .

The element of malice aforethought in implied malice murder cases is therefore derived or "implied," in part through hindsight so to speak, from (i) proof of the specific intent to do some act dangerous to human life *and* (ii) the circumstance that a killing has resulted therefrom. It is precisely due to this nature of *implied malice* murder that it would be *illogical* to conclude one can be found guilty of conspiring to commit murder where the requisite element of malice is implied. Such a construction would be at odds with the very nature of the crime of conspiracy—an "inchoate" crime that "fixes the point of legal intervention at [the time of] agreement to commit a crime," and indeed "reaches further back into preparatory conduct than [the crime of] attempt" (Model Pen. Code & Commentaries,

supra, com. 1 to § 5.03, pp. 387–388)—precisely because commission of the crime could never be established, or be deemed complete, unless and until a killing actually occurred.

. . .

Similarly, in *People v. Collie (1981) 30 Cal. 3d 43 {177 Cal. Rptr. 458, 634 P.2d 534}* (*Collie*), we applied the above noted reasoning of *Murtishaw, supra, 29 Cal. 3d 733,* to the crime of attempted murder. To constitute an attempt, there must be (i) proof of specific intent to commit the target crime and (ii) a direct, ineffectual act done towards its commission. (*1 Witkin & Epstein, Cal. Criminal Law, supra, Elements of Crime, § 143,* p. 160.) Concluding in *Collie* that the trial court erred in instructing the jury it could convict the defendant of attempted murder on the basis of implied malice and without a finding of intent to kill, we explained: "'Specific intent to kill is a necessary element of attempted murder. It must be proved, and it cannot be inferred merely from the commission of another dangerous crime.'"

. . .

We conclude that a conviction of conspiracy to commit murder requires a finding of intent to kill, and cannot be based on a theory of implied malice.

II

The question remains whether the instructions on implied malice in this case were prejudicial, requiring reversal of defendants' convictions of conspiracy to commit murder designated by the jury as murder in the second degree. We conclude the convictions must be reversed.

The jury was instructed on theories of both express and implied malice. They returned general verdicts, which do not inform us on what theory they found the requisite element of malice necessary to convict on the charges of conspiracy to commit murder. Under the implied malice instructions, the jury could have found malice without finding intent to kill. (*Pen. Code, § 188*.) The prosecutor repeatedly referred to implied malice in the closing arguments, stating at one point that ". . . this could very easily be an implied malice case."

On this record, under the harmless error test traditionally applied to misinstruction on the elements of an offense, namely, whether it appears "beyond a reasonable doubt that the error complained of did not contribute to the verdict obtained" (*Chapman v. California (1967) 386 U.S. 18, 24 {17 L. Ed. 2d 705, 710, 87 S. Ct. 824, 24 A.L.R.3d 1065}*; see *People v. Harris (1994) 9 Cal. 4th 407, 424–425 {37 Cal. Rptr. 2d 200, 886 P.2d 1193}*, and cases cited), reversal is required, for it cannot be determined beyond a reasonable doubt that the erroneous implied malice murder instructions did not contribute to the convictions on the conspiracy counts. Nor is there anything else discoverable from the verdicts that would enable us to conclude that the jury necessarily found the defendants guilty of conspiracy to commit murder on a proper theory, i.e., based on express malice or intent to kill. (*People v. Harris, supra,* 9 Cal. 4th at p. 419.) Defendant Chatman was convicted of second degree murder, which conviction itself could have been based on a theory of implied malice; defendant Swain was found not guilty of murder and its lesser offenses.

That portion of the Court of Appeal's judgment affirming defendants' convictions of conspiracy to commit murder must therefore be reversed.

. . .

CONCLUSION

To the extent the judgment of the Court of Appeal affirmed defendants' convictions of conspiracy to commit murder, it is reversed. In all other respects the judgment of the Court of Appeal is affirmed.

PEOPLE v. SAUGSTAD et al.

COURT OF APPEAL OF CALIFORNIA, THIRD APPELLATE DISTRICT

203 Cal. App. 2d 536; 21 Cal. Rptr. 740

May 15, 1962

OPINION BY: SCHOTTKY, J.

O. E. Saugstad, James Quirk, and William Kimball were tried by a jury on six counts, each charging a conspiracy to file false reports with the Department of Motor Vehicles and two counts of conspiracy to obtain money by false pretenses. All were found guilty of the six counts charging a violation of section 182, subdivision 1, of the Penal Code, in that they conspired to violate *section 20 of the Vehicle Code* by making a report of sale of a new vehicle although it was a used vehicle. Only Kimball was found guilty of the conspiracy charges relating to obtaining money by false pretenses. Probation was denied. Each was sentenced to the county jail, and in addition Saugstad and Quirk were ordered to pay a fine on each of the conspiracy charges relating to the filing of false reports. The conspiracy charges relating to false pretenses against Kimball were dismissed. This appeal is from the judgments of the court and from the orders of the court denying appellants' motions for a new trial.

O. E. Saugstad was the president of the O. E. Saugstad Company, a Ford dealer in Roseville. Kimball was the general manager and Quirk a deskman.

It was a practice of the company to assign stock numbers and prepare stock cards for each new car obtained. When a customer selected a new car, the salesman would obtain the proper stock card, and when the order was complete the stock card and the order would be pinned together. The salesman was essentially an order taker. The transaction was then handled by a closer. If the closer were successful, the contract was prepared, the car was delivered to the customer, and the stock card and the accompanying papers were sent to the office for processing. In many instances the car which had been delivered to a customer would be returned, or in the parlance of the trade "rolled back." In such cases the cars were cleaned up and replaced in the new car stock. The stock cards were returned to the new card file without any notification of the fact that the car had been delivered. This procedure was authorized by Kimball.

When a new car is sold sets of forms provided by the Department of Motor Vehicles must be completed. The forms consist of a paper license plate and an original, duplicate and triplicate form of the "Dealer's Report of Sale and Application for Registration of New Vehicle." The original form, which is an application for registration, is to be completed by the dealer and purchaser at the time of sale but not later than the next business day. (Cal. Admin. Code, tit. 13, § 460.) The report of sale is to be forwarded to the department within 10 days of the date of sale. When through error a report of sale must be voided, all copies must be marked void and (except the copy retained for the dealer's record) returned to the department with a written explanation and the dealer's certificate that the vehicle covered by the report did not leave the possession of the dealer and was at no time operated under the paper license identification.

The second copy, the notice of sale, is blue and is in two parts. The stub of this copy is required to be forwarded to the department not later than the next business day following the sale. The body of the form is attached to the windshield of the new vehicle which is delivered.

The third copy remains in the book supplied by the department.

Sales meetings were held every morning at which Quirk and Kimball addressed the sales force. Kimball gave Saugstad a daily report on the conduct of the business.

Kimball did not order the original report of sale sent to the department on the sale of the cars which were rolled back. He testified that he knew that if the original were sent in the car could not be resold as a new car.

Quirk, Kimball, and Saugstad were familiar with the fact that cars were being rolled back. Quirk and Kimball received commissions on each car sold.

In many cases in the operation of the Saugstad Company cars delivered were returned for various reasons after having been operated for varying periods of time and for varying mileage. In each case the application for the registration of a new vehicle had never been forwarded to the Department of Motor Vehicles (although the notice of sale had been forwarded). Upon the return of the car the stock card for the car was returned to the new car inventory without any notation that the previous transaction had been cancelled, the papers evidencing the transaction were cancelled, and the car itself returned to the new car lot. At the same time the previously completed but not forwarded application for the registration of a new vehicle was voided.

The evidence relating to the charges of conspiracy to violate *section 20 of the Vehicle Code* was similar as to each count. For that reason the evidence will be set forth only as to one of those counts because it suffices to illustrate the evidence as to all.

On June 29, 1959, Pablo Carillo purchased a 1959 Ford Fairlane, serial number C9RT169017, from the O. E. Saugstad Company. Carillo took delivery of the automobile and drove it between 600 and 700 miles. He was subsequently called in by somebody from the Saugstad Company and told that he could not keep the car because he was not a citizen of the United States. Carillo then returned the car to the Saugstad Company. The triplicate copy of the "Dealer's Report of Sale and Application for Registration of New Vehicle" was filled out by an employee of the Saugstad Company, stating that the vehicle was "Sold to Carillo, Pablo Vences." It also stated with respect to the vehicle: "Date first Sold 6-29-59" and "Date first operated 6-29-59." The conditional sales contract between the O. E. Saugstad Company and Pablo Carillo was dated "6/29/59." The duplicate of the dealer's report of sale, bearing serial number 627063, dated "6/29/59," was filled out and forwarded to the Department of Motor Vehicles. Stamped on this was the word "VOID."

On July 12, 1959, Edward Krumenacher purchased the same 1959 Ford Fairlane, serial number C9RT169017, from the O. E. Saugstad Company, paid the consideration therefore and took delivery. At the time he purchased the automobile the mileage registered on the speedometer was approximately 14 miles. The conditional sales contract between the O. E. Saugstad Company and Edward Krumenacher was dated July 12, 1959. This contract was accepted on behalf of the Saugstad Company by the appellant Quirk. The stub of the duplicate dealer's report of sale, serial number 659143, was filled out with the date sold as "7/12/59" and forwarded to the Department of Motor Vehicles. The original of the "Dealer's Report of Sale and Application for Registration of New Vehicle" was filled out, reporting the vehicle sold to "Ed B. Krumenacher," and stating with respect to the vehicle: "Date first Sold 7-12-59" and "Date first operated 7-12-59." This document stated the dealer's name as "O. E.

Saugstad Co." and opposite the dealer's name as authorized agent was the signature of appellant Quirk.

Appellants' first contention is that the court committed prejudicial error in instructing the jury that motive was not an essential element of the crime of conspiracy. The instruction complained of was as follows: "Proof of a motive for an alleged crime is permissible and often is valuable, but never is essential. If, after a consideration and comparison of all the evidence, you feel an abiding conviction to a moral certainty that the defendant committed (any) crime of which he is accused, the motive for its commission becomes unimportant. Evidence of motive is sometimes of assistance in removing doubt and completing proof which otherwise might be unsatisfactory. Motive may be shown by positive evidence or by facts surrounding the act if they support a reasonable inference. When thus proved, motive becomes a circumstance, but nothing more than a circumstance, to be considered by you. The absence of motive is equally a circumstance to be reckoned with, but on the side of innocence, tending to support the presumption of innocence, and to be given such weight as you deem proper."

Appellants argue that a corrupt motive and a joint evil intent are necessary to constitute the crime of conspiracy and rely heavily upon a statement in *People v. Eiseman, 78 Cal. App. 223 {248 P. 716}*, at page 247, "that a corrupt motive was an essential element of the crime of conspiracy." The quoted phrase is a loose statement of the law. We believe that the rule is correctly stated in *1 Wharton, Criminal Law and Procedure (Anderson), section 85,* as follows: "Analytically a dual mental state is present in the case of conspiracy. There is both (1) the intent or agreement of the parties to act together, and (2) the intent to commit an unlawful act or to commit a lawful act by unlawful means, or to do an act jointly which the law makes illegal when done by two or more persons."

In his work on the General Principles of Criminal Law (2d ed.), Professor Hall states at page 92: "In some cases of conspiracy where knowledge of illegality is part of the relevant *mens rea*, the language of the decisions is also in terms of 'corrupt motive,' but it is again clear that this is often the evidentiary basis upon which the material knowledge of the law is determined."

The instruction complained of must be read together with the other instructions given, and the jury was adequately instructed on the subject of intent in the following particulars: the jury was instructed that in every crime of the type charged in each count of the indictment there must exist a union or joint operation of act and intent; the jury was instructed with respect to the conspiracy counts of which the appellants were convicted that it must have been shown beyond a reasonable doubt and to a moral certainty that they wrongfully and intentionally conspired to make false statements or conceal material facts in documents filed with the Department of Motor Vehicles and that it must have been shown that the appellants performed or caused to be performed certain overt acts toward the accomplishment of the objects of the conspiracy; the jury was instructed that common design is the essence of the conspiracy; and the jury was instructed as to the definition of *section 20 of the Vehicle Code* and all other words defined by statute that were pertinent. Such instructions adequately informed the jury of the law applicable to the case. (*People v. Bucchierre, 57 Cal.App.2d 153 {134 P.2d 505}.)*

It is significant that none of the appellants made any request for an instruction that a corrupt motive and joint evil intent are necessary to constitute the crime of conspiracy.

Appellants' next contention is that the court committed prejudicial error in instructing the jury as to the difference in meaning between "vehicle" and "automobile." The instruction complained of was as follows:

"I instruct you that in Counts one, three, five, six, seven and eight of the indictment the terms 'new vehicle' and 'used vehicle' are used, whereas in counts two and four of said indictment the words 'new automobile' and 'used automobile' are used."

"You are instructed that the terms 'new vehicle' and 'used vehicle' are defined by law, whereas the words new automobile and used automobile are not. You are therefore instructed to construe the words new automobile and used automobile in their usual acceptance in common language."

The term "automobile" was used only in counts two and four which charged conspiracy to obtain property by false pretenses. The appellants Saugstad and Quirk were acquitted on these counts and the indictments on counts two and four were dismissed as to the appellant Kimball. Since the term "vehicle" was only used in counts one, three, five, six, seven, and eight of the pleadings, and since the court at the request of appellants instructed the jury as to the meaning of the terms "new" and "used" vehicle as set forth in the Vehicle Code in compliance with their request, and since there was a dismissal or acquittal as to those counts in which the term "automobile" was referred to, we are unable to understand how appellants could have been prejudiced by the instruction given, which appears to have been in accordance with appellants' theory of the case.

. . .

Appellants' final and most serious contention is that the evidence is insufficient to support their convictions. The gist of appellants' contention is as follows: "Appellants all contend the evidence is insufficient in that there is an absolute failure of proof as to the overt act charged in each of the counts of which appellants were convicted. Each overt act charges that appellants on a certain date made a report of sale of a new vehicle to a certain person although the vehicle covered was a used vehicle. As hereinbefore stated the terms 'new vehicle' and 'used vehicle' are defined by statute."

The principal question that we must determine is whether appellants could properly be found guilty of conspiracy to violate *section 20 of the Vehicle Code* by filing false reports, where the overt act charged was filing a report of sale of a new vehicle when in fact the vehicle was a used one.

Appellants were convicted on six counts of violation of section 182, subdivision 1, of the Penal Code, conspiracy to make false reports to the Department of Motor Vehicles in violation of *Vehicle Code section 20*. Subdivision 1 of *section 182 of the Penal Code* provides as follows: "If two or more persons conspire: 1. To commit any crime."

Section 20 of the Vehicle Code provides as follows: "It is unlawful to use a false or fictitious name, or to knowingly make any false statement or knowingly conceal any material fact in any document filed with the Department of Motor Vehicles or the Department of the California Highway Patrol."

The essential element of the crime of conspiracy is the unlawful agreement between two or more persons to commit an offense prohibited by statute, accompanied by some overt act in furtherance of such agreement. (*People v. Sears, 138 Cal. App.2d 773 {292 P.2d 663}; People v. Goldstein, 136 Cal. App.2d 778 {289 P.2d 581}.)* The unlawful agreement may be established by circumstantial evidence, and it is rare when the conspiracy can be established by direct evidence. (*People v. Garcia, 187 Cal. App.2d 93 {9 Cal.Rptr. 493}; People v. Reed, 188 Cal.App.2d 395 {10 Cal.Rptr. 536}; People v. Robinson, 43 Cal.2d 132 {271 P.2d 865}.)*

In the instant case the evidence discloses with respect to the various counts that it was the practice of the appellants to sell new cars, prepare a report of sale, retain the report, and then if the transaction did not go through recover the vehicle, return it to the new car lot and resell the car as a new one. In each instance the first purchaser had operated the vehicle and had driven distances ranging from 200 miles to 3,000 miles. In each instance the first report of sale was not filed with the Department of Motor Vehicles as required by the Administrative Code, title 13, section 460, and the instructions appearing on the form of the Department of Motor Vehicles to be filled out in transactions involving the sale of new cars. In this connection the evidence discloses that the appellants, Saugstad, Kimball, and Quirk, were familiar with the administrative regulations on the subject, and in fact had discussed the so-called "roll back" situation and the penalty provisions incurred in this practice.

In each instance the vehicle which had been originally sold and returned was again sold to a second or subsequent purchaser. The report of sale to the second or subsequent purchaser, filed with the Department of Motor Vehicles, was false in that it reported that the date the automobile was first sold, and the date it was first operated, was a date subsequent to the date it had in fact been sold to and operated by the previous purchaser.

Appellants argue that since the term "new vehicle" is defined in *section 430 of the Vehicle Code* as one which has never been registered and the term "used vehicle" is defined in *section 665 of the Vehicle Code* as one that has been registered, and since none of the vehicles had been registered at the time of sale to the ultimate purchaser, the overt act alleged in each count was not proved within the meaning of *section 1104 of the Penal Code.*

We do not agree with this contention. It is true that *section 1104 of the Penal Code* requires that in charging a conspiracy at least one overt act must be alleged and proved. However, it is well established that the overt act need not be a criminal act in itself . . . . It is sufficient if the overt act represents any step in furtherance of the conspiracy. It may be an otherwise lawful act and it may be merely a part of the preliminary arrangement for the commission of the ultimate offense. (*People v. Buono, 191 Cal. App.2d 203 {12 Cal. Rptr. 604}; People v. Garcia, supra; People v. George, 74 Cal. App. 440 {241 P. 97}.*) In each of the counts on which appellants were convicted the evidence shows that the reports filed with the Department of Motor Vehicles concealed and falsified facts as to when the vehicle had been first sold and when it had been first operated in violation of *section 20 of the Vehicle Code.* The making out of the report of sale to the second purchaser was the essential overt act in furtherance of the conspiracy to violate section 20. The documents as to each count were admitted into evidence as proof of the commission of the overt act charged.

The purpose of the overt act is simply to show that the agreement has proceeded beyond the meeting of the minds stage to some direct or physical act, however innocent in itself, tending toward the furtherance of the objective of the conspiracy. As was said by the Supreme Court of the United States, "The function of the overt act in a conspiracy prosecution is simply to manifest 'that the conspiracy is at work,' *Carlson v. United States, 187 F.2d 366, 370,* and is neither a project still resting solely in the minds of the conspirators nor a fully completed operation no longer in existence." (*Yates v. United States, 354 U.S. 298, 334 {77 S.Ct. 1064, 1 L.Ed.2d 1356}.*)

Furthermore, we believe that while words in an indictment are, if they have a technical meaning, ordinarily construed according to such meaning, the rule does not apply where the technical word has both a limited meaning and a broad significance in the popular sense and where the whole indictment makes clear that it was used in the latter sense. (*27 Am. Jur., Indictment and Information, § 62,* p. 626; *Dealy v. United States, 152 U.S. 539, 545–546 {14 S.Ct. 680, 38 L.Ed. 545}.*) In the technical sense a new vehicle is one that has never been registered. In the popular sense a new vehicle is one that has not been previously sold and if previously operated then no more than necessary to prepare the vehicle for sale. Any vehicle that had been operated several hundred miles or more would not be a new automobile to a lay individual. Construing the words of the indictment broadly and not in their technical meaning, a new vehicle would be one that had not been operated. A used vehicle is one that had been operated. The appellants falsified the reports to the Department of Motor Vehicles by not stating the actual date the vehicle was first operated. They reported the sale of a used vehicle as a new one. In the sense that the vehicle had previously been sold and operated it was a used car, or a car that had been used; and in this sense the pleading was sufficient. The fact the Vehicle Code defines a new vehicle would not prevent the words of the indictment from being used in their popular sense.

. . .

We are satisfied that the evidence is sufficient to support the judgments of conviction. Indeed, it is difficult to understand how the jury could have rendered any other verdicts. It is clear from the evidence that it was a common practice of appellants to sell new automobiles, prepare a report of sale, retain it, and then if the deal did not go through recover the vehicle, return it to the new car lot, and resell the car as a new car. In each instance the first purchaser had operated the vehicle. In each instance the first report of sale was not filed with the department as required. In each instance the report of sale filed with the department was false. It would be incredulous to think that such activity could go on without the knowledge and connivance of the top officials, namely, appellants Saugstad, Quirk, and Kimball. By permitting the practice and by permitting the filing with the Department of Motor Vehicles of reports of sales of new vehicles when in fact the vehicles had been operated, the named parties formed an agreement (implied perhaps) to file documents with the department which contained false statements. From the evidence introduced at the trial the jury could and did find such a conspiracy to have existed and could and did connect appellants with it.

The appellants were represented at the trial and upon the appeal by able and experienced counsel and received a fair and impartial trial. The jury was fully and fairly instructed and the instructions are singularly free from error. Because of the numerous contentions of error made by appellants, we have made a careful examination of the entire record and are convinced that even if appellants are correct in some of their contentions of error no miscarriage of justice has resulted.

The judgments and orders are affirmed.

PEOPLE v. RUSSO

SUPREME COURT OF CALIFORNIA

25 Cal. 4th 1124; 25 P.3d 641; 108 Cal. Rptr. 2d 436

June 28, 2001

OPINION BY: CHIN, J.

In California, a conviction for conspiracy requires proof that at least one of the conspirators committed an overt act in furtherance of the conspiracy. We granted review to decide whether the jury must unanimously agree on a specific overt act. We conclude the jury need not agree on a specific overt act as long as it unanimously finds beyond a reasonable doubt that some conspirator committed an overt act in furtherance of the conspiracy.

I. FACTUAL AND PROCEDURAL HISTORY

On the night of July 14, 1994 (all dates are to the year 1994), a Fresno County deputy sheriff found David Russo's body, dead from a gunshot wound to the back of the head, wrapped inside a sleeping bag in the backseat of David's car in a remote rural location. David's wife, defendant Susan Lee Russo (hereafter defendant), and codefendants Bobby Morris and Jason Andrews were tried together for conspiring to murder and murdering him.

A. EVIDENCE AT TRIAL

The prosecution presented evidence that defendant knew she would receive over $200,000 in the event of David's death from his employer, the United States Navy. Circumstantial evidence, including a comparison of bloodstains found in the bedroom of the Russo house in Riverdale with bloodstains found near the body, indicated that David had been killed in that bedroom. Other evidence showed that David had possessed a nine-millimeter Beretta handgun.

Defendant told the police the following: She let some people into her house around 1:00 a.m. on July 14, and after that she saw David's nine-millimeter Beretta gun. She had given the gun to someone on July 12. She told the people who had entered her house that her husband was asleep and they should keep their voices down. The people were making hand signals. Someone shot David with his own gun. The shot was muffled and occurred while she was checking on one of her children. After the shot, she saw her husband lying on the bed and the other persons still in the bedroom. The gun was wrapped in a towel. She picked up the gun and handed it to one of the others. She and the others then wrapped David's head in a garbage bag and his body in sleeping bags, tied ropes around the body, and put it into David's car. The others talked about a meeting place and then left. She was told the car would be "torched." She later cleaned up the bedroom.

Defendant admitted that she had previously talked about her husband's killing and that "outside people" would be hired to do it. She had the impression it would be done that night. Defendant knew that David was insured. She had planned to buy a house and pay bills with the insurance proceeds. Regarding the killing, she said, "It was just an easy out. It was stupid."

Travis Hayes testified that on July 13, in defendant's presence, Andrews solicited him to kill David. Andrews had a nine-millimeter handgun strapped to his side. Defendant told Hayes she could get him whatever money he wanted. Hayes said he would consider it. Defendant and Andrews gave Hayes $100. Later, Hayes told Andrews he could not go through with the crime. Two days after that, Andrews told Hayes that David had already been killed and asked Hayes to burn David's car. Hayes did not do so.

James Plantz testified that a few days before David's death, Morris asked him if he or anyone he knew would kill someone for $100. Morris said he would help, but the other person would have to do the actual killing. Plantz refused to help Morris. The day before the killing, Morris made statements to Plantz indicating involvement in the plan to kill David. Later that day, Andrews told Plantz that he had hired someone to do a killing for $100, but that the person had backed out. The next day, Morris told Plantz that Andrews had killed the intended victim by shooting him. Morris took out a nine-millimeter pistol, ejected a spent casing from it, and said, "Oh, there it is."

Morris testified on his own behalf. He said that Andrews had talked to him about killing David, but Morris thought the proposal was "bullshit." He never intended to help

Andrews kill David. The night of the killing, defendant asked him to come to the Russo home in order, he assumed, to pick up some drugs. At the house, Andrews handed him a gun and told him he could have $100 if he killed David. Morris declined and returned the gun to Andrews. Andrews then took the gun, wrapped it in a towel as a silencer, and entered David's room with defendant. Morris heard a muffled shot. He then helped Andrews and defendant dispose of David's body and the gun. He felt he had to because his fingerprints were on the gun.

Andrews also testified on his own behalf. He said he had become sexually involved with defendant before David's death. She had talked about possibly divorcing David but never about killing him. Before the killing, defendant gave him some of David's guns, including the nine-millimeter handgun. She told him David wanted the guns out of the house before someone used them in the house. The evening of the killing, defendant asked him to come to her home and drop off some drugs. He and Morris went to the Russo home shortly after midnight and gave defendant some drugs. Morris asked where David was. Defendant told him he was in a back room. Morris disappeared down the hall and Andrews heard a gunshot. Morris then came out of David's room and pointed the nine-millimeter gun at Andrews. Morris told Andrews and defendant to help dispose of the body. Andrews did not think defendant was involved in the shooting. She never asked Andrews to kill David.

B. PROCEDURAL HISTORY

The prosecution charged defendant, Andrews, and Morris with David's murder under the special circumstances of murder for financial gain and lying in wait, and with conspiracy to murder David. (*Pen. Code, § § 182, 187, 190.2, subd. (a)(1) & (15).*) (It also charged defendant with another count not relevant to the issue before us.) As part of the conspiracy charge, the prosecution alleged the three committed 10 overt acts: (1) Morris asked Plantz if he knew anyone who would kill David; (2) defendant gave Andrews David's handgun; (3) Andrews and defendant asked Hayes to help them kill David; (4) defendant told Hayes she would pay him whatever he asked if he would help kill David; (5) Andrews gave Hayes $100 after he and defendant asked him to help kill David; (6) defendant contacted Andrews after David went to sleep the night of the killing; (7) Andrews and Morris went to the Russo house that night; (8) defendant let Andrews and Morris into the house; (9) defendant let Andrews and Morris into the bedroom of her sleeping husband David; and (10) defendant, Andrews, and Morris fatally shot David in the back of the head with the nine-millimeter Beretta while he was asleep.

During argument to the jury, the prosecutor asserted that the jury did not have to agree on any specific overt act as long as it agreed unanimously that at least one was committed. Later, out of the jury's presence, the trial court expressed the same view. Accordingly, it instructed the jury that all the jurors had to agree on the verdict but not also that it had to agree unanimously on a specific overt act.

The jury convicted defendant of first degree murder and conspiracy to murder and found the special circumstance allegations true. The verdict form for the conspiracy charge stated the jury unanimously agreed that at least one overt act was committed. The jury was unable to reach a verdict as to Andrews. It found Morris guilty of David's first degree murder but was unable to reach a verdict on the special circumstance allegations and the conspiracy charge. The court sentenced defendant to prison for life without the possibility of parole.

On appeal, defendant argued, among other things, that the trial court erred prejudicially in not requiring the jury to agree unanimously on at least one specific overt act. The Court of Appeal agreed that the court erred, but it found the error harmless. It modified the judgment in a way not relevant here and affirmed it as modified. We granted defendant's petition for review, limited to the issue regarding jury unanimity as to a specific overt act.

II. DISCUSSION

At common law, and still today where unchanged by statute, conspiracy consisted of the unlawful agreement, and no overt act was required to establish the crime. (See generally Perkins & Boyce, Criminal Law (3d ed. 1982) § 5.B.3., pp. 685–687; 2 LaFave & Scott, Substantive Criminal Law (1986) Conspiracy—Limits of Liability, § 6.5(c), pp. 93–94.) Today, many jurisdictions, including California, require proof of an overt act. (*Ibid.*) In California, "No agreement amounts to a conspiracy, unless some act, beside such agreement, be done within this state to effect the object thereof, by one or more of the parties to such agreement. . . ." (*Pen. Code, § 184*; see also *id.* § 182, subd. (b).) Thus, "A conviction of conspiracy requires proof that the defendant and another person had the specific intent to agree or conspire to commit an offense, as well as the specific intent to commit the elements of that offense, together with proof of the commission of an overt act 'by one or more of the parties to such agreement' in furtherance of the conspiracy." (*People v. Morante (1999) 20 Cal. 4th 403, 416 {84 Cal. Rptr. 2d 665, 975 P.2d 1071}.*)

One purpose of the overt act requirement is to provide a *locus penitentiae*—an opportunity to repent—so that any of the conspirators may reconsider and abandon the agreement before taking steps to further it, and thereby avoid punishment for the conspiracy. (*People v. Morante, supra,* 20 Cal. 4th at p. 416, *fn. 4; People v. Zamora (1976) 18 Cal. 3d 538, 549, fn. 8 {134 Cal. Rptr. 784, 557 P.2d 75}.*) Another purpose is "to show that an indictable conspiracy exists" because "evil thoughts alone cannot constitute a criminal offense." (*People v. Olson (1965) 232 Cal. App. 2d 480, 489 {42 Cal. Rptr. 760};* see also *People v. Jones (1986) 180 Cal. App. 3d 509, 516 {225 Cal. Rptr. 697}.*)

In a criminal case, a jury verdict must be unanimous. (*People v. Collins (1976) 17 Cal. 3d 687, 693 {131 Cal. Rptr. 782, 552 P.2d 742};* see *Cal. Const., art. I, § 16* [expressly stating that "in a civil cause three-fourths of the jury may render a verdict" and thereby implying that in a criminal cause, only a unanimous jury may render a verdict].) The court here so instructed the jury. (See *CALJIC No. 17.50.*) Additionally, the jury must agree unanimously the defendant is guilty of a *specific* crime. (*People v. Diedrich (1982) 31 Cal. 3d 263, 281 {182 Cal. Rptr. 354, 643 P.2d 971}.*) Therefore, cases have long held that when the evidence suggests more than one discrete crime, either the prosecution must elect among the crimes or the court must require the jury to agree on the same criminal act. . . .

This requirement of unanimity as to the criminal act "is intended to eliminate the danger that the defendant will be convicted even though there is no single offense which all the jurors agree the defendant committed." (*People v. Sutherland (1993) 17 Cal. App. 4th 602, 612 {21 Cal. Rptr. 2d 752}.*) For example, in *People v. Diedrich, supra,* 31 Cal. 3d 263, the defendant was convicted of a single count of bribery, but the evidence showed two discrete bribes. We found the absence of a unanimity instruction reversible error because without it, some of the jurors may have believed the defendant guilty of one of the acts of bribery while other jurors believed him guilty of the other, resulting in no unanimous verdict that he was guilty of any specific bribe. (*Id.* at pp. 280–283, *182 Cal. Rptr. 354, 643 P.2d 971.*) "The [unanimity] instruction is designed in part to prevent the jury from amalgamating evidence of multiple offenses, no one of which has been proved beyond a reasonable doubt, in order to conclude beyond a reasonable doubt that a defendant must have done *something* sufficient to convict on one count." (*People v. Deletto (1983) 147 Cal. App. 3d 458, 472 {195 Cal. Rptr. 233}.*)

On the other hand, where the evidence shows only a single discrete crime but leaves room for disagreement as to exactly how that crime was committed or what the defendant's precise role was, the jury need not unanimously agree on the basis or, as the cases often put it, the "theory" whereby the defendant is guilty. (See generally *People v. Jenkins (2000) 22 Cal. 4th 900, 1024–1026 {95 Cal. Rptr. 2d 377, 997 P.2d 1044}.*) The crime of burglary provides a good illustration of the difference between discrete crimes, which require a unanimity instruction, and theories of the case, which do not. Burglary requires an entry with a specified intent. (*Pen. Code, § 459.*) If the evidence showed two different entries with burglarious intent, for example, one of a house on Elm Street on Tuesday and another of a house on Maple Street on Wednesday, the jury would have to unanimously find the defendant guilty of at least one of those acts. If, however, the evidence showed a single entry, but possible uncertainty as to the exact burglarious intent, that uncertainty would involve only the theory of the case and not require the unanimity instruction. (*People v. Failla (1966) 64 Cal. 2d 560, 567–569 {51 Cal. Rptr. 103, 414 P.2d 39}.*) Other typical examples include the rule that, to convict a defendant of first degree murder, the jury must unanimously agree on guilt of a specific murder but need not agree on a theory of premeditation or felony murder (*People v. Pride (1992) 3 Cal. 4th 195, 249–250 {10 Cal. Rptr. 2d 636, 833 P.2d 643}*), and the rule that the jury need not agree on whether the defendant was guilty as the direct perpetrator or as an aider and abettor as long as it agreed on a specific crime (*People v. Santamaria (1994) 8 Cal. 4th 903, 918–919 {35 Cal. Rptr. 2d 624, 884 P.2d 81}*).

We must now decide where the requirement of an overt act fits into this dichotomy between a specific crime and a theory of the case. Must the jury unanimously agree on at least one *specific* overt act, or does it suffice if it agrees there was at least one such act? The first Court of Appeal decision to consider the question, *People v. Jones, supra,* 180 Cal. App. 3d 509, concluded "that the jury only need be unanimous in finding *an* overt act was done in furtherance of the conspiracy, not in finding a particular overt act was done." (*Id.* at p. 516.) Accordingly, "a trial court need not instruct the jury they must unanimously agree as to the overt act done in pursuance of a conspiracy." (*Id.* at pp. 516–517.) Several subsequent cases have agreed with this conclusion.

. . .

The Court of Appeal here held that the jury must unanimously agree on a specific overt act. It and other courts have interpreted *People v. Brown (1991) 226 Cal. App. 3d 1361, 1367–1370 {277 Cal. Rptr. 309]*, and *People v. Ramirez (1987) 189 Cal. App. 3d 603, 611–615 {236 Cal. Rptr. 404},* as supporting that conclusion. (E.g., *People v. Godinez, supra,* 17 Cal. App. 4th at p. 1367.) However, neither of these cases clearly holds such unanimity is required. *Ramirez* seemed to assume this form of unanimity is required, but it actually concluded only that "any error in failure to give a specific unanimity instruction was harmless." (*People v. Ramirez, supra,* 189 Cal. App. 3d at p. 615.) Although *Brown* stated that "an overt act is an essential element in the crime of conspiracy," its actual holding was "that a conspiracy conviction cannot stand if the only overt act found occurred after commission of the criminal offense which was the conspiracy's object." (*People v. Brown, supra, 226 Cal. App. 3d* at p. 1369.) That holding is not at issue here. In any event, we agree with *People v. Jones, supra, 180 Cal. App. 3d 509*, and those cases following it, and disagree with any interpretation of *Ramirez* and *Brown* that is contrary to those decisions.

. . .

In this case, the question thus becomes whether the evidence suggested two discrete crimes, i.e., two discrete conspiracies, or merely possible uncertainty on how the defendant is guilty of a particular conspiracy. The overt act, although necessary to establish a punishable conspiracy, need not itself be criminal. (*People v. Robinson (1954) 43 Cal. 2d 132, 139 {271 P.2d 865}; People v. Jones, supra, 180 Cal. App. 3d* at p. 516.) If only one agreement existed, only one conspiracy occurred, whatever the precise overt act or acts may have been. The evidence here showed but one agreement, and hence but one conspiracy—the agreement by defendant and at least one other person (Morris or Andrews or both) to murder David. Although the jury had to find at least one overt act, whether it was one or another of several possible acts only concerns the way in which the crime was committed, i.e., the theory of the case, not whether discrete crimes were committed. Thus, if the jurors disagreed as to what overt act was committed, and agreed only that *an* overt act was committed, they would still have unanimously found defendant guilty of a particular conspiracy. No danger exists that some jurors would think she was guilty of one conspiracy and others would think she was guilty of a different one.

Moreover, any one of the conspirators, and not necessarily the charged defendant, may commit the overt act to consummate the conspiracy. (*Pen. Code, § 184; People v. Robinson, supra, 43 Cal. 2d* at p. 140; *People v. Jones, supra, 180 Cal. App. 3d* at pp. 515–516.) Disagreement as to who the coconspirators were or who did an overt act, or exactly what that act was, does not invalidate a conspiracy conviction, as long as a unanimous jury is convinced beyond a reasonable doubt that a conspirator did commit some overt act in furtherance of the conspiracy. When two or more persons combine to commit a crime, the jury need not agree on exactly who did what as long as it is convinced a particular defendant committed the crime regardless of what that defendant's precise role may have been. Sometimes there may be uncertainty as to which of two persons did what, but no doubt that each, or at least a particular defendant, was guilty of the crime. "If 12 jurors must agree on the role played by the defendant, the defendant may go free, even if the jurors all agree

defendant committed the crime. That result is absurd." (*People v. Perez, supra, 21 Cal. App. 4th* at p. 222, *26 Cal. Rptr. 2d 691,* and quoted in *People v. Santamaria, supra, 8 Cal. 4th* Not only is there no unanimity requirement as to the theory of guilt, the individual jurors themselves need not choose among the theories, so long as each is convinced of guilt. Sometimes . . . the jury simply cannot decide beyond a reasonable doubt exactly who did what. There may be a reasonable doubt that the defendant was the direct perpetrator, and a similar doubt that he was the aider and abettor, but no such doubt that he was one or the other." (*People v. Santamaria, supra, 8 Cal. 4th* at p. 919.) This case is a good illustration. Here, the jury clearly had no doubt that defendant—who essentially confessed—was guilty of conspiring with someone to murder David. But Morris and Andrews each professed innocence and blamed the other. The jury's inability to reach a conspiracy verdict as to either Morris or Andrews suggests at least some juror or jurors had a doubt whether either was a coconspirator. This doubt might extend to who committed the overt act or its exact nature. However, the jury could reasonably have agreed that defendant conspired with at least one of them and that some conspirator committed some overt act in furtherance of the conspiracy. Indeed, here the purpose of the conspiracy was not just furthered but fulfilled— David was actually murdered. To prohibit a conspiracy conviction for want of a specific overt act under these circumstances would be, to borrow the term from *People v. Perez, supra, 21 Cal. App. 4th* at p. 222, absurd.n2

> n2 In some cases, the trial court may have to give some form of a unanimity instruction. For example, if there is a question regarding the statute of limitations, the court might have to require the jury to agree an overt act was committed within the limitations period (see *People v. Zamora, supra, 18 Cal. 3d* at p. 548), or if evidence existed that the defendant had withdrawn from the conspiracy, the court might have to require the jury to agree an overt act was committed before the withdrawal. No such circumstance exists here, so we do not consider these questions.

III. CONCLUSION

Because the Court of Appeal found harmless what it perceived to be error, we agree with its conclusion, although not its reasoning. Accordingly, we affirm the judgment of the Court of Appeal. We also disapprove any interpretation of *People v. Brown, supra, 226 Cal. App. 3d 1361,* and *People v. Ramirez, supra, 189 Cal. App. 3d 603,* that is inconsistent with this opinion.

PEOPLE v. GORDON

COURT OF APPEAL OF CALIFORNIA, SECOND APPELLATE DISTRICT, DIVISION TWO

47 CAL. APP. 3D 465; 120 CAL. RPTR. 840

APRIL 24, 1975

OPINION BY: COMPTON, J.

Defendant was indicted by the Grand Jury of Los Angeles County for one count of violation of *Penal Code section 653f* (solicitation of a bribe). Prior to trial defendant moved under *Penal Code section 995* to set aside the indictment. That motion was denied and in the jury trial which followed defendant was found guilty as charged. She appeals the judgment of conviction and among other things contends that her motion under section 995 should have been granted.

The indictment alleged that on or about the 3d of January 1973, the defendant did "willfully and unlawfully and feloneously solicit another to offer, accept and join in the offer acceptance of a bribe." According to the evidence the person alleged to have been solicited was Officer Joseph Stanley of the Los Angeles Police Department who was at the time in question assigned to the narcotic detail.

FACTS

Defendant was an attorney at law and shared office space with another practitioner Mr. Bane. Mr. Bane had formerly been a member of the staff of the City Attorney of the City of Los Angeles. During that tenure he had become acquainted with Officer Stanley.

At some point late in the year 1972, defendant contacted Mr. Bane and stated that she knew where there was a two- or three-pound quantity of cocaine to be seized. She inquired whether Mr. Bane believed Officer Stanley would be interested and whether he could be trusted. Mr. Bane replied in the affirmative. Defendant asked Mr. Bane to contact Officer Stanley.

Mr. Bane mentioned the matter to Officer Stanley and the officer expressed an interest in seizing the cocaine. Mr. Bane advised the defendant of Officer Stanley's interest.

In late December of 1972, the defendant called Officer Stanley at the Administrative Narcotics Division of the Los Angeles Police Department and inquired if he had discussed with Mr. Bane the two or three pounds of cocaine and whether he was interested in seizing the cocaine and making an arrest. Officer Stanley stated that he was and arrangements were made for the defendant and Officer Stanley to meet. Defendant gave the officer her business and home telephone numbers.

On January 3, Officer Stanley called defendant at her office and a meeting was arranged at the building of the Los Angeles Community College Board of Trustees. That same afternoon Officer Stanley went to the agreed location. He saw the defendant sitting in the gallery observing a meeting of the board. Defendant nodded to Officer Stanley and the two went to a coffee shop located in the building.

In the conversation that followed defendant told the officer that she had a client who "wanted someone taken care of." The officer asked her if she meant "killed" and she replied "no" that she meant "discredited." She identified the person whom her client wanted discredited as Monroe Richman, a member of the Los Angeles Community College Board of Trustees. She stated that her client was highly politically oriented and that he, the client, had inquired of her if it could be arranged to have Mr. Richman "planted" with a quantity of narcotics and then arrested. Defendant also stated in that conversation that "she wouldn't even consider a situation like this unless it was worth money for everybody concerned." Defendant suggested that narcotics be planted either on Mr. Richman's person or in his car. Defendant offered to provide Officer Stanley with information upon which to effect the arrest of a person in possession of two or three pounds of cocaine and then asked if it would be possible to take a portion of that seized cocaine and plant it on Mr. Richman. Officer Stanley replied that it was possible. Defendant indicated that "it might be worth around $10,000." There were subsequent conversations between the two concerning the acquisition of the cocaine. On January 10, 1973, Officer Stanley called the defendant at her home and surreptitiously recorded the conversation which in part went as follows:

> Stanley: I wanna talk about the original 2 to 3 pounds.
>
> Gordon: Um-hum.
>
> Stanley: All right. We gotta have that for our supply.
>
> Gordon: I don't know if I'm gonna be able to get that.
>
> Stanley: You don't think—you don't think you're gonna be able to get that?
>
> Gordon: I'm not sure about that. Assuming I can't get that, can we still do this other thing?
>
> Stanley: Well, assuming you can't get the 2-3 pounds of coke, I don't know how we can come up with any other cocaine.
>
> Gordon: Maybe the price will just raise a little bit on the whole deal.
>
> Stanley: Well, can your man bear the traffic?
>
> Gordon: I don't know what the traffic is.
>
> Stanley: Well, I don't either. What do you think?
>
> Gordon: Well, *I'm thinking in terms of 10 grand.*
>
> Stanley: For the whole—For the whole thing 10 grand?
>
> Gordon: Um-hum. That too little?
>
> Stanley: Well, then what do you and I do with it?
>
> Gordon: *I don't care. I'll take a third, you can take three-quarters. You can take—give me a quarter. I don't care. What-ever you think is fair.*
>
> Stanley: All right.
>
> Gordon: Uh—You know I'm not out to—to take 50. I'm not out to take very much at all. It depends.
>
> Stanley: Okay, well—
>
> Gordon: I'd like—I'd like—uh—you know—a couple—$2500.
>
> Stanley: All right. But I—
>
> Gordon: I didn't—matter of fact I would like to—if you think that's not enough we may have to go out and make a purchase and let's up it.
>
> Stanley: Well, I don't know. You're right. We may have to make a purchase. (Italics added.)

The following day the officer called defendant at her office. In that conversation defendant told the officer that she had decided not to be a party to this scheme, that she felt she had a political career ahead of her and she did not want to take a chance on ruining that career. Subsequently the officer made several more contacts with the defendant in an effort to get her to introduce him to her client who originally proposed the scheme. Such meeting, however, was never consummated.

CONTENTIONS ON APPEAL

Defendant contends that there was insufficient evidence to sustain the conviction because there was no evidence that on January 3 she actually solicited the officer to accept the bribe, the argument being that she was "merely feeling out" the officer.

Solicitation consists of the asking of another to commit one of the specified crimes with intent that the crime be committed. The intent may be inferred from the circumstances of the asking. (*People v. Shapiro, 170 Cal. App.2d 468 {338 P.2d 963}.*)

"The solicitation of a bribe need not be stated in any particular language; such a solicitation may be in the form of words which carry the import of a bribe and were evidently intended to be so understood." (*People v. King, 218 Cal. App.2d 602,* at p. 610 *{32 Cal.Rptr. 479}.*)

The jury by its verdict found the defendant did in fact, and with the requisite intent, ask the officer to accept a bribe. On appeal from the judgment of conviction we view the evidence in the light most favorable to supporting the jury's determination and indulge in all reasonable inferences—which the evidence will support. (*People v. Reilly, 3 Cal.3d 421,* at p. 425 *{90 Cal.Rptr. 417, 475 P.2d 649}; People v. Redmond, 71 Cal.2d 745, 755 {79 Cal. Rptr. 529, 457 P.2d 321}.*)

Officer Stanley testified to statements by the defendant from which it could be reasonably inferred that the defendant was asking the officer, in return for the lion's share of $10,000 to arrange to falsely arrest Monroe Richman for possession of narcotics. The jury's verdict is well supported by substantial evidence. The jury could consider defendant's statements subsequent to January 3, in determining her intent on that earlier date. In fact, since the indictment alleged that the crime was committed "on or about January 3," the jury could have based its verdict on the aggregate of the conversations between defendant and Officer Stanley.

Defendant next contends that even if the words used by defendant amounted to a solicitation the officer was not solicited to act in his "official capacity."

Penal Code section 7, subdivision 6, states: "The word 'bribe' signifies anything of value or advantage, present or prospective, or any promise or undertaking to give any, asked, given, or accepted, with a corrupt intent to influence, unlawfully, the person to whom it is given, in his action, vote, or opinion, in any public or official capacity; . . ."

It is ludicrous to suggest that the solicitation by the defendant was not intended to affect Officer Stanley's action in his official capacity as a police officer for the City of Los Angeles. While it is true that it is not the official duty of a police officer to "frame" innocent persons by planting narcotics on them, it is generally within a police officer's official duties to make arrests. The solicitation here was for the officer to wrongfully and corruptly use his power of arrest in return for money.

The defendant sought out Officer Stanley because he was in fact a police officer and presented the matter for decision by him in his official capacity. (*People v. Finkelstin, 98 Cal.App.2d 545 {220 P.2d 934}.*)

In any event "'The giving or receiving of money . . . for the purpose of influencing official conduct is not deprived of its criminal character by the fact that the action contemplated is not within the officer's jurisdiction.'" (*People v. Lips, 59 Cal.App. 381, at p. 389 {211 P. 22}; People v. Megladdery, 40 Cal.App.2d 748 {106 P.2d 84}.*)

. . .

Since the crime was fully committed on January 3, it is no defense that the defendant later withdrew or failed to consummate the crime which was the object of the solicitation. The offense of solicitation "is complete when the solicitation is made, and it is immaterial that the object of the solicitation is never consummated, or that no steps are taken toward its consummation." (*People v. Burt, 45 Cal.2d 311, at p. 314 {288 P.2d 503, 51 A.L.R.2d 948}.*)

. . .

Defendant makes a number of other claims of error, none of which have merit. The evidence in this case is overwhelming and defendant was fairly tried. There was no miscarriage of justice.

The judgment is affirmed.

PEOPLE v. SAEPHANH

COURT OF APPEAL OF CALIFORNIA, FIFTH APPELLATE DISTRICT

80 Cal. App. 4th 451; 94 Cal. Rptr. 2d 910

April 28, 2000

OPINION BY: HARRIS, J.

STATEMENT OF THE CASE

A single-count information filed on August 12, 1998, in Kings County Superior Court charged appellant Lou Tong Saephanh with solicitation of murder in violation of *Penal Code . . . section 653f,* subdivision (b). On October 7, 1998, after a 2-day jury trial, appellant's motion for acquittal pursuant to section 1118.1 was denied, and appellant was subsequently found guilty. . . . On November 5, 1998, after consideration of the probation officer's report, the court denied probation. The court sentenced appellant to the upper term of 9 years. On November 23, 1998, appellant filed a notice of appeal.

FACTS

In October and November 1997, appellant had consensual sexual intercourse with Cassandra Y. Cassandra became pregnant and, in January 1998 while appellant was in prison, she informed appellant of her pregnancy. Appellant first asked if the baby was his and, when told it was, exclaimed, "Oh, I've been wanting a baby for a long time." Cassandra and appellant spoke about the baby every week and appellant was excited.

In May 1998, while still incarcerated, appellant wrote a letter dated May 22, 1998, to his friend and fellow gang member Cheng Saechao, also known as O. Dee. In pertinent part, it stated, "By the way loc, could you and the homies do me a big favor and take care that white bitch, Cassie for me. ha, ha, ha!! Cuzz, it's too late to have abortion so I think a miss carrage would do just fine. I aint fista pay child sport for this bull-shit loc. You think you can get the homies or home girls do that for me before she have the baby on Aug. 98" (*Sic.*) At the time he wrote the letter, appellant was upset. He did not want to pay child support.

Vicki Lawrence, a correctional officer at Corcoran State Prison working for the investigative service unit, testified that when an indigent inmate wishes to send a letter, he puts it into a night drop for processing through the mail room where the letter is stamped for delivery. Lawrence found the letter in her "in box." The investigative unit reviews inmate correspondence placed in the institution's mail system. According to Lawrence, she opened and read the letter appellant had written. She immediately notified her supervisor, Sergeant Basinger. The letter was thus intercepted by the institution's internal investigative unit and never reached the addressee.

Rick Bellar, an investigator with the Kings County District Attorney's Office, read a copy of the letter that Basinger provided him and thereafter interviewed Cassandra, Cheng Saechao and appellant. Bellar interviewed appellant on June 2, 1998, at Corcoran State Prison. Appellant admitted writing the letter and that he was serious when he wrote it. Appellant told Bellar that when he wrote the letter, he was thinking that if Cassandra did not let him be a part of the baby's life, he wanted to "get rid of the baby." Appellant did not want to pay child support. Appellant was angry because Cassandra did not seem to love him, and there was an argument in which Cassandra told appellant he could not see the baby. Appellant expected Saechao and other gang members to punch Cassandra in the stomach during a fight or have her fall, thereby causing a miscarriage.

Appellant told Bellar he later called Saechao and told him to ignore the letter, but Saechao did not know what letter appellant was talking about.

Appellant presented no evidence on his behalf.

DISCUSSION

I. THE SOLICITATION CONVICTION

Appellant contends there is insufficient evidence to support his conviction for solicitation of murder because the evidence establishes that the soliciting communication was not received by the intended recipient and, in fact, establishes no one was solicited. He asserts that California's solicitation statute, section 653f,n2 requires proof of a completed communication. He suggests a "completed communication" occurs only when the intended recipient of the communication receives it.

> n2 Section 653f, subdivision (b) provides: "Every person who, with the intent that the crime be committed, solicits another to commit or join in the commission of murder shall be punished by imprisonment in the state prison for 3, 6, or 9 years."

Appellant acknowledges no published California case has so held and notes the issue is one of first impression in California. According to appellant, however, "two other states which have considered the issue under solicitation statutes similar to [California's section 653f], Oregon and New Mexico," concluded solicitation requires a "completed communication," i.e., one which was received by the intended recipient. He contends these authorities should be applied in California.

In *State v. Cotton (1990) 109 N.M. 769 {790 P.2d 1050}*, the defendant was convicted of two counts of criminal solicitation. While he was incarcerated in New Mexico, he wrote two letters to his wife in Indiana suggesting that she warn their daughter not to testify against defendant on molestation charges and that she persuade their daughter to leave New Mexico and go to Indiana. Neither letter ever reached defendant's wife, both having landed in the hands of law enforcement. On appeal, the defendant claimed insufficient evidence to support the solicitation convictions because the letters never reached the intended recipient, the defendant's wife. (*Id.* at p. 1051.)

The New Mexico Court of Appeal agreed. First, it noted that New Mexico's criminal solicitation statute "adopts in part, language defining the crime of solicitation as set out in the Model Penal Code promulgated by the American Law Institute." (*State v. Cotton, supra,* 790 *P.2d* at pp. 1052–1053.)n3 The court distinguished New Mexico's statute from the Model Penal Code, noting that New Mexico's solicitation statute "specifically omits that portion of the Model Penal Code subsection declaring that an uncommunicated solicitation to commit a crime may constitute the offense of criminal solicitation. The latter omission, we conclude, indicates an implicit legislative intent that the offense of solicitation requires some form of actual communication from the defendant to either an intermediary or the person intended to be solicited, indicating the subject matter of the solicitation." (*790 P.2d* at p. 1053, fn. omitted.) Thus, by adopting in part the Model Penal Code section defining solicitation but omitting language from that section criminalizing uncommunicated solicitations, the New Mexico Legislature intended that the New Mexico statute not criminalize uncommunicated solicitations.

n3 According to the opinion, New Mexico's criminal solicitation statute provided, in pertinent part:

"'[A] person is guilty of criminal solicitation if, with the intent that another person engage in conduct constituting a felony, he solicits, commands, requests, induces, employs or otherwise attempts to promote or facilitate another person to engage in conduct constituting a felony. . . .'" (*State v. Cotton, supra,* 790 *P.2d* at p. 1052; see *N.M. Stat. Ann. § 30-28-3(A)*.)

Model Penal Code section 5.02 provides in pertinent part:

(1) A person is guilty of solicitation to commit a crime if with the purpose of promoting or facilitating its commission he commands, encourages or requests another person to engage in specific conduct that would constitute such crime or an attempt to commit such crime or would establish his complicity in its commission or attempted commission.

(2) It is immaterial under Subsection (1) of this Section that the actor fails to communicate with the person he solicits to commit a crime if his conduct was designed to effect such communication.

The court observed that one scholar suggests uncommunicated solicitations may have to be prosecuted as attempted solicitation. (*State v. Cotton, supra,* 790 *P.2d* at p. 1054.) The court rejected the state's argument that uncommunicated solicitations nonetheless constitute solicitations because New Mexico's criminal solicitation statute expressly provides that one is guilty of solicitation where he "'otherwise attempt[ed] to promote or facilitate another person to engage in conduct constituting a felony. . . .'" (*Ibid.*) The court declined to read that provision "so broadly." (*Ibid.*) The court reversed the judgment. (*Id.* at p. 1055.)

In *State v. Lee (1991) 105 Or. App. 329 {804 P.2d 1208}*, the Oregon Court of Appeal reached a similar result. There, the defendant, while in jail, wrote letters to an acquaintance in a juvenile center outlining plans to rob a store and residence. Authorities in the juvenile center intercepted the letters, which never reached the intended recipient. The defendant was convicted of solicitation to commit robbery. On appeal, he argued lack of evidence to sustain the conviction because the letters were never received by the intended recipient.

Citing *Cotton* and apparently following its reasoning, the Oregon court noted Oregon's criminal solicitation statute n4 "was based, in part, on the Model Penal Code." (*State v. Lee, supra,* 804 *P.2d* at p. 1210.) As did the court in *Cotton,* the *Lee* court noted the omission of Model Penal Code language criminalizing uncommunicated solicitations in

Oregon's criminal solicitation statute. "Significantly, the legislature did not adopt the provision of the Model Penal Code that specifically provides that solicitation may be based on an incomplete communication." (*State v. Lee, supra,* 804 P.2d at p. 1210.) The court concluded a completed communication is required to prove the crime of solicitation. The court determined attempted solicitation is a necessarily included offense of solicitation and remanded for entry of judgment of conviction on that crime. (804 P.2d at pp. 1210–1211.)

> n4 According to the opinion, Oregon's solicitation statute provided: "'A person commits the crime of solicitation if with the intent of causing another to engage in specific conduct constituting a crime punishable as a felony or as a Class A misdemeanor or an attempt to commit such felony or Class A misdemeanor the person commands or solicits such other person to engage in that conduct.'" (*State v. Lee, supra,* 804 P.2d at p. 1210; see *Or. Rev. Stat. §* 161.435(1) (1999).)

Respondent agrees no California authority has directly addressed the issue of whether one may be found guilty of solicitation where the intended recipient of the soliciting communication never received the message. Respondent notes there is a split in authorities from other jurisdictions addressing the issue.

. . .

Does California's section 653f include in its ambit solicitations not received by the intended recipient? *Cotton* and *Lee* concluded the New Mexico and Oregon Legislatures intended their solicitation statutes to require a solicitation be received by the intended recipient for criminal liability to attach on the basis of the omission from their statutes of language contained in the Model Penal Code on which those statutes are based. Section 653f, enacted in 1929, is not based on the Model Penal Code. (See Model Pen. Code & Commentaries, com. 2 to § 5.02, p. 367 & fn.11.) Thus, we disagree with appellant that *Cotton* and *Lee* examined "solicitation statutes similar to *California's Penal Code section 653f,*" at least in terms of legislative history and intent. We find *Cotton* and *Lee* unpersuasive on the issue of whether section 653f criminalizes the making of soliciting communications not received by the intended recipient.

. . .

As have the parties, we have located no California case squarely addressing the question of whether the intended recipient of a solicitation must receive the solicitation for liability to attach under section 653f.

. . .

As noted, section 653f, subdivision (b) provides: "Every person who, with the intent that the crime be committed, solicits another to commit or join in the commission of murder shall be punished by imprisonment. . . ."

The plain language of section 653f, in particular the phrase "solicits another," demonstrates that proof the defendant's soliciting message was received by an intended recipient is required for liability to attach. The facts of this case are illustrative of the plain meaning of the statute. Here, appellant intended to ask Saechao and the "homies or home girls" to kill Cassandra's fetus. However, neither Saechao nor the "homies or home girls" ever received the soliciting message. Thus, appellant did not solicit Saechao or the specifically designated others.

Respondent nonetheless contends the harm is in the asking and suggests the crime of solicitation was complete when appellant "deposited the correspondence with the requisite criminal intent." According to respondent, solicitation has two elements, a request to do a crime and intent that it be completed. Thus, respondent asserts, "appellant's letter was the murder request and, when he dropped it off to be mailed, he possessed the requisite criminal intent, thus satisfying both the elements to criminal solicitation."

We disagree that the letter, never received by any person appellant intended to solicit, in itself constitutes a "request" as that term may be applied in interpreting section 653f. Evidence appellant wrote the letter to Saechao is insufficient to show appellant actually requested Saechao, or the "homies or home girls" commit murder, in the absence of evidence any one of them received the letter. This is so even though appellant posted the letter. The crime of solicitation defined by section 653f requires that two or more persons must be involved, at least one being necessarily a solicitor and the other necessarily being the person solicited.

We agree with appellant that solicitation requires a completed communication.

. . .

Section 653f has the two-fold purpose of protecting the inhabitants of California from being exposed to inducement to commit or join in the commission of crimes and preventing solicitations from resulting in the commission of the crimes solicited. (*Benson v. Superior Court* (1962) 57 Cal. 2d 240, 243 {18 Cal. Rptr. 516, 368 P.2d 116}; *People v. Burt* (1955) 45 Cal. 2d 311, 314 {288 P.2d 503, 51 A.L.R.2d 948}.) Uncommunicated soliciting messages do not expose others to inducements to commit crimes. Nor is there a likelihood that an uncommunicated message would result in the commission of crimes. Thus, letters posted but not delivered do not give rise to the dangers from which section 653f seeks to protect society.

However, messages urging commission of a crime which are received expose individuals to invitation to crime and create a risk of criminal activity. Criminalizing completed solicitations furthers the policies of protecting individuals from exposure to inducements to commit crimes and preventing commission of the crimes solicited. Thus, a conviction for a violation of section 653f requires proof that the person solicited received the soliciting communication. One cannot "solicit another" without a completed communication. The communication is only completed when it is received by its intended recipient.

Appellant did not ask Vicki Lawrence to kill Cassandra's fetus and appellant was unsuccessful in asking Saechao (or, for that matter, the "homies or home girls") to do so because his letter was intercepted. Appellant did not "solicit another" to commit murder within the meaning of section 653f, subdivision (b). Thus, his conviction for solicitation of murder cannot stand.

II. ATTEMPTED SOLICITATION

Appellant next contends he is guilty of no crime. He asserts attempted solicitation is not a crime in California because there is no reference to attempt in section 653f. He cites other criminal and noncriminal statutes containing attempt language and suggests the absence of such language in section 653f is a clear manifestation of legislative intent attempted solicitation is not a crime.

We disagree. "Every person who attempts to commit *any crime*, but fails, or is prevented or intercepted in its perpetration, shall be punished where no provision is made by law for the punishment of those attempts, . . ." (§ 664, italics added.) Solicitation is a crime, and thus falls within section 664, which applies to the attempted commission of any crime. The plain language of section 664 makes clear the Legislature is aware of specific provisions regarding attempt in the context of some crimes, and it expressly applies to those crimes which do not address attempt. Attempted solicitation of murder is a crime in California.

. . .

The crime of solicitation is complete when the solicitation is made, i.e., when the soliciting message is received by its intended recipient. It is immaterial that the object of the solicitation is never consummated, or that no steps are taken towards its completion. (*People v. Cook (1984) 151 Cal. App. 3d 1142, 1145 {199 Cal. Rptr. 269}*.) . . . The Legislature presumably was aware of section 664, criminalizing an attempt to commit *any crime*, when it enacted section 653f. We conclude the absence of language expressly *exempting* section 653f from the ambit of section 664, in effect at the time section 653f was enacted, suggests the Legislature did not intend to foreclose convictions for attempted solicitation.

Pursuant to the plain language of sections 653f and 664, attempted solicitation of murder is a crime. We will direct that appellant's conviction be modified to a conviction of attempted solicitation of murder. This resolution of the matter renders moot appellant's claims of instructional error.

DISPOSITION

The judgment of conviction for solicitation of murder is vacated. The matter is remanded to the trial court with instructions to enter a judgment of conviction for attempted solicitation of murder and thereupon to re-sentence appellant.

KEY TERMS

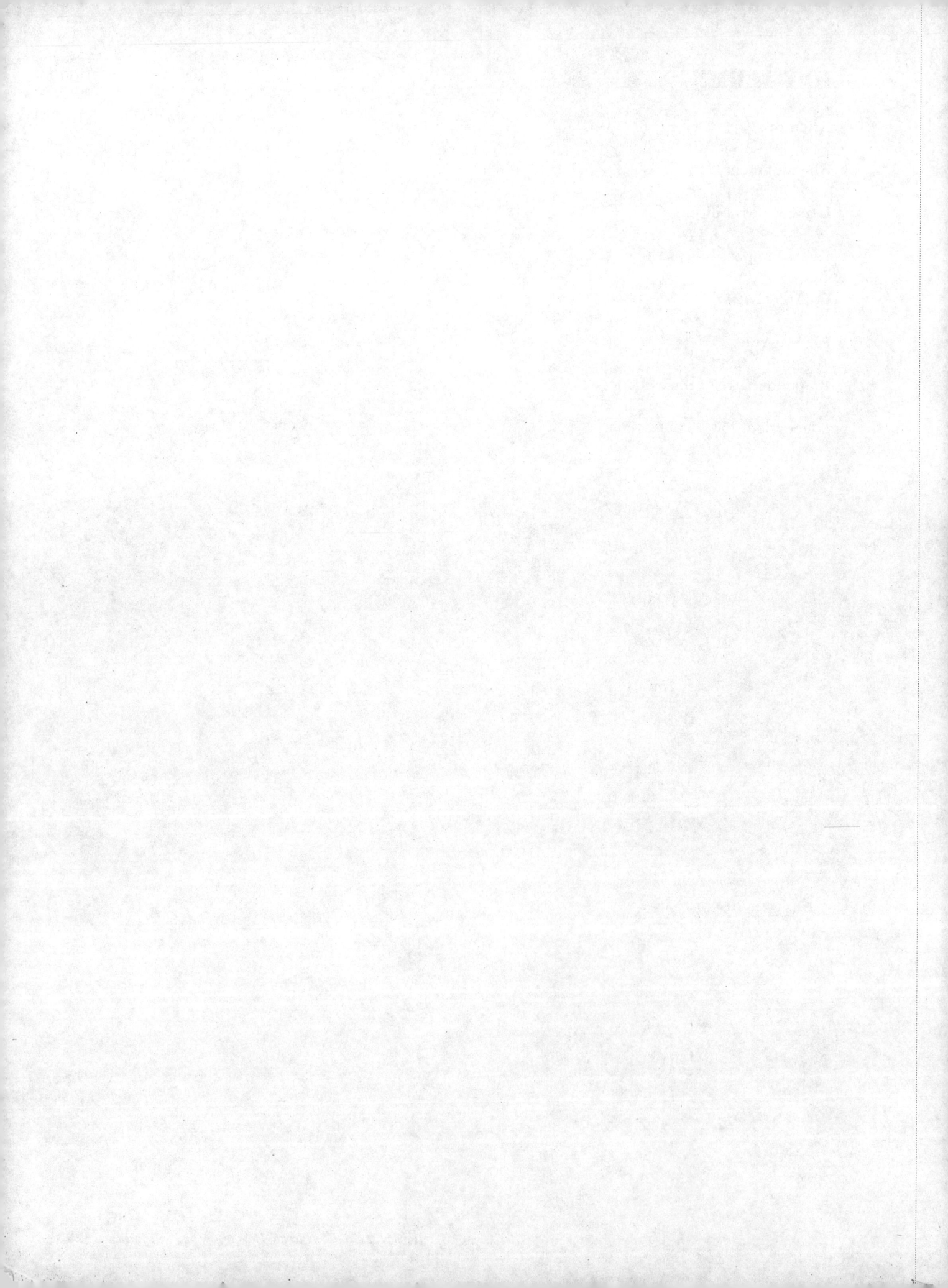